MONEY
DYNAMICS
FOR THE 1980s

MONEY DYNAMICS FOR THE 1980s

Venita
VanCaspel, CFP

President
VanCaspel & Co., Inc.
1540 Post Oak Tower
5051 Westheimer
Houston, Texas 77056
(713) 621-9733

Reston Publishing Company, Inc.
A Prentice Hall Company
Reston, Virginia

*To the VanCaspel Team, whose daily dedication
and delightful spirit make it possible
for me to help others become financially independent.*

Drawings by Jan Smulcer

Library of Congress Cataloging in Publication Data

VanCaspel, Venita
  Money dynamics for the 1980s.

  Includes index.
  1. Finance, Personal.   I. Title.
HG179.V36   332.024   80-16799
ISBN 0-8359-4618-5

© 1980 by
Reston Publishing Company, Inc.
A Prentice-Hall Company
Reston, Virginia   22090

10   9   8   7   6   5   4   3   2   1

Printed in the United States of America

CONTENTS

13 LIFE INSURANCE—THE GREAT NATIONAL CONSUMER DILEMMA 403

14 PROTECTING AGAINST THE UNEXPECTED 457

PREFACE

Our country's per capita income is one of the highest ever known to mankind; yet of every one hundred of our citizens who reach the age of 65, ninety-five are flat broke! Of every one hundred who reach their "golden years," only two are financially independent; twenty-three must continue to work; and seventy-five are dependent on friends, relatives, or charity.

They lost the money game. The money game is unlike any other game. You cannot choose whether you'll play. You cannot choose to sit out a hand or move to another game. For this game—the money game—is the only game in town.

Since you have no choice but to play, the only intelligent thing for you to do is to learn the rules and play to win! Losing means spending twenty to thirty years of your life in angry frustration in a state of financial insecurity.

If you have no choice but to play the money game, and if it is so essential to win, why weren't you taught how to play it successfully in school?

I really don't know. There is an educational void in our country. We are spending millions of dollars teaching both our young people and our adults to earn dollars; yet we are not teaching them what to do with these dollars once they are earned. I find that they are making some tragic mistakes.

Somewhere, somehow, back in the dark pages of history, a false idea germinated and grew. This sinister concept was that "money is the root of all evil." This is not true. Money is not "the root of all evil." It is the misuse of money that brings corruption and human suffering. The proper use of money provides the necessary food for your family; it helps build hospitals to aid them in regaining their health when they are ill; it helps build churches in which they may worship; it provides wood and bricks to be used in constructing a roof over their heads; and it provides

fabrics to make the clothes that will protect their bodies from the cold winds of winter and the blistering heat of summer.

Upon you falls the responsibility to be a good steward of every dollar that comes your way.

I feel I should warn you now that applying the information contained in this book will not give you instant wealth. If I knew how to do that, as committed as I am to helping others become financially independent, do you really think I would be willing to sell that secret for so small a sum as the price of this book or to let you subscribe to any handy dandy investment advisory service that I might establish?

On the other hand, what are your choices? I see only three:

1. Try to make it fast, with limited hopes for success. (Look around you and unemotionally calculate your odds.)
2. Try to make it slowly, with a rather good chance for success.
3. Don't try at all. This is the choice that is being made by the majority of your fellow citizens.

I am convinced that if you are granted a reasonable amount of time, the ability and willingness to earn an average wage, the discipline to save a small portion of your earnings, and the intelligence to apply the principles taught in this book, you can become financially independent. Attainment of this desirable state does not require brilliance or luck. It requires discipline, agility, and the ability and willingness to make your dollars work for you as hard as you had to work for them.

I have found that financial planning is like navigation. If you know where you are and where you want to go, navigation is not difficult. It's when you don't know those two points that arriving at your destination becomes unlikely. To illustrate this point, let's assume that you are boarding a large luxury ocean liner with its mighty engines running in preparation to leave port. You go into the chart room and ask the captain to show you on his charts your present location, your next port of call, your destination, and the route he is planning to take. He shrugs his shoulders and answers, "I really don't know." Would you be confident of his reaching his destination? Would you want to be a passenger on his ship?

If your answer is no, use this same intelligence in plotting your own financial course. For you are the captain of your vitally important financial ship.

Enter now your chart room to plot your financial future. Here you will learn how to determine your present position, where you want to be on a certain date, and alternate courses that are available for arriving at your destination.

In my years of financial planning I have never met a person who planned to fail, but I have met many who failed to plan. Unfortunately, the results have been the same.

I have dedicated a large portion of my life to helping others develop and successfully execute their plans for financial independence.

Through the pages of this book I shall endeavor to do the same for you.

To ensure that you will have a solid foundation upon which to build, it will be necessary to begin the book with some tables and charts that may at first glance not seem as exciting as we both would like for them to be. But do persevere, devour them, and let them seep deeply into your subconscious mind. You'll find them invaluable benchmarks to the successful attainment of your predetermined worthwhile goal of financial independence.

ACKNOWLEDGMENTS

So many have touched my life and helped me toward my goals that this page could not possibly cover them all. I would like to express my special thanks to Helen Fourmy, who has been my faithful, motivating, and excellent associate for many years; to Jolieta Davis, whose immense talent and personal dedication smooths the ripples of my personal and business life; and to Yvonne Ingram, her very talented assistant; to Donah Shaw, my delightful and efficient secretary, who brings order and fun into my life; to Susan Streich, whose calm and lovely presence gives me a sense of continuity; to Kathy Owen, our bright and capable "Maggie"; to Nancy Claire, who greets our clients in a special way; to Jan Smulcer, who is no longer on our staff, but whom we still claim and who did the fun drawings in this book; to Patsy Dobson, whose speedy and efficient fingers typed parts of this manuscript; to John Weatherston, who brings us the wise maturity that comes from experience; and most especially to Walt Burton, Wally Garrett, and Terry Albin, who, along with Helen, make up the most talented team of financial planners in the country today.

TO WIN THE
MONEY GAME

Welcome to the decade of the '80s! It will be a decade of dynamic, challenging, frustrating change—in family relationships, international affairs, living patterns, and most especially in the nurture and investment of your money. That is why this book is titled *Money Dynamics for the '80s*. To win the money game in this decade—and win you must—you will have to develop a special kind of expertise, mental attitude, agility, and determination. It is the purpose of this book to teach you all the strategies that you'll need to know to win.

If you are doing anything with your money the way you did it just a few years ago, you are doing it wrong. All the old rules have changed. New rules have dramatically thrust themselves upon your universe. It will do you no good to cry for the return of the money principles of the past, resisting the pains of change; your resistance will not only be in vain, but it will be disastrous to your wealth.

YOUR REACTION TO CHANGE

It will not be change, but your reaction to change, that will determine your financial future. Change can greatly enhance your fortune, or it can destroy it; make you a millionaire or a pauper; delight you or disappoint you; exhilarate you or depress you. Change brings with it heightened potential and devastating crevices of danger.

FINANCIAL SURVIVAL

How you cope with this inevitable change will determine whether you'll win or lose. This book is dedicated to you, to teach you not only how to survive, but how to prosper. It is designed to help you become financially independent, if you have not already arrived at that happy state. If you have, it will help you multiply your money many times over.

This book is written to you in first person because the only concepts I can share with you that will have any validity are those I have experienced and observed from my years as a Certified Financial Planner.

For the past nineteen years, it has been my privilege to have helped a vast number of individuals and couples just like you to become financially independent and to make their money grow. During this time I have conducted hundreds of public financial planning seminars in Houston and in our major cities across the nation, been the lead speaker for a large number of national conventions, spoken to innumerable service and social clubs, appeared as a guest on numerous television and radio shows, been interviewed by our national news-

2

papers and magazines, written numerous articles, and had published two top selling investment books. For eight years, I was the author and moderator of a thirty-minute television show called "Successful Texans" shown on Houston's CBS affiliate station. Each week on this show, I interviewed a Texan who had attained success in his or her chosen profession under our free enterprise system.

I am in daily contact with some of our nation's top policy makers, the most expert observers of the money scene, our leading financial planners, and a large number of successful business and professional people who make decisions that affect us all. From this vast exposure to information, my training, and my years of experience, I have developed a certain expertise for helping others become financially independent. I am dedicated to helping all with whom I come in contact to reach this desired state. I feel that this is my calling—my justification for having passed this way.

This book is written to make you knowledgeable about money matters—to inspire you, to give you hope, to motivate you to act. For, unless you apply this knowledge, I will have left you financially where I found you.

Throughout this book I will use the masculine pronoun in a neutral way to mean "he or she." I have found that God has been very fair in His apportionment of brains. He has made women as intelligent and as capable as men, so in this book I'll not bother myself with all this "he-she" business, but will rather devote myself to the order of the day: helping you make your money work effectively for you.

FINANCIAL PLANNING IS PERSONAL

Financial planning must be personal. You are different from any other person. You were created as a unique individual and have developed in your own unique way. You have different financial objectives, different assets, a different tax bracket, and a different temperament from even your closest friend. Your financial program, therefore, must be designed for you and for you alone because you are special.

If you and I could sit down and plan your financial future, I would ask you many pertinent questions about you and your money. I would then endeavor to design a program that fits not only your financial needs, but your emotional needs as well. To design a program for your financial needs is relatively simple, once I know all the facts; but mapping a course that fits your temperament and your prejudices and then communicating these ideas to you in such a way that you will understand and then act upon them is a continuous challenge.

Since you and I may never have this opportunity, I have designed this book to give you a step-by-step guide to be used in designing your own financial blueprint.

DEAR INVESTOR

My greeting to you is "Dear Investor" because you are an investor. You are either investing all of your wealth in today's goods and services or you are reserving a portion of it to invest in tomorrow's goods and services. You do not have the choice of whether you will invest, but you do have the choice of how you will invest. The wisdom you bring to bear on these choices will have a greater influence on your financial future than the amount of money that comes your way.

Do you want to consume all that you earn today and hope that somehow tomorrow will take care of itself? As short-sighted as this may seem, it is the course being taken by the vast majority of your fellow citizens. Today, of every 100 or our citizens who are reaching the age of 65, only 2 percent are financially independent; 23 percent must continue to work; and 75 are dependent on friends, relatives, or charity. Of every 100 reaching 65, 95 are flat broke!

According to the National Council on Aging, the total liquid assets per capita of those 65 years of age in the U.S. was only $3562 in 1978. What a tragedy! This need not happen to you.

SUCCESS ASSURED

Financial independence can be yours if you learn and apply the information contained in this book. My first two books, *Money Dynamics* and *The New Money Dynamics*, have launched thousands down this road. Sales of these two books have soared as financial planners have used them with their clients both here and abroad. My mail detailing successful results has become an avalanche of joy to me. For nothing delights me more than receiving testimonials of success.

You may ask, if my first two books have been so successful, why I don't just rest on my laurels and let their advice stand. The reason is that the world of money changes, and it changes daily. That's what I love about my profession. Every day when I get up it's a new day. Changes take place that make old concepts and strategies obsolete; but opportunity is still there in abundance. Just the rules for capturing those opportunities have changed.

Are you wondering if you can win the money game? Of course you can. Do you know why? Because there are so few people out there trying. That's why success is so easy. There is so little competition. You can be a winner, and you will!

THREE FINANCIAL PERIODS

Now let's look at your financial life. It will most likely be composed of three periods: the "Learning" Period; the "Earning" Period; and the "Yearning" or "Golden" Period, depending on the decisions you make in your "Earning" period.

Let's examine each of these financial periods!

The Learning Period

I hope that you begin learning at birth and never cease to learn until you bid this world good-bye. However, your formal learning period will probably last for your first twenty-five years, depending on your choice of a vocation.

If you are considering whether a college education is a good investment for yourself, your children, or your grandchildren, the answer is yes. It will cost between $15,000 and $50,000, depending on your choice of schools, vocation, and number of years before entering college. But the investment can yield a good return. Studies show that a college graduate earns $250,000 to $400,000 more during his life than does a person with only a high school diploma. Time, money, and effort invested in education increase the productivity of the individual. This investment in human capital is similar to an investment in capital equipment for a plant that increases productivity, which in turn yields an increase in profits. A college education can bring more than just financial rewards. The ability to think and to plan is stimulated in college. There are fewer divorces among college graduates. It can add a greatly enlarged dimension to life. And it is an asset that cannot be confiscated through taxation or other means.

In my years of financial counseling I have found that there are many who want to believe that financial gains come by luck. I do not believe in luck. "Luck" comes when preparedness and opportunity get together. I personally have found that the more I place myself in the path of opportunity, the luckier I become. I have found that I have never learned a new tax law or mastered a new investment concept that I haven't had an opportunity to use advantageously immediately.

As I observe many around me, I am reminded of the man who stood in front of a wood-burning stove and said, "Give me some heat and I'll give you some wood." But that's just not the nature of a wood-burning stove. The wood must come first. The same is true of preparation, so do not skimp on this important ingredient. Put adequate wood in your burner, and it will yield to you the warmth of financial security.

However, never make the mistake of thinking that you can rest on your laurels of accumulated knowledge, for you are living in a dynamic world of change that makes it absolutely essential that you obtain new information every day. I hope you did not end your education upon your graduation, but that yours is truly a commencement exercise where you begin your education.

The Earning Period

The second period of your financial life will be your "earning" period. This will probably last for around forty years, from age 25 to age 65. This is when you apply the vocation that you have learned during the first period of your life.

Have you ever thought of just how much money will come your way during those forty earning years, or have you just thought of your earnings as so much money a month? Add it up and you'll see that a tremendous amount of money will pass your way. As a matter of fact, if you never earn more than $525 a month, over a quarter of a million dollars will pass your way. If you earn $1050 a month, over half a million dollars will pass your way. If you earn as much as $2100 a month, over a million dollars will pass your way.

Monthly Income	10 Years	20 Years	30 Years	40 Years
500	60,000	120,000	180,000	240,000
600	72,000	144,000	216,000	288,000
800	96,000	192,000	288,000	384,000
1000	120,000	240,000	360,000	480,000
1500	180,000	360,000	540,000	720,000
2000	240,000	480,000	720,000	960,000
2500	300,000	600,000	900,000	1,200,000

. . . at only $1500 per month,
$720,000 will pass through your hands
during your earning years . . .

As you can see from the above chart, there is no question that a lot of money will come your way. What's the problem? It's how to keep some of it from passing through your fingers, isn't it?

The Secret of Accumulation of Wealth

Let me share with you a very simple secret for the accumulation of wealth. The secret has only ten words in it and is so simple you will be tempted to discard it. But if you remember it and put it to use, it will be of great value to you for the remainder of your life. The secret is this: "A part of all I earn is mine to keep."

You may be tempted to say, "Everything I earn is mine to keep." It isn't so, is it? It belongs to the IRS, the baker, the butcher, the mortgage company, the church. If you were to place in a line, in the order of their importance to you, all those whom you wanted to receive a portion of your paycheck, would you place yourself at the head of the line? Is that where you have been putting yourself? If you are like so many others, you've put yourself at the end of the line, trying to save what is left over and finding that your ability to spend

up to and beyond your income is utterly amazing. You must learn to pay yourself first or, if not first, at least along with all the others.

If you were to save one-tenth of all you earned and did it for ten years, how much money would you have? A whole year's salary at one time, of course. And that's not all, for you would put this money to work, and before long you would have much more working for you.

The Yearning or Golden Years

The third period of your life will be your retirement years. These will either be your "yearning" years or your "golden" years, depending on the financial decisions you make during your "earning" years.

If you are a male and live to age 65, you will probably live to around 80 years of age. If one of we females make it to 65, please be

prepared to have us for a very long time. You can hardly kill off an old woman—we are sturdy! My oldest client is 96 years of age. Three years ago I got her to quit investing for growth!

Will this period of your life take care of itself? The answer is NO. The future belongs to those who prepare for it—and how tragically few are preparing!

Why, in a nation with a high per capita income and unparalleled prosperity, do 98 percent of our citizens reach 65 without having made adequate preparation to retire in financial dignity?

Perhaps they—and you—have been lulled into a false sense of security by the cozy sound of the words Social Security. (Doesn't Social Security, especially if you say it softly and slowly, sound like a warm puppy?) Don't wait until you find that it should have been called "Social Insecurity," for by that time it will be too late to alter your financial fate.

Actually, Social Security was never meant to provide you with financial independence. It was designed to prevent mass destitution. If you count on it at all, which I don't recommend, treat it as a very miniscule part of your financial plan.

It may surprise you to learn that when you reach the age to qualify for Social Security benefits, if your income from it and other sources is insufficient for you to live in financial dignity, making it necessary for you to continue to work, you will forfeit all or most of your Social Security benefits each month until you reach age 72.

Today more than 2¼ million of our citizens over 65 are caught in this financial trap, forcing them to lose their Social Security benefits. Most of them paid into the system their hard-earned dollars all of their working years. But they are disqualified from receiving their benefits because these are not enough to keep body and soul together, for their average Social Security payment is only $254 per month.

If they had made provisions outside of Social Security, they could be receiving unlimited income from capital in the form of dividends, interest, and royalties and still receive their Social Security checks.

You may live a long time; yet longevity may be a mixed blessing. You may decide how long you will work, or it may be decided for you, but the decision of how long you will live is not in your hands.

Present-day medical science is getting so good at making us live longer that for every ten years we live, they add another four years to our life expectancy. Medical science may be adding years to your life, but it is still up to you to add some life to those years. Money is a necessity. It will not of itself bring you happiness—it will only give you options. However, I have yet to meet a person who found joy in poverty.

3 FINANCIAL PERIODS

Age 1–25	25–65	65–?
LEARN	EARN	YEARN or GOLDEN

Have you ever considered what the difference in the eyes of the world is between an "old man" and an "elderly gentleman"? It's no other than income.

THREE SOURCES OF INCOME

If you'll stand back and objectively analyze sources of income, you will find that there are three chief sources.

The first is you at work. However, there will come a time that regardless of how badly you want to work, the world will not let you. It will retire you.

The second source is your money at work. If you make proper preparation and turn some of your income into growing investments, a time will come when you will no longer have to work for your money, but you can trade places with your money and let your money work for you. I have found that income from capital is immensely more secure than income from labor.

The third source of income is charity.

Man at work, money at work, charity—which source do you want to depend on at age 65? Since "man at work" may not be an option open to you and "charity" has rarely brought happiness, apply your intelligence toward assuring yourself that there is sufficient "money at work" to retire in financial dignity.

During my years of financial counseling, I've searched for the reasons so many are failing to become financially independent. I felt if

I could discover the answer to this question, I could help thousands of people avoid living twenty to thirty years of their lives in the tragic state of financial insecurity and enable them to retire in financial dignity.

SIX REASONS SO MANY FAIL

I believe I have found the reasons. There are six, and here they are: (1) procrastination; (2) failure to establish a definite financial goal; (3) ignorance of what money must do to accomplish that goal; (4) failure to understand and apply our tax laws; (5) investment in the wrong kind of life insurance; and (6) failure to develop a winning mentality about money. When you have completed reading this book, you will know how to avoid all these reasons for failure and have a definite blueprint for financial success.

Procrastination

Procrastination can be your greatest deterrent to reaching your goal of financial independence. Time can be your greatest ally. If you have a sufficient amount of time, you will not need as large an amount of money to put to work. The less time you have, the more money it will take. Do not waste this precious commodity—a commodity that is distributed to each of us equally.

Procrastination is a deadly enemy of your obligation to be able to retire in financial dignity. Sometimes you may confuse goals and obligations. A larger home, a boat, travel to foreign lands—all of these can be your goals. But preparing to retire in financial dignity is more than a goal. It is your obligation, a debt that you owe yourself and others—your family, your community, and other taxpayers. With proper financial planning and sound money management, it is a debt that you can pay, making your retirement years happy instead of haphazard, comfortable instead of dependent.

I have observed that in the early years of life, when spending habits are formed, thoughts of retirement are far away and have little relationship to current needs and even less to future needs. The habit becomes reinforced with the same passing of time that brings retirement closer. Then when retirement time is so near as to be of immediate concern, it is often too late to make adequate preparation.

Procrastination always stands in the shadows, awaiting its opportunity to spoil your chance for success. You will probably go through life as a failure if you wait for the "time to be right" to start doing something worthwhile. Do not wait. The time will never be "just right" to start your journey down the road to financial independence.

Failure to Establish a Goal

The second reason so many fail to become financially independent is that they fail to establish a goal. If you aim at nothing in life, you are just liable to hit nothing. I've never had anyone come to me and say, "Venita, I plan to fail." Yet I've observed many who failed to plan, and unfortunately the results will be dismally the same.

When I was the moderator for my television show "Successful Texans," I made a very interesting discovery. My guests were very different in their appearances, voices, heights, weights, educations, and family backgrounds. But they always had one thing in common: each of them knew where he was going. Each had a goal. If anything sidetracked them or if something didn't work the way they had planned, they just dusted themselves off and went right back in the direction of their goal. After many years of observation, I am in complete agreement with the famous psychologist William James, who said, "anything the mind can believe and conceive, it can achieve." Visualize your financial goal right now. For your mind will not let you conceive what you cannot achieve.

A cook will never bake an apple pie until he decides to bake an apple pie. The recipe book will stay on the shelf and the apples will stay in the fruit bowl. The same is true of you. You'll never become financially independent until you decide to become financially secure.

The Plan. Success in money management is not a will-o'-the wisp that comes to some and not to others because of fate, chance, or luck. If you've held this idea in the past, do get rid of it now. Success in money management can be predicted, but you must have a plan and you must follow that plan.

If you give a blueprint to a skillful builder, do you think that it will be a matter of chance, or luck, that he will complete the structure successfully? Of course not. He merely begins at the beginning and follows the plan step by step to its completion.

This book is your blueprint for success. If you follow it, financial independence will be yours.

Ignorance About Money

The third reason that I have found that so many are failing is ignorance of what money must do to accomplish a financial goal.

There is an educational void in our nation. As a matter of fact, we are raising a nation of financial illiterates. Even our college graduates cannot figure simple percentages.

The tragic mistakes they are making because of these deficiencies in our system are destroying their dreams, their hopes, their families, and their pride in themselves and their country. Their hoped-for rewards from their talents and skills are disappearing like vapor. From my years as a stockbroker and later a financial planner, I have observed daily the devastating effect of this void.

Our schools are doing a tremendous job of teaching the know-how of a vocation. They are offering their students a vast array of opportunities to prepare themselves for the career of their choice, from basic mechanics to electronics. They are offering them the opportunity to acquire knowledge in a vast array of fields such as engineering, chemistry, computer technology, sales, distribution, management, and accounting. They are even offering students courses that will prepare them to live enriched lives through the study of music and the various arts.

Yet it is not teaching them the one subject that they will need to live well in our free enterprise system—and that is how to manage their money. This vacuum is so great that the average couple cannot begin to defend themselves against the financial uncertainties of our complex society.

This lack of financial know-how is destroying the American dream and causing these financially illiterate citizens to vote to destroy our free enterprise system. Any person is against anything he does not understand and in which he feels he cannot participate. The destruction of this system would be one of the greatest tragedies to beset our world.

The free enterprise system is not perfect by any stretch of the imagination, but it is the best system yet devised for bringing the greatest good to the greatest number of people.

As Josh Billings, the nineteenth century American humorist once said, "The trouble with most folks isn't so much their ignorance, as knowing so many things that ain't so."

Failure to Learn Our Tax Laws

The fourth reason so many fail to achieve financial independence is their failure to learn and apply our tax laws. The only money you'll ever get to spend at the grocery store is what the government lets you keep. Every investment you make must be carefully correlated with you tax bracket or you are making the wrong investment. You must learn to avoid taxes—not evade them. There could be a difference of around fifteen years if you make that decision—learn to defer taxes, convert to classifications where the taxes are lower, and learn to think in terms of tax equivalents. You'll find throughout this book how to invest for "keepable" income, especially in Chapters 12 and 21, "Avoiding the One-Way Trip to Washington" and "Your Diagram for Financial Independence."

Contrary to any misleading headlines you may read, your taxes will not be cut appreciably in the decade of the '80s. Even without further legislation, taxes will go up, thanks both to the Social Security tax, increases already enacted, and inflation pushing your income into higher tax brackets. The massive tax increase in the guise of a mislabeled "windfall-profits tax" (on which there can be a tax without a profit) is really a sales tax on gasoline, heating oil, and other petroleum products.

The real burden of taxes is what the government spends, not what it takes in as taxes. If government spends more than it takes in, you and I pay the difference in the form of inflation and the interest expense on the national debt.

The Wrong Kind of Life Insurance

The fifth reason I have found that people fail to become financially independent is that they were sold the wrong kind of life insurance. I say "sold" because if they had received sufficient information about the purpose of life insurance and how each policy was put together, they would not have made the tragic mistakes that they have made.

My publisher excerpted and made available for distribution Chapter 13, "Life Insurance—The Great National Consumer Fraud," from my two previous books. Over a million copies are now in circulation across the United States. I am delighted with the fantastic impact this chapter has made and is continuing to make, and the number of families that will have a better opportunity to achieve financial independence because they have followed my instructions. I have changed the title of this chapter slightly for this book because those who profit so handsomely from selling the wrong kind of insurance have been able to get it banned or its use curtailed in eight states. It is my hope that the change from "fraud" to "dilemma" will somewhat reduce their success and make it possible for more families to benefit from the information it contains. You'll learn all you need to know about life insurance when you read Chapter 13 of this book.

Failure to Develop a Winning Mentality

The sixth reason that I have found that people fail to win the money game is their failure to develop a winning mentality. The demarcation line between success and failure is often very narrow and can be crossed if the desire can be stimulated, competent guidance made available, and sufficient encouragement and incentive provided.

There are many vital parts to the psychology of winning. Some of the most important when it comes to becoming financially independent are attitude, effort, enthusiasm, lack of prejudice, and persistence.

Attitude. There is a truly magic word that you should place not only in your vocabulary, but also in the very fiber of your being if you desire to be successful in the realm of money or any other important area of your life. That magic word is ATTITUDE!

Everything in life operates on the law of cause and effect. You must produce the causes; the rewards will take care of themselves. Good attitude leads to good results; fair attitude, to fair results; bad attitude, to bad results.

You will shape your own financial life by the attitudes that you hold each day. If you have a poor attitude toward learning about money management, you will not learn very much until you change your attitude. If you have an attitude of failure, you are defeated before you start.

Sometimes a prospective client will say, "If I invest, the market will go down. I've never made any money in the market." Until he can change his attitude, he will not become a successful investor. I have found that truly prepared, working optimists always make money. I have also found that pessimists rarely do.

Look around you. Study successful people. You'll find that they go sailing through life from one success to another. These people have the attitude that they can accomplish whatever they set out to do. Because of this attitude, they do accomplish their goals. They achieve some remarkable things and the world calls them successful, brilliant, lucky, and so on.

Luck. As I've already mentioned, I do not believe in luck. Luck happens when preparedness and opportunity get together. If you are prepared, you will be lucky. A close friend of mine, who is a well-known and respected business consultant, studied a particular company and bought shares of stock while it was still in its infancy. These shares have now grown tremendously in value and have made him a very wealthy man. There are those who would scoff and say, "I should be so lucky." It wasn't just luck. He was prepared. When he and his wife were first married, they scrimped and saved and lived in a modest apartment. They even sold their car and rode the bus to work so they could save a nest egg. It was this nest egg, which they had so painfully saved, that was used to make their "lucky" investment.

Had they not prepared, they would not have had the means of availing themselves of all this "luck." Remember our example of the wood burning stove: you must put in the wood before you can warm yourself.

Prejudice. We all have prejudices, but we should continually work to rid ourselves of them. In counseling, I sometimes encounter a couple who seem to be saying to me, "Please don't confuse us with facts." They do not want to know the truth. The truth will not make them free, regardless of how carefully or intelligently it may be presented to them.

Lack of Concentrated Efforts. To become a good investor, you must seriously apply your intelligence, use your ability to acquire knowledge, and give your attention to details and timing. If you cannot, will not, or do not have the ability to do these things successfully for yourself, do not take a distorted ego trip by not admitting that someone may be able to do something better than you can do it. Put the professionals to work for you.

Desiring Something for Nothing. If I were to distill all the wisdom I've ever learned into nine words, they would be: There is no such thing as a free lunch. I have observed two drives where this is evident. One is the gambling instinct, which has driven many to failure in the market. Investing, properly approached with constant supervision, is in my opinion the safest long-term thing that can be done with money. Speculation, on the other hand, can be risky.

This desire for a "free lunch" is often seen working in the opposite manner by those who will leave their funds in a savings institution because they refuse to pay a brokerage commission to get their funds invested. The money that they "save" is often very costly.

In making an investment decision, the important factor is not what it "costs." You do not care what it costs, but you are truly concerned with what it pays.

Lack of Enthusiasm. I do believe I can forgive almost any shortcoming a person may have except lack of enthusiasm; and it is especially essential in the acquisition of money. Enthusiasm is contagious; if you have it in sufficient quantities, others will welcome you into their group. You will be more in touch with the needs and thinking of the people around you, and you can profit from the investment opportunities that will become obvious to you.

Guessing Instead of Thinking.   Information is available about almost any subject you need. Don't let indifference or plain laziness keep you from acquiring the facts essential to making good judgments. Acquire the major points of information you need—you'll never have "all" the information. If you wait that long, you'll probably make your decision too late for maximum profit. I find that most decisions are made too late rather than too soon. We all have a tendency to have a good laugh when someone says, "Do something, even if it's wrong." I have found that there is usually more merit in this than is apparent on first blush. As Emerson said, "Do the thing and you will have the power."

Lack of Capital.   Build up your nest egg, and do it while you are young. Don't spend the nest egg, but use it for collateral to leverage for a larger egg and then a larger one. Never consider any earnings on your investments as spendable until you have reached your goal of financial independence. Your banker will also usually welcome you with open arms if you have collateral to back your bankable idea.

Being Overinfluenced by the Opinions of Others.   I have observed that those who fail to accumulate sufficient amounts of money are easily influenced by the opinions of other people. Opinions are cheap. You will find them everywhere. There are always those who are just waiting to foist their opinions on you if you will accept them. If you let others overinfluence you when you are reaching decisions about your money, you will not succeed.

Lack of Persistence.   Are you a good "starter" and a poor "finisher," as so many are? Each year we must close our reservations early for our January financial planning seminars because we cannot seat all those who want to come. This year our overflow seminar in addition to our regular three-session seminar had 700 people in it.

If you begin a financial planning program and happen to experience a temporary setback, do not give up. I've observed this at times when a client starts a monthly investment program. If the market goes up after he starts his program, he'll happily put in his investment each month, but if the market goes down, he'll abandon the program, regardless of how I've tried to explain that dollar-cost-averaging results can benefit from stock market fluctuations. There is no substitute for persistence. If you make persistence your watchword, you'll discover that "old man failure" will finally become weary of you and will make his exit. Failure cannot cope with persistence.

Inability to Make a Decision. I have found over and over again that those who succeed in making large sums of money or in a chosen profession reach decisions promptly and change them, if at all, very slowly. I have found that those who fail reach decisions, if at all, very slowly and change them frequently and quickly. Procrastination and indecision are twins. Pluck this grim pair out of your life before they bind you to the treadmill of financial failure.

Yesterday is past, tomorrow is only a promise. Only today is legal tender. Only this moment of time is yours. Where you will be financially next year or ten years from now will depend on the decisions that you make today—or the ones you don't make.

Of the many studies of successful people, near the top of the list of characteristics is their ability to be decisive. Of the many studies of failures, at the top of the list of reasons for their failure is procrastination.

Making a decision is a privilege. No one can make your decisions for you. You will find that free advice about your money is always available. It's usually those who lean back and give you the most "positive" advice whose finances are bordering on catastrophe. They are often wrong, but never in doubt.

There are times when I, or one of our team of financial planners, have counseled a couple who have attended all three sessions of our investment seminar and thus have listened to me for at least five hours. They have asked for an appointment, and one of us has spent two hours with them in an uninterrupted personal conference. When it comes time to apply this information to their own personal finances, they will say, "This sounds fine, but let us go home and think it over." On the surface this sounds like a prudent, sensible thing to do, doesn't it? However, I find that it usually is not. They already have all the information they need. They will not be "thinking it over" after they leave. Dozens of other matters will require their attention. They are trying to avoid making a decision, not realizing that no decision is a decision. They are deciding that where their money is now is the best place for it to be—for that is the result brought about by their lack of action. Always remember, indecision is decision—usually against you.

Overcaution. The person who takes no chances generally must take whatever is left over after others have finished choosing. Overcaution is as bad, if not worse, than lack of caution. Both should be

avoided. Life will always contain an element of chance. Not to win is not a sin. But not to try is a tragedy.

If you've never missed when investing, you've not been in there trying, or you've been holding your losers far too long for maximum profits. Play the money game well, but never safely. Avoid a life of no hits, no runs, no errors!

The reason many are not successful investors is that they are afraid to do anything with their money, so they leave it in the bank or savings and loan for years, where inflation destroys it. That's not playing it safe. That's playing it dumb.

Lack of Self-Discipline. Another cause of failure is lack of self-discipline. The secret of financial independence is not brilliance or luck, but the discipline to save a part of all you earn and to put it to work in shares of American industry, real estate, natural resources, collectibles, etc.

To be a winner, you must practice self-discipline. Self-discipline achieves goals. There are those who think of self-discipline as "doing without." To me, it is "doing within." It's a mental and physical process. It's your own vivid visualization of financial independence. Winners are those who are doing within while they are doing without.

Expectations. The successful people with whom I have visited seem to find their accomplishments not too difficult and often surprisingly easy, simply because it seems so few are really trying.

Winners look at life as a game—one they expect to win, are prepared to win, desire to win, and know how to win. They have conscientiously nurtured and developed the habit of winning.

Money. Rid yourself of the old myth, if it has been plaguing you, that money is not important. It is important—vitally important! It is just as important as the food it buys, the shelter it provides, the doctor bills it pays, and the education it helps to procure. Money is important to you as you live in a civilized society. To split hairs and say that it is not as important as other things is just arguing for the sake of the exercise. Nothing will take the place of money in areas in which money works.

What is money? Money is the harvest of your production. The amount of money you will receive will always be in direct ratio to the need for what you do, your ability to do it, and the difficulty of replacing you.

I'm amazed at the number of people who tell me that they want money but don't want to take the time and trouble to qualify for it. Until they qualify for it, there's no way they can earn it.

All you need is a plan—a road map—and the courage to arrive at your destination, knowing in advance that there will be problems and setbacks, but knowing also that nothing can stand in the way of your completing your plan if it it backed by persistence and determination.

Keep money in its proper place. It is a servant, nothing more. It is a tool with which you can live better and see more of the world around you. Money is necessary in your modern life. But you need only so much of it to live comfortably, securely, and well. Too much emphasis on money can reverse your whole picture and make you the servant and your money your master.

You do want to have money and the things it can buy, but you also must check up continually to make sure that you haven't lost the things that money cannot buy.

HOW MUCH MONEY WILL YOU NEED?

Since one of your objectives is to have sufficient funds to retire in financial dignity, you might ask how much will it take? I really don't know, but let's see if we can get a bit of a handle on the situation.

The amount of money you will need at retirement time will depend on the standard of living you wish to maintain, the number of years before you retire, the amount of destruction inflation will have brought to the purchasing power of money, your ability and willingness to apply what you'll learn in this book to produce the maximum income and growth during retirement, and the number of years you will live.

To get some idea of the amount that may be required, let's begin with what you would need if you were retiring today and then adjust your figures by what you feel the future rate of inflation will be.

Table 1–1 shows rates of inflation from 5 to 15 percent (18 percent was the rate that greeted you as you entered the decade of the '80s).

To make your calculations, subtract your age from 65 to obtain the number of years before retirement (if this is the age at which you plan to retire). Read across the top and find the rate of inflation you feel it is safe for you to assume. There you will find how many dollars

TABLE 1–1. ADDITIONAL INCOME NEEDED (IN DOLLARS) AT RETIREMENT, WITH VARIOUS INFLATION RATES

Years Until Retirement	5%	8%	10%	12%	15%
10	1.63	2.16	2.59	3.11	4.05
11	1.71	2.33	2.85	2.48	4.65
12	1.80	2.52	3.14	3.90	5.35
13	1.89	2.72	3.45	4.36	6.15
14	1.98	2.94	3.80	4.89	7.08
15	2.08	3.17	4.18	5.47	8.14
16	2.18	3.43	4.60	6.13	9.36
17	2.29	3.70	5.05	6.87	10.77
18	2.41	4.00	5.56	7.69	12.38
19	2.53	4.32	6.12	8.61	14.23
20	2.65	4.66	6.73	9.65	16.37
21	2.79	5.03	7.40	10.80	18.82
22	2.93	5.44	8.14	12.10	21.64
23	3.07	5.87	8.95	13.55	24.89
24	3.23	6.34	9.85	15.18	28.63
25	3.39	6.85	10.83	17.00	32.92
26	3.56	7.40	11.92	19.04	37.86
27	3.73	7.99	13.11	21.32	43.54
28	3.92	8.63	14.42	23.88	50.07
29	4.12	9.32	15.86	26.75	57.58
30	4.32	10.06	17.45	29.96	66.22
31	4.54	10.87	19.19	33.56	76.14
32	4.76	11.74	21.11	37.58	87.57
33	5.00	12.68	23.23	42.09	100.70
34	5.25	13.69	25.55	47.14	115.80
35	5.52	14.79	28.10	52.80	133.18

it will take then to buy the same amount of groceries that a dollar buys today.

For example, assume that you would need $2000 per month if you were retiring today, that you are age 45, that you plan to retire in 20 years at age 65, and that you feel the government can slow inflation to 5 percent. (Unfortunately, not many economists today would agree.) Go down the left-hand column to 20 and across four columns to 2.65, your adjustment factor. Now let's adjust: $2000 × 2.65 = $5300. This would be the amount you would need per month in 20 years to obtain the same housing, food, and clothing as you do with $2000 today.

Inflation will probably not accommodate you by stopping when you retire, so you should plan for an additional amount to cover continued inflation.

How Much Capital Does This Require?

What goal should you set for yourself to have a monthly income of approximately $5300 per month at age 65? Assume also that you will not receive a pension from your company. How much capital will it take to produce $5300 per month?

Shall we use a 6 percent yield? If so, we will need $1,060,000 of capital ($5300 × 200 = $1,060,000). At an 8 percent yield, we can reduce this amount to $795,000. That's a lot of capital. Before you become discouraged, remember that you have 20 years before you need it, and if you decide to use a portion of your principal each month during retirement, this amount can be reduced. There is nothing sacred about principal. The sacred thing is to make you and it come out together!

Incidentally, since my first book was published back in 1975, we have received thousands of calls asking why I multiplied the monthly income desired by 200 to obtain the amount of capital required. If you'll take 12 and divide by the rate of return and multiply your answer by the monthly amount, it will give you the amount of capital required to produce that monthly income. For example, 12 ÷ .06 = 200. $5300 × 200 = $1,060,000, the capital needed to produce $5300 per month at 6 percent. At 8 percent, you would multiply by 150 (12 ÷ .08).

Monthly Savings Needed

How much will you need to invest each month if you average 6 percent on your investment (see Table 1–2)? (Surely when you've completed this book you will be able to at least double that amount.)

As you can see, time is a powerful ally in accomplishing your goal.

TABLE 1–2. MONTHLY SAVINGS NEEDED AT SIX PERCENT INTEREST
(COMPOUNDED ANNUALLY) TO ATTAIN PREDETERMINED
AMOUNT OF CAPITAL

AGE NOW	YEARS TO RETIRE-MENT	MONTHS TO RETIRE-MENT	*Desired Amount*			
			$200,000	$300,000	$500,000	$1,000,000
25	40	480	$ 102	$ 153	$ 255	$ 510
30	35	420	140	210	350	700
35	30	360	198	297	495	990
40	25	300	286	429	715	1430
45	20	240	426	639	1065	2130
50	15	180	674	1011	1685	3370
55	10	120	1192	1788	2980	5960

If your goal is $300,000 and you begin when you are 25, you can reach
it by saving $153 per month. If you wait until 40, you will need to save
$429 per month.

If you put your money to work at 12 percent, and you must, you
can either reduce the amount you must invest by half or your goal can
be $600,000 when you retire.

TIME, NOT INSTANT PUDDING

Time can be a great ally in accomplishing your financial goal. Use
it to your advantage, rather than trying to reach your goal fast, as tempt-
ing as that may be.

You will be tempted, for we live in an age of "instants." We drink
instant coffee, eat instant pudding, spoon instant soup. Do not make
the mistake of trying to carry this over to your money world. It takes
time to accumulate a living estate. Many have difficulty accepting this
fact of life. Many of our citizens have adopted an attitude of impatience,
perhaps at the cost of serenity and physical and mental well-being. On
the other hand, impatience to get things done deserves much of the
credit for the achievements of Americans in building the wealthiest nation in the world.

Time is important. As a matter of fact, it is the first ingredient of
my formula for financial independence.

FORMULA FOR FINANCIAL INDEPENDENCE

This is my formula that I have used over the years that has been so valuable to me and my clients:

Time + Money + American free enterprise =
Opportunity to become financially independent.

Let's take a good look at what effect time, the rate of return, and the amount of money you have to put to work will have in accomplishing your financial goal.

Time—The First Ingredient. If you are young and have only a small amount of money to invest, don't despair, for you possess one of the most important ingredients for financial independence—the ingredient of TIME. It doesn't take much money to compound to a tidy sum if you have time for it to grow. A savings of $20 per month started at age 25 is equivalent to $60 a month started at age 35, $200 at age 45, and $850 at age 55 (as pictured in Figure 1–1). Or, if we calculate the importance of time in reverse, a savings of $50 a month for ten years at 12 percent is less than $25 a month for fifteen years.

Perhaps you have a lump sum of $10,000. Let's look at the difference time makes in your results:

Years	At 6 Percent
10	$ 17,908
20	32,071
30	57,434
40	102,857

These figures point out the importance of starting as early as you can to reach your predetermined goal. I hope you are granted a large amount of this first ingredient, and that you learn early the importance of putting each day of it to maximum use.

Money is the second ingredient—an ingredient that you have every payday or that you have acquired through previous paydays of your own or your industrious and generous forefathers.

Your next challenge is to put this money to work for yourself as hard as you no doubt had to work to get it. To become financially independent, you must save and let your money grow. Unfortunately, I observe many people who save and let savings institutions grow, building magnificent skyscrapers that add impressively to our skyline.

Rate of Return

The rate of return that you receive on your funds will be determined by how skillfully you put your money to work under our free enterprise system.

You've earned your "gold stars"

You have looked at how important time is in the accomplishment of your goal; now let's introduce another important factor, the rate of return, and look at the difference an additional 6 percent can make:

$10,000 LUMP SUM INVESTED AT 6 PERCENT AND 12 PERCENT

Years	At 6 Percent	At 12 Percent	Difference
10	$ 17,908	$ 31,058	$ 13,150
20	32,071	96,462	64,391
30	57,434	299,599	242,165
40	102,857	930,509	827,652

If we assume that you can invest $100 per month, your results would be:

$100 PER MONTH INVESTED AT 6 PERCENT AND 12 PERCENT

Years	Amount Invested	At 6 Percent	At 12 Percent	Difference
10	$12,000	$ 16,766	$ 23,586	$ 6,820
20	24,000	46,791	96,838	50,047
30	36,000	100,562	324,351	223,789
40	48,000	196,857	1,030,970	834,113

Don't Fight the Battle Alone. Are you amazed at the difference an additional 6 percent can make in your results?

At 6 percent you contributed $48,000 in forty years, and the savings institution contributed $148,857 from their profits by investing your money in American industry, real estate, and natural resources.

On the other hand, if you obtained 12 percent on your investment, you contributed $48,000, and you let American industry, real estate, and natural resources contribute $982,970 to your wealth, for a difference of $834,113.

It is not necessary to fight the battle alone if you will apply the information contained in this book so that American free enterprise can be of help to you.

THE EIGHTH WONDER

One of the best ways to obtain a graphic picture of the importance of the rate of return is to study compound interest tables. Compound interest tables are fascinating. In my opinion, the "eighth wonder of the world" is not the Astrodome, but compound interest. Tables 1 through 6 in the Appendix show compound interest results and will be of immeasurable help to you in your financial programming. Don't yield to the temptation of saying, "Oh, I probably can't understand them," and flip casually by. Take a moment now to study them and you'll be surprised to find some real jewels of information. I'll help you apply the information so you won't have to go it alone.

Lump Sum Investment

Table 1 in the Appendix will show you how much a $10,000 lump sum will grow over the years at varying rates of return. If you haven't yet saved $10,000, just keep dropping zeros until you reach your category. If you are fortunate enough to have $100,000, just add a zero.

For example, if you have $10,000 to invest for a goal that is twenty years away and you can average 12 percent on your money, you will have $96,462 when that time arrives, exclusive of taxes. If you have thirty years, that $10,000 will grow to $299,599; in forty years it will be $930,509.

Monthly Investment Results

Let's assume you do not have a lump sum, but can invest $1200 a year, for an average of $100 per month.

Again, if you average 12 percent over a twenty-year period, your results will be $96,838; in thirty years, $324,351; and in forty years, $1,030,970. As you can see, the secret of financial independence is not brilliance or luck, but the discipline to save a portion of all you earn and put it to work aggressively.

Annual Investment Required

In the Appendix you'll find two other very interesting compound interest, or yield, tables. Table 3 enables you to determine how much you'll need to save per year to accomplish your predetermined goal. This table is done on a $100,000 basis. Just multiply to adjust to your goal. For example, you've determined you'll need $500,000 when you retire in twenty years, and you feel you can average a minimum of 12 percent on your investments. That would mean that you must save $6195, or $516 per month to accomplish your goal. If you started thirty years before retirement, you could reduce this to $154 per month.

Lump Sum Required

Further, let's assume you would like to know what lump sum you would need to invest at various rates of return to equal a given amount at the end of a specified period.

Again, if you have twenty years before retirement and you can average 12 percent on your investments and desire $500,000, you will need to make a lump sum investment of $51,835. To point out the importance of time, if you had started thirty years before you would only need a lump sum investment of $16,700.

THREE THINGS YOU CAN DO WITH A DOLLAR

There are only three things you can do with a dollar—spend, loan, or own. If you decide to spend your dollars, I hope you've had a good time, but you have cut off our conversation. The only money that I can help you invest is the money you decide to keep. If you decide you are not going to spend it now, but are going to keep it to spend at a later date—not that you are never going to spend it, since that's just too cruel a thought—there are only two things you can do with a dollar: loan or own.

You may "loan" it to a savings institution, placing it in what is commonly called a "guaranteed" fixed position. We'll look at ways this can be done in Chapter 11, "Lending Your Dollars."

You may also place your dollars in a position so that you can "own." You may own shares of American industry, real estate, commodities, energy, diamonds, precious metals, rare stamps, art objects, antiques, and precious gems. We shall discuss the many ways that you can "own" throughout this book.

Let me now share with you the Rule of 72. It's a very simple one that you can use without elaborate compound interest tables.

THE RULE OF 72

I have a degree in Economics and Finance, yet I was never taught this rule in college. It's an extremely valuable rule and you'll find it very useful. The Rule of 72 gives you the answer to the question of how long it will take to double your money—to make $1 become $2—at various rates of return.

If you obtain 1 percent on your money, it will take 72 years for $1 to become $2. If you obtain 1.3 percent, it will take 55.4 years; if

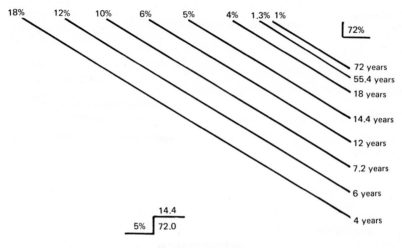

Figure 1–1.

you obtain 6 percent, it will take 12 years; if you obtain 12 percent, it will take six years; and at 18 percent, four years (see Figure 1–1). When you came to 1.3 percent in the example above, did you say to yourself, "In these enlightened times no one would loan money at 1.3 percent." Unless you are one of the informed minority who have read and applied Chapter 13 of this book or my last two books, you are probably loaning your money at 1.3 percent or less on the cash surrender value portion of your life insurance.

With the Rule of 72, you can see that at 6 percent $1000 becomes:

$2000 in 12 years
4000 in 24 years
8000 in 36 years

At 12 percent, $1000 becomes:

$ 2000 in 6 years
4000 in 12 years
8000 in 18 years
16,000 in 24 years
32,000 in 30 years
64,000 in 36 years

As you can see, it does make a difference how well you invest your money.

A couple of variations on the Rule of 72 are the Rule of 144 and the Rule of 116.

THE RULE OF 144

This rule is applicable to annual investments, not lump sum investments. This rule will show you at what time the total amount of money you have invested will approximately double at various rates of return. Divide the interest rate into 144 to find the number of years it takes to approximately double the total amount accumulated. For example, let us assume that you invest $1000 per year at 6 percent. Divide the interest rate into 144, and it equals 24. In 24 years you will have saved $24,000; this should double to $48,000 in 24 more years.

THE RULE OF 116

As inflation becomes more rampant, you may want to think in terms of how long it takes to triple your money. You can calculate the number of years it takes to triple a sum by dividing the rate of return into 116. For example, if you average 12 percent on your money, it will triple in 9.7 years.

WHICH RATE IS SAFER?

Which is the "safest" thing to do with your money—"loan" or "own"?

In the past, has it been safer to "loan" your money to a savings institution at 4 to 6 percent (or even for a brief period of time at 12) or to "own" shares of American industry, real estate, and energy, with the hope of averaging 12 to 30 percent or above? We shall take an in-depth look in this book at which way has truly been the "safest" long-term approach to money management. Suffice it to say here that if you have to wait eighteen years at 4 percent or twelve years at 6 percent for $1 to become $2, you have lost the fight, because inflation has more than doubled your cost of living—to say nothing of your loss through the tax bite.

At 6 percent, your exercise has been similar to the little frog who was trying to hop out of the well. Every time he hopped up one foot, he slid back two. If you ignore that insidious thing called inflation, your money exercises may prove to parallel those of the little frog in the fairy tale of the frog and the princess, but without the kiss of the princess to miraculously make you an affluent prince.

"STABILITY" vs. "SAFETY"

In Chapter 11, "Lending Your Dollars," I'll discuss the matter of stability and safety in more detail, but suffice it to say here that one of the most common mistakes I see made regarding the investment of money is that people confuse two very similar words that have very different meanings. These two words are "stability" and "safety." Stability is the return of the same number of dollars at a point of time in the future. "Safety" is the return of the same amount of food, clothing, and shelter. You can be "stable" and be far from "safe."

THE $200,000 ESTATE

I require my clients to have as their minimum goal a $200,000 estate. I'll have to admit as soon as they reach it, I raise the ante. Your goal must be a minimum of this amount; and the younger you are, the higher your goal must be because inflation will continue to erode your purchasing power. A 6 percent yield on $200,000 is only $1000 per month, and that's not easy street today.

Figure 1–2 is a handy chart showing how much you need to invest annually or monthly to reach a goal of $200,000 at 12 percent.

To all my good engineering friends, let me say that I am quite aware that money does not compound in a straight line, but in a curve. However, I have learned that only a few people can relate to a curve, but almost everyone can relate to a straight line—hence the straight lines. You will find a chart with the proper curves in Chapter 13, "Life Insurance—The Great National Dilemma." In that chapter, I also tell you how to buy time.

PENNIES BECOME MILLIONS

You may have seen this vivid illustration before, but let me repeat it, for it is such a graphic example of compounding.

Let's assume you had a choice of working thirty-five days with a pay of $1000 per day or working for a penny the first day and doubling the amount each day for thirty-five days. Which job offer would you take?

If you took the first choice, at the end of the thirty-fifth day you would have received $35,000. What would you have received if you had made the second choice? You would have received

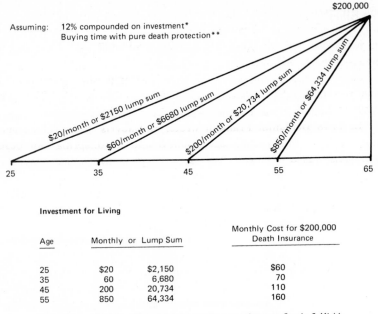

$200,000

Assuming: 12% compounded on investment*
            Buying time with pure death protection**

$20/month or $2150 lump sum

$60/month or $6680 lump sum

$200/month or $20,734 lump sum

$850/month or $64,334 lump sum

25   35   45   55   65

Investment for Living

Age	Monthly	or	Lump Sum	Monthly Cost for $200,000 Death Insurance
25	$20		$2,150	$60
35	60		6,680	70
45	200		20,734	110
55	850		64,334	160

*University of Michigan, Bureau of Business Research. *Common Stocks & Yields.*
**Based on rates of a leading insurance company.

Figure 1–2.

$339,456,652.80. As you can see, one penny compounded at 100 percent per day produces over a third of a billion dollars by the thirty-fifth day. I realize this is an exaggerated example, but your rate of earnings is very important today in your quest for financial independence.

Get to know and fully comprehend interest rates, leverage, and how to compound your capital through good investments.

To Be More Specific

Perhaps your timetable does not fit into neat little five- and ten-year segments, and the money you have to invest is not blocks of $10,000 lump sum or $100 per month. In the Appendix you'll find tables that give you the necessary numbers to calculate a lump sum investment at various rates of return from 2½ to 15 percent and from one to fifty years. The first is Table 5, titled "One Dollar Principal Compounded Annually." For example, if you have seventeen years before retirement and have $14,000 you can put to work for that purpose, your factor would be 6.8660. $14,000 × 6.8660 = $96,124 in seventeen years at 12 percent.

Let's assume that you can invest an additional $160 per month.

Look at Table 6, titled "One Dollar Per Annum Compounded Annually." Go down the 12 percent column until you are opposite seventeen years and you will find your factor of 54.7497. $160 per month times 54.7497 is $105,119.

So in seventeen years with a $10,000 lump sum investment to which you added $160 per month, you would have $201,243 (exclusive of taxes).

In 1748 Benjamin Franklin wrote, "Money is of a prolific, generating nature. Money can beget money, and its offspring can beget more." His was a definition and joyous explanation of the nature of money and one that can be of great value to you. Franklin's words "Money is of a prolific, generating nature" have a biblical ring to them, as well they may, because it is in the Bible that we first become aware that we are required to be good stewards of money.

YOU ARE THE STEWARD

I firmly believe that every dollar that comes your way comes there for a purpose. A portion of that dollar should be spent for the necessities of life, a portion for luxuries, a portion should be given away, and a portion should be invested for tomorrow's goods and services. I am also thoroughly convinced that you are the steward of every dollar that comes your way, and if you are not a good steward of that money it will be taken away from you.

The story of the talents in the Bible are as true today as they were when they were recorded. In Matthew 25:14-29 you will find these words:

Again, the Kingdom of Heaven can be illustrated by the story of a man going into another country, who called together his servants and loaned them money to invest for him while he was gone. He gave $5000 to one, $2000 to another, and $1000 to the last—dividing it in proportion to their abilities—and then left on his trip. The man who received the $5000 began immediately to buy and sell with it and soon earned another $5000. The man with $2000 went right to work, too, and earned another $2000.

But the man who received the $1000 dug a hole in the ground and hid the money for safekeeping. After a long time their master returned from his trip and called them to him to account for his money. The man to whom he had entrusted the $5000 brought him $10000.

His master praised him for good work. "You have been faithful in handling this small amount," he told him, "so now I will give you many more responsibilities. Begin the joyous tasks I have

assigned to you." Next came the man who had received $2000, with the report, "Sir, you gave me $2000 to use, and I have doubled it."

Good work, his master said. "You are a good and faithful servant. You have been faithful over this small amount, so now I will give you much more."

Then the man with the $1000 came and said, 'Sir, I knew you were a hard man, and I was afraid you would rob me of what I earned, so I hid your money in the earth and here it is." But his master replied, "Wicked man! Lazy slave! Since you knew I would demand your profit, you should at least have put my money into the bank so I could have some interest. Take the money from this man and give it to the man with the $10,000. For the man who uses well what he is given shall be given more, and he shall have abundance. But from the man who is unfaithful, even what little responsibility he has shall be taken from him."

Let's analyze what the master considered good stewardship. He praised the two who "bought and sold" with the money entrusted to them, and gave them more. He severely reprimanded the one who dug a hole and buried the money, saying, "You should at least have put the money into the bank so I could have some interest." Note, however, that this was not what he recommended. Had the servant lived in the United States during the period when our banks paid 3 percent interest, in order for the money to have doubled, the master would have to have taken a twenty-four-year trip. Even if he had earned up to 5 percent, it would have taken 14.4 years. And at 8 percent it woud have been a nine year trip. By most standards these would be very long trips.

Table 1–3 shows the rates paid by savings and loan associations and by banks from 1947 through 1979.

SUMMARY

In this first chapter you and I have come a long way toward determining what your goal must be to attain financial independence. We've had to cover a few charts and tables to give a perspective to your challenge and to give you the assurance that you'll win the money game.

You've already seen that it will be necessary for you to save for the future so that you can fulfill your obligation to yourself, to your family, and to society. But you've also seen that you have all the requirements for financial independence and that you will not have to fight this battle alone. Your dollars can have fantastic earning power if you employ them properly—and this book will teach you how.

APPLICATION

All the knowledge in the world will do you no good unless you apply it to your own particular set of circumstances. So at the end of each chapter I'll give you some questions to answer, some financial data to collect, and some specific tasks to perform.

TABLE 1–3. INTEREST RATES (PERCENT) PAID BY SAVINGS
AND LOAN ASSOCIATIONS AND BY BANKS

Year	Savings Accounts in Savings Associations	Deposits in Commercial Banks
1947	2.3%	0.9%
1948	2.3	0.9
1949	2.4	0.9
1950	2.5	0.9
1951	2.6	1.1
1952	2.7	1.2
1953	2.8	1.2
1954	2.9	1.3
1955	2.9	1.4
1956	3.0	1.6
1957	3.3	2.1
1958	3.38	2.21
1959	3.53	2.36
1960	3.86	2.56
1961	3.90	2.71
1962	4.08	3.18
1963	4.17	3.31
1964	4.19	3.42
1965	4.23	3.69
1966	4.45	4.04
1967	4.67	4.24
1968	4.68	4.48
1969	4.80	4.87
1970	5.06	4.95
1971	5.33	4.78
1972	5.40	4.65
1973	5.50	5.12
1974	5.55	5.15
1975	5.25	5.00
1976	5.25	5.00
1977	5.25	5.00
1978	5.50	5.25
1979	5.50	5.25

May I suggest that you obtain a loose leaf notebook and that you paste these words on the outside:

(Your name)   's Progress Report Toward Financial
Independence.

Begin your notebook by listing the following questions and your answers to them. This notebook is for your eyes only, or for yours and those of your spouse if you are married, so be very honest with yourself and very specific.

1. What source or sources of income do I want to depend on at age 65?
2. How many years before I plan to retire?
3. What monthly income would I like to have if I were retiring today?
4. What inflation factor do I feel best applies to me?
5. How much will I need per month at retirement?
6. If I choose the guaranteed route, how much capital will be required?
7. What rate of growth on my investments is my minimum objective?
8. If I choose the variable route, how much capital will be required?
9. How much can I put to work today? (a) Lump sum (b) Monthly.
10. What books am I going to read to assure myself that I'll develop and keep a winning attitude about money? (To start, you may want to read Dr. Maxwell Maltz' *Psycho-Cybernetics* and Dr. Dennis Wateley's *The Psychology of Winning*.)

2

INFLATION,
THE ROBIN HOOD
OF THE 'EIGHTIES

There are four prime reasons you must learn to invest.

1. To put inflation to work for you.
2. To increase your income.
3. To make your capital grow.
4. To learn to turn your tax liabilities into assets.

In this chapter we'll take an unemotional look at inflation and the devastating path it has cut across the face of the United States, bringing havoc to many a financial plan.

INFLATION, THE ROBIN HOOD OF THE 'EIGHTIES

Inflation was the Robin Hood of the 'seventies and will continue to be the Super Robin Hood of the 'eighties. Accept this fact of life and make your decisions about money accordingly. If I can leave only one thought with you, from your having read this book, it is this: Deal with life as it truly is and not the way you wish it were. This chapter will give you the facts about inflation. This book will enlighten you as to ways that you can make it work for you rather than against you. There is probably nothing in your economic life that can make you as much money as inflation if you understand how it works, learn to embrace it rather than fear it, and harness its energy.

Inflation does not destroy wealth. It does not reduce the number of houses that builders can build, the amount of wheat that farmers can produce, nor the number of telephones that Ma Bell can install. Inflation redistributes wealth. It takes it from those who do not understand how it works and gives it to those who do.

Inflation takes from the ignorant and gives to the well informed. You will either be its victim or its beneficiary. It will make you a winner or a loser. The choice is yours. It's much more fun being a winner. All you need to do is accept the fact that inflation is a fact of your life, an economic force in the world in which you live and that you must protect yourself against it or suffer its dire consequences. It has been your constant companion since the day you were born, and from all indications it will continue with you for the remainder of your life. This problem does not belong to the United States alone, but has been felt worldwide. Tolstoy chronicled that every civilized nation that has ever existed has experienced the ravages of inflation.

Do not be deceived when the nightly news gives a glowing report that inflation has decreased by a percentage point. Inflation will accelerate and decelerate, but the pattern is still upward. Perhaps 12 percent inflation is better than 13 percent, but it still means that your cost of living is doubling every six years!

POOR RICHARD HITS THE FAN

I was raised in the dust bowl of Oklahoma under the Puritan ethics embodied in *Poor Richard's Almanac*—"Work hard, be thrifty, don't borrow."

Were you raised under Poor Richard's guidelines? If you were, throw off his shackles this very minute. He'll drag you down to the bottom of inflation's ocean, and you won't surface in time for resuscitation.

Have you been exposed for years to the "Prudent Man's Rule," so dear to the hearts of regulatory agencies who decide if you have prudently managed pension funds under your trusteeship or other fiduciary responsibilities? If you have, and have faithfully followed the old guidelines of 40 percent in corporate bonds and the remainder in very, very blue chip common stocks, you and the beneficiaries of your pension plan have been losers and from all indications will continue to be losers. The "Prudent Man's Rule" has now become the "Stupid Man's Rule" with the continued battering of double-digit inflation.

You will find the "Poor Richard" and "Prudent Man's" philosophy very hard to escape, for it is all around you. Today as you drive down the freeway to work, strategically positioned at a curve in the road, in brilliant lights, you may see a billboard emblazoned in bold print that reads:

"INVEST IN SERIES E BONDS TO GUARANTEE YOUR FUTURE"

Is this false advertising? Can you name a ten-year period in the past thirty years when investing in a Series E bond has "guaranteed your future?" Can you name even one year in the past decade when, after inflation (and later after taxes), your money maintained the only value worth maintaining—its purchasing power?

I read an interview recently where the U.S. Savings Bonds people were asked, "Does it pay to save with the inflation rates exceeding 18 percent and Savings Bonds paying 6 percent?" And the added question was put to them, "Under these circumstances can you really say you are saving?"

The Savings Bond spokesman's reply was, "Yes, for if you didn't save, you'd be that much farther behind." It would appear that he was conceding that a loss was involved, but he insisted a loss could be a gain.

If it doesn't pay to save, you might be asking, does it pay to spend? Often it does, if you have exchanged your paper money for something more durable that has an opportunity to retain its value—if you have moved your money out of paper and into things in other words. Once you have brought yourself to making this decision, you have opened yourself to a wide range of other decisions: Which things? When? At what price? At what location? This book should give you some of the answers. You live in a world of change. Every day is a new day. That's why my profession as a Certified Financial Planner is such an exciting one and why I love it so much. That's why this book has "dynamics" in its title. Financial survival requires the best use of your intelligence, experience, agility, continuous study, daily diligence, and discipline. But your rewards can be so great that the investment of your time and energy in this endeavor can make it all worthwhile. There will be times, if you are not always on guard, when you may be lulled into a false sense of security, and you'll temporarily let down your defenses. You may hear one of the government's "Inflation Fighters" make an optimistic announcement, or you may have received something comparable to the big WIN button to wear, but don't be deceived. (In case you don't remember, WIN stood for Whip Inflation Now.)

WHAT CAUSES INFLATION?

Your government itself is the chief cause of inflation. It does this not by trying to give you what you hate, but by trying to give you the goodies you want—such as full employment or health insurance that you won't buy for yourself. I truly believe that if our forefathers were writing the Bill of Rights today, after having lived in our conditioned atmosphere for a number of years, they would put in the Bill that every person is entitled to a job. Before World War II this was not a commonly held belief. Before then prices went up, but they also went down, so prices remained essentially stable. Now, with so many believing in their right to job security and abetted by the philosophy of a host of Congressional members that you can solve any problem if you'll just cover it with enough appropriations, inflation is on the rampage not only here but abroad, for we have exported this concept.

The year after World War II, Congress passed the "full employment" act declaring that our government would vigorously promote both price stability and full employment. Even a college freshman with no more exposure to economics than Economics 101 should know that these are two inconsistent goals.

The Employment Act of 1946 was to be the embodiment of Utopia, and brilliant government administrators would do a balancing act whereby high employment rates could be generated by accepting higher inflation. But what has the implementation of this theory wrought? We have found that employment that results from inflation only lasts for a short period of time, and in order to restimulate employment, inflation must again be accelerated. Always remember that full employment brings the politicians more votes than licking inflation, therefore the majority of politicians will opt for full employment.

Inflation also makes it easier to meet any economic liquidity crises that may occur. For example, look at what happened with regard to Penn Central and Franklin National Bank. There was a time when bankruptcies, like unemployment, were natural phenomena. Today, Washington abhors such an occurrence, so it loans money to Lockheed, becomes Franklin National Bank's low-cost supplier of funds, and guarantees Chrysler's loans. The possibilities are great that the frequency of these rescues may increase, for bankrupt companies have few employees.

I know you must find it as incongruous as I do that the government of what is billed as being a capitalistic free-enterprise system is taking badly needed capital from other areas of our economy and subsidizing what specialists agree is one of our worst-managed companies, Chrysler, in the name of preservation of jobs, when that same money in other more efficient areas would create more jobs. To add to this unbelievability, the support comes at a time when one of the most efficiently run industries in our nation is being criticized and penalized for making profits. When we reward the inefficient and penalize the efficient, we increase inflation by disrupting the natural forces of supply and demand.

What has been the history of inflation in the United States?

SINCE 1900

Let's examine the past by beginning at the turn of the century— 1900. Figure 2–1 plots the purchasing power of our dollar from 1900 through 1979.

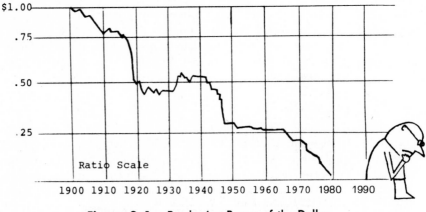

Figure 2–1. Purchasing Power of the Dollar

An even more graphic way of looking at the effect of inflation is to look at a dollar composed of quarters that you have held since 1900. You now go to the grocery store to make a purchase. How much do you think it will buy in the form of goods and services in comparison to what it bought in 1900?

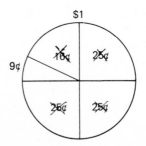

Your dollar has lost over 90 percent of the only value it has— what it will buy. A dollar has no value in and of itself. Its only value is what you can exchange it for in the marketplace. What you want to store for the future is not so many dollars, but so many pairs of shoes, tubes of lipstick, and hamburgers.

THINK OF BREAD

In 1940, you could go to your local grocery store and buy ten loaves of bread for $1. By 1950, you could buy only six loaves. By 1960, it would buy only four, and by 1970 only three. How many will it buy today? It is the same dollar, but it has lost the major portion of its only value.

If I can do nothing else for you in this book but to help you to convert your thinking from dollars into bread, I will have done for you an immense favor. I warn you, it is an emotional transition that only a few can make. If you can make it, you will be in the minority—but remember, it's only the minority that become financially independent.

During the years between 1940 and 1979, the dollar held its own in only two years, and then by less than 1 percent. Not even a professional gambler would accept those odds. Yet, if you are holding a dollar today, you are betting against those odds. If you are a saver, placing your savings in a "guaranteed" savings account, you are a gambler, and if the past is any indication of the future, you are "guaranteed" to lose!

What if I were to say to you, "I want to recommend a stock for your serious consideration. I know that its record has not been very good, but I have faith that it will improve. It was selling for $100 in 1951; by 1956 it had dropped to $96; by 1961 to $88; by 1966 to $79; and by 1971 to $63. Today it is at $40, but don't let that discourage you. I still have faith in this investment, and I want you to invest in it." If I were to make such a "buy" recommendation to you, what would

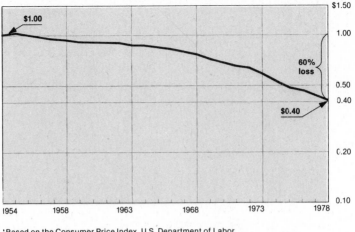

*Based on the Consumer Price Index, U.S. Department of Labor
December 1953 = $1.00

Figure 2–2. Purchasing Power of the U.S. Dollar, 1953–1978

you say to me? Before you say, "You've got to be kidding!" I want you to know that this investment is recommended by most of our state and national banks, by all of our savings and loans, by all of the nation's life insurance companies that sell cash surrender value policies, by your city, and by the federal government itself. What is this investment? It is the U.S. dollar! (See Figure 2–2.)

IT IS THE U.S. DOLLAR

"Guaranteed" dollars are recommended as a good, "safe" investment for you by all savings institutions and insurance companies that sell cash surrender value life insurance; yet they never want a "guaranteed" dollar for themselves. They want to "guarantee" your principal, "guarantee" your rate of return, and "guarantee" that your dollar will

" IT IS THE U.S. DOLLAR!"

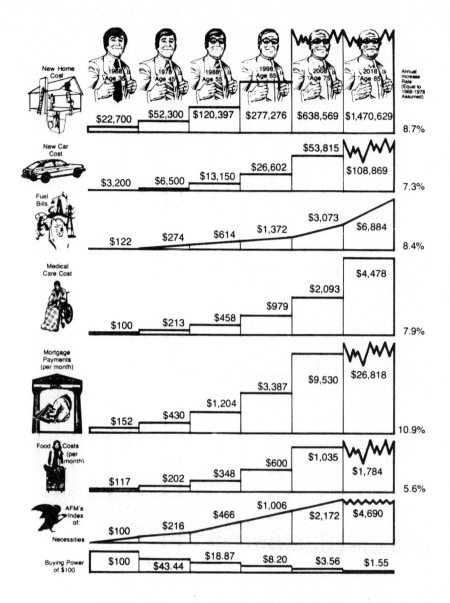

Figure 2–3. Effect of Inflation on Purchases

work for them—usually harder than it works for you. You will receive a "guarantee" that you can always get back each deflating dollar you have placed with them (excluding "your" savings account with the life insurance company). You are also guaranteed that you can never receive any more than that dollar, plus any compound interest you may have left with them, regardless of how much your money has earned for the institution to which you loaned it, and regardless of what the cost of living has become.

In my seminars I sometimes hand out the chart shown in Figure 2–3 that gives a visual picture of inflation as it relates to the things we buy. I remember a lady looking at it and saying, "I think these figures are exaggerated and I just can't accept them." I asked her if she could accept the 1968 to 1978 figures. Her answer was, "Oh yes, because they actually happened." These figures are only an extrapolation of what happened from 1968 to 1978. You may use them as you see fit.

If you are still in a state of shock, here is another table that will not help you regain your composure; it shows prices at a 6 percent inflation rate and a 13 percent inflation rate for the 'eighties.

INFLATION FOR THE 'EIGHTIES

Name	1980 Price	1990 Price @ 6% Inflation	1990 Price @ 13% Inflation
Yale University (tuition, room & board)	$8,090	$14,500	$27,500
Public college, yearly cost avg.	3,350	6,000	11,400
Avg. taxi ride, NYC (before tip & abuse)	2.95	5.30	10.00
Movies (first run)	5	9	17
Slice of pizza	0.65	1.20	2.25
Broadway musical, ticket	25.00	45.00	85.00
Beefeater Gin (qt.)	9.59	17.20	32.50
Bottle Budweiser Beer (3rd Ave. bars)	1.25	2.25	4.25
Barron's	1.00	1.75	3.50
New York Times	0.25	0.45	0.85
Cadillac Coupe de Ville (with extras)	14,000	25,000	48,000
U.S. new car, avg. sticker price	8,750	15,700	29,700
Radial tire	42.00	75.00	142.00
Hardcover book (avg.)	12.50	22.50	42.50
Paperback book (avg.)	2.75	5.00	9.25
First-class postage stamp	0.15	0.27	0.50
19" Sony Trinitron color TV	630	1,125	2,150

INFLATION FOR THE 'EIGHTIES (*Continued*)

Name	1980 Price	1990 Price @ 6% Inflation	1990 Price @ 13% Inflation
Median price (Oct.) existing homes	56,300	101,000	191,000
Run-of-the-mill suburban $150,000 house, NYC	150,000	270,000	510,000
New York Hospital, private rm. per day	337	600	1,150
Obstetrician's delivery fee	1,200	2,150	4,100
Dinner, inexpensive Chinese restaurant	6.50	11.65	22.00
Dinner, expensive place (La Grenouille)	34.75	62.25	120.00
Lunch, intimate Italian place (Giovanni's)	14.00	25.00	47.50
McDonald's qtr.-pounder with cheese	1.45	2.60	5.00
McDonald's shake	0.75	1.35	2.55
Gasoline, per gallon	1.16	2.10	4.00
Subway & bus fare	0.50	0.90	1.70
Razor haircut (Nino's)	6.20	11.00	21.00
Hotel room with bath (first-class hotel)	80	145	275
Christmas tree (89th & 3rd Ave., NYC)	40	72	135
Bacon per lb.	1.75	3.15	6.00
Coffee per lb.	3.50	6.25	12.00
Brooks Bros. neckties	14.00	25.00	48.00
Brooks Bros. suits	290	520	1,000
Maximum Social Security deduction	1,587	2,840	5,395
Median family income (1978 = $17,640)	22,000 (est)	39,400	75,000
Marginal tax rate (married, jt. ret., 2 Dep., itemized ded. equal to 17% of gross income and no change in tax law)	22%	36%	50%

Inflation averaged 2 percent in the 'fifties, 2.3 percent in the 'sixties, 6.1 percent in the first half of the 'seventies, and the government admits to 13.7 percent the latter part of the 'seventies; but most accredited economists admit to a level in excess of 20 percent in the 'eighties. I do not believe that history always repeats itself, but I have found that if I ignore the past, I often condemn myself to repeating the same mistakes in the future.

50

TABLE 2–1. 8% INFLATION

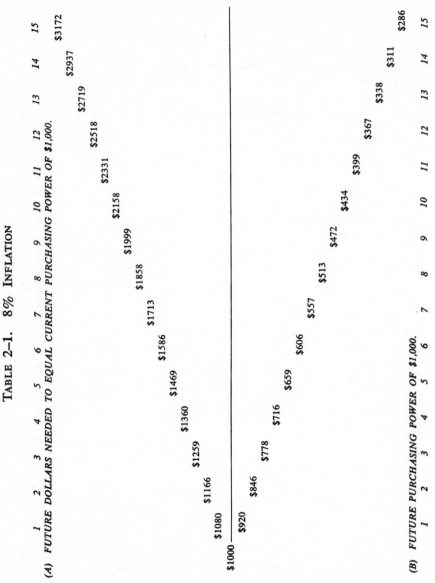

(A) FUTURE DOLLARS NEEDED TO EQUAL CURRENT PURCHASING POWER OF $1,000.

1	2	3	4	5	6	7	8	9	10	11	12	13	14	15
$1080	$1166	$1259	$1360	$1469	$1586	$1713	$1858	$1999	$2158	$2331	$2518	$2719	$2937	$3172

$1000

(B) FUTURE PURCHASING POWER OF $1,000.

1	2	3	4	5	6	7	8	9	10	11	12	13	14	15
$920	$846	$778	$716	$659	$606	$557	$513	$472	$434	$399	$367	$338	$311	$286

"GUARANTEED INCOME FOR LIFE"

Avoid being enticed by advertisements for endowment policies that proclaim "an income that you can never outlive" when that income is $1,000 a month. Let's assume we can slow inflation to 8 percent. What future dollars would you need to equal the current purchasing power of $1,000? (A on Table 2–1). Or looking at it in another way, what will be the future purchasing power of $1,000? (B on Table 2–1).

OBTAINING A REAL INCOME OF 2 PERCENT

If you were to say to me "Venita, I think I deserve a 'real' income after income taxes and inflation of 2 percent," how much would I have to be sure you obtained on your investment to reach what you have decided you deserve?

My answer to you will be influenced by two factors: the rate of inflation and your tax bracket. Table 2–2 will probably be an eye opener to you. As you will see, if we can slow inflation to 8 percent and you are in a 20 percent tax bracket (I jokingly tell my seminar audiences that they're at least in a 20 percent bracket if they're warm), you must receive 12.5 percent on your money. If you are in a 30 percent bracket and we have inflation at 10 percent, you must earn 17.1 percent. In a 40 percent bracket and 11 percent inflation you must

TABLE 2–2. RATE OF RETURN REQUIRED TO PRODUCE
A "REAL" 2% INCOME AFTER INCOME TAXES AND INFLATION

INCOME TAX RATE	Inflation Rate										
	2%	3%	4%	5%	6%	7%	8%	9%	10%	11%	12%
60%	10.0	12.5	15.0	17.5	20.0	22.5	25.0	27.5	30.0	32.5	35.0
50%	8.0	10.0	12.0	14.0	16.0	18.0	20.0	22.0	24.0	26.0	28.0
40%	6.7	8.3	10.0	11.6	13.3	15.0	16.7	18.4	20.0	21.7	23.3
30%	5.7	7.1	8.6	10.0	11.4	12.9	14.3	15.7	17.1	18.6	20.0
20%	5.0	6.3	7.5	8.8	10.0	11.3	12.5	13.8	15.0	16.3	17.5

INSTRUCTIONS:
1. First, select the column which matches the inflation rate (2% to 12%).
2. Second, select the line which matches the income tax rate (20% to 60%).
3. The number which appears at the intersection of the column and line indicates the rate of return necessary to offset the combined effect of income taxes and inflation. (For example, if you assume inflation will continue at 6%, a 50% taxpayer must earn a 16% rate of return per annum in order to show a 2% real growth after adjusting for both income taxes and inflation.)

earn 21.7 percent; and in a 50 percent bracket and 12 percent inflation you must earn 28 percent. As you can see, you really have to run very fast today to be 2 percent ahead. If you are brave enough to want 5 percent real income after taxes and inflation, look in the appendix. At 14 percent inflation and a 59 percent bracket, the rate of return required is 46.3 percent.

THE TAX BRACKET CREEPER

There is a hideous monster lurking in the Internal Revenue Service Tax Rate Schedule that you may not be aware of that can bring devastation to your financial planning. It's not the "Cookie Monster"; it is the "Bracket Creeper Monster." This monster hides out in the fine print of the I.R.S. tax schedule, and he especially feeds on inflation. In the past ten years, the prices you have had to pay for your daily living expenses have doubled, but you might not feel so used because you've been receiving cost of living raises to help you maintain your purchasing power. This might be true except for the "Bracket Creeper Monster." Your higher income has pushed you into a higher tax bracket. For example, if your taxable income was $20,000 and you filed a joint return ten years ago, you paid $4,380 in federal income taxes, leaving you $15,620 after taxes to enable you to keep pace with inflation. Your employer has by now raised your salary until your taxable income is $40,000, making you owe a federal income tax of $10,226 and leaving you $29,774 after taxes. But to keep even, you would need $59,548. Your federal income taxes increased 133 percent while your cost of living increased 100 percent.

The average working couple earning $20,000 to $25,000 a year will pay more than one-third of their income in taxes. On a national level, federal and state income taxes after all exemptions and deductions will average 12.2 percent of personal income; but other taxes such as sales, excise, customs, property, Social Security, and franchise more than triple the bite.

Taxes have risen a massive 46 percent as a share of personal income in the past three decades. Americans today are taxed 38 cents for every dollar earned. Social Security is our fastest rising federal tax.

Unless Congress periodically "cuts" tax rates because of the "Bracket Creeper Monster," an ever larger share of our Gross National Product will automatically flow to Washington.

United States federal tax collections from its citizens who do not take steps to protect themselves through proper planning increases an average of 16 percent for every 10 percent of increase in personal income. If you live in a state with progressive state income taxes, such as California and New York, inflation causes an increase in the state tax bite as well. This results in the government having a vested interest in maintaining inflation, since our laws permit a windfall tax bonus every year we have inflation.

INDEXING

There is increased interest by some of our more conservative Congressmen in a system called indexing. This is a system already in use in Canada. Under this system, as the cost of living goes up, indexing raises the dollar limits of the tax brackets and also the exemptions and standard deductions that the taxpayer can subtract from his taxable income. In 1979, a ranking Senator who is a member of the Senate Finance Committee and a member of the Joint Committee on Taxation addressed the Senate in these words:

> Despite all the political rhetoric about tax cuts during the 95th Congress, more than 80 percent of the American taxpayers can expect a tax increase this year. The increase, which will approach $10 billion, comes after Congress passed a major tax reduction in hopes that it would pacify taxpayers crying out for lower taxes.
>
> Inflation is our number one tax problem. As inflation increases, a taxpayer's income must also increase to enable the family to buy the same amount of goods and services. But, as nominal income rises, the taxpayer is pushed into higher and higher tax brackets—thus paying a larger tax bill—despite the fact that no gain in purchasing power has been realized. . . .
>
> The legislation I introduced today is designed to insulate taxpayers from the tax impact of inflation by automatically adjusting tax liabilities each year to reflect increases in the cost of living.

This legislation had already been proposed a year before and has become known as the "Tax Equalization Act."

The Senator continued his address by saying that the Federal government will reap a $15.6 billion "windfall profit" in 1980 due to inflation. He estimated that the government benefited from this "taxation" by $9 billion in 1978 and $11.5 billion in additional revenues in 1979.

You may have heard that no one benefits from inflation. That's obviously not true. The federal government benefits very much from inflation. Under the present system, the money that taxpayers lose by being pushed into higher tax brackets goes to the Treasury at a rate of more than $1 billion for each percentage point of inflation. Not only does the government benefit at the expense of the taxpayers, but by spending the extra billions it receives, the government also increases inflationary pressures. As long as the government profits from inflation, it has a vested interest in continuing it.

THE NEW MATH OF INFLATION

Poor Richard advised "don't borrow," but inflation has made his advice obsolete. Inflation rewards those who owe money, not those who pay cash. I'm not talking about plastic money—your VISA, Master-Card or American Express cards. Never charge anything you can't pay for in thirty days. Never borrow for your daily living or luxuries. Only borrow long-term for investing—never for spending.

Let's look at the balance sheet of three families and see which family was the most prudent in an inflationary economy.

The Anderson family's balance sheet looks like this:

Cash	$10,000	Mortgage	$ 5,000
Home	10,000	Net worth	$15,000

Net worth is the difference between your assets and your liabilities and is a measure of how rich you are.

Now let's assume that prices double. The Andersons' balance sheet will now look like this:

Cash	$10,000	Mortgage	$ 5,000
Home	20,000	Net worth	25,000

The Andersons' net worth has now increased from $15,000 to $25,000, which at first glance appears good; however, their net worth has not doubled, as prices did. Therefore, this family has fallen behind in the inflation race. Their wealth or purchasing power has been reduced by inflation.

Now let's examine the Barton family's balance sheet:

Cash	$ 5,000	Mortgage	$ 5,000
Home	10,000	Net worth	10,000

A doubling of prices has this effect on their balance sheet:

Cash	$ 5,000	Mortgage	$ 5,000
Home	20,000	Net worth	20,000

The Bartons have held their own. They have exactly kept pace with inflation.

Now let's look at the Calloway family's balance sheet:

Cash	$ 3,000	Mortgage	$10,000
Home	12,000	Net worth	5,000

When prices doubled the Calloways' net worth looked like this:

Cash	$ 3,000	Mortgage	$10,000
Home	24,000	Net worth	17,000

The Calloways' net worth increased from $5,000 to $17,000, or more than tripled, while prices only doubled. The Calloways beat inflation.

What lesson about inflation have you learned from these three families? Is it this sad commentary: "Inflation rewards those who owe money, not those who pay cash"?

You don't have to be on the verge of bankruptcy to benefit from inflation. You can and should have cash, but you will want to have a large amount of your assets invested in things—hard assets. To win the inflation game in the years ahead, you will have to be leveraged in this way. Your assets must be primarily in investments whose prices can rise as fast as the general price levels at each stage of the inflation cycle. Large amounts of cash do not fit into the inflation-benefiting category, for a dollar is still a dollar whose purchasing power shrinks with inflation. There was a time when families did not feel comfortable unless they had cash in the bank. Today many families feel uncomfortable with money in the bank.

INFLATION DOES NOT HURT THE KNOWLEDGEABLE

Inflation will not hurt you if you become knowledgeable and act to protect yourself from it. But you will be saddened as you look around and see the tragic faces of the hard-working, thrifty, sacrificing persons who have faithfully saved and put their money where they have been told it would be safe and have lost their money's only true value—its purchasing power. With it they also lost the privilege of retiring in financial dignity. At least the spendthrifts had the fun of spending their money until they got off the inflation train. During their working years, raises usually matched or exceeded their increases in their cost of living. But when they got off the inflation train and it went on without them, they had no chance of keeping up with the inflationary spiral.

THE TOTAL PORTFOLIO

To take advantage of the transfers that inflation makes in wealth you must begin by thinking in terms of a total portfolio that you will have positioned efficiently at the proper time to beat inflation. Your portfolio must maximize your after-tax return balanced against a level of risk that provides you with peace of mind. You will want to avoid fads unless you are equipped emotionally to act rapidly. As inflation pushes up the price of your assets, faddists will start jumping in with both feet. At this point prices will begin to overdiscount inflation. The faddist will be selling as prices drop. You will want to be in a position to buy at that time.

To beat inflation, you will always want to be holding the right combination of assets. There is an investment for each season, but not an investment for all seasons. This means that nothing you have can be just put away in your safe-deposit box and forgotten. You must learn to be flexible and alert.

You should classify all the investment vehicles available to you as to their appropriateness for accelerating inflation or decelerating inflation. Then decide whether inflation is about to accelerate or decelerate.

I often find that many who come to me for financial counseling have already accumulated sufficient assets, or could easily do so within a few years, to enable them to reach or work toward financial independence, if these assets were properly put to work. This is, or probably will become true with you. You may be, or will be, working extremely hard for your money, but unfortunately once it is obtained, instead of putting it to work for yourself, you have unknowingly given away its earning power. You cannot afford to have your money working for others. If you do, you'll lose the money and tax game!

SUMMARY

Inflation will be a part of your life for as long as you live. You can fear it, hide your head in the sand, and say that it doesn't exist or that it will go away, but you are only kidding yourself and inviting financial disappointments. Inflation can be your valuable ally. You can use it to increase your wealth by applying your intelligence and energy to studying the inflation cycles and positioning your assets at the proper location at the proper time. You must face the reality that you will probably never own an asset that is immune to the inflation cycle.

The facing of this reality and your determination to use these forces can be a challenging and profitable undertaking.

APPLICATION

1. Have you mentaly made the necessary transition from dollars into bread?
2. Go to the library and check out a 1940 *Life* Magazine or *Saturday Evening Post* and study the ads.
3. Do you think the Full Employment Act of 1946 will be repealed?
4. Are you still living under the *Poor Richard's Almanac* theory of working hard, saving, and not borrowing?
5. What steps will you take today to throw off Poor Richard's shackles and move into the real world?

3

SUCCESS IN THE STOCK MARKET

In my opinion, selected common stock equities will be a viable choice, intermittently, for around 25 percent of your investment dollars during the decade of the 'eighties. I make this statement without my usual hedge clauses, because intelligent analysis leads me to no other conclusion.

In the first chapter of this book I gave you my formula:

Time + Money + American Free Enterprise =
Financial Independence

In this chapter I'll substitute "Industry" for "Free Enterprise." Once I've done this, your next question will be, "Which American companies should I invest in, when should my money be committed, and for how long should it be invested?"

I'm sure that you are aware by now that I do not have a crystal ball that shows the future. (Those who claim they do most probably will have to become accustomed to eating ground glass.) However, there are some valid reasons why the time you spend learning to become a successful investor in the market should be a very rewarding experience for you in this decade.

"PLAYING THE MARKET"

I often have people come up to me at our seminars or at social occasions and say almost smugly, "I play the market," as if the market were a game. They seem to think I should be pleased and give them a loving pat on the head.

Investing is not a game. It is a very exacting science that requires skill, training, knowledge, and discipline. Even with these qualifications you will not always be right. This dynamic and fast-moving world we live in changes every minute of every day. Successful investing is a skill that you must either learn yourself or hire the professionals to do for you. You have no choice.

THE LANGUAGE OF INVESTING

To become a successful investor, you'll need to know the language of investing and the kinds of securities that you'll find in the marketplace.

There are three basic types of securities. They are:

1. Common stock
2. Preferred stock
3. Bonds or debentures

Common Stock

All corporations have common stock. If you organized a corporation for the purpose of buying a popcorn stand at the corner of Main Street and First, and sold one share of common stock to nine persons at $100 per share and one share to yourself at $100, the corporation would be capitalized at $1000 and would have ten stockholders. In buying one of these shares, you became a shareholder of the corporation. You took an equity position and will participate in the future gains or lack of gains of the corporation for as long as you hold your share.

Preferred Stock

Preferred stock is a stock on which a fixed dividend must be paid before the common shareholder is entitled to a dividend each year. The dividend is usually higher, and if it is a cumulative preferred stock, any past dividends that have been omitted must be paid before the common shareholder is entitled to a dividend. If the preferred is also convertible, it will have a conversion ratio into the common.

There is much confusion about preferred stock. The uninitiated seem to feel that "preferred" means "better." This is rarely true. Unless it's convertible, it has neither the growth potential of a common stock nor the relative stability of a bond. The word "preferred" relates to dividend precedence only. I personally believe there are better ways for an individual to invest.

Bonds or Debentures

The third type of securities is bonds or debentures. A corporate bond may be a mortgage bond. For example, if you were to invest in equipment trust certificates, you would hold a mortgage on specific freight cars.

A much larger area of the bond market is debentures. Your security for this type of bond is the general credit rating of the issuing corporation. For example, you may buy an American Telephone and Telegraph debenture at 8.70 percent due in 2002. In this instance, you do not acquire a mortgage on specific telephones, but instead your security is based on the tremendous assets and credit of AT&T.

Characteristics of common stocks and bonds can be oversimplified by stating them in this manner:

STOCKS

1. Not guaranteed as to principal.

2. Not guaranteed as to rate of return.

3. Guaranteed to participate in the future destiny of the company.

BONDS

1. "Guaranteed" as to principal if assets are available at maturity.

2. "Guaranteed" as to rate of return if funds are available.

3. Not guaranteed to grow, regardless of any increase in the profits of the corporation.

Convertibles

There are those who feel that convertible bonds give the best of two worlds—offering you the third characteristic under stocks, and the first two under bonds; however, they frequently fall short on both scores.

A convertible bond is a bond that usually carries a lower interest rate than a regular corporate bond, but is convertible into common at a specified ratio. For example, if a convertible is bought at par, which in a bond is usually $1000, and is convertible into 100 shares of common at the holder's option and the common is selling at $10, there would be no incentive to exchange, for the bond will usually carry a higher yield than the common. However, if the market price of the common should increase to $15, you would now have a bond with a value of $1500. If, on the other hand, the common goes below $10, you still have your bond with its higher yield acting as a cushion under the bond.

How have they performed? Not well enough for any gold stars. The size and quality of the convertible market has left much to be desired. In severe market declines, they have suffered along with their common neighbors.

My emphasis in this book will be on common stocks. They will offer you the greatest potential for gain (or loss). You will find a vast array of them in the marketplace, which may seem confusing at first. However, we'll take a step-by-step approach, and your learning should progress rapidly.

To be successful in the stock market, you will need to know how to use the mass network of facilities available to you for trading securities. And you need to keep accurate records; Figures 1 and 2 in the Appendix are suggested forms for keeping records of your buys, sells, and dividends.

LISTED STOCKS

Stocks that are publicly held are classified as either listed or un-listed (commonly referred to as over-the-counter). "Listed" means that a stock is listed on a national or regional exchange. Listed stocks represent, in dollar assets, the largest segment of the American economy. There is probably no asset that you will ever own that you can so readily turn into cash as a stock that is listed on a national exchange. It offers almost instant liquidity.

Our four largest exchanges are the New York Stock Exchange, the American Stock Exchange, the Pacific Stock Exchange, and the Midwest Stock Exchange.

The Big Board

The New York Stock Exchange is the oldest and largest. It began very informally near the time of the birth of our nation. Our first Secretary of the Treasury needed to set up a monetary system. To have a monetary system in this new nation, he needed to establish banks. To establish banks, he needed stockholders who were willing to invest capital. However, no one was willing to invest capital in bank stocks if there was no way to sell their shares. To make a market for these bank stocks and other issues, a group of eleven men used to meet under a buttonwood tree at the foot of a street called Wall, and trade among themselves and as agents for their clients. They eventually moved inside, and from this humble beginning grew the mighty New York Stock Exchange.

How Wall Street Got Its Name

It might interest you to know how Wall Street got its name. The Dutch, who first settled Manhattan Island, were very fond of pork, so they brought hogs from the Netherlands. To confine the hogs they built a wall to make a pig pen—hence the name Wall Street. It's fun to note that some of our stock market history goes back to pigs and hogs. Unfortunately, we still have a few investors who get piggish. It is always good to remember an old saying, "In Wall Street, the bulls sometimes make it and the bears sometimes make it, but the hogs never do." *

THE OVER-THE-COUNTER MARKET

Another vast area of the stock market is the "unlisted" market, called the over-the-counter (OTC) market, that has no "counter" or meeting place. Once, I had a lady become confused and ask me for an "under-the-counter" stock. After she told me which stock she had in mind, I decided she had accidentally hit on a good description. It was a very speculative stock.

The over-the-counter market is a vast negotiated market. For many years there was no central marketplace for these stocks. Various brokerage houses would "make a market" in a particular stock. This means that they would inventory the stock they bought and sold. There are now over 50,000 stocks traded in the over-the-counter market, through a network of telephone and teletype wires linking the various brokerage houses. There is a daily "pink sheet" giving "bid" and "asked" quotations of the market makers from the previous day reporting to the National Daily Quotation Service. ("Bid" means what someone is willing to pay for the stock. "Asked" is the amount for which someone is willing to sell, subject to confirmation or change in price.) When you see a market report on a listed stock in the paper, you know that a trade actually took place at that price. In the over-the-counter market, you could have a quote with no trade taking place.

There is a wide range of quality in the stocks traded in the over-the-counter market. Traditionally, bank and insurance company stocks have been traded there, even though they have substantial assets. On the opposite end are "penny stocks" (those that sell for a nominal amount per share), which also trade there.

---

* Evan, Esar, *Twenty Thousand Quips and Quotes*. New York: Doubleday, 1968.

Often a stock is traded over-the-counter for years, and as it grows in assets and popularity, it may apply for listing on a national exchange and be accepted.

In the past, I have warned that if you are new to the market, you probably should avoid the over-the-counter market until you become more knowledgeable, but with the establishment of NASDAQ, the whole complexion of this market has changed.

NASDAQ

In February, 1971, the National Association of Security Dealers Advanced Quotations appeared on the scene. Various market makers of OTC stocks feed in the changes in their markets to Bunker-Ramo Central Control, which updates the "bid" and "asked" quotes on each issue every five minutes, showing the best "bid" and "asked" offers available.

NASDAQ has had a profound effect on the OTC market, making current markets available to all parts of the country at the same time and enabling dealers to give prompt and accurate service.

YOUR BROKERAGE ACCOUNT

How do you use this mass network of facilities? How do you open an account with a stockbroker? It's just as easy as opening a charge account. As a matter of fact, your prospective broker will probably ask fewer questions than the department store where you applied for your last charge account. He will need to know your address, home and office telephone numbers, occupation and company for whom you work, if you are over 21, spouse's name (if married), social security number, if you are a U.S. citizen, bank reference, and how you want your stocks registered.

A good financial planner will ask much more information about your assets, your age, your tax bracket, your financial objective, and your temperament. (A financial planner is a stockbroker, but a stockbroker is not necessarily a financial planner—unless he or she is trained to treat your complete financial planning needs.) If in doubt, you may want to choose one who is a member of the International Association of Financial Planners and perhaps has earned the Certified Financial Planner designation. You'll learn more about this growing profession in Chapter 20.

When you make a purchase or sale, it is a firm commitment, regardless of whether the stock goes up or down. A confirmation is mailed to you showing the number of shares of stock purchased or sold, price, commission and fees, net amount due, and settlement date. Within five business days from the trade date, you must pay for stocks you have bought. If you have sold a stock, you must deliver your stock certificate within the same period of time, and receive payment.

Commissions Are Low

Stocks carry one of the lowest commission rates for the exchange of property in the United States. Remember the commission you paid when you sold your last house? Was it 6 percent to the realtor, plus all the closing costs, making your total between 10 percent and 12 percent? You can sell 100 shares of a $40 listed stock for a commission of around 1¾ percent, and this rate will probably go lower. Quite a difference, isn't it?

How Your Order Is Executed

After your account has been opened, you may place your orders by telephone with your broker and ask him to buy or sell securities for you. For example, let's assume that you place an order to buy 100 shares of General Widgets "at the market." Your broker then gives the order to his company's trader. The trader immediately contacts its floor broker on the floor of the exchange, who quickly walks (it's against the rules to run) to the post where General Widgets is traded. Since you want to buy, the floor broker tries to buy at the lowest price.

At the same time, there may be a farmer in Vermont who must have funds to pay for his son's college tuition. He contacts his broker, his broker contacts his floor broker, and the two of them meet at the General Widgets post. The exchange is an auction market, and bids and offers are made by outcry. That's why the floor of the exchange is so noisy and may look and sound like a madhouse. Your company's floor broker will be trying to buy for you at, say, $50 per share. The farmer's broker will be trying to sell at $50¼. Your broker finally decides he can't buy for you at $50, and the Vermont farmer's broker decides he can't obtain 50¼, so $50⅛ is agreed upon. Millions of dollars of stock change hands daily. However, no contracts are signed, and there is no shaking of hands. In this business, your word is your bond; and when it isn't, you're no longer in this business. A record of the trade is written on a slip of paper and handed to a runner, who places the slip in a pneumatic tube that carries it to the tape operator. Within approximately three minutes, if you are sitting in front of a tape in a brokerage office, you will see your trade coming across the screen: GWI 50⅛. This is for 100 shares. If the trade had been for 200 shares, it would have shown GWI 2s 50⅛. If the trade was for 1000 shares, it would appear GWI 1000s 50⅛.

Round Lot, Odd Lot

All transactions shown on the tape and reported in the financial section of your newspaper are for round lots (100-share trades or multiples of 100). This does not mean, however, that if you want to own some shares of General Widgets, you have to have $5,012.50 plus commission. For instance, if you want to buy ten shares, you certainly may. You would give your ten-share order to the broker, who would contact the odd-lot broker. The odd-lot broker buys in round lots on the exchange and divides it into odd lots. You pay an odd-lot differential for his service. In this example, it would be an additional ⅛ of a point, or $.125 per share. This is not a commission. It is an odd-lot differential. Your commission would be in addition to the differential.

The amount you pay per share for your odd-lot purchase is determined by the price of the next round-lot trade after your order is received. For example, if the next round-lot trade is $50⅛, you would pay $50¼.

If you buy an odd lot on a round lot—for example, 125 shares—you pay an odd-lot differential on the 25 shares if you trade on the New York Stock Exchange. If the stock is traded on the Pacific Stock Exchange, it trades with the round lot without the odd-lot differential. No odd lot differential is charge on orders entered before the market opens. As you can see, the odd lot charge is not enough difference to discourage you from buying in odd lots.

RATIOS

Ratios can be quite confusing to the investor who is new to the marketplace. To give you a better understanding of them, let's examine two well-managed companies, X and Y. They both manufacture an excellent product for which there has been an increasing demand. For ease of comparison, assume that the stock of both companies sells for $10 per share and that both earn $1 per share.

Stock X pays a 50¢ dividend, and stock Y pays a 10¢ dividend. What is the yield of each, and what is the price–earning ratio?

Stock	Market Price	Earnings per Share	Dividend	Yield	Price—Earnings Ratio
X	$10	$1	50¢	5%	10:1
Y	$10	$1	10¢	1%	10:1

Yield is the relationship of the dividend to the market price. Therefore, a 50¢ yield on a $10 stock would be 5 percent per annum. A 10¢ dividend would then be a 1 percent yield.

The *price–earnings ratio*, often referred to as the P/E, is the relationship of the market price to the earnings. It indicates how much the investing public is willing to pay for $1 of earnings. In both stocks, the amount is $10, making the P/E ratio 10:1.

Which Stock is Best?

Which stock should you buy? When I ask this question in the seminars, the majority choose stock *X*. The savings institutions' advertising campaigns have made them very income-conscious.

Did you answer *X* or *Y*? The correct answer for you depends on your financial objective. Do you need income now, or do you need income later? If you need it now, you may want to choose stock *X*; if you need it later, you should choose stock *Y*. If the company pays out 50¢ to you and you are in a 30 percent tax bracket, you lose 15¢ to Washington. If you are in a 50 percent bracket, you lose 25¢. If your need is for income later, then you very well may come out better if the company plows back the 90¢ into enlarged plants and facilities, with the hope that someday stock *Y* will grow in value to perhaps $15 per share. Sometimes it's better to get your eyes off the extra 4 percent income and on to the 50 percent potential in capital gains.

There is often another factor to be considered, and that is your temperament. There is a triangle in finance as there may be in romance. Let's look at the financial triangle and see where you should place yourself for your mental comfort and for the best correlation with your financial objectives.

TRIANGLE OF FINANCE

At the top of the triangle I have placed Growth, at the left Income, and at the right Stability. (I used to call this corner Safety, but with our present rate of inflation if you are "stable," you are certainly not "safe," so I have changed it to Stability.) By stability, I mean a guarantee of the same number of dollars at a future date, not the return of the same purchasing power.

As you can see, the farther you move toward Growth, the farther you move from Stability and Income. You may be young enough to invest for Growth, but when you move in that direction, you could have increased volatility. This may disturb your peace of mind, and peace of

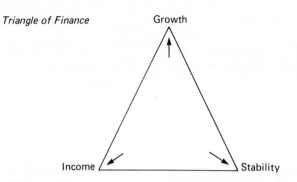

Triangle of Finance

mind is a good investment, too. If you were my client, I would try to determine your peace of mind level, because regardless of how well the investment fits your financial objective, if you are uncomfortable with it, it's not right for you and you may abandon it before it has had time to achieve the desired goal.

Let's assume your chief reason for investing in stocks is for income. What characteristics should be of importance to you?

HOW TO SELECT INCOME STOCKS

Income stocks are relatively easy to select as compared to growth stocks. However, there are some important points you'll want to consider before you give your broker a buy order.

Good Dividends That Keep Increasing

You want stocks that not only pay good dividends, but also have a record of increasing their dividends rather consistently. If you are dependent on your dividends for your groceries and the price of food continues to rise, you must either increase your income or reduce your intake. Most of us would probably be a lot healthier if we did the latter, but we have a tendency to reject this alternative.

Dividends That Are Earned

You should carefully determine if the corporation is earning the dividend. Years ago many of the bank trust departments were putting shares of Sinclair Oil in trust accounts that they managed for widows who needed income. Sinclair was paying a liberal dividend. Unfortunately, the trust officers did not look to see if the company was earning the amount they were paying. They were not. The day of reckoning came, as it usually does, the dividend was cut, and many a widow's account suffered capital losses. Do not reach too far for yield and jeopardize your capital.

Often I have calls from someone who is going through a *Standard and Poor's Stock Guide* and spots a stock paying a 12 to 14 percent yield. They'll excitedly call to buy it, assuming that no one else has been so observant as to have spotted this bonanza. Usually the reason for the high yield is the poor evaluation that the market has given to the future prospects of the company.

Resistance to Business Cycles

A characteristic of all good income stocks should be that they have a good measure of resistance against cyclical waves in the economy. The consumer demand for the products produced by these companies should continue through all phases of the economic cycle.

Long Dividend Record

In selecting stocks for dependable income, it is obvious that you will want to choose quality issues, since younger, less tested companies have not been around long enough to establish an extended dividend payment record.

Income stocks usually pay out 65 to 75 percent of their net earnings in cash dividends. Once a regular dividend rate has been established, it is unlikely that it will be reduced because of poor earnings in a single year.

During times of market corrections, I often have calls from less sophisticated holders of income stocks who are worried that their dividend will be cut because the market price is down. If all is well with their company, I try to calm them with the explanation that short-term market prices often have no relationship to earnings. (In the long term they usually do.)

Who Decides the Amount of the Dividend?

The amount remaining after the expenses and taxes have been paid by a company is the amount available for dividends. The decision as to whether a dividend should be paid and how much it should be is made by the board of directors. The amount of the earnings, the need for retained earnings, and the past dividend record all influence the directors' decision.

Yield on Original Purchase Price

As you learned above, the yield on a stock is the relationship of the dividend to the market price. Every shareholder is entitled to the same dividend per share. However, the market price paid by one shareholder may be different from that paid by another. If you paid $50 for a share of stock and the dividend is $2, your yield on your original investment is 4 percent ($2 divided by $50). If you paid $35, the $2 represents a return, or yield, on your original investment of slightly more than 5.7 percent.

Most yields, however, are calculated on current market price. If the price per share is now $60, still with a $2 dividend, the yield would be slightly over 3.3 percent.

Looking Ahead

If you do not need income now, consider companies with slightly lower yields. Often these companies are plowing back a larger portion of their earnings into expanded facilities that should in time yield higher earnings that would allow them to pay out higher dividends. Over a ten- to fifteen-year period, many growth stocks have actually had a larger cash pay-out than income stock. One percent on $10,000 is only $100. But let's assume the growth stock continues to grow and reaches a value of $100,000. (One percent on $100,000 is $1000, or 10 percent on your original investment.)

A booklet that you may find of help if you are interested in selecting stocks for income is one published by the New York Stock Exchange, entitled "Investment Facts—Cash Dividends Every Three

Months From 25 to 100 Years." The booklet points out that the widespread ownership of stocks listed on the New York Stock Exchange is due in large part to a growing awareness that surplus dollars can be put to work in investments that will reflect the ever-changing economic conditions of our country.

The ability of common stocks to mirror these developments constitutes their greatest attribute. Of course, it is also their greatest risk. On the plus side is the fact that over the years the yields from good common stocks often have helped their owners keep in step with living costs. There is no such phenomenon as a "sure thing," and past performance does not guarantee the future. But the facts that history has recorded may serve as a clue to the future. If so, it may be of help to look at the long-time dividend payers listed in this booklet.

The booklet lists recent prices of the stock, the dividend record, and its yield. Of these common stocks, 466 have paid a cash dividend every single quarter for 25 years, and 100 have paid a dividend for every quarter for 50 to over 100 years.

Preferred Stocks

Preferred stocks are equities senior to the common, but junior to indebtedness of the issuer. Preferred stock dividend income is 85 percent tax-exempt for corporations, which often makes them attractive corporate investments. This fact tends to raise the price of the preferred in the marketplace, which will generally make them less attractive to you for your individual investment program. You will normally receive a higher rate of return from a high-quality corporate bond than from a preferred stock.

Blue Chips, Red Chips, White Chips? The stocks I have described above would generally be called blue chips. What is a "blue chip" stock? First, the name can be traced to the game of poker, in which there are three colors of chips: blue for the highest value, red for next in rank, and white for the lowest value.

Sometimes people will come up to me after a seminar or a television appearance and say, "I only invest in blue chip stocks and throw them in the drawer and forget about them." They stand there seemingly anticipating my approval. I consider this approach a risky one. I would prefer to see them invest in more volatile stocks and watch them carefully than to have them plant their garden and not tend it. The blue chips of today may be the red chips of tomorrow, the white chips of the next day, or merely the buffalo chips. (I'm a rancher—you do know what pasture frisbee is, don't you?)

However, there are some characteristics of the so-called blue chips that are worthy of your consideration, such as:

1. A long history of cash dividend payments in bad times and good.

2. A long history of good earnings in both booms and recessions.

3. Leadership in an established industry.

4. Good prospects for continued good earnings growth and dividends should pay off in the years ahead.

INCOME vs. GROWTH

The equities market provides a wide spectrum of alternatives with respect to rates of return. When investing in growth companies, you must pay a premium in terms of P/E relationship and, therefore, receive less in the way of current income. Growth companies have an opportunity to reinvest their earnings at higher rates than are available to you as a stockholder if the earnings were paid out to you and you had only the after-tax amount to invest. Therefore, growth companies have very low pay-out ratios.

It is too simplistic, but there is some truth in the fact that the highest-yielding common stocks have lower expectations of future growth and, therefore, lower P/Es.

If you do not expect growth of the company, you should ask yourself why the price is so low, making the yield so high. Is the company in serious financial straits? Is the company likely to cut its dividends? Is the regulatory environment likely to be adverse so that the company may have to reduce its dividend to conserve its cash for working capital needs? What is the outlook for the industry, etc.?

It is clear that investing for income is not without risk. If you had bought certain steel company issues a few years ago for income, you would have had your dividends reduced and in some instances eliminated. Not only did the income go down, but the principal loss was also substantial. It is also clear, however, that investing for high income can have its rewards. In periods of high merger activity some cash-rich income stock companies became the targets of acquiring companies. Some of those acquired had spectacular rises in their prices, and if you had sold your shares at the proper time, you could have realized substantial capital gains.

In summary, if your desire is for income:

1. Look for companies that have a long unbroken dividend record.

2. Don't reach too far for yield and jeopardize principal.

3. Remember that too high a yield can be dangerous and misleading.

4. Favor companies producing consumer goods and services.

5. Select sound companies that continue to increase their dividends.

Income stocks are not too difficult to select after you've conscientiously done your homework. However, selecting growth stocks can be one of the greatest challenges you have ever undertaken.

GROWTH STOCKS—THE ROYAL ROAD TO RICHES

During the surging 'sixties, the magic word on Wall Street, Main Street, Podunk Street, or almost any street you happened to be traveling at the time, was "Growth"! Investing in "growth" stocks was the royal highway to riches. So greatly did some "investors" become enamored of that magic word that they were willing to pay fantastic prices for new and relatively untested electronic and scientific issues. So unrealistic did they become that they actually paid as high as 70 times earnings. In some instances, there were no earnings at all.

Growth Stocks—What Are They?

What are growth stocks, and why should you consider investing in them?

A growth company is usually one that is increasing its sales and earnings at a faster rate than the growth of the national population and business in general. The long-term annual growth rate of our population has been about 3 percent. In recent years, large families have become taboo, and we are beginning to move toward zero population growth; however, we shall probably not reach ZPG until around the year 2000. A growth company, as a rule of thumb, should be increasing its sales and net earnings at least as fast as the combination of the two, and preferably much faster.

Growth companies are usually producing goods and/or services in dynamic and new industries. The 1940s saw the surge of oil stocks, television shares, and pharmaceutical companies. The 1950s continued the drug stocks' popularity, with flurries in uranium, cameras, electronics, missiles, and automation.

The 1960s saw leisure-time industries; baby products; continued popularity of electronics, with computer-oriented stocks keeping pace;

technology-related industries; life insurance companies; drugs; retail; convenience goods; soft drinks; and, most especially, the surge of the conglomerates trying to leverage their balance sheets, many times using what became known as "funny money." Ling-Tempco-Vought, Gulf and Western, Textron, and International Telephone and Telegraph all brought visions of investor "sugar plums" during their heydays of mergers and acquisitions. There was a short period of time when there were jokes in the investment community of investment decisions becoming a matter of which one of the few conglomerates to choose. The tinsel began to tarnish, the craze passed, and we returned to sound investment evaluation based on realities rather than the new math of Wall Street, which seemed to say that 2 plus 2 equals 5.

THE MID-'SEVENTIES

During the first part of the 1970s, the market suffered a major correction. This correction was much more extensive than the widely followed Dow Jones Industrial Average revealed. The decline of the Dow, though sizable, was not bad enough to explain the awful sense of despair that gripped Wall Street during the latter part of 1973 and on through 1974 and 1975. It did not tell how hard the overall stock market was hit. The only averages that showed declines approaching the true magnitude were the superbroad unweighted ones, such as the *Value Line Composite* and the *Indicator Digest* average.

The bull market of the 1960s was in the supergrowth stocks—the franchises, the computer leasers, and the like—not the staid, less volatile Dow 30. The Dow went up during those years, but the broader averages went up more rapidly and also went down more rapidly when the high flyers fell out of favor.

Why was the market plunge so severe in 1973 and 1974? There are many reasons, all interrelated. Let's look at a few of them.

Many market declines are in direct relationship to the junk some stockbrokers "peddle" on the way up. Being a broker is a volatile vocation, but it is made more so by the short memories of a large portion of its personnel. It was another case of too much sizzle and not enough steak.

The Federal Reserve Board instituted extremely restrictive money policies in an effort to slow down runaway inflation. The results of its actions could be compared to taking a man who has been accustomed to three gourmet meals a day and throwing him into solitary confinement, giving him only bread and water, and then beating him with a stick. The market must have a steady flow of money to function properly. Historical studies show a direct relation between the supply of money in the economy and stock market prices.

The ugliness of Watergate disillusioned the American public as nothing else had in many a decade. Their faith in their leaders was badly shaken. A sense of uneasiness and gloom settled over our nation.

During the Ford administration, a certain confidence was renewed and continued for the first part of the Carter Administration. But as faith in Carter's leadership declined, and with the administration's capitulation of the direction of the economy to what many consider the ill-advised and counterproductive actions of the Federal Reserve Board, the market again was thrust down. When people feel bad inside, they sell their stocks. When they feel good, they buy. Gut-level feelings have no correlation with earnings. Human emotion took over, and they sold and sold.

It is at times such as those that we need to read these words: ". . . even in the general moment of gloom in which this . . . is written, when many begin to wonder if declines will never halt, the appropriate abracadabra may be: 'They always did.' " *

HOW TO SPOT GROWTH STOCKS

To become good at selecting for growth, you must be aware of current events: current trends, supply, demand, psychology, and money markets. In fact, you must be truly current. One of the most stimulating characteristics of being a financial planner is that every day is a new day in the market. Nothing remains static. There is no way you can be a truly top-notch investor by buying blue chips and throwing them in a drawer and forgetting them. This only increases your risk and lowers your opportunity for gain.

Be in the Right Industry

If I were to choose the most important consideration for selecting growth stocks, I would have to say that it is to be in the right industry at the right time. There is always an industry moving up, regardless of the general overall trend of the market. You should endeavor to predict a trend before it happens and to move out before the trend runs out. You should try to be aware of technological changes and opinions of the buying public. It will not pay you to be right if nobody cares. Sitting

---

* Bernard M. Baruch, October 1932.

with money in a stagnant "correct" situation while other stocks are moving up just doesn't take the place of making money.

Fantasy Stocks

Do not buy what I call fantasy stocks—stocks based on an idea yet to come. The idea may be great—even correct—but how do you know there will be adequate financing, good and honest management, marketing ability, and public acceptance of the product? (What people want and what they need are different things.) You might say, "But look at Haloid that later became Xerox." There is no way that those who bought Haloid could have known it would become one of the best-managed sales organizations that the country had seen for many a year. Also, you could have bought Xerox many times since its beginning and made just as much money with proper timing on buys and sells. If you will wait until some of the results are in, it may save you some heart-aches. (Of course, you will also need to be astute enough to avoid getting on at the front of the bus while the informed are getting off at the back.)

This is different from a story stock from which good results have already been realized, but even better results are expected. The best story is the "Good Earnings Story."

Management Is the Key

There is no substitute for energetic, intelligent, dedicated, and en-thusiastic management. They should be a stock-minded management team that is interested in increasing the market price of their stock, and this can only be sustained in the long term by increased earnings.

With good management and an average product, it is possible to make money. A superior product with poor management may well yield very disappointing results. The key is good management and a superior product together.

Self-Generating Earnings

Select a company that has self-generating rising earnings and re-serves with expectations for continued increases over the foreseeable future. Few companies really shine solely by acquisitions, as many seemed to believe during the conglomerate era of mergers. Pre-tax earn-ings on assets of growth companies should be between 10 and 30 per-cent. Companies that have enjoyed such gains are Tampax, Avon, Merck, Coca-Cola, Eastman Kodak, Minnesota Mining, Proctor and Gamble, IBM, Xerox, and Hewlett-Packard.

Technological Research and Development Are a Must

A growth company must retain a large portion of its earnings for research and development that will produce a salable product that offers excellence in quality, design, or performnace, and preferably all three.

Flair for Salesmanship

A growth company must have a dynamic, aggressive sales department. A good example of salesmanship is Revlon. They are masters at selling "hope in a jar." Their ads are so compelling that it takes restraint to read their brilliant magazine ads and not dash to the nearest cosmetic counter.

Consistently Superior Growth of Earnings

A growth stock is not just a stock that has gone up in price. You want stocks that have shown a consistent, year-after-year, superior growth in earnings even in the face of business reverses and that have a consistent year-in, year-out market for their products or services.

Leaders in a Fast-growing Field

You will want to search for the companies that dominate their markets or are leaders in fast-growing fields. These can be companies

in emerging fields or companies that have developed new ideas in established fields.

Offer a High Return on Equity

A high return on equity means that the company's net profit related to the equity of the stockholders is high in comparison to that earned by other firms in the same industry. The average on all stocks today is about 11¢ per dollar committed. Your growth stocks should exceed this.

In entering the market for trading purposes, timing is all-important. This must be finely tuned.

Cyclical Stocks

Most short-term speculators use the so-called "cyclical" stocks. These share are found in those industries most sensitive to swings in the business cycle. They include the heavily capitalized industries such as steel and heavy machinery. These areas are traditionally strongest in periods of prosperity and at a low ebb in times of recession. The trick is to buy cyclical stocks in the early stages of a business upturn and sell them as closely as possible to the crest. This is not easy.

Popular Favorites

Another trading technique is to move along with the popular stocks of the moment. You can make as much money, short term, on what others think a stock is worth, as on what it is really worth. In the long term we have always returned to basics.

Following the fashions in finance is hazardous. However, if by using good logic you are convinced that a new industry is about to boom, then cautious selections of a stock in that industry may prove rewarding. The trick is to buy early and then, when everyone is clamoring for shares in that industry, sell! Almost invariably the stock market darlings, at the height of their popularity, will sell above sensible valuations.

Special Situations

Another area of speculation is the area of special situations. This can cover a great many areas: mergers, sudden increase in the price of a valuable asset, a new mineral find, a new venture, and so on. Your success will depend greatly on your getting accurate information ahead of the pack. Is the product or service in the mainstream of a rapidly

"That valve controls the Dow Jones Average"

growing demand? Is the demand likely to last? If it is a new venture, determine if it is well capitalized. At least half of all new ventures fold because they run out of capital before they can get into full-fledged operation.

Who will be managing the company? Innovators may have a highly functional idea or patent, but they'll fail because they do not know how to run a business. Creative design people often are very poor at manufacturing techniques, cost control, merchandising, financing, and record keeping. Check to see if those who will run the business are personally solvent and have adequate practical or technical background. The key man may be a fantastic salesman and a poor production man, or vice versa. He may know sales promotion but have no idea about cost controls.

The third thing to consider in a new company is superiority of product or service. New products should be advanced, unusual, and ahead of the field.

Finally, can you afford to lose everything you put into the new company and not miss the money?

On the record, the chances of a new company's growing from zero to great substance are very slim. But if this kind of speculation adds zest to your life and you can afford it, happy hunting!

INVESTOR OR SPECULATOR

We have covered some of the basic characteristics that you must consider in becoming an investor for growth. Should you ever speculate in the stock market? Are there categories between being an investor and being a rank speculator?

The Trader

In even the most valid growth stock selection, there is a time to buy and a time to sell. However, there is another area of the stock market that I would classify between the growth stock investor and the rank gambler. It is that of the trader. I must admit that the line of demarcation does get hazy at times.

There appear to be at least three classes of people who fit this category. If you do not have ample capital, I hope you will resist the temptation to join their ranks, as most out-and-out traders die broke. These three classes are:

1. The constitutional speculators: not necessarily gamblers, but people willing to "take a chance"—to take big risks in hope of great gain.

2. Those who truly think they can supplement their income by modest trading in and out of the market.

3. People with large amounts of income to whom fully taxable income is unattractive, but to whom long-term caital gains, usually taxed at a lower rate, are most alluring.

RIGHT STOCK ACTION

Don't Be Greedy

One characteristic that I have observed about the timing of all good traders is that they never try to squeeze out the last point in a stock. When the great financier Bernard Baruch was questioned on how he made so much money in the stock market, he answered, "I always sold too soon." He always tried to leave a little in it for the next buyer.

Cut Losses Quickly

In trading, it is absolutely necessary to cut your losses quickly. If you've made an error in judgment, don't wait around to find out just how wrong you really were. You can't afford an ego trip. If a 10 percent drop occurs, seriously consider getting out.

Some of my clients act as if the stock knew they owned it or what they paid for it. The stock doesn't even know that your cousin, once removed, works for the company.

Don't think about an impending dividend, or that you have a loss in the stock, or that you just bought it. Also, don't hesitate to buy it back, even at a higher price, if you made a mistake in selling. Above all, don't fall in love with a stock—don't marry it. Be objective. Be flexible. Don't be guilty of prejudices in stock. We all have them occasionally, but the sooner you recognize them and shed stocks that hinder your investment judgment, the better investor you'll become.

Tax considerations should be the furthest from your mind. You are only trying to use $1 to make $2, not to do tax planning while in front of a stock board watching the "horses" run.

Don't Cry

Two other cardinal rules are "Don't cry" and "Don't look back." Lick your wounds and charge forward.

FLEXIBILITY IN SELECTING STOCKS

Common sense will be your greatest ally. You probably will not be able to produce a superior investment performance all of the time. Some of the most respected professionals do not, and they occasionally lag behind the averages. First of all, you'll want to search for bargains. If you can buy stocks at a fraction of what you think they are worth, in the long run most of them should turn out better than if you had paid all you thought they were worth.

To decide what a stock is worth, you will want to use what is called security analysis. The best book on this subject is *Security Analysis* by Graham and Dodd. After you've used standard security analysis to decide the value of a stock, you'll want to compare it with the price of other stocks and buy those stocks that have the lowest price in relation to what you think they are worth.

You will also need to be flexible. There are those who will only buy famous stocks. I know others who will buy only those stocks that the analyst designates as fast-growth stocks.

The fact that you have been in the right kind of securities for several years does not mean that they will be the right kind for the future.

You'll be tempted when you've had unusually favorable performance to be self-satisfied and think you've found the answer to stock selections and continue with those stocks. But if a particular security or industry has had a superior performance for five years, it may be time to get out of it. It probably won't be in the right industry for the next five years. Flexibility must be your policy. To achieve this, look around to find the cheapest stock in relation to value.

It is extremely difficult to buy a bargain if you are buying what other people are buying. If you want to buy the same thing that is popular with your friends or popular with the other investment security analysts, you won't get a bargain. If you buy the same things they buy, you'll have the same performance they'll have. If you're going to have a superior performance, you've got to buy what other people are not buying, or even what other people are selling. Therefore, you'll want to search for those areas that are extremely unpopular and then determine if that unpopularity is permanent. Things don't get low for no reason at all. They get low because other people are selling them. You'll want to search for those stocks that other people are selling, and then if you determine that this problem or adverse outlook is temporary, you will want to buy them and patiently hold them until the public changes its mind. Some of the ancestors of the Rothschilds of Europe were asked questions on this subject and they said, "We always buy cheap and sell dear." You'll want to become a philanthropist. If people are extremely anxious to sell things and trying to find a buyer at any price, you accommodate them; and at other times when people are extraordinarily anxious to buy something and bid it up to a high price, you'll again accommodate them by selling to them.

Uncertain Outlook

You might be saying to me, "But, Venita, the outlook right now is so uncertain." That's true, but you must accept the fact that it is always uncertain—you could have made that statement every day for the past forty years.

We don't have the same uncertainties that we had in the past, but we do have our own very serious uncertainties. Therefore, nobody can promise you that you're going to get good investment performance in anything, no matter what investment you choose. One of the great uncertainties is socialization. Around the world there has been a tendency for the government to interfere more and more with free enterprise and the competitive system; and that does lead to a lot of problems, especially for investors. It burdens the producers with a lot of unnecessary work and expense. It raises the cost of almost everything. It reduce the growth rate. So, in your investment research, one of your major problems will be to find out which stocks are not likely to be greatly hurt by socialization.

SHOULD YOU BUY ON MARGIN?

From years of observing margin account investors, my answer to you is No. Leave this area to the large, sophisticated—whatever that means—investors who are active in the market and who understand the risks as well as the rewards of this type of account. I find that it is usually best if you discipline yourself to the use of only your investable funds. To lose some of your savings in the market is one thing. To lose your future savings as well is another. Yes, I know if it goes the other way your potential for gain is greatly enhanced. It's not that I don't believe in leverage. I believe very strongly in using leverage in real estate and other areas, and in using stock as collateral for funds to purchase capital items.

If after these warnings you still want to open a margin account, here is how it works. First, the Federal Reserve Board sets the margin requirements. These requirements have ranged from 50 to 100 percent in the post-World War II period. For example, if the margin rate is 70 percent, it means that if you want to buy $10,000 worth of stock you would need to put up $7000 in order to make the purchase. You would deposit the required cash or securities with your broker within five business days after the purchase.

You will pay interest for the amount you have borrowed. This has ranged from 6½ to 20½ percent. The amount of interest will be posted on your statement monthly.

To open the account you deposit $2000, or whatever minimum your brokerage firm requires, and sign a margin agreement and a securities loan consent form. This agreement gives your broker the power to pledge or lend your securities. Your securities will be held in what is called "street name," meaning that they are registered in the name of the brokerage house and you do not receive delivery of the certificates. Your broker will, however, credit you with all the dividends received, send you all the reports, and vote your stock in the manner that you direct. You must also abide by the margin maintenance requirements. This usually requires that your margin equity be at least 25 percent. For example, if you bought $10,000 worth of stock with an initial margin requirement of 70 percent, you put up $7000 and received credit of $3000. Let's assume the stock drops to the point where it is worth $4000. Since you owe your broker $3000, your equity in the securities is only $1000 and you are right at the 25 percent limit. At this point you will receive a margin call and you'll be asked to put up more cash or securities. If you cannot meet the call, he will sell your securities, retain the $3000 you owe him, and credit you with the balance.

SHOULD YOU BUY OR SELL OPTIONS?

The use of options has increased greatly in the past ten years. You may have attended a seminar, read newspaper ads, or received a call from an aggressive broker extolling options as the way to lock in additional income if you are on the selling side and to make a large return on a small investment if you are on the buying side.

Buying Options

It's not all that easy, but in order for you to not feel left out when the conversation turns to "puts" and "calls," let's take a brief look at the world of options.

A "call" option is a contract that gives you the right to buy 100 shares of a given stock at a fixed price for a fixed period of time. The period of time usually runs nine months and ten days (for tax reasons), but can run 30, 90, 120 days or other lengths of time. The premium that you pay for the option usually runs about 10 to 15 percent of the value of the stock.

A "put" option is the reverse of a "call" option. You now have the privilege of selling 100 shares of the stock at a fixed price within the option period. These usually cost a few percentage points less than call options and are not as popular.

Why would you ever buy an option? The main reason is that it gives you a chance to make a sizable profit on the move of a stock while limiting the amount of possible loss. For example, you think that General Widgets Company stock selling at $40 may surge to $80. It would cost you $4000 to buy the shares, and you may not want to risk $4000 or you may not have $4,000 to invest. Still, you would like to take the chance that General Widgets will jump and as a result you'd make a large profit. In this case you might go the option route, buying an option for $400. Let's assume your anticipations are correct and the stock hits $70 within the option period. You exercise your option, buy the 100 shares at $40, and then turn around and sell the shares for $70. You have received $7000 from the sale of the shares. From this you would subtract the $4000 you paid for them, the $400 premium for the option, and about $110 for the brokerage commissions, and you would wind up with a profit of $2490.

Now let's assume that your expectations did not materialize and General Widgets goes to $30. What do you do? You do nothing. You simply let your option expire. You are out $400. Your loss is limited to the cost of your option and you are thankful that you didn't buy 100 shares at $4000 and watch your investment shrink.

"Put" options work in reverse. (There are also some very fancy devices called "straddles"—a combination of a put and a call; "strips," which are composed of two puts and one call; and "straps," which are one put and two calls.)

Selling Options

What is a call option? It is a contract that allows the buyer of the option the right to purchase a particular stock at a specific price during a defined period of time, regardless of the market price of the stock. A covered call option is an option written by a seller who owns the underlying security. When you write a covered call option, you receive an option premium and also continue to receive any dividends on the underlying portfolio stock.

The combination of the income from the option premium plus the dividends from your stock may be two or three times the amount of dividend income alone. Option writing can substantially increase your income from the stock without a commensurate increase in risk.

You may also lock in a profit. If you have bought a block of stock with the goal of making $5 per share profit and sell an option at $5, you lock in that profit.

Your overall objective when you sell call options is to utilize various strategies to produce higher current income, lessen your portfolio's volatility, and hopefully reduce your risks in down markets.

Now let's return to portfolio basics.

A PROFITABLE PORTFOLIO

There are three important areas in choosing and maintaining a profitable portfolio of stocks: diversification, proper selection, and constant supervision. Let's examine the first, diversification. Diversification means spreading the risk. The old adage of not putting all your eggs in one basket has considerable merit in assembling a good investment portfolio.

Diversification

Don't put all your faith in only one company, for it may disappoint you. You may be well informed on sales figures, competitive situations, or whatever, but always be prepared for a disaster. Going for broke on a winner could make you rich, but no one knows which stock will be the big winner. If you buy a diversified group of fundamentally sound stocks with good earnings, the chances are that in a good market you will catch at least some of the big winners. Most big money in a diversified portfolio comes from one or two big winners.

Don't be deceived into thinking that ten oil stocks is diversification; it is not. You should have a portfolio covering a wider range of industries. For example, you may have some stocks in the soft drink industry, the retail area, drugs, home furnishings, electrical equipment, brewing, agricultural machinery, gold mining, and others.

When managing your own portfolio, you may find it extremely helpful to limit yourself to ten stocks, regardless of the amount of money you have to invest. I'm surprised to find that investors think they can only own 100 shares of each company's stock. If the capital you have available for investing is sufficiently large, perhaps you should consider owning 1000 shares of each stock.

Moving to Strength

Don't overdiversify. You cannot be truly current on more than ten stocks at a time. If you limit your holdings to ten stocks and a stock comes to your attention that you feel you should buy, what will this force you to do? To eliminate one. So you go down through your list and sell the one that is doing the poorest job for you. Now, won't you? I wish this were true of all my clients. Many go through and pick out their winner to sell and smugly say, "You'll never go broke taking a profit." They are keeping their losers and selling their winners. That's not the way to upgrade a portfolio. Sell the poorest performer. This allows you the possibility of continuously moving to a position of strength.

Timing Is the Key

There is a time to buy and a time to sell. The old adage about buying low and selling high is easy to say and very hard to do. Often you never know what the high or low is until it's too late for maximum advantage.

But how do you determine when to buy and when to sell? Let's look at buying first.

When to Buy. Buy stocks only when you think you can make a profit. The only reason to be in the market is to make money. Buy only when you anticipate a substantial rise within one year. Look for 25 percent appreciation per year. Buy for investment gain, not dividends.

When the Federal Reserve Board is escalating the prime rate, money will earn more in mutual money market funds than in the stock market, so you might as well move there and sit out the storm.

When to Sell. I have a very simple rule for judging when to sell a stock I own. It's so simple you'll probably dismiss the whole idea. However, I've found over the years that it has helped me cut through the tinsel and fog and to reach good decisions as to when to sell.

I do not look at what price I paid for a stock unless selling it would cause me to incur a large capital gains tax liability. I simply ask myself, "If I had the money this stock would bring in my hands at this moment, would I buy this stock at this price?" If my answer is Yes, I hold. If it is No, I sell. The only difference between my owning this stock and having the money is a small amount of commission which I should not let affect my judgment.

You may have great difficulty selling. Most people do. If you have a gain, you may not be able to bear the thought of selling and paying the capital gains tax. When you analyze the situation, there are only two ways to avoid eventually paying it, neither of which you are going to like. You can hold it until it goes back to what you paid for it; or hold it until your death, and let your heirs worry about the tax when they sell it.

On the other hand, if you have a loss, you may say, "I won't sell, for I just can't afford to take a loss." You already have the loss. There are only two questions now that you should ask yourself. Can you deduct the loss advantageously on your income tax, and where are you most likely to make up your losses—where you are or in another stock?

Lay your hand over the cost basis of your stocks and judge them individually on their potential over the next six months.

When you no longer anticipate a worthwhile rise, when the outlook for earnings is no longer favorable, when the stock is clearly overpriced in relation to its normal price–earnings multiple or to that of companies of similar quality in the same industry, sell.

Don't Average Down

I am not in agreement with a large number of stockbrokers who advise their clients to average down. What is meant by averaging down? Let's assume that you bought 100 shares of a stock at $30 per share, and it has dropped in price to $20. There are those who recommend that you buy another 100 shares at $20. This would give you an average cost per share of $25 on the 200 shares.

I feel you can average yourself right into the basement of the poorhouse. I never mind paying a higher price than my original purchase price if there is earnings justification. It just means the market has confirmed my own good judgment.

No One Rings a Bell

Are you bearish or bullish for the next two months? How about the next eight months? What about the next eighteen months? (That's long term for the dynamic market we have. As a matter of fact, I find that most people consider twelve months and one day long term.)

Are you bearish for the short term and bullish for the long term? If so, you probably have lots of company. The only problem is that no one rings a bell when the bottom (or the top) of the market has been reached, and those who wait often continue to wait until the market has climbed to new highs. Then they panic on the up side and say, "What a fool I was not to have bought back when the market was low. I've already waited too long, but there must be plenty of good buys left." And they hop in with both feet.

With the continuously growing appetite and importance of the institutional investor, it is well to consider if the individual investor can compete successfully.

THE INSTITUTIONAL INVESTOR

The institutional investor is one who usually buys in large blocks at advantageously lower negotiated commissions. He is the large life insurance company, the large bank, the large pension fund manager, the large college endowment fund manager, the large mutual fund.

There is considerable evidence that their demand for stock will be a strong force in the marketplace. Projections show that in the 1980s nonprofit institutions will have in their portfolios $4 billion worth of stocks, life insurance companies $5.5 billion, private pension funds $13.3 billion, open-end investment trusts $90 billion, and state and local government retirement plans $1.5 billion (even under our new pension laws).

There are just not this many new quality issues coming into the market to fill the demand. As we learned in basic economics, if demand is greater than supply, the price will rise.

Logic would seem to indicate that with this much money in the hands of trained, informed, unemotional money managers would lend a high degree of stability to the market. I'm sorry to say that I don't think this is what will be happening. Their equipment for becoming better informed has reached a high degree of electronic sophistication. Unfortunately, they all seem to be availing themselves of the same tools. They are all reading the same computer printouts from their very advanced monitoring equipment. This shows all of them the same buy and sell signals at the same time, causing simultaneous buying and selling that results in sudden and often precipitous price changes.

An example might be found in the stock of Wrigley. Their commercials may have been a bit staid—"Double your pleasure, double your fun"—but you always knew Wrigley was there. Then suddenly at 1 P.M. on that fateful day in October, trading was halted by the New York Stock Exchange. When it reopened around 2:30, there was no pleasure and no fun. Wrigley was off 27 points, almost a 20 percent drop. Just like that. By year's end it had shed another 15 points. (I'm happy to report that it has now come back.)

Had the bottom suddenly fallen out of the chewing gum market? No, as a matter of fact, third-quarter earnings were well above the previous year's earnings, but they were not what Wall Street expected. Wall Street becomes nervous when its expectations are not met, and 20,000 shares were dumped. That is what is called "bombing" a stock.

YOU CAN COMPETE

Can you as an individual investor compete with so many institutional buyers in the market?

Yes, you can probably beat all but the well-managed mutual funds if you will conscientiously do your homework and keep reasonably calm. One of your greatest assets is flexibility. There will be times when the economy is such that you can't make money in the stock market. At such times, get out.

It may be more difficult for the professional money manager to unload a block of 200,000 shares of the kinds of stocks institutions hold without depressing the market in that stock.

For example, suppose you decide that IBM's multiple (the stock's price relative to its earnings per share) is too high, and you'd like to sell your 50 shares. Fine—no problem. But if Morgan Guaranty held $2 billion of IBM stock, could they do the same? No, they are locked in, unless they want to see their last shares sold at prices much lower than their first.

Very often, the way to make big money in the market is to find small, well-managed, rapidly growing companies. Most institutions are too big to be able to take advantage of that strategy. You can buy meaningful positions in smaller companies that the "big boys" cannot touch. You would hope, however, that as the company grew, the institutions would be able to move in, which in turn should help move up the price of the stock you "discovered."

KEEP YOUR PERSPECTIVE

When news seems at its worst, remember that good news has always followed bad news. Things do move in cycles and waves. (I know you feel some of them may engulf you.) Interest rates do adjust downward as well as upward. The crisis shortages can be solved. A nation that can go to the moon can also produce energy, good food, and unpolluted air and water if business is freed from unnecessary interference. Inflation, however, is something you must learn to live with. It may slow slightly, but you must accept it as a continuing fact of life.

It's important to be in the stock market, for it offers you opportunities for gains, favorable tax treatment on these gains, and liquidity. Yes, there are risks. But all of life is a risk. Investing will always be a delicate balance between risk and reward.

WHICH STOCKS FOR THE DECADE AHEAD?

Don't I wish I knew! And don't you wish I knew and would pass on the secret to you?

From all indications, the decade ahead can be a very good one, but emphasis will be in different areas than before. It will probably be an economy of shortages of natural resources with higher capital investment requirements than in the 1970s. While the 1970s were consumer-oriented, the 1980s will probably be investment-oriented. We will have greater emphasis on how to manufacture products more cheaply and to conserve our natural resources such as oil and gas, lumber, iron ore, and copper. Greater emphasis will be on technology —of building smaller cars that consume less fuel; of contructing homes that are smaller and better insulated and probably located nearer to places of employment; of producing heating and air conditioning units that are designed to consume less electricity. "Recycling," "recovery," and "reuse" will be words that we'll use often in our day-to-day conversations.

Now that you have studied the fundamentals of how stocks are traded, what to look for in income stocks and in growth stocks, and the areas to be cautious about in speculative issues, let's determine what the 'eighties should hold for the market.

To obtain a better perspective for the 'eighties let's take a few minutes to look at what preceded the decade, where we are now, and what we might anticipate in this decade.

Era of Stability

During the years 1949 to 1966, our country experienced an era of stability. Inflation was at a low to moderate rate, our gross national product showed a comfortable increase each year, and capital and labor worked together in relative peace.

Then President Johnson decided to bring us the Great Society without paying for it. He attempted welfare and warfare without the wisdom or the courage to increase taxes. The gold backing of our dollar was removed, the Treasury printing presses began to hum, and before long too many dollars were chasing too few goods, and inflation with its terrible devastation was unleashed on an unsuspecting citizenry.

Era of Pendulum Economics

Beginning around 1966, we entered an era of pendulum economics that continues today. Government bureaucrats, thoroughly indoctrinated in the Keynesian theory, began playing with the money supply under the guise that by doing so with their great wisdom, they could finely tune a balance between full employment and inflation. (Keynesian economics has destroyed every economic system upon which its theories have been imposed.)

Pendulum economics is comparable to the pendulum on a grandfather clock. If you are riding on the pendulum, you may fare very well as you ride back and forth. However, if you are standing in its path frozen by confusion or indecision, it will knock you to the ground. This is exactly what has been happening to many stock investors the past fifteen years.

Hedge Against Inflation

According to the old rules, stocks were supposed to provide you with a hedge against inflation. However, if you invested fifteen years ago and have done no better than the Dow-Jones Industrial Average (most investors do not do as well) your portfolio not only has not shown a gain, but a 4 percent loss. If stocks have had such a poor performance for so long, you may be asking me why I'm recommending equities as viable investments for you to consider.

First, I believe circumstances have changed and will continue to change during the 'eighties. And second, one of the most common mistakes I see investors make is to extrapolate. If stocks have been rising two or three years, investors extrapolate and conclude they will rise the next few years. If they have been going down, they extrapolate downward. This could, of course, happen, though I find it rarely does.

I am convinced that the stock market will be an excellent place in which to invest intermittently for growth and income during the 'eighties. There are many reasons for my conviction. Some will be obvious, and others not so obvious. Let's begin with the obvious.

Basic Relative Value

The basic relative value of American stocks is at its highest compared to present market price. Stocks represent investment values that you have not seen for the last half-century. By virtually all yardsticks—like price earnings ratios, dividends, growth, book value, and return on equity—a large number of stocks are selling at unusually low prices. While the market values of the majority of stocks has not increased, the corporations behind them have prospered, and their earnings have climbed. There are many sound and profitable companies selling at dramatic discounts.

Stocks are bargains when compared to other investment possibilities. Over the past decade, real estate, precious metals, antiques, and other collectibles (all of which we'll discuss as we progress through the book) have provided a hedge against inflation because their prices have increased. Stocks have not participated. Yet these stocks aren't just pieces of paper called stock certificates; they represent shares of ownership in real businesses that have assets that can produce growing earnings and dividends.

Corporations Are Repurchasing Their Stocks

Some of the smartest and best qualified investors in the world know that these stocks are a bargain. How do I know? I know because these same businessmen are repurchasing their own stocks.

Even in the Great Depression, on the market's worst day, stocks were not as cheap in relation to replacement value. That is why the people who know their companies best are using their cash to buy their own shares at a fraction of what they know they are worth.

Mergers and Acquisitions

There has been a large increase in the number of mergers and acquisitions by American businessmen. Stocks of many of these companies are being acquired for less than the value of their production facilities, trained personnel, and established outlets. Rather than spend money to set up new plants and marketing programs to expand their company, cash-rich companies are making tender offers that may represent as much as a 40 to 100 percent mark-up over the current price of the company's stock, and still feel they are getting a steal.

Political Environment

Tax Reform Act.   With the passage of the Tax Reform Act of 1978, for the first time in forty years Congress gave token recognition that it may make more sense to invest than to spend. They voted a small break in capital gains taxes, made the 10 percent Investment Tax Credit permanent (I'll tell you about this later), and gave token tax cuts for individuals and corporations. There is a glimmer of recognition that capital formation is an essential ingredient of business and industry; that plant and equipment can't be built if all their profits are taken away; and that capital is necessary to create employment. These greater incentives to invest will enable corporations to build new facilities or modernize old ones, which should, in turn, increase worker productivity.

Proposition 13.   Proposition 13 in California is another encouraging sign. Californians voted themselves a 50 percent tax cut and got away with it. And they followed this with Proposition 2, which limits the amount of money that the state government can spend. It can never again be higher than it was in 1979, adjusted for inflation and population growth. These are important trends in the political environment.

Defense of the Dollar.   On November 1, 1978, a decision was made to defend the dollar. This was a monumental decision. We had been letting the dollar "go to hell in a hand basket," but finally the decision was made that the dollar was important, that it was the currency of the world, and that we would defend it. That's an important political decision and bodes well for business.

Federal Budget. The 'eighties began with the first Democratic budget in my lifetime that did not have any new social legislation in it. This is truly a historic turn of events.

Supply and Demand

As you learned in Basic Economics 101, to be a successful investor you must invest your money where demand is greater than supply. Let's look at the demand/supply situation regarding common stocks.

I believe there is a critical shortage of common stocks in this country, and they are not making many more of them. What few new stocks have come on the market have been more than overshadowed by the repurchases and acquisitions. Major companies are buying up other whole companies, taking millions of shares of stock out of circulation. Therefore, the supply is dwindling while demand is growing.

Availability of Money

One of the most important criteria for appreciation of stocks is not always the possibility of their selling at higher prices because of value, but the availability of cash. The majority of work I see security analysts do is on what the company is worth. However, I find that another very important factor that affects the market is how much cash is available. There is a large amount of capital waiting in the wings to buy stocks at the right time. Institutional investors like banks, insurance companies, and pension funds have sizable amounts ready to go into the market.

Pension Funds

As we entered the 'eighties, over $600 billion were in pension funds. Over the years, more than 50 percent of new money has been placed in stocks. In fact, in the early 'seventies, this moved to almost 100 percent of new money, and then dropped to only 9 percent of new money in the early 'eighties.

Pension funds began the 'eighties with approximately 45 percent of their funds in common stocks. That's the lowest in fifteen years. Cash flow of pension funds exceeds $20 billion a year. Also, pension funds began the decade with $35 billion of the securities they own that will mature within four years. Take $20 billion a year cash flow for four years that's $80 billion; add in $35 billion—that's $113 billion available cash even if they don't increase their percentage.

Property and Casualty Companies

Property and casualty companies are usually enormous holders of common stocks. They began the decade with only 15 percent of their assets in common stocks. That's the lowest in 25 years.

Individual Investors

Individual investors invested only 10 percent of total assets in stocks at the beginning of the decade. That's the lowest in near-term history. At the same time, over $50 billion was parked in mutual money market funds.

Foreign Investors

Foreign investments in the U.S. were at a low point at the beginning of the 'eighties. There is an enormous amount of foreign money available for investment in the U.S. Foreign investors' interest is two-fold. Our stocks are attractive values, and our U.S. dollar is severely depressed in comparison to other currencies.

There has also been a change in foreign legislation. Mrs. Thatcher in England was able to change restrictions so that Englishmen can invest more easily in foreign securities. Now they can invest what they choose where they choose. Japan for the first time is allowing their pension funds to go outside the country to make 10 percent of their investments.

There appears to be a tremendous amount of funds held by pension plan managers, institutions, foreign investors, and by the American investors that are poised ready to go into our stock market. In addition, there is a large amount of funds invested in fixed income investments (that are definitely losing the inflation race). Even if only a small amount of that money is moved into equities, it will have a significant impact on stock prices.

New Issues Not Coming to the Market

This comes at a time when very few new issues are coming onto the market. Who wants to sell his stock for three to four times earnings, which is the ratio many excellent companies are selling for today? When you buy a company that trades at three times earnings, you are buying it at a 33 percent after-tax return and about a 66 percent pre-tax return. Not a large number of investments provide rewards of this magnitude.

Return on Assets

There are many who have made the assumption that, even though the rate of return of corporate earnings has been around 12 percent through most of the postwar period, when these capital assets would have to be replaced they would cost more in "real dollars" because of inflation; therefore, the rate of return in constant dollars was dropping. In-depth studies I have made do not substantiate this theory. Return on corporate assets has been fairly stationary even with rising inflation. The companies have been earning these returns on replacement values, not on original cost, thereby offsetting inflationary penalities. After adjusting for inflation, there does not appear to be a long-term decline in profitability.

I feel that those who argue that they should adjust earnings down to take into account the swollen profits of inventory and inadequate depreciation of plant and equipment are forgetting that a large portion of corporate assets come from borrowed money, which in our inflationary times can be repaid with cheaper and cheaper dollars .

The assets they purchase with borrowed funds will appreciate compared to the shrinking dollars that will be required to repay the debt. However, I find many investors concentrate only on the first adjustment, which reduces profitability, while ignoring the latter, which can improve it. This results in their undervaluing the earnings of a vast majority of stocks.

Stock Earnings vs. Bond Interest

During the past ten years, investors have been placing too low a valuation on stock earnings relative to the interest rates they could obtain on corporate bonds. To calculate the earnings yield on common stock, you simply take the earnings per share and divide it by the market price. For example, if you have a stock that earns $1 and the market price is $10, your earnings yield would be 10 percent.

A common mistake that I see investors make in inflationary times is to calculate bond interest at the rate presently in effect rather than the real rate (the present rate minus the current rate of inflation). If bonds have a rate of 9 percent and inflation is running at 7 percent (and don't you wish it would slow to this), then the real rate is 2 percent before taxes. However, I find that many investors tend to ignore the real rate of interest and focus only on the current rate; therefore, they demand too high a dividend rate on common stocks.

For example, if the Dow trades at seven times earnings, the earnings yield on the Dow is 14.2 percent. (To calculate the earnings yield from P/E ratio, place the numerator 1 over the P/E ratio. If it is 7, the earnings yield is 1/7 or 14.2 percent.) When inflation runs at the same rate as bonds, their real rate is zero. To obtain a real interest rate on stocks, they too must have an earnings yield in excess of the rate of inflation.

Higher Costs Are Passed to the Consumer

Have corporations been able to pass on increases in wages and materials and maintain their profit margin on sales? The answer appears to be yes. For the past ten years, the profit margin has been 14.9 percent of sales, compared to 15.4 percent the previous ten years and 14.9 the ten years before. You can see that profit margins have held up very well despite accelerating inflation, credit crunches, recessions, and periods of price and wage controls.

As a matter of fact, corporate earnings have increased faster than the rate of inflation in the last decade. Therefore, common stocks have provided a hedge against inflation in terms of real purchasing power, despite their poor showing in the stock market.

Return on Equity on the Dow

The return on equity on the Dow has not varied substantially over the past twenty-five years, running about 10 percent. The poor performance of the stock market appears, then, to be largely attributable to the inability of the individual investor, the institutional investor, and the brokers to understand the effect of inflation on corporate profits.

Expected Slowdown in the Economy

A brief slowdown in the economy can be a constructive move for the market in that it tends to moderate interest rates and inflation. The market has a tendency to look beyond the valleys to the peaks beyond. The market is usually a leading indicator, anticipating the resumption of sound economic growth.

WHERE WILL THE DOW BE BY 1990?

Where will stock prices be toward the end of the 'eighties? I really don't know, but I can look at where it is estimated the Gross National Product will be by then. It appears that the GNP will double within the next eight years, if for no other reason than inflation. The cost of

living in the U.S. has doubled in the last eleven years, and it is estimated that it will more than double in this decade, so that the rise in
the cost of living alone will double our GNP. When we add to this
the increased population and the possibility of increased output per
person, it is conservative to say that the GNP of the United States will
double in this decade. If the GNP doubles, the sales volume of the
corporation should also double. If the sales volume doubles, what will
happen to profits? They will double unless there is a change in the profit
margin. There could be and there sometimes are temporary changes
in the profit margin, but it would seem reasonable to assume that the
profit margins won't be any lower than now. There's a less than 50–50
chance that they'll be higher. Therefore, profits should double. Now,
if profits double, what will happen to share prices?

The Dow Jones Industrial Average entered the decade selling at
only slightly above six times earnings. Over the past eighty years stocks
have averaged selling at fourteen times earnings, and for many reasons
it is very likely that they will again sell for at least average price–
earnings ratios. If they do, that's fourteen times earnings, which is more
than double where they are now. So if their earnings double and the
price earnings ratios double, stock prices should quadruple. There are
several reasons that this is not too optimistic. One is that the price–
earnings ratios are extraordinarily low. In forty years, there has never
been a time when the ratio between the price and the earnings was
below 6 for more than two or three months. Also, price–earnings ratios
are low compared to what they are in other nations. In Japan, the
average P/E ratio is twenty times earnings. In most of the world, P/E
ratios are far higher than they are on the New York Stock Exchange.
So our common stocks are cheap in relation to earnings. Also, they
are low in relation to book value. There have been very few times in
the history of the U.S. when you could buy shares of oil stocks on the
exchange below their book value. This is one of those few times.
(Book value is the value of all assets less all liabilities.) Even when
the stock market reached its all-time low in 1932, the Dow did not
trade below book value for more than a few months.

To me, the stock market appears cheap by every historical standard as we enter the decade of the 'eighties. Even though inflation will
continue, companies are proving they can not only survive, but also
prosper in this climate.

There is no question that our economic system does face new and
challenging problems. There will continue to be energy shortages and
the OPEC cartel, a government that taxes business profits and capital
gains excessively, prohibitive ecological costs, and a large uninformed
citizenry that is anti-business.

But I am convinced that the U.S. stock market is destined for explosive growth. In the 1980s we should move away from planned obsolescence and should begin to build things to last. Eating habits may change. As the prices of animal feeds increase, we may see more meat substitutes. There will be a rash of changes. But is this bad?

The decade ahead will offer you a dynamic challenge—a challenge that you cannot afford to turn down. It is a challenge you must accept. Do so with intelligence, knowledge, vigor, and enthusiasm!

APPLICATION

1. A good way to become knowledgeable about growth industries is is to be alert to current trends. In which areas should you be attuned as you read the daily newspaper?

2. How will you become informed about the management of the corporations in the industries that you feel offer the most growth potential?

3. How do you determine the right time to invest?

4. How will you time your sales?

5. What is the Gross National Product today?

6. What is your prediction of what the GNP will be in ten years?

7. What is your prediction of the price–earnings ratio of the stocks on the Dow in ten years?

8. What action will you take to apply your predictions to benefit your own financial future?

   a.

   b.

   c.

9. Sit down and draw the financial triangle. Place yourself on the triangle. Are you emphasizing income when your real objective is growth of capital?

10. Order the booklets "Investment Facts—Cash Dividends Every Three Months From 25 to 100 Years," "The Language of Investing," and "How to Get Help When You Invest" from the New York Stock Exchange, 11 Wall Street, New York, N.Y. 10005.

4

LETTING THE PROS
DO YOUR
INVESTING

Now that you've had a good look at some of the basic requirements to becoming a successful investor in the stock market, you may be saying to me, "I'm an engineer [or accountant or salesman or doctor]. I'm good at what I do because I devote many hours a day to my vocation, but I have neither the time nor inclination to study the stock market. Yet I know that I need to have my money working for me. I may have children who will need funds to go to college, and I'll need to have funds to retire in financial dignity someday. What can I do?" If you don't have what I call the three *T*s and an *M*, put professional money managers to work for you.

TIME

The first *T* is for time. Do you truly have the time to study the market trends? I'm not asking if you have a moment before you settle down to watch the next murder mystery or police or hospital drama on TV to take a quick glance at the evening newspaper to learn whether your stocks went up or down during the day.

Do you really have the time to spend studying balance sheets, profit and loss statements, market trends, economic indicators, changes in monetary policies, increases in government expenditures, decreases in other areas of government expenditures, shortages, surpluses, consumer buying trends, international competition due to lower labor costs, acecss to raw materials, and so forth?

If you can answer that you do have this time and feel that it would be more rewarding financially and emotionally to spend this time being a professional in the market than spending it developing more expertise in your profession, pursuing a hobby, or engaging in recreational activities, then you have the first *T*.

TRAINING

The second *T* is for training. What is your educational background—accounting, statistical analysis, money and banking, marketing, economics, finance, human psychology? Even if you have the first *T* of time, can you properly translate this knowledge into action? If you can, and if you are thoroughly schooled in these areas and have developed some reasonable expertise in them, you qualify for the second *T*.

TEMPERAMENT

The third *T* is for temperament. Are you temperamentally suited for successful investing in the stock market? Have you worked very hard for your money? Were you a child of the Depression? Does your memory of hard times make you squeeze every nickel until it screams loudly?

I was raised in the hard times of the dust bowl of Oklahoma. That trying experience made an indelible impression on me. In my counseling I have observed many others from a similar background. In most of them I have found that it has caused their emotional decisions about money to be more black and white than they should be. Money decisions must often be based on various shades of gray. I find that if a person has experienced bad times, he either clutches a dollar very tightly to his bosom for fear of losing it, or determines that once he gets a dollar, he is going to put it to work aggressively to see if he can turn that dollar into an additional dollar. My reaction to my dust bowl experience was and still is the latter. It's not that I enjoy hoarding money or even spending it. My challenge has been to take one dollar and make two, and then take the two and make four, and so on. Money is like a flower. If you squeeze it you will crush the life out of it. You must let it blossom forth to reveal its full beauty.

Analyze your own personality. This is not an easy thing to do. Some basic books on psychology may be of help to you. One I have enjoyed is Dr. Muriel James' book on transactional analysis entitled *Born to Win*. I also recommend Dr. Maxwell Maltz's book, *Psycho-Cybernetics*. The whole field of psychology can be fascinating, and through it you may discover why you and others react to certain stimuli and conditions the way you do. In the world of finance, this knowledge can pay handsome dividends.

Can you act when you have reasonable facts before you? You'll never know all the facts. If you wait until you are 100 percent sure, your decision will invariably be too late. I find that most investment decisions are made far too late rather than too soon. Don't ever deceive yourself into thinking that if you don't make a decision, you haven't made a decision. You have. You have decided that where your money is right now is the best place for it to be.

I've found the difference between mediocre and superb performance in the market is the ability to evaluate and then take the appropriate action quickly.

I observe many who plant good fruit trees in the form of good stocks and refuse to harvest the fruit, letting it rot on the trees.

Don't become enamored with a stock because it has been good to you by making you an unrealized capital gain (meaning it went up). Don't be afraid of taking a profit if it appears that the stock has topped out and will probably be flat for six months to a year. Don't back off from taking a profit just because you'll have a capital gains tax to pay.

There is a time to buy and a time to sell—regardless of which stocks you own. Can you unemotionally move when it's time to do so? If so, you have the third *T*, temperament.

MONEY

You have analyzed your three *T*s. Now let's look at how you fit the *M*. *M* represents money. Do you have enough money to diversify your holdings? Diversification is one of the first rules of successful investing. Do you have sufficient funds to enable you not to put all your eggs in one basket, but to have at least ten baskets—one basket for office equipment, another for natural resources, still another for beverages, another for retail stores, another for automobile stocks, etc.?

It is difficult to obtain adequate diversification with less than $100,000. There are many institutions and other fiduciaries who do not consider sufficient diversification can be obtained with less than $250,000.

You may feel the need to subscribe to an advisory service. You should calculate this cost in money and in the time needed to digest and apply the contents.

If you have the three *T*s and an *M*, you will find being your own

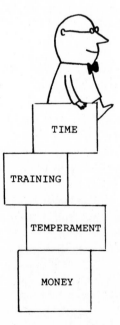

pro fun and rewarding. Therefore, you should plan to devote considerable time and energy to this important facet of your financial future. If not, let the pros do it for you.

LETTING THE PROS DO IT

You may find letting the professionals do your investing for you very hard to do. It is especially hard for some professionals. You would think it would be otherwise, since they are so aware of how much time, training, and experience it took to bring them to their present level of proficiency. The admission that someone can do something better than they can do it often is just too hard an admission for some persons to make. The same doctor who would be aghast if I should suggest diagnosing my own pains will hop into the stock market arena without any more preparation.

Even when the professional becomes a pro in the market, I usually find that the good full-time pros outperform the part-time pros.

Let's assume that you are willing to let the professionals help you. What choices are available to you?

Private Professional Management

There are two ways to obtain professional management. If you have a large amount of money to invest, you may qualify for private professional management through an investment advisory service. There are some that will accept as small an account as $50,000 for a fee of 1 percent of the net assets per annum. Most of the top services will not accept an account of less than $250,000. Some services will not accept a private account of less than $20 million. On this size account one-half of 1 percent of the net asset value is the usual management charge.

Let's assume that you have sufficient funds to qualify for private professional management. What should you do?

First, do an in-depth study of the professional teams available. Become acquainted with their personnel, and take a good hard look at their past performance. After all, you are buying brains. You might as well get the best "brains" you can for the money you are paying.

Second, you will sign an agreement giving the management service discretionary power to buy and sell for your account. This can be cancelled or amended at your discretion. In the agreement you should designate the stockbroker of your choice.

Third, you will need to transfer the agreed amount of money or stocks to the bank or broker that is to act as the custodian of the assets in the account. They will then make the proper delivery of stocks and money at the direction of the advisors.

After these necessary steps have been taken, you will begin to receive confirmations from your broker on each buy and sell. Your service will also make a monthly or quarterly report to you, giving you a resumé of all transactions, a report on gains and losses, and often a comparison of your portfolio's performance against that of the popular averages.

You may withdraw the account at any time.

Public Professional Management

If the amount you have for investment in equities is less than $250,000, you should consider using public professional management, through the investment medium of the investment company trusts, commonly called mutual funds.

I would prefer calling them by another name. Not that the term "mutual fund" does not give an indication of their nature, but I find that so many confuse them with mutual savings and loan or mutual insurance companies, and worry that they can be assessed, which of course is not true.

The Feeling Is Mutual. "Mutual" means you may mutually benefit from pooling your resources with others. For example, let's say you have $1000. Alone you could not obtain diversification or professional management. But let's assume there are 999 others who each have $1000 and have the same financial objective that you do. If all of you pooled your funds, you would have a million dollars. With a million dollars, you would have sufficient money to spread your risk among a number of different industries. You would also have enough money to hire some top professional money managers to select and constantly supervise your holdings. A mutual fund, then, should do for you what you would do for yourself if you had sufficient time, the proper training, the right temperament, and sufficient money to diversify. It offers the same advantages to the small investor that the wealthy have always had. The wealthy have enough money to diversify and enough money to hire the pros.

In a previous chapter, we concluded that there are three basic requirements for successful investing: diversification, proper selection, and constant supervision. Let's examine these three to see if a quality mutual fund with excellent management could fulfill these requirements. There is a wide range of expertise in mutual fund managements. There are a large number of them that I would not use. There are a select group of management teams that have consistently produced superior performance. You should spend considerable time and study choosing the one or ones you will use.

THE SEMINAR FUND

For the past eighteen years I have conducted financial planning seminars in Houston, Texas. At the second session of each seminar, I discuss mutual funds and how they work. As an example, but not necessarily as a recommendation, I usually use the same mutual funds. It is middle of the road in its financial objectives, has a good 46-year record, and has averaged approximately 12 percent compounded over its lifetime with all distributions reinvested. It's not always the top performer among funds, but its record is consistently good. (Sometimes I use another fund with a very good 53-year record, which obviously has excellent management.)

Incidentally, I remember using this fund one night at a seminar when a lady, evidently impressed with the possibilities of what the fund could offer, came up to me and blurted out, "Whatever will the savings and loans do?" When I asked her what she meant, she said she feared that everybody would now take their money out of them, and they would not have sufficient money to lend for home mortgages. I calmed her fears by assuring her that much of the money would remain there, so she need not be so concerned.

I always use a fund that has averaged at least 12 percent over the long term, for I'm convinced that that's the minimum long-term performance you should accept on your money. With our present rate of inflation and progressive tax bite, you have to obtain that performance to make any reasonable progress. This 12 percent has not been enough to keep you even the past few years, but by using a system I'll show you, you should be able to hold your own.

In this book I'll call this fund the Seminar Fund. That's not its real name. If I were to use its real name, I would have to hand you a prospectus before I could tell you about it, and send you a new one each year. I do encourage you to go to your broker and get the prospectus of a real fund. Most prospectuses are pretty much the same. The funds they describe differ as to financial objective, investment advisors, and performance, but their fees, commission, and structure will be similar.

In our chapter on selecting stocks, we agreed that one of the first requirements of successful investing was diversification—spreading your risk. Mutual funds uniquely fulfill this requirement.

Diversification. The Investment Company Act of 1940 provides that a mutual fund may not have more than 5 percent of its assets in any one company, nor own more than 10 percent of the outstanding shares of any one company. Because of this regulation, if you own a mutual fund you know that you will always have at least twenty stocks in your fund's portfolio, and also that any one of the twenty will not represent more than 10 percent of the outstanding shares of that company. This in itself ensures a fair degree of diversification.

You will find as you explore the large number of funds available that most of them have from 100 to 150 different stocks in their portfolio, and cover a wide spectrum of industry groups.

For example, Table 4–1 shows the way $10,000 would have been

TABLE 4–1. LARGEST INDIVIDUAL HOLDINGS

Philip Morris	$385	NCR	289
Boeing	356	Conoco	240
International Business		Ford Motor	239
Machines	315	SmithKline	232
MCA	311	Union Oil of California	218
General Dynamics	294		

OTHER PORTFOLIO SECURITIES IN THE SEMINAR FUND

Abbott Laboratories	$133	Delta Air Lines	48
Ahmanson (H.F.)	43	Diamond Shamrock	68
Alcan Aluminum	176	Digital Equipment	102
Alco Standard	67	duPont	43
Allis-Chalmers	108	Eastman Kodak	31
American Airlines	25	Federal National Mortgage	213
American Broadcasting	128	Federated Department Stores	41
Amfac	53	Firestone Tire & Rubber	9
Armco	52	First Charter Financial	31
Avery International	48	First Chicago	36
BankAmerica	74	GEICO	58
Bethlehem Steel	29	General Electric	71
Boise Cascade	17	General Motors	112
Braniff International	41	General Telephone &	
Bristol-Myers	87	Electronics	26
Canadian Pacific	75	Goodyear Tire & Rubber	14
Capital Cities		Great Northern Nekoosa	110
Communications	154	Great Western Financial	137
Carolina Power & Light	21	Halliburton	92
Clark Equipment	45	Hanna Mining	50
Colt Industries	119	Hart Schaffner & Marx	21
Communications Satellite	62	Hewlett-Packard	74
Connecticut General Insurance	148		

TABLE 4–1. (*Continued*)

Hilton Hotels	77	Reynolds Metals	58
Holiday Inns	50	Richardson-Merrell	65
Host International	19	Roadway Express	20
Intel	183	Rohm & Haas	124
INTERCO	11	St. Joe Minerals	42
Jonathan Logan	11	Safeway Stores	27
K mart	76	Santa Fe Industries	81
Kaiser Aluminum & Chemical	143	Scott Paper	22
Knight-Ridder Newspapers	102	Searle (G.D.)	13
Leaseway Transportation	7	Shell Oil	132
Manufacturers Hanover	22	Southern Railway	20
Masco	53	Sperry	94
McDermott (J. Ray)	28	Squibb	16
McDonald's	91	TRW	107
McDonnell Douglas	86	Tenneco	27
Mohasco	17	Texaco	23
Morgan (J.P.)	46	Texas Instruments	40
National Semiconductor	55	Tidewater	78
Northwest Airlines	144	Times Mirror	127
Northwestern National Life		Transway International	33
Insurance	39	UAL	79
Norton Simon	57	Union Camp	29
Outboard Marine	16	United Technologies	12
Owens-Corning Fiberglas	75	Westvaco	94
Penney (J.C.)	73	Xerox	138
Phillips Petroleum	187	Other Stocks	264
Pitney Bowes	67	Total Stocks	9,666
Polaroid	126	Net Cash and Equivalents	334
RCA	31		
Reynolds Industries (R.J.)	38	Total	$10,000

spread if you have invested in the Seminar Fund on December 31, 1979, and lists the ten largest individual holdings separately.

Sometimes in the seminar in describing the diversification, I mention Philip Morris and that the fund had its largest holding there on December 31. I tell my audience about the time when the first tobacco warning was issued by the Surgeon General and one of my lady clients called to see if she should sell her Philip Morris stock and that my answer to her was, "No, never sell sin short." I then go on to comment that they've added another popular "sin"—Miller High Life Beer.

Diversification such as this can permit you to own your slice of the U.S. economy by becoming a part owner of the major companies whose products and services you use regularly. At the end of 1979, the Seminar Fund's portfolio was diversified into 107 common stocks.

Such diversification is essential if you want to build a prudent investment portfolio. Even if you had many thousands of dollars to invest, you would find it difficult to achieve this broad diversification. To purchase 100 shares each of just ten of the largest holdings in the Seminar Fund would have cost nearly $53,000 at year-end 1979.

I'm sure you'll agree that this array of 107 plus a few other stocks and cash and cash equivalents should fulfill the first requirement for successful investing—diversification.

Proper Selection and Constant Supervision.   The Seminar Fund often has a picture in its guidebook of some very learned looking men and women sitting around a large conference table with research reports in front of them. They are having one of their daily conferences to determine which stocks to add and which to take out of the portfolio, or to just be as certain as they can that the stocks they presently hold fulfill the requirements that the shareholders designated when they chose this particular fund.

A staff of analysts, each a specialist in his own field, constantly reports to this committee. There will be specialists in the oils, the chemicals, the automotives, and so forth. Not only do they read, analyze, and project figures on each company in their industry specialty, but they also make on-the-spot studies and conduct fact-finding interviews with the top officers of these companies. They often have research staffs worldwide.

I remember an officer of an oil company calling me to invest in a particular fund after one of the fund's analysts had called on him. He was very impressed with the analyst's thorough knowledge of the oil industry and especially of his company.

Successful investing is a full-time job. In a dynamic and competitive economy, the fortunes of individual companies—and often entire industries—can change very rapidly. Professionals who can stay abreast of these changes and capitalize on them are likely to achieve superior results.

These financial analysts log hundreds of thousands of miles a year visiting corporations and talking with their key executives, their competitors, their suppliers, their bankers, and their customers. The analysts also study the industry, as well as the economic and regulatory climate in which each company operates. They review trade publications, company reports, and financial journals; confer with leading business consultants and economists; and analyze reports from scores of investment and statistical services. The information gathered by these financial professionals flows continuously into their offices, where it is evaluated and converted into investment decisions.

Successful investing is a continuous problem-solving process. As in any problem-solving situation, the individual or group who, first, has access to the best information concerning the problem and, second, can apply the best combination of judgment, experience, imagination, and financial resources to this information is the one most likely to consistently come up with the best solutions.

The thoroughness and training of these specialists fulfill the two other requirements of successful investing—proper selection and constant supervision.

In addition to these three requirements of successful investing, the properly selected mutual fund can provide other valuable benefits. These benefits include:

1. Convenience
2. Dollar-cost averaging
3. Ease of record keeping
4. Matching your financial objectives
5. Passing on professional management
6. Ease of estate settlement
7. Lower costs
8. Quantity discounts and Rights of Accumulation
9. Exchange privilege
10. Timing
11. Performance
12. A check a month

Convenience, an Essential Ingredient. The first is convenience. We all do what is convenient for us. Mutual funds can offer this convenience with a plan that will fit almost any pocketbook. You may start an investment program in a mutual fund with a relatively small amount of money; in fact, some funds have no minimum initial investment. Others will accept as small an amount as $100. You may then add in some funds any amount or as small an amount as $25. In addition, you have the privilege of automatically reinvesting both your dividends and your capital gains, usually without commission. Some funds charge to reinvest dividends. None charge to reinvest capital gains. If you were to receive these same dividends from individual stocks in your private portfolio and you realized capital gains from your buys and sells and wanted to reinvest, you would be charged a commission.

With a mutual fund you can have immediate reinvestment of small or large amounts of money, giving you an opportunity to speed up your compounding potential.

Dollar-Cost-Averaging as You Earn.   The second item in the list of twelve additional advantages that a mutual fund may offer is that you can truly dollar-cost average. This means putting the same amount of money into the same security at the same interval. One certainty of the stock market is that it will fluctuate. So put this characteristic to work for you instead of worrying so much about it. Choose an amount you can comfortably invest each month (not too comfortably or you may not save anything) and invest that amount on the same day each month.

Many funds provide a bank draft authorization so that the bank can automatically draft your account each month. I find this to be an extremely satisfactory arrangement for my clients. Banks never forget! I find my clients often do.

The mutual funds will carry your share purchase out to the third decimal point, which allows you to truly dollar-cost-average. This makes this investment medium a good one to use for this purpose.

The chapter entitled, "Is There an Infallible Way to Invest?" covers this point in more detail.

Record Keeping Made Easy.   Another characteristic of the mutual fund is that you have professionals doing your record keeping. You will have five choices when you open an account. Regardless of which choice you make, the fund will provide you a historical record of your account.

1. Reinvest all distributions.

2. Reinvest all distributions, and you may add amounts systematically or when you desire.

3. Receive dividends in cash and reinvest capital gains.

4. Receive dividends and capital gains in cash.

5. Receive a check a month.

All you need to do is keep the last confirmation you receive that year, and you will have a complete record of your account. The mutual fund also will send you (and IRS) a Form 1099, showing the dividends and capital gains paid to you for the year. This you will want to keep and attach to your federal income tax return.

You will receive a confirmation statement every time there is any activity in your account. You do not need to worry about the safety of your share certificates. They will be held for you by the fund's transfer agent, or sent to you if you wish.

Where Do You Fit on the Triangle?   Do you remember our triangle of finance that we used when we were discussing individual stocks? It is applicable here, too. A fund must state in its prospectus its financial objective. This objective cannot be changed without the consent of the shareholders. The fund rarely changes its objective. If it is presently an income fund and management also desires to manage a growth fund, they will establish a new fund and add it to their family of funds. The financial triangle would look something like this:

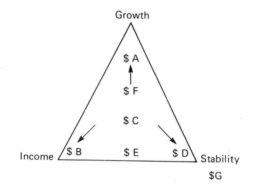

As you can see, you can't be a Paul Revere who hops on his horse and rides off in all directions. You must decide in which direction you want to go. When you maximize Income you move farther from Growth. The same is true if you select Stability as your primary concern.

A fund management group may have a family of funds, attempting to provide a fund for each place on the triangle, or it may have only one or two.

KINDS OF MUTUAL FUNDS

There are approximately eleven kinds of mutual funds: growth (aggressive, quality with income), income, tax-advantaged trusts, corporate bond, balanced, convertible bond, specialty funds, option, municipal bond, and money market funds.

Growth Funds

Under the growth designation you could have four subheadings: "go-go," very aggressive growth, quality growth, and growth with income funds.

If you invest in a quality growth fund, you will be placing your dollar nearer to the top of the triangle at *A*, because its objective is long-term growth. Intermittent volatility should not be of great concern. Nor should you be interested in dividends. As a matter of fact, if it were possible for the fund managers to select stocks that paid no dividends and just grew in value, with no need to buy and sell and realize capital gains, this would be ideal for you. What you really want is for $1 to grow to at least $3 in ten years. You would prefer not having any tax liability in the meantime if this is possible.

When I've asked a prospective client his financial objective and he has answered that it is growth, I may recommend a particular quality growth fund to him. When he asks me, "How much does it pay?" meaning what are the dividends, I know I have not communicated properly what a growth fund is designed to do.

Common Stock Funds

The middle-of-the-road fund that seeks growth with income is the stronghold of the mutual fund industry. It would fit in the middle of your triangle and is the place where most investors feel the greatest comfort.

When deciding where you should be on the triangle, you should remember that your temperament is important in your investment program. I find in my counseling that once I have sufficient information about a client's time schedule, assets, and tax bracket, it is not difficult to choose the investment I feel would fulfill his needs financially, but it may not fit his temperament. Regardless of how much I think he should invest for maximum growth, if I detect that volatility would disturb his peace of mind, then the best investment for him will probably be in the middle. Peace of mind is a good investment, too.

Our Seminar Fund fits in the middle, and it is letter F on the triangle. Let's say that F stands for "just fine" for most investors. Trying to make it too fast is what causes most failures. Remember, those who make it to their goal of financial independence have usually done it slowly. If you select your fund well from this category, you should be able to obtain your 12 percent compounded over a twenty-year period. (12 percent is $96,462.) The Seminar Fund has in the past averaged 12 percent or better in seventeen of the twenty-seven twenty-year periods. The entire record appears in Table 7 of the appendix.

In this category also are funds that invest in stocks only from the list that are legal for investment of trust funds in the District of Columbia and meet the "prudent man's rule" for investing. This means that an attorney, a fiduciary, or you could place an orphan child's money in it and it would be difficult to question you as to whether you had acted as a prudent fiduciary.

Income Funds

There is a good selection of quality income funds. Their portfolio managers choose stocks that have paid good dividends in the past, have a record of increasing dividends, and have a reasonable expectation of continuing good dividends and market stability of their shares. If your need is for income now, rather than later, this is the type of fund you should consider. Your location on the triangle would be *B*.

Bond Funds

When you invest in a bond fund, you are placing your dollar in the lower right-hand side of the triangle (*D*). Bond funds have been around for many years; however, during the growth craze of the 1960s, they attracted very little attention. With the agonizing reappraisals in the stock market in the seventies they became popular.

Bond funds invest most of their funds in debt-type securities. These are corporate bonds and debentures, perhaps a few convertible bonds, treasuries, commercial paper, etc. Instead of taking an equity position in the market, you become a lender of money.

When you invest in a bond fund, do not think that the price of the shares will remain fixed. It will not. It does exhibit some fluctuation, though usually not as great as in other security investments.

If your fund is composed of bonds with an average yield of 9 percent and the going interest rate is 10 percent, then the fund will not be able to sell their bonds at par; therefore, the price of your shares could decline. On the other hand, if the going rate drops to 8 percent, they probably can sell the bonds at a premium (above par) and the price of your shares would increase. If they purchased a bond at par (usually $1000) that carries a rate of 9 percent, which matures January 1, 2000, this does not mean that they must hold the bond until the year 2000 to turn it into cash. It means that on January 1, 2000, the person holding the bond is guaranteed $1000. Between now and that date, the value will usually fluctuate with the country's going interest rate.

Balanced Funds

In position *C* on the triangle, you will find balanced funds. These are funds that invest approximately 60 percent of their funds in high-quality bonds and the remainder in high-quality, income-producing "blue chip" stocks. In periods of market decline, if that decline has not been caused by extraordinarily high interest rates as occurred in

1979–80, they could experience less volatility than the growth funds. Conversely, in a rising market they usually lag behind.

Convertible Bond Funds

In an effort to obtain the best of two worlds, some management groups have established convertible bond funds. These funds were designed to have a relatively good yield—around 5 to 6 percent—and have the potential for growth. They listed the characteristics of their fund by showing the advantages and disadvantages of bonds and stocks, and proposed that they would combine the best from both. Your dollar with them would be placed around E on the triangle. As discussed earlier, its characteristics are supposed to offer you the best of two worlds: the guarantee of principal and rate of return of a bond, and the potential for growth of common stock.

The theory runs that, even though you may be placing a bit of a damper on maximum growth potential, there is down-side protection, for the convertible bond should only drop in price to a level where it will take on the characteristics of a bond yielding the current interest level.

The number of quality convertible bonds available in the marketplace has been limited. This tends to make a thin market (not enough traders to make it competitive). Also, many of the firms offering convertibles bonds are not the blue-chip companies. They had to offer convertibles to "sweeten the kitty" to sell their bonds to the investing public. So the convertible bonds may be tied to less stable securities, which can cause more volatility than some shareholders are willing to accept.

Specialty Funds

Specialty funds may concentrate in insurance, bank, utilities, or gold stock. I have not placed them on the triangle because their characteristics are not easily categorized. Utility shares may be popular from time to time for those who want income. Gold stocks can be a very interesting approach in times of worldwide economic instability. In 1979, we began using a mutual fund that invested almost entirely in South African gold stocks. Political unrest and a rapidly eroding dollar made it fairly obvious that gold would be in higher demand. Since the stocks usually lag behind the bullion itself, this gave us an opportunity to capitalize on a diversified professionally managed portfolio of gold stocks while having liquidity with no storage problem and the ability to buy in small units. (I'll cover gold in Chapter 9, "All That Glitters and Gold.") Our performance was superior, more than doubling our money in less than six months.

Tax-Managed Trusts

In recent years a new type of fund has appeared that is attracting considerable attention. It is a fund that elects to be taxed as a corporation rather than act as a conduit, as a regular mutual fund does. You are not given a choice of whether or not you will receive your dividends in cash. They are reinvested for you. The fund pays the tax, if any is due. Usually the fund can avoid the tax by conscientious portfolio management. If you've held your shares for over a year and want some cash distribution, just liquidate some shares. The gain will be treated as a capital gain for tax purposes.

One of these funds with a large amount of utilities in their portfolio will from time to time let you exchange certain of your utility stocks for shares, thereby avoiding the commission on their sale. Another tax-advantaged trust offers a unique feature that can be most helpful if you find yourself locked into 7 to 8 percent certificates of deposit while interest rates have escalated to above 13 percent. If you have a certificate of deposit that matures in eighteen months or less, carries an interest rate of 7 percent or higher, that has been issued by a federally insured bank or savings and loan, they will accept the certificate at its current value in exchange for shares of either their growth fund or their utility fund. In this way you avoid the horrendous penalty for early withdrawal, increase your yield by as much as 5 percent, and also avoid ordinary income tax on the earnings after the exchange.

Flexible Funds

There is another category of funds that is difficult to place in any one position. Their chief characteristic is that they are allowed by charter to invest all or a portion of their funds outside the United States. This can be a valuable feature because there are times when there are good buys in other countries and not here. The majority of the few funds following this approach have done very well.

Municipal Bond Funds

These are covered in more detail in Chapter 3, "Lending Your Dollars." They provide tax-free income, permit additions in small amounts, and provide reinvestment privileges to allow you to compound tax free.

Money Market Funds

During the extremely high interest rates of the mid-1970s, a new kind of fund appeared called the Money Market or Reserve Funds. Do you remember seeing advertisements in your newspaper back in 1974 offering 12 percent on $100,000 certificates of deposits. Well, some people didn't have $100,000, so some of the funds established money market funds whereby investors with as little as $1,000 could take advantage of these higher rates by pooling their money with others in the fund. The management would in turn invest in $1 million CDs, treasury bills, etc. These grew in popularity so by the end of 1979, there was over $60 billion in these funds. There is no cost to deposit your funds with them and none to withdraw. You may reinvest your dividends and have check writing privileges in amounts of $500 or more. Their management fee is small. I personally use this type of fund extensively for my liquid cash needs and encourage my clients to do so. The only place that I keep dollars I need liquid are in checking accounts and money market funds issued by mutual funds (not the so-called money market funds issued by the saving and loans. They do not have these features.) These funds are represented by the letter G and is outside the triangle, since it would be out of the market. Here G could represent "Good" if money is tight and is attracting interest rates of 10 to 14 percent.

"WILL SOME BRAINS"

Another characteristic of a mutual fund is that it allows you to choose professional management for those dependent on you. I have a client who has been an excellent stock trader for years. We have made very good profits together. He has thoroughly enjoyed the challenge of predicting trends before they happened, buying the leading stocks in those industries, moving out of them before the trends ran out, and moving into the next trend ahead of the other traders. A few years ago he said that he wanted to invest in a particular mutual fund. Since he had never shown any interest in mutual funds over the years that he had been my client, and since he obviously was very good at selecting his own portfolio, I asked him why he had now decided to avail himself of outside professional management. He said, "I want to will some brains to my wife and daughter." He was not being derogatory. He described his wife and daughter to me. He obviously loved them very much and was proud of their accomplishments. Then he added, "They know nothing about money management. It's probably my own fault. Stock analysis and projections have been my avocation for many years, but I've never attempted to share this information with them. On the other hand, I don't really think it's their cup of tea. They are both creative, artistic, very social people who have taken delight in the luxuries my talent has provided for them, but I don't think they have ever given much thought to the source of the funds that provide these luxuries. I'm getting up in years now and want to will some brains to my wife and daughter so that they may continue to have professional management of their money in the event that I'm not here to provide it for them."

The selection he made was good, and his reasoning was sound. He selected a management team with a long and consistent record of good performance.

You may want to consider if professional management is something you desire to have readily available to members of your family.

EASE OF ESTATE SETTLEMENT

Another reason that my client chose to place some of his funds under professional management as he grew older was the ease of estate settlement. He knew that upon his death the individual stocks in his portfolio would be frozen and could only be changed with the permission of the courts.

For example, let's say that shares of U.S. Steel had been in this portfolio at the time of steel's confrontation with the Kennedy administration, when for all practical purposes they were told they would not be allowed to make a profit. There had been earlier storm warnings on the horizon. Quick action to sell looked prudent. But if the estate had not been probated, the shares could not have been sold quickly enough to protect the estate.

Now let's assume that U.S. Steel had been in the portfolio of his fund. The fund's portfolio managers were free to sell U.S. Steel from the fund and replace it with another stock. The shares of the fund were frozen in the estate, but not the securities that made up the portfolio of the fund. Therefore, the mutual fund could have provided professional management of his assets while awaiting settlement of the estate, which can take several years.

DIVERSIFICATION MAINTAINED AFTER PROBATE

Another advantage that the fund makes available is the ease with which an estate can be divided with no disruption of diversification.

Let's assume that there were four heirs instead of two, that he wanted them to share and share alike, and that the securities in the estate were in the form of 4000 shares of the Seminar Fund. Each heir would receive 1000 shares. There would be no disruption of diversification in each of the four portfolios. Each would still own a proportionate share of 100 to 150 stocks, all professionally selected and managed as if they belonged to one billionaire.

LOWER COST

Mutual funds should not be used as trading vehicles, for the initial commission can be higher to buy than for individual stocks. However, there is no commission to sell regardless of how much the shares may have grown in value. Also, most funds do not have a commission to reinvest dividends or capital gains.

A study conducted by the National Association of Security Dealers indicated that an investment of $5000 in sixteen individual issues, which is what they deem necessary for adequate diversification, would cost 7 percent in commissions, assuming an "in and out" transaction in listed securities. If you conclude that dividend reinvestment at asset value is worth 1 percent to the average investor, that rights of accumulation are worth 0.5 percent, and that the exchange privilege is worth 0.4 percent, the commission of individual stocks would be 8.9 percent. They also found that the average sales charge on fund sales is only 4.4 percent because of the discounts obtained on purchases of over $10,000 and cumulative discounts.

On the basis of prevailing commission rates, $5000 invested into twenty different stocks at $25 per share would pay commissions around $474 each time, or 9.5 percent of the amount involved. The average fund has over 100 stocks, or five times this diversification, plus a team of professionals selecting the stocks.

For example, a $100,000 investment in a fund with 100 stocks in its portfolio would carry a 3½ percent cost in and no cost to come out. Compared to purchasing and selling a 100 shares of $20, the commission would be around $102, or a little over 2½ percent. That's for just one trip and one stock. It's difficult to trade for as low a cost. The funds also pay commissions, but with negotiated rates you would find it difficult to match their lower costs.

Also, the Seminar Fund over a fifteen-year period would have reinvested more distributions for you without charge than your original investment on which you paid a commission. So you might feel you had your second go-around for free.

WHAT DOES IT PAY?

I find that many people get hung up on what something costs them. I hope you do not. I never worry about what something "costs" me, but I am vitally concerned about what it "pays" me. It makes no difference what it "costs."

Let's assume that you turn over $1 to me to manage for you. I charge you no sales charge to do this. I will charge you, however, one-half of 1 percent yearly management fee. At the end of ten years, I return to you $2 net after all costs are taken out.

Now let's assume that you turn over another $1 to me, and on the $1 I charge you 8½ pennies. Again I charge you one-half of 1 perecent yearly management fee and at the end of 10 years I return to you $3. Which was the best investment for you? Which really cost you the most? Did your efforts to save 8½ pennies "cost" you $1?

DISTILLING THE WISDOM OF THE AGES

If I were to distill all the wisdom that I have acquired over the years reading and observing, I could put it all in just nine words. "There is no such thing as a free lunch."

For example, let's assume you had $10,000 in 1950. A savings institution would not have charged you to open a savings account with them. As a matter of fact, they may have given you a handy Teflon skillet or a fuzzy wuzzy blanket for doing so. But how much did it cost? At the end of 1979, 30 years later, your $10,000 would have grown to $37,178 with them if all distributions had been reinvested. However, in that same period, had your $10,000 been in the Seminar Fund with all distributions reinvested your results would have been $280,990 (see Figure 4–1. Which would you rather have—3.7 times your original capital, as in the savings account, or 28 times your original capital in the Seminar Fund? (I'm required by regulation to put in this disclaimer about it being a period of "rising stock prices" and "may be no indication of the future." Incidentally, the Dow Jones Average was not up but down 4 percent over the past fifteen years. Incidentally, most investors do not beat any of the popular averages. Bankers are now try-

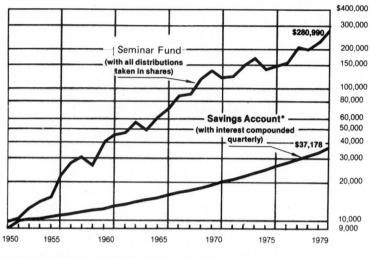

Figure 4–1. Growth of a $10,000 Investment in the Seminar Fund and in a Savings Account

ing to "index," which means their trust departments are trying to do as well as the indexes by investing in the same stocks.

"OPPORTUNITY FEE"

I call the mutual funds sales charge an opportunity fee. My reason for doing so is this: Let's assume that you want to travel from Houston to Dallas. You find that the only way to get there is by bus. You go to the bus station; the clerk writes out your ticket and says, "That will be $14.65, please." You answer, "I'm just not going to pay that." If you don't, you're just not going to Dallas. It's not what something costs you, but what it pays you that should be your chief concern.

There are, however, a few well-managed funds that do not make a sales charge. Carefully examine their performance, too. Remember, though, you will not have the help of a financial planner in selecting stocks and in timing their purchase or exchange, and lack of cash flow may affect their performance. You will be buying them very much as you would a suit of clothes from a mail order catalogue or Sunday supplement of your newspaper.

BUYING BRAINS AT A DISCOUNT

Earlier I said that mutual funds enabled the smaller investor to obtain the same advantages as the wealthier investor. The investor who has larger amounts does obtain quantity discounts on his original purchases. Table 4–2 gives some typical acquisition costs.

TABLE 4–2

Amount of Purchase	Total Acquisition Cost
Under $10,000	8.50%
$ 10,000 but less than $ 25,000	7.50%
$ 25,000 but less than $ 50,000	6.00%
$ 50,000 but less than $ 100,000	4.50%
$ 100,000 but less than $ 250,000	3.50%
$ 250,000 but less than $ 500,000	2.50%
$ 500,000 but less than $1,000,000	2.00%
$1,000,000 but less than $2,000,000	1.50%
$2,000,000 and more	1.00%

Letter of Intent

Perhaps you do not have a sufficiently large sum today to cross one of the discounts, but you will during the next thirteen months. Then you may want to consider buying under a letter of intent. The letter of intent is not a commitment to buy, but a privilege to buy at a discount during the thirteen-month period. For example, let's assume that you have $10,000 to invest today, but anticipate having an additional $15,000 to invest during the coming thirteen months. You would then invest under a $25,000 letter of intent. When you do that, you receive the same discount on your $10,000 purchase as if you had invested $25,000. The custodian bank then escrows some of your shares. When the additional $15,000 is added, they release your shares. If you decide you do not want to add the remaining $15,000, that is your privilege. If the thirteen months pass and you have not completed your letter, you have two choices: return the discount, which you would not have received anyway without the letter, or the custodian bank will sell enough of your escrowed shares to return to the fund the second discount you received and will send you the remaining shares. Your discount would be adjusted back to the $10,000 level. Therefore, the letter of intent never costs you more and can save you money. You are not required to return the dividends and capital gains on the extra shares you received during the period they were in escrow.

THE LARGE INVESTOR

As you reached the $500,000 level in Table 4–1, you may have said, "Big deal. Who has that kind of money?" Contrary to what many people think, many large investors buy mutual funds. Many financial planners report that their clients' average mutual fund purchase is over $27,000. Many pension funds invest far in excess of a million dollars with the funds and receive the original discount plus continuing to receive additional discounts. The Seminar Fund has many large investors with more than $5 million invested, and one company has 27 million dollars in the Fund.

Adding More at a Discount

Under what is called "rights of accumulation," you may also qualify for additional discounts. Let's assume that you own shares that have a value of $20,000 and that you have $5000 you would like to add to your account. You may do so under the "rights of accumulation" at the $25,000 discount level. As your account grows, you may continue to add at progressively smaller opportunity fees as you cross each discount. One of the reasons pension and profit-sharing plans use mutual fund shares is their lower cost of acquisition, diversification, ease of record keeping, and to meet the "prudent man" rule and fiduciary requirements.

THE EXCHANGE PRIVILEGE

An important characteristic of most mutual funds is that they offer you the privilege of exchanging one of their funds for another one of their funds. There would be no commission and there would either be no charge or a $5 exchange fee that would go to the transfer agent for his expense in doing this for you. This could be of interest to you if your financial objective has changed.

For instance, if your financial objective has been growth but you are retiring, you may now be more interested in income. You have the privilege of changing from one fund to the other without a sales charge. You should be aware, however, that if you realize a gain on your shares, the IRS considers this a sale, and you'll have to pay a capital gains tax on your profit. A better way may be for you to just begin your check-a-month from your growth fund, hoping that appreciation will replace the value of the shares redeemed.

You may also establish a loss for tax purposes using the exchange privilege. Let's assume that the market has dropped below your cost. You are still confident of the investment ability of the management team and believe that temporary market conditions have adversely affected anticipated performance. You are nearing the end of the year and have some capital gains already established for the year. You many want to exchange the fund that you own for one of their other funds, thereby establishing a loss for tax purposes. Even without a capital gains, you could establish a $6000 loss to be used against $3000 of ordinary income. If you do not use all of the loss in that year, you may carry it forward indefinitely until you have used all of it.

You would need to wait at least thirty-one days before moving back to your original fund, or the IRS would disallow the deduction, calling it a "wash sale." Again, there is no commission to exchange it back to your original position.

Timing

The greatest advantage to the exchange privilege is that it gives you the opportunity to move in and out of the market without a commission. If the Federal Reserve is severely tightening the money supply, which looks as if it will choke the market, and your fund is part of a family of funds that has a money market fund, you may want to move over to this safer harbor, ride out the storm, and draw a tidy interest in the meantime.

You may be wondering why the fund managers do not take this action for you. They do move into as defensive a position as they can under the regulations by which they must abide. However, to qualify as a regulated investment company, which is important to you in terms of your taxes, less than 30 percent of their gross income in any fiscal year can be derived from holding securities less than three months. This regulation may inhibit moving from stock to cash on a short-term basis, which for your purposes may be the most prudent action to take. The exchange privilege gives you the opportunity to take advantage of the strengths of top professional management while avoiding the weakness caused by these regulations. This can make it possible for you to exploit their offensive ability by holding their funds during rising markets and avoiding what may be short-term weakness by moving out of the funds entirely during down markets.

Timing Services

You can attempt to time your own moves in and out of the market or you can use a timing service to do this for you. Our firm makes timing services available to our clients. Timing services have become very viable considerations during the past few years, due to the fact that there has been a change in the rate of inflation. During the twenty-year period between 1946 and 1966, we experienced an Era of Stability in our economy. Inflation was moderate, the fiscal authorities were not tampering unduly with the money supply, and for the most part the U.S. was dedicated to the profit system under free enterprise. Our standard of living was going up, and our gross national production was increasing steadily. Then in 1966, the Johnson administration attempted welfare and warfare without the courage to increase taxes. They wanted to create the Great Society without paying for it. This ended the Era of Stability and launched us into the Era of Pendulum Economics. Up until that time our stock market indexes resembled the man with the yo-yo walking up the stairs. If you got your eyes off the yo-yo the man eventually climbed the stairs. With the coming of pendulum economics, the market become like the man with a yo-yo standing on the stairs. You'd make it and lose it, make it and lose it. It became more and more obvious that there were times when it might be too risky to be in the market and other times when it was risky to be out of it. If the drops could be avoided, the gains could be accelerated. This brought the birth of the timing services.

A sketch of this might look something like this:

Era of Stability   Era of Pendulum Economics

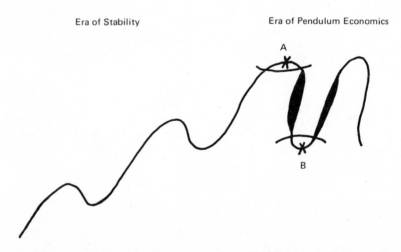

Our company and others went out to find a service that would get you out at point *A* and back in at point *B*. I wish I could report to you that we found one. We did not. But we did find more than one that had a good record of getting you out in the *A* area and back in around the *B* area. Obviously, this would not guarantee you against a loss. For example, if you went in at the high at $10 and the timing service triggered you out at $9, you would have suffered a $1 loss. What the timing service attempts to do is to avoid your investment going to say $6 before you start your climb up again. Even if your climb up starts at $9, your potential is greater than if you had come down to $6 before starting up again.

Timing services are not a panacea. In sideways markets they can be very disappointing. They should be used, if you so choose to use them, over at least a four-year period. Figure 4–2 shows the results using a particular timing service with a growth fund in the same family of funds as the Seminar Fund. The future may be better or it may be worse.

What Kind of Funds Work Best With Timing?

If you are convinced that the timing service can help in keeping you out of the market when you ought to be out and in the market when you ought to be in, then your logical choice would seem to be an aggressive high-quality growth fund. It should go up faster in an up market when you are in and should go down faster in a down market when you are out.

Charges for Timing

Fees charged by the various timing services usually average about 2 percent a year. The performance shown for the fund above is before the 2 percent fee; however only a 5 percent figure was used for income while out of the market, and interest rates during some of those periods ran over 13½ percent in the money market funds where the money was placed when out of the market. If you are interested in timing, you should select a family of funds that has an aggressive growth fund and a money market fund. The timing service will then move your funds between the two.

Disadvantages of Timing Services

First, they can only try to get you out near the top and back in near the bottom. They will not be infallible. Though the fund does not charge a commission to make the exchange, the IRS does get into the act. If a gain has occurred, you will have realized either a long- or a short-term capital gain, and they'll want what they feel is their share. However, if you are using timing with a tax-sheltered vehicle such as a Keogh, Individual Retirement Account, IRA Rollover, pension or profit-

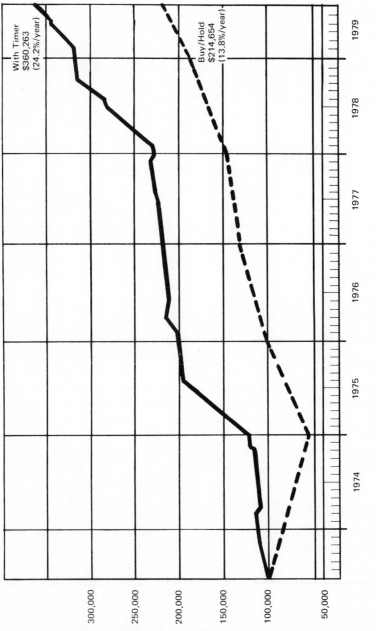

Figure 4–2. Results of Using Timing Service with Growth Fund in Same Family of Funds as Seminar Fund

sharing plan, or a wrap-around annuity (all of which will be discussed later), all of these compound tax-sheltered, and no tax will be due.

PERFORMANCE

You've heard the expression, "It doesn't mean a thing unless you pull that string." The same is true of your mutual fund. What has been its past performance (knowing that whatever it has been, there is no guarantee it will be the same in the future)? But perhaps you can obtain some wisdom from the past.

I will be disappointed for you if it does not do as well as 12 percent average. There will no doubt be times when this will be an unattainable goal and other times when you'll vastly outperform this objective. Figure 4–3 shows the 46-year record of the Seminar Fund without superimposing a timing service, but using the expertise of their professional management. During this period, many seemingly catastrophic events have occurred, as you can see by the notations titled "There have always been 'reasons' not to invest." You will note, however, during its 46 years from January 1, 1934, to December 31, 1979, it had a compound rate of return of 12.09 percent. You can see for yourself the years it did that well and the years it did not. As a matter of fact, 19 one-year periods were below that average and 27 one-year periods were above that average.

Is Its Performance Guaranteed?

As you look at this record you may be asking, "Is this investment guaranteed?" I'm happy to tell you it is not! If you want a "guaranteed" dollar, you should take it to an institution that has a gold emblem on the door that declares that your funds are "guaranteed" (up to $40,000) by the F.D.I.C. What does F.D.I.C. stand for? That's right—the Federal Deposit *Insurance* Corporation, a guaranteeing arm of the government. (They also bring to you the post office and Amtrak.)

Have you ever bought an insurance policy for which you did not pay a premium? What if I came to you and said, "I want to guarantee that you can always have your $10,000 back at any time regardless of what increases may have occurred in your cost of living and regardless of how much money I have made on your money, and all I want to charge you is $820.58 per month every month you leave it with me, or $10,064.33 per year"? What would you say to me? You'd say "the cost is too high," wouldn't you? That's what would have been your average per-month cost the past 46 years to have had your $10,000 guaranteed.

"Total Return"

A meaningful way to compare the return on an investment in The Seminar Fund with the return on other investments.

"Total return" is simply a percentage figure which shows the change in the value of an investment when income dividends and capital gain distributions are taken in additional shares; it is a combination of income return and capital results.

Income return is represented by the Fund's income dividends. Capital results are the change in net asset value of the Fund's shares, adjusted for capital gain distributions. Together, these add up to a percentage return that can be compared to those provided by other investments.

The chart below illustrates an assumed $10,000 investment in the Fund from January 1, 1934 through December 31, 1979. The table depicts the Fund's total return in each of those 46 years. For example, it shows that in 1979 the Fund had an income return (with dividends reinvested) of 4.3% and an increase in adjusted net asset value of 14.7% for a total return of 19.0% for the year.

The boxed figures in the lower right-hand corner sum up the entire lifetime of the Fund. They show that an investment

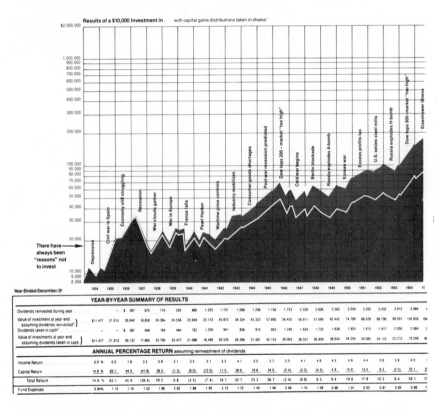

Figure 4–3. 46-Year Record of Seminar Fund Without Timing Service

in the Fund has provided a compound annual investment return of 12.09%.

One more point. If you look at the third line of the table ("Dividends taken in cash"), you will see that the Fund shareholders who have chosen to take their dividends in cash have received a growing stream of income that more than offset the constantly rising cost of living.

During the period illustrated, stock prices fluctuated and were higher at the end than at the beginning. These results should not be considered as a representation of the dividend income or capital gain or loss which may be realized from an investment made in the Fund today.

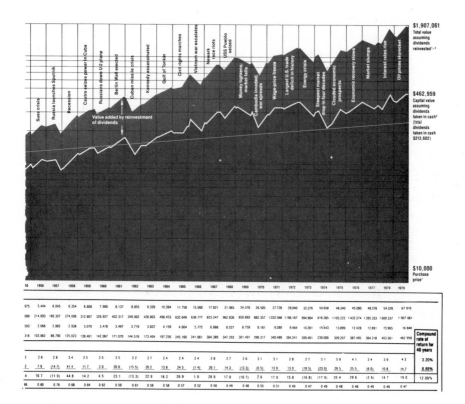

	55	1956	1957	1958	1959	1960	1961	1962	1963	1964	1965	1966	1967	1968	1969	1970	1971	1972	1973	1974	1975	1976	1977	1978	1979	Compound rate of return for 46 years
975		5.444	6.045	6.354	6.808	7.900	8.137	8.855	9.339	10.394	11.758	15.060	17.821	21.985	24.576	26.505	27.728	29.040	32.376	50.656	48.340	45.080	48.378	54.328	67.910	
089		214.893	189.307	274.006	312.807	326.927	402.317	349.002	428.803	498.453	632.649	638.777	823.247	962.836	859.893	882.357	1.032.568	1.196.167	994.964	816.385	1.105.222	1.432.274	1.395.333	1.600.337	1.907.061	
503		2.666	2.882	2.938	3.070	3.478	3.497	3.719	3.822	4.159	4.604	5.772	6.668	8.027	8.759	9.161	9.289	9.464	10.261	15.443	13.899	12.428	12.891	13.965	16.840	
316		103.862	88.790	125.023	139.461	142.067	171.070	144.516	173.404	197.256	245.160	241.661	304.389	347.293	301.491	299.317	340.489	384.241	309.461	239.000	309.207	387.495	364.318	403.361	462.959	
2		2.8	2.8	3.4	2.5	2.5	2.5	2.2	2.7	2.4	2.4	2.4	2.8	2.7	2.6	3.1	3.1	2.8	2.7	5.1	5.9	4.1	3.4	3.9	4.3	3.20%
2		7.9	(14.7)	41.4	11.7	2.0	20.6	(15.5)	20.2	13.8	24.5	(1.4)	26.1	14.3	(13.3)	(0.5)	13.9	13.0	(19.5)	(23.0)	29.5	25.5	(6.0)	10.8	14.7	8.89%
4		10.7	(11.9)	44.8	14.2	4.5	23.1	(13.3)	22.9	16.2	26.9	1.0	28.9	17.0	(10.7)	2.6	17.0	15.8	(16.8)	(17.9)	35.4	29.6	(2.6)	14.7	19.0	12.09%
66		0.80	0.78	0.68	0.64	0.62	0.59	0.61	0.59	0.58	0.57	0.52	0.50	0.49	0.48	0.55	0.51	0.49	0.47	0.49	0.48	0.46	0.49	0.49	0.47	

A guaranteed dollar rarely pays. Most of the time it costs, and costs dearly.

To calculate this cost for yourself, note that the $10,000 has grown to $462,959 with no reinvestment of dividends. (You're taking the interest in cash from your guaranteed investment, too.) Subtract $10,000, your original investment, and this leaves $452,959. Divide this number by 552 (46 years x 12 months per year) to obtain $820.58 per month.

To get a visual picture of the difference between the "guaranteed" and the nonguaranteed, take your pencil and start at the left side of the chart at $10,000 and draw a line to the right side at $10,000, and you will note that the difference is $452,959.

THE YO-YO AND THE STAIRS

Now that you've studied the chart of the Seminar Fund, what are your reactions? Remember, it covers a long period of time. As a matter of fact, it covers a 46-year period from 1934 through 1979. Do you agree that this is a fairly graphic picture of a man with a yo-yo going up the stairs? What difference did it make to him how many times the yo-yo yo-yo'd during the life of the fund? The stairs he climbed reached quite a height. If you had invested $10,000 on January 1, 1934, reinvested all your capital-gains distribution (classified as part of capital by regulation), and on December 31, 1979, decided to cash in your shares at that lower spot in the market, you would have received $462,959 net to you after all costs had been taken out, with the exception of your federal and state income tax responsibility. If you had reinvested both your capital gains and dividends, your $10,000 would have grown to $1,907,061.

Just think how many life insurance policies, by contrast, have been sold to men age 19 or to their parents or grandparents with the idea that the $10,000 placed in the cash value would be growing for their retirement incomes at age 65. For example, if they had placed $10,000 into an insurance contract with one of our largest companies 46 years ago, the guaranteed cash value by December 31, 1979, would be $26,021. In addition, their projected dividends (not guaranteed) were $14,523, for a total of $40,544. To give you a point of reference, $10,000 compounded at 3 percent for 46 years is $38,950; at 5 percent, it is $94,343. You can make these calculations for yourself by looking in the Appendix at Table 5, "One Dollar Principal Compounded Annually."

We, of course, do not know what the next 46 years will bring, but if our economy is no better or no worse than the past 46 years, surely this performance can be one of the possibilities you should consider.

WHAT ABOUT INFLATION?

Inflation is the economist's way of saying "rising prices." The experts can all explain how it happened and what it means, but no one has been able to make it go away. To keep even with rising prices, you will need a constantly rising income. How much income will you need in the future? One word tells it all: more. You will need more take-home pay from your job and more dividends from your investments.

Under the mountain chart you've just been studying, look at the line entitled "Dividends taken in cash." It shows how much cash, in income dividends, your $10,000 investment with capital gains reinvested would have generated during each of the past 46 years. Note that in 36 of the past 43 years, the dividends paid by the Seminar Fund increased over the prior year. From a modest $387 paid in 1936, the dividend payments have increased to $16,840 in 1979—that's more than 168 percent of your original investment. This increase in income would not have been possible from a like amount invested in bonds or placed in a savings account.

THE BERKLEYS AND THE CAMPBELLS

Another way to examine the cost of the guarantee is to take the hypothetical case of Sally and Jim Berkley and Vicki and Jack Campbell. Both inherited $10,000 on January 1, 1950, and each couple invested their $10,000 for retirement and to provide some income to help with current expenses.

The Berkleys placed theirs in a guaranteed position where they could obtain a 9 percent return with the principal guaranteed. (This was no small feat, since the rate being paid by savings and loans in the U.S. in 1954 was 2.5 percent. Perhaps they invested in Lower Slobovia Sewer Bonds.) The first year and every year thereafter they earned $900 interest on their investment—$75 a month, never less, never more. The Berkleys felt safe and said, "With an investment that pays 9 percent a year, we have no worries. We are safe for life."

But were they really? What happened to their purchasing power? In 1950 they could feed their family for a whole month on $75. Today their grocery bill is that much each week. Of course, they still have their original nest egg, but that, too, will buy only a fraction of what it used to. The Berkleys didn't understand how savagely inflation could eat away at the purchasing power of their dollars. Their "safe" investment had turned out to be not so safe after all. There is no fixed-income investment available with a yield high enough to offset long-term inflation.

The Campbells, on the other hand, understood that the only "safe" investment was one that would protect their purchasing power. They realized they would need more and more income in the years ahead and that their original investment would also need to grow. The Campbells decided to invest in the Seminar Fund. Like the Berkleys, they took their income in cash.

The Campbells knew that the value of their investment and the size of their income dividends would fluctuate. But they recognized the fact that a rising income is the best hedge against rising prices. And they felt that, over the long haul, an investment in the Seminar Fund and the income that it produced should continue to grow, reflecting the growing earnings and dividends of the companies in which the Fund invested.

Figure 4–4a & b show what happened. Year after year, the Campbells received more income—rising income to help them keep pace with the rising cost of living. By 1964, their dividends for the year totaled $994; by 1969, they totaled $2094; by 1974, they were up to $3692; and in 1979, while the Berkleys were still getting only $900 a year, the Campbells received $4026 in dividends from their Seminar Fund.

The Campbells had another enormous advantage over the Berkleys. At the end of 1979, the Berkleys' investment was still worth only $10,000, but the Campbells' investment in the Seminar Fund had grown to more than $110,000!

Perhaps you should think about the Berkleys and the Campbells as you plan your financial future. Remember that a fixed return—no matter how high it is—is never "safe." Not as long as prices keep going up.

Do you believe that prices will continue to rise?

Do you believe you'll need a rising income to offset those rising prices?

Should some of your investment dollars be put to work in an investment like the Seminar Fund?

DIRECT OR INDIRECT INVESTING?

All money is invested in American industry either directly or indirectly. The direct method can be accomplished by putting your money to work in an investment similar to the Seminar Fund. An indirect method would be to lend your funds to a savings institution and let it

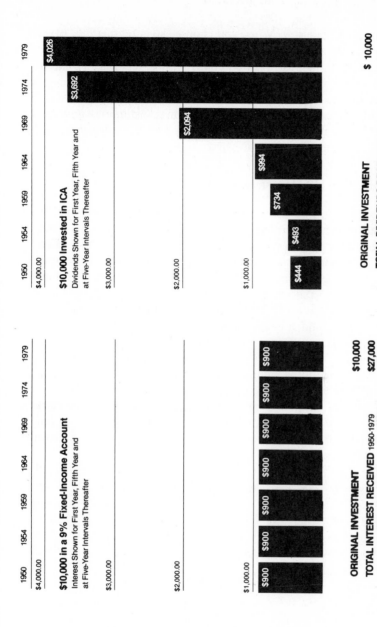

Figure 4–4. (a) Sally and Jim Berkley's "Guaranteed" Account; (b) Vicki and Jim Campbell's Investment Account

135

invest in American industry. When you choose the latter method, you in effect place a filter along that $10,000 line in our example. The screen in that filter has in the past been equipped with a very fine mesh, and very little has filtered through to you.

Remember, to become financially independent you must save and let your money grow. Many save and let savings institutions grow. To participate in the profits of American industry, you must get your eyes off the yo-yo and on the stairs.

ALL ASSETS FLUCTUATE IN VALUE

Why should you let daily fluctuations bother you? Everything you own fluctuates in value. The market value of any asset you own is only what someone is willing to pay you for it.

Your home fluctuates in value every day, but the newspaper doesn't carry a market page quoting its value. What if it did? You come home on Monday, pick up the newspaper, and find that the market value of your house is quoted at $60,000. On Thursday evening you come home, pick up the paper, and find that it is quoted at $55,000. Would you panic and begin crying? Would you be alarmed and begin to weep over your $5000 loss? The loss is just as real if you need to sell. Fortunately for your peace of mind, the values of your home and other assets are not published every day; therefore, you are unaware of their fluctuation in value, and you are saved the agony of existing in a state of panic as some do when they own securities.

Don't succumb to the yo-you panic! If you do, you may find it very costly.

CONSISTENCY OF PERFORMANCE

Table 7 in the Appendix is a record of four time periods. It shows the span in each that was best, that was worst, and the median period.

For our purposes here, let's consider the median to be fairly typical. Here are the compound growth rates for each of the median periods shown:

Median Period	Ending Value	Compound Rate
10 years (1955–64)	29,537	11.4%
15 years (1946–60)	52,022	11.6
20 years (1947–66)	104,215	12.4
25 years (1947–71)	168,537	12.0
Lifetime		
46 years (1934–79)	1,907,061	12.1%

A FAIR RATE OF RETURN

If I were to ask the average investor what he considered a fair rate of return, he most likely would answer, "At least as much as the banks and savings and loans pay on six-year certificates of deposit." Let's look and see how many times the Seminar Fund has performed that well.

In ten years, $10,000 invested at 8 percent grows to $22,080. During the 37 ten-year periods shown in Table 8 of the Appendix, the Seminar Fund failed to do that well only nine times—28 times it did better. Seventy-six percent of the time it exceeded 8 percent.

In fifteen years, $10,000 invested at 8 percent grows to $32,810. During the 32 fifteen-year periods, the Seminar Fund failed to do that well only five times—26 times it did better. Eighty-four percent of the time it exceeded 8 percent.

In twenty years, $10,000 invested at 8 percent grows to $48,754. Of the 27 twenty-year periods, the Seminar Fund failed to do that well only once—26 times it did better. Ninety-six percent of the time it exceeded 8 percent.

In twenty-five years, $10,000 invested at 8 percent grows to $72,446. During the 22 twenty-five-year periods, the Seminar Fund easily surpassed this amount every time. One hundred percent of the time it exceeded 8 percent.

At this point you may be ready to say to me, "Venita, do I have to keep reinvesting forever? Don't I ever get to spend any of my money?" You've been working hard for your money and now it's time to change places with your money and let your money work for you. One very good way to do this on an orderly basis is to establish a systematic withdrawal plan, commonly called a check-a-month.

HOW TO RECEIVE A CHECK A MONTH

Let's assume you began investing in the Seminar Fund on December 31, 1950, by beginning with a lump sum of $10,000 and that you added $100 a month for the next twenty years. On December 31, 1969, you would have made a cumulative investment of $33,900 and you would own 16,910.266 shares with a market value of $223,385 (see Appendix for details).

Let's now assume you are ready to start enjoying the fruits of your labor and investment program. You would then deposit your 16,910.266 shares with the transfer agent (or you may have left them with him all along as unissued shares), and you complete and send him a withdrawal application stating how much a month or quarter you would like to receive. He would begin sending you a check each month or quarter. You are free to increase, decrease, stop, and start whenever you like. Each time with your check will be a complete report on the status of your account.

If you had started a 6 percent withdrawal on December 31, 1970, you would have received monthly withdrawals of $1,116.93, or $13,403 per year. Ten years later, on December 31, 1979, you would have withdrawn a total of $134,030, and your remaining shares would have had a value of $265,130.

Your net results would have been:

Amount withdrawn	$134,030
Amount remaining	265,130
	$399,160
Amount you contributed over 20 years	33,900
American industry contributed	$365,260

(See the Appendix for details.)

Again, you don't have to fight the battle alone, if you'll let American industry work for you.

Source of Your Monthly Check

Your monthly checks may come from one or a combination of four sources. These are:

1. Dividends
2. Realized capital gains.
3. Unrealized capital gains.
4. Original investment.

If the amount you requested the fund to send each month is more than the dividends the fund is earning, the second source of funds would be your realized capital gains—the profits the fund has made buying and selling stocks. If your withdrawal is more than these two, they will need to use some of your unrealized gains. (This occurs when the fund has bought a stock, and it has increased in value, but they have not yet sold it. Thus the gain is unrealized.) If the amount per month you have requested is greater than these three, you will then start using a portion of your original investment. But don't be overly concerned about doing so. You have saved it for this purpose. Your concern should be with making you and it come out together.

The check-a-month can be an excellent way to use your acumulation in an orderly fashion while keeping the remainder at work in a diversified, continuously managed portfolio of common stocks.

As hard as it may be for you to believe, it was not until the mid-1960s that mutual funds were allowed by our regulatory agencies to show a check-a-month withdrawal record.

THE KETTLE OF NUTRITIOUS BROTH

You might picture your withdrawal program like a kettle filled with nutritious broth. This broth represents housing, clothing, food, etc., for your retirement years.

Your kettle might look something like this:

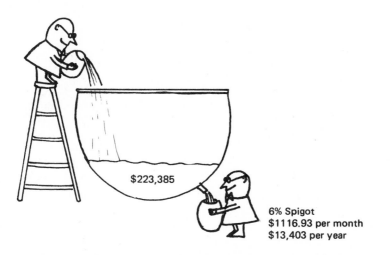

$223,385

6% Spigot
$1116.93 per month
$13,403 per year

As the fund needs dollars to send you your check each month, they will redeem shares. When the fund distributes dividends or capital gains, they reinvest them into additional shares. Therefore, the number of shares you own will change with any activity in your account. This is the reason that you deposit your shares with the transfer agent when you begin your withdrawal program. Your concern should not be with the number of total shares in your account, but with the net asset value of the shares in the account.

Your performance record if you begin it today may be better or it may not be as good. But don't you like to visualize American industry ladling in the nutritious broth at the top while you withdraw at the bottom?

How Long Will Capital Last?

Let's assume that instead of the level of the kettle increasing, it decreased. There is nothing sacred about principal. There is nothing that says you are obligated to leave an estate to your heirs. The "sacred" thing is to make you and it come out together.

If you used capital at 7 percent while it was only earning 6 percent, do you know how long your capital would last? Thirty-three years! If you begin your withdrawal at 65, in 33 years you'll be 98 years of age!

Figure 4–5 is a handy chart to use in programming how long capital will last:

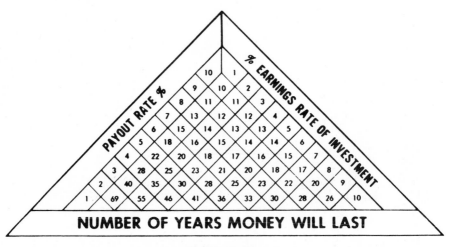

Figure 4–5.

Another way to visualize how long capital will last is to use Table 4–3.

Suppose you have $100,000 that is growing at the rate of 7 percent a year, and you withdraw at an annual rate of 8 percent—$8000 a year or $666.67 per month. Look at the box where these two percentage figures intersect, and you will see that principal will last thirty years.

YOU'RE NOT SPENDING, BUT REPOSITIONING

I find that often a prospective client feels that he is spending his money when he makes an investment.

TABLE 4–3. HOW LONG WILL YOUR MONEY LAST?

PERCENTAGE OF ORIGINAL PRINCIPAL WITHDRAWN PER ANNUM	Total return per annum on balance of principal						
	3%	4%	5%	6%	7%	8%	9%
	PRINCIPAL WILL LAST . . .						
4%	46 yr						
5	30	41 yr					
6	23	28	36 yr				
7	18	21	25	33 yr			
8	15	17	20	23	30 yr		
9	13	14	16	18	22	28 yr	
10	12	13	14	15	17	20	26 yr

If you make an investment by withdrawing funds from a savings account, you are not spending your money but repositioning it, so that it will work for you rather than for the savings institution.

If you should desire to redeem your shares, you may do so on any business day. You may cash in all or part of your shares. When you sell your shares back to the fund, you will receive an amount representing your share of the value of all the securities and other assets of the fund at the time. It could be more or less than your cost. The amount you receive will depend on the investment performance of the fund and the market value of the stocks in the funds portfolio that day.

If your need for money is temporary or if it is not a favorable time in the market, you may want to consider using your shares as collateral at your bank. You can usually rent time in this way with the hope that the value will increase at a later date.

Even if the market is progressing nicely, you may decide to borrow against the value of the stocks instead of disturbing the goose that you feel is producing satisfactory eggs.

The rent (interest) is deductible on your federal income tax return.

WHO INVESTS IN MUTUAL FUNDS?

A recent New York Stock Exchange study compared twenty-two million investors who owned only common stocks with nine million investors who owned mutual funds. (Five million owned both mutual funds and common stocks; four million owned funds only.) It contrasted the "stock only" investors with the fund investors and found:

1. Fund investors are the better-educated clients; 65 percent are college graduates vs. 50 percent of the "stock only" clients.

2. Fund investors are the wealthiest clients, with the largest assets; 23 percent have portfolios of more than $25,000 vs. 15 percent of the other clients.

3. Fund investors are the highest-income clients. Nearly one-half have incomes of $15,000 vs. only one-third of the other clients.

4. And finally, to put away the idea that mutual fund investors lock up their money forever, fund investors are the most active clients, with one-fourth making more than six transactions per year vs. only one-tenth of other clients.

IF IT'S A "BETTER MOUSETRAP"

If quality mutual funds have performed in the way I've enumerated in my examples, why haven't investors embraced them with great enthusiasm and in massive numbers?

The chief reason is that state securities boards, the Securities and Exchange Commission, and the National Association of Securities Dealers have prohibited them from telling their story. About all they have allowed those recommending mutual funds as a valid way to invest to do legally is to warn you that you might lose your money. That's not the best way to spread the good word, I'm sure you will agree. It has been said that it is easier to get an ad for pornographic literature approved than it is an ad for a mutual fund.

A mutual fund prospectus giving full disclosure of all pertinent facts was rejected by one of the states because it showed a loaf of bread in color. Even though it had in bold print on the front of the prospectus these words:

THESE SECURITIES HAVE NOT BEEN APPROVED OR DISAPPROVED BY THE SECURITIES AND EXCHANGE COMMISSON, NOR HAS THE COMMISSION PASSED UPON THE ACCURACY OR ADEQUACY OF THIS PROSPECTUS. ANY REPRESENTATION TO THE CONTRARY IS A CRIMINAL OFFENSE.

I've had many clients call panic-stricken when they reread the packet of material after they had made an investment. One in particular was a lady for whom I had made an investment in a fund that contains

---

We are indebted to *Wiesenberger Financial Services Marketer* (an excellent publication) for this breakdown on mutual fund clients.

shares only in common stocks and/or securities convertible into common stocks that are legal for the Investment of trust funds in the District of Columbia. It is a fund that qualifies under "the prudent man rule" and is often used by attorneys who are in a fiduciary capacity. After reading this caption again she called and was incensed that I would have the audacity to recommend an investment that was not "approved by the Securities and Exchange Commission." No amount of explaining ever convinced her that the SEC neither approved or disapproved, so we cancelled the trade. What she missed in income is pictured in Figure 4–6.

I pride myself on having informed investors, but a prospectus has often been a deterrent to intelligent investing.

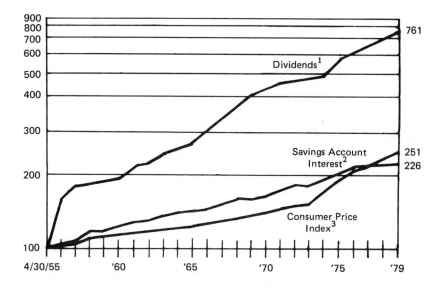

[1] Dividends on an investment assuming capital gains distributions taken in shares. Dividends for the 12 months ended April 30, 1955 = 100.

[2] Interest on an investment, based on effective annual rates of interest combining both passbook and longer term certificate accounts as reported in the United States Savings and Loan League Fact Book. Interest for the 12 months ended April 30, 1955 = 100.

[3] Consumer Price Index average for 12 months ended April 30, 1955 = 100. (U.S. Department of Labor, Bureau of Labor Statistics.)

Figure 4–6.   Dividends vs. Savings Account and the Cost of Living

The regulatory agencies also have not allowed sales literature that pictures people who showed any signs of reasonable solvency. I remember one brochure that was rejected because the man had cuff links in the cuffs of his shirt. They were not diamond-studded but looked more like the dime store variety.

PERSPECTIVE ON PERFORMANCE

With respect to performance, the mutual fund industry's long-term record has been very good, even when we add into the industry total the dismal record of the go-go funds. There is no question that you should be selective in your choice of fund management, just as you are with any investment. Some managements have historically outperformed others. Your charge for management will be approximately the same for each, so choose the ones that have depth of management, an excellent long record of past performance, and a fund or funds that fit your financial objectives. You may also want to consider having some of your money under one management and some additional funds under another. There is great merit in your considering diversification of "brains." Don't get hung up on an extra 1 percent or so cost for the "opportunity fee." Diversification can add safety and perhaps increase your net worth.

Compared to What?

Beginning in 1971, it became fashionable among financial writers to give a sharp jab to the stomach of the mutual fund industry. There are at least two reasons for this. First, I think the writers just got tired of reporting the same old news each day, which in substance said the market went down again. Second, the mutual fund industry had been a knight in shining armor. When spots of tarnish began to show, it was much more fun to kick the knight than to polish away the tarnish to let the shining metal beneath show through.

The incongruous part of this development was that these same financial writers were the ones who had placed the crown of victory on the heads of some of the "go-go" fund managers with such headlines as "_____ Fund up 113 percent for the Year!" (Regulations require that I omit the name of the fund.)

Headlines such as these and interviews quoting the "bright" young men who were managing a very small number of "hot" funds brought on a performance race like we've never seen before and, it is to be hoped, will never see again. The older, well-managed funds, with seasoned money managers at the helm and with true dedication to sound investment principles, did not engage in these wild excesses as did the few gunslingers who had their field day in the speculative heat of 1967.

I'm convinced, as I've mentioned, that many of the agonizing reappraisals we have had in the stock market (that's stockbroker jargon for saying that the market went down) are in direct proportion to the amount of junk peddled by stockbrokers during speculative periods.

As a financial planner dedicated to faithfully helping my clients accomplish their long-range plans, I had one whale of a time trying to justify why I recommended a fund that only increased 39 percent in 1967, after they have read a headline that year stating "_____ Fund up 113 Percent." My warning about "letter stock" (stock that could not be sold until a certain time had elapsed) fell on deaf ears. I had to either sell the fund to the client or know that he would buy it from some other broker. With us, we could at least warn him when we saw the storm warnings.

A large number of funds were sold to life insurance companies during this period. The more sophisticated investors were beginning to see the error of placing their savings in cash surrender value of life insurance policies. This caused the insurance companies that had built their vast empires on high-cost, low-protection, cash surrender value policies to become extremely nervous. They were beginning to lose the "savings" dollar. They began to look for equity products, with possible hedges against inflation, that their agents could sell. They hoped to keep their agents and to train them to add this new product to their line of wares. They found, however, that it was very hard to undo all the indoctrination they had subjected their agents to when they had taught them to sell "guarantees."

The Gunslingers of the Go-Go Era

There were excesses in 1967. The young gunslingers who were the "portfolio managers" of a minority of "go-go" funds, as these performance-crazed funds were called, were too young to remember a severe market decline. They thought the only direction the market could go was up.

Even the more temperate managers were tempted to chase rainbows. Fortunately, the majority did not succumb to the temptation. When the plug was pulled in 1969–1970, the go-go era went down the drain. Along with it went its idols and much of the capital of those who

idolized them. While only a small perecntage of industry assets was engulfed in the go-go era, regrettably this portion was very visible. The press had a field day.

Don't be too sure that you would have avoided these excesses if you had been in the thick of the 1967 frenzy.

When I have someone say to me, "Mutual funds are not doing so well," again, I ask, "Compared to what?" Compared to what the average speculator did on his own—even as badly as these few funds did—they still fared better than he did, due mostly to the funds' diversification. So again I ask, "Compared to what?" Compared to the man who bought Ling-Tempco-Vought (LTV Corp.) at 169½ and later sold for 8¾?

We'll skip such "delicacies" as Four Seasons Nursing Home and National Student Marketing and look at some others:

Stock	Highs	Later Lows
Wyly Corporation (formerly University Computer)	$187	$1⅛
Kalvar Corp.	176½	1½
Tex-Sym (formerly Westec)	67⅛	⅜
Levitz Furniture	60½	1¼
Winnebago Industries	48¼	1

Did You Know the Dow Jones Average Is Not for Sale?

In some financial publications, you may find mutual fund performances lumped together and actually compared to the Standard and Poor's 500 Stock Index, as if the Index were for sale. It's not for sale. Neither is the Dow Jones Industrial Average.

Your problem may be not what the Dow has done performance-wise, but how you can intelligently put to work $10,000.

The most common comparison I've seen in the press matches Standard and Poor's 500 Stock Index and the Lipper Average of 530 mutual funds. All the comparisons I've seen wholly ignore the critical fact that the S&P index is weighted by the value of each company's common stock. Twenty-five giant "blue chips" account for about one-half of the weight of the Index, with the 475 remaining securities accounting for the other half.

Comparing Index Apples and Lipper Oranges

In the fund figures, the situation is reversed. While 52 percent of industry assets are represented by the 25 largest funds, they have a weighting of only 2 percent in the Lipper Average. Conversely, 209 small growth funds, generally highly volatile, account for 40 percent of the weight of the average, but only 2½ percent of industry assets.

Does it matter? Of course it does. For while it purports to compare "the market" with "the fund industry," it is really, to use a trite phrase, comparing "apples and oranges." Thus, in a year such as 1972, when large companies were the best market performers and small funds were the worst industry performers, we had a comparison showing a 15½ percent gain for "the market" (the Standard and Poor's 500) and only 9½ percent for "the industry" (the Lipper 530). And on the basis of that comparison, despite its obvious unfairness, a theory gained credence in the press that might be described as the "idiot theory of performance" —if fund managers fall that far short of the market, they must be idiots.

But if market "apples" can be compared with fund "oranges," so can market "oranges" be compared with fund "apples." This would then give the "genius theory of performance." Using 1972 as a criterion, the fund managers could claim brilliance. In 1972 the average stock on the New York Stock Exchange (unweighted by inflation) rose by just one-half of 1 percent. The fund industry, taking into account all its assets and weighting each fund's performance by its assets, rose by 13 percent —a gain 26 times larger than the New York Stock Exchange Index. If we were so foolish as to rely on this comparison, the fund managers could be acclaimed as geniuses. This comparison never made any headlines.

Obviously the fund managers are not geniuses, nor are they idiots. However, most of them did outperform what the average person did on his own in the same period.

CURRENT PERFORMANCE

How have mutual funds done as a whole the past few years? Remember, you can't buy the average, nor would you want to. You'll want to be more selective.

According to Lipper Analytical Services, the value of a mutual fund investment would have increased on average 23.48 percent in 1979. This estimate is based on the investment results of 492 mutual funds of all kinds and assumes that capital gains and dividends were reinvested. It compares with an increase of 18.65 percent in the Standard and Poor's Index of 500 stocks, also including an estimate for reinvested dividends. The 1979 figures for equity funds alone, using the same method of calculation, were:

Capital Appreciation	36.95%
Growth	30.19
Growth & Income	22.55
Equity Income	16.69
Average of Equity Funds	28.69

In the five years to the end of 1979, termed by Lipper "an extraordinarily difficult and widely varied investment environment," the average increase of 492 mutual funds of all kinds was 134.09 percent, again with capital gains and dividends assumed to have been reinvested. The S&P 500 index, including dividends, rose 99.02 percent. Using the same method of computation, equity-fund figures were:

Capital Appreciation	227.46%
Growth	151.94
Growth & Income	125.89
Equity Income	128.42
Average of Equity Funds	157.04

THE HINDSIGHT GAME

Let's play a game to test your performance in stock selections. I'm even going to let you choose the winner after the race has been run. Below are the thirty stocks in the Dow Jones Industrial Average. I grant you $30,000. You are to select three stocks and invest $10,000 in each as of December 31, 1933. Now go down the list and make your selections.

Now look at Table 9 in the Apendix and you will find the amount each of your stocks would have grown to in that period of time. Add up their totals and divide by three to get your average. What is your figure? How close does it come to $462,959, the performance figure for $10,000 invested in the Seminar Fund? Are you surprised to find that only three stocks out of the thirty in the Dow Jones Industrial Average outperformed the Seminar Fund? Minnesota Mining & Manufacturing was the top performer of all. Ten thousand dollars in it grew to

Dow Jones Industrial Stock	Your Selection	Estimated Market Value
Allied Chemical		
Aluminum Company of America		
American Brands		
American Can		
American Telephone and Telegraph		
Bethlehem Steel		
Chrysler		
duPont		
Eastman Kodak		
Esmark		
Exxon		
General Electric		
General Foods		
General Motors		
Goodyear Tire & Rubber		
INCO		
International Harvester		
International Paper		
Johns-Manville		
Minnesota Mining & Manufacturing		
Owens-Illinois		
Procter & Gamble		
Sears, Roebuck		
Standard Oil Company of California		
Texaco		
Union Carbide		
United States Steel		
United Technologies		
Western Electric		
Woolworth, F. W.		

$6,030,000, or 60,200 percent. The second best performer was Merck, which grew to $3,392,612. The poorest only grew to $14,394. The Seminar Fund outperformed all but three of the thirty stocks on the Dow Jones Average. Investing in common stocks does require skill.

INCOME

At this point you might be saying, so much for growth, income is the important thing. Let's look at the dividends. Have you ever said, "If I had just invested in General Motors or American Telephone and Telegraph, I would have received a lot of cash dividends." After all, General Motors is the nation's second most widely held stock and AT&T is number one. However, had you been an investor in the Seminar Fund for the same period of time, you would have received more dividends. Here are the figures, assuming a $10,000 investment made on December 31, 1933:

	Market Value 12/31/79	Total Cash Dividends	Total Results
The Seminar Fund	$462,959	$213,602	$676,561
General Motors	84,507	186,999	271,506
AT & T	28,018	50,312	79,657

When someone tells you he wished his grandfather had set aside some shares of GM or AT&T for him in the thirties, tell him you would have preferred that your grandfather had put the same amount of money into shares of the Seminar Fund.

CAN YOU BEAT DOW JONES?

The average person does not do as well as the Dow Jones Industrial Average when investing on his own. This does not mean, of course, that you are average. You should use the system which best serves your temperament, lifestyle, and pocketbook.

Let's take a look at Table 4–4 and see how the Dow Jones Average of 30 Industrial Stocks, the Standard & Poor's 500 Composite Index, and the New York Stock Exchange Composite Index did in comparison to the Seminar Fund.

TABLE 4-4

Summary	Latest 15 Years (to 12/31/79)	Latest 20 Years (to 12/31/79)	Latest 30 Years (to 12/31/79)	Latest 46 Years (to 12/31/79)
The Seminar Fund	+115.0%	+204.7%	+1,003.8%	+4,529.6%
Standard & Poor's 500 Composite Index	+ 17.2	+ 80.2	+ 544.0	+ 968.7
Dow Jones Average of 30 Industrial Stocks	− 4.0	+ 23.5	+ 319.1	+ 739.6
New York Stock Exchange Composite Index †	+ 35.7	+ 92.7	+ 525.1	na

* Figures reflect changes in net asset value per share adjusted for capital-gain distributions.
† Prior to June 1964 this index was calculated weekly. Therefore, some of the "years" before 1964 actually represent periods of 52 or 53 weeks.
(na—Index not computed for this period.)

You can compare the Seminar Fund's performance each year for the past 46 years by looking at Table 10 in the Appendix.

FAMILY OF FUNDS

I would encourage you to have a portion of your funds under the management of a group that manages a family of funds with funds of varying objectives plus a money market fund.

You may be having difficulty choosing which fund when you are in the market. One solution might be to use several within the same family. You receive the quantity discount and the cumulative discount privilege, and you can move from fund to fund or completely out of the market without commission.

The Seminar Fund is one of a family of fourteen different mutual funds. Three of these funds in the Seminar family have growth of capital as their primary investment objective. But each of the three approach growth of capital in a different way. Investing some money in all three could be the answer to the problem of finding a way to take advantage of the dynamic stock market of the 'eighties. Here's how it works.

Fund No. 1   Invests primarily in larger growth companies selected from around the world. This fund has the flexibility to invest up to 50 percent of its assets outside the United States. Astute investors realize that half the world's total corporate capitalization is outside the U.S. There are more billion dollar companies overseas than there are here in America. With half the opportunities for capital growth existing elsewhere in the world, it makes good sense to take advantage of them.

Fund No. 2   Seeks growth of capital by investing primarily in smaller, rapidly growing companies with histories of consistently rising earnings and profits. Over the past few years, the stocks of companies of this type have done exceptionally well.

Now you have some dollars invested in large companies around the world and some in small companies that are highly profitable. Common sense dictates, however, that sometimes it makes sense to have more money in larger companies than in small and, at other times, more money in small companies than large. Also, there are a great many opportunities in what we call "turnaround situations"—in other words, a company that has not been profitable in the past but could well be in the future. This need for flexibility and shifting emphasis leads us to

Fund No. 3   This fund seeks growth of capital through investment in any type of company that looks promising. Based on the management's evaluation of changing market economic conditions, the fund may invest in large companies or small ones, established leaders or young companies. It may diversify broadly or focus its attention on just a few industries. This fund is the swing portion of your growth investment program.

All three of these funds have had excellent investment results. Fund No. 1 was formed early in 1973, and since that time the U.S. stock market has been virtually unchanged. Yet, Fund No. 1 appreciated over 78 percent—not counting any dividends paid—during the same period.

Fund No. 2 ranked #5 in ten years and #3 in five years among funds with the same investment objective of long-term growth and income secondary. The fund appreciated over 50 percent in 1979 alone.

Fund No. 3 came under the management of the Seminar family in 1973. By late August of 1979 it had appreciated over 128 percent, while the Dow Jones appreciated slightly over 6 percent. It appreciated almost 46 percent in 1979.

We do not know the future, of course, but you may want to consider the possibility of investing in all three funds.

WHEN THE PROS FAIL YOU

Look for depth of management and performance over long periods of time when you select your family of mutual funds. But what if you have been faithful about doing your homework and have selected a family of funds that has had a good past performance record with good management? Now let's assume that the management changes. They lose some of their top pros, or they are bought out by an industry that has more experience in managing debt instruments than equities. What do you do? If, after you have given the new management a reasonable amount of time to prove their professional management abilities, they are failing to perform, get out. Deal with reality—not with what you hoped would be or will be.

I should warn you that regulatory agencies may make it very difficult for even the most dedicated and conscientious financial planner to be of maximum help to you. The regulatory personnel may not be trained in money management and look only at cost, not results, and may reprimand him for moving you from a "sacred" investment. (It becomes "sacred" to them when you pay a commission.) Ask him, before you become his client, if his first allegiance is to you, or if his fear of being questioned on "suitability" will make him leave you in an investment that has changed in suitability for your purposes.

UNDERLYING VALUE IS THE KEY

I personally believe that the 'eighties hold great promise because by the end of the decade of the 'seventies the Dow Jones Industrial Average was selling at only 6.2 times earnings.

To put this into perspective, if you could buy all the outstanding stock of a company that's selling at five times earnings, you'd be getting a 20 percent return on your investment. Even if you were to assume a decline of 25 percent, this would still mean a price-earnings ratio of only 6.7, or an earnings return of 15 percent.

Companies create wealth, and, in the past, successful investing in common stocks has resulted from becoming one of the owners of the companies creating this wealth. Stock prices in the long term are determined by the earnings and assets of these companies.

Do not make the mistake so many investors do of taking the short-term view of the stock market when providing for your long-term goals. I find that so many predict the future by making straight-line extrapolations of the latest three- or five-year periods. When the market has gone down over a period of several years, instead of welcoming it as a buying opportunity, they sit on their hands. When the market has been going up for a period of years, they assume the opposite and eagerly jump in with the full anticipation that this happy condition will continue for the next three to five years.

Watch for times in the market when good solid values are available, and have the courage to buy at bargain prices.

SUMMARY

A mutual fund can do for you what you would do for yourself if you had sufficient time, training, and money to diversify, plus the temperament to stand back from your money and make rational decisions. It should make available to you what the very wealthy have always had: sufficient money to diversify and sufficient money to buy some of the best brains in the country.

If you can do better than the professionals and can spare the necessary time from your full-time vocation, by all means do your own buying and selling. If not, don't let your ego keep you from hiring these professionals to work for you for $5 per thousand or less.

APPLICATION

1. How much can you invest today in a lump sum to begin your journey toward a minimum $200,000 living estate?
2. Should your goal be higher? $300,000, $400,000?
3. What amount can you invest each month?
4. Should you use the convenience of the bank draft system so that your investment schedule will be systematic? The bank never forgets. You might.
5. Analyze your performance record on your stocks, using a record similar to the one in the Appendix. What has been your percentage of gain?

	Your Record	Your Chosen Fund's Record
Last year	_____	_____
Last 5 years	_____	_____
Last 10 years	_____	_____
Last 15 years	_____	_____
Last 20 years	_____	_____

6. Rate yourself with regard to the three *T*s and an *M* as they relate to investments:

	Excellent	Good	Poor
Temperament	_____	_____	_____
Time	_____	_____	_____
Training	_____	_____	_____
Money to diversify	_____	_____	_____

7. Which type of fund best fits your financial objective and temperament?

Aggressive growth	_____
Growth	_____
Growth with income	_____
Income	_____
Corporate	_____
Convertible bond	_____
Balanced	_____
Specialty	_____
Flexible	_____
Tax-Advantaged Trust	_____
Municipal bond	_____
Money market	_____

8. Should you hire a timing service?

9. Write to the Investment Company Institute, 1775 K Street, Washington, D.C. 20006, Telephone 202-273-7700, and ask them for their booklets describing the various uses for mutual funds. They are an excellent source of information and will provide you without charge a complete list of all funds keyed to their investment category. This list will include addresses and in many instances toll-free telephone numbers.

10. The address of Wiesenberger Financial Services is 870 Seventh Avenue, New York, New York 10019. Telephone 212-977-7453

THE INFALLIBLE
WAY TO INVEST

DOLLAR-COST-AVERAGING

Is there an infallible way to invest in the stock market? Perhaps not. But then, what in life is infallible? However, there is one way of investing I've found that comes closer than any other. It's called dollar-cost-averaging.

This concept has been widely practiced by astute investors for years. Instead of trying to time the "highs" and "lows" for their purchases (which, as we've learned already, is a lot easier said than done, since you never seem to know what the low is until it's too late to do anything about it), they have learned the value of investing a fixed amount of money on a regular schedule and letting the principle of dollar-cost-averaging work for them.

This plan does not require brilliance or luck, but the discipline to save and invest over a long period of time. How dull—no brilliance or luck, just discipline. That doesn't make your adrenal glands surge, make bells ring in your cerebrum, or bring a sparkle to your eyes. Nor will it lend itself to sharing enticing tidbits at the "happy hour" about your marvelous astuteness in the market.

But let's assume that you are going to get your kicks in other ways and that you feel becoming financially independent does have some compensating features. Just what is dollar-cost-averaging, and why should you consider it as one method for attempting to build your living estate?

When you dollar-cost-average, as you will remember, you invest the same amount of money in the same security at the same interval over a long period of time, with the assumption that the stock market will fluctuate and eventually go up. (These two things have always happened in the past. We don't know what the future holds.)

Let's assume that you can discipline yourself to save $100 a month, or a quarter, or at any regular interval, and that you have the earning capacity and the discipline to do this for a long period of time. Then get started immediately, because it makes little or no difference in your end results whether the market is going up, down, or sideways when you start.

If you are paralyzed into a state of inertia as to when to buy, what to buy, and when to sell, which has caused you to be in the delay–linger–wait syndrome, skip buying a particular stock and choose a mutual fund that has an excellent reputation for good management and a commendable record of past performance. A fund is especially adaptable to dollar-cost-averaging because under an accumulation plan you can buy fractional shares carried out to the third decimal point. You may also invest monthly or quarterly in a Monthly Investment Program (MIP) Plan in a stock listed on the New York Stock Exchange. However, you may find the MIP Plan in the end more costly and without sufficient diversification.

Let's assume you have $100 per quarter to invest. For the sake of simplicity, we will assume that you have chosen an investment company trust and it is selling at $10 per share. You invest $100 and receive 10 shares. Then a correction occurs in the market and the fund in which you are investing goes down to $5 per share. You still plop in your $100 for the quarter. (You're not masterminding this program, once you've made your decision regarding the investment to be used; but you are investing each quarter, regardless of what the market is doing.) At $5 per share you would receive 20 shares for your $100. Let's assume by the next quarter the market has returned to where it was when you started and is now selling at $10 per share. You will now receive 10 shares for your $100.

An overly simplified illustration would look something like this:

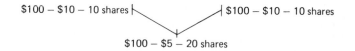

$100 – $10 – 10 shares $100 – $10 – 10 shares

$100 – $5 – 20 shares

Let's take an inventory:

	Regular Investment	Share Price	Shares Acquired
	$100	$10	10
	100	5	20
	100	10	10
Totals	$300	$25	40

Results: Total invested $300. Total shares owned 40.
Ending market price per share $10: 40 × $10 = $400.

You have made a $100 gain with the market dropping 50 percent and only returning to where it started. Average price per share $(25/3) = \$8.33$. Average cost per share $(\$300/40) = \$7.50$. You bought more shares (20) at a low cost ($5) than at a high cost ($10) and received an average cost for your securities.

If you are investing in a mutual fund, it should have a tendency to fluctuate with the market because of its wide diversification, and if our long-term upward trend continues, you should benefit from this fluctuation.

If you are one of those who enjoys playing with numbers, here are three hypothetical examples started at different points in varying business cycles. I've simplified and somewhat exaggerated the examples to more clearly demonstrate the principles of dollar-cost-averaging. In actual application you should take into consideration the period of your overall program.

In a Declining Market

Regular Investment	Share Price	Shares Acquired
$ 300	$25	12
300	15	20
300	20	15
300	10	30
300	5	60
Totals $1500	$75	137

Average price per share ($75/5) = $15.00
Dollar-cost-average per share ($1500/137) = $10.95.

This example shows the importance of continuing your investment program throughout a declining market. When the share value dropped from $25 to $5, the greatest number of shares was acquired. So any recovery above the dollar-cost-average of $10.95 would establish a profit.

In a Steady Market

Regular Investment	Share Price	Shares Acquired
$ 300	$12	25
300	15	20
300	12	25
300	15	20
300	12	25
Totals $1500	$66	115

Average price per share ($66/5) = $13.20
Dollar-cost-average per share ($1500/115) = $13.04

Even in a relatively steady market, dollar-cost-averaging can work to your advantage, as the example above shows, the actual per share cost is 16¢ less than the average price of $13.20 per share.

In a Rising Market

Regular Investment	Share Price	Shares Acquired
$ 300	$ 5	60
300	15	20
300	10	30
300	15	20
300	25	12
Totals $1500	$70	142

Average price per share ($70/5) = $14.00
Dollar-cost-average per share ($1500/142) = $10.57

As the above example shows, the dollar-cost-average per share of the five regular investments is $10.57. When compared with the current $25 per share value, it does demonstrate the importance of fluctuations in prices to the success of dollar-cost-averaging.

The practice of dollar-cost-averaging does not remove the possibility of loss when the market is below the average cost, but it clearly demonstrates that the successful pursuit of the system will lessen the amount of loss in a declining market and increase the opportunity of greater profit in a rising market.

So you see, dollar-cost-averaging doesn't give you the fun of sharing your brilliance at the coffee klatch; but if it helps you to increase your assets, it could make it possible for you to enjoy a fattening, gooey Danish pastry later.

If your real reason for investing is to make money, dollar-cost-averaging is the most infallible way that I have found to approach the market.

INVESTING FOR GAIN?

You would be surprised how many people are in the market not to make money but for the thrill it offers!

One afternoon a dentist and his wife came to my office to open a brokerage account. They said they did not expect or want my advice. All they would require of me were good executions. They explained that his profession kept him extremely busy with little time off and "playing the market" would be their diversion. Their chief goal was not to make money but to use their brokerage account as a mini-Las Vegas. (This type of account brings joy to the heart of a broker who enjoys receiving a good income. No investment responsibilities, just the delight of taking the commission checks to the bank.)

This case history reminds me of another. One of my young CPA clients stopped me on the street one day to tell me he would be calling me in about a month to make an investment of some funds he would be receiving. A month passed; then two months passed. One afternoon our paths crossed again, and I asked, "Tommy, have you received your money yet?" A sheepish grin appeared on his face. He said, "Yes, but tax time was so busy, we just couldn't get away for our planned trip to Las Vegas, so I put the money in the commodity market and lost it."

I'm going to assume that you are reading this book because you want to become financially independent and not for the kicks gambling may give you.

EGO, THE DETERRENT

Let me again remind you that one of the greatest deterrents to successful investing is the three-letter word, EGO. Dollar-cost-averaging will not do a thing to bolster your ego. Ego causes investors to hold a stock long after it has gone sour because their ego will not let them admit that they could have made a mistake. They harbor the hope that by some miracle it will return to what they paid for it; then, they tell me, "I'll sell." Don't say to me, "I've never had a loss," and expect me to be impressed. It means to me that you've probably never been in there trying or that your ego made you hold long past the time when you should have let go. When you make a mistake in the market, don't just hold. If you do, you may find out just how wrong you really were.

One of the major reasons many refuse to use professional management is that it's an admission that someone can do something better than they can do it. Again, EGO.

Let's assume that your masculine or feminine prowess is not threatened by the admission that someone can do something better than you and that you've decided to let the professionals managing the Seminar Fund do your investing for you.

JOHN WORKED FOR THE TELEPHONE COMPANY

Let me share with you the account of John and Martha. John worked for the telephone company and he reached the historic day when he became 50. His wife, Martha, gave a big birthday party for him, and loads of friends came to help him celebrate. They had a great time that evening.

However, the next day, John began to have some somber thoughts. "I'm 50. I'll retire from the company in 15 years. We haven't saved much toward retirement. I wonder what my pension will be?" John went to the personnel office the next day to inquire about his pension and found it would be only $350 per month.

That night, as they sat at the kitchen table, John told Martha of his unhappy findings and said, "Martha, even with Social Security, our pension will not be enough to allow us to retire in dignity."

The children were all out on their own by then, and, after scrutinizing their budget, they decided that they could save $100 a month. So each month after that John sent the custodian bank of the Seminar Fund a check for $100 and requested that they invest it for him in shares of the Fund.

John and Martha did this for 15 years. Then came John's happy retirement day, and on that day he sat down at the same kitchen table and wrote a letter to the same bank, saying, "I've been sending you a check for $100 a month, but I'm retiring now and won't be able to send you any more money. Would you be so kind as to now send me a check for my dividends each quarter and to also send to me any capital gains you make each year." This the bank did. John lived 20 more years, and when he was 85 he departed this life.

A few weeks later, Martha's friend Julia also lost her husband. She came to Martha saying, "I've received these life insurance proceeds, and I have such a strong sense of stewardship about their use that I'm endeavoring to invest these funds as prudently as I can. I've been considering a particular mutual fund and remembered that you and John owned it. I need to know if you have been happy with the results? Martha said, "Oh yes, and I still own the fund." Julia answered, "I know it's a personal matter, but would you tell me how well you have done?"

Martha began walking toward a drawer in the kitchen saying,

"I don't mind sharing this information with you at all. John kept excellent records, so let's take a look."

When they looked at John's records, this is what they found. John and Martha had received $44,224 in dividends and $53,933 in capital gains distribution during the 20 years of John's retirement. Martha said, "I especially remember these capital gains distributions because John liked them the best. He kept reminding me that they were 'half tax-free' and, of course, now they would be 60 percent tax free." Then she added, "Would you believe that I still have all the shares we had at the time John retired? We often looked up their net asset value in the paper together, so I know how to calculate their value."

When Martha and Julia multiplied the number of shares times the net asset value per share, they found they had a value of $96,510.

All John and Martha had ever done was save $100 a month from age 50 to 65!

Table 11 in the Appendix gives the record of the Seminar Fund, showing a beginning investment of $250, adding $100 per month for 15 years for a total investment of $18,150, and then taking in cash the dividends and capital gains for the next 20 years.

Perhaps you are five years older than John and have only ten years before you reach retirement age. Let's assume that you can begin with $250 and can faithfully add $100 a month, rain or shine, market going up, market going down, Elliot Janeway's predictions of bust, or Kiplinger's *Changing Times* headline of "Boom Ahead!" For 119 additional months, you faithfully send in your money to the custodian bank or service corporation. How will you come out? I don't know. I can show you on Table 10–2 in the Appendix how you would have done during each of the thirty-six ten-year periods between 1934 and 1978 using the Seminar Fund. The last column on the right shows the results.

Age 45

If you are 45 years of age, five years younger than John, you can see the twenty-six twenty-year periods of the fund in the Appendix. Again the last column shows each twenty-year period.

Does Life Begin At Forty?

Perhaps you are only a tender 40. Does life begin at 40? I don't know that it does, but I do know that if you come to me at that age and do not plan to retire until 65, I have twenty-five years to be of help to you.

In the last forty-five years, there have been twenty-one twenty-five-year periods, and Table 12 in the Appendix shows what happened during each of those twenty-five-year periods. Again, the right-hand column tells the results.

Are You a Tender 19?

Let's assume that you are a mere 19 years of age. Table 13 in the Appendix is the total record that was attained by dollar-cost-averaging over a forty-six-year period. The total results from January 1, 1934, to December 31, 1979, after all costs were taken out with the exception of federal income taxes, was $1,611,547. Over a million dollars dollar-cost-averaging with $100 per month.

The secret of financial independence is not brilliance or luck, but the discipline to save a part of all you own and to put it to work in a good cross-section of American industry, energy, and real estate.

SAM STEADY AND GEORGE GENIUS

Are you asking yourself, "Is this the right time to invest? If I wait, could I buy at a cheaper price?"

Let's look at two investors and, just for fun, let's call them Sam Steady and George Genius. Sam Steady began investing $100 each month, reinvesting all his dividends and capital gains for thirty years. When he calculated his results on December 31, 1979, he found that he had invested $36,000 and he held shares with a market value of $234,708.

George Genius, on the other hand, was truly a genius. After long, tedious hours of study and agonizing decision making, he successfully picked the absolute low of the year each year for thirty years and invested $1200 at that point beginning on March 13, 1950. When he calculated his results he found that he had invested $36,000 and that his value was $261,121. He was sure his performance would be so far superior to Sam Steady's that he was eager to tell him about it. When they sat down to compare their results, George was deflated to learn he had outperformed Sam by only $26,413, or around 11 percent, while Sam had done no agonizing and had enjoyed many hours of leisure that he had not had. In Table 14 in the Appendix, you can see Sam and George's record.

When is the best time to start a monthly investment program? Answer: As soon as possible.

OTHER USES FOR DOLLAR-COST-AVERAGING

Perhaps there is no other vehicle that you can so conveniently use to dollar-cost-average as a systematic investment program in a mutual fund. This is true because you can actually put the same amount of money, at the same interval, in the same investment because the fund will sell fractional shares carried out to the third decimal point. However, you can use the general system to acquire paintings of a particular artist, gold and silver coins, antiques, and other collectibles over a period of time. This should prevent you from making all your purchases at the peak of a craze. Of course, it may prevent your obtaining a large quantity at the low as well.

LUMP-SUM INVESTING

You can also use dollar-cost-averaging for larger lump-sum investments. For example, you have $25,000 to invest, but you are uncertain whether this is the right time to commit so large a portion of your assets to the market.

You may select the fund or list of stocks that fits your financial objective. If you are using a fund, you may file a Letter of Intent with the fund, as discussed in Chapter 4, "Letting the Pros Do Your Investing." This gives you the privilege of investing at two discounts over the full offering price. There is usually a discount at $10,000 and a second one at $25,000. You have thirteen months to cross one of these discounts.

The lump-sum method is also helpful when you do not have the $25,000 now but will have it within the 13-month period. You may be selling some of your assets at a capital gains or cashing in some government bonds with a large amount of accrued interest. If you space their disposition over two tax years, you may be able to save some tax dollars.

Realize that dollar-cost-averaging takes time because it means placing your investment dollars in your chosen securities month after month, year after year, sweating out recessions, confidence crises, and so forth. Compared to the horse races or a turn at the crap table, it's disgustingly dull. If the thought of retiring in financial dignity and enjoying the Golden Years brings you joy, perhaps dollar-cost-averaging is for you.

Our formula still remains:

Time + Money + American Free Enterprise =
Opportunity To Retire in Financial Dignity

SUMMARY

You will find as you go through life that there are very few things that you can consistently count on to be true over long periods of time. But I am convinced that if you have the ability to earn a reasonable income, have the discipline to systematically save and invest the same amount of that income each month, have the intelligence to select a fund as good or better than the Seminar Fund, are granted a sufficient number of years, and if our economy is no better or no worse than it has been in the past, you should become financially independent. Substitute DCA (dollar-cost-averaging) for EGO and do it NOW. Again I repeat: The secret of financial independence is not brilliance or luck, but discipline!

APPLICATION

1. How many years do you have before retirement?
2. How much can you save each month for this purpose?
3. Which day of the month is most convenient for you to make your investment?
4. Should you send in your check each month or let the bank draft your account automatically?
5. If you decide to use mutual funds, which fund best fits your objectives?
6. What other method have you found to attain financial independence that has a greater likelihood for success?
7. What is the secret of financial independence?

6

THE REAL
REWARDS
OF REAL ESTATE

There are three major areas you should consider when determining how best to employ your investment dollars. The first area is shares of American industry. You have looked at the criteria you must learn and follow to realize success in this area. The second major area is real estate, which we will examine in this chapter. The third is natural resources, with which you will become more familiar in a later chapter.

In times of uncertainty, such as occurred in the early 1970s, investors tend to "return to the earth." This phenomenon exhibits itself in revived interest in investments closely allied with the land—either under, in, or attached to the land. Let's first consider which, if any, of these areas offers a valid investment medium for you.

RAW LAND—THE GLAMOUR INVESTMENT

Often a young couple who has attended one of my seminars will come to our office for counseling, as each person who attends a seminar is entitled to do. They will be very starry-eyed about their future and say, "We want to invest in land. They're not making any more of it, you know."

Yes, I know they're not making any more of it—with perhaps the exception of the Dutch reclamation from the sea. That does not mean, however, that land is a valid investment consideration for them. To begin with, young couples usually have no more than $5000 in liquid assets, they frequently have two or more children, and they have a very small equity in their home. It will be very difficult for them to take a meaningful position in raw land. Larger tracts—which they do not have the resources to secure—offer the best profit potential. Taxes must be

paid while they wait for the land to "mature"—meaning waiting for the ultimate commercial user. Also, if they borrow money to finance the purchase, interest payments must be paid. Because of their lower tax bracket, the deductible characteristic of interest is not of significant help. They must also forego liquidity while waiting. Investing in "land" becomes more of a wistful dream than a valid investment possibility for this couple.

Your financial situation may be quite different. You may possess liquid assets and have a high cash flow from other income sources to service the interest on the loan and to pay taxes while you wait. You may be in a higher tax bracket, allowing you to shift a significant portion of the carrying charges to the IRS. This makes an investment in raw land a valid possibility for you. Your next consideration should be whether to invest on an individual basis or to join others in a land syndication.

Historical Perspective

Although America has built most of her cities, building is still going on at a rapid pace. Far more vacant land remains available than you might think. Not counting reserves of government property or the Alaskan wilderness, there are more than five acres of land per person in the United States. Much of this land is usable and accessible.

Our present land boom began after World War II and appears to have years to run. Most of the war babies who made such a demand on school facilities in the 1950s and the colleges in the 1960s now have families of their own and need shelter. This is causing a great demand for places to live and for the land upon which to build. Demand for housing is steadily increasing and should continue to do so for the next decade. Housing construction brings other real estate activities. Shopping centers, office buildings, and industry follow new centers of population into expanding suburbs. There are many indications that land and its development hold great profit potential for the eighties.

Land has always been the glamour growth area of real estate. It comes unfettered of buildings to manage and tenants to satisfy. However, you must also realize that an investment in empty land is the most speculative kind of real estate venture.

Principles to Follow

If you decide that investing in raw land is for you, there are six basic principles you should remember. The first principle is: Don't follow the population. Get out in front of it. Put your dollars in advance of a population or business trend. The second is to realize that timing of land purchases is all-important. The third is to be prepared financially to service your holdings. The cost of property taxes, liability insurance, and interest on financing makes it necessary to have around a 20 percent a year increase in the price of the land just to cover expenses, to say nothing of what the money you have invested could be earning in another investment.

It is important that you fully comprehend the nature of the ultimate land use, which will determine what a developer can afford to pay for your property. It is also necessary for you to understand the timing of the return of your invested capital. For a property to double in value may seem to be good; however, if the property should take twenty years to double, it will not be quite so attractive. (Remember our Rule of 72. You've only averaged 3.6 per annum percent on your money.) Successful real estate investment requires a forward-looking investigation and an understanding of the nature and character of the property being considered.

Fourth, keep your down payment low—paying down as little cash as possible. Sellers are often willing to accept 29 percent or less down and to finance the remainder to spread out tax payments on capital gains.

If you want to take the risk of maximum leverage, you should endeavor to negotiate the smallest down payment you can get—perhaps as low as 10 percent. If you take this course, you will need to obtain over a 20 percent annual appreciation. In other words, you would be counting on the price of the land's doubling in less than four years.

Fifth, be prepared to wait. The price of raw land seldom climbs steadily over a long period. Instead, values tend to remain fairly level for years.

When prices are rising, it may be easy to sell land, but if the price doesn't rise, money invested in land may be tied up for years while the expenses of ownership roll on. Even if a buyer can be found, financing may be difficult for long periods of time. Many banks will not carry mortgages on undeveloped land. You, the seller, may have to finance the buyer over a period of years. This may very well make land the least liquid of investments.

Some of the saddest plights I have seen have been widows who could not find a buyer for their raw land and had to sacrifice essentials to pay the taxes and interest on the land.

Sixth, if you make a land purchase and incur a large debt, be sure to buy adequate term life insurance to cover the indebtedness to avoid a possible hardship on your heirs. Even if you own the land outright, without any indebtedness, land is not liquid. Insurance proceeds will allow your heirs to have enough ready cash to pay inheritance taxes and avoid a forced sale at the wrong time.

If you have already accumulated a substantial net worth with some liquidity, raw land may be a viable investment consideration for your investment dollars. If not, as glamorous as owning raw land may appear, you should probably pass up the temptation.

Raw Land Syndications

In recent years raw land syndications have enjoyed considerable popularity. Should you consider owning a small interest in a syndication? It all depends. Here are some criteria you should examine carefully:

1. Who is the general partner or syndicator? What is his track record? Is it excellent or just fair? Syndications can be good or very poor depending on the know-how of the syndicator to buy right and to find a satisfactory buyer when it's time to sell.

2. Who are the other investors? Can they meet their portion of the payments on principal, interest, and taxes when they are due? If they can't, and you and the other syndicators can't pick up the tab, the property will revert back to the mortgage holder.

3. Ask yourself, "Is it a good investment?" If the answer is yes, then look at the tax savings potential. Too many syndications are structured to save taxes and have slim chances of earning you a good return on your invested dollar. Too many syndications have been put together on the "greater fool theory"—meaning, "I'll find a greater fool than I am and sell it to him." Raw land can become an alligator—an alligator that eats money. Avoid alligators.

4. Examine what your after-tax cost will be on the investment, and then calculate what you feel your yearly return will be on your cost basis.

Recreational Lots

Should you buy recreational lots at the seashore, on the lakes, in the desert, in the mountains? Probably not. Some work out well, but the majority have been marked up so much before being offered to the investor that the opportuntiy to sell at a profit is minimal. Liquidity is a definite problem after all the lots have been sold and the aggressive sales force has moved on to other developments.

INVESTING IN COMMERCIAL INCOME-PRODUCING REAL ESTATE

Indirect Investing

It has been an interesting psychological study to me during my many years as a financial planner to find that many who make deposits in savings and loan institutions are convinced that the officers of those institutions are rigidly standing there, guarding their little nest egg to guarantee its safety. It never seems to occur to them that while they are depositing their hard-earned money at the teller's window, the loan officer at a desk a few steps away is lending out the same money to be invested directly into real estate.

If you are a depositor in a savings and loan association, you are an indirect investor in real estate. You are "guaranteed" your sliver of the interest the borrower pays plus your original deposit, and the institution is entitled to what very well may be the larger portion of the pie. Let's say, for example, that you have $100,000 and you place it in a savings and loan and are willing to leave it there for one year in a certificate of deposit. Also, let's assume that you are in a 40 percent tax bracket. Your mathematics at the end of the year could look something like this:

$100,000	Deposit
7,500	Interest for one year
$107,500	Total at the end of the year
3,000	Taxes due at 40%
$104,500	Net after taxes
4.5%	After-tax return

And what was the rate of inflation last year? The government admits to 13.7 percent in the C.P.I. (Consumer Price Index) by the end of 1979 and over 18 percent by the early 1980s.

You were like the little frog that hopped up one step and slid back two; you didn't make it out of the financial well.

Direct Investing in a Nonmortgaged Building

Let's say instead that you become a direct investor by taking the same $100,000 and buying and paying cash for a building. You then lease that building for $10,000, or 10 percent per year, under an arrangement that is called a triple-net lease or a net-net lease. In a triple-net lease, you would be a nonoperating owner, and the lease holder would be the operator and would pay all variable costs such as taxes, insurance, and maintenance (from whence comes the triple name), as well as a lease rental each month.

The company doing the leasing may find this arrangement advantageous, for it enables them to free capital for inventory or other activities related to their business. It may also offer tax advantages. You as the owner, on the other hand, may like the arrangement because you have no variable costs to surprise you and you should have a predictable income stream from the lease for a period of years.

As a direct investor, not only do you place yourself in a position to obtain the full earning power of your money, but you introduce the vital ingredient of tax shelter on all or a portion of your cash flow due to allowable depreciation.

Depreciation

Depreciation deductions for income tax purposes are allowed as if the building is decreasing in value with use. This may be true. Often the contrary is true. In fact, it may actually be increasing in value as replacement costs escalate. Depreciation is a bookkeeping entry. No checks are sent, and it does not reduce the actual cash flow.

There are varying kinds of depreciation schedules, but for now let's assume that we are using what is called straight-line depreciation, meaning that the building is depreciated in equal amounts over its expected life (you are not permitted to depreciate the land on which the building is built.) Let's see how allowable depreciation affects the taxation of your cash flow.

Your mathematics might run something like this if you had purchased land and building for $100,000, with a cash flow of $10,000, or 10 percent, and your accountant had set a value of $75,000 on the building and determined that it had a thirty-year life. He allocated $25,000 as the cost of the land. The example below is grossly oversimplified, but should introduce to you the basic effects of depreciation on your taxable cash flow. In this example I've assumed a tax bracket of 40 percent.

HYPOTHETICAL EXAMPLE OF A $100,000
NONLEVERAGED BUILDING, TRIPLE-NET-LEASED

$100,000 at 10% cash flow	$10,000
Building $75,000 — depreciation	2,500
Taxable cash flow	7,500
Taxes at 40%	3,000
Cash flow	$10,000
Minus taxes	3,000
Net after taxes	$ 7,000 or 7%

At an after-tax return of 7 percent, you've improved your situation, but considering our present rate of inflation, you may feel you are just holding on with your bare knuckles if you include any appreciation that may have occurred.

Direct Investing in a Mortgaged Building

Again let's buy a building for $100,000, but this time let's only put down $25,000 of your money and borrow the remaining $75,000 from a life insurance company, and let's assume we can borrow the money at 10 percent interest per annum. You have now introduced another deductible item—interest expense.

Your savings from this deduction will be determined by your tax bracket. In our example, you are in a 40 percent bracket, so Uncle Sam picks up 40 percent and you pick up the remaining 60 percent. In other words, you have been able to shift a portion of the burden of carrying the mortgage. Shifting the burden back to the government is a vital lesson that you must learn in order to survive financially.

In addition to being able to deduct interest payments, you are also allowed to deduct depreciation on the entire $75,000 allocated to the price of the building, not just on that portion represented by your $25,000 down payment.

Let's look at some possible mathematics that illustrates the possible effects of depreciation and interest deductions. (This is intentionally oversimplified with amortization of the loan and salvage value omitted.)

HYPOTHETICAL EXAMPLE OF A $100,000
LEVERAGED BUILDING, TRIPLE-NET-LEASED

$100,000 at 10% — cash flow	$10,000
$25,000 down payment	
$75,000 mortgage at 10% interest	7,500
Net cash flow after interest	$ 2,500
Minus depreciation	2,500
Taxable income	0
Net after tax cash flow	2,500
$2,500 on $25,000 equals 10%	

At 10 percent after-tax cash flow, you are beginning to make progress.

After studying the above mathematics, you may have been inspired to go look for a building to buy and then lease. After long searching, you may have come away bewildered, finding that you lack the expertise to select the building and/or sufficient funds to make an economically viable investment in a commercially leasable building. If this has occurred, don't give up the idea of investing in triple-net-leased buildings, because the shortage of capital for business expansion that is a current condition in our economy today makes this type of investing one that you should consider.

Let me now introduce you to a method of investing that may offer you one of the best approaches to investing today under our present tax laws. This method is called the limited partnership. The more you learn about the limited partnership approach to investing, the more you will probably want to use this method.

LIMITED PARTNERSHIP

A limited partnership is composed of one or more general partners who have professional expertise and who are willing to assume unlimited liability and several or a large number of limited partners, usually without expertise, but with some investable funds, who do not want liability beyond the extent of their investment. The limited partners are treated, from the standpoint of taxes and income, as individuals, with all the benefits flowing directly through to them, if certain IRS criteria are met. This is called the *conduit principle.*

A limited partnership may be diagramed in this manner.

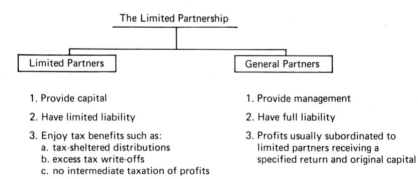

The Limited Partnership

Limited Partners	General Partners
1. Provide capital	1. Provide management
2. Have limited liability	2. Have full liability

3. Enjoy tax benefits such as:
  a. tax-sheltered distributions
  b. excess tax write-offs
  c. no intermediate taxation of profits
	3. Profits usually subordinated to
	limited partners receiving a
	specified return and original capital

REGISTERED LIMITED PARTNERSHIPS

A limited partnership offering made on a national public basis must be registered with the Securities and Exchange Commission and with the Securities Commission of any state where it is offered.

The Securities and Exchange Commission neither approves nor disapproves the offering. They do not rule on its investment merits, but attempt to see that those making the offering make "full disclosure" of all material facts relative to the offering in the prospectus, which may be interpreted by the particular SEC examiner as full disclosure of all the possible *negatives* that could possibly occur. (In Chapter 18, "How to Read a Prospectus," you may become painfully aware of the difficulty you may have in obtaining a clear understanding of just what is being offered.) You will rarely become aware of any of the positive attributes of the offering from reading the prospectus, especially if you do not read to the end of a usually very long document. After reading it, you may be completely stunned and wonder how your financial planner ever had the audacity to recommend such a "risky" investment. Don't stop there. Continue to investigate and study, and find out if there are merits to the investment that may outweigh the negatives. Look to see if these are truly negatives. Often you will find there are not, despite the prospectus. The other day a regulatory officer declined to let an issuer use a copy of an article that was an extremely informative and true account of the investment because there were no, or very few, negative comments about the investment. You will usually be allowed to learn only the negatives—none of the attributes. Personally, I feel "full disclosure" should include both.

Some states, in addition to determining if there has been full disclosure, will attempt to judge the merits of the offering and also to determine suitability guidelines for the residents of their state. Some government employees are empowered to take it upon themselves to decide "what is good for you," or what is "fair, just, and equitable," what is the minimum you can invest, and what assets you must own for it to be "suitable" for you.

It may appear ironic to you that the proverbial little old lady in tennis shoes can open a trading account with a swinging brokerage firm, can trade in such commodities as pork bellies and cocoa futures, can trade options—naked or covered—and can speculate in computer and uranium stocks, with or without any hopes of future earnings. But when the same little old lady wants to invest in a limited partnership that invests in a diversified portfolio of professionally selected triple-net-leased buildings from corporations that have assets of millions of dollars and are publicly traded, such as General Motors, Sears, and Safeway, she must in most states have $20,000 in income and $20,000 in net worth, exclusive of home and furnishings for her to be a "suitable" investor. In other states, she may be required to have assets in excess of $100,000 for it to be "suitable" for her to make an investment of as small an amount as $2500.

You should carefully consider the limited partnership as an investment medium. Under the expert management of the *right* general partners, in the *right* investment area, at the *right* time, you may find that it offers excellent potential for tax-sheltered cash flow, excess deductions to shelter other income, equity buildup, and appreciation. This is not to say that all limited partnerships are without risk. Everything that has to do with investing or not investing money has risk. Doing nothing with your funds during periods of accelerated inflation is extremely risky.

You should look into publicly registered income-producing triple-net-lease limited partnerships:

1. If you are willing to give your investment a bit of time to mature.

2. If you do not demand instant liquidity on all your assets.

3. If you do not have an emotional need to tally up your net worth daily by looking up quotations in the daily newspaper.

4. If you are in a tax bracket of 25 percent or above.

5. If you are willing to forego ego and admit that there might be those who, through economy of scale and expertise, can do your real estate investing for you better than you can do it for yourself.

These real estate limited partnerships usually can be divided into two broad classifications: nonoperating and operating. Each offers different types of properties, different potential benefits, and different exposures to risk. Let's first look at the nonoperating partnerships.

NONOPERATING PARTNERSHIPS

In 1973 and again in 1979, the Federal Reserve Board adopted a very restrictive money supply policy in an effort to slow inflation. These restrictive periods brought about such shortages of capital that only corporations with the assets of a company like General Motors could go into the market and successfully float a bond issue, and then only at very high interest rates. And in the '79 credit crunch, even the mighty IBM had to abort an offering. This left many large, very credit-worthy corporations who had expansion plans already on the drawing boards with no or limited access to capital needed for these plans. In order to continue their pattern of growth, these corporations began selling their buildings and then leasing them back under a triple-net-lease arrangement. This freed their capital to continue their expansion and inventory as they had originally planned.

TRIPLE-NET LEASES

The mechanics of the triple-net lease work something like this. Let's say that the J.C. Penney Company builds a building for $3 million, pays $1 million dollars down and obtains a $2 million mortgage. Penney's then sells its buildings to a limited partnership and leases it back under the triple-net-lease arrangement, whereby they agree to pay the partnership a monthly lease payment and also agree to pay all the variable costs, such as taxes, upkeep, and insurance. Sears, Safeway, Federated Department Stores, and others have done the same. If many companies take this approach, a demand is created for large pools of capital, and this is just the economic condition that occurred in the periods described above. To fill this great need, an organization of real estate experts whom I highly respect registered with the SEC for national distribution units of a large limited partnership to invest in the triple-net leases of these major U.S. corporations. For their buildings to be eligible for purchase by this partnership, each corporation must have a sizable net worth, be credit-worthy, and be publicly traded. Thirty to fifty of these buildings were then placed in each partnership. The partnership was divided into $500 units, and investors were allowed to purchase as few as five units ($2500). They have now been doing this for over ten years.

Each offering is usually for $60 million of capital, which allows the general partners, with three-to-one leverage, to invest approximately $180 million in triple-net-leased buildings each year.

Actually, the investments are made as the money comes in from the offering. If you make an investment in this type of partnership, you may not know which buildings will be purchased. The general partners will notify you as purchases are made. This procedure is known as investing in nonspecified properties, or a "blind pool."

Blind Pool

"Blind pool" means you do not know which General Motors building or which J.C. Penney's building the general partner will buy. I much prefer a blind pool because the general partner has much more bargaining power when they have the money in hand. For example, let's assume they have found the building that meets their investment criteria and they go in to negotiate for its purchase, but the owner knows the sale will be contingent on the general partner's ability to raise the capital to make the purchase. What kind of hard negotiating do you think they'll be able to do? But, let's assume they enter the bargaining room with millions of dollars already in hand. Do you think they are in a more advantageous bargaining position? I do. So when you are investing with a general partner with an excellent past performance record, I believe it will be to your advantage to choose a blind pool offering, despite the HIGH RISK caption on the front cover.

Leverage

If there are any long-term mortgages used in the investment, this will also trigger the HIGH RISK caption. Sure, leverage can work against you in adverse circumstances, but remember what Bernard Baruch said when they asked him how he made so much money. He said "OPM"—"Other People's Money." Also, inflation rewards those who owe money, not those who pay cash, because the borrower is allowed in an inflationary economy to repay the debt with cheaper and cheaper dollars. (I'm not advocating short-term debt, only long-term secured debt, so put away your credit cards.) You are solvent as long as what you own is greater than what you owe.

I have often wondered if money market instruments such as U.S. government bonds and certificates of deposit of large commercial banks and savings institutions were to be the investment, but at the time the investor made the investment he did not know which instruments, and if leverage was going to be used, whether the caption HIGH RISK would be required on the front of the prospectus.

In my opinion, this type of investment is not high risk. I would personally rather own J.C. Penney's buildings than own its bonds. Any court in the land will throw out a tenant for nonpayment of the rent. Of course, recourse is also available to a bondholder if the interest is not paid when due, but this is a much slower process, and there is less potential for full recovery. Also, there is not a specific building that can be rented to another tenant in the meantime.

The potential benefits of an investment in a nonoperating real estate limited partnership are:

1. Potential cash distributions paid quarterly or monthly.

2. Current tax shelter of a portion or all of your cash flow.

3. Equity buildup (mortgage paydown).

4. Appreciation.

Let's look at some oversimplified mathematics that could occur if the partnership that I've been using for my clients continues to meet its financial objectives. It has in the past, but it may not in the future. Let's assume that after careful study you feel this investment meets your financial objectives and fits your temperament. Let's further assume the following: You make a $10,000 investment; the partnership, on the average, pays you a 9 percent cash distribution each year, with 75 percent of it tax sheltered; the properties are held for ten years, and they appreciate 1 percent per year. (We are currently receiving tax shelter on 98 per-

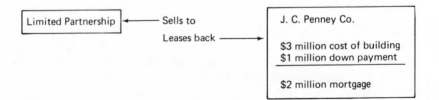

cent of the distribution, and our appreciation has been far in excess of this amount.)

Original Investment		Mortgage		Real Estate at Work
$10,000	+	20,000	=	$30,000

Per Year:

NOW

Benefits	$900	75% sheltered

LATER	$500	Equity buildup (average)
Benefits	300	Appreciation at 1% × 3 times the original investment

Or, if we use percentages, here's another way of picturing their objectives for you:

	Quarterly Cash Distributions	Excess Deductions
NOW Benefits	9% (cumulative average) (75% tax sheltered)	0
	Equity Buildup	Appreciation
LATER Benefits	4–6%	3–9% (1% to 3% × 3 times of leverage)

In this oversimplified example, to your $10,000 investment the mortgages the partnership assumed would add an additional $20,000, for a total of $30,000 in real estate working for you.

Let's further assume that you are in the 30 percent tax bracket. If your cash distributions are $900 per year and 75 percent is tax sheltered, the remaining $225 will be taxed. At 30 percent, you would lose $67.50 to Washington, leaving you with $832.50, or an 8.32 percent after-tax cash flow. (You would have to earn 12 percent fully taxable to equal this return.) This would be your NOW benefit.

LATER BENEFITS

Equity Buildup

Every month when the lessees pay the rent, the general partner in turn pays a portion of the amount received to you and a portion to the mortgage company. This builds up your equity.

Equity buildup through the reduction of mortgage balances is one of the primary sources of your potential gain in this type of partnership. This is the reason that the partnerships usually hold properties long enough to provide a meaningful reduction of the mortgage balances. You do not, of course, receive this equity buildup until the building is sold for a profit, or for at least the original purchase price. However, a big plus for you is the fact that any buildup that occurs does so from funds paid by the lessee.

Let's look at the mathematics if the partnership in which you may have invested sells all the buildings in its portfolio in ten years and is able to sell them for just their original purchase price:

HYPOTHETICAL EXAMPLE OF POSSIBLE RESULTS

	Investment		Mortgage		Real Estate
	$10,000	+	20,000	=	$30,000
NOW					
Benefits	9,000	Cash distributions ($900 × 10 years)			
LATER					
Benefits	5,000	Equity buildup ($500 × 10 years)			
Total					
Benefits	$24,000	Total cash distributions, equity buildup and original capital before capital gains taxes			

Over the ten years you would have received a total of $9000 cash distributions paid out on a quarterly basis, and would now cash in on your equity buildup of $5000. This plus your original investment of $10,000 would total $24,000. Therefore, your benefits would have been 9 percent NOW and 5 percent LATER, or a total of 14 percent per year before taxes.

Appreciation

The example above does not include any appreciation. Let's now assume that some appreciation occurs because of escalating replacement costs and the increased cost of strategically located commercial land. If the buildings appreciate 1 percent a year and you are leveraged three-to-one, (meaning you invested $10,000 and the general partner borrowed $20,000 on your behalf) this would provide you with another $300 per year, for a total of $3000 appreciation in ten years. This sum added to the $24,000 would bring your total to $27,000. If a 2 percent appreciation occurs, this would add $6000, for a total of $30,000. Capital gains taxes would then be due based on the amount that your sales price exceeds your adjusted cost basis. Adjusted cost basis is arrived at by taking your original investment, which was $10,000, and subtracting losses and cash distributions not taxable and by adding any taxable gains. The government never forgives a tax, but it will allow you to defer it and oftentimes it can be turned into the more favorable capital gains. It is usually to your advantage to defer taxes for a number of reasons. The chief reason is we have inflation and you can pay it off with cheaper and cheaper dollars. At only 7 percent inflation and a 40 percent tax bracket, in ten years you could pay off the original $1 tax liability with a 48¢ dollar; and if you can then convert it to a capital gains, which real estate lends itself to doing, you could pay it off with a 19¢ dollar. The game you must learn to play if you are to survive financially is the D.C. Game. You'll either be sending your money to Washington, D.C. or you'll learn to defer and convert!

Possible Disadvantages

You should be aware that the long-term triple-net leases that contribute so much to the dependability of your cash distributions can have an adverse effect on appreciation potential. The partnership may not be in a position to raise rentals, and current cash flow is the most important item in determining the sales price of your property when it is sold. (However, today more and more leases contain escalation clauses.)

This type of partnership usually must also use a more conservative straight-line depreciation schedule; therefore, the distributions may be only partially sheltered and will not provide excess deductions that can save taxes on income from other sources.

Investing in triple-net-leased properties is not without risk. While the management need not be concerned with fluctuations in occupancy rates and operating expenses, nor with variation in rent schedules, it does need to be concerned with the credit-worthiness of its corporate tenants. Great expertise is necessary to evaluate the properties as well as the financial strength of the corporate tenant.

If you are a conservative, income-seeking investor desiring some tax shelter and some opportunity for appreciation to hedge against inflation, you should consider committing some of your investment dollars to this type of partnership.

We've been appraising here the characteristics of partnerships that are nonoperating. Let's now turn our attention to those partnerships where the general partners actually operate the properties purchased.

OPERATING LIMITED PARTNERSHIPS

An operating partnership usually invests in multitenanted properties, such as apartment buildings, office buildings, and shopping centers, and operates these properties. In this type of real estate investment, leases are generally of shorter duration, which can be a major advantage. Rents can be raised as the leases are renewed. This provides appreciation potential. However, it can also be a major disadvantage if your buildings do not stay fully rented. If the vacancy factor goes up, the cash flow goes down and can go down to the point where there is no income. This could occur when 20 percent or more of the units are vacant and there are large mortgage payments to be met.

MULTIFAMILY HOUSING

I know of no area today where demand does, and from all indications will continue to, outstrip supply more than in the area of multifamily housing. The vacancy rate for garden-type apartments is below 4.8 percent. This is the lowest rate in the 20 years that records have been kept. A conservative estimate of the need for new housing in the U.S. over next five years is 2,300,000 units per year. However, housing starts are estimated at only 1.35 million.

In addition, because of the dramatic increase in construction and land costs, the average family can no longer qualify for a mortgage on the average American home. The family income today is approximately $15,500, the average existing home cost $67,900, and the average new home is $75,000 (in many areas such as San Francisco, it is higher). Even if these families were to be offered interest-free mortgages, they could not qualify. This leaves them only three choices: to live in mobile homes, to live with relatives, or to rent garden-type apartments. If these families want to live in the more desirable areas of their city, want access to such facilities as swimming pools, tennis courts, and recreation centers, they have no other option but to live in garden-type apartments. They may be frustrated potential homeowners, but home ownership is not one of the options open to them.

Also, there usually is a twelve- to eighteen-month lag between demand and the appearance of new construction, with severe shortages in the interim.

Rents are currently increasing approximately 7 percent per year, while at the same time building costs have been increasing at the rate of 12 to 15 percent. Rent today is one of the consumer's best buys. Historically, rents have run 36 to 40 months behind inflation. Also, the

Tax Reform Act of 1976, which required capitalization of interim financing, will eliminate many potential apartment builders, and apartments will now be built on the basis of dire need and profitability rather than on the amount of money savings institutions have available to loan.

Figures 3 and 4 in the Appendix will give you a startlingly graphic picture of the collision course toward which we are headed regarding adequate housing for our citizens. The cost of apartment construction has escalated around 150 percent since 1967, while vacancy rates plummeted rapidly. You will note from Figure 5 that the median cost for new homes has escalated 190 percent since 1970, while the median family income has only increased from under $10,000 to around $15,500. The third chart in Figure 5 combines these figures with the plummeting percentage of families able to buy a new home. As you can see, the purchase of a home is becoming more and more difficult to attain.

The alternatives to renting apartments are mobile homes, condominiums, townhouses and single-family homes, all of which require substantial down payments. This leads to the conclusion that demand for apartments will be increasing at a time when supply is decreasing.

Now that you have been apprised of this situation, how can you best turn this knowledge into a profit? Should you go out and buy some apartments? Probably not, unless you have a large amount of money to invest, because economy of scale is often necessary for maximum profitability. Probably not, unless you are either very talented at repair and upkeep, or have the ability to supervise others, and truly want to be bothered about repairing a renter's commode. You may very well enjoy a larger return on your money by investing, along with a large number of others, in very selected limited partnerships that invest in garden-type apartments, selected shopping centers, and office buildings across the growth areas of the United States, with chief emphasis on the Sun Belt. In this way, you can invest as small an amount as $5000 ($2000 for some partnerships) or in multiples of $500 above that amount, and can have the potential for quarterly distributions, tax-sheltered. You also may have excess deductions to save taxes on other income, equity buildup, and possible appreciation with no effort on your part but to deposit the hoped-for quarterly distributions into your bank account and to enter the proper amounts for excess deductions in the proper place on your income tax return each year. You do not have to report your tax-sheltered quarterly distribution.

Management Is the Key

For many years, I have recommended to my clients several registered offerings by general partners whose expertise I greatly respect and with whom my clients and I are very comfortable. These partnerships have an offering each year that allows them to acquire in excess of $100 million of properties. Their past performance has been excellent. They have exhibited the ability to buy excellent properties at the right price and location, and have been able to manage these properties with outstanding expertise and to sell them profitably at the right time for maximum profits. This may or may not continue, but the quality and depth of their personnel, their very conservative approach to financing, and their stringent reserve requirements encourage me to think that this trend will continue.

YOU AS AN INVESTOR

Let's assume that you are in the 30 percent tax bracket. Let's further assume that you have $10,000 you do not need to grab back over the next five to seven years, and that you are investing in a limited partnership that has leverage of around four-to-one and has as its objective a 3 to 6 percent cash flow. In this type of investment, your cash flow may vary. You are investing in an operating business, and like other business operations, cash flow can fluctuate. Some months, for example, a carport may need to be added to enhance a property or other improvements may need to be made. It's not like the partnership investing in triple-net leases, where all the costs are paid by the lessees. Here they are paid by the partnership. Cash flow should not be your chief concern, but appreciation potential from their plowing back the cash to obtain a higher sales price later. If current cash flow is important to you, the triple-net lease may be best for you.

Let's further assume that not only will the cash flow be sheltered from current taxation, but that there will be excess deductions of 5 to 10 percent that you can use to save taxes on other income. This is produced because the apartments may be on a 125 percent accelerated depreciation schedule (200 percent if they were new, which they usually are not; 125 percent if they are not). But the key ingredient is the depreciation allowed on certain component parts—drapes, carpets, refrigerators, etc., which can be depreciated over very short periods of time.

These quarterly distributions and excess deductions can provide you with your NOW benefits. Your LATER benefits can come from equity buildup (mortgage paydown) and appreciation. Equity buildup in these partnerships will probably be smaller per year than in the triple-net-lease partnerships, because the properties are usually held for shorter periods of time. If you've ever looked at the amortization table on your own home, you will have discovered that equity buildup occurs in a

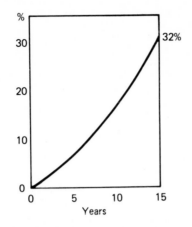

Figure 6–1.   Equity Buildup of 25-Year Mortgage at 9.5%

curve. It is small at the beginning, with most of your payment going to interest, and larger as you get further into the schedule. Figure 6–1 gives you a picture of how equity buildup escalates the longer the property is held.

The equity buildup may be only around 3.5 percent if the apartments are held for only brief periods of time and more if they are held longer.

This type of partnership offers greater appreciation potential than the triple-net leases. Sears, Safeway, General Motors, and others have tremendous bargaining power when it comes to negotiating lease terms. Apartment renters, in sharp contrast, have no bargaining power at all when there is a shortage of housing. Because current vacancy rates are at the lowest level they have been in the twenty years records have been kept, the apartment owners should be able to raise the rents to keep up or ahead of inflation. This should increase the cash flow, which, in turn, usually increases the sales price.

MULTIPLE-TENANT MATHEMATICS

If we assume a 5 percent cash flow, a 9 percent excess deduction, a 3½ percent equity buildup, a conservative 6 percent inflation, your tax bracket at 30 percent, a $10,000 investment, and four-to-one leverage, your mathematics could look something like this each year while investing in this type of partnership:

HYPOTHETICAL EXAMPLE OF $10,000 INVESTED IN A
LIMITED PARTNERSHIP INVESTING IN MULTIPLE-TENANT REAL ESTATE

	Original Investment	Mortgage	Real Estate
	$10,000	+ 30,000 =	$40,000
NOW	500	Tax sheltered, paid quarterly	
Benefits	270	9% excess deduction ($900 × 30%)	
	$ 770	Current after-tax benefit (or 7.7%)	
LATER	350	Equity buildup (mortgage paydown)	
Benefits	2400	Appreciation ($600 × 4 of leverage)	

Using percentages, the following might give you a better visual picture of what the partnership hopes to accomplish:

HYPOTHETICAL EXAMPLE OF THE ABOVE USING PERCENTAGES

	Quarterly Cash Distributions Tax Sheltered	Excess Deductions
NOW Benefits	3–6%	5–10%
	Equity Buildup	Appreciation
LATER Benefits	2.5–3.5%	10–24%

NOW Benefits

Your $500 cash distribution, tax sheltered, plus your excess deductions would make up your NOW benefits. In a 30 percent tax bracket, you would keep $500 plus another $270 if depreciation, interest expenses, etc., brought you a total of a 9 percent excess deduction. This would provide you with a total after-tax benefit of $770 (the $500 they paid to you plus the $270 you did not have to send to Washington). How much would you have to earn on $10,000 to have $770 left after taxes? You would have to earn $1,100 taxable income, or 11 percent per annum, to obtain an equivalent to your current keepable income here. In a 40 percent bracket, you would have to earn $1433, or 14.3 percent; in a 50 percent bracket, $1900, or 19 percent; and in a 60 percent bracket, $1925, or 26 percent. These would be your NOW benefits, and they can be most attractive. However, your chief reason for investing should be your LATER benefits when the apartments are sold and you hope to cash in on the equity buildup and appreciation.

Later Benefits

When the properties are sold for as much or more than the original purchase price, and only then, do you reap any later benefits. Various payout arrangements are provided by the general partners, so you should study each carefully and see which ones appear to give you the fairest return. A typical arrangement may be that when you have received back your original investment plus 12 percent per year, the general partner then receives 10 percent of the profits in excess of your original capital contribution, and you and the other limited partners receive the other 90 percent. Other programs may provide that this split or other arrangements, such as an 86–14 percent split, shall occur once you've received back your original investment plus 10 percent. Your net results may be as great in one as the other. It all depends on the sale price.

On receiving your proportionate part of the sales proceeds, you will owe a capital gains tax (and perhaps a small ordinary income tax if accelerated depreciation has been taken) on any gain above your adjusted cost basis unless you take steps to shelter it again. Remember all those distributions that you have been receiving without current taxation and the excess deductions that have saved you taxes on your other income? Now the IRS wants its due. Taxes are rarely forgiven, but they can be postponed with good tax planning. In the interim you have the earning power of the money, and when and if you do have to pay, you can make the payment with cheaper dollars if inflation continues. Also, it gives you time to plan with the hopes of converting ordinary income into capital gains, lowering your tax bite, and giving you time to figure out how to postpone paying the tax until an even further point in the future. Tax avoidance or postponement must be a vital part of your program for economic survival.

Performance: Past and Projected

Past performance of the partnerships my clients have used have been most gratifying. I do not know the future. However, I do know that this performance was obtained when our country was experiencing lower rates of inflation and excessive overbuilding. We are now experiencing well-documented underbuilding and double-digit inflation. We have underbuilding, and we have no rent control in the areas in which these partnerships purchase properties. The partnerships are still able to buy properties on the basis of current cash flow rather than replacement costs, and these are rapidly escalating. Rent is still one of America's best buys, and I feel it must increase before sufficient new building will occur. This should allow the partnerships to continue to make substantial rent increases while maintaining high occupancies. You should consider investing some of your "hard" after-tax dollars in large, well-managed limited partnerships investing in multifamily housing:

1. If you thoroughly understand that investing in income-producing real estate entails giving up some liquidity, and that the past is no guarantee of the future.

2. If you are in a 30 percent tax bracket or above.

3. If you want your funds invested where demand is greater than supply.

SHOPPING CENTERS AND OFFICE BUILDINGS

In addition to multifamily housing, the general partner will usually have the option to invest in shopping centers and office buildings in addition to apartments. These can also be most rewarding and can offer excellent tax-sheltered cash flow, some excess deductions, and equity buildup and appreciation potential. The general partner will usually diversify the portfolio as to kinds of properties and their locations. Past results on these have been very pleasing to our clients. Your leverage would be similar to the multifamily housing partnerships. Some are structured with some first-year write-offs going in. Others are not.

Choose management with an excellent past performance record. That doesn't give you a guarantee for the future, but it gives me a lot of comfort when I'm making this type of investment, which I do in both registered and private placements.

You may want to use this type of partnership or the triple-net lease, or you may use both, as many of my clients choose to do. The triple-net lease is the more conservative of the two and should pay out higher current cash distributions. The latter should pay out distributions completely tax sheltered with excess deductions to save taxes on other income. If growth of capital is your primary objective, multifamily housing and multiple-tenant properties should offer you greater potential.

PRIVATE PLACEMENTS

If you are in the 50 percent tax bracket or above, have assets in excess of $200,000 excluding home and furnishings, and your temperament does not require greater safety of diversification, you may want to consider investing in a private placement if it is offered by a general partner with high integrity, a very large net worth, and a long and excellent performance record. Never, never invest in one that does not meet these criteria. A private placement is offered under SEC Rule 146 and can, under certain provisions, qualify for exemption from registration. However, the private placement documents, called the offering memorandum, must disclose all pertinent information as they would if they were registered. They may contain even more.

An SEC regulator will not have scrutinized the offering memorandum, but our laws are such that all the negatives and disaster possibilities that they can possibly think of will be in the offering memorandum, and it will be a very long and weighty document with pages and pages of dire warnings.

The maximum number of investors can be only 35 and in some states fewer, and they must be "sophisticated and wealthy" or have a "sophisticated offeree's representative and be wealthy." (You'll find further information in Chapter 12, "Avoiding the One-Way Trip to Washington.")

A private placement usually contains only one property. One in which I have invested required that I make investments over a three-year period. The first year I invested $13,062.50, writing off 55.4 percent of the investment. The second year I invested $13,433.33, writing off 99.7 percent, and the third year $14,473.33, writing off 64.5 percent. This made my average investment approximately $13,670 per year over the three-year period. I will not be required to make further investments, but I anticipate receiving write-offs for an additional six years, with a total anticipated write-off of 122 percent of the amount I have invested. My cash flow the second year was 3.2 percent tax sheltered (in reality it was over 5 percent, since this was 3.2 percent on the total three-year investment and I did not make the third-year investment until the third year and was actually earning on the funds in another position) with equity buildup at 4.2 percent. By the fourth year, tax-sheltered cash flow moved up to 8 percent, and the equity buildup was 4.9 percent that year.

By the end of the third year I calculated that my benefits in a 50 percent tax bracket had been:

	Year	Cash Distribution Tax-Sheltered	Tax Savings From Excess Deductions
NOW	1st	Minimal	3,636
	2nd	1,262	6,480
	3rd	2,614	4,190
		3,876	14,307

	Year	Equity Buildup	Appreciation
LATER	1st	$ 48	
	2nd	155	?
	3rd	169	

My first three years:

$ 3,876   Cash distributions received
 14,307   Tax savings from write-offs
    372   Equity buildup
_____
$18,555 ÷ 3 years = $6,185 average benefits per year.

The average benefits per year, $6185, divided by $13,670, the average investment per year, gave me 45 percent average *after-tax* benefit per year. To obtain the same current equivalent net after-tax benefit on a taxable cash flow, I would have had to earn 90 percent annually on a certificate of deposit. In addition, I anticipate six more years of tax write-offs without any additional investment, and I anticipate receiving tax-sheltered cash distributions of 8 percent or more from the fourth year on, plus capital appreciation.

I've only pointed out the plus side of what I hope for from this investment, but let's also look at the possible negatives. The chief one is lack of diversification. I do not have ten to fifteen properties, as I would have had in a good diversified public offering. If, for example, the area should suffer a sharp decline in employment, such as happened in Seattle a few years ago, I could suffer a negative cash flow. For that reason, I must be sure I have staying power—meaning other funds to carry me through if this should happen.

DEDUCTIONS

Perhaps you already know how "write-offs" or deductions occur, but let's look at the four most important sources for my deductions in the above investments:

1. Depreciation. I was allowed my proportionate part of the depreciation of the apartment complex's total purchase price, even though the mortgage company provided approximately four times as much capital as I did. The buildings can be depreciated on a 125 percent depreciation schedule, since we are a second owner of a multifamily housing investment. Plus we can use component part depreciation—drapes, carpets, etc.

2. Interest expense. Interest payments on the mortgage (subject to some restrictions) are also allowable deductions.

3. Operating losses, if any should occur.

4. Charges that can be legitimately expensed in the year paid.

Because of borrowed funds, I will be allowed to deduct more

than I have invested. (The Revenue Act of 1978 modified the at-risk rule to apply to all activities except real estate investments. This is another plus for investing in real estate.)

If you are financially able to assume greater risks and you meet the suitability requirements, private placements by the right general partners are investments you should consider. They can be structured for greater tax benefits so that you can invest some "soft" before-tax dollars, and the burdensome expense of registration can be reduced.

Let's now turn to another form of real estate that can be income producing—mini-warehouses.

MINI-WAREHOUSES

From all indications, the decade of the 'eighties will bring to you many investment opportunities. One type that has particularly appealed to our clients the past four years have been registered limited partnerships that invest in mini-warehouses. Private placements in these areas had been available previous to this, but not registered ones that could be purchased by the average investor in small units.

Again we return to our demand/supply criteria. Why has demand for mini-warehouses greatly escalated? And why do I think that this demand will continue?

As home prices continue to rise, many would-be buyers are being priced out of the market and forced to live in apartments. Even those who are able to buy must settle for smaller homes or condominiums. The cost of constructing new office buildings also has escalated, limiting more and more businesses in the amount of space they can afford to rent. Manufacturing representatives likewise are finding conventional warehouse space costly or nonexistent.

These factors have combined to create a need for temporary storage space, opening the way for investment opportunities in mini-warehouses. These structures are inexpensive to construct and designed to offer accessible storage space for personal and business use at a relatively low cost. Space may be required on a long-term or short-term basis, but the typical rental period is less than one year, and spaces are rented usually on a month-to-month basis.

Mini-warehouses are ordinarily built in locations that are highly visible from main roads and expressways. They have brightly painted doors and neon signs in eye-catching positions. Several complexes can be situated within a metropolitan area. Managers who live in the complexes provide security and ongoing rental information and services.

The cost per square foot of building a mini-warehouse is roughly half that of an apartment building. But a mini-warehouse can be rented for a comparable amount of money per square foot, and it has a much lower operating cost.

By investing in units of a public offering, you can become an investor in as many as eighteen to twenty mini-warehouse complexes in four to five major "metroplexes" with as small an amount as $2500. The units are usually $500 and most offerings require a minimum investment of five units.

As investments are made in the units, the general partner obtains land and builds the mini-warehouses with no financing. The elimination of interim financing costs and mortgage payments makes it possible for mini-warehouses to produce a positive cash flow with only a 30 percent occupancy. In a good location, this level is often reached within 60 days of completion of the facility.

At 95 percent occupancy, mini-warehouses can begin producing a cash flow of 12 percent or more by the fifteenth month.

As an owner, you receive your proportionate part of the depreciation that is allowed on the warehouses, which could shelter 20 to 25 percent of your cash flow from taxes.

Also, your cash flow has the potential of increasing annually. I have found that management in the past has been able to escalate rents approximately 10 percent per year without causing the renters to move. This 10 percent usually can be translated into a 2 percent increase per year in cash flow to our investors. (We are a nation of packrats, and a 10 percent increase in cost usually is not enough to make us move our junk.)

Most partnerships are set up with the arrangement that when you have received your original investment back, the general partner can either mortgage or sell the building. If they obtain a mortgage, you would receive your proportionate part of these borrowed funds. These funds would not be taxable to you since they are borrowed. You would still own your proportionate part of the warehouses, less the mortgages, so you should continue to receive some cash flow after mortgage payments. If the mini-warehouses are sold, you would receive your proportionate part of the profits, if any are realized. Forty percent of these profits would be taxable as a capital gain.

BUDGET MOTELS

Another area of investment we have recommended to our clients is the area of budget motels through registered limited partnership where the general partner is one that heads a fast-growing budget motel chain.

As inflation continues, the commercial travelers' cost for transportation, food, lodging, etc. is escalating. Not travelling is not an option open to them, since they usually cover a large territory, so their alternative is to seek lower cost accommodations. The old "mom and pop" motels are fast losing ground to the new, well-managed national budget motel. You can become an investor for as small an amount as $2500 in units of $500. Cash flow projections are excellent beginning the second year. You should only anticipate bank interest or less during the first year while the motels are being constructed. They may be constructed for cash and, after a steady cash flow has developed over two to three years, a mortgage may be obtained on the motels. These funds could be used to increase the number of rooms of the original motels or to build additional motels in other selected locations.

This is an investment you may want to consider if you are interested in cash flow with some tax shelter and the potential for appreciation. However, prolonged gas rationing could reduce the cash flow from this type of investment.

FARMLANDS

Should you consider investing in farmlands? Your answer probably depends on the amount of money you have to invest, your tax bracket, your temperament, and what you enjoy doing. Farmland properly bought and financed in the right location has in the past enjoyed excellent price appreciation and since 1976 has increased around 20 percent a year. (Note Figure 6 in the Appendix.)

In addition to inflation, there are other factors that can cause an increase in farmland values. Some of these are:

1. Increasing demand and ability to pay for food that can be produced from farming the land.

2. The scarcity of good crop-growing land. This scarcity increases as urbanization takes more and more farmland and converts it to housing subdivisions.

3. Increasing demand for U.S. food items and commodities, especially by the OPEC countries as we enrich their coffers.

Should you consider investing monies in farmland as an inflationary hedge and to produce an income stream? If so, what investment strategy should you use?

If you are knowledgeable in farming and have sufficient time and the desire, you may want to consider buying some farmland and putting it into production. This takes great expertise, usually fairly large amounts of money, and may not offer you the amount of diversification needed to reduce risks.

Limited Partnerships in Producing Croplands

A program you may want to consider is a limited partnership in producing croplands in which you can invest as small an amount as $5000, and which has as its financial objective the following:

1. The prediction of the demand for specific food items and the availability of land for their production.

2. The minimization of production variations and fluctuation of market prices by crop diversification.

3. The purchase of only improved and income-producing farm-land to avoid negative cash flow.

4. The control of labor costs by mechanization.

5. The professional selection of the land best suited for the crops to be grown.

6. A management team that has had success in growing all of the crops they plan to grow.

A limited partnership, where you can pool your funds with other investors, may be able to offer you the potential of profitable farmland investing that only a few wealthy investors could afford in the past.

If you do decide to invest in this type of partnership, what should you anticipate? I don't know, for this type of partnership is a new one that has no performance history, and there is no guarantee that they can accomplish their objectives. I can only state what they hope to do.

First, they hope to be able to give you 40 to 50 percent write-off on your original investment. This comes from reimbursing the former owner that year for his growing crop, fertilizer, and seed consumed; depreciation of vines, trees, and irrigation equipment; and cultivation, spraying, and weeding the crops. If you are in a 50 percent tax bracket, you would receive approximately a $5000 deduction on a $10,000 invest-ment. Beginning the second year, they hope to be able to pay out to you a minimum of 8 percent, or $800, on a $10,000 investment with approximately half of the distribution tax sheltered. In addition, they hope to build your equity each year by 2 to 4 percent through amortiz-ing the mortgage used in purchasing the land. They also hope to provide you with capital appreciation of at least the average amount of increase in farm values that has occurred over the last 35 years. This has been around 7 percent per year. If they leverage two to one, then 7 percent doubled should give you approximately 14 percent appreciation.

If all of these possibilities seem feasible to you, then you may want to consider investing in limited partnerships that invest in producing croplands in this manner. This could offer you the potential of participating in the production and growth in the value of croplands.

The minimum investment in these limited partnerships is usually $5000, and suitability requirements for this type of investment may require $25,000 of income and $25,000 in assets exclusive of home and furnishings.

REAL ESTATE INVESTMENT TRUSTS

All of the types of participation in commercial income-producing real estate we have discussed so far may appeal to you, but at this point in your financial life you may not meet all the suitability requirements, or you may not choose to invest this amount of money in a less liquid limited partnership. By suitability I mean that the regulatory agencies may require that investors in limited partnership offerings have an income of $20,000 and $20,000 of net worth, exclusive of home and furnishings, or a net worth of $75,000 with no income requirements. Are there ways you can participate with smaller amounts of money? Yes, you can, through what are known as real estate investment trusts. This type of real estate investment was developed in response to the needs of those who wanted to invest small amounts of money in the profit potentials that real estate investing had to offer, but wanted at the same time to maintain the liquidity of a stock. To fulfill this desire, the modern equity trust was created to acquire and hold income properties of all types, yet have the shares publicly traded.

The REIT (Real Estate Investment Trust) industry expanded dramatically in the late 1960s and early 1970s, when many financial institutions, with the encouragement of Wall Street, established affiliated mortgage trusts in order to provide additional sources of capital. Though a few trusts used little leverage, many aggressively sought higher yields by lending to builders for construction. Their yields, together with their price per share, escalated and they became the darlings of the brokerage industry and of our largest national banks. Some of these REITs bore the prestigious names of such banking institutions as Chase Manhattan Bank and Bank of America. The nation's largest brokerage firms brought forth underwritings in REITs and held many public seminars extolling their virtues. Unfortunately, neither they nor others ever anticipated the drastic steps that would be taken by the Federal Reserve Board shortly thereafter to restrict the nation's money supply, causing a disastrous money crunch and sending interest rates reeling skyward. Many of the mortgage REITs had loaned funds for longer terms while borrowing for short terms and making a tidy sum on the spread between the two. But suddenly their cost to borrow money escalated beyond the rates at which they had made their loans. This spelled immediate and devastating trouble. Also, rapid inflation caused construction costs to mushroom and made many projects uneconomical to complete. Many builders were forced out of business, leaving numerous REITs with unfinished or unsold projects, nonearning loans, and overinflated assets. These disasters had great repercussions in the banking industry and on Wall Street, both of which were partly responsible for the creation of the problem in the first place. The difficulties of the REITs were widely publicized in the newspapers and trade journals, with the result that still today the very mention of the word sends shudders down the spines of many potential investors.

Even in less perilous times, REITs may have a rough time. A REIT, for example, may have made an excellent purchase of property, but it may be what is known as a "turn-around situation." During the period when needed improvements are being made, the REIT's earnings may be lower. A drop in earnings of a stock frightens traders and often causes them to virtually bomb a stock, driving down its price and causing general chaos and disappointment to the investor.

I'm convinced that my beloved Wall Street has never really understood real estate investing and that, properly structured, REITs can offer a valid investment opportunity for those who want to participate in commercial income real estate while being able at the same time to maintain liquidity.

Open-End REITs

There are some new *equity* REITs that have come forth in recent years that are struggling to overcome the notoriety of their namesake. The new equity trusts (as opposed to mortgage REITs, which loan funds and do not own the property) are designed to be offered and available on as continuous a basis as is permitted by law. Their open-endedness, their low price per share, their small minimum investment requirements, and no suitability standards extend the possible benefits of real estate investing to many who would not otherwise be able to participate. Some of these REITs have distribution reinvestment privileges and monthly automatic check plans, making them a good flexible accumulation vehicle. They are also providing special packaging arrangements that qualify these trusts for use in Keogh and IRA plans.

REITs may fit your needs. Their shares can be freely transferable, in contrast to limited partnership interests. The trust must by regulation be a passive entity and must employ outside agents to perform required services. So long as it meets certain asset and income tests and distributes at least 95 percent of its net taxable income each year, it will not be separately taxed. However, distributions may be partially or wholly tax sheltered, but net operating losses cannot be passed through to you as an investor to be used to shelter income from other sources, as can occur with the limited partnership arrangement.

You may find the operation of a REIT very much like that of a limited partnership with the exception that more emphasis will be placed on cash flow and equity buildup because of their inability to pass through excess tax losses. However, the increased liquidity of their shares and the restrictions on resale of their properties may encourage them to periodically refinance their properties, which in turn could allow current realization of some of the equity buildup.

Possible Disadvantages

What are some of the risks and disadvantages of investing in registered limited partnerships that invest in income-producing commercial real estate?

First, there can be delays between the time you make your investment and the time the money is actually invested in properties. During the interim you will receive interest, but you will not be receiving tax-sheltered cash flow from real estate.

Second, any accelerated depreciation, if such a schedule is used, leaves smaller amounts to be deducted in later years, and can also be classified as a "preference item" under the Tax Reform Act of 1976.

Third, partnership units can only be transferred with the consent of the general partner. (In the past this has not been withheld unreasonably.) Therefore, there will usually be no public market for the units.

Fourth, borrowing money permits the acquisition of more properties, but it also requires that the mortgage be paid regardless of whether the partnership is netting that amount each month after expenses. This therefore increases your potential exposure to loss. This would be true whether you were the owner through a partnership or individually.

THE IDEAL INVESTMENT?

I have never found an ideal investment. If you do, please let me know. However, I have found that the right kind of commercial income-producing real estate limited partnerships under the guidance and management of the right general partners has in the past contained some of the characteristics of an ideal investment. These are

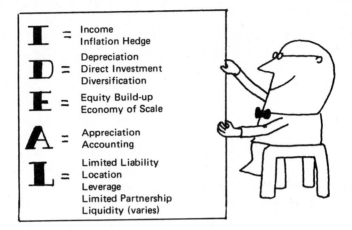

I	=	Income Inflation Hedge
D	=	Depreciation Direct Investment Diversification
E	=	Equity Build-up Economy of Scale
A	=	Appreciation Accounting
L	=	Limited Liability Location Leverage Limited Partnership Liquidity (varies)

Let's consider each in summary:

Income With Tax Shelter

The only money you'll ever spend at the grocery store is what the IRS lets you keep. Income-producing real estate limited partnerships investing in triple-net leases have in the past paid out cash flow quarterly with the major portion sheltered. This has come about because they are allowed to pass through to the limited partners the depreciation and interest expense on the properties. Those investing in multiple-tenant properties have been able not only to shelter the cash distributions paid quarterly, but to provide excess deductions to save taxes on income from other sources.

Inflation Hedge

If you have received no other message from this book, I do hope the one you have not missed is the absolute reality that inflation came thundering in with our government's dedication to full employment and will never go away until this philosophy is changed. My advice to you is to quit worrying about inflation and get on the right side of it. Inflation can make you a lot of money if you place your funds intelligently in those areas where demand is greater than supply.

Depreciation

The limited partnership form of investing permits the pass-through of the depreciation expense deduction allowed by the IRS. Another important characteristic of real estate is that depreciation is allowed on the total cost of the building—not just on your investment. You may have only put in $10,000 and the mortgage company $30,000, but your depreciation is based on the total $40,000. You are allowed a deduction for depreciation even when your asset is actually growing in value.

Direct Investing

All money placed in a savings and loan association is invested in real estate. If you are a depositor, you are an indirect investor in real estate, and you will receive a portion of the return on the real estate investment. If you invest in a limited partnership, the partnership may borrow the mortgage money from the savings and loan, but you have a direct investment and are in a position to receive your money's full earning power (but you also give up the fixed dollar guarantees). In my opinion, your only hope of staying even after inflation and taxes is to be a direct investor.

Diversification

One of the first rules of successful investing is diversification. Never put all your eggs in the proverbial one basket. Spread your precious eggs out in several baskets of various kinds of real estate and in various locations. Ten properties located in ten locations should offer more safety than one property in one location.

Equity Buildup

If you own a home on which you have a mortgage, you are already familiar with equity buildup (mortgage paydown). The difference between the equity buildup in your home and the equity buildup in the commercial properties of the limited partnerships is that you had to build up the equity in your home by your monthly mortgage payments, but in the limited partnerships the renters build up your equity by their monthly rent payments. Equity buildup is also occurring without current taxation providing deductions are in excess of cash flow.

Economy of Scale

I can't emphasize enough how important economy of scale can be in the purchase, management, and sale of commercial real estate. The truly significant profits are more often made on the very large real estate properties. They can buy the carpeting, paint, refrigerators, etc., directly from the factory. As a limited partner, you have the opportunity to participate in a proportionate part of larger properties than you may be able to do on an individual basis.

Appreciation

"Capital gains" has always been and still remains the golden word of the investment world. No federal income taxes are paid on the appreciation of real estate until the properties are sold. The properties can just sit there and grow in value without taxes. (They can go down in value, too.) Appreciation is realized when and if the properties are sold for a larger amount than was paid for their purchase. If the properties have been held for over a year, the profit on the sale is considered a capital gain and usually 60 percent of it is not taxable, except under certain circumstances under the new tax laws.

As inflation pushes up replacement costs, appreciation in real estate has a good likelihood of occurring.

Accounting

My clients especially enjoy the accounting done for them by the general partners for their real estate investments. They are sent a completed Schedule K-1 (schedule used for limited partnership), as well as a blank one to complete and attach to their income tax returns, plus a guide with red lines and arrows stating, "Put this figure on this line." By following their detailed instructions, the clients can complete their own returns if they desire. (However, I find that truly creative CPAs are worth more than they cost.)

Leverage

Again, as mentioned before, remember Bernard Baruch and his answer to the question of how he made so much money. He said, "O.P.M.—Other People's Money." Let other people's money work for you. Inflation rewards those who owe money, not those who pay cash. Here I am talking about long-term real estate mortgages, not revolving charge accounts. When and if appreciation occurs, the total value of the building appreciates, including the borrowed portion. Leverage can work for you if properly used. It can spell disaster if it is abused or if the economy of the area turns against you.

Limited Liability

As a limited partner you could not be called upon for additional funds.

Liquidity

Real estate investment trusts provide you with liquidity. Many of the other forms of investing in real estate curtail liquidity. Do not place funds into real estate that you want to be free to grab back on very short notice.

Location

The three most important rules in selecting the right piece of real estate are location, location, location. Your objective should be to be a proportionate owner of a diversified portfolio of properties selected and managed by top professionals who have established a long record of success and who have large pools of money for investing. This enables them to purchase properties that have the necessary characteristics of good location and the right terms.

CONCLUSION

If you are willing to give up instant liquidity, are in a 25 percent tax bracket or above, and can forego the pleasure of looking up the market value of your properties in the paper each day, you may find that the limited partnership is a good way to prevent double taxation and to allow you to participate in investments that, if made individually, would require large amounts of capital.

Investing in real estate should be considered in any program designed to build financial independence. In my opinion, the opportunity for relatively high leverage with relatively low risk makes it a viable inflation hedge. Unusual tax benefits also can enhance its attractiveness, but they should not be your principal motivation.

Current tax-sheltered cash distributions can also be attractive. If your income stream needs to be steady, then be prepared to sacrifice some of the growth potential. If current income is not your chief objective, then look at the operating partnerships where income may fluctuate but where the potential for appreciation is greater.

Our formula for financial independence should now add real estate and might read this way:

Time + Money + Real Estate = Opportunity for
Financial Independence.

APPLICATION

1. Which areas of real estate investing best fit your tax bracket and your temperament?
2. List the steps you will take to become better informed of investment alternatives.
3. Make a list of all your alternative investment possibilities. Calculate your expected rate of return, your loss to taxes, your keepable funds after taxes, your potential to hedge against inflation, and your potential for equity buildup and growth of capital.

YOUR WORKSHEET FOR COMPARING REAL ESTATE INVESTING
WITH OTHER TYPES

$ _____ investment, _____% tax bracket.

Indirect Investing

	INCOME	TAXES	KEEPABLE	INFLATION HEDGE	EQUITY BUILDUP	APPRECIATION
Savings & loan						
Corporate bonds						
Municipal bonds						
Single-premium deferred annuity						

Direct Investing

Triple-net leases   _____

Multiple tenant   _____

4. List here the areas of our economy where you feel demand will be greater than supply over the next three years:
   a.
   b.
   c.
   d.

5. List here the course of action you plan to take to profit from these shortages:
   a.
   b.
   c.
   d.

7

THE ROOF
OVER YOUR HEAD

There is one kind of real estate about which you have no option—you must have a place to live during every period of your life. You do, however, have a number of choices about how you allocate your funds to meet this and other needs.

Food, clothing, shelter—the three essentials of life! That's what you learned in grade school, and as an adult you probably do not question these necessities. Since shelter is a necessity, but only one or your necessities, it behooves you to approach its provision as coolly and economically as possible, for you will want to have funds left over for a few of the other goodies that put a bit of frosting on the cake of life.

There is much fuzzy thinking about the best way to provide shelter. Many couples, particularly young ones, hate to rent even for a short period of time. They are convinced that rent receipts are pure waste, not realizing that rent money is no more wasted than the money spent for food or medicine. Many view house payments as almost pure "savings" and rent money in terms of a leaky faucet.

You may be one of those who are deliberately closing your mind to economic realities in order to own your own home.

SINGLE-FAMILY DWELLING— HOBBY OR INVESTMENT?

To put this matter of renting versus owning into proper perspective, let's look at the landlord–tenant relationship. A landlord renting a one-family dwelling would probably earn a net of 6 percent on his equity—the market value of the home less the mortgage. This could happen only if he kept the home rented most of the time and the renter paid the rent promptly. (He may, however, be enjoying considerable tax shelter by way of depreciation while owning an appreciating asset.)

If the landlord has a $10,000 equity in a $50,000 home, he might hope to earn about 6 percent net on his $10,000 each year, or $600, or $50 per month. Or, put in another way, if you had that much equity in your own $50,000 home, you'd be saving $50 per month by not renting the house from the landlord. However, you may not save that much because you can't claim as many deductions as the landlord.

Real estate ads often cite the fact that homeowners can deduct interest on their house loan and real estate taxes from their income taxes. The ads are true but do not give the whole story. The landlord also can deduct these items, plus many more that the IRS will not allow the homeowner to take. These cover insurance, repairs, painting, the green shrubbery, depreciation, and so on.

Every house has a potential rental value—the sum that could be realized by renting to a tenant. As a rule of thumb, the rental value is about 10 percent per year of the market value. A $50,000 home then has an approximate annual rental value of $5,000, or a little over $400 per month.

A single-family dwelling may not be a good investment, in the real sense of the word, for either the landlords or the homeowners who are in the lower income tax brackets (with the exception of the time between the mid-1970s through the present, when high interest rates and high replacement costs have greatly escalated home values). Homes often are more of a hobby than an investment unless you have chosen a home in what later becomes a growth area where land values accelerate rapidly. This could then be an excellent investment. However, don't go overboard; inflation or a shift in location desirability may not bail you out of a costly real estate purchase. While you're waiting for the property to inflate in value, taxes and interest may put a very bad dent in your family budget.

The Real Cost

The real cost of home ownership includes upkeep and repair, fire and homeowner insurance, property taxes, equity investment, and depreciation (value loss). These expenses are just as real if you are a homeowner as if you are a landlord. The big difference often lies in the fact that a landlord recognizes them and includes them in the price he charges for the use of his property, whereas you may be tempted as a homeowner to pretend that these expenses do not exist.

The landlord knows that he must get at least 10 percent per year in rent on his property to cover his expenses and net him a profit. You, as a potential or present homeowner, would be wise to think as he does.

If you have been living in an apartment, feeling you just must buy your own home and save all that rent money, do slow down and take heart. The drain on your solvency may not be as bad as you have been thinking.

Avoid the Apples and Oranges Comparison

The rather unemotional approach I've given home ownership should do one thing for you, and that is to make you aware that the monthly payments have little to do with the real cost of owning a home.

How do you go about comparing the cost of renting an apartment with the cost of buying a home? One way is to compare the annual rental for an apartment with 10 percent of the value of the home whose purchase you are considering. If you foolishly compare the monthly payments on the house with the monthly payments on the apartment, you are, in effect, comparing apples and oranges. There is no compara-

tive relationship. Mortgage payments have nothing to do with the cost of home ownership. Mortgage payments only relate to debt reduction.

Study Figure 7–1 and you will see that homeownership costs have escalated rapidly since 1970. While apartment rents have escalated around 55 percent, home ownership costs have escalated around 160 percent. Rent is one of the best buys today, having gone up less than the Consumer Price Index. As you'll note, it has gone up around 75 percent during the same period.

BUY OR RENT?

Should you buy or rent your shelter? Your answer should be determined by a number of factors. Chief among these would be: your tax bracket, need for space, temperament, savings in the bank, investment possibilities, familiarity with the various neighborhoods, current home prices, availability of financing, and likelihood of being transferred.

Tax Advantage

Much has been said about the tax advantages of home ownership and there are some excellent advantages, but these advantages are not

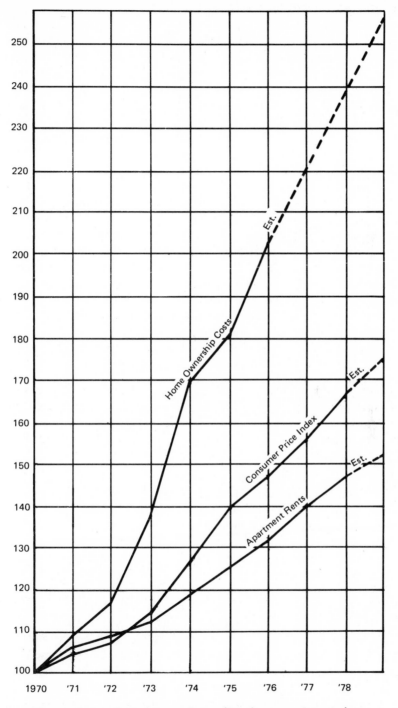

Figure 7–1. Cost of Home Ownership, Consumer Price Index, and Apartment Rents, 1970–1979

as clear-cut as they may appear at first. Interest and property taxes have both soared the past few years. Interest rates alone on a typical home are over twice what they were just a few years ago. Because these are allowable deductions on your tax return, they can be important to you if you are in a sufficiently high tax bracket. If you are in a 30 percent bracket, you are able to shift $30 out of every $100 you pay in interest and property taxes back to the IRS. In a 50 percent bracket, it's $50. As you can see, the higher your bracket, the greater the "subsidy" from the government.

This does not mean, however, that renters do not get tax breaks, too. The landlord is permitted to deduct interest and property taxes also. In addition, he is allowed to deduct two other important items the home owner is not allowed. He can deduct depreciation on the total cost of the property and also operating expenses. We learned how important depreciation deduction can be from Chapter 6, "The Real Rewards of Real Estate." If landlords were required to pay these bills without treating them as expenses, rents would have to be higher. By permitting treatment of these items as operating expenses, renters pay lower rents and find more apartments available.

In the lower tax bracket, the tax relief may be just an illusion. If your income is $15,000 per year, you may not get much of a tax break from the extra deductions. Even if you are in the middle income bracket, you will probably save no more than 15 percent of the net cost of your interest and property taxes by deducting them from gross income.

The IRS allows each family a standard deduction anyway, and unless you have enough deductions to itemize, including interest and property taxes, these last two costs become pure expenses.

If you have ever had a really aggressive real estate agent pull out his form entitled "Analysis of Home Ownership Costs," he may endeavor to persuade you that owning your own house will cost practically nothing, since the monthly charges consist almost entirely of tax-deductible interest and property taxes, and the remainder is your contribution to your equity, which will, of course, increase. He will then proceed to tell you that all you need is a down payment, which will be the best investment you have ever made. He will attempt to persuade you that you should be a wise house hunter and buy, and not a foolish house hunter and rent, with nothing to show for it but rent receipts.

But this arithmetic omits two crucial elements. One of these is the loss of income that the down payment might produce if invested elsewhere. Another is the transfer costs—the expense of buying and selling a house, which can amount to over 8 percent of its value. When these costs are put into your analysis, they can turn the calculations around in favor of renting.

However, our whole U.S. housing system encourages buying, not renting. Spouses, children, pets, neighbors, politicians, and bankers all argue for home ownership. It has become one of those fundamentals we look to as securing the nation. Our tax laws favor ownership. The Brookings Institution estimates that homeowners get $7 billion worth of federal tax breaks annually.

The IRS also exempts you from the capital gains tax when you sell your house, as long as you buy another house that is as expensive within a year or build another within eighteen months. This all encourages home ownership to become a habit. With exceptions, these rules also apply to a condominium and stock in a cooperative.

Gains that are not taxed reduce the basis on your new home. (Losses are not deductible.)

A second rollover of gain within eighteen months is also permitted without tax if you are an employee or are self-employed and the gain is from the sale of a former residence in connection with starting at a new principal place of work, provided the tests applicable to the deductions allowed for moving expenses are met.

Also, if you are 55 years of age or older (or your spouse is) before the date of sale of your home, you may elect a one-time exclusion of up to $100,000 of gain ($50,000 on the separate return of a married person) if you have owned your home and used it as a principal residence for periods aggregating three years or more during the five-year period ending on the date of your sale.

Mobility—The American Way

Another consideration that may recommend renting is that we are a very mobile society. Renting allows you to move more easily without the worry and delay of selling a home and the expense of sales commissions and horrendous closing costs.

At this point you may be thinking that if you owned a home, you would have built an equity in return for your payments as the years go by, whereas now you have nothing but rent receipts.

But remember, I've been comparing the cost of renting with the cost of owning. You can save money and acquire net worth in other ways than by paying on a mortgage. You could open a savings account or start a monthly investment program with the difference.

The Case of Mrs. Bailey. An elderly widow client of mine lives in a house that is debt free and has a market value of $50,000. She asked if she should sell her house and rent an apartment. I told her that if she would bring me a list of her expenditures for the past year, I would be happy to advise her from a financial point of view. She gave me a list of her utilities, yard-work expenses, house repairs, insurance, and taxes. I then added the 6 percent "guaranteed" return she could obtain on the $50,000 that would be available for investment after the sale of the house. When we added all of these together, we found that she could live in a $500 per month apartment more cheaply than she could live in her own home. In addition, she did not have to worry about watering her yard or possible vandalism during trips out of town.

I advised her, however, not to rush into selling her home. Answering a question on a financial basis is one thing and answering it on an emotional basis is quite another matter. Sometimes you need to consider that some expenditures are an investment in living.

Your Temperament

Home ownership may have great psychological benefits for you. Pride, a sense of belonging, having a place to put down roots—all of these can be very important. You may change, improve, and convert your home and grounds as you wish.

However, you now have an asset that may demand much from you. It will take your or someone's time, energy, and money. Home repairs and upkeep can be costly. You have now become your own landlord, garbage man, and repairman. Yards will probably have to be mowed and shrubbery planted, watered, and trimmed. This may take away some of your freedom to play golf and tennis or to travel.

Is your income variable? Could it drop by a large amount? Are you subject to transfer? If so, you could have difficulty selling your home if this happened in a recession or a period when mortgage money had either dried up or had become very expensive. When you rent, your commitment lasts only as long as your lease.

Your Need for Space

If you have a growing family, they may need more space than renting would provide. Small children will need a place to play. The number of apartments that accept children or provide them with sufficiently large play areas is limited. Schools may be better and not as crowded in the suburbs. Investigate thoroughly the schools and recreational and cultural facilities.

WHAT PRICE HOME CAN YOU AFFORD?

If you decide to purchase a home, it may be the largest single investment that you will make in your whole lifetime; therefore, invest carefully and within your budget.

There is no magic rule as to what percentage of your income should be spent for a roof over your head; however, I have found that usually this expenditure should not exceed 30 to 35 percent of your income. We've already concluded that there are other things in life as important as housing. You may desire good clothing, nutritional and tasty food, excellent medical care, a sporty or at least adequate automobile, and an annual vacation. This makes it necessary to apportion your income.

There are certain guidelines lenders will use in determining the maximum mortgage they will grant. A rule of thumb used by many lenders is two and one-half times your gross yearly income. For example, if your family's gross annual income is $20,000, your range is $40,000 to $50,000. If it is $30,000, then $60,000 to $75,000. If you are in a higher tax bracket, you may want to consider spending less than two and one-half times your income. After all, there are other things you'll want. A large home may not be as important to you as other pleasures and comforts.

As interest rates escalated in the early 1980s, the rule of thumb became that the housing costs of the purchaser should not be more than one-fourth of his income. As you will note from Figure 7–2, if you are purchasing a $50,000 home with a mortgage over a thirty-year period at 10 percent, the monthly principal and interest payments are $438.78. Using the 25 percent of income formula, you would need a monthly income of $1752, or $21,024 annually, to qualify for a home loan.

But as interest rates escalate, you will need a larger amount of income to qualify. At 13 percent, your monthly principal and interest payments are $553.05, and your family would need an income of $2212 a month, or $26,544 a year, to qualify for the mortgage. This means you would need $5520, or 26.2 percent more, annual income with a 13 percent rate than a 10 percent rate.

As you can see, the amount of income required escalates as you go on up to, say, 14 percent on a conventional loan for the same period of time and price of home. Your payments would be $592.44, requiring that you have a monthly income of $2368, or $28,416 a year. This means you would have to be earning $7392, or 35 percent more than you would at the 10 percent rate.

These figures only take into consideration the principal and interest mortgage payments, and do not include other housing costs such as insurance, taxes, utilities, maintenance, and repair. Inclusion of these, of course, would mean that you would be required to have a higher annual income to qualify for a loan.

Estimates of these housing costs for each home with a $50,000 mortgage vary widely, especially in costs for insurance and taxes, depending on the location of the home (Figure 7–2). But the percentage of additional income needed is about the same.

Another rule of thumb used by some lenders is that it will probably cost you one and one-half weeks take-home pay for each month's total housing expenses. This would include insurance, taxes, repairs, heat and utilities, garbage collection, mortgage principal, and interest.

In my opinion, you should be a little more conservative and use only two times your annual salary so that you will have funds for other household improvements. Costs are escalating and you probably consider a built-in dishwasher, garbage disposal, ovens (both conventional and microwave), trash mashers, and central air conditioning as essentials. These conveniences can increase your maintenance and utility bills. If you are in a lower income bracket and your family is large, the amount you should spend should probably be less.

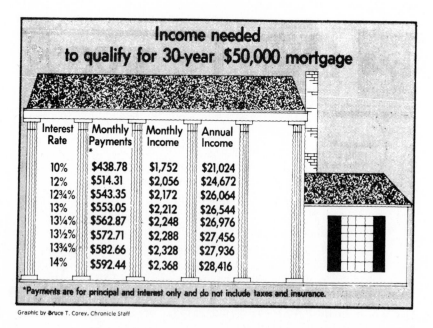

Income needed to qualify for 30-year $50,000 mortgage

Interest Rate	Monthly Payments *	Monthly Income	Annual Income
10%	$438.78	$1,752	$21,024
12%	$514.31	$2,056	$24,672
12¾%	$543.35	$2,172	$26,064
13%	$553.05	$2,212	$26,544
13¼%	$562.87	$2,248	$26,976
13½%	$572.71	$2,288	$27,456
13¾%	$582.66	$2,328	$27,936
14%	$592.44	$2,368	$28,416

*Payments are for principal and interest only and do not include taxes and insurance.

Graphic by Bruce T. Corey, Chronicle Staff

Figure 7–2. *(Courtesy of Houston Chronicle)*

SHOULD YOU BUY A NEW OR OLD HOME?

Advantages of the Old

New and used homes appreciate at about the same rate if the neighborhood is good. The rate in recent years has been between 10 and 15 percent a year. The possibility of your buying a used home is greater because more of them are available.

Also, you may be able to buy the older one for less. The rooms may be more spacious. The construction may be of higher quality. It may be nearer shops, schools, churches, and transportation. The neighborhood will be established, and the landscaping has probably been done. Taxes tend to rise less for older homes and you may avoid assessments for such things as utilities and water systems.

Disadvantages of Buying an Older Home

It may be more difficult when purchasing an older home to obtain the maximum mortgage, and the duration of the mortgage could be less. Repairs and remodeling can be expensive. Upkeep can be greater. The older home may lack central air conditioning and new built-in appliances; adding them now may be costly. There has been increased interest in older, close-in homes in recent years as the cost of gasoline soars and traffic congestion increases.

WHERE TO BUY?

I once interviewed the head of the real estate department for Prudential Life Insurance Company. When I asked him what the most important considerations in choosing real estate were, he drew himself up to his quite considerable height and said that there are three requirements you must never forget. They are "location, location, location!" (Another time when I asked a very successful real estate investor this same question, his answer was "terms, terms, terms.")

The same is true in selecting your home. The three requirements you should never forget are neighborhood, neighborhood, neighborhood. (As the cost of money escalates and inflation destroys purchasing power, you may also want to add "terms.") The homes and people around you not only affect the resale value of your home, but also your enjoyment of it.

The Least Expensive in the Neighborhood

Resist the temptation to buy the most expensive home in the neighborhood. It is much wiser to own a modest home in an expensive neighborhood. Your modest home may gain in value by being surrounded by more expensive homes, but an expensive home in a less expensive neighborhood will probably suffer.

Distance from Work

Distance from work should also be seriously considered. Before you yield to the temptation to move far out from town to escape high land and tax costs, consider the cost of driving long distances to work. This cost can easily wipe out any savings.

Savings of $4500 on the price of a home 30 miles from work could be used up in a few years if it were necessary to drive an extra 1500 miles a year.

The time required to drive the extra distance should also be of prime consideration. Time is money. Extra time spent in driving may subtract from your earning power and sap your energy.

If you find, after considering all of these factors, that you still want to live farther out, may I suggest that you utilize your commuting time by installing a tape cassette in your automobile. There are excellent educational and motivational tapes on almost any subject.

LARGE OR SMALL DOWN PAYMENT?

If you do decide after looking at all the facts that buying a home of your own is best for you economically and/or emotionally, then should you make a small down payment or a large down payment?

From the point of view of a financial planner, there is no doubt that the down payment should be as low as possible. There are a number of reasons you should make this choice.

1. Any money tied up in a mortgage is a dead asset. The house doesn't know whether or not it has a high or low down payment on it. It will increase or decrease in value just the same.

This is especially true in a state that has a homestead law like Texas. Once you've moved in, you cannot refinance this home and get that equity out. It is locked in until you sell. It's almost like having that much money sitting in a checking account not drawing interest.

2. Interest is deductible. As you've seen, you don't want to miss this subsidy.

3. Inflation rewards those who owe money, not those who pay cash. You can pay off the mortgage with cheaper and cheaper dollars as inflation continues. (Remember the new math of inflation.)

4. If you need to sell, it's easier to find someone with a small down payment than a large one.

The Allens and the Bakers

To help you make your comparison, let's look at two families. Each found just the right home, and each home cost $60,000. Each, fortunately, had $60,000, an income of $30,000 a year, and two healthy children of approximately the same ages.

The Allens. The Allens were reared by parents who programmed them with such admonitions as "Always pay cash;" "Never owe money;" "You might come upon hard times, so have your house paid for so you'll have a roof over your head"—the Poor Richard guidelines.

When it was time to close on their home, the Allens felt that the most prudent way was to pay cash, which they did. They then complimented themselves on saving "all that interest" and not having to make house payments each month.

The Bakers. The Bakers were reared by parents who were business oriented and held the earning power of a dollar in high respect. They had taught their children to use or rent each dollar they could and to put it to work at its maximum potential. So when it came time to close on their home, they felt that the prudent course for their family was to move in with the minimum down payment and to obtain the best mortgage available.

Then they began shopping for terms and rates. First, they went to a life insurance company—choosing the kind that has enticed their policyholders to do their "banking" with them in the form of cash surrender value. These companies, consequently, have large sums to lend. In fact, they are the largest single underwriters of real estate mortgage money in America today.

The Bakers also shopped at savings and loan associations, which also have vast sums of lendable funds. These funds have been placed on deposit with them by those who wanted a "guarantee" of only a portion of the earning power of their money. These depositors were willing to settle for indirect investing in real estate by investing in the mortgage of the Bakers' home. The Bakers found that the rates and terms varied from one savings association to the other, depending on the amount of lend-able money each had at that particular time and the value judgment of each of their loan officers as to the Bakers' ability to pay.

They also shopped mortgage companies and found that the rates varied by the same criteria as did those of the savings and loans.

The Bakers decided on a financing plan (Table 15 in Appendix) that would allow them to make a $12,000 down payment, with a $48,000 mortgage for thirty years at 12½ percent from a life insurance company, with monthly payments of $512.29, principal and interest. (Their taxes were estimated to be around $100 per month and the in-surance around $40. This makes a total of $652.29).

Assuming a Mortgage. Since the homes were new, it was neces-sary for the Allens and Bakers either to buy with cash or obtain a new mortgage. Had the homes been "used," a third option might have been available and desirable. This is to "assume" a mortgage—that is, to take over responsibility for the mortgage that the seller has on the house. Frequently an older mortgage has a lower interest rate than a new mort-gage, and the closing costs are considerably less if the home is in a community in which banks charge "points" for a loan (a "point" is 1 percent of the amount of the loan). The purchaser pays the seller for his "equity" (the difference between the sale price and the mortgage) and then assumes the monthly payments. Ultimate legal responsibility for the mortgage, however, lies with the original buyer, so it is impor-tant for the seller to check the buyer carefully. If the owner's equity is high, it will usually be advisable to obtain a new loan commitment in order to avoid a high down payment.

Which Couple Made the Right Decision? Let's look at the Allens. They will not have a monthly house payment, and they will not have to pay interest on $48,000. They reasoned that over the thirty-year period they will "save" $136,424 in interest on the $48,000 loan. They felt smugly proud of their decision.

The Bakers, on the other hand, felt that they had made the right decision.

Which do you think made the right choice? Measure your value system against each of theirs and see where you feel you will be the most comfortable. This will help you to decide which course would be best for you.

But do remember what I said about inflation rewarding those who owe money, not those who pay cash. I realize that this is a sad com-mentary on life, but it is fact you must learn to accept. You must learn to be a realist. Look at life the way it truly is, rather than the way you wish it were.

If the government is successful in slowing the rate of inflation to 4 percent (do you really think they will?), you would be paying off your "loaned" dollars in ten years with 60¢ dollars, in fifteen years with 40¢ dollars, and in twenty years with 20¢ dollars.

Think how long your dad had to work for a dollar thirty years ago, and then compare it with the minutes of work you have to do today. Any time you can postpone paying back a dollar that you have obtained on a long-term basis at a reasonable rate, always avail yourself of the opportunity. You must, of course, invest the money you have not paid down on the house in such a way as to earn more than the after-tax cost of renting it.

Making the House Payments.   The Allens do not have to concern themselves with paying monthly house payments; the Bakers do. The Bakers also have the responsibility of investing $48,000. How should the Bakers invest these funds to provide the extra $512.29 needed monthly for house payments?

There are various investment possibilities that they should consider. One approach that they could use is to make a $48,000 investment in a middle-of-the-road quality mutual fund, similar to the Seminar Fund, and then take a check-a-month withdrawal. If $512.29 per month is withdrawn, that would be a 12.8 percent withdrawal. These withdrawals may come from four possible sources: (1) dividends, (2) realized capital gains, (3) unrealized capital gains, and, if these are insufficient, (4) the original investment. You cannot know what the future will bring. For example, if your fund grows at 14 percent and you take out 12.8 percent, or $512.29 per month, your original investment will grow. If it does not grow at 12.8 percent, you will use a portion of your original investment and, in time, perhaps all of it. If all of it is consumed, you obviously would have to look to other sources for your monthly house payment.

Had the Bakers placed their $48,000 in the Seminar Fund on December 31, 1950 and then had the custodian send a check to the mortgage company for $512.29 each month for the next 30 years, the fund would have paid the mortgage company $184,410, and they would have had $101,725 left in their account on December 31, 1979. The Baker's house is worth just as much as the Allens', plus they have securities worth another $101,725. In the meantime, if they had needed some liquidity or collateral it would have been more accessible.

I've used an example of putting the total $48,000 in a mutual fund (incidentally I probably would have had them add another $2,000 to obtain the $50,000 discount); while I probably would have recommended diversifying a portion of the funds into oil and gas income, triple-net-lease real estate, multifamily real estate, etc., I have used the mutual fund because it is possible to determine exactly what would have happened in the past. Of course, if you were to follow the example of the Bakers, you might not do as well, or you might do better.

Meeting an Emergency. The Allens paid cash for their home, remembering their parents' warnings about possible hard times. However, if the Allens have an emergency, they will not be able to redeem a few square feet of their house. If they live in a state with a homestead law, they can't even pledge it as collateral for a loan. The loan-free home may have given them joy at the time of purchase, but if they should have a real emergency, they may find that their home is a dead asset that does not offer liquidity.

The Bakers, on the other hand, could redeem a few shares of their stock or take their shares to the bank and use them for collateral to borrow any needed funds.

AVAILING YOURSELF OF AN OPPORTUNITY

In money management, always put yourself in the driver's seat. Leave options open to yourself. Using your stock as collateral at the bank does not necessarily require an emergency. A good business opportunity may present itself. You'll have to pass it up if you don't have available funds. With collateral you can obtain these funds.

Interest Is Deductible

To give you an idea of how much of the Bakers' monthly payment is interest, which is deductible, the percentage schedule for the first five years of their loan was: 99.6%, 99.2%, 98.8%, 98.2%, and 97.7%. For the first year, .996 × 512.29 × 12 = $6122.89 interest out of a yearly payment of $6147.48.

The IRS lets the Bakers deduct interest payments, so if they are in a 40 percent tax bracket, Uncle Sam bears 40 percent of their interest cost.

Of the 12½ percent interest they are paying, their net cost is 7.5 percent.

Salability

We've mentioned earlier, as one of the reasons you should consider renting, the fact that Americans are a mobile lot. Recent studies show that the average family moves every seven years. The letters IBM, in our neighborhood, stand for "I've Been Moved." If moving is necessary, you may find it easier to find a buyer with $12,000 for a down payment than one with $60,000. A $12,000 equity is a salable equity, whereas the $60,000 one is probably not. Of course, the house can be refinanced, but this might cause them to bear seller's points on a new mortgage, which could run several hundred dollars.

There are reasons other than transfers for moving. The children may have grown and left the nest, making a large home a burden rather than a necessity. The desirability of the neighborhood may have changed, or your company offices may have moved to another section of town. The reasons for moving can make a lengthy list.

Rate of Gain on Invested Capital

It is estimated that homes have appreciated an average of 10 to 12 percent per year over the past 10 years.

The Allens have $60,000 invested in their home. Twelve percent appreciation would increase their net worth by $7200 per year.

The Bakers' $60,000 home has also appreciated the same 12 percent, or $7200, but they have only $12,000 invested. An increase of $7200 is 60 percent on their invested capital, as compared to the Allens' 12 percent. (The figure for the Bakers must be adjusted for their net after-tax interest expense.)

SHOPPING FOR TERMS

Money is a commodity. It is a commodity like peanuts, warehouses, and even houses. Never be emotional about money. If you do, you won't make rational decisions about it. Put it in its proper commodity status. Therefore, go in a businesslike manner to secure your mortgage.

If you have a contact at a lending institution, be sure to avail yourself of any help this person can give you; it does make a difference whom you know. Do not accept the first loan offered to you. Shop for rates and terms. Each institution's circumstances vary from time to time, so their lending conditions and rates will vary accordingly.

Rates are important; but, as I will discuss later, the down payment and length of payment period far outweigh a slight differential in rates.

There was a time when the very word "mortgage" was tainted, and melodramas such as "Damsels in Distress" were presented from theater stages across the land portraying the villain as the man who held the mortgage. (There is still a delightful rendition of this melodrama presented nightly on a riverboat moored on the banks of the Mississippi River in St. Louis. It's fun to hiss the villain and cheer the hero and heroine.)

Today, instead of evoking visions of "The Perils of Pauline," mortgages are an acceptable and honorable way of American life; so go ahead and rent money, but do shop for the best terms available.

TIMING YOUR PURCHASE

No doubt, some years are better than others for buying a home. If you buy your home when money is abundant, your interest costs will be lower, which will result in lower monthly payments for you. The quantity of money, which influences the cost, is regulated by action of the Federal Reserve Board, which in turn is based on consumer borrowing demands and whether the current objective is to try to slow inflation or to increase employment. If the main thrust is to slow inflation, money will be tighter and interest rates higher. If the latter, credit will be more available and will cost less.

But what if you decide that you've reached that period in your family's life when you should buy a home, and it turns out that this is the time the Federal Reserve Board's money policies are restrictive and have driven money rates to a high level? Should you postpone your purchase?

The answer is probably no. Such Federal Reserve Board action is usually taken only to slow down inflation. This means that you are looking for a house during a period of constantly rising building costs. During these times costs are probably rising faster than the carpenter can drive a tenpenny nail. If you wait until interest rates are lower, the price of the house will by then have inflated, and your monthly payments will be just as great or greater. Since the part that is interest is tax deductible and the part that is principal is not, you may be better off with the combination of lower price and slightly higher interest. So if you feel you must buy a home, go ahead regardless of present interest rates.

THE HYBRID HOMEOWNER

If you want the advantages of owning your home and the advantages of an apartment, perhaps you should consider owning your own apartment.

This can be done either in a co-operative apartment or townhouse, or a condominium. What's the difference?

In a co-op, you buy "shares" in the building and facilities, including recreational facilities. When shares are sold in co-ops, it must be by vote of the majority of the shareholders. You become both landlord and tenant, which means that you take your share of both economic and managerial responsibilities.

Co-op ownership does give the tax advantages of home ownership together with recreational facilities and maintenance at a lower cost than an individual family dwelling.

In a condominium, you own your own apartment and a pro rata share of the facilities rather than stock in the building. This means that you have the same responsibility for common areas, but you may sell your apartment to whomever you wish. The tax and facilities cost advantages are identical to the co-op.

The methods of financing for both are similar to financing a one-family home.

What are some of the problems with these forms of home ownership? First, in co-op apartments, owners have occasionally had problems with the co-owners vetoing the sale of their shares, which means, effectively, they could not sell their home. More important, poor maintenance of an apartment complex seriously lowers the value and salability of your apartment, so it is imperative to buy in a well-located, well-maintained building, just as you should buy a home in a well-located and well-maintained neighborhood.

You may need to have an income above $20,000 to approach any meaningful break on your tax return through home ownership.

There are many legitimate reasons for buying a home. You may feel that it is a better place to raise your children. It may give you a sense of security, of belonging, or of status. A lovely home can be a true joy and a prestige symbol that adds to your self-confidence.

However, don't plunge into home ownership only because others are doing it—a kind of follow-the-follower pattern of thinking—without truly weighing the pros and cons. Even though there are a number of valid reasons for home ownership, I find that most of them are sociologic and very few are based on genuine economic facts. The 1970 census established that 62.9 percent of U.S. families live in houses that they own. This still leaves a substantial minority who rent.

If you truly feel that owning your own home will bring you greater enjoyment of life, will make you a more responsible citizen, and will offer you that additional privacy that may be important to you, then consider buying a home. But if your reasons are to boast about all the money you are saving, be careful not to boast to an economist.

MORTGAGE REFINANCING

Before we summarize some of the highlights regarding home ownership, let's discuss whether you should ever refinance your home. The answer may very well be yes.

Your home could be an excellent source of capital. With your equity increasing each year due to inflation and brisk demand, you may be living in a giant savings account. If you want money to pay for college costs or medical bills or to invest, one way would be to refinance your morgtage. This approach not only frees capital, but it gives you the advantage of paying off your new mortgage with a new level of inflated dollars.

Your home doesn't know whether it has a mortgage on it or not. It will inflate just as much with a small equity or a large, and if you use the funds obtained from refinancing, you could have two assets escalating with inflation, rather than just one. Always look at the reverse possibility, too.

SUMMARY

1. It can be less or more expensive to rent a multifamily dwelling than to own a single-family dwelling. Rental frees down payment money for other investments and also allows you mobility to move to larger or smaller quarters or another location quickly and easily.

2. Calculate your true housing costs unemotionally, remembering that the mortgage payment is only one of several major items in your housing costs.

3. Monthly house payments should not exceed one week's earnings.

4. If you anticipate moving, buy a home similar in style to that of your neighbors. This does not do much for your sense of creativity, but it may help you avoid taking a shellacking on resale. A good rule to remember when making an investment in any asset of considerable value is "Be a conformist." The more conventional you are, the better your chances are of increasing the value of your assets. Preserve some of your individuality, but don't go overboard. You may find it quite expensive if you do.

5. Avoid paying too much for gimmicks. The builder may have spent an extra $1000 on gadgets for flashy first-impression eye appeal and be able to sell you the house for an extra $3000. As the years go by, you will want to build in your own charm, and the "gook" the

builder originally added may turn out to be a hindrance rather than an enchantment.

      6. Avoid paying too much for a view. Surroundings are important, but after a year you'll probably take the view for granted and wish that this extra expenditure had been avoided.

      7. Keep your down payment as low as possible: inflation lets you repay with cheaper dollars; resale should be easier; return on invested capital can be higher; and liquidity or pledgability can be available in times of emergency or investment opportunity.

      Your home can be your castle or, under unfortunate circumstances, your prison, so use both your heart and your head in choosing how you'll provide that roof over your head.

APPLICATION

1. Should you rent or buy?
2. How long do you plan to live there?
3. If you decide to buy, should it be a house, a cluster home, a condominium, or a townhouse?
4. How much is available for a down payment??
5. Emotionally do you identify with the Allens or the Bakers in this chapter?
6. On the basis of our formula, what price home can you afford?
7. What kind of neighborhood best fits your way of life?
8. Is availability of a clubhouse with social facilities, tennis courts, and swimming pools important to you?
9. Whom do you know, or what contacts can you make, to obtain favorable financing?
10. Is the prime interest rate rising or dropping at this time?
11. If you have chosen to make a low down payment, how will you employ the remaining funds?
12. Items to include in your housing checklist:
    a. First and foremost, remember location, location, location. How is the location?
    b. Accessibility to work?
    c. Accessibility to schools?
    d. Accessibility to shopping facilities?
    e. Access to recreational facilities?

f. Rate of price increase of homes in the neighborhood? Percent per year.

g. Neighbors?

h. Traffic patterns?

i. Noise?

j. Smells?

k. How does the cost of the home that you are considering compare with recent sales in the neighborhood?

l. Conditions of the maintenance fund for upkeep of the neighborhood?

m. Determine whether or not is it located within the bounds of the 100-year flood plain as determined by the National Flood Insurance Program. (If it is, to obtain a loan you must buy flood inurance at a cost of $125 per year.)

n. Towns grow and values tend to increase west, north, uphill, and away from rivers. Where is the house in relation to these?

o. How old is the home?

p. If the home is 10 years old, are you a good handyman on repairs?

q. Does the home fit your style? Yard work? Entertaining?

8

ENERGIZING
YOUR
INVESTMENTS

You'll remember that a major requirement for successful investing is to place some of your funds where demand is greater than supply. One commodity that is already in great demand, and most certainly will increase, is energy. The developed nations of the world continue to increase their demands while the emerging Third World nations are rapidly joining the throng.

You will discover as you begin to study energy-related investments that energy is a broad category and not all areas will be viable considerations, especially if your investment funds are limited.

THE ENERGY CRISIS—ITS CAUSE

In 1974, the average man on the street came face to face with the fact that energy is not a magical manna that drops from heaven and runs into his electric light switch and into the tank of his automobile. With the Arab oil embargo, he discovered that he could no longer drive into the corner gas station, say, "Fill 'er up," receive a sheet of green trading stamps (double on Tuesdays) plus a drinking glass with the insignia of his local football team, and be merrily on his way in a few minutes.

The "energy crisis" did not just suddenly arrive on the scene, although it may have appeared to from listening to and reading the news media. In 1967, I interviewed Michael T. Halbouty, a highly respected independent oil producer, on my CBS affiliate television program, "Successful Texans." He warned then, as he had been doing since 1960, of the impending energy crisis if steps were not taken to allow a reasonable return on capital invested in the oil industry. At that time, he was making warning speeches across the nation, and he has continued to do so. I interviewed J. Hugh Liedtke, Chairman of the Board of Pennzoil. He also warned of the problems that were imminent if proper action was not taken. He quoted extensively from comprehensive government studies on the subject and brought charts to illustrate graphically the seriousness of what must surely happen.

I interviewed George Mitchell, Chairman of the Board and President of Mitchell Energy and Development. He gave the same warning and continues to do so. (I again interviewed Mr. Mitchell before my trip to the White House October 4, 1978, where I, along with other community leaders, was briefed by President Carter and his staff regarding the need for the passage by Congress of the Natural Gas Policy Act.)

These knowledgeable oilmen and others with expertise in the industry pointed out over and over again that the flow of new oil could not possibly meet the new and increasing demands.

The need to encourage production seemed obvious to those who

232

were in production, but the opposite view was taken by those who controlled the legislation to fulfill the need.

The Federal Power Commission continued to hold down the price of natural gas to the 10¢ to 16¢ per cubic foot price to which they had arbitrarily rolled it back, despite the continuous pleas of the oilmen. The Commission took the pose of the three little monkeys, put their hands over their eyes, and said, "Hear no evil, see no evil, speak no evil," and all these bad, bad predictions will "fade away." Of course, the big bad wolf, called energy shortage, did not fade away.

The attitudes of the eastern congressmen also aggravated the picture as they took the attitude. "How dare you talk of raising the price of the natural gas used to bake the bread for the dear families residing in my state?" And then they added, "And don't you muss our scenic coastlines with refineries either; keep them down in Texas and Louisiana where they belong."

They also insisted that the federal government allow massive amounts of foreign oil to be imported into the United States at prices so low that domestic producers could not compete.

At this time a shortage of risk capital to be used to drill oil wells also occurred.

In the 1950s, the corporate tax rate was 60 to 70 percent, and the individual rate could go as high as 90 percent. At these confiscatory levels, there was a tremendous incentive to search for ways of turning tax liabilities into potential capital assets. Oil drilling programs fit this possibility because of the 100 percent write-off potential of intangible drilling costs. Large amounts of risk capital, therefore, were made available.

But in the 1960s, the maximum corporate tax level was reduced to around 48 percent and the individual's to the 50 to 70 percent level. This greatly reduced the tax incentive. All of these factors conbined to reduce the profitability of searching for oil and gas reserves.

The number of independent oil operators dwindled from 35,000 to 5000, and the number of rig operators from 3500 to around 900.

As the supply of oil and gas was decreasing, the demand was increasing. A collision course was already in the making when the Arabian bloc discovered our great vulnerability and decided that their best bargaining tool against Israel was the U.S.'s dependence on their oil.

Will the government take a more intelligent approach throughout the eighties? To date, their batting average has been zilch. Instead of taking steps to lessen our dependence on foreign oil, they have concentrated on making the oil companies the scapegoat and blaming them for all of our problems. The explanations of the energy crisis I've heard gushing forth from government officials, newspaper reporters, and TV commentators have been tantamount to blaming the gynecologist for the baby.

Our profit-minded and efficiently run oil companies did not produce the gasoline shortage. Our wasteful consumers did not produce the gasoline shortage. Severely cold winters in the North did not produce the shortage. Not even the OPEC countries produced the gasoline shortage.

The oil industry has been around for a long time and they have always had the obligation to make a profit for their stockholders. Our consumers have not suddenly become more wasteful. The North has had hard winters before. Sheiks have always desired wealth. Why, then, for a century or more before 1971 were there no energy crisis, no gasoline shortages, no problems about fuel oil?

We have an energy shortage for only one reason. The government decreed that there would be one. Of course, this was not done openly. The administration didn't send a message to Congress asking them to legislate long gasoline lines. But when President Nixon, on August 15, 1971, imposed wage and price controls, maximum prices on crude oil, gasoline, and other petroleum products were instituted. However, when these controls were later lifted on other commodities, but remained in force on crude oil and its by-products, the journey to shortages was greatly accelerated.

As an economist, there is one thing I have learned very well, and that is how shortages and surpluses are created. If a surplus is desired, all that is necessary is to have the government legislate a minimum price that is *above* the price that would otherwise prevail. That is what has been done to produce surpluses of wheat, sugar, butter, and many other commodities. Perhaps the most tragic of all is the creation of a surplus of teenage labor. The minimum wage is a legislated price above the price that would otherwise prevail for the labor of teenagers. Like every minimum price, it enhances the amount supplied and reduces the amount that is demanded, thereby producing a surplus.

If you want a shortage, do the opposite. Have the government legislate a maximum price that is *below* the price that would otherwise prevail. A good example is New York City and other cities that have unwisely legislated rent controls, causing a shortage of rental dwellings. The energy crisis and the gasoline shortage has come to us in the same way.

I firmly believe that the elimination of all controls would cause the gasoline lines to disappear. Petroleum prices could temporarily be higher but would not produce the disorganization and confusion experienced under past controls.

The true cost of gasoline to us as consumers may even go down, for even if the price of gasoline goes up at the pump, we could eliminate the waste of time and gasoline that is consumed in waiting in lines or looking for stations that are open or without a line. We could also hope to eliminate the estimated $12 billion annual budget of the Department of Energy, which adds, conservatively, another 9 cents per gallon to our cost of gasoline at the pump. The D.O.E. employs over 20,000 people, and its budget exceeds the total profits of the ten largest oil companies and is more than double the profits of the next 20 largest. Its budget is about the same as the total dollars spent annually exploring for oil and gas in the U.S. by all participants. This includes all the major oil companies, smaller oil companies, independents, and individuals. It costs you and me over $3.60 for every barrel of oil produced in the U.S. just to have the D.O.E. As a comparison, the average selling price of domestic crude oil was only $3.92 in 1972. This does not include all the costs to comply with all the regulations, allocation requirements, pricing systems, and other overhead generated by the D.O.E.

The government's attention has been so preoccupied by "windfall profits" that few, if any, steps have been taken to increase production in order to reduce our dependence on imports from the OPEC countries. As a matter of fact, the tax bill amounts to protectionism for the Persian Gulf. It's frightening to me to realize that the value of all our Big Board (NYSE) companies is around $900 billion—a value that has taken 200 years to create—and that over the next four years we may be paying half of that to OPEC. This is not a sustainable position. We can't continue a policy whereby much of our real estate, many of our companies, and a large amount of our equities will be bought in exchange for oil.

Over the next few years, more than a trillion dollars will go out of the Western world to pay for oil. I don't believe our national and international monetary system can sustain such a drain.

TURNING LEMONS INTO LEMONADE

There is no question that the government's ostrich-like policies created the energy crisis of 1973–74 and have perpetuated its continuation. But instead of wasting our energies condemning their actions, let's examine ways that you may benefit from the existing situation. Let's consider it an "Energy Opportunity" rather than an "Energy Crisis."

How can you best avail yourself of these opportunities? There are three areas that you should consider: investing in energy-related securities, investing in oil and gas producing wells, and investing in oil and gas development and exploration.

Energy Stocks

I believe that we may be at the beginning of a new Sputnik-like era. Our reaction to the Sputnik shock in 1957 caused a big boom in technical equipment. Fortunes were made in semiconductors. A similar opportunity may now exist with regard to energy-related securities. Our petroleum engineers lead the world in hydrocarbon expertise. I have high hopes that those billion-dollar brains at NASA in Houston will soon be turned to alternative energy research. A nation that can put a man on the moon can surely solve her energy problems, especially in view of the fact that we are blessed with an abundance of two additional great energy sources, coal and uranium. With the proper investment incentives, other natural resources such as hydrogen, thermal energy, solar energy, and wind-generating power offer great potential but very little impact for several decades. Unfortunately, the government to date has floundered and, instead of providing sufficient incentives for private investment, it has enacted punitive laws that discourage research and development by industry, especially in oil, gas, coal and uranium, which is necessary to supply our energy needs until other sources prove significant.

Nuclear power makes the cheapest and best use of our natural resources and, despite some of the emotional outcries against it, our top scientists maintain that with proper safety precautions, it can be a blessing to an energy-demanding world.

Much emphasis has been placed on solar energy and what a boon harnessing it will be to the world. The data I've gathered from the energy engineers I've talked with indicates that this is just a popular pastime for politicians, and that in the near future solar power will have as much impact on the energy business as a mosquito bite on the epidermis of an elephant.

The U.S. has enough uranium for the production of significant supplies of nuclear energy. A large number of the oil companies have entered the field. You would think this would delight the government, but instead legislation has been proposed to prevent them from doing so. Uranium may some day overshadow oil as a source of energy.

Oil- and Gas-Producing Wells

Another energy source is the gasification of coal, which, if done on a large enough basis, should be no more expensive than importing

oil. Likewise, the western United States has vast quantities of oil in the form of shale rock. Concentrated technology should be able to devise economical means of extracting this oil on a basis that would be competitive with the world market of crude oil. If this industry was allowed to develop without governmental intervention, there are strong indications that our gap between domestic oil production and consumption could be narrowed significantly. Additionally, we still have untapped sources of hydroelectricity and geothermal energy.

The industries that will benefit from the new push to be self-sufficient in energy will offer a vast range of investment opportunities. Study each carefully, and pick the leader in the industries you choose.

To take advantage of this rare investment opportunity, you should use the same basic criteria that I've outlined earlier in the selection of your stocks. Some of the older, more heavily capitalized companies should fit the income category if this is your financial objective. The smaller, more aggressive companies may be involved in more venturesome drilling programs, or research and development activities that place them into the growth or speculative categories.

Oil and Gas Development and Exploration

Many companies will broaden their base and engage in exploration, production, refining, and distribution. They may even go into the manufacture of products that use petrocarbons as their base.

You should consider not only these companies, but also those that build offshore drilling rigs and those that build refineries. Oil without refineries is of no use. We faced a refinery bottleneck long before there was a Middle East bloc.

Management skills, company's assets, and consumer demand are vital areas for study, whether you are selecting an oil company or a company in a related field.

ENERGY PRODUCTION

We have been examining investing in oil and gas and other energy through the stock market. This is a legitimate consideration for your investment dollars. But let's look at other ways. One way that I feel is worthy of your consideration is participation in energy through investing in oil and gas income limited partnerships.

To help you make a decision on whether to invest in companies that produce oil and gas or to invest directly in production by investing in limited partnerships that buy only producing wells (no drilling), let's take a look at Exxon's figures the year I did my first Energy Seminar.

EXXON 1972 FIGURES PER SHARE

22.39	Earnings before depreciation and taxes
4.72	Depletion and depreciation
17.67	Pretax earnings
10.83	Corp. taxes (including minority interest expenses and excise taxes
6.84	After-tax earnings
3.80	Dividend (taxable to the shareholder, thus double taxation)
3.04	Retained earnings (corp. decides how they will be used)

As you can see, if you had owned a share of Exxon in 1972, only $6.84 of cash flow was left after taxes to allow them to perpetuate the business. Of this amount, $3.80 was paid out to you as a dividend. You probably paid federal income taxes on these dividends, therefore suffering double taxation. The company retained $3.04. The company did not ask you whether you would like to have these funds reinvested. This was decided for you by the board of directors. You did hope, however, that these funds would be used to find more oil and gas, which should increase the profitability of the company and eventually be reflected in the price of the stock.

Exxon is a corporation; therefore, as an investor, your liability is limited to the amount of your investment. If you have invested $10,000, that is all you can lose, even if their stock were to become nonexistent. It is also readily salable, since it is listed on the New York Stock Exchange. Its value may fluctuate, but it is a liquid investment.

Is there a way that you can obtain the same limited liability while avoiding some of the double taxation, get the benefits of the depreciation and depletion allowance, and for the minimal sacrifice of accepting some limited liquidity avoid the worry of market fluctuation? Yes, there is, through the investment medium of oil and gas income limited partnerships.

OIL AND GAS INCOME LIMITED PARTNERSHIPS

In making any investment decision, you should attempt to find a vehicle that will supply a product that everyone wants, that everyone needs, and that is in short supply. There is no such thing as an ideal investment, but oil and gas income limited partnerships fit a number of the criteria that you will want in your investment program.

Oil and gas drilling programs have been offered to high-tax-bracket investors for many years, but it has only been since 1970 that you have had the opportunity to invest in production without the risks of drilling. This is accomplished through a product designed for both the smaller, lower-tax-bracket investor as well as the higher-tax-bracket investor.

The concept of owning oil and natural gas reserves is more than 100 years old, but before the advent of oil and gas income limited partnership, ownership in production was limited almost entirely to oil companies, wealthy individuals, and institutional investors.

These oil income partnerships are based on a simple concept. A series of limited partnerships acquire existing, producing oil and gas properties for the income that they generate. The production from these wells is sold, and the income flows back to the limited partners and to the managing general partner. They offer good income potential, substantially tax-sheltered in the early years, with a continuing partial shelter in later years, an opportunity for appreciation to stay abreast of inflation, and first-year deductions that may be used to reduce your other taxable income.

As in real estate limited partnerships, you, the limited partner, have limited your liability to the amount of your investment. The general partner who possesses the management expertise has unlimited liability. He secures the proper producing properties and has the responsibility of operating them on a profitable basis. For doing so, the general partner usually shares 15 percent of the costs and the revenues.

Despite the oil business's reputation for riskiness, in my opinion a well-managed oil income program has less risk than most stock investments. This is true because oil income programs are not particularly subject to stock market fluctuations. The value of the programs depends upon the value of their reserves and the level of income that they produce. The partnership does no drilling. If an opportunity exists for in-field drilling, such drilling is contracted for by the general partner on a farm-out basis. This means that none of the limited partners' money is subjected to any drilling risk.

This type of partnership is structured similar to the diversified concept of a mutual fund, and the oil income programs acquire a variety of already-producing oil and natural gas wells for the income or profit they can generate as the natural resource is produced over the economic life of the properties. The properties acquired by the general partner for these programs have generally experienced several years of production. This is desirable because after sufficient time has passed, oil reservoirs have enough production history and reservoir data so as to allow reasonably accurate estimates of the reserves. Such producing properties can be evaluated within an acceptable margin for error. It is at that stage that oil income programs become buyers of producing properties.

If you become an investor in oil and gas income limited partnerships, the major portion of the revenues will flow directly to you. You will receive the depletion and depreciation allowance that shelters part, and sometimes all, of your cash flow. You'll pay taxes only once on the remainder that is not sheltered. To date, we've had almost all of the cash flow sheltered.

Cash Flow Investment Options

Some programs offer three options for the disposition of your quarterly distributions.

The first option is to reinvest all of your quarterly distributions into subsequent partnerships. This gives you the opportunity to increase your capital base if your objective is asset growth rather than current income. (Approximately 75 percent of our clients make this choice.) If your financial objective changes, you are always free to choose one of the other two options.

A second option is to receive a portion of your distributions quarterly or monthly in cash and to reinvest the balance into future partnerships. This method is designed to provide you with a way to use a portion of your income currently while maintaining your capital base. We have found that if you limit your cash withdrawal to no more than 10 to 12 percent, you should be able to maintain your capital.

But you might say to your financial planner, "I think my ball of twine is about to unwind, so just send me the total cash distribution." If you choose this third option, you will receive all your distributions in cash quarterly. Each distribution will contain a portion of original capital as well as income earned on the capital.

Past Performance

How would you have fared if you had made an investment of $10,000 in the October 1970 partnership of a management company that we frequently use and were appraising your results on December 31, 1979 (see Table 8–1)? (I always use $10,000 in my examples because the math is easier, but you may invest as small an amount as $2500.)

Investors generally experience a gradual increase in distributions over the first two or three years of a partnership's life. This is due primarily to the amount of time required to invest the partnership's funds in producing properties plus the need to dedicate a part of the cash flow to repay loans made by the partnership to acquire their properties. Since each partnership is a depleting entity, once it has reached its maximum distribution level, an investor should see a gradual decline in the distributable cash flow over its remaining economic life. As Table 8–2 illustrates, to date there have been exceptions to this rule. Because of increases in the price of oil and gas sold, improved recovery

TABLE 8–1. HYPOTHETICAL INVESTMENT OF $10,000 IN AN OIL AND GAS INCOME PROGRAM

As of *December 31, 1979*	
Option I—All Distributions Reinvested:	
Distributions Reinvested	$ 54,366
Purchase Price	$125,702
Option II—Accepting 12% Withdrawal:	
Distributions in Cash	$ 10,800
Distributions Reinvested	$ 33,368
Total Distributions	$ 44,168
Purchase Price	$ 98,319
Option III—All Distributions In Cash:	
Distributions in Cash	$ 34,183
Purchase Price	$ 58,291

TABLE 8–2.   HISTORIC QUARTERLY DISTRIBUTION SUMMARY FOR
1970 PARTNERSHIP INVESTMENT OF $10,000

Year	Quarter	Amount	Year	Quarter	Amount
1971	first	$ 585			
	second	587	1976	first	$ 750
	third	302		second	650
	fourth	447		third	650
				fourth	650
1972	first	$ 414			
	second	425	1977	first	$1621
	third	425		second	1621
	fourth	350		third	1621
				fourth	1621
1973	first	$ 350			
	second	300	1978	first	$1621
	third	350		second	1621
	fourth	400		third	1621
				fourth	1621
1974	first	$ 800			
	second	1000	1979	first	$1621
	third	925		second	1621
	fourth	900		third	1621
				fourth	1621
1975	first	$ 900			
	second	875	Inception to Date Total		$34,187
	third	875			
	fourth	825			

techniques or enhancements of the properties owned by the partnerships, and expert management of the partnerships in general, distributions have continued to increase more and remain constant longer than
one might reasonably expect.

What Should You Expect Today?

Should you expect to do this well if you were to invest in an oil
and gas income limited partnership today? I really don't know. I do
know that the 1970 timing was exceptionally good and that this is an
excellent management team. There is no question that they have reaped
the advantage of greatly accelerated oil prices, for which they cannot
claim credit. I truly hope that oil prices won't accelerate as rapidly in
the future; however, it appears to me that there will still be significant
price increases.

Leveraged and Nonleveraged Programs

Oil income programs can be of two types: leveraged and non-leveraged. Leveraged oil income programs use bank production loans to finance a portion of the purchase price.

In the first example above, leverage was used; it works something like this. For every $1 that you invest, about 80¢ remains after start-up costs for doing the research on production and general expenses. (It's actually running about 84¢. Many of the start-up costs are fixed dollar items. So if the general partner can generate sizable subscriptions, the start-up costs, as a percentage of the investor's dollar, are reduced.) This 80¢ is supplemented by borrowing up to 80¢, to provide total purchasing power of about $1.60 for each gross dollar invested. The bank loans allow the general partner to purchase larger reserves from which to obtain cash flow. The loans are usually paid back to the banks over a period of years, dedicating less than 50 percent of the cash flow from the properties for debt service. For a well-managed program, this should still allow ample cash flow to insure good distributions to the limited partners. You also have the potential for an increase in cash flow after the bank borrowings are repaid. This type of financing can produce favorable results. We all know that our country runs on energy. We also should be aware that the energy business runs on money. Several companies have done a superb job of combining the two.

From my studies of the leveraged and nonleveraged programs, I believe it is reasonable to anticipate a higher return on the leveraged programs.

Restored Liquidity

Restored liquidity is a difficult concept to understand. This means the amount of your original investment that has been "restored" to you —in other words, how long did it take for you to get your money back? For example, if you had invested $10,000 in the first program discussed above, your restored liquidity is as shown in Table 8–3.

Perhaps you did not need current income, chose not to reinvest in the next program, and could not think of anything more constructive to do with your checks than to put your quarterly distributions into a passbook savings accounts at your bank. If you did, by the first quarter of your fourth year you would have put all of your funds back into your savings account, where it would be drawing interest, plus you would be receiving cash flow from your oil and gas program.

To Table 8–3 we can now add two additional columns. Column I

TABLE 8–3. $10,000 INVESTMENT

Year	Annual Cash Flow	Cumulative Cash Flow	Restored Liquidity
2nd	1921	1921	19.21%
3rd	1614	3535	35.35
4th	1400	4935	49.35
5th	3625	8560	85.6
6th	3475	10,335	103.3
7th	2700	14,735	147.3
8th	6484	21,219	212.2
9th	6484	27,703	277.0
10th	6484	34,187	341.8

would show earnings on your cash flow from your program plus 5¼ percent interest in your savings account all compounded annually, and Column II would show restored liquidity from the program plus interest from your savings account:

	Column I	Column II
1971	0	19.2
1972	100	36.3
1973	190	52.2
1974	269	91.2
1975	478	130.7
1976	686	164.6
1977	864	238.0
1978	1249	315.4
1979	1520	395.4

I think it's interesting to note that your cash in your savings account would now be $39,540 and your repurchase price for your oil program would be $58,292, for a total of $97,832. You now have the potential for two incomes from the original $10,000. Had you chosen to reinvest in future oil and gas programs instead of withdrawing the cash, your repurchase price would be $110,612, or an additional $12,780. It rarely pays to take a working dollar and make it become a loaned dollar that works for a savings institution.

Compare this restored liquidity with an investment of $10,000 in a corporate bond paying 10 percent. It would have taken you 10 years to receive interest checks totaling $10,000 (to say nothing about the loss of purchasing power that has occurred to your principal due to two-digit inflation). Always keep indelibly pressed on your mind the time use of money. Money received today is always more valuable than receiving the same amount in the future.

BUYING RESERVES

How does the general partner determine how much to pay for oil and gas properties? Oil and natural gas are often found in sand and rock formations, so the energy cannot be extracted from beneath the earth's surface in a matter of days, months, or for that matter sometimes many years. Because of this natural delay, the expected revenue to be returned over time is discounted to present worth when petroleum engineers are determining the price that should be paid for an acquisition.

The first thing the engineers determine is the amount of oil or gas a reservoir will produce annually and the estimated cost of producing that reservoir. They must then determine what they expect to sell the production for per barrel or per Mcf, which allow them to calculate the gross revenues to be realized over the property's economic life. By subtracting the costs of operations from the gross revenues, the operating profits may be determined for each year of the well's economic production.

You wouldn't invest a dollar today for a dollar to be paid back to you at some time many years later. Neither would a petroleum engineer. Consequently, after the general partner has determined his objective rate of return for the partnership, he must discount each year's revenue by that factor to a present worth figure. The total value of each year of revenue's net worth becomes the price that may be paid to achieve the target result. This is the "time-use of money" concept that we've already discussed.

Discounting is nothing more than compounding in reverse. When you learned the "Rule of 72" earlier, you learned that money that is invested and compounded at 12 percent per year will double every six years. Conversely, if we wish to see our money compound at 12 percent per year, we would pay only half today what we would expect to realize in six years. With this in mind, we would only be willing to pay 50¢ for a dollar of net revenue to be realized in six years. If a dollar of revenue would not be realized for twelve years, we would only be willing to pay 25¢ today for that future dollar of revenue. If the dollar of revenue is not to be realized for eighteen years, we would only pay 12½¢ today for that future dollar of revenue. With this formula, we would only be willing to pay 87½¢ for $3 of future revenue that would be realized $1 in each of the sixth, twelfth and eighteenth years (see Table 8–4).

TABLE 8–4. PURCHASE PRICE PER $1

Years Before Recovery	Amount Would Pay		Reserves
1			
2			
3			
4			
5			
6	$.50		$1.00
7			
8			
9			
10			
11			
12	.25		1.00
13			
14			
15			
16			
17			
18	.12½		1.00
	.87½	for	$3.00

For Your Added Protection

For your added protection, the discounting does not stop here; the general partner, who is acquiring the production on your behalf, then begins what is called "haircutting," or applying a risk factor. They do this because they know that engineering of reserves is more of a scientific art than an exact science, so they want to build in protection by haircutting what they will pay for reserves. This discounting of future net reserves and haircutting the resulting figures provides a substantial degree of protection to an investor acquiring producing oil and gas properties.

The actual risks hinge on two elements: (1) Is the engineering accurate? (2) Will the energy be sold for the prices anticipated? However, it would seem that the error in either of these areas would have to be extremely large in order for an investor not to realize a return of his capital over the partnership's life. Therefore, if you are considering this as a viable investment, to me the real risk is not so much if you will get your money back, but rather if the profitability will be as large as anticipated.

Companies offering oil and gas income programs attempt to minimize errors in engineering by using several different experts to estimate reserves. If multiple evaluations arrive at comparable results, then the risk of surprises should be minimized.

First, they look at the history of the wells they are considering for purchase for the program. If this looks promising, their in-house engineering staff does an in-depth study. If it still looks good, they submit it to one or more independent engineering firms for study and calculation of reserves. Once they, too, feel that the properties are attractive, the general partner submits the properties for study to the oil and gas department of the bank that will be doing the matching financing, if leverage is to be used. If all of these agree, then an offer is made at a price that they feel will allow them to fulfill their financial objective for their investors.

All of these studies do not guarantee that errors of judgment will not be made, but I do know from discussing this matter with independent oil consultants that they make very conservative estimates for banks and then discount these estimates sometimes as much as 30 percent.

The general partner spreads each partnership's investments into a number of different acquisitions with as many as 150 to 1000 wells to maximize diversification.

In analyzing the risks you may be taking in any investment, always look at potential supply and demand. From all the projections I have so diligently studied, I am convinced that demand should exceed supply, which in turn should be translated into higher oil and gas prices over the next ten- to fifteen-year period.

Depreciation and Depletion

Depreciation in an oil and gas program is similar to that which you obtain in a real estate investment. The depreciation schedule for each piece of equipment depends on its expected life.

Depletion allowances are unique to natural resources and have been allowed because the resource is being depleted; therefore, a portion is considered to be a return of capital.

As you are probably aware, percentage (statutory) depletion has been under attack by Congress constantly for several years. With the Tax Reduction Act of 1975, percentage depletion is no longer allowed for those buying already-producing oil and gas properties. However, investors are allowed cost depletion.

If Congress continues to chip away further at percentage depletion allowance, then you should anticipate paying even more for gas at the pumps.

Since the oil and gas income funds now use cost depletion instead of statutory or percentage depletion, their tax-shelter benefits should not be greatly affected, particularly in the earlier years. Cost depletion works similarly to any other depreciation schedule.

TAX-SHELTERED CASH FLOW

What should you anticipate in the way of cash flow if you should invest in an oil and gas income program? The figures we presented when we first started recommending this program are as follows. (We still use the same figures even though results have been far superior to our projections.)

	Cash Flow Investor	Write-Offs
1st year	7–9%	13–15%
2nd year on	10–12%	

If your cash flow is greater than 12 percent and you take all your distributions in cash, a portion of your cash flow probably represents a return of your own capital and you may be gradually liquidating your holdings in oil and gas.

The goal of any investment program is to obtain cash flow, tax-sheltered with appreciation potential. To date, tax-sheltered cash flow has been a delight to many owners of previous income programs. They must realize, though, that the IRS never truly forgives a tax. The limited partners are reducing their tax basis and will have a capital gains tax on selling if the sales price is above the cost basis that is left. My philosophy is to take the tax-sheltered cash flow now. In the meantime, you'll have the time-use of your money, and we will surely be able to think of a way to avoid paying the tax later, or at least reduce it when and if that time should come.

INVESTMENT UNITS

Most states require a minimum investment of $2500. New partnerships are available for investment every month or every quarter, depending on the programs selected. Some states require that the minimum be invested in each new partnership one wishes to invest in, while other states let you add as little as $50 into new partnerships as you go along once you've met the original minimum per offering. The wells in each partnership are selected for a broad blend of pay-outs. Some wells should have a high cash flow and deplete more rapidly. Others should deplete over a much longer period of time. The operators work continuously to increase production. The reason for this is that the general partners' interests in these programs parallel that of the limited partners. As they increase productivity for you, they increase their own revenues.

MINIMUM REPURCHASE PRICE

Some programs offer you the guarantee that if within ten years after you invested in one of their partnerships your total distributions plus your repurchase price does not equal 100 percent of your investment, they will add an amount necessary to reach that minimum repurchase price. In my opinion, the general partners should never have to dip into their coffers to meet this guarantee.

DISADVANTAGES OF OIL AND GAS INCOME PROGRAMS

There are two disadvantages to oil income programs of which you should be aware. These are investment lag time and liquidity.

Oil income programs may raise all of their money before they identify the properties that they intend to buy. (They may also have properties inventoried and ready for placement.) If they do this, the funds are usually invested in Treasury bills or certificates of deposit while the program management searches for suitable purchases. They may be able to find the right properties immediately, or it may take as long as a year to do so. During that year, you would not be receiving oil income, although you would be receiving interest on your funds. However, in recent years as the amount under management has grown, very large purchases are being made in advance. A recent purchase of some of Ashland Oil's production by one of the general partners was in excess of $120 million.

A more important disadvantage to you of some oil income programs is their limited liquidity, since there is no ready market for the limited partnership interests.

You should always view your investment as a long-term one, but of course, you never know when you might need to convert your investment into cash.

In the programs we prefer, the general partner is contractually obligated to repurchase your program from the partnership's inception, subject to its financial ability to do so, at their determined purchase price.

After the acquisitions are completed, the general partner may give you a cash selling price each quarter or each year, depending on the program involved. You may choose to cash in your interests or continue to retain them. We find that our clients usually choose to retain them, since they do not know of another investment that has offered them a comparable cash flow, with tax shelter and potential for appreciation.

In summary, if you desire a relatively low-risk investment in energy, give serious thought to oil and gas programs for your "hard" after-tax dollars.

These programs have made it possible for investors to join together and combine their resources in order to acquire a diversified portfolio of producing oil and gas properties that are managed professionally. Typically, the programs are designed for the generation of immediate income, but may, through reinvestment of distributable cash flow, offer an excellent opportunity for asset accumulation.

"HARD" AND "SOFT" DOLLARS

Above, I used the term "hard dollars." There are two kinds of dollars—"hard" and "soft," as you will learn from Chapter 12, "Avoiding the One-Way Trip to Washington." For now, suffice it to say that your "hard" dollars are the ones that you have left after you have sent to the IRS the portion of your income that they require. "Soft" dollars are the dollars that you are going to lose to taxes if you don't take some constructive steps to prevent the journey.

Every taxpayer who has income in excess of $7000 on a joint return has some "soft" dollars; however, our security laws are such that there is very little a financial planner is allowed to do to help you shelter those dollars until you reach the 49 percent tax bracket and have a certain net worth.

You hit the 50 percent (technically 49 percent) bracket at $45,800 in 1979 on a joint return, and you'll have a tax liability of $12,720. If you are single, you'll reach the "magic" number at $34,100, losing $9766 to taxes. If you have reached this bracket, you may want to consider placing some of your funds into limited partnerships that invest in oil and gas drilling programs.

If your taxable income is below these figures, you may want to skip to the applications at the end of this chapter. If you want to get a preview of the possible tax incentives with which you may want to become familiar when you cross into the 50 percent tax bracket, do read on. As inflation continues its destructive path, more and more of our citizens will move across that line. Inflation is "taxation without representation," and that provoked a little tea party in Boston once upon a time. With inflation, you are thrust into a higher and higher tax bracket even without Congress increasing the tax rate schedule. We are one of the few nations that taxes inflation. "Indexing" has been discussed in Congress, but may have little chance of passage, for this would slow down the increase of revenues and prevent some of the proliferation of spending programs so dear to some.

OIL AND GAS DRILLING LIMITED PARTNERSHIPS

There are two basic classes of drilling programs, and each of these can be structured in a wide variety of ways.

The majority of the programs you'll be offered will be registered programs, meaning the general partner has gone to the time and considerable expense of registering the program with the Securities and Exchange Commission and the various states in which they will be offered. This means these programs can be offered publicly to those who meet the suitability requirements in those states in which they have been approved for sale. These requirements vary from state to state. Some states only require full disclosure. Other states' securities personnel take it upon themselves to determine what is "good for you."

Historically, oil drilling programs have raised far more money than income programs. In recent years, public and private drilling programs have attracted more than $1.5 billion per year, whereas the newer income programs have attracted less; but the amount is increasing rapidly as many more investors have received such pleasing results as energy prices continue to rise.

You may be asking, "Isn't it risky to drill for oil and gas?" The answer is, "Yes, it is." Searching for oil does involve considerable risk. (Paying taxes does too.) Most oil programs attempt to reduce your risk by drilling a large number of holes in different areas on which a large amount of geological study has been done.

Should you invest in a drilling program? Your answer should be determined by your tax bracket, the source and regularity of your income, and your temperament. The question was much easier to answer before the passage of the Tax Reform Act of 1976 and its many provisions to reduce incentives for investing in energy. However, let's assume that you have earned an additional $10,000 and that it will be taxed at the 50 percent level. If you don't make an investment that provides a $10,000 deduction, you will have only $5000 left after taxes. If, however, you invest this $10,000 in a drilling program that entitles you to 100 percent write-off, you will be investing $5000 of your money and $5000 of IRS's money. Your question now is, "Am I willing to risk my $5000 for the potential of keeping IRS's $5000 and possibly a larger return?" If your answer is "yes," go ahead and make the investment. If it is "no," then you'll be more comfortable paying the tax or seeking other ways to turn your tax liabilities into assets.

Always keep in mind that striking oil is not simply a matter of drilling a hole in the ground until the elusive oil pool is discovered, whereupon the oil gushes out like a broken water main. Nothing could be further from the truth. Despite the high level of U.S. petroleum technology, there remain many situations where trial and error is the only method that can be used to determine if there is oil at that location and if it can be raised to the surface and transported to the refinery economically.

Exploration Economics

With the emergence of the OPEC cartel in 1973, dramatic changes have been forced upon the world scene regarding supply and cost of energy. Our governmental policies of disincentive had discouraged exploration and development, making us more vulnerable than even OPEC realized when they first tested the waters to see if they could make their controls effective. Unfortunately, today we are no closer to a solution to our energy problem.

Even the most junior student of basic economics should be able to come to grips with the realization that decontrol of prices must be the cornerstone of any program to increase supply.

Price has always been and will continue to be the only common denominator for the many daily decisions that will have to be made about production and, for that matter, conservation of energy. No government has the omnipotence to make these decisions efficiently. Decontrol would create a climate that would provide the incentive to search for oil and gas.

The Natural Gas Policy Act of 1978 is a good example of what even limited decontrol can accomplish. Though the act is a nightmare of undecipherable regulations, it did allow the price of newly discovered gas to increase to the range of $2 per thousand cubic feet at the wellhead the early part of 1979. The resulting improvement in economics of gas exploration is shown by the table below which was provided to us by the *National Tax Shelter Digest*. Realize when looking at Table 8–5 that these economics apply to a successful well only and make no

Table 8–5. Exploration Economics
Typical Western Oklahoma Gas Well

Year		Costs	Revenue	Discovery Ratio for Break Even
1970	Drilling Cost	$ 150,000		
	Operating Cost	30,000		
	Royalties at 12.5%	85,000	4,000,000 Mcf	Profit—$ 373,000
	Prod. Taxes at 7%	41,700	@ $.17 per Mcf	Risk — 150,000
	Total	$ 306,700	$680,000	Ratio—3:1
1979	Drilling Cost	$ 430,000		
	Operating Cost	77,000		
	Royalties at 22%	1,760,000	4,000,000 Mcf	Profit—$4,773,000
	Prod. Taxes at 12%	960,000	@ $.17 per Mcf	Risk — 430,000
	Total	$3,227,000	$8,000,000	Ratio—12:1

253

reference to the wells that may need to be drilled to find this successful one. (Magazine subscription address in the Appendix.)

You can see from the example of a typical 10,000-foot gas well in western Oklahoma that in 1970 it cost $150,000 to drill and a total of $306,000 to bring the gas to production and to sell the gas. With reserves of 4 million Mcf and a price of $.017 per Mcf, this well would yield gross revenues of $680,000, or a profit of $373,000. But the decision of whether to drill is made on the ratio of return divided by risk, and this was a return/risk ratio of 3 to 1. This means the exploration driller would have had to hit one out of every three to pay for his unsuccessful wells and show a profit on his total drilling program. A 33 percent exploratory success is very difficult to achieve; therefore, drilling rigs in the U.S. declined from 5000 in the 'fifties to only 900 in the early 'seventies.

With improved prices by 1979 of $2 per Mcf, gross revenues from this same well would have been $8,000,000. By then inflation had also taken its toll and tripled drilling costs, and royalties and production taxes had increased 2000 percent. However, the resulting return/risk ratio increased substantially to 12 to 1. The base economics of exploration for this type of well became four times better in 1979 than in 1970, exclusive of any tax benefits.

Under the 1978 gas act, gas prices at the wellhead for newly discovered reserves increased to around $2.28 per Mcf with the provision that prices will be allowed to increase at a rate of 2 percent above the average inflation rate. This increase in the price ceiling has already provided an improved economic climate for gas exploration, and the number of drilling rigs have tripled.

Eighty percent of this activity has been by the independents, not the majors, and much of the capital employed by them comes from outside the industry from investors in the 50 percent tax bracket or above. As these investors become more and more aware of the improved economics and the tax benefits, even more capital should be forthcoming.

How should these improved economics affect your investment decisions? If you have some of your earnings that will be taxed at 50 percent or above, you may decide that exploration for petroleum is a viable consideration for you. If so, you will want to know more about some of the programs that may be offered to you.

EXPLORATORY OR DEVELOPMENT PROGRAM?

Exploratory

An exploratory drilling program is composed primarily of wildcat wells in areas where there has been no established production. Oil and gas may be there only in the minds of the geologists, since there is no proof of its existence. Such exploratory drilling is usually done in locations that are unexplored, often remote, very deep, and with no pipelines in place to transport the product if any is found.

A well is also considered exploratory if it is drilled where production has been established at, say, 5000 feet and the geologist thinks there might be additional production at 20,000 feet below that and drills to either prove or disprove his theory. In exploratory drilling, your chances of finding anything commercially profitable are 1 in 20.

Development Wells

After a discovery has been made, there are reasons to believe other production can be found in close proximity. If wells are drilled at this point, it is called development drilling. Your success ratio on development wells could move up to 60 to 70 percent. Of course, your lease costs will be higher, making the wells more expensive, if you have to acquire such leases in order to drill.

How They Differ

The chief difference between an exploratory and development program, aside from the risks of drilling, is the length of time you may have to wait before you start receiving a cash flow.

Development programs will usually have cash distributions sooner than exploratory ones. This is true because the wells may be shallower so they take less time and money to drill, or the pipelines are already in place so they can be hooked up for delivery more quickly. Good roads will probably already have been built, which should greatly speed up transporting the oil if trucks are used for hauling.

In an exploratory program, if production is found, additional capital may be needed for further development. If all or most of the original capital has already been spent, additional capital must be secured. This can be done by using revenues from the first well, but the process will probably be time consuming. Money can be borrowed from the bank, providing further deductions, but this debt would need to be paid by the cash flow from the productive wells before you begin receiving distributions. Thus, you would own an asset but would probably have to wait for cash distributions. Another means is for the general partner to assess the limited partners. If you are one of the limited partners, this may or may not fit your financial circumstances in the year the assessments may be made. As you can see, one of the characteristics of an exploration program may be slow cash flow, but your ultimate returns could be greater.

How to Choose a Program

You and your financial planner will need to do some in-depth "due diligence" to determine which program best fits your needs and temperament. Choose a program offered by general partners who have good past records or, if no past records exist, become familiar with the expertise of their geological staff, the net worth of the general partners, and the fairness of the "pay-outs." Determine if you can make money with the compensation schedule if the drilling programs are successful.

TAX BENEFITS

There are three important tax benefits available to you if you invest in an oil drilling program. These come from the deduction of intangible drilling costs, the depletion allowance, and the potential for partial long-term capital gains treatment upon the sale of the investment. Your program may also be structured in a way that will provide additional tax benefits due to investment tax credits and depreciation of capital equipment.

Your major costs in drilling can be expensed as intangible drilling expenses. These include well-site expenses and actual drilling costs, etc., and can be expensed in the year incurred if a dry hole is drilled. These items become preference items under the new law if the well is productive. This should mean that from 60 to 90 percent of your investment may be deducted in the year you make the investment and up to 100 percent within a two to four year period.

The extent of your tax benefit will depend upon the type and amount of your income.

Sheltering Ordinary Income

Let's assume you have a taxable income of $75,000. In the first column of Table 8–6, we will assume the total $75,000 is classified as earned income and in the second column as unearned income. (Earned and unearned income will be more completely explained in Chapter 12, "Avoiding the One-Way Trip to Washington.")

If you are attempting to shelter capital gains, especially if they exceed $100,000, be sure to go over the various tax implications with your financial planner and a competent C.P.A. before using oil and gas drilling programs.

Depletion

The best known tax benefit is the depletion allowance. This allows for a portion of your income from the sale of oil and gas production to

TABLE 8–6. TAX BENEFITS FROM OIL DRILLING INVESTMENTS

First Year	Earned	Unearned
Taxable income	$75,000	$75,000
Less: Deductions from gas and oil program investment (80% of $10,000)	8,000	8,000
Taxable income with investment	$67,000	$67,000
Federal tax without investment (on $75,000)	$27,178	$27,778
Federal tax with investment (on $67,000)	23,178	23,458
Tax savings with investment	$ 4,000	$ 4,320
Cost of investment	$10,000	$10,000
Less: Tax savings	4,000	4,320
After-tax capital at risk after first year	$ 6,000	$ 5,680

Second Year	Earned	Unearned
Taxable income	$75,000	$75,000
Less: Deductions from gas and oil program investment (20% of $10,000)	2,000	2,000
Taxable income with investment	$73,000	$73,000
Federal tax without investment (on $75,000)	27,178	27,778
Federal tax with investment (on $73,000)	26,178	26,698
Tax savings with investment	$ 1,000	$ 1,080
After-tax capital at risk after second year	$ 5,000	$ 4,600

TABLE 8–7. DEPLETION ALLOWANCE RATE

Year	Production Exempted		Depletion Rate
1980	1000 barrels a day or	6.0 million cu. ft. gas	22%
1981	1000	6.0	20%
1982	1000	6.0	18%
1983	1000	6.0	16%
1984 and thereafter	1000	6.0	15%

be tax-sheltered provided that you qualify as a small producer. Table 8–7 shows the depletion allowance rate by year and by production volume.

To determine the tax-sheltered amount, apply the depletion rate to your gross income before separating expenses that will result in the tax-free amount (assuming they do not exceed 50 percent of the net income). Typically, 30 percent or so of the cash flow in a drilling program would be tax-sheltered, as the following example illustrates:

Gross Income	$2000
Less Separating Costs	600
Net Income	$1400
Depletion Allowance (22% of gross income)	440
Taxable Income	$ 960 (31.43% of Net Income)

In this example, you would receive a check for $1400, with $440 or 31.43 percent being tax-free because of the depletion allowance. A maximum of the amount, $440 would have to be included as a tax preference item, but would not be taxed at the minimum tax rate unless you had other items of tax preference that would exceed the exclusions ($10,000 or ½ tax liabilities). However, preference items do reduce the amounts of earned income applicable to the 50 percent maximum tax rate on a dollar for dollar basis without any exclusions. In certain types of program structures, an even larger percentage of income may be tax-free due to depreciating capital expenditures.

REDUCING RISKS

Drilling limited partnerships use various means of distributing their drilling dollars in an attempt to reduce risks.

Some divide each program's capital into three parts. One-third goes into development wells, where they feel the odds on finding reserves are 1:2, with the value of the reserve ranging from 5:1 to 20:1 and return on risk on invested dollars ranging from 1:1 to 1.5:1. Another third is invested in controlled wildcats, where they feel the odds on finding reserves are 1:4, value of reserves 5:1 to 30:1, and return on risk on invested dollars 1:1 to 5:1. The last third is invested in wildcats, with odds on finding reserves moving up to 1:15, value of reserves 5:1 to 50:1, and return on risk on invested dollars 0:1 to 10:1.

If all their odds worked perfectly, they would drill a minimum of twenty-one wells and find three producers and eighteen dry holes. However, it would have been worth the risk they took, for the three producers should return to them one to three times their investment.

As you can see from the above, it should greatly enhance your potential if each drilling program in which you invest has sufficient capital to drill a large number of wells. Drilling for oil and gas takes skillful geologic research, but your chances are greatly increased as you increase the number of wells drilled.

STRUCTURE OF A DRILLING PROGRAM

There are many ways to structure a program with regard to who bears the cost, who receives the tax advantages, and who receives the income.

In a large number of programs, the general partner trades the limited partners (which would be you if you chose this medium) all of the tax advantages and 60 percent of the revenues for a free look at the bottom of the hole.

Let's use an example of a successful well drilled at a cost to the partnership of $200,000. The limited partner would provide $120,000, but would be entitled to deduct all the intangible drilling costs of the dry holes, capitalize the drilling costs on the successful ones, and receive 60 percent of all revenues. The general partner would bear all other tangible costs of $80,000 that are capitalized over the life of the assets, and would receive 40 percent of all the revenues. Many oil and gas managements offer four to five drilling programs per year. Others offer larger but fewer programs.

In no sooner than 18 months to 3½ years after the initial investment has been made in a drilling program, the company has had time to complete a cycle that consists of the following: (1) drilling the wells in each prospect, (2) arranging financing for any subsequent drilling or making assessments if permitted by the program, (3) carrying out subsequent drilling, (4) being evaluated and (5) perhaps offering to exchange for stock or cash a buy-out at a stated amount. Some programs exchange for stock that did not previously exist; hence there is no way of establishing a true market value for it. If this course is used, no taxable gain is made at the time of exchange. Another way is for the limited partners to be offered registered stock in exchange for partnership interest. When this is done, a capital gain is realized, and you would have a tax liability. When the latter course is followed, the price is determined by the average of the bid and asked prices of the stock for two months previous to the exchange. There is no question of the market value of the stock for which it is exchanged, while in the case of new stock this can certainly be a factor. In the past, this has been a very definite shortcoming with too ambitious pricing on the new stock based on reserve values discounted and unescalated prices for reserves.

You must usually decide within a specified period of time whether to make the exchange for stock. If you do not, you will continue to received the oil income but you may not have an opportunity to exchange at a later date.

A third choice may be offered, and that is for the general partner to buy your production for cash. The value will be based on the evaluation placed on the reserves by an independent geological engineering firm and discounted back to give credit for the earning power of money, then further reduced for risk by probably 30 percent. Your choice will probably be dependent on your income needs at the particular time and your tax considerations.

The program described above is only one of the ways a drilling program can be structured by a sponsor. There are six additional ways commonly in use. Let's first look at these other ways.

Tangible—Intangible Sharing

For income tax purposes, the IRS refers to two basic types of costs in connection with drilling for oil and gas: tangible costs and intangible costs. Tangible costs are expenditures for items that can be salvaged. The intangibles, the nonsalvageable costs, may be deducted as described above. In the tangible–intangible sharing, the general partner bears the tangible expenses, and the limited partners bear the intangible expenses.

Working Interests

In this structuring, the general partner shares in the operating expenses and net profits of the producing wells. This formula may or may not entail investment by the general partner. If the general partner pays no part of further costs, it is called a "carried working interest."

Net Profits Interests

This formula entails no expenses on the part of the general partner. The investor pays all drilling costs and bears all expenses of operating the wells. The general partner receives a stated percentage of net profits.

Carried Interests

In this case, the investor carries the general partner, usually to the casing point, at which time the general partner is permitted to buy into the partnership at the original price.

Disproportionate Sharing

This is a common feature. The investor bears one-third of the total cost of a program and in return receives one-fourth of any profits.

Overriding Royalty Interest

Under this formula the investor pays the cost of drilling and completing wells, and the sponsor receives a percentage of gross revenues. Generally speaking, I prefer programs in which the general partner bears some portion of the risk along with the limited partners. It seems more equitable and also tends to make the general partner more careful in his expenditure of partnership capital.

CORPORATIONS

Corporations did not bear the brunt of TRA 1976, so if you have a profitable corporation you may want to consider a drilling program for the corporation. The corporate tax rate presently is 17 percent on the first $25,000 of taxable income, 20 percent on the next $25,000, 30 percent on the next $25,000, 40 percent on the next $25,000, and 46 percent on over $100,000.

Importance of Management

As in any business venture, management is the single most important consideration in choosing the drilling program. Determine before you invest if the general partner has substantial assets, a good reputation in the industry, and an excellent performance record.

You will find drilling program management difficult to evaluate, because future performance cannot be directly related to past success. Management's drilling success ratio does not lend itself to making a judgment regarding profitability potential. A company that drills successful wells 90 percent of the time, for example, may have only marginally profitable wells, but a company with only a 10 percent record of drilling success can be extremely profitable.

I try to avoid both high and low success ratios (not that I consider this very scientific, but it has been effective). A balanced drilling program that consistently achieves a success ratio of 85 percent to 95 percent may be concentrating on low-risk/low-return prospects. On the other hand, if the company has a low success ratio, it may indicate that they are drilling too many high-risk prospects or that they are not successful oil finders.

Even this approach does not lend itself to accurate selectivity. The majority of drilling programs now in existence have been started since 1968. This means that many of the programs have not been in operation long enough for you to judge their success record adequately. Drilling programs take time before all prospects have been developed and transportation channels worked out, to permit production of the reserves discovered.

In addition, the Securities and Exchange Commission requirements for publishing reserve estimates for past programs in prospectuses are extremely hard to comply with. Cash pay-out tables can often be very misleading, especially if the program is a nonassessable one that relies heavily on bank borrowings to finance their development work. This could mean that a large portion of the initial revenues has been used to repay loans; therefore, the investor has not yet realized much of his potential return.

REGISTERED PROGRAMS

Registered programs, as you will remember, have been registered with the S.E.C. and, because they can be publicly offered, usually have a large amount of capital to be used for drilling. This allows them to drill more wells, thereby spreading your risks and increasing your potential for gain in each program. Most registered programs are offered early in the year, with the last programs offered before October. January programs can offer 90 to 100 percent write-off and later programs 40 to 60 percent, with most of the remainder deductible the next year.

PRIVATE PLACEMENTS

As you will remember, private placements are exempt from registration if certain requirements are met. These programs can have no more than 35 "sophisticated" investors with net worth sufficient to meet suitability requirements (usually those investing $150,000 or more are exempt from this maximum). Because of the limitation on the number of investors, the amount of capital available will usually be smaller, and your diversification will probably be less. However, these programs can be specially structured to fit particular needs and are often available later in the year.

Most registered drilling programs are nonleveraged, so that the write-off on exploratory drilling will not be over 1 to 1 and somewhat less on development drilling (drilling on proven acreage).

Private placements can be structured using recourse financing that may provide you with a 2 to 1 or greater write-off on the capital you invest that year. Remember, however, that recourse financing means if the program does not produce sufficient revenues to pay off the note, you must pay the note on its maturity, if the maturity date is not extended. Even if it is paid off for you, it can be taxable to you. Several development programs that drill shallow wells in proven fields have used this approach successfully.

Some of the private placements doing exploratory drilling may require sizable investments of as much as $150,000 to be made up of cash and recourse notes. Others have much smaller minimums.

ROYALTY PROGRAMS

Another approach to participating in oil and gas is to invest in a program that acquires royalties and overriding royalty interests for leases on which others are expected to drill. These royalty payments are generally made to those who hold a working interest. If a dry hole results and the well is plugged and abandoned, the partnership is permitted to write off its investment as an abandonment loss cost; if you are an investor, you would receive your proportionate write-off. If the drilling is successful, the partnership capitalizes the investment, and the program is entitled to depletion over the years.

SHOULD YOU INVEST IN EXPLORATION?

Not everyone should invest in drilling programs. You should look at your personal finances very critically before reaching a decision. Factors you should consider are:

1. *Do you have a stable high-level income with some of that income taxed in the 50 percent or above bracket?* It might be advisable to wait until you are at the 60 percent level. I would recommend that you should anticipate this high income for at least three years, for even good program managements will have bad years. You should plan to diversify your drilling program investments over several years with the same company. Consistent investment with the same company increases your chances of overall success.

2. *Do you have substantial assets?* Most programs have a "suit-

ability" requirement of assets of $50,000, exclusive of home and furnishings, plus a 50 percent tax bracket or, in the absence of the latter, a net worth of over $300,000. This should be a minimum requirement. In addition, you should have adequate life, medical, casualty and disability insurance, cash reserves, and other assets.

3. *Are you temperamentally suited to investing in exploration?* That is, are you willing to assume the risks involved, and do you have the patience to wait for the exploration to be done? If you should draw a blank in your drilling program, will it cause you to lose sleep? You should invest in anticipation of gains, but you must be prepared to accept losses.

Drilling programs are relatively illiquid, and if you are forced to sell your interest in a hurry, you may have to do so at a substantial discount. You should anticipate being locked in for a period of time sufficient to allow the completion and development of most of the drilling prospects. Otherwise, until drilling is completed, the program's value cannot be accurately determined.

Before investing in any tax shelter, discuss the matter with your C.P.A., but do find one who has tax savings for you as his chief concern, not just tax tallying.

I have a doctor client in a very high tax bracket who had needed some tax-sheltered investments every year I had had him for a client. Whenever I would suggest a particular shelter to him, he would ask that I submit it to his C.P.A., which I was happy to do. Unfortunately, his C.P.A. was an uncreative soul who could tell him to the penny how much he owed in taxes at the end of the year, but he could not imagine taking any "risks" to prevent paying taxes. So the C.P.A. always turned down each proposal. Finally, I told the doctor I would not send any more offerings to his C.P.A. because he was only going to say no and tell him just to pay his taxes. The doctor admitted that this was true and joined with me in investing in the oil and gas drilling program that discovered a major gas field in Louisiana.

COAL IN YOUR ENERGY FUTURE

Another area of energy is coal. To date the government has only given lip service to its potential for helping solve our energy problems. They admit there is a shortage of oil and gas and an abundance of coal, but continue punitive regulations and disincentives so great that our vast coal reserves are still virtually untapped.

Vast Resources

Our country has vast resources of coal. Our domestic coal reserves are equal to one-half of the known reesrves in the entire world and have five times the energy value of our domestic recoverable oil and natural gas.

Of a total of 1600 billion tons of identified coal resources (plus an equal amount believed to exist), reserves of 434 billion tons are considered mineable under today's economic and technological conditions. Yet, we consume and export only about 600 million tons a year.

Technology Development Required

Whether we can continue to maintain a way of life that depends on a high rate of energy consumption will no doubt be determined by how successfully we are able to take advantage of our coal. Today three-fourths of our energy comes from oil and gas. A principal objective of U.S. energy policy should be to develop the technology that will enable coal to be substituted for fuels in short supply.

The U.S. has enough coal that is recoverable under present economic and technological conditions to last 360 years at current rates of consumption. Moreover, technology now being developed by industry can enable us to recover and use a larger portion of our coal resources. Several forecasts project a tripling of the U.S. demand for coal by the year 2000 if certain technological and environmental problems are overcome.

Substitute for Other Energy

In expanding the use of coal the primary near-term challenge between 1975 and 1985 is to recover and burn more of this fuel with less environmental impact. Electric utilities, which already use almost two-thirds of all U.S. coal produced, also account for 9 to 10 percent of the oil and 16 to 17 percent of the natural gas consumption. So generating plants need to rely even more on coal (and nuclear energy) to conserve scarce quantities of domestic oil and gas.

Need for Coal Gasification and Liquefaction

The importance of coal to the nation's energy future will continue to rise during the next quarter of a century.

Projections of our midterm energy needs require the establishment of an industry to make synthetic fuels from coal and oil shale.

According to the 1976 National Energy Plan for Research, Development and Demonstration, the United States will probably need a synthetic fuel production capacity of five million barrels or more per day by 1985, if oil imports are to be held at current levels. This would probably require 100 to 200 synthetic fuel plants, costing $1 billion or more each.

How can you make investments that can participate in the development of our needs for coal utilization? This is a difficult question to answer. Some of the private placements offered for coal mining have produced excellent results. Also, unfortunately, this need has attracted those who do not have the necessary expertise to select, negotiate, and mine the proper leases. Some of these have offered private placements that do not appear to me to have economic viability.

Several of our international oil companies emphasize that they are not just in the oil business, but are in the energy business. They are doing vast amounts of research and development on the best ways to mine and use coal as well as process oil shale, capture solar and geothermal energy, and safely use nuclear energy.

Your conscientious study of the various emerging companies and established companies pursuing these solutions should bring you rewards

SUMMARY

An intelligent approach to financial planning cannot ignore the potential rewards of investing in energy. If you are in the 25 to 50 percent tax bracket, the oil and gas income programs may best fit your investment needs. Even if you are in a 50 percent bracket or above, you'll still have some "hard" after-tax dollars that you may want to put to work in the income programs.

If you are in the 50 percent bracket or higher and have "soft" dollars to invest, you may want to consider investing some of those dollars in exploration programs. Oil and gas account for three-fourths of all the energy we consume, and the demand is growing at an unprecedented rate, both here and in foreign countries. It is estimated that on a worldwide basis, there will be more oil consumed during the decade of the eighties than has been consumed since petroleum was discovered.

Do your tax planning early. This gives you an opportunity to look over the many viable possibilities. It also gives the companies time to do the drilling before year end and possibly provide you with a larger write-off for the year. It also gives you the additional benefit of having your annual investment deductible in advance against your estimated quarterly tax liability. You should consider investing smaller amounts in several partnerships rather than all of your funds in one. This allows you to spread your risk over a large number of wells.

APPLICATION

1. Should some of your "hard" dollars be invested in oil and gas income-producing programs?
2. What other investments compare favorably for after-tax return and potential for appreciation?
3. What dollar amount should you invest this year?
4. Should you invest in energy stocks? If so, which four offer the greatest potential for price appreciation?

Stock	Market Price	Yield	Price/Earning Ratio
1. _____	$_____	_____%	_____
2. _____	_____	_____	_____
3. _____	_____	_____	_____
4. _____	_____	_____	_____

5. If you have some income that will be taxed at 50 percent or above, how much of it should be invested in drilling programs? Do some preliminary figures by using the worksheet in the Appendix. Under TRA 1976, I have not been able to design a worksheet that seems to fit all of my clients.

9

ALL THAT
GLITTERS
AND GOLD

As the value of your paper currency erodes, you must of necessity turn your attention to tangible assets that have the potential of retaining their exchange value without being diluted by the government's currency printing presses.

What choices of tangible assets are available to you? There are many. Chief among them are art, antiques and other "collectibles;" gold; silver; rare coins; rare stamps; and gemstones. Rarity is one of the chief characteristics of the tangible asset sought by those striving to protect their wealth.

In this chapter let's take a look first at gemstones, chiefly diamonds, and second at precious metals, chiefly gold and silver. In our next chapter we'll examine other collectibles.

THE ECONOMICS OF DIAMONDS

The brilliance and durability of diamonds have always fascinated humans, and the desire for them has not diminished over the years but has become more widespread. However, in the last few decades the beauty of diamonds has become secondary, and they are being viewed more and more in terms of their investment potential. Those of us who live in the U.S. have been slow in catching up to the awareness of this potential, but Europeans and Third World businessmen have recognized it for years.

In typical fashion, once alerted to the possibilities, U.S. investors have jumped into the market with enthusiasm and vigor. Too often, though, they have done so without sufficient information or the background to make wise decisions.

Since I believe investment-grade diamonds should be a part of most diversified portfolios, my goal in this chapter is to help you become more knowledgeable about this fascinating area of investing. This information will not be sufficient to make you an expert on the subject, but it should make you more knowledgeable, teach you a few dos and don'ts, and whet your appetite to seek further information.

Diamonds have always been a haven for the assets of the very rich. Worldwide affluence is a relatively recent phenomenon. Europeans have a much longer tradition of mistrust of governments and fiat currencies than do we Americans. Consequently, gemstone investing has a much older history in Europe. This demand has accelerated during the past few years, raising the prices and pulling the better quality stones to markets outside our country. This stepped-up demand here and abroad caused a doubling of prices from 1975 to 1978.

Beauty, Durability, Rarity

All gems have three attributes in common. They are beautiful; they are durable; and they are rare. Beauty may be in color, irridescence (as in pearls or opals), or fire (as in diamond). Durability is necessary for a valuable gem—pearls are soft, yet durable. A diamond is the only colorless, transparent gemstone that has all three of these qualities. It stands alone in its ranking of gemstones for its transparent, colorless beauty, as well as its rarity and durability.

Since the nineteenth century, the major mining center for diamonds has shifted from India to South Africa. South Africa experienced a "Diamond Rush" in the 1860s very much like California's Gold Rush. The rarity of diamonds is underlined now by the fact that fewer and fewer of the finest gemstones are being found.

Costly to Mine

Searching for the diamond of high value is not unlike looking for the proverbial needle in the haystack. It is estimated that current procdures may require mining from 45 to 200 tons of rock or sand to uncover one carat (2/10 of 1 gram or 1/142 of an ounce) of quality diamond, an extremely costly and arduous process. Approximately 80 percent of all diamonds found are unsuitable for jewelry or investment and are used for industrial purposes. The industrial diamond, because of its color, structural defects, size, or shape, does not meet the high standards required for gemstones. Of the remaining 20 percent, only about 3 percent are considered to be of investment grade. And of this 3 percent, only 1 percent will yield a gemstone of at least 1 carat in size.

Today diamonds are mined not only in South Africa, but also in South West Africa (Namibia), Angola, Australia, Russia (20 percent of the world's supply), Brazil, and India. The United States' production so far has been quite modest.

Monopolistic Control

The major control for distribution of diamonds is by the DeBeers Consolidated Mines of South Africa, Ltd. Since the 1930s, DeBeers has held an ironclad monopoly on the diamond industry that amounts to from 60 to 85 percent of the world's supply. The Central Selling Organization (CSO), the wholesaler arm of DeBeers, purchases rough diamond not only from DeBeers mines (18 percent of world's supply), but also from other producers. The distribution of the diamond is controlled through "sights" or sales which are held ten times each year by DeBeers. At these sights, packages are made up of the rough high-grade stones, as nearly as possible according to the requirements that have been previously stated to DeBeers, which insures a firm control on the price. DeBeers' stated policy is "to maintain a high degree of price stability for gem diamonds at all times." While this method of control has been questioned, it has not been broken. Major producers and cutters cooperate with DeBeers because they agree that control and stability are as good for the industry as for DeBeers.

The select group of 230 buyers invited to the "sights" may refuse to purchase a packet, but they rarely do, as hundreds of other buyers could easily replace each one. After the purchase of the parcels from DeBeers, the buyers, if they are dealers, sort the package into categories for their own customers. If they are cutters, they will divide the rough package into the group they plan to sell, and the stones that will be cut under their supervision. Each stone must be evaluated, and the master cutter must use his skill and professional judgment in deciding the most practical shape and size for that particular stone before the work is begun. Then cutting, shaping facets, and polishing will all be a part of the process.

The Four Cs

Cut. The "cut" of a diamond refers to its proportions and dimensions, based on certain measurements. The brilliance of the diamond depends not only on the light reflected from the surface, but on the rays that have been partly absorbed before being refracted. The diamond is exceptionally reflective: about 17 percent of the light falling directly on its surface will be reflected back, accounting for its "life" (compared with about 5 percent of light falling on a transparent glass stone). Diamond will also absorb 80 percent of the light entering before it is refracted, creating the diamond's "fire." The perfectly cut diamond maximizes the amount of light returned to the viewer; hence, the more finely proportioned the stone, the higher the value.

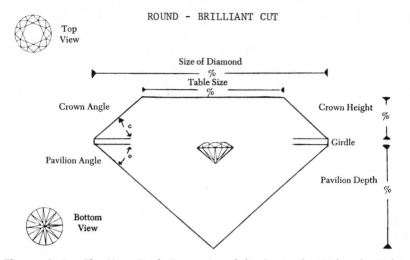

Figure 9–1.   The More Finely Proportioned the Stone, the Higher the Value

The word "cut" is also used to mean the "shape" of the stone, or the design of its finished form. While unusual shapes may be used, many cutters choose one of the five most popular shapes or cuts:

1. The familiar Round-Brilliant with 58 facets has been a favorite in rings and other types of jewelry for centuries. In tiny sizes, with only 18 facets, it may be used as a side stone in the setting, when it is called a single cut. Eighty percent of all polished diamonds are Round-Brilliants.

Three modern variations of the Brilliant cut are also among the most often selected:

2. The Marquise-Brilliant is usually long and narrow, in a pointed boat shape. In the setting of a ring, this shape tends to make the fingers look slim. Because of the additional labor required for the cutting, it may be more expensive than a Round-Brilliant stone of the same size and quality. Also, the Marquise may be chosen by the cutter to maximize the unflawed portion of a stone.

3. The Pear-shape Brilliant is another popular cut for jewelry. The world's largest fashioned diamond, the Cullinan I, or the Great Star of Africa, is pear-shaped. The original size of the rough diamond was 3106 carats.

4. The Oval-Brilliant is also an adaption of the Brilliant-Round. It may appear to be even larger than a Brilliant-Round of the same carat weight.

5. The Emerald cut, so called because emeralds are often cut this

Oval   Marquise

Pear-shaped

Round brilliant

Emerald

Figure 9–2. The Most Popular Diamond Cuts

way, is rectangular or square. It facets are polished diagonally across the corners.

After the diamond has been cut and polished, the finished product will be sold to importers, wholesalers, or distributors. There are about ten exclusive cash markets, or Bourses, in the world, one of which is the Diamond Dealers Club in New York. The diamond trade is extremely secretive and security conscious. (I still have my security badge with my photograph on it from my trip to the floor of the Club.) Once a grudgingly bestowed membership is gained for the clubs, business is conducted on the principles of trust and credit. The loss of that trust by simply refusing to purchase a stone once accepted can ruin the perpetrator forever in diamond circles.

Purchasers select stones from the cutter with the greatest care. Other features in addition to the cut and proportion which increase the value of a gem are the color, clarity, and carat weight.

Color. Diamonds come in a full range of colors, including red, pink, blue, and yellow, with the highest grade of color for a diamond the whitest possible, or colorless. As color is detected in a stone, its value decreases as the hue deepens. This is true until the diamond reaches the optimum point—when the shade is so rich that the value rises precipitously. This rare and quite valuable color is termed a "Fancy." Fancy diamonds are in great demand for investment stones as well as for jewelry.

Techniques and systems for color grading of polished diamonds may vary to a significant extent among diamond exchanges and dealers throughout the world, but the determination is becoming increasingly scientific because of the spectrophotometer. This instrument measures the nitrogen content of a stone; more nitrogen means a deeper color. The spectrophotometer is an instrument commonly used in research by industry for measuring absorption and directional reflectance. Specially modified for diamond-color grading, it is used to measure specific wave lengths of reflectance, comparing the diamond to pure barium sulphate powder as a standard of whiteness.

Clarity. The third C is clarity. The clarity of a stone is another factor that governs its price. Clarity is defined as the degree of internal perfection, or the degree to which the stone possesses inclusions, or irregularities, which may diffuse or scatter light. Undesirable reflections may be caused by the presence of foreign matter within the stone, surface defects, minute cracks, natural strains in the crystals, or certain other imperfections. The method of quantifying clarity is a point system generally based on the size of the inclusion, its position, and the extent to which it interrupts the optimum passage of light. The terminology established by the Gemological Institute of America is generally used; it runs from FLAWLESS to VERY VERY SLIGHT INCLUSIONS, to VERY SLIGHT INCLUSIONS, to IMPERFECT. For a diamond to be regarded as FLAWLESS, it must be free of external blemishes as well as being clean internally. While FLAWLESS is the top grade for clarity, it is something of a misnomer, for rarely if ever is a stone completely flawless This grade may possess some modest irregularities that cannot be considered to materially affect the brilliance of the diamond. Figures 7 and 8 in the Appendix show a GIA Color-Grading Scale and a chart of color grading systems for polished diamonds.

Carat. The fourth factor affecting value is the carat weight. This is a familiar standard, but must not be confused with the "karat" used to describe the fineness of gold. The origin of the carat measurement was the seed from the carob tree. This tiny seed was so uniform in weight and shape that Middle Eastern gem traders used it as a gauge in weighing diamonds. The international standard of the carat weight is .2 grams, while each carat is divided into 100 points. For example, a ¾ carat stone would weigh exactly 75 points, or 75 percent of the weight of one carat, or .15 grams. In determining carat weight, laboratories use extremely accurate caratronal electronic scales which can weigh to one-thousandth part of a carat. This sophisticated equipment is believed essential to proper evaluation, since carat size is a prime factor in assessing the value of the diamond.

After a stone has been chosen for purchase because of its maximum value in the categories of cut, color, clarity, and carat weight, the higher grade diamonds will be sent to an independent laboratory for analysis and certification. This could be the fifth *C*. These certificates give an exact description of the stone, making evaluation an easy matter. If a retail value is placed on the diamond at this point, it will usually be about double the wholesale value.

Cost

The passage of a stone from the cutter to wholesaler to jewelry manufacturer to jewelry wholesaler to retailer creates a chain of markups which escalates the price to the ordinary buyer. Also, the price spread is not linear or predictable by carat weight. A small stone may have a 200–300 percent spread, whereas a large stone of two or more carats may have no more than a 20 percent spread. In Figure 9 in the Appendix you'll find the prices of 1 carat flawless diamonds for the past seven years.

Thus the value of a diamond as an investment is best realized when dealing at the cutter's level. The diamond as a collectible or hard currency has a long history of price stability not found in gold or silver, which are subject to market swing and governmental control. In recent years there has been an unceasing upward spiral of diamond prices and value, a trend which is likely to continue because of limited supplies and increasing consumer demand. It has been estimated by one source that without new discoveries, the world's entire supply of diamond will be exhausted by about the turn of the century.

Liquidity

Suppose you need to turn your stones into cash. Liquidity of diamonds falls somewhere between that of gold coins and real estate. They are more liquid than real estate but less liquid than gold coins. Diamonds are a relatively long-term investment and should not be purchased with a speculator's eye for quick, overnight profit. On the other hand, diamonds do represent a tremendous opportunity for concentrated wealth that occupies a minimum amount of space and causes a minimum amount of nervousness when reading the financial page of the newspaper each morning.

Inflation Hedge

Have investment grade diamonds properly bought offered a hedge against inflation? The answer is yes. Not only has their value kept pace with the rate of inflation, but they have far outstripped even current inflation rates. This could make the purchase of diamonds one of the best hedges against the current trend in monetary depreciation. De-Beers sets the price of diamond against the world's strongest currency, with an eye on the inflation charts. Since the United States accounts for approximately 55 percent of the world's market for diamonds, the rate of inflation in the U.S. is a large factor in the pricing. Worldwide inflation, of course, must also be considered. For example, a country with major cutting centers, such as Israel, must be taken into account. Inflation has run over 280 percent in Israel in the past four years.

Stable Stores of Value

The wild fluctuations in the gold and silver markets in the early weeks of 1980 spotlighted what has become a highly unstable condition for some collectibles. In times of political unrest, collectibles become more appealing to some investors. Diamonds so far have been immune to this instability, but of course we do not know if they will continue to be. The enormous interest in buying diamonds as investments now requires a careful consideration of the present market and a chary look at the future.

Fundamental to the dependability of the diamond market has been the power of DeBeers. As stated above, the cartel has controlled up to 85 percent of the world's diamond supply through controlled distribution. The percentage is not fixed, however, and has been known to slip to as low as 60 percent, as it did as recently as 1977. The continued maintenance of stability is based on the belief by the world's suppliers that the cartel serves the best interest of the industry as a whole. It is difficult to argue with the success of the past, but it is also impossible to predict who will attempt to break the monopoly in the future. The huge outreach of DeBeers makes it unlikely that its grasp will be loosened in the near future, but challengers will be seeking ways to sell independently. One likely development in the next decade will be more companies attempting a vertical control of their own. In trying to crack the market, they could easily flood it with supplies that would send prices tumbling. Once again it must be emphasized that any investment brings an element of risk. To succeed, DeBeers must continue to balance the needs of producers against those of major cutters, as well as to convince both groups that continued control is in their best interest as well as possible. On balance, the danger of undercutting the cartel is not sufficiently dire to warrant withdrawal from diamond investing. DeBeers has not gained its position without learning how to maintain that status. Recent manipulation of the market that ended the 1978 wave of speculation buying of rough diamond was impressive evidence of the scope and resources of the cartel and made any prospective toppling of DeBeers seem a very unlikely prospect indeed. On the contrary, the plan of the company is to extend its influence further, even in the areas of cutting and marketing. Nevertheless, there will continue to be both smuggling operations and small governments' determined efforts to market diamond independently. DeBeers expects this. You should also.

The wild card in this scenario is the Soviet Union. Up until now, Russians have worked primarily through the cartel. The fine reputation of the Russian polished diamonds, however, creates the possibility of an independent marketing effort on their part or a price war generated by their unilateral offering of rough stones. The Russian intent in marketing diamonds is as unpredictable as Russian foreign policy right now, but it would seem that stability would be in their best interest, since diamond constitutes a major export for them.

The politics of any of the producing countries could potentially affect the diamond market. Past unrest in South Africa created some apprehension on the part of distributors. It should be remembered in this regard that the DeBeers Central Selling Organization has had extensive experience negotiating with many different regimes. A shift in government would not alter the need for marketing, while temporary disruption of the producing mines would only enhance the value of investment diamonds.

Scarcity

A much more crucial future certainty is the eventual depletion of the world's natural diamond supply. While too much may be made of this, since there is obviously a limit to "the world's supply" of any natural resource, the fact remains that diamond supplies are dwindling. The estimate mentioned above, that without new finds the entire world's supply will be marketed by the year 2000, is one of several estimates that vary between twenty to forty years. All are based on known supplies. The recent find in Australia which was widely reported has so far produced disappointing results. The result of exploratory mining in the western United States is still undeclared.

For the investor, the most important aspect of this reality of shortage is that there has been in recent years a marked reduction in the number of highest quality stones, particularly in the larger sizes. This is both good news and bad. The good news is that scarcity creates value in gemstones. The bad news is that it is difficult to obtain the finest investment-quality stones. One possible result of this could be a lowering of standards for what is considered "investment-quality" diamonds. As the demand for gemstones continues, this will perhaps inevitably occur. Already the requests for lower quality stones are increasing. Another possibility for expanding the market for investment, however, is the secondary purchase (or exchange buying) which speculators in diamond may create by their resale of the existing stones. This trend is already evident.

The DeBeers organization has had a curious love/hate relationship with the investment market. As a matter of fact, a pattern of reluctance regarding investment has developed among most of the old stalwarts in the diamond industry: DeBeers, jewelers, and even the Gemological Institute of America, which was created to serve the needs of jewelers, but is now inundated with calls for certification of investment diamonds. All these agents see their livelihood in the lucrative jewelry business and not in investment diamonds. DeBeers, for example, is reluctant to see small stones siphoned off to the investment world; hence their desire to maintain the standard of one carat or above for "investment size" and the best colors of D-E-F as "investment quality." Even with these standards, DeBeers apparently is fearful that investment buying will drive up the price of diamond to such an extent that the long-standing emotional and aesthetic appreciation and ownership of diamond will be beyond the reach of the average consumer. DeBeers has spent an enormous amount of advertising money in the past few years on diamond jewelry, with an emphasis on "diamonds are a girl's best friend" and "a diamond is forever." Preservation of the jewelry business and the diamond mystique is one reason for DeBeers' determination to maintain control of the world's diamond supply and diamond prices. Also, as long as it maintains the distribution monopoly, the investment-grade diamonds which exist will be rationed.

Consistently Rising Prices

Diamond salespersons have regularly touted the fact that diamond prices have consistently risen since World War II. The prices to which they refer, of course, are the DeBeers prices for rough diamond. Can this trend continue? The best analysis, based on the continuing control of DeBeers and the nature of inflation, would say yes. Only catastrophic economic upheaval could disrupt the entire market. If that eventuality occurs, the portability and concentrated form of diamond would then make it the asset least likely to lose value in the transition to a new economy. This has always been one of the distinct advantages of collectibles as investments, and of diamond especially. Table 16 in the Appendix gives a comparison of annual rates of return for a ten-year period.

How to Invest

After learning what you have thus far about diamonds, if you feel they are worthy of some of your investment dollars, there are certain criteria to follow and pitfalls to avoid.

First, deal only with reputable persons or firms. This is the first, primary, and essential criterion for choosing wisely. Unfortunately, the recent upsurge of interest in diamond has brought the usual pack of charlatans who capitalize on consumer fads and naiveté. The publicized stories of zirconium switches and telephone sales tend to make buyers uneasy. But reputable firms do exist. Care should be taken to get recommendations and to investigate past records. A gemstone should not be bought from a person or firm without strong backing. Also, as a general rule, one should not buy an investment stone from a jeweler. The jeweler is at the end of the escalating price chain within the industry and seldom can give the best prices. In addition, jewelers rarely have access to the quality of stone that would be considered investment grade.

Second, the selection of a stone must be made with care. This does not mean merely looking at the beauty of gems displayed on black velvet. It means, rather, the selection of a stone that maximizes the qualities described above (color, clarity, cut, carat weight, and proportion) in line with the amount of money you have to invest. The best investment is still the Round-Brilliant cut in *H* or better color, with at least ½ and hopefully one carat or more in size. Once the parameters of the possible choice have been defined, it will be your pleasure to see a selection of stones within these guidelines and appreciate the beauty of the diamond chosen. This, however, is not completely necessary. More important is the transaction with the trusted broker, mentioned above, *and* the most important aspect, the certification of the stone by an independent laboratory such as the Gemological Institute of America.

Certification

If you have taken the first precaution (in choice of broker), certification will be an automatic procedure, with the cost probably absorbed by the company. You should be very careful in dealing with any sellers who claim to do their own certification. In addition to the independent certification, many companies offer a period of thirty days or more in which a stone may be returned without question. Within that period, if there is reason to want it, you may get a second certification of the stone, which, of course, should duplicate the first description if both are done properly. A possible trend in diamond security is the use of sealed packages for gems, once certified. While this may seem an ideal solution to the potential problem of switching stones, it really does not eliminate the possibility, since the seal must be broken in any case if verification is absolute, and packets may be switched as easily as stones.

Certification of polished diamond is one of the most important developments in the industry. It moves the sale of diamonds within the purview of a person such as yourself who may have minimal geological expertise. It is of special significance for investment goods, since each diamond has its own "fingerprints" which make it unique. The importance of securing independent certification cannot be overemphasized.

Third, you should plan carefully with your financial planner the percentage of your total assets that should be in hard assets.

Fourth, think of diamond as a long-term investment, not a short speculative venture. Two years should be a minimum time for you to consider holding a stone; much longer is better.

Fifth, in case it should be necessary to liquidate your investment in the future, check beforehand how to resell. Many companies make a resale-on-consignment service available to their diamond customers, although they will not guarantee a repurchase because of the risk of having the sale classified as a security by the S.E.C. Also, diamond marketing is carried on in the United States through computer listings, brokers, and companies that sell investment stones. Just as you should not purchase your investment diamonds from the typical jeweler, neither should you sell them through that avenue.

Sixth, plan to protect your investment through careful maintenance. Diamonds are the easiest of all hard assets to store and care for. Vaults or safety deposit boxes are available, and adequate insurance is easy to obtain. Of course, careful records and safekeeping of the certificates are vital. Though it's best not to, if you choose you can have your diamonds mounted and enjoyed as jewelry. Even though we recommend storage in a safety deposit box, I dare say the majority of owners will be wearing them on their next visit to our offices.

Summary

Diamonds can be a viable part of your total portfolio of investments. You will not be able to look up their value daily in the newspaper, but you can subscribe to such monthly publications as *Precioustones Newsletter* that will give you a price range (see Appendix for other sources). Certified diamonds have recognized value the world over; they are the epitome of portability and concentrated wealth; they can bring the added pleasure of rarity and beauty; they are convenient to store and can be bought in small units of measurable value; they have been an excellent hedge against inflation, and demand is increasing while supply is diminishing. These are excellent criteria for an ideal investment.

GOLD

Reports of spectacular increases in the price of man's most treasured metal, gold, flashed across your television screen almost every evening as you entered the eighties. In five wild and erratic trading days in January of 1980, the value of gold leaped by an incredible 34 percent and closed at $808 in New York, at $823 in Hong Kong, and at $835 in London and Zurich.

This dazzling run-up has underscored the enduring psychological lure of the yellow metal as a haven in times of strife and uncertainty. This gold rush has been fueled by a deep feeling held by many that the only thing that will survive is gold. Also, there is deep within many a fear of being too late and being left out. This causes them to stampede whether it's for the Who concert in Cincinnati or to buy gold.

Even in normal times gold has held a special attraction. Charles de Gaulle spoke lovingly of "gold, which never changes, can be shaped into ingots, bars, coins, has no nationality, and is eternally and universally accepted as the unalterable fiduciary value." From biblical reference to the gift of the Magi to the gold medals awarded at Olympic competitions, gold has been held in high esteem.

Should gold have a place in your total financial planning? The answer is probably yes. Now the question is, should you use it as your "fail safe" plan in the event other more conventional approaches fail, or regard it one of the items you should value for its investment merits alone? Should you treat gold as you do fire insurance on your home?

If your home doesn't burn down, you probably wouldn't cancel your fire insurance. Or should you treat it as a viable investment for profit? This you will need to answer for yourself.

Let's say you've determined that a portion of your assets should be in gold or gold-related investments. What approach should you take? Should you invest in gold bullion, gold coins, gold medallions, gold jewelry, gold mining stocks, or mutual funds that invest in gold mining stock?

The method I have used personally and recommended to my clients has been a mutual fund investing in South African blue-chip gold mining companies.

Mutual Fund Investing Gold Mining Share

Up until 1979, I recommended the use of this mutual fund as a "fail safe" plan in the event that some of the more conventional ways of investing were adversely affected by more catastrophic events. This served its purpose very well.

However, in 1979 as I observed inflation growing more rampant and the OPEC countries stacking up more and more eroding U.S. dollars, our objective changed from preservation to a profit motive. So, I sent out a letter and a prospectus of the fund and recommended purchase of its shares. Many of our clients responded and were rewarded with a 235 percent gain in a year's time. (Please know that my batting average isn't this good most of the time.) I did have an interesting call from one of my clients, however, after the tremendous increase in the price of the shares, asking why I hadn't badgered her into making an investment. I told her the most "badgering" I ever do is to send out a prospectus, an application blank, and instructions on how to make out the check.

I personally prefer gold mining shares for a number of reasons. Usually their price lags slightly behind the bullion itself, giving me an opportunity to see the direction gold prices are moving. Most of the time the shares outperform the bullion, plus they also pay a dividend, which in the past has run as high as 10 percent. There is daily liquidity by wire or mail. Also, the government could ban the ownership of gold and could require that it be turned in for less than its market value.

South African Political Stability

Many have expressed a fear of political instability in South Africa, and others have expressed a dislike of some of their race policies. In regard to their political stability, it is interesting to note that almost every nation except South Africa has replaced its political leaders over the past four to five years either by scandal or a vote of no confidence. Also, the Republic of South Africa has never had a bank failure. They are also working on an improvement in the standard of living for everyone in their nation.

Patriotism

On a few rare occasions I've been questioned about how patriotic it is to invest in South African gold shares. That's a question you may have and should answer for yourself. I personally believe if we have monetary turmoil and economic disruption, I have a patriotic duty to maintain my purchasing power in real money so that I will have the means of helping rebuild our country in the event an economic disruption should occur. Historically, gold-related investments have been a good mechanism for the preservation of capital in times of monetary and economic uncertainty.

Each of us, I believe, has a stewardship responsibility for that which is available to us. To preserve buying power is an obligation of all of us who are socially minded because those who have capital always dictate the ethics and morality of our nation through the type of investments that they make.

Gold Demand

There are five types of gold demands today: the monetary demand, the industrial commercial demand, the political demand, the hedging against dollar fluctuations, and the inflation-hedging demand.

Monetary Demand. Even though politicians like to condemn the backing of gold or silver for paper currency in circulation as archaic, it does have the advantage of limiting the amount of currency and credit governments can create. The supply of money today is growing worldwide at a compound rate of 16 percent per year, while the gold supply is increasing only around 1½ percent.

I will not go into how the U.S. has arrived at this point in our history, nor how our country unilaterally abrogated the Bretton Woods Treaty on August 15, 1971, when we closed the gold window and refused to exchange any more dollars for gold. Suffice it to say, since that time the world has been pushed into floating exchange rates which have caused highly unstable fluctuating currencies.

Today, in spite of our often repeated U.S. position that gold is being demonetized, European monetary authorities believe the opposite—that gold is being remonetized. Some 51 percent of the monetary reserves of the world's central banks are held in gold bullion. Arab and Japanese central banks have become particularly active in acquiring gold. The OPEC oil producers are now accumulating $45 billion per year in excess paper currency reserves and are believed to be purchasing much of the gold being offered at our U.S. Treasury auctions. They are thereby swapping our depreciating U.S. dollars for appreciating gold bullion. The grim fact is that the Arabs could purchase all U.S. and IMF reserves with just three years' excess oil profits.

Industrial Demand. In 1978 industrial and jewelry demand for gold absorbed approximately 1293 tons of gold. There were only 1379 tons of newly mined gold. This is about 93 percent of total world production. This demand is growing, and it appears that a real supply-demand disparity will be developing throughout the 'eighties comparable to the shortage that already exists in silver.

Political Demands. This factor could be the most important. Political demand for gold occurs when there is political turmoil in the world as "smart money" of a particular region moves out of the currency of that region and into the world's most liquid and anonymous instrument, gold.

Inflation Hedge

With inflation now at double-digit levels here and throughout much of the industrialized world, inflation-hedge demand for gold is picking up. Government officials love to blame inflation on the bankers, businessmen, middlemen, consumers, truckers, farmers, and OPEC. If these are the culprits, we might ask why Switzerland and Germany, who both import oil from OPEC, have only 2½ to 4 percent inflation.

Inflation is really more simple than this. Inflation is not rising prices or wages; it is the expansion of the monetary base by our federal government. If you'll just remember to substitute "dilution" for "inflation," you'll get a clearer picture of what has been happening. Government is causing inflation and blaming everyone else.

Ways to Invest in Gold

There are five ways you may want to consider when considering gold as an investment. I've already discussed gold stocks. Four others are gold bullion, gold coins, gold futures, and gold mining ventures.

Gold Bullion (Bars and Wafers). You probably should not consider this way, since it would generally have to be assayed prior to resale. You could consider this method if you are buying a large amount of gold and plan to leave it on deposit at a bank and eventually sell it without ever taking possession.

Gold Coins. One way you might consider is low-premium bullion coins that trade within a few percent of their bullion content. These coins, such as the 1 ounce Krugerrand, 1.20 ounce Mexican 50 peso and the .98 ounce Austrian 100 Corona are very liquid, require no assay upon resale, and are concentrated forms of wealth in a convenient and anonymous bearer form. These can be purchased at a 3 to 7 percent premium.

Gold Commodity Futures. These are highly speculative and very difficult to trade successfully. Go this route only if you are willing to take very speculative risks.

Gold Mining Ventures. This is covered in Chapter 12 "Avoiding the One-Way Trip To Washington."

Gold in Financial Planning

I believe gold should be a part of your well-diversified financial program. There appears to be a strong long-term upward trend in gold-related investments. Certainly over the past decade this type of diversification would have provided you with an excellent inflation hedge and could have provided ballast to your portfolio and also brought you a profit.

If you are the manager of a pension or profit-sharing plan, last year's liberalization of ERISA regulations now makes it easier for pension and retirement funds to be invested in gold, diamonds, and other tangible assets. Our company's pension plan holds investments both in a mutual fund investing in South African company shares and in investment grade diamonds.

Gold-related investments tend to be contra-cyclical to other investments, and could therefore tend to iron out swings in the value of your portfolio. They offer liquidity also, as well as a measure of privacy and flexibility since they are anonymous bearer instruments. If you believe that gold is in a long-term uptrend, you should consider dollar-cost-averaging just as we discussed when investing in stocks. In so doing, you should buy at various price levels. This should give you a good average price.

SUMMARY

The ground rules you've used over the past years have all been changed. Remember, Poor Richard has bitten the dust. What was considered prudent in the 'sixties and 'seventies will not work in the 'eighties. Conversely, investments that many considered speculations then are now "conservative" and "prudent" in these turbulent 'eighties.

Being in the right place at the right time will not be easy, but it will be necessary if you are to profit and win the money game. Gold, diamonds, silver, copper, strategic metals, and other tangible assets will no doubt play a very important part in your battle for financial survival in the 'eighties.

Remember the Golden Rule: "He who has the gold makes the rules." This is true whether it's black gold (oil) or yellow gold.

APPLICATION

1. What plan do you have for obtaining additional information about investment-grade diamonds?
2. If you do decide to make an investment in diamonds, should you store them or wear them?
3. How do you plan to become more knowledgeable about gold?
4. What investment media best fits your assets, temperament, and time frame?

INVESTING IN COLLECTIBLES

As inflation continues its rampage, you will want more and more to consider the advisability of getting some of your money out of paper and into "things." Once you've made that decision, there will be some other decisions you'll have to make: Which things? Where do you find them? What should you pay for them? How do you become knowledgeable? Should they be collectibles?

Let's take a look at collectibles or "collectimania"—the investment trend sweeping the country that involves the purchasing, collecting, and investing in items commonly referred to as "collectibles," or sometimes "investibles." More specifically, collectibles are things that have had a history of rising in value after purchase.

WHAT ARE COLLECTIBLES?

You may find collectibles a new concept as a viable consideration for your investment dollar. Just what are collectibles?

Collectibles include a very broad and fascinating range of tangible goods that usually have in common some degree of: (1) rarity, (2) scarcity, (3) demand, (4) popularity, (5) craftsmanship, (6) antiquity or age, (7) aesthetic qualities of beauty and taste, (8) absolute and/or classical value to our society and culture. Collectibles include the serious investments such as rare coins, rare stamps, rare books, antiques (furniture, dolls, and classic antique cars), art (oil paintings, prints and sculpture), and oriental rugs and carpets. On the other hand, collectibles also include the more faddish, perhaps less prudent, and yet irresistible nostalgia items—toys, Mickey Mouse watches, beer cans, gum machines, movie magazines, table radios, old opera records, baseball cards, old cameras and "photographia" parts and photos, stock certificates, tea and tobacco tins, Coke signs, Coke trays, penny arcade machines, coin-operated flip-card peep shows, Beatles albums, memorabilia of singers of the 'fifties, old *Life* magazines, "Peanuts" memorabilia, patriotic items, cast iron and tin toys, zeppelin toys, old radio giveaways (Tom Mix, Jack Armstrong, The Lone Ranger, etc.), movie posters, memorabilia of the moon landing, and the list goes on and on.

Because the objective of this book is to help you increase your net worth, let's take a serious look at investing in collectibles rather than collecting collectibles. This you can do on your own just for fun. My main focal points will be on the methodology of investing in this area: how it came to be an important aspect of a complete investment portfolio; its viable outlook and longevity as a major investment alternative in today's inflated and stormy economy; the advantages and disadvantages of investing in collectibles; a list of guidelines that will serve as pointers in the science and art of collectibles; and last, but not least, a section describing each of the "serious" collectibles—those with excellent annual growth rates, excellent demand, and a proven track record of consistent profit, growth, and long-term value.

From my studies I have found that there are at least six areas with which you'll want to become familiar since they have the best investment success record. These are: rare coins, rare stamps, famous oil paintings or paintings by famous artists, and antique furniture, cars, and oriental rugs.

INVESTING vs. COLLECTING

Of course, collecting for investment purposes is an entirely different game from collecting collectibles merely for the sake of collecting. The latter practice is considered more of an exhilarating hobby, a treasure hunt, and a means to exhibit a display case of proud possessions. Investing in collectibles is the method by which money is made and is a calculated and serious business, as are investing in stocks, real estate, and energy. In fact, investing in collectibles has reached such a peak that many large brokerage houses, financial planners, and others have established a full gamut of services for the collector-investor who wishes to enter the collectibles marketplace. Experts are available to advise their clients on how to make a prudent investment in a collectible specialty area, how to diversify, and how to make profits in collectibles both in the short term and over the long term.

A number of trust companies that manage the finances of many wealthy individuals now recommend that some of their clients put as much as 20 percent of their funds into art, antiquities, and other tangible holdings in order to protect their funds from ever-rising inflation and the ever-bigger tax bites. Trust companies that act as custodians for clients' investments for Keogh, IRA, pension and profit-sharing plans are now accepting rare coin and stamp portfolios into these plans. We have a portfolio of rare coins in our pension plan and they have performed superbly.

A number of the larger brokerage firms are establishing collectibles departments. The "rush" by the financial establishments to become serviceable in this alternative investment field is an indicator of the seriousness of the investors' concern over rising inflation. A partner of an old and highly respected brokerage firm recently said, "Obviously, investors are more impressed with the return on things that continue to outperform traditional investments." In their last study on comparaive yields of tangibles, they reported that Chinese ceramics headed the list with a ten-year compound rate of return of 19.2 percent per year. Next in line were high-grade American stamps, producing 15.4 percent per year; then paintings by old masters, yielding 13 percent per year; as well as nongold U.S. coins, producing 13 percent per year, all for a period of ten years.

THE FASCINATION WITH TANGIBLE ASSETS

This boom in investing in collectibles and tangibles can be attributed to several factors: affluence, nostalgia, inflation fears, confiscatory taxes, increased leisure time, disenchantment with other forms of investment, and well-publicized accounts of "soaring" prices of collectibles. Much of the fascination with collectibles appears to be as related to stiff taxes as it is to inflation, for profits on them often elude the tax collector, unlike the gains on securities. The collectible marketplace operates in a free-market atmosphere. There is little or no regulation. There is a free wheeling-dealing atmosphere where markets are cornered to make a sale at a profit and where there is no S.E.C. to interfere.

You will find that dealers in collectibles are similar to stockbrokers, except their credentials are not regulated in the conventional stock brokerage ways. You will find a significant number of excellent dealers, both small and large, who are totally honest. However, you must be cautious, for any area as unregulated as this one will also attract the opposite type of dealer—one who is dishonest, one who may even receive your payment without delivering your purchase to you, or who may sell forgeries and counterfeits as if they were the "real things."

DISADVANTAGES vs. ADVANTAGES OF INVESTING IN COLLECTIBLES

Besides the apparent disadvantage of some "wheeler dealers" in the marketplace, there are other disadvantages and pitfalls you'll want to know about before making a commitment of any kind to this type of investing. Because the positives tend to outweigh the negatives, I'll present the disadvantages first:

1. There is no spot price for collectibles—a collectible has a spread between the bid and ask prices which can run as much as 30 percent per item.

2. There is a sales tax on the collectible item added to its price when you keep it in the state in which you purchased it, and this can turn out to be a sizable amount.

3. The extra money spent on the spread and the sales tax means that the collectible must be bought with the idea of holding it for at least eighteen months to two years, and selling it then only if the market is right.

4. Not all collectibles have kept pace with inflation. Generally speaking, high-grade coins and art and antiques, when professionally selected, have done as well as the very best kinds of investments available, and continue to do so.

5. Prices of collectibles can "skid." For instance, the value of some timepieces and stringed instruments fell by 30 percent in 1975.

6. The collectible market is fraught with fakes and flawed merchandise. When a collectible starts coming into demand, the forgers may grind out reproductions in massive quantities.

7. Many hundreds of "get rich quick" and other spurious investment schemes have occurred in the collectibles market. All are risky, some are rip-offs.

8. Collectibles do not pay interest or dividends. They often entail such costs as insurance and storage. They may be difficult to sell within the timetable you have set.

9. Their profits may be a bit deceptive. For instance, the collector-investor may have bought a Victorian clock for $1000 and sold it at an auction five years later for $1500. On first blush, that may seem good. But after paying the auction $300, he only has $1200 left; so his net gain is only $200, or 4 percent a year. So he didn't win the money game.

THE ADVANTAGES

None of these disadvantages should necessarily discourage you from becoming better informed about collectibles. Investibles can and do pay off, both in enjoyment as well as in financial rewards.

1. Especially at the present time, the collectibles market has outperformed by a very big margin many more conventional types of investments, and there are indications that unless inflation is brought under control this will continue.

2. With the recent lifting of exchange controls in Britain, which enabled British individual investors and pension funds to invest abroad, there should be a larger number of potential buyers of American collectibles and antiquities. This should help support prices.

3. The willingness on the part of financial planners, banks, investment firms, brokerage houses, and auction houses to inform and advise their clients makes expert advice much more available to you and to others interested in collectibles as investments.

4. The proliferation of investment syndicates formed by doctors, lawyers, and other professional groups in our country has made it possible for quality items to be bought by many more persons than just the wealthiest tycoons in America.

5. The prices of most serious collectibles have averaged a gain in excess of 10 percent per year over the past two decades.

6. The spectacular mega-exhibits on tour in the United States, such as King Tut, have promoted and publicized antiquities and rarities, and are probably accountable for much of the new popularity in rarified Egyptian art treasures. Other exhibits have had similar good effects on art investments.

7. When you sell your collectible your profits, if you have held them for a year, you will be taxed at the more favorable capital gains rate. Another tax advantage that may fit your tax planning needs and philanthropic nature is to give your collectibles to a museum or a university. This will entitle you to take deductions of as much as 30 percent of your adjusted gross income for up to five years.

8. Because the tangibles' trading market has not been tapped yet by federal regulation, you have greater freedom. This in itself can be very advantageous by affecting their investment potential.

GUIDELINES ON INVESTING IN COLLECTIBLES

1. Purchase only what you wish to specialize in; if it is something you like, all the better, as it will maintain your high level of interest over the next ten years and decades thereafter.

2. Buy the best you can afford, even if you must accept limited quantities at first. If possible, purchase your collectibles from a dealer who will guarantee your purchase price back in the future if you trade in for a higher quality.

3. Confine your purchases to collectibles in excellent condition. These will always enjoy outstanding resale value. Look for quality— to be a fine buy, it should be in mint condition. Find out its rarity and its value, as well as was its most recent price; verify its date; and determine how many of such items were made.

4. A collectible of any real value should carry a ticket guar-

anteeing its origin and, in the case of very fine items, its travels as well.

5. The authenticity of the collectible should be guaranteed against a full cash refund.

6. Read as much literature as you can on the subject. The bimonthly newsletter from Sotheby Parke Bernet is an excellent source of information (Write Sotheby Parke Bernet, 980 Madison Avenue, New York, New York 10021)

7. Attend auctions, wander through antique stores, talk to people, and familiarize yourself completely with the area of interest before you buy anything. Study your line of collectibles for quality, art form, and all aspects of its category.

8. Buy only from reputable dealers and/or reputable auctions.

9. Become attuned to holding your collectibles for long periods of time. You must allow time for the mark-up to cover the difference between wholesale and retail prices.

10. If you are a novice, purchase and specialize in collectibles of known and proven work with a history of regular price appreciation.

11. Avoid galleries that operate on a commission basis. This situation encourages pressure tactics by the salesmen in the gallery.

12. Be aware of antique shops with large selections and fancy frames. These angles can lead to overvaluation of the piece itself.

13. Undergo a "comparison-shopping" spree before you actually purchase your item. If you are considering a major purchase, call in a professional appraiser.

14. Be informed and up to date on all prevailing economic and political trends that will influence the collectibles market. A rising stock market can result in extra discretionary income for investors and, therefore, a likelihood of surplus funds for items such as antiques.

15. At auctions, try to spot the dealers in the crowd. Generally they bid inconspicuously, but the auctioneer usually knows them. Look for "quick glances" between the auctioneer and his known customer. It may pay to outbid the dealers. They are planning to pay wholesale prices.

16. Regarding sealed bids, bid what you are ready to pay, and don't expect to get the item at a lower price.

17. When bidding from the floor, start high. Continued bidding from a low level stirs up crowd interest. On the other hand, a high bid can knock competition out of the game before the crowd knows what is happening.

18. Don't be afraid to go to the top for advice, even if you are a small investor. Such establishments as Sotheby's and Christie's of New York have been known for their extreme courtesy to all clients, big and small. (Christie's has started a quarterly newsletter. Write Christie, Manson & Woods, Int'l, Inc., 502 Park Avenue, New York, New York 10022, and ask to be put on their mailing list.)

19. Always arrange and investigate trucking arrangements, insurance, storage areas such as bank vaults or safety deposit boxes, storage fees, pick-up terms, burglar alarms, and other security precautions, etc., before buying the actual items.

20. When choosing the collectible you wish to invest in, apply the old truism, "Follow the smart money." This means that one way to find a shrewd investment is to observe the actions of the wealthy, the sophisticated, and those who have demonstrated beyond question their acquisitive abilities.

THE COLLECTIBLES—SMART MONEY INVESTS IN SERIOUS COLLECTIBLES

Rare Coins

You will find as you study collectibles that of all the traditional collectible objects, the rare coin is probably the best suited to survive and succeed as an investment during the periods of great economic and political uncertainty. Gold coins when cautiously purchased probably provide the ultimate in safety: protection against both inflation and depression.

If you have chosen gold coins as your collectible, you would be wise to acquaint yourself thoroughly with the numismatics (rare coin trading) investment field. Great care in studying rare coins is not difficult, and is very entertaining. The grading system in numismatics will reflect your coins' condition and appearance. Collectors wish their coins to be as nearly perfect as possible; the highest prices are paid for the most perfect coins of a specified type or date.

What Makes a Coin Valuable?   You may ask, What makes a coin valuable? It is more than age, condition, date, type, or metal content. A great deal depends on its rarity and its supply and demand. There are approximately fifteen grades of excellence recognized by the American Numismatic Association, ranging from *Proof,* the mirror-like finish of a coin that was manufactured by the Mint and then carefully preserved from any nicks or scratches, all the way to the fifteenth grade,

Good, which actually means "Very heavily worn with portions of lettering, date, and legends worn smooth. The date may be barely readable."

Prices of rare coins have been rising steadily, year after year, at the rate of about 20 percent annually. In the past five years they have soared even faster. It appears that this trend will continue, for there is a static supply of coins—and there will never be very many more available than there are now—while there is an increasing demand as more and more collectors crowd into the field. As you've learned by now, when demand is greater than supply, prices rise. This is why a Proof-like uncirculated 1796 quarter which sold twenty-four years ago for $200 is worth $30,000 today.

The most expensive coin ever sold in the U.S. to date was sold in November 1979, at the auction of the Garrett coin collection owned by Johns Hopkins University. The coin, a gold 1787 Brasher Doubloon, was sold for $725,000. It was minted by a well-known New York silversmith who lived next door to George Washington on Cherry Street. (Note: The entire Garrett collection, which was auctioned by Bowers & Ruddy, was sold last November for over $7 million.) The coin was only one of six made exactly alike by Brasher.

Rare Coins Limited Partnership. At this point in our discussion you may have been impressed with the investment potential of rare coins, but do not have the interest or perhaps the time to develop expertise in them. If this is where you find yourself, you'll be very pleased to know that a firm in Boston (from whom we bought our coin portfolio for our pension paln) is now offering a Rare Coin Limited Partnership. Each unit is $500 and the minimum purchase is five units, or a minimum investment of $2500. This is a $10,000,000 offering and has as its chief financial objective capital appreciation. The very emergence of a fund such as this establishes the credibility of rare coins as a financial vehicle. The identity of the fund as a security enables all financial planners' clients to enjoy the benefits of rare coins in their Keogh, IRA, and pension/profit-sharing plans.

Rare Stamps

Another area you may want to familiarize yourself with is rare stamp collecting. It is one of the most popular hobbies in our nation, with over twenty million collectors here and fifty million around the world. Most people who collect rare stamps consider it a hobby, but there are growing numbers of persons who are buying stamps as an investment and are finding it very profitable.

Stamp investing, highest quality of course, has yielded about a 12 percent per year rate of return on investment for the past two decades.

In order to realize profit from this type of collectible, you should count on holding onto them for at least three to four years before being able to sell them at a profit, as it will take at least that long to recover the dealer's mark-up.

The price appreciation in rare stamps in recent years has been very gratifying to their investors. While the cost of living increased over 112 percent between 1954 and 1977, the value of all 1882 to 1909 issues of stamps went up 786 percent. The return from selected stamps was even greater.

Philately, as stamp collecting is referred to in trade circles, is a fairly big business. Around a billion dollars in sales occur each year, and it is estimated there are in excess of fifty million collectors world-wide. There appears to be no scarcity of willing investors, but dealers are beginning to complain that they cannot obtain enough quality stamps to sell—again a situation where demand exceeds supply.

The top-priced stamp presently is the British Guyana 1856 one cent, appraised at $280,000.

Some rules you may want to follow when investing in rare stamps are:

1. Begin as a collector, and work into becoming an investor.

2. Diversify in stamps.

3. Choose only top quality stamps.

4. Look for stamps that are old, clean, undamaged, and of course, rare! If you do not have the inclination or time to do this on your own, work with a financial planner who is knowledeable in this area.

Collecting Art

Another area that merits your study and research is collecting art. In this area there tends to be agreement among the experts that those who collect art primarily for profit frequently lose, but that those who collect what they love usually make a substantial profit. You will find that collecting art—paintings, drawings, prints and sculpture—can be a delightful, affordable, and profitable investment. Paintings used to be the classic rich man's collectible, i.e., the Mellons, the Fricks, and Guggenheims. Now we Americans are behaving much like these millionaires and much like the Europeans—seeking both pleasure and profit in the investment of art.

The necessary components of a good art investiment are: rarity, condition, and historical importance. Taste, which is of course subjective, should also be considered. A beautiful picture by a good artist

will usually bring more money over a period of years than a great picture that is ugly by a more important artist.

You will probably find as you study this medium that a good art collector is one who buys with both his eyes and his heart. Underlying every collection that turns out to be a lucrative investment is almost always an undeniable urge to enjoy art.

Collecting and Investing in Antiques

Perhaps you have talent for collecting and a love for antiques. Like other collectibles, they can be fun to own and they can turn into a very good investment over the years. They also have an immediate practical value. You can furnish your home today with reasonably good antiques for less than the cost of high-quality new furniture. The irony is that new furniture will immediately depreciate and lose value, whereas antiques will usually retain and appreciate in value.

Antique shops, shows, and garage sales sometimes offer bargains. But if you are a budding collector, you may be better off spending most of your time at auctions. Auctions have three major advantages: 1) volume and variety, 2) no mark-ups, and 3) usually more affordable prices. It is amazing to many people that auction houses such as Sotheby Parke Bernet advertise that in New York, Paris, and London auctions, 75 percent of their items are sold for under $1000.

Oriental Rugs

Another area you'll want to consider for both their investment potential and beauty are oriental rugs. You can rest assured that oriental

rugs have reached the investment category when *The Financial Planner Magazine* devotes a large section with pictures in color to this investment media.

Oriental rugs come from one of the six schools considered oriental: 1) Persian (or Iranian), 2) Caucasian, 3) Turkoman, 4) Turkish, 5) Indian, or 6) Chinese. Valuable handcrafted carpets and rugs are named "oriental" because most of the great craftsmen down through history have operated east of Europe.

Rugs of investment quality are handmade and most are fifty years old. The price of a fine antique rug, with dimensions of four feet by six feet, from Turkey, Persia, or the Caucasus, can range from $2000 to $10,000 and more. It is important for you to know what types of rugs come from which areas, i.e., a Turkish village rug is coarser in weave than a Persian rug.

In appraising an oriental rug, experts take into account the following considerations:

1. Age

2. Condition (how are the edges and fringes, and is there any luster?

3. Knot count (how many per square inch)

4. Tightness of weave (the tighter the weave the more valuable the rug)

5. Definition of pattern (the more definite a pattern, the more valuable the rug)

6. Singularity (How unique is the rug?)

7. Resale value of the rug (What price will the rug command upon resale or trade-in?)

Generally, the rug's resale value depends upon its overall quantity, as determined by the above criterion.

SUMMARY

You no doubt will find it profitable to get some of your assets out of paper and into things, but I advise you to go very slowly when you move toward collectibles.

It takes two to three years of concentrated effort to become even a high-class amateur of any collectible. Even then, you will be competing with the old hands, including the "collectiholics," and as with any "————holic" reason does not always reign supreme. Perhaps one of the best descriptions of a true collector was made by Jules Fleury-Husson, a Parisian collector in the nineteenth century, when he said: "Do not occupy yourself with politics; never go to the theater; forbid yourself to open a book; scorn the pleasures of family; always have money in your pocket. This will lead to a full life as a perfect collector!"

APPLICATION

1. Do any of the areas of collectibles interest you? If so, which one or ones?

2. Would a limited partnership with a general partner with the expertise be a better solution for the funds you feel should be invested in collectibles?

3. Next time you are in a large city, go to Sotheby Parke Bernet or Christie's. You'll find it enjoyable and perhaps profitable.

4. Are you adding new furnishings to your home? Should you consider using a few pieces of antiques of investment quality and design?

5. Oriental rugs can add beauty to a room and be an appreciating investment at the same time. Go look at them. Even if you don't invest, it should be a pleasurable experience—and that in itself would be an investment in living.

11

LENDING
YOUR DOLLARS

It is your responsibility to be a good steward of every dollar that comes your way. A part of each dollar should be invested in today's goods and services and used to feed, clothe, house, transport, provide health care, and entertain your family and yourself. A part of each dollar should be given away, and a major portion of your dollar will be taken away by the IRS if you do not take constructive steps to prevent it. A part of your dollar should be saved and invested for tomorrow's goods and services.

In an earlier chapter, you learned that there are only three things you can do with a dollar—spend, loan, or own. You will always need to have some of your funds in a "loaned" position. How much should this be? There was a time when I taught that you should keep three months' expenses in cash reserves. Now I teach that you should keep as much of your funds in an idle position as it takes to give you peace of mind, for peace of mind is a good investment. Your peace of mind may require that you keep a lot of what I call "patting money," money that you can mull over and pat like a Linus security blanket. If it does, keep it idle. I'll never disturb your peace of mind. However, I warn you that I'll try to educate you to such a point that you won't have any peace of mind if you leave too much of your money idle. Determine where your level is and place those funds into a "loaned" position, knowing full well that they will be working for someone else and that they are guaranteed to lose with our present rate of inflation and taxation. In this chapter we'll cover the various ways that you can "loan" your money.

YOUR BANKER

A very important consideration in your plan to become financially independent is the selection of the right banker. He can play a vital role in its accomplishment. Take the time and effort to select one who is knowledgeable and creative and whose bank has sufficient assets to finance any bankable project you may want to undertake. Then open your checking account with him.

CHECKING ACCOUNTS

You will always need one or more checking accounts to be used for convenience and for ease of record keeping. Keep a sufficient amount on deposit to enable you to write a check whenever you choose. Feeling "poor" is not an emotionally satisfying feeling and does not contribute to the necessary psychology of winning that you must have to win the money game.

However, do not keep your balance too large. I remember one lady who came in for counseling who had $159,000 in her checking account. I asked if she had a reason for keeping this amount there and she said, "Well, I've been thinking of taking a little trip." I suppressed the desire to ask her which planet was her desired destination.

OTHER WAYS OF "LENDING"

When you move from a checking account to other ways of "lending" your funds, you will find a wide array of choices. These are what are commonly called fixed-income instruments. As evidence of your loan to the borrower, you usually receive securities or instruments that represent contracts to pay back your money at a specified time and at a specified rate. These borrowers may be corporations, the federal government, or financial institutions.

Let's now examine some of the fixed-income instruments that may be available to you.

Passbook Savings Accounts

You may open a passbook savings account in any amount at either a bank or a savings and loan. Interest is earned from date of deposit to date of withdrawal or to "dividend" date. The maximum rates are fixed by the Federal Reserve System or the Federal Home Loan Bank Board. These rates (usually slightly higher at savings institutions) have ranged in recent years from 4½ percent to 5½ percent. Deposits and withdrawals can be made at your discretion. Deposits, in most instances, are federally insured to a maximum of $40,000.

Certificates of Deposit

This is basically a deposit account opened for a minimum amount of $1000 to $5000. Certificates of deposit are issued by both commercial banks and savings and loan associations in maturities of from thirty days to eight years. Interest is paid from the date of deposit to maturity at the stated rate. Interest rates are usually higher than those for regular savings accounts and have reached 7.75 percent for the longer maturities for amounts less than $100,000. Rates will vary depending on going rates at the time of issue. Maximum rates for CDs under $100,000 are fixed by law. Savings and loan rates may be one quarter of a percent higher than those of commercial banks. The rate obtainable on $100,000 and up is usually negotiable, whether with a bank or a savings and loan institution. During 1977, when the Federal Reserve Board was expanding the money supply and demands for commercial loans did not keep pace, $100,000 30-day CDs dropped to 4⅝ percent. During the tight money markets of 1980, they rose to 15 percent.

I personally could never feel comfortable with a long-term certificate of deposit. I feel that I would be betting against the following four odds, with a great likelihood of losing on one or all of them:

1. I am betting that I will not need the money for four to eight years. If I do need the money, my rate will revert back to passbook, and I will be penalized three months' interest.

2. I am betting that long-term interest rates will not rise above 7½ to 8 percent for four to eight years.

3. I am betting that we will not have inflation over that period of time.

4. I am betting that my after-tax return will be greater than the rate of inflation. (In recent years I would have lost on the last three, even if I did not need to use my money.)

Here are some examples of penalties that you could have incurred on a $10,000 certificate if you had made early withdrawal on a six-year certificate of deposit paying 7¾ percent:

PENALTIES ON SIX-YEAR DEPOSIT

Year	Penalty
1	2½ % + 90 days
2	5%
3	7½ %
4	10%
5	12½ %
6	15%

If you renew a six-year certificate twice, there were only three days out of 6,570 that you could have withdrawn your money without a penalty: It's like saying, "Mr. Banker, I liked that penalty so well, may I please have another?"

The banks and savings and loans themselves have come to realize that this is a very severe penalty. Their new disclosure statement for time-deposit contracts reads as follows:

You have agreed by opening this account to keep these funds upon deposit until the above due date and for the full maturity of any subsequent renewals.

Under government regulations, your deposit may not be withdrawn prior to maturity, except with our consent, which may be given only at the time such request is made, unless * (see below)

If we permit you to withdraw all or part of your account before maturity, we are required to impose the *following substantial penalty*: * See Exception Below.

(1) Time deposit with original maturity of one year or less: Forfeiture of three months' interest on the amount withdrawn at the rate being paid upon the deposit. If the amount withdrawn has been on deposit for less than three months, all interest is forfeited.

(2) Time deposits with original maturity of more than one year: Forfeiture of six months' interest on the amount being withdrawn at the rate being paid on the deposit. If the amount withdrawn has been on deposit for less than six months, all interest is forfeited.

A "guaranteed" dollar today is a guaranteed loss! You'll never win the money game with guaranteed losses.

The tragedy of inflation is that many of our elderly citizens are not knowledgeable about how to protect themselves against inflation or must, because of their age, use "guaranteed" accounts.

At 7-percent inflation and a 40-percent tax bracket, what are the net after-tax and after-inflation results on a $10,000 four-year certificate of deposit paying 7½ percent? Here are the tragic results:

Deposit

$10,000

Income		750.00
Inflation	− 700	− 52.50
Taxes		−300.00
	$9,300 +	397.50 = $9,697.50

---

* Where necessary to comply with (1) or (2) above, any interest already paid to or for your account will be deducted from the amount requested to be withdrawn.

First year: $10,000 − 9,697.50 = $302.50 negative interest
Fourth year: $302.50 × 4 years = $1,210.00 negative interest
Results: $10,000 − $1,210 = $8,790.00 purchasing power

Can you bring yourself to try a 14 percent inflation rate? Just think, what have you bought this past year that went up any less than 14 percent?

Deposit

	$10,000		
Income		$750	
Inflation	− 1,400	− 105	
Taxes		− 300	
	$ 8,600 +	$345 = $8,945	

First year: $10,000 − $8,945 = $1,055 negative interest
Fourth year: 1,055 × 4 years = $4,220 negative interest
Results: $10,000 − $4,220 = $5,780 purchasing power

New 2½-Year Certificates

The smaller saver has never received as high an interest rate as the larger saver. (This condition brought the mutual fund money market funds into being.) In 1980, the Federal Reserve Board authorized that there be no legal minimum investment and that savings institutions could accept as little as $100. When the certificate is issued, its 2½-year interest rate is set at slightly below the average interest rate on treasury securities maturing 2½ years later. If you cash in the certificate before it matures, you lose six months' interest.

INTEREST RATES ACROSS THE SPECTRUM

The variety of accounts and rates became so varied during February of 1980, due to the Federal Reserve Board's tight money policies, that one savings and loan listed their accounts and rates in a full page ad (Figure 11–1).

CDs Are Not Withdrawable on Demand

Contrary to what you may have thought, CDs are not demand deposits. They can be redeemed before maturity only at the option of the bank, even if you are willing to suffer the substantial penalties described above. This feature was recently brought to our attention when the Roslyn Savings & Loan in Long Island, New York, refused to grant early withdrawal.

Higher interest rates than any bank.

ANNUAL RATE	**13.013%**[**] (182-Day) Money Market CD	**10.650%** (2½-year) Money Market CD	**8.000%** 8-Year CD	**7.750%** 6-Year CD	**7.500%** 4-Year CD
ANNUAL YIELD	**13.673%** $10,000 min.	**11.402%** $100 min.* (thru Feb. 29, 1980)	**8.449%** $100 min.*	**8.175%** $100 min.*	**7.901%** $100 min.*

6.750% 2½-Year CD	**6.500%** 1-Year CD	**6.000%** 90-Day CD	**5.500%** Money Box Account	**5.500%** Savings Account
7.083% $100 min.*	**6.812%** $100 min.*	**6.272%** $100 min.*	**5.735%** $300 min. (Earn interest on transferred checking dollars)	**5.735%** $5.00 min.

** Annual rate and yield subject to change at renewal. Assumes reinvestment at maturity. Substantial penalty for early withdrawal. The rate is good from Feb. 21 thru Feb. 27, 1980.

Federal regulations prohibit compounding of interest on 6 month Money Market Certificates.

Figure 11–1.

SAFETY

When you lend your money to a bank or savings and loan, it is well to follow the same procedure that a bank would: check out your borrower. How can you do this? In the case of a bank, look for the gilded seal applied to the entrance door of the bank or on the window near the door. Does it contain the letters FDIC? This means that the bank is a member of the Federal Deposit Insurance Corporation and that your account is insured up to $40,000. The Federal Deposit Insurance program insures deposits in national and member state banks, both commercial and mutual savings banks. What this means to you is that if a bank gets into financial difficulties and is closed, your savings up to $40,000 will be reimbursed by the federal government. Although the process begins soon after closure, it may take some months before you receive your money.

All national banks in the United States are required to be members of the system, and state banks may become Federal Reserve System banks by meeting stringent requirements.

All FRS banks have stringent requirements with regard to the structure of their board of directors, interlocking directorates, their relationship with security and investment companies, the payment of interest on deposits, and their relationship to branch banks. They must keep reserves in cash or on deposit with their Federal Reserve bank equivalent to a certain proportion of their various types of deposits, and they are also required to subscribe to the capital of the Federal Reserve bank of their district equal to 6 percent of their capital surplus.

There are no similar requirements for savings and loan associations, although they may operate under federal regulations with guarantees. Federal regulations do not preclude bank failure. In fact, the entire nation is familiar with the failure of the Sharpstown Bank in Houston in 1971. Sharpstown was a state bank with FDIC insurance for savings accounts up to $20,000 (which was the limit at that time). However, many people had more than that amount on deposit.

The risk varies with some savings and loan associations. It is extremely important to learn as much as you can about an association before making a deposit. However, a superficial check may not protect you. The *National Observer* in its December 15, 1973, issue gave an account of a widow "still in shock" who deposited $42,509 in benefits from her late husband's insurance in a Virginia savings and loan corporation. She never doubted the money was safe. The 57-year-old corporation was well regarded. Its officials were among the most esteemed men in the community. There were two things she did not know: the savings and loan corporation was insolvent, and its deposits were not insured. Seven days later, Virginia banking authorities closed the institution and placed it in receivership. Her money, along with that of nearly 3,500 other persons, was frozen. Unfortunately, all those people could end up with losses.

Virginia's inadequacies are not unique. In Louisville, Kentucky, savings of 22,100 persons were jeopardized when two large building and loan associations failed in 1972. Their depositors are expected to recover no more than 30 percent of their money.

If you decide to use a savings and loan association, be sure to look for the gilded seal with FSLIC on the door, for this guarantees that you will have your deposit returned *someday* (not always on demand) up to $40,000.

In Chicago, some 14,000 savers were cut off from their funds when a large savings and loan association went under in 1964. And in Maryland, an estimated 50,000 depositors lost all or part of their funds when some uninsured savings and loans passed into oblivion during the 1960s.

Such misfortunes are unusual in these times of prosperity, but nothing can entirely prevent even national bank collapses. The biggest in U.S. history was in October 1972, when a national bank located in San Diego was declared insolvent. Nearly half of the $940 million on deposit were not covered by the FDIC insurance because of the then-$20,000 maximum. (All depositors were later reimbursed by a government rescue plan.) The difficulties experienced by the Franklin National Bank of New York City in 1974 are also well chronicled.

In Galveston, Texas, an old, well-respected bank was closed by the Securities and Exchange Commission in September 1972. Thanks to the affluence of some of the relatives, who paid off depositors, no one lost any money.

COMMERCIAL PAPER

Corporations finance much of their short-term working capital requirements by issuing commercial paper short-term notes with a fixed maturity of one to 270 days. Paper is normally issued in a minimum amount of $25,000 or as small as $10,000 at some banks for thirty days or longer, and it can be purchased on either a discount or an interest-bearing basis. The investment return is determined by the current level of short-term interest rates and, therefore, can fluctuate significantly over relatively short periods. The returns on commercial paper historically have been about ½ percent below the bank prime lending rate. Paper can be purchased with or without arrangements allowing prepayment of the amount initially invested plus a return at the original investment rate. Without such arrangements, paper can be sold in the short-term market at current rates, resulting in a yield greater or less than the acquisition rate.

GOVERNMENT OBLIGATIONS

Treasury obligations are guaranteed by the U.S. government. Federal agencies, unless specifically indicated, are not technically government guaranteed but are still considered to be of very high quality.

Series E Bonds

The government obligation with which you are probably the most familiar is the Series E Bonds. The bonds are issued on a discount basis. The minimum available is $25. When held to maturity, the investment return is equivalent to 6 percent compounded semiannually. These bonds may be redeemed at any time after two months from issue at a fixed redemption value that results in a return of less than the 6 percent rate. Interest is not taxable until received.

Series H Bonds

Series H Bonds are ten-year income bonds. They are issued at par with interest paid semiannually on a scale graduated to produce a return of 6 percent compounded semiannually when the bonds are held to maturity. The minimum amount available is $500. These bonds may be redeemed at par at the owner's option after six months from the issue date. Redemption prior to maturity results in a yield under the 6 percent rate.

If you have held Series E Bonds for some years and are now in need of income, you may want to consider exchanging them for Series H Bonds. There will be no tax liability on the accumulated interest on your Series E Bonds when the exchange is made, nor will there be any until you decide to redeem the Series H Bonds. At that time, a tax liability will be incurred.

Series EE and Series HH Government Savings Bonds

These bonds are now being offered as substitutes for the old Series E and H bonds. If you have a Series E bond that is maturing, you can trade it for the Series HH bonds in multiples of $500 and defer the taxes on your interest. Notations will be made on your HH replacement bond showing that the interest has been deferred. The tax will be due when the new bond matures.

This tax deferral does have value, even though the return is meager when you compare it with other fixed-dollar alternatives.

Tax-free savings for children are also made possible by buying the Series EE bonds in the child's name to build a fund for, say, college costs. (Not that I recommend them as a good way to build funds for college. Never try to make a fixed dollar accomplish a variable-dollar goal.) File a return the first year establishing the interest as the child's income. If the amount is small, no tax will be due. Also, no state or local taxes are due on government bond interest.

The new EE bonds are now called "Energy Savings Bonds," which suggests that the government is promoting them as a patriotic gesture.

Treasury Bills

Treasury bills in the past were normally issued in maturities of 91 days, 182 days, and 1 year, and were available in a minimum amount of $10,000, directly from any of the twelve Federal Reserve Banks or through a commercial bank or broker.

These treasury bills in the past were bought by persons with larger amounts to lend, but during the abnormally high rates of 1980, even our middle-income citizens lined up at the bank to buy them. The minimum amount required was lowered to $1000 and purchases could be made directly from the Treasury Department or from the local Federal Reserve Bank or branch. An even simpler way of purchasing them, for a small fee, was through a stockbroker or bank.

Treasury bills are issued weekly on a discount basis, under competitive bidding, with the face amount payable at maturity. The investment return on bills is the difference between the cost and the face amount. Bills may be sold prior to maturity at a competitive market rate, which can result in a yield greater or smaller than the original acquisition rate. Yield on bills, like other short-term money market instruments, can fluctuate greatly, but it is generally lower than other nongovernment, short-term securities.

As you will note from the Figure 11–2, the percentage rate has shown a steep rise since 1978.

A number of financial seminar speakers and editors of newsletters are currently advocating the complete avoidance of certificates of deposit because they fear that the small reserves required by the F.D.I.C. against deposits are not sufficient to give your certificates of deposits enough protection. They recommend that cash be kept only in treasury bills or in money market funds that invest only in treasury bills. I am not at this moment that fearful of the collapse of our banking system. However, I do reserve the option to change if our government's fiscal policies deteriorate further.

Treasury Notes

Notes have a fixed maturity from one to seven years and bear interest payable semiannually at fixed rates. They are available in minimum amounts of $1000. Selected notes are auctioned competitively through the Federal Reserve System on a periodic basis. Buyers can

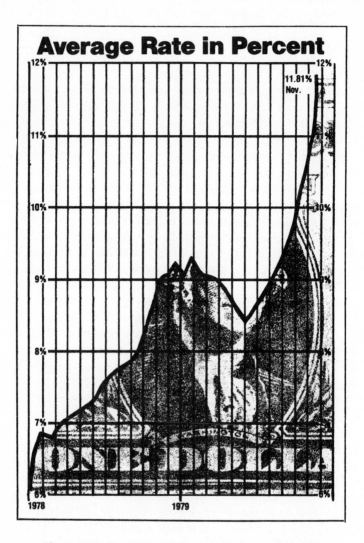

Figure 11–2.   Rise in Treasury Bill Rate, 1978–1980

subscribe through a commercial bank or a broker. Yields on notes are determined by the acquisition price. These notes may be sold prior to maturity at the current market rate, resulting in a yield greater or smaller than the original acquisition rate. Again, yields on Treasury notes generally are lower than their corporate counterparts because of the excellent marketability and credit rating of government securities.

Treasury Bonds

Bonds have a fixed maturity of over seven years and are the longer counterpart of Treasury notes. Yields on Treasury bonds, because they are of longer maturity, sometimes are higher than those of Treasury notes.

Federal Agency Obligations

Agency obligations are issued by federal authorities such as the Federal National Mortgage Association, the Federal Home Loan Bank, the Government National Mortgage Association, and others. These instruments are varied and are tailored to meet the financing needs of the individual issuing agency. Types of issues are similar to U.S. Treasury bills, notes, and bonds. You can acquire these obligations through investment banking houses. Normally, the minimum amount available is $1000 to $5000. Yields are usually one-quarter to one-half of a percent higher than U.S. Treasury obligations. These issues can be sold prior to maturity at current market rates, resulting in a return greater or smaller than the acquisition yield.

There is one group of securities that you may want to consider in this category. They were called "mortgage backed securities guaranteed by the Government National Mortgage Association" when they were first established. Since then, they have received the friendlier nickname "Ginny Mae." Ginny Maes offer a number of special attractions, but one in particular is that they pay a fixed return that is often higher than you can get from a long-term bond.

Probably the main reason they aren't better known is that when the certificates first appeared in 1970, the minimum unit that you could buy from most brokers was $100,000. Consequently, the buyers were banks, insurance companies, pension funds, and other institutions. Soon thereafter, the minimum purchase was cut back to $25,000. Since then, one brokerage firm has created a unit trust that allows individuals to start their investment in Ginny Maes for as little as $10,000.

Ginny Mae pass-throughs were hatched during the credit crunch of 1969–70, when mortgage money was as tight as it has become from time to time since. The Government National Mortgage Association (GNMA), established by an act of Congress, said, in effect, to savings and loan associations, banks, and mortgage bankers, "When you have closed enough mortgages, collect them into a pool; then issue certificates, backed by the mortgages, to raise cash so you can loan out more mortgage money. We'll guarantee the pool, so investors will buy the certificates without worry." The packager of the mortgage pool then "passes through" the mortgage payments he receives to certificate holders.

Why should you buy a Ginny Mae pass-through instead of a corporate bond? Well, it does give you a way of spreading a portion of your money into mortgages without any of the worries of collecting payments, defaults, or bookkeeping. Full payments, on time, are "backed by the full faith and credit of the United States Government," and no corporate bond can make that statement. Bonds can be called back by the issuer, some within five years of issue date, and you would lose the high interest return you were counting on. Ginny Mae certificates usually assure you rates for twelve years.

But perhaps most important, you are buying a mortgage, and the pool sponsor sends you a monthly check. Part of the payment represents interest and part return of your principal. (The principal portion, since it is a return of your capital, is not taxed as income.) With a bond, of course, you have to wait until it matures before your principal is returned. This feature may be of special value to you if you are retired and need a monthly check. If you do not need to use the earnings for monthly expenses, you can reinvest. The effect of monthly compounding is a return higher than that of a bond that pays the same return but sends you interest checks only twice a year.

A number of firms make a secondary market in Ginny Maes so there is no liquidity problem. There is the risk, however, that interest rates may go up. Therefore, since a prospective buyer can get a higher return if he buys a new pass-through instead of yours, your certificate will bring a lower figure than you paid for it. If the interest rate goes down, the reverse occurs and your pass-through can probably be sold for more than you paid for it.

Gilt-Edge Theft

Will you win buying any of these government credit instruments? Analyze this question rationally and then formulate your answer. Inflation reduces the purchasing power of your money, which has the effect of lessening the repayment of your loan. You would seriously protest if you loaned the government $10,000 and they returned $5000. That's exactly what will happen to you if we have a mere 7 percent inflation rate over a ten-year period. Should you demand that in a free economy interest rates fully reflect the inflation rates?

Beginning with Franklin Roosevelt, our federal policy has been to manipulate interest rates in favor of the borrower—and the federal government, of course, has been chief among the borrowers. If you will analyze the relation of rates to inflation, you will find that since

1940 the investor in Treasury bills has lost money in all but six years. With long-term government bonds, he lost all but three years.

Losses by investors in government securities constitute direct gains for Washington. As the purchasing power of your dollar declines, the government can pay you back in cheaper dollars. Moreover, far from being an innocent party, the Federal Reserve plays the key role in generating inflation as a part of its interest-rate manipulation policies.

Since 1940, the Federal Reserve has acquired in excess of $100 billion of government obligations, paying for them with checks drawn on itself, thereby converting paper into primary reserve assets of our banking system. As the money passes through our banking system, which operates on a fractional reserve basis, these are converted into over $700 billion of money and credit. As more money is pushed through the system, this massive infusion of funds lowers the interest rates.

When you lend money to the government and the rate you are paid is less than the rate of inflation, you have set yourself up for the confiscation of your property. A lowering of the rate, however, is announced by the White House Press in dulcet tones using such phrases as "stabilizing the economy" or "fighting inflation."

Before you are tempted to vote for the Congressman whose chief claim to fame is the advocacy of cheaper interest rates (my state has had some very vocal Congressmen who have had this as the chief cornerstone of their political platform), you should be aware that "cheap money" favors the spenders at the expense of the savers. This realization by more and more of our citizens is bringing about a breakdown of financial discipline, of families living beyond their means, and a general disruption of our economy. These factors can lead to unemployment of men and equipment and uneconomic allocation of our resources.

Our constitution provides that "No person shall be deprived of life, liberty, or property without due process of law." This constitutional right is being violated when interest rates are manipulated for the benefit of the government.

MUNICIPAL BONDS

Municipal bonds are issued by local governments (cities, states, and various districts and political subdivisions) instead of the federal government and its agencies. Municipals usually, but not always, provide lower returns or yields than government bonds, primarily because of the special feature they provide. The interest paid on municipal obligations is totally exempt from federal income tax and usually from state income taxes if you are a taxpayer in the state that issued the bond.

Yields on municipal issues are determined by the current level of interest rates, the credit rating of the issuer, and the tax laws.

Most municipal bonds are issued in serial form, some maturing each year for several years, with maturities as high as thirty years. Interest is normally paid semiannually. Investors tend to buy them as they are issued and hold them until maturity. However, municipals, like other bonds, can be sold prior to maturity in the secondary market at the prevailing market rates.

There has been talk from time to time about Congress eliminating the tax-exempt privilege inherent in municipal bonds. If such a change should be legislated, it should not have an effect on those bonds issued prior to the legislation, and their scarcity could easily enhance their value. Before the onerous Tax Reform Act of 1976, we always assumed that the government would not change the rules after the game had been played. Now retroactive legislation has become a reality and a future threat. However, federal taxation of state and municipal bonds does require an amendment to the Constitution ratified by two-thirds of the states. Heavily indebted states are not likely to look favorably on such an amendment.

Another important feature of municipal bonds has been their relative stability. Next to U.S. government bonds, municipal bonds have been the "safest" of all securities. The New York City and Cleveland fiscal debacle has placed a cloud on bonds of cities that do not practice prudent financial policies. Puerto Rican bonds also have received lower ratings in recent years.

I was amazed at the surge of interest in municipal bonds after all the publicity about The Big Apple and its fiscal problems. Even the proverbial "little old lady in tennis shoes" asked for them. This seems to have been caused by several things:

1. Many people were not aware of the existence of tax-free bonds before this publicity.

2. This interest in municipals occurred at a time when the stock market had not been a rewarding place to have money, chiefly because of the tight money policies of the Federal Reserve.

3. These policies pushed the market down and interest rates up on corporate bonds, attracting funds from the market and into fixed-dollar "guaranteed" investments.

4. Since the return from these corporate bonds was fully taxable, the next step was to look for tax relief.

5. Then along came the Tax Reform Act of 1976, making it possible to have managed municipal bond funds with monthly distributions, systematic additions, and reinvestments. A large number of mutual fund distributors then formed municipal bond funds and began active advertising campaigns in our daily newspapers. Since that time the interest of the lay public in municipal bonds has greatly increased.

If you are selecting your own bond portfolio, it will be essential for you to learn something about quality ratings. If you are letting the professionals select them through municipal bond funds or trusts, a knowledge of ratings will still be helpful as you study their portfolios. Moody's Investor Service and Standard and Poor each rate municipal bond obligations according to relative investment qualities.

Using the Standard and Poor's notation system, the following rough definitions can be given to the more prominent categories for corporate bonds, with similar logic applying to municipal bonds:

AAA   Prime or highest-grade obligations, possessing the ultimate degree of protection of principal and interest.

AA   High-grade obligations, differing from AAA issues only in small degree.

A   Upper-medium grade with considerable investment strength, but not entirely free from adverse effects of changes in economic and trade conditions.

BBB   Medium-grade category bonds on the borderline between definitely sound obligations and those in which the speculative element begins to predominate. These bonds have adequate asset coverage and normally are protected by satisfactory earnings. This is the lowest category that qualifies for commercial bank investment.

BB   Lower-medium grade, possessing only minor investment characteristics.

B   Speculative, with payment of interest not assured under difficult economic conditions.

Types of Municipal Bonds

Municipal bonds fall into three main categories:

Full faith and credit bonds of a state or political subdivision of the state have the full taxing power of the issuing local government available to pay both the principal and the interest.

Special tax bonds have a designated tax (gasoline, liquor, cigarettes specifically pledged to pay the interest and principal.

Revenue bonds are backed by the earnings generated in a particular facility and do not have the taxing power of a local government upon which to draw. Many of those bonds are of a very high quality and are often rated equal to or higher than some bonds backed by taxes.

There are also a limited number of hybrid bonds that are paid from both taxes and revenues. Industrial revenue bonds have also appeared in recent years. These bonds generally are secured by a corporation that has entered into a lease agreement with a community. The bond issuer is normally a public authority that issues the bonds under its municipal title but receives annual installments sufficient to pay the principal and interest on the bonds from the corporation that is using the facility.

Municipal Bond Trust Funds

If tax-free income fits your financial plans but you do not have the expertise to select, the time to supervise, or sufficient funds to diversify, you may want to consider investing in a municipal bond trust fund. They are usually sold in units of $1000, plus accrued interest to settlement date. Most of them contain a well-selected diversified portfolio of municipal bonds selected from the top four categories. They provide a tax-exempt yield between 6 and $8\frac{1}{2}$ percent, which they will pay to you on a monthly basis. The funds are closed-end and self-liquidating, and usually do not carry a management fee (because they are not managed), though a nominal sales charge of around $3\frac{1}{2}$ percent is charged when they are purchased. Although the sponsors are usually not required to do so, they do make a secondary market in the trusts, thereby giving you liquidity if you should so desire.

Municipal Bond Funds

The Tax Reform Act of 1976 made it possible for brokers to offer municipal bond funds. These are managed funds that allow additions of smaller amounts of money; a check a month; and the various other conveniences of a regular mutual fund, such as redemption at net asset value, reinvestment of distributions, etc. The municipal bond trust places bonds in a portfolio where they remain until maturity. The bond funds have professional managers who buy and sell bonds in an attempt to maximize yield and safety.

Tax Equivalents

I find that many investors become confused and do not understand the difference between yield and tax equivalents. The other day I had a dentist tell me he was getting 12 percent on his "muni" as he called it. I knew that this was unlikely and asked for a description. It was a 6-percent bond, which of course was equivalent to a 12-percent corporate bond in his 50-percent tax bracket. Table 17 in the Appendix gives all the tax equivalents on municipal bonds.

A simple comparison would look like this for a 6-percent bond on a joint return:

Tax Bracket	6% Municipal Bond Equivalent to
43%	10.53%
49%	11.76%
54%	13.04%
59%	14.63%
64%	16.67%
68%	19.53%

Should You Invest in Municipal Bonds?

When I am asked that question, my answer is, "It depends on what you are going to do with the money if you do not." If you are planning to put it into a savings account at 5½ percent or a corporate bond at 9 percent, and you are in a 43 percent bracket, you can see from the tax equivalents you would receive more keepable income from municipal bonds. As you will note, you would have to receive an income of 10.53 percent to equate a 6 percent tax-exempt income in a 43 percent bracket; and in a 54 percent bracket, you would need to receive a 13.4 percent yield to be equivalent to 6 percent tax exempt. I should warn you if you are considering borrowing money and you own or are planning to buy municipal bonds, the interest you pay on money borrowed to make investments which pay you tax-free income is not deductible. If your investment in tax exempts is substantial (more than 2 percent of your portfolio), the IRS may examine all your investments to determine whether there is "sufficient direct relationship" between your other borrowing and your investment in tax exempts.

CORPORATE BONDS

Another way you can lend your money is through the purchase of corporate bonds. Corporate bonds (or notes) can be broken down into a number of categories depending on the type of corporation issuing the bond. But from your point of view, there are essentially only two types: straight bonds (or debentures) and convertible bonds. Straight corporate bonds, like most government and municipal bonds, pay semiannual interest to maturity, whereupon you receive the principal amount. Convertible bonds offer one additional feature—they can be exchanged, at any time you wish, for a fixed number of shares of the issuing company's common stock. Therefore, convertibles have dual characteristics of fixed-income securities (like any other bonds) and equity securities that may appreciate (or depreciate) in accordance with the stock price movement of the company's common stock. If a convertible bond trades at a price above that which it would as a straight bond for the same company, maturity, etc., it is usually thought of as an equity security rather than as a bond.

Corporate bonds are usually sold in minimum amounts of $1000, although there are some $500 bonds. The yield is subject to the current level of interest rates, the maturity, and the credit standing of the issuer. Because no corporation is considered to be as credit-worthy as the federal government, corporate bonds generally pay a slightly higher return (usually ½ percent to 2 percent higher) than comparable government bonds. Obviously, even when comparing one corporation to another, some are riskier and therefore have to pay more to borrow money.

Bonds are issued in registered form "interest mailed to holder" or in bearer form with coupons to be clipped and mailed to a paying agent through the bearer's bank. Many bonds permit the issuing corporation to redeem them early, usually for a price slightly higher than the maturity value. This call privilege gives the borrower an element of protection, in that he can call in his bonds and issue new ones at a lower interest rate if rates have declined since the time the original bonds were issued. Actually, only bonds trading at a premium over par (indicating that interest yields are now lower than they were at time of issue) are liable to be called. Like other bonds, corporates can be sold prior to maturity at prevailing market rates.

Because bonds represent a fixed stream of income, their market value will fall when the general interest rate rises, and their market value will rise when the interest falls.

Suffice it to say that, although most bonds are issued at par of $1000 and may sell there or at a premium or discount on the day they are issued and will be redeemed at par on the day of maturity, their market value wanders considerably during the interim. Because the cost of money has risen so dramatically since the mid-1960s, the market values of virtually all bonds issued prior to that time have declined to well below their $1000 face values. This kind of market risk in the bond market is very real and exists regardless of the credit-worthiness of the borrower.

Bond interest rates fluctuate for a number of reasons. Probably chief among them during the past few years has been price inflation and expectations of future inflation. As inflation rates increase, consumers and businesses are willing to increase their borrowing to buy at today's lower prices, and individuals become less willing to save at existing interest rate levels. Therefore, interest rates rise to compensate the saver for the expected erosion in the purchasing power of the dollar and to wipe out the advantage to the borrower of speeding up his purchases.

Another key factor has been the policy of the Federal Reserve to control the supply of money—increasing and decreasing it in an effort either to stimulate or decelerate the economy or to obtain money at a lower rate, as we've discussed. In the short run, an acceleration in the rate of growth of the money supply will produce lower interest rates, but over time it has promoted a higher rate of inflation that has resulted in higher interest rates.

Fluctuation of economic activity also has influenced interest rates. The demand for credit rises as economic activity picks up, and therefore interest rates tend to rise; the demand for credit falls as economic activity slows, and this pushes interest rates down.

Bond Ratings

Like municipal bonds, Moody's and Standard & Poor's rate corporate bonds. Their ratings indicate their opinion of the company's ability to meet its principal and interest payments under adverse economic conditions. Two measures of this ability are the amount by which earnings exceed interest payments over a period of years and the amount of stock equity in a corporation in relation to borrowed funds.

If these rating services rate a bond in one of the top four categories, the bond is considered to be of investment-grade quality. To merit the top rating the speculative element is very low. By the fifth rating, it is significant. By the seventh, it predominates.

Corporate Bond Funds

If you have limited funds, it will be difficult for you to buy and sell small quantities of bonds because of the spread between "bid" and "asked" prices in these small purchases. It is also difficult to diversify adequately. For this reason, if you are considering investing in bonds, you may want to use professionally managed corporate bond funds. They offer a savings of the time and talent required to judge the merits of individual issues, their ratings, their maturities, coupon rates, a determination of how much to invest in each issue, the clipping of coupons (it has always sounded like fun, but it's really quite a nuisance), watching for called bonds, safekeeping securities, and year-end accounting.

The specialists managing the fund select the bonds to obtain a special combination of yield, proper diversification, marketability, suitability, and call protection. They also follow the financial progress of all the issues in the fund. You pay an initial sales charge, which is included in the offering price, plus a management fee of around ½ percent annually of the net asset value on the fund.

Current market prices are published daily, and you can redeem your shares whenever you desire.

I find the average person does not realize that when national interest rates go up, bond prices go down. Why would anyone pay you par for a bond paying 8 percent when they can buy one paying 10? They won't, so you must discount your bond until it pays 10 percent.

DISCOUNT BONDS

There are times, such as in the mid-1970s, when low-rated bonds, commonly called "junk bonds," reached yields as high as 14 to 16 percent.

The cut in late 1978 in the capital gains tax rate attracted the interest of some investors to discount bonds. These bonds have a tax advantage over other bonds, since part of their yield comes from built-in capital gains, which will be taxed at the lower capital gains rate.

These are bonds that came out years ago at much lower rates than we have today. In order to compete in today's marketplace, they must sell for less than their $1000 face value. Profits on these bonds come from two sources:

1. The low annual interest these old bonds yield

2. The difference between the price you pay for the bond and the $1000 you will receive when you redeem it at maturity.

For example, in 1956, Southern California Edison issued 25-year AA bonds at 3⅝ percent interest (about $36.25 a year, per bond). One bond might sell today for $885, a $115 discount from its $1000 face value. If you were to buy it, you would still get only $36.25 a year in interest, a meager 4 percent current return on an $885 investment. But two years from now when you cash the bond in for $1000, you'll realize a $115 capital gain. That's the equivalent of another 5.5 percent a year on your investment, raising the total yield—interest plus capital gain—to 9.5 percent.

New AA bonds due in 1985 may have slightly higher current yields. But discount bonds still come out ahead after tax. If you are in the 40 percent income-tax bracket, for example, net return from new bonds may be 6½ percent; from discount bonds, 9 percent.

Discount bonds won't make you rich. Their yields are reliable but unexciting, and their current interest payments may be low. Whenever inflation runs faster than the rate you are receiving, you are losing purchasing power. But the very predictability of a discount bond's profit at maturity could have some uses in financial planning.

For example, if you have a capital loss that you have been carrying forward year after year, you may want to buy some discount bonds a year or two before maturity. When they mature, you'll reap the capital gains and then shelter it by charging it against the capital losses you already have on your books.

Or let's assume that you are in the 50 percent tax bracket or above. You could buy discount bonds maturing in a couple of years and buy them on margin, paying 35 percent of the price yourself and borrowing the rest from your broker. The net interest cost is deductible from income, hence reducing your taxes; all the profit comes as capital gains, deferred until maturity, and because you put up only a small amount of your own money, the built-in capital gain gives you a higher return on your investment. The 3⅝ Southern California Edison bought this way would yield about 7.7 percent after federal taxes, compared with less than 6.5 percent from discounted tax-free municipal bonds.

I have two suggestions if you take this approach. Buy bonds listed on an exchange; they're easier to sell than unlisted bonds if you want to get out before maturity. Also, if you own a lot of tax-free municipals, again check with your accountant before buying bonds on margin; borrowing money for investment may endanger their tax-free status.

Another approach to discount bonds would pertain if you want to try to speculate that long-term interest rates will drop. Discount bond prices usually rise faster than bond prices in general. This activity should attract investors who are more interested in capital gains than in modest, predictable yields, which could increase the market price of your bonds. However, when interest rates are declining, the stock market may be a better speculation than discount bonds.

BONDS AND INFLATION

Bonds give us one of the clearest examples of how inflation creates and destroys wealth. Let's take the example of a AAA-rated American Telephone and Telegraph bond—still highly recommended for widows and orphans by some fiduciaries who ignore reality—that was issued in

1946 at par ($1000) with a rate of 2⅝ percent, maturing in 1986. True to their promise, AT&T has never missed paying $26.25 annually on this bond and in 1986 it will faithfully pay the owner $1000. However, if the widow needs her funds today, its market price is only $632.

What happened? Why did the AT&T bonds which were recommended as "prudent" investments by banks and trust companies turn out so dismally? AT&T was not trying to take advantage of anyone. They didn't force investors to buy 2⅝ percent bonds. They themselves didn't realize what a bonanza they would reap. The real reason that the widows were hurt and AT&T was helped was that inflation greatly accelerated, bringing disastrous results to the bondholder.

American Telephone and Telegraph bonds are rated AAA, the highest-quality rating, yet they did drop tremendously in value. However, their drop was minor in comparison to bonds with lower ratings and, was therefore considered riskier. Two examples of these lower rated bonds are:

1. Bonds issued by Pan American World Airways, at 4½ percent, with maturity in 1986, dropped from a par of $1000 to $570.

2. Bonds issued by Eastern Airlines, at 5 percent, with maturity in 1992, dropped from a $1000 par to $460.

Inflation transfers wealth from the lender to the borrower. The bondholder is hurt in three ways. He is receiving less in terms of interest than he could on newly issued securities. Also, since the market value of the bond has fallen, he has suffered a decline in wealth. When he receives back his principal, his purchasing power will be less.

Under the Poor Richard rules of yesteryears, bonds were investment vehicles that you put at the bottom of your safe-deposit box, whose coupons you clipped semiannually, and which you redeemed on redemption date. Although not exciting, these rules were fine when prices were stable.

History shows that bonds have been a bad buy even if your investment horizons are relatively short. Periods when inflation has accelerated have lasted longer than periods in which inflation rates have decelerated.

During the 1974 market decline, there developed a tremendous interest in bonds and bond funds paying around 9 percent. A large number of both were placed with investors at the investor's insistence. Table 11–1 shows the long-term effect that inflation can have on these bond yields even if a miracle could be wrought and we could return to the 5.2 percent inflation rate that prevailed back in 1974.

Table 11–1 illustrates the loss of purchasing power and effective yield of a $10,000 investment in a corporate bond with a yield of 9 percent if that yield is adjusted for an annual inflation rate of 7.4 per-

TABLE 11–1.   EFFECT OF A 5.2% INFLATION ON
YOUR PURCHASING POWER

Number of Years	Annual Dividend	Loss of Purchasing Power (%)	Adjusted Purchasing Power of Dividend	Effective Yield
5	$900	30%	$630	6.3%
10	900	51%	441	4.4%
15	900	66%	308	3.1%
20	900	76%	216	2.2%
25	900	83%	151	1.5%

cent. If I adjusted these figures to reflect the inflation rate of the eighties, the results would be even more startling. If it were possible to have a "floating" or "self-adjusting" yield based on a 7.4 percent annual rate of inflation, what yield would you need to maintain your purchasing power, based on a beginning yield of 9 percent with 7.4 percent annual inflation rate over 25 years (see Table 11–2)?

TABLE 11–2.   PERCENTAGE YIELD NEEDED TO
MAINTAIN PURCHASING POWER

Number of Years	% Increase in Cost of Living	% Yield Needed to Maintain Purchasing Power
5	43%	12.9%
10	104%	18.4%
15	192%	26.3%
20	317%	37.5%
25	496%	53.6%

For several years, we have cautioned against buying corporate bonds because we felt interest rates would escalate, pushing down bond prices. A large life insurance holding company in Houston sold the largest bond mutual fund offering that had ever been made right in the middle of the time we were expressing this opinion. We did not sell any of the fund and, of course, missed receiving sizable commissions. However, we felt we could not in good conscience encourage the purchase of bonds at a time when interest rates were about to soar. I know our clients are grateful they missed the disastrous debacle that has occurred in the bond market since that date. Had they invested, they would have suffered a 35 percent loss. In just six weeks, a 20 percent skid occurred.

CORPORATE BONDS IN A RETIREMENT PORTFOLIO?

Almost daily I see one of the question-and-answer type financial advice columns in the newspaper advising a couple who are reaching retirement age to buy "high quality corporate bonds." Why, oh why? They may live another fifteen to thirty years. Look at Table 11–3 and see what has happened in the last thirty-six years. You won't have a chance against inflation if you succumb to this advice.

TABLE 11–3. STANDARD AND POOR'S
HIGH-GRADE CORPORATE BONDS

1970–79	−27%
1969–78	−27%
1968–77	−23%
1967–76	−25%
1966–75	−38%
1965–74	−41%
1964–73	−34%
1963–72	−32%
1962–71	−29%
1961–70	−32%
1960–69	−33%
1959–68	−27%
1958–67	−28%
1957–66	−19%
1956–65	−19%
1955–64	−18%
1954–63	−16%
1953–62	−15%
1952–61	−17%
1951–60	−22%
1950–59	−25%
1949–58	−17%
1948–57	−11%
1947–56	−16%
1946–55	− 8%
1945–54	− 2%
Average of 26 periods	23%

Source: Johnson's Charts, Inc.—bond interest not included.

Fixed-income securities may be safe short-term investments and risky long-term investments. In all of the twenty-six ten-year periods from 1945 through 1979, there was not one period when the Standard and Poor's rated composite of high-grade corporate bonds did not show a loss. These losses ranged from 2 percent to 38 percent.

Figure 11–3 gives you a visual picture of bond yields and interest rates from 1968–78.

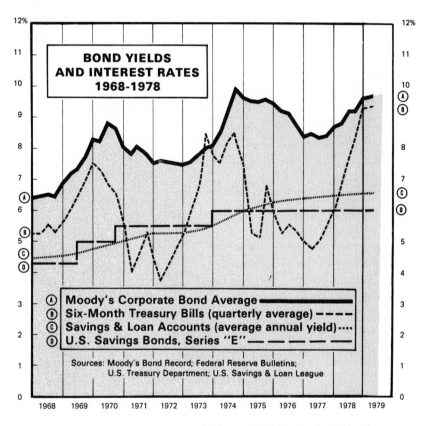

The chart records the yields of (A) Moody's Corporate Bond Average as compared to interest earned on (B) U.S. six-month Treasury Bills and (D) U.S. Savings Bonds "E", and to the average yield paid on (C) Savings and Loan accounts.

Figure 11–3.

CASH SURRENDER VALUE

Another way that many families lend money, probably without realizing it, is by banking with life insurance companies by buying protection that contains a savings program. Of all the ways that you can "lend" money, this is perhaps the least rewarding. The policy does indicate earnings of 2½ percent to 3½ percent on the cash reserve, but, if the policyholder dies, his family receives only the face amount, not the face amount plus the cash reserves. I counsel with many who are under the impression that the face amount plus their "savings account" goes to their beneficiary. The estate planner Norman F. Dacey has published a pamphlet entitled "To the Great Northern Insurance Company I Bequeath the Cash Value of All My Life Insurance Policies." It makes provocative reading. In Chapter 13, "Life Insurance—the Great National Dilemma," you will find the results of a study made by the Federal Trade Commission regarding the rates of return on whole life policies held for various periods of time. For policies held ten years, they found the rates were a minus 9 percent to a minus 19 percent; for twenty years, a minus 4 percent to a plus 2 percent; and for over twenty years, 2 percent to 4.5 percent, with the average for all policies between 1 and 2 percent.

ANNUITIES

Annuities are another way some have chosen to save for the future. What about annuities? Should you take the beautiful full-page color ads in your weekly magazines seriously and "invest" in an annuity for your happy golden years?

The best answer to this question can be found by looking at the past advertisements of insurance companies trying to entice you to buy an annuity. Go to your local library and request that they bring to you their *Life* magazines. You might start with the February 1, 1943, issue. There you will find a half-page ad with a bold headline that reads, "$150 a Month as Long as You Live." The familiar logo at the bottom reads "_____ Mutual Retirement Income Plan Guarantees Your Future." The fine print does not say how much you would need to invest to retire at 60 with $150 per month, but it does hint that the smiling couple in the picture began at age 40, twenty years previous to the time it showed them in happy retirement. Now ask the librarian for the January 16, 1950, issue of *Life*. It also carried an ad by the same company headlined "How We Retired with $200 a Month." The ad shows another mature, well-dressed couple. There is a sandy beach with waving palm trees in the background. This one also does not mention the amount of investment that they would have had to make over that period of time. The same logo appears, however: "_____ Mutual Retirement Income Plan Guarantees Your Future."

Now ask for the January 15, 1951, issue of *Life*. It carried a picture identical to the January 16, 1950, ad and the same script, except the headline had been changed to "How We Retired with $250 a Month." Yes, it had the same guarantee at the bottom. The January 23, 1956, *Life* magazine ran another ad by the same insurance company. This headline read "How a Man of 35 Can Retire at 55 with $300 a Month." This time they did not even bother to change the picture of the smiling, delighted couple. The inflation train continues to run faster and faster, but the ad department seems to be able to keep up by increasing the ante each time.

"Retire on $150 a Month" sounded pretty good back then, so this dollar figure was commonly used in offering fixed-dollar retirement plans. But the story kept changing. The changes in these figures provide unique evidence that there is no such thing as a "guaranteed, riskless" way to achieve financial independence.

Have you ever wondered why the annuity ads often show a man fishing? Do you think it's because he wants to eat?

Single-Premium Deferred Annuities

Single-premium deferred annuities are a different breed entirely from the old annuity contracts, and they can play an important part in your "guaranteed" dollar investment program. Income is accrued to your account tax-deferred. For example, if you invest $10,000 in a single-premium deferred annuity that is earning 9 percent, at the end of a year your account will be $10,900. Until you withdraw the $900 no tax is due, and it compounds tax-sheltered.

If you want some of your funds guaranteed and do not want the income from these funds to be taxed currently, you may want to consider a single-premium deferred annuity. It offers:

1. Guaranteed principal.

2. Interest guarantees.

3. Tax deferral.

4. Special tax treatment at retirement if annuitized. (I do not recommend annuitizing.)

5. Tax-free exchange from one custodian to another.

6. No tax is payable until the withdrawals equal the full original investment.

7. Probate, with its publicity, delays, and costs, are avoided with proceeds being paid to the beneficiary.

Some charge an acquisition fee with no charge for early withdrawals. Other do not charge an acquisition fee, but if you withdraw more than 6 percent in any one year during the first five years, they charge you a percentage on the amount. Table 11–4 gives the after-tax results you would have received in a 30 percent and in a 50 percent bracket if you had placed $10,000 in a savings and loan at 8 percent interest, as compared with having placed $10,000 in a single-premium deferred annuity at 8 percent with interest accumulating without current taxes. Rates on a single-premium deferred annuity are available that guarantee 12.5 percent through December 31, 1981, and they anticipate 11¼ percent until 1986. (It will, however, be taxed on withdrawal at your then-current rate.)

TABLE 11–4. HYPOTHETICAL EXAMPLES OF $10,000 ACCOUNTS

NO. OF YEARS	$10,000 At 8% * Interest (Interest taxed as accrued)		$10,000 Single Premium Fixed Annuity (Interest accumulated without current tax)	Hidden Cost of Taxes	
	30% TAX BRACKET	50% TAX BRACKET	@ 8% *	30%	50%
5	$13,131	$12,166	$ 14,693	$ 1,562	$ 2,527
10	17,244	14,802	21,589	4,345	6,787
15	22,644	18,009	31,721	9,077	13,712
20	29,735	21,911	46,609	16,874	24,698
25	39,047	26,658	68,484	29,437	41,826
30	51,276	32,433	100,626	49,350	68,193
35	67,334	39,460	147,853	80,519	108,393
40	88,421	48,009	217,245	128,818	169,236

* Assume level 8 percent interest throughout the savings period.

Another illustration that may be of interest to you is tabulated in Table 11–5. You could have placed $20,000 in a single-premium deferred annuity, let it compound at 8 percent for ten years, and then started withdrawing $2000 per year for ten years (10 percent on your original investment). This $2000 per year is not taxed, because it is a part of the original $20,000 after-tax dollars you invested. At the end of this second ten years, after you have withdrawn $20,000, you would still have $64,246. Any additional withdrawal would be taxable, but you had not been burdened with taxes for twenty years.

If you want funds quarterly, purchase four different contracts for

TABLE 11–5. ILLUSTRATION OF AN ASSUMED
$20,000 SINGLE PREMIUM DEFERRED ANNUITY INVESTMENT
@ 8%* INTEREST FOR 20 YEARS

End of Year	Value at End of Yr.	Withdrawal at End of Year	Net Amount
1	$21,600		
2	23,328		
3	25,194		
4	27,209		
5	29,385		
6	31,737		
7	34,276		
8	37,018		
9	39,980		
10	43,178		
11	46,632	$2,000	$44,632
12	48,203	2,000	46,203
13	49,899	2,000	47,899
14	51,731	2,000	49,731
15	53,710	2,000	51,710
16	55,846	2,000	53,846
17	58,846	2,000	56,154
18	60,647	2,000	58,647
19	63,338	2,000	61,338
20	66,246	2,000	64,246

* Assume level 8 percent interest throughout the life of the contract. Currently in excess of 10 percent.

the same amounts and schedule a withdrawal from each once a year, timed so you will have quarterly checks.

If you feel that you must have your funds guaranteed, are in a tax bracket of 25 percent or above, and do not plan to disturb the funds for a few years, then you may want to consider a fixed deferred annuity. Rates the past few years have ranged between 8 and 12½ percent, with your funds compounded tax-deferred until withdrawal.

In Table 18 in the Appendix you will find an accumulation program using a $100,000 single-premium annuity showing the minimum guaranteed interest rates and the current interest rate values. You will note that $100,000 has grown to $646,757 in twenty years, tax deferred, at the current interest rate. Table 19 in the Appendix is an example of a $100,000 single premium annuity with a once-a-year 6 percent withdrawal of $6000. Withdrawals were made for the next sixteen years without tax, total withdrawals at the end of twenty years were $120,000 with a remaining value of $303,107. Withdrawals plus end value totals $423,107.

POOLS OF MONEY OR POCKETS OF MONEY

If you are considering lending your money to an insurance company through a single-premium deferred annuity, you will need to determine which type of investment program the company has and which will best fit your needs.

Some companies pool all their monies together. If you choose this type, your interest will fluctuate with the going rates. There is another type that puts your money in pockets of investments—meaning all the money received in a particular period of time is invested in a portfolio and stays invested in that pocket. During times of high interest rates, you can lock in these high rates if you choose this type of account. For example, short-term interest rates have fluctuated rather wildly since 1973, as you will note from Figure 11–4. If you had used a "pocket of money" annuity between September 1, 1974, and January 31, 1975, you would have been receiving 10 percent all along, even though rates plunged during that period. If you had been in a pooled account, your rates would have fluctuated with the going rates.

If you should decide to use a single-premium annuity, then you should decide if these are rates you want to lock in. If you do decide

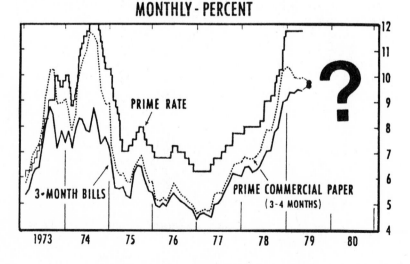

Figure 11–4. Short-Term Interest Rates

on the "pocket" approach and rates go up, you'll be sorry. If rates go down, you'll be glad you did. Since my crystal ball gets a bit hazy, I leave it up to you to decide.

CREDIT UNIONS

I find many of my clients who work for corporations, the city, or our public schools use their credit union for a portion of their savings dollar. You may have a credit union available to you. It can be extremely handy for making deposits. In fact, your company may offer the service of depositing the amount you designate directly into your account. The credit union also provides a handy way to borrow.

I find, however, that many mistakenly think that they offer a less expensive way to borrow. This often is not true. Many credit unions charge 1 percent of the unpaid monthly balance, which is 12 percent per annum. Others charge ¾ percent; this amounts to 9 percent. If you have acceptable collateral, you may be able to borrow at a lower cost from your banker. Check both sources of funds before you borrow.

MORTGAGES

Another way to lend money is to carry the mortgage balance on a home or other real estate you are selling. Many consider this quite an acceptable way to lend money. On the whole, I would not agree. The rates are frozen throughout the life of the mortgage, and the mortgage is a nonliquid instrument except when sold at a considerable discount. As inflation continues its upward thrust, your wealth will be transferred to the person who bought your real estate, and you will have lost the battle with inflation.

If you are selling a piece of property and are convinced that the only way you can get the extra few thousands you desire for your property is to take a second lien for that amount, go ahead and do so. If you collect on the loan, fine. If you do not, don't worry, for you could not have sold it for the full amount you desired anyway. I have done this when selling my home on two occasions and have received payment on both second liens ahead of schedule and for the full amount.

HISTORIC RATES OF RETURN

The rate of return that you will receive by "lending" your dollars through any of the above methods will vary with economic conditions.

Table 11–6 shows yields on various fixed-income instruments over the past 47 years.

TABLE 11–6. AVERAGE ANNUAL YIELD ON SELECTED TYPES OF INVESTMENTS, 1930–1977

Year	Savings Accounts in Savings Associations	Time & Savings Deposits in Commercial Banks	United States Government Bonds	Corporate (aaa) Bonds
1930	5.3%	3.9%	3.3%	4.6%
1931	5.1	3.8	3.3	4.6
1932	4.1	3.4	3.7	5.0
1933	3.4	3.4	3.3	4.5
1934	3.5	3.0	3.1	4.0
1935	3.1	2.6	2.8	3.6
1936	3.2	2.0	2.6	3.2
1937	3.5	1.8	2.7	3.3
1938	3.5	1.7	2.6	3.2
1939	3.4	1.6	2.4	3.0
1940	3.3	1.3	2.2	2.8
1941	3.1	1.3	2.0	2.8
1942	3.0	1.1	2.5	2.8
1943	2.9	0.9	2.5	2.7
1944	2.8	0.9	2.5	2.7
1945	2.5	0.8	2.4	2.6
1946	2.2	0.8	2.2	2.5
1947	2.3	0.9	2.2	2.6
1948	2.3	0.9	2.4	2.8
1949	2.4	0.9	2.3	2.7
1950	2.5	0.9	2.3	2.6
1951	2.6	1.1	2.6	2.9
1952	2.7	1.2	2.7	3.0
1953	2.8	1.2	2.9	3.2
1954	2.9	1.3	2.6	2.9
1955	2.9	1.4	2.8	3.1
1956	3.0	1.6	3.1	3.4
1957	3.3	2.1	3.5	3.9
1958	3.38	2.21	3.43	3.79
1959	3.53	2.36	4.07	4.38

TABLE 11–6. (*Continued*)

Year	Savings Accounts in Savings Associations	Time & Savings Deposits in Commercial Banks	United States Government Bonds	Corporate (aaa) Bonds
1960	3.86	2.56	4.01	4.41
1961	3.90	2.71	3.90	4.35
1962	4.08	3.18	3.95	4.33
1963	4.17	3.31	4.00	4.26
1964	4.19	3.42	4.15	4.40
1965	4.23	3.69	4.21	4.49
1966	4.45	4.04	4.66	5.13
1967	4.67	4.24	4.85	5.51
1968	4.68	4.48	5.25	6.18
1969	4.80	4.87	6.10	7.03
1970	5.06	4.95	6.59	8.04
1971	5.33	4.78	5.74	7.39
1972	5.40	4.65	5.63	7.21
1973	5.55	5.71	6.30	7.44
1974	5.98	6.93	6.99	8.57
1975	6.22	5.90	6.98	8.83
1976	5.25	5.00	6.98	8.01
1977	5.25	5.00	6.98	8.08
1978	5.25	10.00	9.95	9.45
1979	5.25	16.00	13.02	13.00

Sources: Federal Home Loan Bank Board; United States Savings and Loan League; National Association of Mutual Savings Banks; Federal Reserve Board; Federal Deposit Insurance Corporation; Moody's Investors Service.

MONEY MARKET FUNDS

You may be asking where is the best place to position funds that you desire to hold as cash reserves, to have available when the right investment comes along, or to pay taxes. In my opinion, the best way is to establish one or more accounts with money market funds offered by the mutual fund companies.

As mentioned earlier, money market funds came into existence when the Federal Reserve greatly diminished the money supply, pushing up interest rates in the early seventies. Those who had $100,000 or more could obtain yields of 12 percent and above from savings institutions, but those who did not were prevented from obtaining these rates by federal regulation.

Consequently, a number of the mutual fund managements offered the smaller investor a way he could obtain the rate of a million-dollar certificate of deposit by pooling his funds with others.

When you use these money pools, you receive the highest interest available on high-quality money market instruments such as large certificates of deposit of major national commercial banks and government agencies. Many of these instruments that pay higher yields are available only in such large denominations that you could not obtain them on your own.

You may use the fund as an interest-bearing checking account (minimum check $500), and if it is offered by a family of mutual funds, you can quickly go from a liquid position to an equity position in one of their stock or bond funds and return without a commission when the exchange is made.

There is no commission to place funds into the money market fund and no commission to take it out and it compounds daily. You will be poised daily to receive the higher interest rates being paid for million-dollar certificates while being able to write a check on the account and collect interest while it is clearing. In my opinion money market funds eliminate the need for long-term certificates of deposit, because here you have liquidity without a penalty for early withdrawal, have check-writing privileges, and receive the going interest rate. During periods when the Federal Reserve is following an easy-money policy, your rate will drop as the large short-term certificates drop, but when money is tight you may obtain the same rate as a millionaire.

SHOULD YOU EVER BORROW MONEY?

Should you ever consider reversing the "lending" process and becoming instead the recipient? Of course you should, if you can put the money to work so that your after-tax cost is less than the amount you will earn on the investment you made with the loan. Never borrow for essentials or luxuries. Borrow only money to invest or to leave in place an investment you already have that is doing a good job for you.

In fact, in these days of high taxes it is difficult to accumulate a large estate without borrowing money. The great financier Bernard Baruch, when asked how he made his fortune, replied, "O.P.M.—other people's money." Another well-known real estate tycoon said the most important factor in his real estate acquisitions was "terms, terms, terms." Terms in real estate purchases usually mean little or no down payment and a big, big mortgage—borrowing from those who want "guarantees" and are willing to lend.

Where, when, and how should you borrow money?

If you have collateral in the form of publicly traded stocks, your least expensive source for loans in normal times will usually be your own bank. You should go to the collateral loan department (never to the consumer loan department unless you lack collateral).

Assume that you want to buy an automobile. You own 100 shares of an excellent stock for which you paid $50 a share, and it is now trading at $100 with excellent growth potential for the future. Why kill the goose that is laying the golden egg, and why realize a $5000 capital gain, 40 percent of which will be taxable.

Take your stock to your banker and pledge it as collateral. You will be required to leave the stock certificate with him and sign a stock power that allows him to sell the stock and keep the amount you owe to him if you do not repay or renew the loan the day it becomes due.

Collateral loans are usually made for 90 days or 180 days. You may pay on the principal in the interim, but you are not required to do so. On the date the loan becomes due you will be required to send your banker a check for the interest, and you may pay all or part of the loan or send him letter requesting that he renew the loan. Usually this will be acceptable to your banker, for banks must lend money to earn a profit. They have already made a credit check on you and found you acceptable.

Sometimes you'll get a rookie loan officer who learned at banking school that borrowers should be reducing their principal periodically. However, after a little discussion with him as to how banks make their profit, he usually will be quite agreeable to renewing your note.

Always go boldly to borrow money—not with head bowed in an apologetic manner. If your banker had a house to rent and you were considering renting one, in what posture would you go to him? In this instance you have come to do him the "favor" of renting his money so that he can make a profit.

Your banker is always happy to rent you money if you can prove you don't need it. What is your proof that you really don't need it? Your stock certificate, of course, for you obviously could sell the stock and have the money.

Another reason for borrowing on your stock rather than cashing it in is that you are more likely to repay the bank than yourself. For example, you want to buy an automobile, but you don't have that amount in savings. Make a collateral loan to pay for the auto. Then when you finish paying the bank the loan, you will have your auto and your stock.

Build up your collateral and you'll always have the wherewithal for borrowing money that you can put to work. You may want to consider, if you have the temperament for it, putting your dollars to work 1 and 7/10 times—since 70 percent is what your banker will usually loan you if you have publicly held stock for collateral.

Interest Deductible

Interest is deductible on your income tax return with certain limitations under the Tax Reform Act of 1976. Assume you borrow at 10 percent and are in the 30 percent tax bracket; your net cost after taxes will be 7 percent. If you are in the 50 percent bracket, net cost is only 5 percent. Can you invest this money so that your after-tax return will be greater than your after-tax cost? If so, rent the money. If not, your answer is obvious.

Servicing the Loan

You will need sufficient funds or income to pay your interest on your loan when due. There are some investments that have a high after-tax yield that you can use to service your loan while you are enjoying equity buildup and appreciation.

Borrowing Against Cash Value of an Insurance Policy

There are many who consider this a low-cost source of loans. In my opinion, the only time you should borrow on your cash surrender value is when your health is so poor that you cannot pass a physical for a new policy. If you can pass a physical and obtain pure protection at a lower cost, do so. When you have the new coverage, redeem the old policy. You will then have the cash you need without paying the insurance company to borrow "your own" money.

If your health is such that you cannot pass a physical, borrow the money out each year from your policy and put it to work advantageously. Let's assume that you can borrow the cash surrender value for 5½ percent. Technically, at the same time, they claim to be building cash reserves at 2½ percent. This is only a 3 percent spread. In addition, the interest can be deductible, thereby lowering your after-tax cost.

Savings Accounts as Collateral

I often find that a person I'm counseling proudly tells me he has found an inexpensive source for a loan by pledging his savings account as collateral. If you need funds and you have them in a savings account, go ahead and draw them out and use them. They are probably paying you 2 percent less than they are charging you; therefore you are 2 percent in the hole by borrowing your own money.

An exception to this would be if you are very near a dividend date. For example, assume that you have a one-year $10,000 certificate of deposit with a rate of 7½ percent that matures December 31. You need funds on November 1. Use your certificate of deposit for collateral. You'll pay them interest at 9½ for two months, but they'll pay you interest at 7½ for 12 months; $10,000 at 7½ for 12 months equals $750. $10,000 at 9½ percent equals $950 ÷ 12 months = $79.17 × 2 months equals $158.33. Therefore, you still salvage $591.67 of your interest and have the funds you need. This $158.33 is deductible on your income tax. (The $750 is taxable also.)

If your certificate of deposit or savings account is at a bank, you can usually borrow 100 percent. If it is in a savings and loan, they will usually loan 90 percent.

SUMMARY

Should you ever put your dollars in a "loaned" position? Yes, if you need a temporary place for your investment dollars or when interest rates reach astronomical heights. But, you should rarely do so on a long-term basis. As you can see from Table 11–3, over the past ten years you would have suffered a loss if you had held bonds and other fixed-dollar instruments for long periods of time. Interest rates have risen, and inflation has taken its toll. You should use fixed-income instruments when it is to your advantage to be out of equities, but do not complacently overstay.

On the other hand, should you ever do the reverse and borrow money? The answer is yes, if your return is greater than your after-tax cost and if you can sell your investment for more than you owe. Always be solvent: that means you own more than you owe.

APPLICATION

1. How much "patting money" do you need for peace of mind?
2. Is the Federal Reserve expanding or shrinking the money supply at this time?

3. What is a good source for this information?
4. How can you best put this knowledge to use?
5. Where should your cash reserve be placed?
6. What is the rate paid on money market funds today?
7. Can you borrow money and still have peace of mind?
8. What collateral do you have?
9. What steps do you plan to take to build up your collateral?

12

AVOIDING THE ONE-WAY TRIP TO WASHINGTON

Keeping your hard-earned dollars from taking a one-way trip to Washington is worthy of your most dedicated attention. Few other endeavors will add more to your net worth. The only money you'll ever have for investing and spending is what the government lets you keep. I am absolutely dedicated to helping my clients avoid taxes. I believe it is much better stewardship of money to invest these dollars in housing, energy, food, strategic metals, entertainment, and transportation than it is to send them through a wasteful bureaucracy with the hope that some day some of the money may filter back into these areas of great need.

Why pay the IRS money you are allowed to keep? You do have a choice as to whether you pay a small or a large amount of income taxes. But you must learn the rules each year and abide by them strictly. You will find them always changing, often contradictory, rarely simple, difficult to understand, and challenging to apply. Winning the money and tax game—and win you must—will require maximum dedication on your and your financial planner's part, a great amount of knowledge aggressively applied, agility, and constant vigilance. The IRS's job is to thwart your every effort. Tax reduction is their enemy—they refer to deductions as "costing" the Treasury.

I've heard it said that "anytime Congress is in session your money is in jeopardy." Perhaps it could be added that "anytime the IRS is in session your money is in double jeopardy."

Perhaps you have previously shied away from tax-advantaged investments, considering them vaguely immoral. If so, you may be confusing tax evasion with tax avoidance. Tax avoidance is using your intelligence. Tax evasion is illegal and severely punishable. But tax avoidance is not only legal, it is also quite proper.

Congress has enacted laws periodically to encourage the shift of funds from taxable sectors of our economy to areas of public need or good by creating tax-free, tax-sheltered, or tax-deferred investments.

There are those who delight in referring to these incentives as loop-holes, inferring that Congress is not intelligent enough to design a proper tax bill. They fail to recognize that without the incentive of potential gain, no funds would be risked in areas where money is much needed for the welfare of our citizens.

Judge Learned Hand, the famous New York State jurist said:

> Anyone may so arrange his affairs that his taxes shall be as low as possible: He is not bound to choose that pattern which best pays the Treasury. Everyone does it, rich and poor alike, and all do right; for nobody owes any public duty to pay more than the law demands.

Senator Harrison of Mississippi, former Chairman of the Senate Finance Committee, expressed the matter in this way: "There's nothing that says a man has to take a toll bridge across a river when there is a free bridge nearby."

Unfortunately, over the years our tax laws have become so complicated that it will take a great deal of study to avail yourself of some of their benefits. Jerome Kurtz, formerly a Philadelphia lawyer and now the Commissioner of the Internal Revenue, told Congress, "Our existing estate and gift tax system could well be characterized as a government levy on poor advice."

So that you will not suffer any more than is absolutely necessary from this government levy, let's look at some of the ways you can legitimately use to turn your tax liabilities into potential net worth. One of the first games you must learn to play is the "D.C. Game." I like to think of tax reduction as a game that I must win, because it makes the endeavor less grim, more fun, and often profitable. Even if it is not profitable, I'll at least have had the satisfaction of knowing I tried.

THE D.C. GAME

The tragedy of your paying a dollar in taxes is that not only do you lose that dollar, but you also lose what that dollar would earn for you if you were allowed to keep it. It is therefore imperative that you learn to play what I call the "D.C. Game." This means that you'll either send your money on that one-way trip to Washington D.C., or you'll learn to Defer and Convert.

Technically, the IRS never forgives a tax, but our tax laws do allow you to defer a tax until a later date and, if you've chosen certain investments, perhaps convert from ordinary income into a capital gains, which can reduce the taxable portion to 40 percent in most instances.

You may be tempted to say, "If I'm going to pay the tax some day, why don't I just pay it now and that way I won't have to worry about it in the future?" The answer to your question is a resounding one—INFLATION! Every year you postpone paying a tax you not only continue to receive the earnings on that money, but when and if

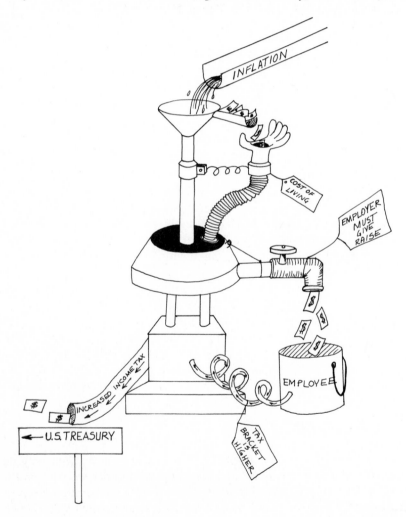

you ever do pay the tax, you can pay it with cheaper and cheaper dollars for which you have worked fewer hours. If you have $1 of taxable income today in a 40 percent bracket, you lose 40¢ of purchasing or earning power if you pay the tax. But if you can postpone the tax for ten years, and if by some miracle the government does change its printing press mentality and inflation slows to 7.2 percent, you can pay the tax with one-half of the purchasing power that you would have to use if you paid it today.

Perhaps you can attain a better grasp of what is happening if you realize that if the printing presses double the amount of money in circulation, the value of your money is cut in half. So when you pay your 40¢ of tax in ten years, it only has the value of 20¢.

Now let's assume you can convert that ordinary income dollar into a capital-gains dollar. You can now reduce your liability to 12¢ of purchasing power in ten years; that is, if you quit the money and tax game at that time, you may want to begin the D.C. game all over and postpone the tax again.

Don't bite the bullet until it is absolutely necessary. Furthermore, you will have an opportunity to generate a return on those dollars during the ten-year period that they are in your hands. At only a 7 percent return, and surely you will do better, each dollar will gain another 97¢ for you, which would still have a purchasing power of 47¢ even after the erosion of a 7 percent inflation rate.

A POSITIVE MENTAL ATTITUDE

The first criterion for winning the money and tax game is a positive mental attitude. If you are getting little twinges of doubt right now that you can ever understand our tax laws—do this. Raise your right hand and repeat after me: "I can understand what Venita is going to tell me!" Did you do it? If you didn't, do it now! Of course you can develop the right mental attitude! William James, the great psychologist, said, "The greatest discovery of my generation is that human beings can change their lives by changing their attitudes of mind." Go to work right now on developing a winning mental attitude. Now let's get ready to meet the challenge.

Step One

The first thing you must do is determine what your taxable income will be for the current year. Do this as early in the year as possible so that you can plan your tax and investment strategy in an orderly

manner. The quality of tax-advantaged investments is usually much higher in the earlier part of the year than in the latter part, and you have time to investigate and judge the quality of the potential investment without an immediate deadline, which could panic you into a poor decision. Don't be desperately looking for a shelter on December 28.

Taxable Income

Taxable income is the portion that is left after you've made all your permissible deductions. Now that doesn't seem hard, does it? You'll find it a bit more difficult than you think. Perhaps one of the best ways is to take the government tax form itself and fill in the blanks. Or you may find it easier to use the worksheet in the Appendix (Figure 10). If all of this is too painful, at least list all the income you anticipate this year on one sheet of paper, and on another sheet list all of your allowable deductions, and compute the difference. This will give you an idea of your problem and where we need to start to solve it. Even if you don't take any constructive steps to shelter—and surely you will—the work you've done gathering this information should greatly reduce the number of hours your C.P.A. will bill you for when he prepares your tax return.

Now that you've tallied your income and your deductions and have a figure for your taxable income, look at Table 20 in the Appendix to obtain an indication of your tax bracket and taxes due. I say "indication" because your tax can vary depending on what portion is classified as "earned" income (called personal service income) and what portion is classified as "unearned" income (income that comes from investments and that is considered passive income).

"Earned" Income

Personal service income is, for the most part, income from your labor in the form of salary, wages, commissions, fees, retirement income, and royalties from personal production. Supposedly your maximum tax on this classification of income is 50 percent.

"Unearned" Income

Unearned income is that from interest from savings accounts, ceritficates of deposit, credit unions, commercial paper, corporate bonds, federal securities, mortgages, etc. You can lose as much as 70 percent of this type of income.

Tax-Deferred Unearned Income

If you invest in tax-deferred annuities, you postpone the taxation on the unearned income until a later date when you are in lower tax bracket. They also provide you with the time-use of money during the deferral period, making it possible to compound a larger sum. Tax-deferred annuities are covered in Chapter 11, "Lending Your Dollars."

Tax-Advantaged Trusts

You read about these in Chapter 4, "Letting the Pros Do Your Investing," and I will also cover them in more detail in this chapter. Tax-advantaged trusts are mutual funds that do not use the usual conduit approach that allows dividends and capital gains to be passed through to you and taxed in your bracket. These funds retain the dividends and capital gains and pay the tax, if any is due after expenses. If you need funds, you redeem shares; and if you have waited a year before doing so, any gain will be taxed at the long-term gains rate.

Tax-Free Income

There is also tax-free unearned income. This can come from municipal bonds, municipal bond funds, and municipal bond trusts. These all produce income that is tax-free and will not be taxed either on your earned or unearned income side. I cover these in Chapter 11, "Lending Your Dollars."

In my opinion, there is no such thing as tax-free income. The spread between the interest you receive on a municipal and the interest you receive on a taxable instrument is in reality your tax.

Do note also what I have to say about the possibility of losing interest deductions if a certain percentage of your portfolio is composed of municipals.

Tax-Sheltered Income

You can receive tax-sheltered income from various limited partnership investments and certain individual investments. This type of income, though probably incidental to the reason you made the investment, will most likely become your favorite type of income. The tax is deferred, but you'll remember how important deferred tax is and how you can convert at least a portion of it into long-term capital gains with their more favorable tax rate. You will find this type of income discussed in Chapters 6 and 8, "The Real Rewards of Real Estate Investing" and "Energizing Your Investments." We'll also discuss tax-sheltered income in this chapter.

INVESTING BEFORE-TAX DOLLARS

The main thrust of this chapter is to teach you how to invest some of your *before*-tax dollars. The tax-sheltered income we've discussed to date, with the exception of the oil and gas exploration and development drilling programs and the real estate private placements, were obtained by investing after-tax dollars. In a 5,0 percent bracket this means that from your last $10,000 of earnings you only had $5000 left to invest. But the goal of this chapter is to show you ways of using tax-favored investments that will let the IRS bear part or all of the cost. Many of the investments I'll discuss will permit you to invest $10,000 of your $10,000 income and in some instances have more money left than if you had paid the tax.

High Risk

Before I cover deductibility and investing tax dollars, let's discuss risk. You may be saying to me, "But Venita, don't tax-favored investments involve high risk?" My answer to you is, "You better believe they do!" As a matter of fact, I will never promise any client that if he makes a tax-favored investment with me he will ever get one penny back. But I am also quick to point out that paying taxes is high risk, too. The return on a tax receipt is zero, and the risk is 100 percent! You may choose. You can invest these funds with me or another financial planner, or you can send them to Washington. All I ever hope to do for any client is to attempt to improve his odds.

There are risks. This is the very reason that Congress has provided the tax incentives. They want to encourage you to invest in high-risk areas that provide for the social good of our country.

There are pitfalls in tax-sheltered investments. These consist of economic risks—such as dry holes, cattle deaths, fluctuating markets. There is also the risk of being a passive investor. As a limited partner you cannot participate in the management without losing your limited liability status. This is why it is so important to evaluate management carefully. Because of the risks involved, you should never invest more than you feel you are emotionally prepared to lose. You should always analyze the economics of the investment carefully and should not be tempted by a tax overkill at the price of eventual returns.

You also have tax risks. There are degrees of certainty that deductions will be sustained. Certain areas are probable; others are gray. You also run the risk of changes in the law, and you always face the risk of an audit.

Whose Money Is It?

There was a period in 1979 when I became quite aware that client after prospective client was coming to my office and saying, "My C.P.A. says I'm paying too much in taxes so I should buy some municipal bonds." After a few months of this I decided I must conduct a seminar for C.P.A.s and clients and talk about "Whose Money Is It?" I did conduct the seminar and continue to have one each year, and it has been extremely enlightening to those attending. To these seminars I invite specialists in the various tax-favored investment fields to make generic presentations of economic potential and deductibility. (Generic means no investment product is presented.)

At this first seminar I handed out the sheet of paper shown in Figure 12–1. It seemed very helpful to those attending, so I've continued its use with clients when we are discussing tax-favored investments. Perhaps you will also find it helpful, so here it is.

WHOSE MONEY IS IT?

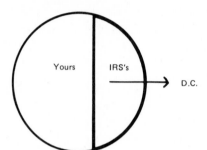

	Deductibility	Approx. 50% Bracket	
		Your Money	*IRS's Money*
1.	0%	100%	0%
2.	50%	75%	25%
3.	100%	50%	50%
4.	200%	0%	100%
5.	Over 200%	0% + investable funds	100% +

2 Choices:

D.C.—Washington

   or

D.C.—Defer & Convert

Figure 12–1. Whose Money Is It?

As you can see from the circle, a portion of your income belongs to the IRS and will be catapulted on its one-way trip if you don't take some action to prevent it. We'll call these your "soft" dollars—the dollars you'll lose to taxes. The ones that are left are your "hard" dollars. (I was giving this explanation to a very hard-working builder the other day and he protested, "but they are all hard dollars. I've worked so hard for all of them.") Regardless of how hard he worked for them, he would not be permitted to keep those dollars unless he made some tax-favored investments. I find that this concept of hard and soft dollars is a very difficult one for clients to comprehend. You must learn to do very different things with your soft dollars than you do with your hard dollars. Even after I've carefully explained all this, time and time again the prospective client will tell me, "Oh, I'm a very conservative person who never takes risks, and this sounds like a risky investment." Again, I have to ask them, "How risky is it to send your money to Washington? What rate of return are you expecting from your tax receipt? How much will your tax receipts increase your net worth?" Yes, I know you may have to pay the piper some day, but with time and inflation perhaps you can improve your odds.

Deductibility

Now look again at our diagram and let's discuss deductibility.

1. *0 percent deductible.* All of the investment was made with your money; none of it was the IRS's. A good example of this would be a municipal bond or a stock investment.

2. *50 percent deductible.* If it's 50 percent deductible, 75 percent is your money, and 25 percent is the IRS's. Good examples of this could be agriculture, marine containers, and certain leasing programs.

3. *100 percent deductible.* If it's 100 percent deductible, 50 percent is your money, and 50 percent is the IRS's. Good examples of this would be programs of oil and gas drilling, cattle feeding, certain real estate, etc.

4. *200 percent deductible.* In this instance, none of it is your money; all of it is IRS's. Cable television, mining, and certain real estate would be good examples.

5. *Over 200 percent.* In this investment not only have you *not* used your money, but you've actually been paid not to do so. Certain mining, video, and real estate investments using recourse financing would be examples of this. (Recourse means you are liable.)

Does this give you a better idea of whose money we are talking about?

PROGRESSIVE FEDERAL INCOME TAX RATES

You will note from Table 20 in the Appendix that taxes begin at the 14 percent level on your first dollar of taxable income above the "zero bracket amount" and run up to 70 percent. (Zero bracket amount replaced the old standard deduction. It is the amount of taxable income on which no tax is levied, and it is built into the tax tables. This figure is $2300 for single taxpayers and $3400 for married individuals filing jointly.)

You reach the 70 percent rate at $108,300 if you are single and $215,400 if you are married and filing a joint return. You reach the 49 percent rate at $34,100 if single and at $45,800 on a joint return.

We all have some hard dollars and some soft dollars. However, most of the tax-favored investments I'll be discussing in this chapter will require that you have some portion of your income in the 50 percent bracket or above and have varying amounts of net worth for the investment to be "suitable" in the eyes of the regulatory agencies. I know that if you are in, say, the 45 percent bracket you don't like paying taxes any more than the person in the 50 percent bracket, but your financial planner's hands are tied by the regulatory agencies, and he'll have to abide by the suitability requirements. But do read on and take hope. We do have some tax-favored investments for the 35 percent bracket investor, and there are more and more being added all the time. Qualifications on some are as low as $30,000 of income and $30,000 of net worth. With inflation and the tax-bracket creep, you may cross the magic 50 percent mark all too soon.

DEDUCTIONS AND HOW YOU GET THEM

I find the majority of those with whom we do tax planning do not understand why or how deductions (write-offs) are allowed against taxable income or against their tax liability. This may be true of you also, so let's take a look at some of their characteristics. This cannot be comprehensive in just one chapter, so you'll need to do some in-depth study on your own.

First of all, you need to understand how limited partnerships and, in some respects, subchapter S corporations are treated for tax purposes. The limited partnership investors are treated as individuals so that all of the tax deductions flow through to the limited partners. The most common sources of these deductions are: investment tax credit, depreciation, depletion, interest deductions, and losses due to various causes.

Investment Tax Credit

The investment tax credit is a credit against your tax liabilities that is allowed on qualified investments in certain depreciable tangible personal property used in a trade or business or for production of income. In a 50 percent tax bracket, ITC has twice the value of a write-off. A tax deduction is applied against your gross income and lowers your taxable income. An investment tax credit is a credit against the tax itself, so you are allowed to subtract it after you come up with the amount of tax due on your taxable income. Congress allows this credit in order to encourage capital investments by business and industry. The Revenue Act of 1978 made the 10 percent ITC permanent. "Permanent" doesn't always mean permanent. It was temporary, and now it's permanent until Congress decides otherwise. In addition, it made permanent a $100,000 ceiling on used equipment eligible for the credit. The ITC can offset the first $25,000 of your tax liability and a percentage of the liability in excess of the $25,000.

In 1980, ITC can be used to offset 70 percent of your tax liability in excess of $25,000, 80 percent in 1981, and 90 percent thereafter. (This means your total credit cannot exceed $25,000, plus this percentage of any tax liability over $25,000, on a joint return.)

If part of your investment tax credit is not used in the current year, the unused credit may be carried back three years to reduce the prior year's income tax liability. If you do not completely absorb the credit in the prior three years, you may carry the credit forward for seven years.

Energy property is eligible for an additional 10 percent investment tax credit. It may qualify for both the regular and energy investment credit if it meets the qualifications for both.

If you dispose of property on which you have taken ITC prior to the estimated useful life used in computing the credit, the tax for the year in which you dispose of the property will be increased by the difference between the credit originally allowed and the credit that would have been allowed if the credit had been based on the actual useful life.

The Revenue Act expanded its availability to a wider range of investors, especially those who make real estate related investments, because ITC can be taken for some personal property used in construction (such as carpets and floor covering, graphics, movable partitions, and decorations). ITC may be taken so long as property is "put into service" prior to the end of the taxable year.

Also, ITC can be taken for certain "qualified rehabilitated expenditures." These are expenditures that are capitalized rather than expensed and have a useful life of five years or more. For example, interior and exterior renovations such as the removal of interior walls and capital expenditures for plumbing, wiring, and heating may qualify.

If your funds are spent on allowable items that have a useful life of seven or more years, you may take the full 10 percent ITC. If they have a useful life of five to seven years, they qualify for 6.66 percent, and those with a useful life of three to five years qualify for a 3.33 percent deduction.

If you renovate a "certified historic structure," you can either take the ITC or amortize your expenses over 60 months.

Depreciation

If you acquire property for use in your trade or business or for the production of income and expect to use it for a period of a year or less, you may deduct the entire cost of the property in the year of purchase. However, the cost of machinery, equipment, buildings, etc., that you expect to use in your trade or business for more than one year must be deducted over the period of time you expect to use the property. The amount you deduct each year is called *depreciation.* You are allowed depreciation on the total cost even though you may have borrowed part or all of the money to make the investment.

The most important thing you need to know about depreciation is that it is a bookkeeping entry. You do not send anyone a check, though you are permitted to deduct the amount of the allowed depreciation on your income tax return. (Actually the general partner sends you a K-1 stating your proportionate part of the deduction, and your CPA puts this information on Schedule E of your tax return.)

Depreciation is allowed because buildings, materials, etc., have a limited useful life and must be replaced. Depreciation allows you to set up a reserve to replace the asset. The amount you will be allowed to deduct will depend on the life of the asset being depreciated and the depreciation schedule you choose. Following are three of the most common depreciation schedules you'll encounter and a brief description of each.

Straight Line.   This is the most frequently used method of depreciation. Annual depreciation under the straight-line method is computed by subtracting the salvage value from the basis and dividing the difference by the estimated useful life. This method results in equal annual amounts of depreciation.

Declining Balance.   Annual depreciation under this method is computed by subtracting the amount of depreciation you claim each year from the basis of the property and multiplying the difference by a constant rate. The same rate applies to the balance each year. Salvage value is not deducted from the basis of the property, but the property cannot be depreciated below its reasonable salvage value. Depending on the type of property, you may be limited to a rate that is 2, 1½, or 1¼ times the straight line rate. To compute the applicable rate, you would divide 200 percent, 150 percent, or 125 percent by the useful life.

Sum-of-the-Years Digits. The sum-of-the-years digits method is based on the application of a diminishing rate to a constant basis. The numbers of the years of useful life are added to obtain the sum of the digits. For example, if the property has a useful life of ten years, the sum of the numbers 1 through 10 equals 55. This becomes the denominator of a fraction, the numerator of which is the number that represents the years of life remaining at the beginning of the year for which the computation is made. Salvage value must be subtracted from the basis when using this method.

As I've mentioned, depreciation is allowed on the total cost of the property, not on the amount you paid down. For example, if you purchased a $60,000 property, paid down $10,000, and the property had a thirty-year life, you would be entitled to a $2000 deduction each year for the next thirty years if you held the property. You put up $1 and will write off $6. This introduces the next most common source of deductions—interest expense.

Interest Expense

If you are an investor in a limited partnership, sole proprietorship, partnership, etc., you may be allowed to deduct your proportionate part of the interest expenses incurred for the investment. Prepaid interest, so commonly used in years past, is no longer deductible. Interest expense occurs any time leverage is used by borrowing funds. (Your deduction for investment interest is limited to your net investment income plus $10,000. This limitation may seem grossly unfair to you, as it does to me, since my father didn't set up a multimillion dollar trust from which to receive investment income, as is the case of a particular senator who pushed for this limitation. What about the hard-working entrepreneur who is still trying to make it?)

Let's take a moment to talk about leverage, for the use of leverage generates interest expense.

Leverage

Advantages. Deductions can often be greatly enhanced by the use of borrowed dollars. This is referred to as leverage and is a very important tool in many tax-sheltered investments. Leverage can entitle you to tax deductions in excess of your cash contributions, but you must be "at risk"—meaning you must pay on the due date if the cash flow from the investment has not paid off the indebtedness or if the due date is not extended.

Leveraging a small equity investment into a substantial tax deduction depends upon an exception to the general rules established by the IRS code concerning your tax "basis." When your aggregate loss equals your basis, no further losses will be permitted until additional basis is added. The basis in your partnership's investment includes your equity investment, your undistributed revenues, and the proportionate part of any partnership debts for which you are personally liable. Despite the "at risk" provisions of the Tax Reform Act of 1976, multiple write-offs are still possible.

Pitfalls of Leveraging.   Repayment of the debt principal creates a call on the shelter's revenue but is not deductible for federal income tax purposes; thus, as the shelter progresses, phantom income is created. These are dollars you never see because they have gone to repaying funds that were borrowed on your behalf, but they are taxable to you. The taxable income will eventually exceed the cash flow that is available for distribution to you. Despite the high initial deductibility, the excess deductions do not create a permanent tax shelter for you, which leaves only your soft dollars at risk.

Also, you should be aware that the day of reckoning for excess deductions cannot be avoided by making a gift of the property or permitting the loan to be foreclosed. This will be treated as a sale.

This is the reason you should also invest the funds you would have sent to Washington. Do not treat these as spendable, but only as assets to build your net worth and to pay a tax, when and if one is due.

Depletion

Certain assets such as timber, oil and gas, and mineral royalties deplete. An oil well, for example, will not flow or pump forever. The oil reserves will deplete. You may qualify for cost depletion, based on the amount of your cost or statutory depletion. Cost depletion is computed by dividing the adjusted basis of the property by the total number of recoverable units in the deposit and then multiplying the resulting rate per unit by the number of units for which payment is received if you are a cash basis taxpayer, or by the number of units sold if you are an accrual basis taxpayer.

Depletion is covered in Chapter 8, "Energizing Your Investments."

If you are an investor in a partnership, the general partner will provide you with a K-1 form to be used for your tax return.

Losses

Although investment and business losses are almost always deductible, there are certain limitations on the timing if they are capital losses. These limitations are covered in the section "Municipal Bond Swapping" in this chapter. The purpose of investing is rarely to obtain real losses. The tax laws are currently structured to give you the incentive to invest in the areas we are discussing through either artificial losses or credits; however, real losses are to be avoided whenever and wherever possible.

DEFERRAL vs. PERMANENT SHELTER

Permanent.   Certain forms of tax-shelter investments generate deductions that are "permanent" in nature. Deductions that are considered permanent are: intangible drilling costs, interest, property taxes, and depreciation. (Accelerated depreciation is subject to recapture. More about that later.)

Deferral.   In deferrals, you have deferred the tax. However, deferral can be an important deduction. It permits you to shift your taxes into future years where inflation allows you to pay with cheaper dollars. It also may allow you to control when you pay the tax, thereby permitting you to do more effective long-range tax planning. One of the most significant benefits is that it allows you to use the government's money interest-free.

Now that you have become more familiar with the areas that permit you to have write-offs against your taxable income, you'll need to become familiar with areas of investing that provide these deductions. There is a wide spectrum of possibilities, but that does not mean that it will be easy to find the right investment at the right time to fit your particular set of circumstances.

Investment offerings will usually be through registered limited partnerships, private placements, sole proprietorships, or by use of subchapter S corporations. Let's briefly examine the characteristics of each.

Registered Limited Partnership

I have covered the structure and characteristics of a limited partnership in Chapters 6 and 8, "The Real Rewards of Real Estate Investing" and "Energizing Your Investments." In a registered offering the general partner has gone to considerable expense and time to register the partnership with the Securities & Exchange Commission (or perhaps if all sales are to be made within one state, only with the state). This registration allows the general partner to offer the investment through a financial planner or other individuals registered with the National Association of Security Dealers, who are allowed to make public offerings to those who meet the suitability requirements. The offerings are usually quite large and may be for amounts up to $100 million. The cost per unit is usually $500 or $1000, though some may be as high as $5000 and the minimum amount of investment is usually from $2500 to $5000. The offerings will usually be open for several months, which should give you ample time to become familiar with the offering, unless you wait until near its closing date.

Private Placements

Effective June 10, 1974, the SEC issued a "Notice of Adoption of Rule 146 Under the Securities Act of 1933—Transactions by an Issuer Deemed Not To Involve Any Public Offering." This ruling exempted from registration certain offerings to 35 investors or less. In most of these offerings, the financial planner has to be very, very careful not to make a presentation to an "unsuitable" prospective investor. Determining suitability was shifted to the general partner and the planner.

My interpretation of the rule boils down simply to this: To be eligible to make an investment in an exempt offering you must be rich and smart or be rich and have a smart friend (technically called an "offeree representative").

Since the maximum number of investors is 35 (usually investors who invest $150,000 or more are not counted against the maximum) and the size of the units will need to be larger, the amount of the investment and the write-off it brings may or may not fit your particular needs. Also, since there can only be a limited number of investors, the whole offering may be completely placed within a few days, which may not give you as much time as you would like to study its investment potential. You will find a more in-depth discussion of private offerings in Chapter 18, "How to Read a Prospectus."

With the increased scarcity of venture capital, Rule 146 may very well prove to be absolutely essential to the maintenance of the free-enterprise capitalistic system in the United States. And I, for one, want to do all I can to maintain it. It is not a perfect system by any means, but it is the best system the world has yet devised for bringing the greatest good to the greatest number of people.

Now that you have become familiar with why certain items are deductible and the manner in which the various tax-favored investments can be structured, let's look at another very important consideration in your tax planning program.

DIVERSIFICATION

A vital requirement for any successful investment program you ever undertake should be diversification—the not-all-your-eggs-in-one-basket rule. This is especially true when it comes to tax-favored investments. Most of them are definitely higher risk than ones without tax advantage; therefore it is prudent to spread this risk within the investment area itself and to various areas. For example, if you have chosen a general partner who offers a number of oil and gas exploration programs throughout the year, spread your investment throughout several of his programs.

Spreading your dollars into several offerings allows you to lower your risks and increase your potential for profit. If one tax-favored investment goes sour, and you should go into each of them with the full knowledge that this could and probably will happen sooner or later, don't spend your time crying and moaning and saying, "I'll never try another tax-advantaged investment." You'll really lose if you do that. You're a "big kid," so act like one. You're smart enough to have earned enough money to put you in a higher tax bracket, so do as you've been doing in your business—dust yourself off, and go out and try again. If you do your homework, you'll win most of the time. You know you are going to lose if you capitulate to the IRS.

Your financial planner will try to prevent any of your investments from going sour. He will have spent many, many hours doing "due diligence" in an effort to obtain as much information as he can about the general partners, their past track records, and the current demand for their products, research, or services. But there is no way that he can guarantee you that any investment will be a success. Always remember that you'll never go down an untraveled path and find it paved, and that many tax-favored investments go down untraveled paths. An investment should be a good investment first and a tax shelter second. Don't be deceived, however, by the poor advice I often hear that an investment must stand on its own without the write-off to be a good investment. This is not true. If you could not risk some of IRS's money along with yours, many tax-favored investments should be avoided.

Different types of tax-sheltered investments may vary dramatically from one another in such characteristics as degree and type of shelter provided, permanency of the shelter, tax consequences down the road, and economic characteristics such as cash flow, appreciation potential, degree of risk, and liquidity. You will find that even inside a given tax-shelter area, the tax and economic characteristics of the investment can vary significantly, depending upon the type of project undertaken and how the investment is structured.

Before investing in any tax-sheltered investment, be sure that you and your financial planner carefully analyze your own particular investment goals and needs in such areas as degree of tax savings needed, cash flow and appreciation potential, liquidity, and the degree of acceptable risk to you. While very few tax-sheltered investments are liquid and all have speculative characteristics, certain types of tax-sheltered investments can provide you with a measure of liquidity and a reduction of risk that others do not possess. Now let's take a look at some of the areas of tax-favored investments with which you'll want to become familiar.

REAL ESTATE

I have covered investing in real estate in an earlier chapter. You may want to reread portions of that chapter at this time.

Our tax laws favor real estate, and the IRS seems to get less uptight when they see a real estate related deduction, although I understand that IRS agents have just been issued a new booklet outlining areas to look for in real estate investments with the hope of disallowing as many deductions as possible. The 1978 Revenue Act exempted non-recourse debt from the "at-risk" limitation on the deduction of losses. (This means that the lending company has a mortgage on the property and must look to the property for obtaining their funds rather than having a claim on your other assets.)

Through the decade of the 'eighties I feel that high interest rates will continue, because long-term mortgage lending is now supported by two- to eight-year certificates of deposit carrying high rates. With the cost of the funds locked into these relatively high-yielding instruments, lenders may be unwilling or unable to roll back rates on new mortgages. New real estate entering the market will be forced to obtain higher rental rates and selling prices because of inflated wages and material costs and these higher interest rates.

Existing vacant housing is at its lowest level in twenty years. The 'eighties began with a vacancy rate for multifamily housing of under 4½ percent and with the cost of single family dwellings so high that the average family could not qualify for a home loan. This should permit significant and frequent rental increases. Locked-in interest rates on the financing means that a large portion of this increase will go down to the bottom line and escalate the price for which properties can be sold. One of the major factors that determines the sale price of a property is its gross rent multiplier (the rent multiplied by a factor from 6 to 14, depending on the demand in the area).

Borrowing by the general partner allows you, the limited partner, to spread your equity and should offer you added diversification, which should, in turn, lower your risks.

Larger down payments may be required by financing institutions in the 'eighties. They may be as much as 30 to 40 percent, in comparison with the 'seventies when the norm was 20 to 25 percent. There may also be less refinancing in the 'eighties because of this. (Refinancing may let you take out some of your equity buildup and allow you to take advantage of the escalating value of your property without selling it. The beautiful thing about cash from refinancing is that it is not taxable because it is borrowed funds.)

The rapid increase in the value of some real estate has brought large capital gains to many owners. This may make some of them very willing to sell their property to you with a lower down payment so as to spread their tax liabilities by spreading the principal payments.

With the average price of a single family home escalating to over $67,000, the majority of new and older families have been eliminated from the home-buying market and pushed into the rental market. It does not appear that the building industry will be able to meet this demand. This should create an outstanding opportunity for investing if you are willing to assume the risks of construction and the lag time that may occur as the units become rented. If you do choose properly, your profit potential should be very good.

If you do not want the added risk of building and the lag in cash flow during the rent-up periods, you may want to look at a private placement of an apartment building that is several years old and already rented with a proven cash flow record. These offerings will most likely be private placements. They can be more creatively structured to give you added write-offs.

You will not have the diversification you do in a public offering because it will be one apartment project, rather than the fourteen to fifteen in the public offering, or one shopping center, or one office building.

An Apartment Building Private Offering

Table 21 in the Appendix is the *pro forma* page from a particular private placement memorandum for an offering we made to our clients. You may want to take a moment to study this page. This is a copy of page 89. The 88 pages before this one were for the most part warning you of all the risks in making this investment. This is what is called "full disclosure."

As you will note from the *pro forma* sheet, you would have invested $6500, $15,500, $13,000, $12,000, and $10,250, for a total of $57,250 over a five-year period. You'll also note that during a ten-year period it was projected that if you were in a 50 percent bracket, your total benefits from tax savings and cash-sheltered cash flow would be $76,042. At the bottom of the page, they have made three assumptions of possibilities that might occur at the end of ten years: (1) abandonment; (2) selling at the original purchase price; and (3) selling at the general partner's projected market price.

It may be difficult to interpret all the assumptions, but let's look at the bleakest—abandonment, or walking away from the property. At first glance you might think that if you had been an investor in this project and abandonment had occurred, you would really have goofed. But let's examine the situation and see how bad it really would have been.

First of all, you do not receive any sale proceeds. That seems pretty grim; after all you did invest $57,250. But let's dig a bit deeper. You received benefits each year during those ten years. Let's assume you did what we advise our clients to do and reinvested your tax savings. (You wouldn't have had that money to spend anyway if you had paid your taxes and sent it on that one-way trip.) For simplicity let's assume you did nothing more creative than place your money into a single-premium deferred annuity at 10 percent. At the end of ten years its value would be $140,299.

On foreclosure you owe the IRS $19,243 in taxes. Incidentally, you won't be able to calculate this from just this one page. If you had the complete memorandum you could. So we now have $140,299 less your tax liability of $19,243, or $121,056—not so bad. In addition, if you invest in another shelter the year of the foreclosure, you may be able to prevent or postpone the $19, 243 tax liability.

Also there is no tax to pay on the first $76,042 when you cash in the annuity, because that's a part of your original investment, and only earnings are taxed when withdrawn.

The second assumption made is that the property was sold in ten years and was sold at the exact purchase price—that no appreciation had occurred in ten years. In this instance, after taxes in a 50 percent bracket, you would have sales proceeds of $44,544 and a tax liability of $30,379, for an after-tax benefit of $14,165, plus the $76,043 previous after-tax benefits you had received, for a cumulative after-tax benefit of $91,042. This is for a sale at cost and does not give credit for the value of your tax-sheltered annuity. Even after withdrawing to pay the tax, you would have $140,299 (the value of the annuity), less $30,379 for taxes, or $109,920 plus the $44,544 sales proceeds, or $154,464.

Now let's assume the general partner sold the property at a future market value equal to 3 percent growth in value per year. Your pre-tax sales proceeds would be $87,186. You would have a tax liability in the year of sale (if you do not shelter your gains and are still in a 50 percent bracket) of $41,040. This would give you an after-tax benefit of $46,146 plus your $76,042 previous after-tax benefits, or a cumulative after-tax benefit of $122,188.

In this instance you would have $140,299 from the annuity, less $41,040 taxes on the real estate sale or $99,259 plus the $87,186 proceeds from the sale of the apartments of $186,445. (You will have some tax on $64,257 of the annuity interest when you withdraw it—but perhaps you won't—or use it for collateral.)

Don't feel because of the above explanation that investing in multi-family housing is riskless. Foreclosure could have come before the ten-year period described above, which would not have given sufficient time for the tax benefits anticipated, nor for the projected cash flow. However, the above is a good example of why you do not want to pay any more taxes any sooner than is absolutely necessary. Again, the tragedy of paying taxes is that not only do you lose that dollar, but you lose what that dollar would earn if you could keep it.

Recapture

"Recapture" is a word that can send shivers down the spines of some, especially if said in an alarmed manner. Let's examine what it is and see if it's something that you could live with if it should occur. Let's assume the general partner failed to bring along a property profitably, and a foreclosure occurred in a limited partnership in which you have invested. Let's further assume that you have written off $40,000 on a cash investment of $16,000. You now have a negative cost basis, and upon foreclosure (or sale) this converts to a long-term capital gains. Forty percent of the capital gains would be taxable, or in this instance $9600. Assuming you are in a 49 percent tax bracket, you would owe $4900 in taxes, yet you did not receive any cash at the time of foreclosure (or sale). This seems pretty bad, doesn't it?

But what is our rule? We don't spend that money that we would have sent to Washington. We invest it so it will be there in the event of just such a reversal as this. Let's assume you invested your net cash in hand in a single-premium tax deferred annuity paying 8 percent in the first example and 12 percent in the second. Your numbers for both the foreclosure and the investment of tax savings should look as follows:

Tax Consequences on Foreclosure:

$40,000	amount you wrote off
16,000	amount you invested
$24,000	negative cost basis that converts to long-term capital gains
× 40%	capital gains tax
$ 9,600	
× 49%	tax bracket
$ 4,900	taxes you would owe

Your investment results if you had invested $8000 the first year and $8000 the second year for a total of $16,000; received a write-off of $20,000 the first year and $20,000 the second year for a total of $40,000; and invested the $1800 each year that you would not have had if you had paid the tax and averaged 8 percent and 12 percent respectively in a single-premium deferred annuity would be as shown in Table 12–1.

TABLE 12–1

Year	Invest-ment	Taxes Saved	Left to Invest	Invest @ 8% (T.S.)	Invest @ 12% (T.S.)
1	$8000	$9800	$1800	$1944	$2016
2	$8000	$9800	$1800	4043	4273
3			$3600	4367	4786
4				4716	5361
5				$5093	$6004

As you will note, if foreclosure had occurred at the end of five years, you would have $5093 at 8 percent ($1493 of which would be taxable) to pay the tax and $6004 at 12 percent ($2404 taxable).

Therefore, you would have $5093 at 8 percent or $6004 at 12 percent to pay your tax of $4900 in the event you did not choose to use another tax-favored investment to shelter your $9600 capital gains the year of the foreclosure.

You should always be aware of the tax consequences of foreclosure, but it should not be so frightening if you've invested your tax savings, and inflation may permit you to pay with a cheaper dollar. The key to any tax-favored investment is whose money you are investing (yours or the IRS's) and what you are doing with your tax savings. I tell my clients that their tax savings belong to me—to invest for them.

Subsidized Housing

I must admit that I've never placed an investor in a subsidized housing program, because I have always worried about his not being in a high enough tax bracket for as long a period of time as most programs require. If the investor is not, he would not reap the maximum tax advantage. Also in most programs I've studied, his potential for capital gains was nil, because when the property was sold he could expect to receive only $1 above the mortgage after twenty to thirty years.

With the advent of the Section 8 Rent Subsidy Program by HUD, there is the possibility that some of the properties now being offered can produce good long-term rentals without the risk of poor occupancy and, in some underprivileged areas, destruction of the property. As a result of Section 8 you may want to take a look at these programs, for they could afford you some capital-gains potential.

Renovation of Certified Historic Buildings

This may not be a tax-favored investment you'll be considering in that there are not too many such buildings available. The building has to be certified as historic and worthy of preservation by the Secretary of the Interior. The tax advantage to this type of investment is that if substantial rehabilitation is being done, the owner may elect to use a 200 percent declining-balance depreciation schedule rather than straight line, or the owner may elect to set up the depreciation schedule on a five-year basis rather than one over the building's useful life.

If you sell the building, this accelerated depreciation could be charged back to you. For example, if the building has a ten-year useful life and you use a 200 percent double-declining balance, you would be entitled to a 20 percent instead of a 10 percent deduction. However, if you sold the building at the end of the first year, this 10 percent would be charged back to you.

You may also be entitled to some other tax breaks from the city, county, and state because of the certification.

OIL AND GAS DRILLING PROGRAMS

In Chapter 8, "Energizing Your Investments," you'll find information and a worksheet that should help you to determine whether this type of investment dovetails with your tax planning needs, temperament, and judgment of economic merit. You will find development drilling programs, exploratory programs, combination programs, royalty programs, completion programs, options to buy production programs, and more. The offerings will be either registered or private placements. The registered programs should allow you to make a smaller investment and give you more diversification. The private offerings will usually require larger minimum investments, but can also be structured to provide larger first-year write-offs using leverage.

What do the 'eighties hold for oil and gas exploration programs? I believe we will gradually emerge from this extended period of utter confusion into what should be a long period of sustained growth. Despite the pressures of inflation; excessive, confusing, counterproductive, and contradictory regulations; political footballing; and punitive tax laws, the oil and gas industry should still be a viable area for your investment consideration. The demand for clean efficient energy is greater than the supply, and this should continue through the 'eighties.

Decontrolled prices must be the cornerstone of our energy policy. Price is the only common denominator for the millions of daily decisions which we must all make about production and conservation of energy.

In choosing a program for your investment dollars, select one that has a general partner who is well capitalized, has considerable expertise, and has a successful track record. His track record does not guarantee that your program will be successful, but I do like to put my money with people who have a record of being winners.

Also, go into programs at the beginning of the year. This should provide you with a larger write-off for the year and give the general partners time for orderly and efficient drilling throughout the year. Drilling rigs and crews may also be more readily obtainable at a lower cost earlier rather than when there are too many out there scrambling for equipment at the end of the year.

CABLE TELEVISION

Cable television offers attractive potential if the program is structured properly and has top-quality management. While cable television is a relatively new and small industry, it has exhibited a consistent growth profile and a remarkable record of stability, and it may offer you a unique opportunity for investing.

Traditional cable systems are built in towns that do not have good television reception due to mountainous terrain or long distances from TV stations. A cable system receives TV signals by using a tall tower and distributes the signal throughout the town on a coaxial cable. Subscribers are charged a monthly fee for the service. After a cable system is built in a community, the maintenance and operating expenses are very low in relation to income. The business is generally very predictable and operates much like a utility company. There is also a potential for cable TV stations to provide current theater movies (already available in some cities), tie-ins to libraries, retailers, and banks—all for the purpose of gathering information and handling transactions with these institutions right in the home.

The capital required to construct or purchase a cable system is substantial, but the investor can leverage his equity investment by utilizing an institutional lender specializing in making first-lien mortgage loans on good cable systems. The collateral on this loan is the cable system itself, and in many cases the personal guarantee of the investor is also required.

The tax shelter is created primarily by the depreciation of the system, the interest on loans, the investment tax credit earned on purchasing the system, and, in the case of a new system, actual operating losses in the first year or two.

A high-quality cable television limited partnership may offer you an investment period of two or three years with an equivalent tax write-off of 200 percent during that period, and with an additional two or three years of tax write-off with no additional investments.

In this same limited partnership, you may look forward to a cash flow starting in the second or third year and continuing throughout the life of the partnership. A total cash return of 200 percent or 250 percent may occur over an eight- to ten-year partnership, in addition to the tax advantages.

One major technological change has come along in the past couple of years that has improved the investment's profit potential, and that is satellites and earth receive stations. With the installation of an earth receive station to receive additional TV programming from a satellite, the cable system can provide additional TV programs. The additional programs attract more subscribers and make the overall service more attractive; hence, higher monthly revenues are possible.

Some of these additional programs that are received via satellite offer uncut movies with no commercials, along with other commercial-free entertainment and sports specials. These channels, called Pay-TV channels, are proving to be very attractive to residents of larger cities. Cable television is growing in larger metropolitan areas where the housing density and family income levels are higher.

Cable television is regulated by the Federal Communications Commission, and in the past few years there has been a noticeable trend toward deregulation, as there has been in the transportation and trucking industries. A part of this deregulating trend is responsible for the ability to provide additional channels via satellites.

One other substantial advantage in these investments is that normal inflation can be expected to also inflate the market value of the cable system, therefore offering a potential hedge against inflation, if and when you and the other limited partners choose to sell the system.

CATTLE-FEEDING PROGRAMS

Cattle-feeding program tax objectives can be summarized in two words: "tax deferral" (postponing a tax liability until a later, more convenient time, or, usually, buying time to figure out a way to avoid the tax altogether). There's no write-off or depreciation on the cattle, but feed costs, interest, and management fees are deductible as they are consumed. Because of the "capital at risk" limitations in the Tax Reform Act of 1976, your deduction will generally be limited to 100 percent or less.

The typical cattle-feeding operation is basically conducted in the following manner. Buyers for the feedlots purchase calves weighing between 400 and 600 pounds. These feeder calves are purchased and placed in feedlot pens of 100 to 200 animals. The feedlot operators feed them a scientifically designed diet in order to maximize their weight gain at the lowest possible cost. In about four to six months, they reach a level referred to as "finished"; they weigh between 900 and 1100 pounds. Finished cattle are sold quickly at prevailing market prices, since additional feed costs make it uneconomical to hold them after they reach their optimum weight.

The price that the general partner must pay to obtain feeder calves, the cost of feed, and the price of finished fat cattle fluctuate with supply and demand. An investment in only a single feeding program, therefore, could generate for you a significant profit or a significant loss. This will depend on timing of purchases and sales. Price changes are the major cattle-feeding risk. However, in recent years many cattle feeders have employed the use of commodity futures hedging their cattle to lessen the impact of rapid price declines.

When the cattle are sold the following year, your net profit, if any,

after loan repayment, sponsor's compensation, and operations expenses, is taxed as ordinary income. This allows you to shift taxable income from one year to the next, giving you the flexibility of deferring the tax into a more favorable year. Most of the programs currently being offered are designed to carry over several years in order to allow more flexibility in your tax planning. Almost all cattle-feeding programs employ borrowed funds. If you are a limited partner, your funds are used for the equity purchase of young feeder cattle. The general partner then borrows additional funds to finance a portion of the cattle purchases, plus the cost of feed to be fed during the period.

Cattle feeding is a cyclical type of investment, but the program that we have used for several years has a seven-year life, which gives the managers time to level out the peaks and valleys.

CATTLE BREEDING

Another tax-favored investment you may want to consider is in a limited partnership that invests in purebred cattle for breeding purposes.

There are two categories of breeders—the purebred breeder and the commercial breeder. The purebred breeder attempts to develop genetically superior breeds of cattle to sell to other purebred breeders or to commercial breeders. The commercial breeder raises unregistered cattle that are intended for slaughter after being grown and fattened.

Purebred breeders concentrate on developing superior seed stock. Champion bulls may sell for ten times more than the average herd sire. The commercial breeder, on the other hand, aims for the greatest number of pounds of acceptable quality beef at the least possible cost to produce.

You may want to consider a limited partnership that breeds purebred cattle. It can offer you appreciation potential, long-term capital gains, tax deductions, and if your timing is right (which I feel it is), favorable marketing factors.

Tax deductions come from maintenance expenses incurred in connection with building up the breeding herd. These are ordinary expenses and create current tax deductions. The resulting herds of cattle, held for breeding purposes more than two years, are long-term capital assets. The sale of the calves from a herd usually results in ordinary income, but the sale of the foundation herd often results in long-term capital gains. When breeding cattle are purchased they are subject to depreciation and investment tax credits. In contrast, when newborn calves are raised through calfhood they often have a zero or near zero basis for tax purposes; therefore they cannot be depreciated. However, the maintenance expenses incurred in raising such cattle are fully deductible and, of course, convertible into long-term capital gains.

The operating profit outlook for beef cattle looks the best it has for many years. Beef consumption per capita has been rising constantly for the last twenty-five years with few exceptions, and last year was more than 120 pounds. Beef consumption is increasing all over the world due to the increase in population and higher personal incomes. The future outlook for demand is strong. Experts have estimated that the U.S. alone will need to add 1,000,000 slaughter cattle each year to keep pace with population growth and living standards.

In the last three years, the supply of beef cows has been cut, but even more importantly the supply of replacement heifers for beef cattle herds has decreased more than 35 percent. Current calf crop is 1 percent under the 1978 crop. This will be the smallest calf crop since 1963 and the fourth consecutive year of decline. This decline, accompanied by the 35 percent reduction in replacement heifer supply, means that the future calf crop will have to decline as old cows leave production and new heifers are inadequate to supply needed replacement. This forthcoming shortage should give a major upward push to prices over

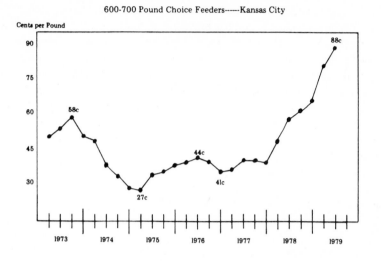

600-700 Pound Choice Feeders------Kansas City

Source: USDA Livestock Meat/Wool Market News
Weekly Reports 1973-1979

Figure 12–2.   Cattle Prices, 1973–1979

the next five years. Figure 12–2 is a graphic picture of what is happening to beef prices.

HORSE BREEDING

Another type of tax-favored investment you may want to consider is one that breeds and produces thoroughbred yearlings or one that breeds trotter horses. Horse racing is the biggest spectator sport in the U.S., and one of the leaders in the entertainment industry. The race itself is only a very small part of the process. It is the culmination of an entire production cycle which is the breeding end of the business. The business of breeding and racing thoroughbreds is like any other industry. It requires careful planning, diligent effort, and intelligence. Because of the complexities of the industry, it can offer an opportunity for substantial risks as well as large rewards.

EQUIPMENT LEASING

Equipment leasing is another area with which you will want to become familiar. You may want to consider becoming a direct purchaser or acquiring an indirect ownership of equipment by investing in a registered limited partnership or in a private placement. Tax benefits in this type of investing come through investment tax credit, accelerated depreciation of the equipment, and interest deductions on loans. Gains can come from rental payments during the term of the lease. In addition, you may receive residual values that may occur when the equipment is sold. Computers are a favorite in this area, although airplanes, ships, trucks, or any other major piece of equipment may be used.

If you go the partnership route, to qualify for the maximum investment tax credit of 10 percent of eligible equipment cost, the partnership must meet the following requirements:

1. The equipment must have a useful life of at least seven years at the time it is placed in service (a reduced ITC is allowed if less than seven years and more than three).

2. The terms of the initial lease, including options to renew, must be less than 50 percent of the equipment's life for purposes of depreciation.

3. The first year's ordinary and necessary trade or business expenses attributable to the equipment must exceed 15 percent of the first year's rental income.

The registered partnership approach could provide for the pooling of your capital with a large number of investors. Thus the partnership would be able to purchase more and more substantial equipment than you would be able to acquire on your own. Of course, the number of different purchases that the partnership could make would depend upon the funds available to it from the offering.

Most partnerships will use accelerated depreciation (200 percent declining balance) on equipment and switch to the straight-line method when it would maximize deductions. In the early years it is possible that depreciation may generate tax losses for you in excess of your tax-sheltered distributions. These may be used to offset other taxable income which could defer some tax liability into the future.

Many partnerships have little or no cash flow during the first three years, if they are highly leveraged. If little or no leverage is used, cash flow occurs earlier.

This type of investment is mainly a deferral and should allow you to take some of your income and tax problems and move them from a year of high tax liability to one that is not as high, perhaps after retirement. The Investment Tax Credit, however, is not a deferral; it is a credit against your taxes, thereby reducing the taxes you pay the year of purchase. Equipment leasing can offer a dual advantage—tax deferral and tax elimination.

You'll want to check thoroughly the quality of the equipment, the creditworthiness of the lessee, and the possibility of sudden obsolescence. Your best opportunities for good equipment leases will be in periods of tight and expensive money.

The risk requirement of the 1976 Tax Reform Act makes it absolutely necessary for you to be very careful about the credit strength of your lessee.

Why Companies Lease Equipment

Many companies now consider leasing to be a viable alternative to purchasing because of the availability of one or more of the following advantages:

1. No Substantial Cash Outlay Required—Since there is no substantial cash outlay for purchase or down payment, the company has additional funds for working capital or other uses.

2. Lower Payments—The lease payments may be lower than purchase financing payments over the same term, and the term is often longer with a lease.

3. Tax Benefits—The entire lease payment is a tax-deductible expense.

4. Flexibility—Lease terms may be tailored to fit the anticipated period that the equipment is needed.

5. Alternate Capital Source—Cash, in effect, has become available from the lessor rather than the company's usual banking source. Also, there is no compensating balance requirement as with bank loans, so that existing bank credit lines are available for other purposes.

6. Lower Cost—Companies that are unable to fully utilize tax benefits may receive a lower interest rate when the lessor retains the tax benefits.

7. Possibility of Off-Balance Sheet Financing—Equipment leased under an operating lease does not have to be capitalized on the lessee's balance sheet.

Equipment Leasing Investment Objectives

The partnership's investment objectives should be to acquire and lease various types of capital equipment which would provide the following to limited partners:

1. Tax Benefits—Provide certain federal income tax benefits including (1) potential generation of tax losses in excess of current "tax-sheltered" distributions during the initial years of the partnership, and (2) the possible availability of the investment tax credit (investment credit).

2. Distributions—Provide quarterly distributions of distributable cash from operations. The amount of cash distributions will vary with the terms of the lease and the kind of equipment involved.

Areas you'll especially want to look at are equipment leasing of aircraft, railroad cars, tractor/trailers, marine containers and machine tools. These could provide you with tax advantage and excellent residual value at the end of the lease term.

Marine Containers. A registered offering I am comfortable with leases marine containers. These are large durable boxes designed to international standards for the efficient carriage and handling of cargo. The containers are built primarily of steel and are in lengths of 20 and 40 feet. (Statistics are cited in "20 foot equivalent units" or "TEUs," wherein one 40-foot container is equal to two 20-foot containers.) They are manufactured in industrialized countries throughout the world.

Due to standardization, containers are intermodal. That means they are compatible with equipment used in the shipment of goods by rail, sea, or highway. The substantial investment in transportation equipment used today to accommodate today's standard containers lowers the risk of their becoming obsolete.

There has been a tremendous growth in world container fleets because the containers eliminate repetitious cargo handling, reduce handling costs, virtually eliminate theft and pilferage, and reduce cargo transit time. The market outlook for containerized cargo should expand for a number of reasons: only half of containerizable cargo is now carried in containers; the inland use of containers is increasing; world trade is expanding; growth in developing areas such as South America, the Middle East, and West Africa is expected to be explosive; and first-generation containers manufactured in the mid-'sixties will be phased out and replaced during the next few years.

This type of equipment leases has the potential for excellent cash flow and annual revenues, as a percentage of original equipment cost can approach 50 percent in the short term.

Tax shelter comes from the fact that our tax laws allow a depreciation over a seven-year life and can also qualify for as much as 100 percent of the 10 percent investment tax credit. This leasing program also offers a good hedge against inflation. Ten-year-old containers are currently selling for what it cost to build them originally.

Table 22 in the Appendix is a hypothetical example of a $10,000 investment. It shows projected cash flow tax savings and the results that could occur if you reinvested your cash flow.

Computers.   I have never placed a client into a computer leasing program, but I do believe you should be familiar with how the programs may be constructed so that you can decide for yourself.

However, I believe there can be considerable risk in computer leasing, as was evidenced when IBM dramatically reduced the price of their new model computers below the price of those already being leased. This caused lessees not to renew their leases on the old computers, leaving the owners with no lease rentals and no residual value.

Large Pieces of Equipment.   Drilling rigs, which may cost as much as $4 million, and river barges, which may cost up to $300,000, can be viable considerations for a leasing program. There should be a continued shortage of this type of equipment, which would keep its residual value very high.

MOVIES

Investing in the production of a movie may be a feasible possibility for you. Until recently, most movies were financed by major studios, syndications, or private placements. Most of these methods required large cash outlays.

The first publicly registered limited partnership program became available in the latter part of 1979 and was structured with a minimum investment of $5000 and a suitability requirement that the investor have an income of $40,000 or a net worth of $100,000 in most states.

There has developed an almost insatiable appetite for feature-length movies by the major television networks. Off-network cable systems, pay television, video tapes, video discs, and nontheatrical outlets also are demanding large quantities of movies. This increasing demand often makes it possible for the movie makers to prelease their movies for from two-thirds to 100 percent of the cost of production, greatly reducing their risks.

ABC moved from $20 million in gross revenue in 1975 to approximately $200 million in 1978 by aggressively bidding for feature films, and they moved to number one among the networks. NBC and CBS are still trying to catch up. This battle for product has increased film revenue by 30 percent per year for the last three years, and we expect this pattern to continue.

To break even on a movie that costs around $2.5 million to produce, the movie would have to gross about $10 million in the theatrical market—meaning the movie houses. This may sound small if you have been reading about some of them grossing over $200 million, but the majority don't net this figure. But the television and other revenues should greatly reduce this requirement. Two million dollars from TV is equal to $8 million in movie box office grosses. According to a recent study, these figures on presales may run between $5 and $7 million.

In a 50 percent bracket I calculate that you are only risking approximately 37¢ on each dollar you invest even without these presale revenues. Also, as income comes in, you will not owe taxes on your cash flow until you have received back your investment. The income-forecasting method of reporting motion picture earnings allows deductions equal to income. For example, if 40 percent of forecast income is earned in one year, then 40 percent of production costs can offset this.

ITC of 6⅔ percent is allowed for movies in the year you make the investment. In a 50 percent bracket this is equivalent to double that of a write-off. In a 40 percent bracket it is equivalent to 2½ times a write-off ($1.00 \div .40 = 2.5$). If the movie is prereleased for two-thirds of the cost, then your risk would be further reduced to approximately 10¢ on a dollar.

For example, if you were investing in a registered offering that offered $5000 units and you invested in two units, in a 50 percent bracket your numbers might look like this if the film was never distributed:

$10,000	investment
(1332)	ITC − 6⅔% = $666 × 2
(5000)	tax savings
$ 3,668	your money at risk

If no revenue came from the theaters and the movie was preleased for 67 percent of the cost to produce:

$10,000	investment
6,700	prelease revenues
$ 3,300	at risk
$ 3,300	
(1650)	tax savings in 50% bracket
(670)	ITC
980	potential loss

If $3300 of revenue comes to you, you are home free, plus you would have received an additional $666 in investment tax credit. If you do not, you can still write off the $3300.

All told, your risk is nearer to 10¢ on a dollar if the movie is presold for 67 percent of its cost to produce.

This type of investment should not give you a tax-preference or a recapture problem, since it is usually the intention of the partnership to lease rather than sell the films. Once you have recouped your investment, you might consider making a gift to a family member in a lower tax bracket or to a charity for additional deductions at the "fair market value."

The sharing arrangement on the first public offering we made to our clients was that 99 percent of disbursable cash would go to the limited partners and 1 percent to the general partners until the limited partners had received 120 percent of their initial investment back; then the proceeds would be split 60 percent to the limited partners, 25 percent to the general partners, and 15 percent to the producer and talent.

Cash distributions from a successful film could start seven or eight months after release, and the payout on your original investment could occur during the second year. After that, income could continue for six to ten years.

The average gross per week of a theater is $6000 with roughly 25¢ on a dollar going to the partnership. If a film appears in 200 theaters for an average of ten weeks with an average $6000 gross, the box office receipts would be $12 million, of which sum the partnership would receive $3 million.

If the downside risk can be calculated to be 10¢ and the upside potential very good, you might compare this with an investment in a $30 stock that cannot lose more than $3 but has the potential to outperform the market substantially.

I'm pleased to see the offering of a registered limited partnership where you and I have an opportunity to become an investor in a movie with as small an amount as $5000.

NEW CROPLAND DEVELOPMENT

If you want to become a sole proprietor or a general partner in new croplands, our tax laws will allow you to write off farm losses against ordinary income and later take a capital gains when you sell the land. You will be allowed to write off most of the cost of establishing a producing orchard or vineyard and then sell the land and productive trees or vines as real property.

The reason given for allowing these deductions only to sole proprietors or general partners is to make the deductions available only to "bona fide farmers" who are taking risks.

Take a fig or pistachio ranch as an example. Ordinarily, the IRS rules state that you can't write off costs of a fruit or nut tree. You have to depreciate the costs you have in it, starting in the year that the tree is ready to bear. A fig tree may cost 50¢ as a seedling and another $3 in costs to bring it to plantable stage.

Next, you can enter into a farm management contract at arm's length with a third-party firm, paying this firm an annual service fee to take care of your trees. You buy the seedlings and each year expense the contract costs of care and management. These costs can be expensed in the year in which they are paid. The drip irrigation system is also leased, and this can be expensed. When you sell the farm there's very little depreciation recapture because you expensed most of the development costs each year.

When your fig ranch reaches bearing age, it can have a substantial cash-flow generating ability and a corresponding capital value. You can sell it or trade it and roll your equity into other land. This is one of the ways you can build up your equity while using tax-sheltered cash.

I'm familiar with one 160-acre fig ranch which showed the following results. The land was purchased with a small down payment and the remainder was financed. The land was prepared, seedlings bought,

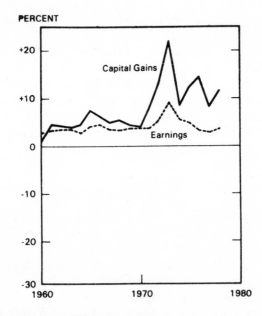

Figure 12–3. Farm and Ranch Earnings and Capital Gains, 1960–1980

and other nondepreciable costs were expensed. The total cost basis in the land after these expenditures was about $1500 an acre. During the next six years an additional $1857 an acre of deductible development costs were expended. Counting investment tax credit, almost all of the out-of-pocket money was written off. By the end of the sixth year the land could have been sold for $6000 an acre. The investors, however, reasoned that the ranch was a good inflation hedge. They projected if inflation occurred at 15 percent in the land over the next six years they could sell for around $14,000 an acre. If that should happen and the investors were in a 50 percent tax bracket, they would have invested only about $900 per acre in hard after-tax dollars to cover development costs. If they sell the fig ranch at $14,000 an acre and subtract their $1500 basis, they will have a $12,500 an acre capital gains.

If you are considering this type of tax-favored investment it is very important that you become familiar with many aspects of farming and the people with whom you'll be investing. (Incidentally, because of the Tax Reform Act of 1969 these write-offs cannot be obtained on citrus and almond groves.)

Figure 12–3 shows farm and ranch earnings and capital gains during the past twenty years.

TIMBER

Another area you may want to consider on an individual or partnership basis is an investment in timber. Some of its profit-potential characteristics are:

1. Low management costs
2. Continuous physical growth
3. Replenishable natural resource
4. Excellent hedge against inflation
5. Actuarial predictability
6. Favorable marketing outlook

A well-tended commercial forest can be a safe and rewarding investment which can provide you with a good cash flow and a potential for excellent capital gains.

Trees grow constantly, both physically and dimensionally every year. One economic benefit of timber is that when the price of timber dips temporarily, the growth in physical volume continues and before long can overcome the effect of the price decline.

It is predicted that the demand for timber will double in the next twenty-five years. By purchasing "uneven-aged" stands of timber, you may benefit from a harvest of mature trees every five years while at the same time benefiting from their growth; with stands of 1000 acres or more, 100-acre parcels can be scheduled for cutting each year, which can provide annual yields of 8 to 12 percent.

Apart from the future impact of inflation on timber prices, the demand–supply outlook for timber is very favorable and should result in an upward push in prices. There is an increasing demand for timber for such conventional uses as building materials, and our energy needs are also putting additional pressure on the timber industry. Studies are now being made on the possibility of using "energy plantations" as a cheaper source of fuel. Figure 12–4 shows the price index of pine sawtimber stumpage for a five-year period.

Work with your financial planner and determine if this is an area about which you should be better informed. Carefully examine what offerings are available through a strong and experienced general partner.

MINING

Another area that may lend itself to tax incentives and offer a good potential for gain is that of mining for precious metals and other hard rock minerals. This industry reminds me of the oil and gas industry back in the 1950s. At that time the large producers and the small independent prospectors represented the vast majority of the activ-

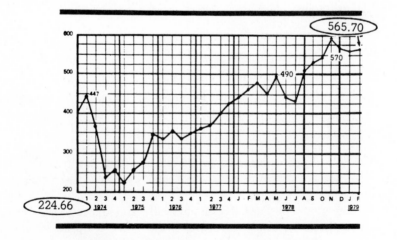

Source: Vardaman's Green Sheet, James M.
Vardaman & Co., Inc., Spring 1979.

Figure 12–4. Pine Sawtimber Stumpage Price Index

ity within the industry. The same is true in certain areas of the mining industry today. Presently, it is possible to find vast mineral reserves which are too small for development by the large mining companies yet require too much capital for the independent "prospector."

If you are in the 50 percent tax bracket or above, you will want to find a private offering being made by a general partner that is a small to medium size corporation with personnel who have outstanding "hard rock" expertise, that has claims with excellent potential, and that is willing to finance the venture with participation from private capital. This can offer an attractive investment from both an economic and tax-incentive viewpoint.

Tax Incentives of Mining

What would be your source of write-offs if you were to become a limited partner investor in a private placement offering in mining?

First are the tax-deductible expenses incurred during the exploration operations, development, and mining phase. Second, claim owners and property owners often require the payment of an overriding royalty in exchange for the right to "mine" the ore body. Advance payment of

this "uniform minimum annual royalty" in the initial years may be in the form of a (corporation or partnership) nonrecourse note issued by the operating entity. If you desire to guarantee your "prorata share" of the minimum annual royalty note, you would be entitled to a federal income tax deduction which could be substantially in excess of the amount of the actual cash you initially invested in the mining program.

This portion of the minimum annual royalty liability payment which is accrued is often paid from the actual gross revenue of the mining operation during the productive life of the mine; however there is no question that you are "at risk" if revenues are not produced.

Economics of Mining

I am familiar with a placer gold mining operation in Montana with geological reports showing reserves of 2 million cubic yards of gravel. This gravel has an average content of .04 ounce of gold per yard which engineers have determined is recoverable through a simple, high volume gravel separation process. Recovery costs should total an estimated $14 per yard of gravel processed. Assuming $600 per ounce of gold, $10 per yard of total profit could result for the investing partners. With an investment of $47,500 in cash over a two-year period, the limited partner could have written off $140,000 on his tax return because of the way the investment was structured.

The projected profit potential on the investment over a twenty-year period is $500,000. Depletion allowance will apply to a portion of this; however, a substantial amount of the cash flow would be taxed as ordinary income as it is received.

Another mining investment I'm familiar with is of a lead/barite/flourspar/silver mine with an estimated 800,000 tons of ore which could yield $72 per ton of gross revenue. It has been estimated that this mine will generate a net profit of nearly $8 million to the investing partners over a six-year period.

Each unit of the partnership was $48,000 plus recourse notes for which the investor was entitled to a $142,000 deduction. Financial projections are that each unit could yield a potential profit of $220,000 over a six-year period. The same taxability of cash flow would apply on the cash flow. These are projections and may never materialize.

PENSION AND PROFIT-SHARING PLANS

If you own or are one of the higher paid employees of a corporation, an excellent way to shelter funds from taxes is to establish a pension and/or profit-sharing plan. Have a specialist design the plans that give you the greatest advantage. These are covered in detail in Chapter 16, "Planning For the Later Years."

There is probably no other vehicle that you can use if you own a closely held corporation, and all the conditions are right, that will provide you with such good shelter without the IRS questioning your deductions, if you follow all the rules. It gives you the flexibility to play the game to your maximum tax advantage. You can balance the funds between the corporation, yourself, and the pension plan.

Not only are your contributions deductible to the corporation, but also all the earnings in your plan compound tax-sheltered. At retirement time you can do an IRA Rollover to postpone taxes, plus funds that are not withdrawn are permitted to continue to compound tax-sheltered. Also, if death should occur, inheritance taxes can also be avoided if the plan is set up properly.

These plans can be funded in a variety of ways. Our company's plan uses investments in mutual funds, stocks, oil and gas income programs, deeds of trust, investment-grade diamonds, wrap-around mortgages, etc. Never fund your plan with any type of life insurance. In Chapter 13, "Life Insurance—The Great National Consumer Dilemma," I point out why.

KEOGH AND INDIVIDUAL RETIREMENT ACCOUNTS

If you are self-employed and do not have a large number of employees, you should consider establishing a Keogh account. Your contribution to your own retirement plan is deductible, and the distributions are allowed to compound tax-sheltered. You are allowed to contribute and deduct 15 percent of your self-employment income up to a maximum of $7500. You can also have a defined-benefit Keogh and perhaps contribute more. This is covered in detail in Chapter 16, "Planning for the Later Years."

If you work for a corporation that does not have a retirement program or is not making a contribution on your behalf, or if you are earning income by working, you are allowed to contribute 15 percent or your income up to a maximum of $1500, deduct it from your taxable income, and let it compound tax-sheltered in an Individual Retirement Account. If $875 is put in a nonworking spouse's name and $875 in the working one's name, $1750 can be contributed and deducted. This is also covered in more detail in Chapter16.

CAPITAL GAINS

Capital gains occur when you sell an asset for more than your cost basis. If you have held it for less than one year, the gain is a short-term capital gain and is taxed as ordinary income if you do not have a long or short term capital loss to offset it. If you have held your asset over a year when the sale is made, then 40 percent of the gain is taxable and is added to any other taxable income. The maximum amount that can be lost to tax on a capital gain is 28 percent. This does not sound so bad if you say it quickly, but often these assets represent a business or a farm on which a couple have slaved many long hours for many years, and it's often very painful to have so large an amount of these inflated dollars snatched away. If the capital gain exceeds $100,000, it is more difficult to provide acceptable shelter because of the alternative minimum tax legislated by the Tax Revenue Act of 1978.

Alternative Minimum Tax

The reduction of the taxable portion of a long-term capital gain from 50 to 40 percent and the elimination of the untaxable portion as an item of tax preference were steps in the right direction by Congress. But there was a blockbuster in this piece of legislation if you had a capital gain in excess of $100,000 and unusually high itemized deductions.

A worksheet is included in the Appendix (Figure 11) for your use in making your preliminary calculations, but I strongly advise you to consult with your tax advisor before entering into any tax-sheltered investments if you have received in excess of $100,000 of capital gains. Briefly, this Act contained two significant factors:

1. Only 40 percent of the gain is tabaxle income for purposes of computing federal income taxes in the regular way.

2. The other 60 percent of the gain is considered a preference item for purposes of computing the new alternative minimum tax. In most instances, this new alternative tax is computed by (a) adding one's taxable income to the 60 percent excluded portion of the gain; (b) exempting the first $20,000; and (c) taxing the first $40,000 of the remainder at 10 percent, the second $40,000 at 20 percent, and the rest at 25 percent.

Now you must pay *either* the regular-way income tax *or* the alternative minimum tax, whichever is *greater*.

A major result of this interaction is that there is a limitation on the amount of a gain that should be sheltered.

For example, if you have no other taxable income and you have a $200,000 long-term capital gain, your regular tax for a joint return would be $30,478. The Alternative Minimum Tax, however, is $37,000. Therefore, your tax liability is $37,000. If you create $10,000 of deductions, only $2500 in tax savings result.

However, if you are already in the 49-percent bracket or higher because of ordinary income, you should shelter a part of your gain if it is $100,000 or less.

STOCKS

Your chief incentive for investing in stocks should be to make a profit. When you can't make a profit in the market, get out. You should sell when you anticipate that market conditions may become unfavorable or that your stock may have topped out for what appears to be a prolonged period of time. If you sell for more than you paid for the stock and you have held it for over a year, you will trigger a capital gain, 40 percent of which will be taxable unless you have offsetting losses.

For example, let's assume that you bought 1000 shares of a gold stock at $5 and that you sold it a year later at $10. You now have a $5000 long-term capital gain, of which 40 percent is taxable. This $2000 will be added to your taxable income and will be taxed at your top rate.

If you have realized capital gains and it's toward the end of the year and you have some losses in some of your other stocks, bonds, or other assets, you should consider selling them, establishing your loss, and charging it aginst your capital gains. Be sure to wait thirty-one days before buying the same asset back or it will be considered a "wash sale" and the loss will be disallowed. For example, if you had a loss in American Telephone & Telegraph you would not want to buy it back before thirty-one days had lapsed, but you could buy General Telephone the same day and still charge off the loss on AT&T.

Don't let the fact that you'll pay a tax keep you from selling a stock that has matured and seemingly reached a plateau. Often I see people plant good fruit trees and let the fruit rot on the trees. Of course, they can avoid the capital gains if they hold it until it goes back to what they paid for it, but this hardly seems like brilliant financial planning.

MUNICIPAL BOND SWAPPING

If you own some municipal bonds and interest rates have risen since you made your purchase, but you still want to own municipals or corporates, you might consider swapping bonds. You must be sure that the bonds you repurchase are either from a different issuer or of a different issue date or coupon maturity.

The swap could work like this. You own bonds with a par value of $10,000, a coupon rate of 4 percent that is due in ten years, and a market value of $7200. You sell these bonds and replace them with $10,000 par value bonds carrying a 6.5 percent coupon rate, due in twenty years at a discounted price of $7200. Your net results would be: (1) your yearly income is increased $250 per year; (2) you have established a capital loss of $2800; and (3) you will recoup your loss in 11.2 years by the increased income of $250 per year. If you have a long-term capital gain to charge your loss against, you'll recoup it sooner. If you do not have a long-term capital gain or if your loss exceeds the gain, $6000 of your excess can be applied against $3000 of ordinary income. If your gain is short-term, $3000 can be applied against $3000 of ordinary income. If your losses are greater than this, they can be carried forward indefinitely to be applied against future gains and/or applied against $3000 per year ordinary income.

If your capital loss is considered long-term for each dollar of loss, only one-half can be offset against ordinary income subject to the $3000 limitation.

DISCOUNT CORPORATE BONDS

Another way to realize capital gains is to buy discounted bonds such as were available at the peak of the high interest rates in 1980. For example, you could have bought:

Alabama Power: 7¼% of 2002 at 60¾ to yield 13¼%
General Motors: 4⅞% of 1987 at 67½ to yield 11.19%
Houston Lighting & Power: 3% of 1989 at 52½ to yield 11.56%

All of these bonds are high grade and should pay $1000 per bond at maturity, providing you with a long-term capital gains. For example, par is $1000 and the current price on Alabama Power is $607.50; therefore you would have a capital gains in the year 2002 of $392.50. (I hope this example also points out the risk of a "riskless" investment —the characteristic often attributed to high-grade corporate bonds by the uninformed.)

An easier way that takes less expertise on your part and should carry less risk because of their professional management and diversification is to invest in mutual funds investing in deeply discounted bonds. When interest rates go down bond prices should go up, and the sale would produce a capital gain; or if the discounted bond matured and par value was received, a capital gain would occur.

MUNICIPAL BONDS

I've covered these in Chapter 11, "Lending Your Dollars." In my opinion you are playing Russian Roulette with inflation if you invest in municipal bonds. You are obviously better off in municipal bonds than in corporate bonds in the higher brackets, but both are guaranteed to lose in this inflationary economy. An alternative you may want to consider is the tax-managed funds.

TAX-MANAGED FUNDS

Tax-managed mutual funds may offer you a better alternative than municipal bonds. These funds usually are invested in high-yield securities with income compounding tax-free inside the fund.

A few minutes of calculations will demonstrate the total cost of inflation and taxes. You may have averaged a 10 percent return from your money market fund, but if your taxable income was $36,000, for example, you would have had only 5.7 percent after taxes, which did not let you keep up with inflation. If you invest in municipals—even those that earn 7½ percent—this will still not be enough to keep up with inflation. In addition, you have the risk of a decline in principal if interest rates rise and you need to sell your bond before maturity.

In a tax-managed fund dividends and capital gains are not paid to you, but are allowed to compound automatically. When you redeem your shares, they are taxed as long-term capital gains if you have held them for a year. These shares can also fluctuate in value.

Most mutual funds elect to be taxed under the special provisions offered to regulated investment companies. As a result, most funds do not pay corporate taxes on dividends or interest as long as they pass through at least 90 percent of income to their shareholders. In turn, the shareholders pay taxes at their individual rates. Tax-managed funds are operated differently. They have elected corporate tax status and do not plan to distribute realized income and capital gains to shareholders. Since income is not distributed, there is no tax to the shareholders. The funds pay taxes on only 15 percent of dividend income less operating expenses. This is made possible because tax law excludes from taxation 85 percent of preferred and common stock dividends paid from one coporation to another corporation.

In basic terms, tax-managed funds pay corporate taxes on only 15 percent of their investment income—and this obligation may be offset with operating expenses. Since they don't distribute the income, the stockholders pay no current tax at all.

You may find that tax-managed funds offer other features that meet your needs. If a regular cash flow is desired, most funds allow for a monthly or quarterly check through a systematic withdrawal plan. Some funds allow for telephone redemptions which improve liquidity. Social Security (Tax I.D.) numbers are not requested by most funds and no forms are sent to the Internal Revenue Service, because annual income tax reports for the shareholders are not necessary. However, you are responsible for reporting capital gains once shares are redeemed.

SINGLE-PREMIUM DEFERRED ANNUITIES

These have been discussed in some detail in Chapter 11, "Lending Your Dollars." However, since we are discussing tax avoidance, or at least deferral, let me share Table 12–2 with you. I call it the "Hidden Cost of Taxes." This table will again emphasize that when you pay a dollar in taxes, not only do you lose that dollar, but you lose what that dollar would have earned for you if you had been allowed to keep it. Let's take an example of $10,000.

Look at the "Hidden Cost of Taxes" which the IRS has taken from you on the earnings produced by your accumulated capital. On just $10,000 in ten years in a 30 percent tax bracket, the cost amounts to $4345. In a 50 percent bracket it is $6787. After twenty years it is $16,874 and $24,698, which amounts to much, much more than your original investment. From that time on, the difference, as you can see, becomes almost unbelievable, and this loss to the "Hidden Cost of Taxes" is just on a single investment of $10,000. How many people do you know who are earning taxable income on many times this amount?

SUBCHAPTER S CORPORATIONS

A subchapter S corporation is a small business corporation that has elected not to be taxed as a corporation. A shareholder of a sub-

TABLE 12–2.   HYPOTHETICAL EXAMPLES OF $10,000 ACCOUNTS

NO. OF YEARS	$10,000 at 8%* Interest (Interest taxed as accrued)		$10,000 Single-Premium Fixed Annuity (Interest accumulated without current tax)	Hidden Cost of Taxes	
	30% TAX BRACKET	50% TAX BRACKET	@ 8% *	30%	50%
5	$13,131	$12,166	$ 14,693	$ 1,562	$ 2,527
10	17,244	14,802	21,589	4,345	6,787
15	22,644	18,009	31,721	9,077	13,712
20	29,735	21,911	46,609	16,874	24,698
25	39,047	26,658	68,484	29,437	41,826
30	51,276	32,433	100,626	49,350	68,193
35	67,334	39,460	147,853	80,519	108,393
40	88,421	48,009	217,245	128,818	169,236

* Assume level 8 percent interest throughout the savings period.

chapter S corporation must include in his income his pro rata share of the corporation's taxable income whether the amount was actually distributed to him or not. This can become a tax shelter when lower-income family members are given or sold stock in such a corporation.

Another use may occur when you have a good bankable idea for a new business that will by its very nature probably be operating in the red for its first few years. By setting up the company as a subchapter S corporation, the losses can flow directly to you, and you can charge them off against your ordinary income. Later when the business becomes profitable, you can convert it to a regular corporation. There are limitations to the number of shareholders permissible in a subchapter S corporation, plus certain qualifications, so be sure you cover your bases if you take this route.

HOME OWNERSHIP

If you are in a tax bracket of 40 percent or above, there is considerable merit to owning a home on which you have obtained the maximum mortgage. As explained in Chapter 7, "The Roof Over Your Head," interest is deductible; therefore your interest cost is subsidized by the amount of your tax bracket. If your interest is 10 percent and you are in a 40 percent bracket, your net interest cost is 6 percent. If your bracket is 60 percent (and surely you'll make some tax-advantaged investments to lower it), your net interest cost after taxes is 4 percent.

THE INSTALLMENT SALE

Perhaps you hold a large amount of stocks or other assets that have greatly appreciated in value. The stocks may be growth stocks that pay out modest dividends, but you need more income, or you may feel you do not have adequate diversification. However, if you sell the stocks you would trigger a capital-gains tax which could reduce your net worth. This may give you a locked-in feeling.

Is there a way to postpone a portion of the taxes, obtain diversification, increase your income, and possibly decrease future inheritance taxes?

Yes, there is through the use of an installment sale. To illustrate the possible advantages of this approach, let's consider the options open to you.

First, you can hold on to your present investments. By taking no action you remain locked in. To avoid capital-gains taxes, you would have to keep these investments for the rest of your life. Also, any additional appreciation will further increase the value of your estate for federal tax purposes, as well as your potential capital-gains tax.

Second, you can sell your investment for cash and reinvest the proceeds. This creates an immediate capital-gains tax on which taxes must be paid. Assume that you have a cost basis of $20,000 on assets that now have a value of $100,000. Upon sale you realize an $80,000 capital gain that will be taxable at the capital-gains rate.

Third, you can make an installment sale. Under this plan you would sell your asset to a buyer at its full market value. The buyer would give you an interest-bearing installment note. In this way you incur capital-gains liability only as you actually receive payments from this note. The provisions of the note establish the amount of money you will receive at specified intervals and the period of years over which the periodic payments will be made.

Advantages to the Seller

There can be advantages to you, if you are the seller, and also to the buyer. Let's examine some of them.

First, you can unlock your gains and spread your tax liability over a period of years, when you may be in a lower tax bracket. Second, you can increase your income over the term of the note. Third, the payments you receive may be substantially taxable as capital gains. Fourth, as the note is repaid and the payments spent, the value of your estate decreases for federal estate tax purposes. Any growth in assets you have sold now belongs to the buyer and will not be reflected in your estate. Fifth, you should be able to obtain more diversification, which should reduce your risk.

Advantages to the Buyer

The installment sale allows the buyer to become the owner of substantial assets without making any large and immediate cash outlay. He can now sell the newly acquired stocks or other assets without the payment of substantial income, gift, or estate taxes and put the proceeds into a more appropriate investment. He may also receive an annual tax deduction for the interest he is paying on the note. In the meantime, all future growth belongs to the buyer. (It should be noted that as this book went to press Congress was considering legislation which would limit the advantages of an installment sale with related parties. If such legislation is enacted, it must be carefully analyzed by your legal counsel in order to avoid any unwanted tax problems.)

The proper legal instruments to accomplish an installment sale should be prepared by your attorney and should be coordinated with the advice of your C.P.A. Remind him that the note should be carried at interest. The interest may be stated or unstated. If stated (which I recommend), it must be at least 6 percent per year. In the event the interest stated is less than 6 percent, or if no interest is stated at all, Uncle Sam will impute 7 percent interest rate.

PRIVATE ANNUITY

Another tool that may fit your financial objective is the private annuity. This type of an annuity involves the transfer of your property to a transferee—an individual, a partnership, or a corporation—in exchange for an *unsecured* promise to make periodic payments to you in fixed amounts for a designated period of time. In most cases, this will be for your lifetime. The assets you may use for this are real property, stocks, bonds, mutual funds, limited partnerships, and so forth.

The advantage to you in using this method is that it can usually increase your cash flow from your assets without substantially increasing your income tax liability. Capital-gains taxation will be spread over the life of your agreement and, as a result, may be reduced in amount.

Since these assets are generally not includable for estate tax purposes, there could be a savings on estate taxes in the event of your premature death. The private annuity can be partially taxable under the estate under certain conditions which your attorney can detail for you.

There are some disadvantages to the private annuity. Let's assume you transferred this property to your son and you die prior to the completion of the agreement. There is the possibility that your son may be subjected to an adjustment in the basis of that property. If your son holds the property for at least a year before selling it, the gain would be subject to treatment as a long-term capital gain. If he sells it immediately and you die, it could be subject to short-term capital gains treatment. If you live longer than the life expectancy table indicates, the payments may be greater than the original value, but the tax savings and appreciation could more than make up for this. Also, there is no tax deduction accruing to your son for interest paid to you. Another disadvantage is the provision that you are unable to secure the annuity payments by collateralizing through a trust or by mortgage.

How to Fund the Installment Sale or the Private Annuity

One excellent way to provide the necessary funds for the monthly payments the buyer will need to make to you is for him to invest the proceeds from the sale of the assets in shares of a high-quality mutual fund that is within a family of funds that also has a money market fund, and to begin a systematic withdrawal program. He might also superimpose a market timing service on the fund so they could move you in and out of the market as market conditions dictate. In this way you could obtain diversification in a quality cross-section of securities that are professionally managed and have the custodian bank send you a check each month.

Other investments you should consider are oil and gas income limited partnerships, income real estate limited partnerships, and quality stocks that pay generous dividends.

In summary, the advantages of the installment sale or the private annuity are:

1. Avoids all the costs of probate in the case of an annuity.

2. Saves on federal estate taxes at death, in case of an annuity.

3. Saves on state inheritance taxes.

4. Spreads the long-term capital gains tax over a number of years.

5. In the case of a private annuity the transfer may incorporate a gift.

6. There is no future appreciation to increase estate valuation.

THE LIVING TRUST

The proper use of the living trust (also referred to as the revocable or the *intervivos* trust) can reduce the cost of passing your assets to your heirs.

With the living trust, a pour-over will should be drawn to cover all assets you have not registered to the trust. You should have the trust drawn in the state in which you reside.

Your trust can be written so as to pass your assets as you would do in a will. Some states will allow you to be your own trustee. Some require co-trustees. You may also use a bank or corporate trustee. All of the assets you want to place in the trust should be listed. As changes are made the list should be changed.

The trust can offer the following benefits:

1. The cost of probate and administration fees saved because the trust assets are not probated through the courts.

2. The prolonged probate time can be saved, as the assets can be passed immediately. All creditors must be paid, and the federal estate taxes and the state taxes can be put into an escrow account with the trustee liable.

3. The problem of incapacity is lessened. Generally, under the will method the individual has no document while he is alive, and, should incapacity occur, the court must be petitioned to declare him incapacitated in order to sell any property. The document can state that three doctors can declare the individual incapacitated and the co-trustees or successor trustee assume trustee role.

4. The trust can afford privacy in death as to the amount of the assets held in the estate, since it does not go through the probate court. No listing of assets is required, which usually ends up in the local papers.

5. A trust can keep the estate under family control. Since assets such as stock, property, or closely held corporations or businesses are not under court control, these can be sold to raise cash for costs and fees and for state and federal estate taxes.

6. The savings of federal and state inheritance and estate taxes may be achieved by splitting the assets between husband and wife into two trusts.

There are some assets that you should avoid placing in the living trust. Some of these are cars, jewelry, furs, and furnishings. You also should not place in the trust professional corporation stock, since most states require that the stockholder be of the same profession as the original stockholder.

Also, you cannot place in the trust tax option corporations and subchapter S corporations, since a trust cannot be the owner of such stock, as it would terminate the election.

The transfer of assets into a living trust is not of taxable consequence. (Gift taxes can occur when assets are placed into short-term or irrevocable trusts.)

INCOME SPLITTING

If you are in a high tax bracket and if you have dependents, you may want to consider income splitting. For example, the interest and dividends you are receiving are being taxed at your higher bracket. If they were shifted to your children, who may have a low or non-existent bracket, you could reduce the family's overall tax burden. To do this, you will have to transfer the income-producing assets to them either temporarily or permanently. This income could be used for such things as summer camp, riding lessons, or college expenses. This arrangement may not be used for items you are legally required to provide.

How should income splitting be done? You probably want to avoid outright gifts or guardianships. Contracts of minors can be voided, and guardianships are cumbersome. Ways you might consider are custodial accounts, special trusts for minors, Clifford trusts, interest-free loans, and gifts.

Custodial Account. Set up an account with an adult as custodian for the child. You cannot use any of the income for the support of your child, for that is your legal responsibility. You will still be entitled to the $1000 exemption for your child, or each child if you have more than one, as long as the child is either a student or under 19 years of age. Each child receives up to $1000 a year tax-free from his own additional exemption added to the $100 dividend exclusion.

Funds accumulated in your children's custodial account may be used for their college education upon their attainment of majority at age 18, with your being taxed on the amount used. If your state has lowered the age of majority to 18, you are relieved of parental support at that time. You may apply the $3000 annual gift exclusion to each child and do this each year. If your spouse joins with you, $6000 each year can be gifted to each child without gift tax. To avoid these gifts being a part of your estate in the event of your death, you should not be the custodian, nor should your spouse if the spouse has joined in the gift.

Special Trust for Minors.   Perhaps you feel it prudent that your child or children not have access to the principal until age 21. Under the Section 2503(c) Trust, you may use your $3000 per child annual gift exclusion ($6000 if joined by your spouse). These assets and income can be used for the child before age 21. If the trust's assets have not been spent by then, the principal must be paid to the child at age 21.

Clifford Trust.   Another method of income splitting is through the use of the Clifford trust. This is a short-term living trust created for a period of the lesser of ten years and a day or the life of the beneficiary. At the end of this period, the trust terminates and your property is returned to you.

A Clifford trust may be used for your dependent children, dependent parents, or others for whom you want to provide income for a period of ten years. Its chief advantage is that it permits you to split income without giving up your asset permanently.

For gift tax purposes, you will be making a gift of the present value of the right to receive income over the period of the trust. This will usually amount to 44.2% of the value of the assets placed in the trust.

Interest-Free Loans.   Another method you may want to consider for income splitting to save taxes is to make an interest-free loan on a demand note. You would not be required in this arrangement to give away your assets permanently, nor even relinquish control for ten years, as in a Clifford trust.

One way you might use to accomplish this is to set up a trust for your children and fund it with, say, $1000. You then lend funds to the trust and take back an interest-free demand note for that amount. The trust then invests the loan proceeds in high-yielding investments. This income can be accumulated in the trust for future use or distributed currently. You should have no gift tax on the transfer. You may recover the funds at any time, and appreciation on the investment is removed from your estate. The note would, of course, be a part of your estate.

The IRS has been trying valiantly to combat this arrangement. The first case of major significance in the area of interest-free loans to family members was *Johnson v. U.S.* In that case, a parent made an interest-free loan payable on demand to his children. The IRS contended that interest-free loans defeated the purpose of the federal estate tax by reducing the parent's estate by the amount of the interest that could have been charged. However, the District Court held that no gift had been made. According to the Court, the purpose of the federal estate tax was not defeated, since balance on the loan would be included in the parent's gross estate. The District Court also stated that a parent had no obligation to charge interest on a loan to children, or otherwise deal with children at arm's length.

Making Gifts.   You may give $3000 each year to as many people as you desire without a gift tax. If you and your spouse join in the giving, this amount can be $6000. Any amount you give above this amount is taxable and counts against your tax credit. This can have the effect of your prepaying your estate taxes. However, if you are gifting an income property to a person in a low tax bracket this could be a reason for gifting above this amount. Another reason might be that the gift is an appreciating asset. By making the gift the appreciation occurs outside of the estate.

CREATIVE, KNOWLEDGEABLE C.P.A.

Do find yourself a creative, knowledgeable C.P.A. who is truly dedicated to helping you *not* pay taxes. I've met some who should be on the IRS payroll. If all your C.P.A. does for you is tally up how much taxes you owe on April 15, the IRS will do this without sending you a bill. You don't want a tax tallier. You want one who conscientiously works for you to lower your taxes. Your greatest single expense last year was probably your tax bill. An excellent C.P.A. is invaluable, and his fees are deductible. Don't, however, shift to him the burden of deciding on the economics of a particular tax-favored investment. That's not his role. I repeat, that's not his function in your life. Your financial planner has that obligation to you. Your C.P.A. should only be concerned with the tax aspects of the investment to determine if it fits your needs and if he agrees with the tax opinion in the offering memorandum. If you mistakenly place on him the burden of determining the investment merits of a proposal, he will almost always object. That way he'll never be wrong—of course, he'll never be right either, and you will have condemned yourself to sending your dollars on that one-way trip. Start paying your C.P.A. for helping you not to pay taxes. He must be willing to devote time to your cause. I've seen many C.P.A.s say no just because they did not want to burden themselves with reading and digesting an inch-thick private offering memorandum. Even if they did read it, the offering may have been about an area in which they had little or no expertise, but they were embarrassed to admit their ignorance to their client. Then I've seen others who got their kicks in life by building a reputation as a "deal killer."

SUMMARY

If you are in a 20 to 30 percent tax bracket, you should consider making investments that give you tax-sheltered income, such as registered limited partnerships investing in triple-net leases of commercial real estate (see Chapter 6, "The Real Rewards of Real Estate") and oil and gas income programs (see Chapter 8, "Energizing Your Investments"). If you are in the 30 to 50 percent bracket, you will also want to consider registered oil and gas income programs and add to those registered offerings of multifamily housing, office buildings, shopping centers, and motels. If you are in the 40 percent bracket, you may want to look at registered programs such as cattle feeding, marine container leasing, and movies. If you are in the 49 percent bracket and above, you will have a wide variety of both registered and private placement instruments to choose from. Present security regulations make it relatively easy for your financial planner to reduce your tax burden. Figure 12 in the Appendix is a simplified worksheet showing the effect of particular tax-favored investments on your taxable income. Unfortunately, he will be limited in helping you if you are below that bracket. You hit that level at $45,800 taxable income on a joint return and $34,100 on a single. If you are not presently earning that amount, look around you diligently. There are many exciting career opportunities that will bring you that amount of income and much more. You'll find that if you search with an open mind it is not hard to succeed, because there are so few people out there trying. As you will remember, we've learned that it's not how hard you work or how many hours. Your rewards in life will always be in direct proportion to what you do, your ability to do it, and the difficulty of replacing you. And when you've reached those loftier income levels and are searching for the best tax-favored investment, seek out areas where demand exceeds supply. Then look for investment packages that have been fairly structured so that if the investment is profitable you will make money. Seek out investments with general partners of unquestioned expertise, high integrity, substantial net worth, and an excellent past performance record. The latter may not always be possible. The area of investment may be a new one. But, if you persist in a spirit of serendipity you should reap great rewards.

As you search for economically sound tax-favored investments, you'll find that you are being joined by an increasingly larger number of your fellow citizens. More and more of them are looking for opportunities to put their hard-earned money into areas of great social need. Also, there is a growing resentment to the ever-increasing tax burden being pressed upon them by the tax bracket creep—a product of escalating inflation. As they are faced with a lowering of their standard of living, they are looking for a better way.

As you look for a better way, you should not be foolhardy in your search for tax relief, but neither should you be obsessed by a fear of risk or a fear of the IRS. I emphasize again that you don't get a write-off for investing in a Series E bond. (Not that I consider such an investment "safe"—it's "stable" but not "safe." Remember, our definition of safety is the return of the same amount of food, clothing and shelter—not the same number of dollars at a point in the future.)

Also remember that it is not "safe" to pay taxes either. The probability of your receiving any income from your tax receipt is quite remote. Payment of taxes means a guaranteed loss, and an expected rate of return of zero. Investing in tax-favored investments also carries great risk, but at least you have a fighting chance of turning some of your tax liabilities into assets.

Not only were tax-favored investments put on our law books by Congress to fill a social need, but by your reduction in the amount of taxes you send to Washington, you can hope to force the government to curtail some spending and leave more investment dollars in the private sector to create jobs and consumer products.

Tax-favored investments are not gimmicks or "loopholes," as some politicians are so fond of calling them at election time. The beneficiaries of these investments are you and me and your fellow Americans. You are financing areas of public need much more efficiently than can be done by the federal government. Free enterprise's record of performance is far superior. Look around you at government's dismal failures in public housing, energy, postal service, and Amtrak, to name only a few.

Congress made conscious decisions to grant tax incentives for investments in key industries rather than through government subsidies or government-owned-and-operated companies. Tax incentives serve the nation's needs as well as your needs. Congress did not enact tax incentives for the benevolent purpose of reducing your tax bill. When you invest in areas of great social need, you should feel patriotic. You are providing venture capital which benefits the country and which you hope will increase your spendable income and your estate.

Most high-income Americans work hard to earn their money and should be permitted to enjoy the rewards of such hard work. More and more of our high-income citizens are discovering that it has been impossible to retain a large portion of their income, and they are reducing the number of hours they work, often in fields where there is great need, such as in the medical field.

You should always keep in mind that, even though the characteristics of the various shelters vary greatly, they are all complex, involve risk, and are usually nonliquid. Even with the tax benefits you may receive, you can lose money as well as make it. Most tax shelters are far removed from the traditional investments such as stocks and bonds, and even if you are an experienced investor, you may find it hard to determine what is glitter and what is gold.

Another characteristic is that they can bring you an adversary—the IRS. This adversary thinking can probably be best described by the answer given by the Commissioner of the IRS to *The National Tax Shelter Digest Magazine* when he was asked to do an interview for the magazine. He stated, "Writing an article about tax shelters would be like a police chief writing an article for a burglary magazine."

This interview request was made at an American Bar Association convention where the Commissioner spoke. Attending were many young, impressionable C.P.A.s fresh out of college. Can't you envision them sitting there with stacks of regulations in front of them being taught the evils of tax shelters. As the instructors graduate these recruits, you can see them dashing out into the far corners of the country armed with wisdom and guidelines ready to save the government from the dangers of those who have the audacity to try to reduce their tax burdens.

Search for the right tax-favored investment. Work with the knowledgeable pros with the hope of keeping some of your hard-earned dollars from taking that long one-way trip to Washington!

APPLICATION

1. Calculate your anticipated taxable income for this year.
2. What is your tax bracket before shelter?
3. Do you presently have a knowledgeable and concerned financial planner who can help you build a living estate? If your answer is no, what steps are you going to take to find one? In the Appendix you'll find the addresses and phone numbers of the International Association of Financial Planners, the College of Financial Planning, the Institute of Certified Financial Planners, and Brigham Young University, which now offers a degree in Financial Planning. Also, you will find the addresses of *The Financial Planner Magazine*, Rich White, Editor; the *National Tax Shelter Digest*, David Groark, Editor; and the *Brennan Reports,* William Brennan, Editor. I recommend that you subscribe to all of them.
4. Do you have a creative, knowledgeable, and competent CPA who cares about your financial future? If not, what steps will you take this week to find one?

5. If your need is for spendable income, compare your after-tax return on municipal bonds, corporate bonds, money market funds, limited partnership programs that invest in oil and gas income, real estate triple-net leases, multifamily housing, marine container leasing, budget motels, mini-warehouses, etc.

6. Would a "guaranteed" single-premium deferred annuity using a yearly withdrawal, discussed in Chapter 11, "Lending Your Dollars," be a good solution? How about a tax-advantaged trust?

7. Should some of your hard dollars be invested in equipment leasing programs?

8. What constructive steps will you take this year to reduce your taxes?

   (1)

   (2)

   (3)

   (4)

Happy Tax Avoidance!

13

LIFE INSURANCE— THE GREAT NATIONAL CONSUMER DILEMMA

THE GREAT MYSTERY

The great mystery of life is the length of it. You should have a plan with the hope you will live a normal lifetime. You should have a plan in the event you should die before you have had time to accumulate a living estate. You do not know which will occur; therefore, you should prepare for either event. It is not difficult to acquire financial independence if you seek competent advice, apply your talents, and are granted sufficient time.

How can you be sure you will have this time? You cannot. There is a way to "buy" time, however, and it is called "life insurance." This is the name given to it by life insurance companies who desire to sell it. A better term would be "financial protection for dependents." There is nothing that can insure your life.

THE PURPOSE OF LIFE INSURANCE

Life insurance is a wonderful thing. There is no substitute for it until a sufficiently large estate has been acquired to protect those dependent upon you. It can provide you with a way to guarantee that your dependents will have the financial means to continue to maintain a standard of living in the event you should die prematurely. It can be an economic extension of yourself. You should attempt to provide this protection for your dependents before you begin an investment program.

At the beginning of this book I stated that there are six main reasons why most of our citizens reach the age of 65 flat broke: (1) procrastination, (2) failure to establish a goal, (3) ignorance of what money must do to attain that goal, (4) lack of a winning attitude, (5) failure to learn and apply our tax laws, and (6) being sold the wrong kind of life insurance. I say "sold" because I believe that had they been told how to obtain protection properly, they would not have made such glaring errors.

So that you will not fall victim to being sold the wrong kind of life insurance, I hope to give you a clear understanding of how policies are constructed. This should enable you to select the proper type of coverage to protect your dependents during the time you will need to acquire a living estate.

There is only one kind of life insurance, and that is pure protection based on a mortality table. All other kinds are pure protection plus a savings account that I call "banking." It is the "banking" portion that can be the culprit, so it is necessary for you to understand thoroughly this part of a vast number of policies that are in existence today and are being so aggressively sold.

As a rule of thumb, you can avoid most of the errors made in the acquisition of life insurance protection if you refuse to "bank" with any insurance company under conditions that you would not bank with your own bank.

The purpose of life insurance is to protect those dependent upon you in the event you should die before accumulating a living estate. After you have accumulated a living estate, your need to protect their livelihood has already been accomplished. You should plan to be self-insured by age 65. Life insurance is to protect an economic potential. You have either made it financially by 65, or you'll probably never make it.

After you have "made it," you have fulfilled your obligation to your dependents and yourself. However, at that point you may have another desire. You may want to pass on your estate intact, or at least partially so, to your heirs. You do not have this obligation, but if it is your desire, it is easy to calculate how much insurance will be needed to pay inheritance taxes.

NAMES GIVEN TO LIFE INSURANCE POLICIES

There are four major names given to life insurance policies sold in the United States today: *term*, *ordinary* or *whole life*, *limited payment life*, and *endowment*. Each can be participating or nonparticipating. In addition, there are special policies that provide combinations of the above.

You will need a clear understanding of how each kind is constructed so that you can avoid being sold the wrong kind. Regardless of what kind of life insurance policy you purchase or what it is called, the true cost of insurance goes up each year. Rates are based on likelihood of death, and each year as you become older you are more apt to die. This is reflected in a mortality table. All life insurance is "pure" insurance, called "term." In some policies there has been added a savings element, so they consist of "term" plus a savings program.

Term Insurance

There are three basic kinds of pure protection, plus some special kinds that contain the basic characteristics.

Annual Renewable Term. Let's first look at annual renewable term. If you have this type of policy, the face amount of your insurance remains the same and the rate per thousand increases each year. You can obtain annual renewable term in most states to age 100. This amount of time will adequately take care of any needs you may have to protect your dependents. However, some states allow you to renew as annual renewable term only to age 75. At that time, if you have purchased the policy properly so that it is renewable and convertible without evidence of insurability, you can convert it into a number of other types of policies.

Decreasing Term. Another type of term insurance you will want to know about is decreasing term. In decreasing term, your rate remains the same and the amount of insurance decreases. This type may fit your family's needs if your family is young and their need for coverage is great. As the children mature and become more self-sufficient and your living assets increase, your need for "outside protection" will probably decrease. Decreasing term insurance can fit this picture very well. Or perhaps you have bought some property on which you have a mortgage payable over a certain number of years that you would want paid if you should die. A decreasing term policy could be obtained to fit this circumstance.

With your decreasing term program, you will want to have an increasing investment program to replace the protection that is diminishing. You are, in effect, substituting a living estate for a death estate, which is the direction you want to go. You don't want a death estate, but until you have had time to accumulate a living estate, buying a death estate is a necessity.

There was a time when a number of very good financial planners recommended decreasing term joined with an investment program with the hope of increasing their clients' living assets. But, when the economy was suddenly hit by double-digit inflation and the stock market suffered a precipitous drop, many of them changed their approach. Fortunately, they had obtained for their clients policies that were renewable and convertible at the clients' option, so they were able to convert them to policies that would retain their coverage.

Decreasing term may serve your purpose very well, but the coverage does diminish each year. Perhaps you should place yourself in the driver's seat, so that you can decide whether or not your coverage should decline rather than have the decision automatically made for you. You can make your annual renewable term policy decreasing term by just dropping the amount of coverage your family no longer needs.

Mortgage insurance is in reality a decreasing term policy. If knowing that your family will have extra funds to pay off the mortgage on your home provides you with greater peace of mind, you can consider mortgage insurance. However, paying off the mortgage may not be the most prudent thing for them to do. They need only to continue making the monthly payments as before. If you have given them the proper investment instructions, using the information obtained from this book, they should be able to invest the funds in a more beneficial manner where these dollars have a chance to grow and at least keep pace with inflation. Why should they place a portion of their assets in a dead position earnings-wise when it is not required of them?

Level Term. Level term means that the face amount of the policy remains level for the term of time chosen. The most common periods are 5, 10, 15, 20, 25, and 30 years, and level term to 65. For example, if you chose a ten-year level term, basically what the insurance company would do is add up the annual renewable term rates for ten years, divide the total by 10, and you would pay the same rate for ten years. You would be overpaying in the early years and underpaying in the later years.

These three are your basic pure term policies. There are some special policies that contain similar provisions as they affect you.

Additional First-Year Premium-Level Term. Additional first-year premium-level term (commonly called "deposit level term") is a term policy, usually of 5-, 8-, 10-, 12-, 15-, or 20-year periods, where you pay an additional first-year premium to the company as evidence of your intent to retain your policy for the specified period of time. The one most commonly used by financial planners is ten years in duration, renewable and convertible at your option without evidence of insurability.

The "deposit term" concept was developed because of the high lapse (cancellation) rate on conventional policies. Reportedly, of every three new policies written today, one is lapsed within two or three years. These lapsed policies are expensive to an insurance company because of the substantial costs to place the policies in force initially. They have paid for your physical examination, paid a sales commission to the agent, and paid other numerous charges in relation to the policy.

If you drop your policy in the first few years of its existence, it is unprofitable for the company. To protect themselves, insurance companies must "load" the premium of each policyholder in order to recapture some of these costs. Since they do not know who will lapse the policy, they include this "loading" for all those insured.

"Loading" is helpful in solving their expense problem, but what about your expense problem? If you are one of the "good" guys who keeps his policy, you are having to pay for the "bad" guy who drops his.

To some insurance companies this did not seem fair. So they constructed a policy so that the "good guys" would not have to pay for the "bad guys."

All three policyholders now make an additional first-year premium. This amount can be lower at younger ages and higher at older ones, or it can be some fixed amount, such as $10 per $1000 of coverage regardless of age. As a result, all three insurance purchasers get a reduced annual premium.

When and if the "bad guy" lapses his policy, he forfeits all or a part of his additional first-year premium, commonly called a "deposit," depending on the length of time he has kept it. However, unlike before, the "good guys" just keep paying the reduced premium and this time the "bad guy" pays for his own mistake.

What happens if you don't lapse your policy? There are two possibilities: you complete the period, or you die within the period. If you live to complete the period, the company will usually return to you double or more the amount of your additional first-year premium, and this increase is tax-free.

In the event of your death, some companies will return the "deposit" to the beneficiary, while others will pay the maturity value as an additional death benefit. (The maturity value is the amount it would have grown to if you had lived to the end of the contract period.)

At the end of the term, you will have various options if you still have a need to protect dependents with life insurance. You may want to renew for the same amount of time or for a shorter period. For example, let's say you have a ten-year policy and your beneficiaries still have need for protection for another ten years. At that time, if you choose to renew, you would again make a "deposit," and your new level premium for the period would be based on your age when you renew.

All premiums for all life insurance policies are based on a mortality table, and as you grow older your rate per thousand increases.

Some companies may require you to pay an extra exchange premium for the privilege of renewing your coverage as "deposit" term, but their total premiums may or may not be any higher. You will have several conversion choices that you may make at the end of each period. Usually, if you do not exercise any choices, it will automatically convert to decreasing term.

Some policies that have the same basic provision are called modified-premium whole life. However, instead of automatically converting to some form of term, they automatically convert to whole life, if no other election is made. (You should exercise other options.)

This type of policy, though it doesn't affect the essential elements you want in your coverage, can be of great help to the insurance company offering it. It can often help the company in clearing the policy for sale in some states. Also, our tax laws are such that this designation may save the company considerable amounts of taxes and increase their net after-tax returns, which could permit them to charge lower premiums.

Whole Life, Straight Life, Ordinary Life

Whole life, also called straight life and ordinary life, is the most commonly sold life insurance policy. If you have bought this type of policy, you own a decreasing term policy, to which has been added a low interest—and for the early years of the policy a no-interest or negative interest—"savings account." (Many experts contend that it basically is always a no-interest account. I have put the term "savings account" in quotes because reserves that are used to develop cash values are often incorrectly, and usually illegally, referred to as "savings" by some salesmen.) The face amount of your policy and your yearly premiums will remain level throughout your whole life, and it will endow or mature at age 100.

With this type of policy, cash-surrender value accumulates from a portion of the premiums you pay. You can obtain this cash in two ways: you may cash in your policy and thereby lose your insurance protection, or you may pay 4½ to 8 percent to borrow out the cash. If death occurs while your loan is outstanding, the amount of your loan and the interest, if it has not been paid as you went along, are subtracted from the face amount of your policy.

If your death occurs with no loan outstanding against your policy, the cash value is not added to the face value of the policy and paid to your beneficiary; rather, only the face amount is paid, regardless of the amount in "your" savings account. *Your cash value is a part of your death benefit—not in addition to it!*

In the past, whole life has been the most commonly sold type of policy. But as consumers have become more knowledgeable and inflation has taken its devastating toll, it has been increasingly difficult to sell, and the number of this type of policy has greatly declined.

Limited Payment Life

Another type of life insurance policy you may encounter is one on which you pay for a limited period of time. This type of coverage is called limited payment life. It provides lifetime coverage, with premiums payable for the specified period of time: twenty years, thirty years, or paid-up at age 65 (which would be a variable number of years depending on your age). At the end of that period it is "paid up" and no more premiums need be paid. The premiums on this type of policy are naturally higher than for a whole life policy, for you are paying premiums for only a portion of your life; hence the term "limited payment life."

A great disservice has been done to you and your family whether you live or die if you have been sold this type of policy, especially if you have several small children for whom you must provide. As a young family, you are likely to have only a limited number of dollars to spend for life insurance, and this type of policy offers your family less coverage in the years when they most need the protection, so that you can pay little or no premiums when your need for protection has lessened and your ability to pay has probably increased. In addition, with our pattern of continued inflation, you have used "expensive" dollars while you were young—meaning dollars for which you had to work many hours—so that you could use less expensive ones later on—meaning dollars for which you have worked fewer hours.

Endowment

Another type of life insurance policy you may have been sold is endowment. In this kind of policy, the face amount will be paid to you if you are still living on a specified date or to your beneficiary if you should die prior to that date. Some are designed to endow in twenty years, others endow at age 65, although I am amazed at the number of policies I come across that endow at age 80. Yes, 80!

In reality, a whole life policy is really an endowment policy that endows at age 100.

In an endowment policy, as well as in other policies that accumulate cash surrender value, you may choose a lump-sum payout or an annuity of a specified amount per month for as long as you live. If you make the latter choice, the monthly payments will cease on your death. You may choose, however, to have your beneficiary continue to receive payments after your death for a set number of years. If you make this choice, your payments will be less per month. The premiums on an endowment policy, as you might expect, are very high as compared to the other forms I've discussed.

Endowment policies are often sold as retirement programs or college education programs. Since these premiums are paid with after-tax dollars and the cash surrender values often compound at a very low rate, they can make an endowment policy an expensive and often inadequate way to invest for retirement or for college.

For example, if you are in a 30 percent tax bracket, you must earn $5690 to have $3983 left to pay insurance premiums on a $100,000 20-pay life policy at age 50. In a 40 percent bracket, you would have to earn $6638; and in a 50 percent bracket, you must earn the princely sum of $7966 to have $4210 left to begin its meager climb in value. Surely your financial planner can design a better retirement program for you.

THE SALES PRESENTATION

In an effort to increase your level of awareness, I feel it would be helpful at this time if I were to pretend that I am a life insurance agent who has come to sell you the life insurance policy that would best benefit *me* and *my* children. (Let me hasten to add this is not a blanket condemnation of life insurance agents. I firmly believe that most of the agents who sell the wrong kind of insurance do so out of ignorance and not malicious intent. This was the conclusion reached by Senator Phillip Hart's committee on life insurance before his untimely death.)

Okay, here I come. Are you ready?

You are a male, age 35, and I come to you and say, "I can obtain for you a $10,000 level term to 65 policy for only $100 per year." You decide the price fits your budget and begin to say, "Yes," but I interrupt you to say, "But your insurance is all gone at age 65, and you don't want that to happen, do you?"

At this point you stammer, "Why, no, I wouldn't want to be without life insurance." (Analyze that statement. "You've either made it financially by 65, or you'll probably never make it.)

So I say, "Well, now here's a policy for only $200 a year that never runs out; it's called whole life." (I don't add, "You must pay premiums your whole life and it endows at age 100.")

Just as you are about to agree to this policy, I say, "You don't want to pay premiums all your life, do you? Here is a policy for $300 on which you can quit paying premiums in 20 years. It's all paid up."

Just before you sign I say, "But let me tell you about another policy. At the end of 20 years you've only put in $9000, we will give you $10,000; you've had your insurance free for 20 years and made $1000 profit. Isn't that great?"

But how great was it? Let's analyze the purpose of your life insurance. Its purpose was to protect those dependent upon you in the event that you do not live long enough to accumulate a living estate. Right?

Let's say that you really did die in ten years. (Take a few minutes here for a thorough study of Figure 13–1, *Four Basic Types of Level Coverage.*)

In the first policy pictured you would have spent $1000 in ten years and your beneficiaries would have received $10,000. In the second, $2000 would have been spent and they would have received $10,000. In the third, $3000 would have been spent and they would have received $10,000. In the fourth policy you had a first-class demise; $4500 would have been spent and your beneficiaries would have received $10,000.

HOW MUCH FOR PROTECTION?

How much of each of your twenty-year endowment premiums went to provide protection, and how much was earmarked for "your" savings account? Look at the two diagrams in Figure 13–2, and you will find that the answer is around $50. You have been paying for two things: protection and savings. But your beneficiary receives only the face amount of the policy.

What if I had told you that for $50 you could have bought a $10,000, twenty-year decreasing-term policy and that if you did nothing more constructive than take the $400 savings in premiums each year to the bank, and your bankers paid you only 4 percent on your savings, in twenty years you would have $12,400 instead of just the $10,000 you would have received from the endowment policy? If you obtained 6 percent from your banker, your $400 savings per year would have grown to $15,596 instead of $10,000. Your "free insurance and $1000 profit" were indeed expensive. (Tax-free municipal bonds and municipal bond funds providing you with the privilege of reinvesting so you can have tax-free compounding if tax considerations are a factor currently pay in excess of this amount. Tax-deferred single-premium annuities paying 12½ percent are also available. Or if you want a "guar-

(1) Level Term to 65

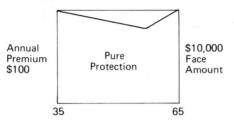

Annual
Premium
$100

Pure
Protection

$10,000
Face
Amount

35   65

(2) Whole or Ordinary Life

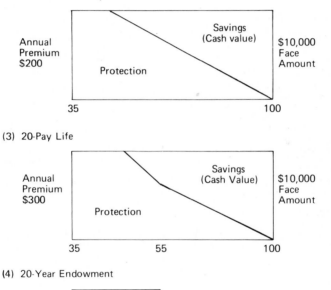

Annual
Premium
$200

Protection

Savings
(Cash value)

$10,000
Face
Amount

35   100

(3) 20-Pay Life

Annual
Premium
$300

Protection

Savings
(Cash Value)

$10,000
Face
Amount

35   55   100

(4) 20-Year Endowment

Annual
Premium
$450

Savings
(Cash Value)

$10,000
Face
Amount

Protection

35   55

Figure 13–1.   Four Basic Types of Level Coverage

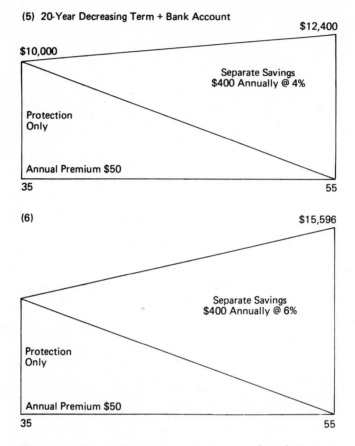

Figure 13–2. 20-Year Decreasing Term and Bank Account

anteed" investment without current taxation, use Series E government bonds. Remember, never combine living and dying—they are incompatible. "Banking" with the insurance company can prove to be very costly to you.

A DIAGRAM OF A WHOLE LIFE POLICY

Since the most commonly sold policy is whole life, let's assume that you own a $10,000 whole life policy on which you pay annual premiums of $200 and that you've had it for a sufficient period of time to have built up $4000 in cash surrender value. A diagram of your policy might look something like Figure 13–3.

The face amount of the policy is $10,000 and is marked (1). This

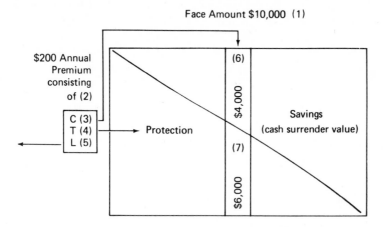

Figure 13–3.   Diagram of a Whole Life Policy

is the amount that would be paid to your beneficiary if you should die, providing that you had paid your premiums and there were no outstanding loans against the policy.

The premium that you would pay would be $200, marked (2). Under (2), you will see that the premium is divided into three parts. The first is *C*, marked (3). This represents "cash." This is the portion of your premium that is deposited into "your" savings account each year. The second is *T*, for "term" or "true insurance" and is marked (4). This is the portion that is used to buy true protection on your life and to pay company expenses and provide the company with a profit. The third, is *L* for "Load" (5) and represents the expenses incurred by the company for sales commissions, administrative expenses, and taxes. Now look at (6). This is "your" savings account. As you can see, as you increase "your" savings account, you decrease your insurance portion, which is marked (7). If cash surrender value (6) increases and the face amount (1) remains the same, then insurance protection (7) must decrease.

Let me repeat again: My objection is not to life insurance; there is no substitute for it if you have beneficiaries to protect. My objection is to the "banking" element. Buying life insurance should be an economic decision, not an emotional one. I don't feel that it is good economics for you to take an after-tax dollar for which you had to earn $1.43 in a 30 percent tax bracket and $2 in a 50 percent bracket and substitute it for an insurance dollar that I can buy for you for a few pennies. Also, once the dollar is there, you lose its earning power. (Yes, I know it's supposed to compound at 2½ to 3½ percent on the reserves,* but if you die with it there, that's small consolation to your beneficiaries, for they receive only the $10,000.) At 6 percent on "your" $4000 savings account, you are losing earnings of $240 per year, and at 7.5 percent, the amount lost is $300. If you were calculating your cost per thousand for keeping such a policy, your costs could be as follows:

TRUE COST PER THOUSAND OF THE POLICY
IN FIGURE 13–3

Premium	$ 200
Lost earnings @ 6% on $4000 cash value	240
Total cost	$ 440
Amount of insurance left in policy	$6,000
Cost per thousand today ($440 ÷ 6)	$ 73.33

When you took out the policy, you were paying $200 per year for $10,000 of insurance, or $20 per $1000. Now it is costing you $73.33 per $1000.

To help you get a clearer picture of the true cost of insurance, let's look at Figure 13–4. The shaded area all the way across is labeled "Insurance." This shows that the cost of insurance in each policy is the same, regardless of the kind you buy. Differences in savings and expenses cause the premiums charged to vary.

Take a moment to study Figure 13–4. Note also the difference in the expense factor and premiums paid between "Nonpar" and "Par" (participating) policies and you can determine your cost to participate.

Why Cost Per Thousand Varies

As you can see, Figure 13–4 illustrates a $100,000 policy at age 35. The first column shows that if you could get your coverage on the 1958 mortality table rate, you could obtain a $100,000 policy for $251 a year. But it's difficult to get a company to sell you insurance at the mortality rate. (Actually, they reinsure you with a reinsurance company to spread their risk for only $1.06 per thousand, or $116 including

---

* The reason I say "supposed to" is that there are some very respected insurance analysts who contend that interest return to the policyholder is always 0 percent, unless cash values should exceed face amount. Also, you should be aware that the percentages shown in your policies are only premium discounts. For example, if you are a male age 60 on a 2½ percent American Experience table, your cash value should be $710.22 per thousand. If you were on a 3 percent table, it would be $666.74. Were you aware of this reverse arithmetic?

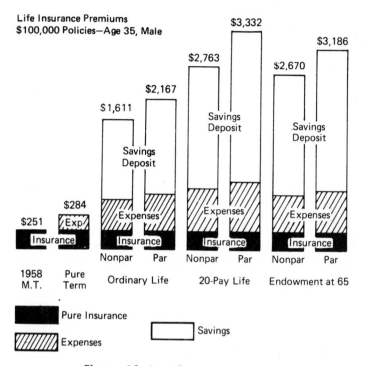

Figure 13–4.   Life Insurance Premiums

policy fee, and the reinsurance company still makes money.) You can, however, find a company that will sell it to you on a pure term basis. This could cost you $284 a year or less. Now, if you want to have a "participating" whole life policy, you can obtain an ordinary life policy for $2167 per year. If you decide you do not want to "participate" in the "profits" of the company, they can sell it to you at a lower premium of $1611. (A portion of this $556 additional premium may be returned as a "dividend" if the Directors vote to do so.)

Let's go on now to the 20-pay life in our illustration. Remember, that's the policy "you don't have to pay on your whole life. It's paid up." Again, if you want to participate in the profits it can cost $3332 per year, but if you're willing not to participate in the profits, you can buy it for $2763.

You can obtain an endowment-at-age-65 nonparticipating policy for $2633 per year; the premium for a participating policy is $3186. (Again, a partial return of the premium could occur.)

As you can see, the true cost for insurance protection is the same in every policy. The amount of premium you pay for this insurance is determined by how wisely you select your policy and how much forced "savings" you desire.

Endowment vs. Decreasing Term

Figure 13–5 shows the difference between buying a $100,000 "endowment" at age 65 and buying "decreasing term to age 65" with premium savings invested separately at 3 percent, 4 percent, 5 percent, 6 percent, and 8.5 percent. At only 8.5 percent (and I would not give you any special awards if that's all you averaged, nor would you win today's money game), you would have $305,662 in savings as compared to $100,000 in the endowment policy.

As you can readily see, it does make a difference where you "bank."

To help you get a clearer picture of the reasons that you should separate living and dying, let's take a look at the difference that it could make to you if you save inside a policy or outside an insurance policy.

LIFE INSURANCE AS AN "INVESTMENT"

Have you ever been told that life insurance is a good investment? Figure 13–6 shows the investment results of compound interest versus ordinary life, with an annual investment of $1000 versus an annual insurance premium of $1000 for a $55,000 face amount policy for a male aged 35. As you will note, cash surrender value of this policy would be $28,380 at age 65 and $55,000 at age 100.

Here are the results of compounding $1000 per annum at various rates of return from age 35 to age 65 (30 years), outside the policy:

3%	$ 49,002
4%	$ 58,328
5%	$ 69,760
6%	$ 83,801
8.5%	$134,772

Here are the results of compounding until age 100—the endowment age for the whole life policy:

3%	$ 200,162
4%	$ 306,767
5%	$ 479,637
6%	$ 762,227
8.5%	$2,551,387

INVESTMENT RESULTS

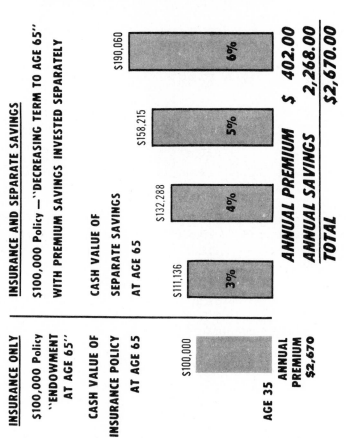

INSURANCE ONLY

$100,000 Policy "ENDOWMENT AT AGE 65"

CASH VALUE OF INSURANCE POLICY AT AGE 65

$100,000

AGE 35 ANNUAL PREMIUM $2,670

INSURANCE AND SEPARATE SAVINGS

$100,000 Policy — "DECREASING TERM TO AGE 65" WITH PREMIUM SAVINGS INVESTED SEPARATELY

CASH VALUE OF SEPARATE SAVINGS AT AGE 65

$111,136 3%
$132,288 4%
$158,215 5%
$190,060 6%
$305,662 8.5%

ANNUAL PREMIUM $ 402.00
ANNUAL SAVINGS   2,268.00
TOTAL $2,670.00

Figure 13–5.   Investment Results

419

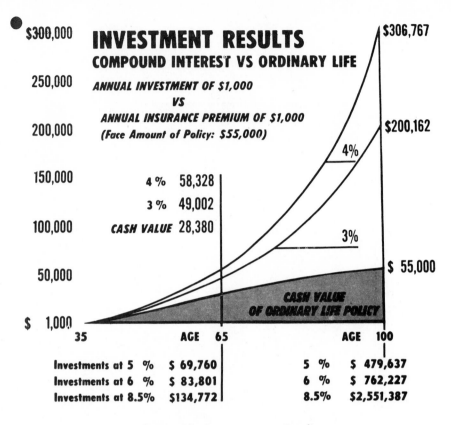

Figure 13–6. Investment Results

Federal Trade Commission Study

In July 1979, the Federal Trade Commission, Bureau of Consumer Protection, printed the results of an exhaustive study done by their staff and titled "Life Insurance Cost Disclosure." In this report they showed the chart in Figure 13–7 to give the consumer a visual picture of the rates of return on various investment choices.

In summary the chart shows the following rates of return on the savings portion of the whole life policies the staff studied:

Years Held	Rates of Return
5	−9% to −19%
10	−4% to + 2%
20	+2% to +4.5%

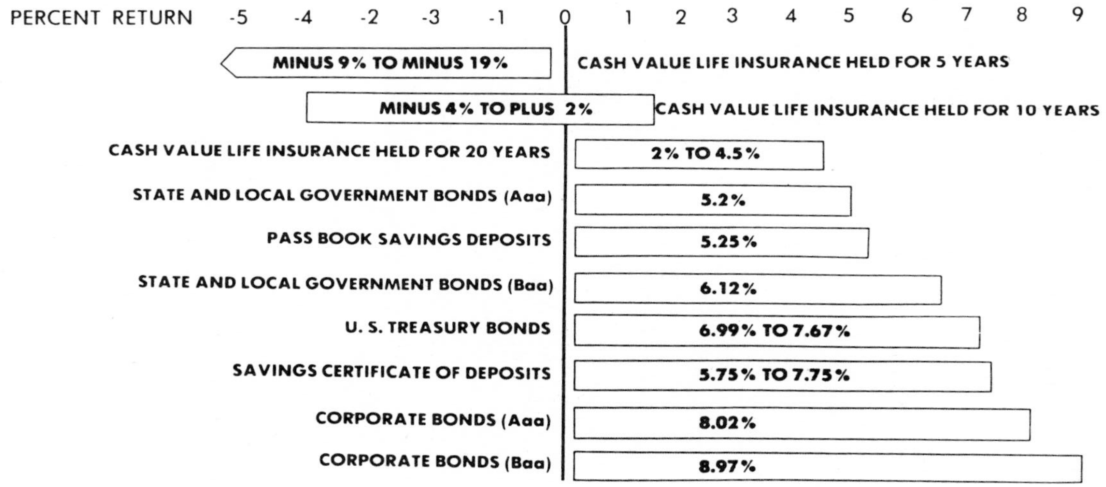

PERCENT RETURN

-5	-4	-3	-2	-1	0	1	2	3	4	5	6	7	8	9

CASH VALUE LIFE INSURANCE HELD FOR 5 YEARS
CASH VALUE LIFE INSURANCE HELD FOR 10 YEARS

MINUS 9% TO MINUS 19%

MINUS 4% TO PLUS 2%

CASH VALUE LIFE INSURANCE HELD FOR 20 YEARS — 2% TO 4.5%

STATE AND LOCAL GOVERNMENT BONDS (Aaa) — 5.2%

PASS BOOK SAVINGS DEPOSITS — 5.25%

STATE AND LOCAL GOVERNMENT BONDS (Baa) — 6.12%

U. S. TREASURY BONDS — 6.99% TO 7.67%

SAVINGS CERTIFICATE OF DEPOSITS — 5.75% TO 7.75%

CORPORATE BONDS (Aaa) — 8.02%

CORPORATE BONDS (Baa) — 8.97%

CAVEAT: PURCHASERS SHOULD CONSIDER TAX ADVANTAGES AND
DISADVANTAGES OF ALTERNATIVE INVESTMENTS.
RETURNS ON CASH VALUE INSURANCE POLICES ARE GENERALLY
TAX FREE. SOME BONDS ARE TAX-EXEMPT.

SOURCE: FEDERAL TRADE COMMISSION

Figure 13–7. Rates of Return on Various Investments, 1977

421

At our present rate of two-digit inflation, not only is the rate of return not keeping pace, but the policyholder has a negative return.

The FTC report claimed that the industry-wide average rate of return to policyholders' cash-value insurance was 1.3 percent, and further claimed policyholders were being deprived of over $3.7 billion in investment income annually that they could obtain by investing the cash elsewhere.

Dividends—Myth or Reality?

A rose is a rose is a rose. But a life insurance dividend is not a dividend, is not a dividend, is not a dividend! It is a partial return of an overcharge. Those policies that pay "dividends" are often called "participating" policies. (On the front lower left-hand side of the policy you may read "PAR" or "NONPAR.") The words "participating" and "dividends" have a nice ring to them. After all, you certainly enjoy your dividends from your 100 shares of General Motors or Exxon or from your Seminar Fund. But what is a "dividend" from an insurance policy? I refer you to no less an authority than the United States Treasury Decision No. 1743. When the Tariff Bill of 1911 proposed an income tax on life insurance dividends, representatives of life insurance companies protested the tax. I quote from the decision arrived at after the protest:

> Reduced to final analysis the contentions of the various companies are. . . .
> That dividends declared by participating companies are not dividends in a commercial sense of the word, but are simply refunds to the policyholder of a portion of the overcharge collected, which overcharge is merely held in trust by the company issuing the policy. Annually, or at stated periods, all, or a portion thereof, is returned to the person holding the policy. . . .
> It was vigorously contended by counsel representing certain of these companies that it was necessary in order to secure new business, to convince the prospective policyholder of the desirability of the same, and that this commercial necessity had resulted in the companies making misrepresentations of facts as to dividends to prospective purchasers of insurance, and that names and designations, having a single specific meaning in the commercial world and which were therefore attractive to prospective policyholders, had been adopted to represent transactions which they now hold are entirely different from that their name implies and represents, and from which the policyholder himself believed he was receiving and that business necessities had caused a continuance of these misnomers. *It was represented that, in fact, there were no dividends, but merely a refund of overcharges,*

which, for reasons above stated, were usually referred to as dividends.

Participation—How Much Does It Cost?

Carefully study Table 13–1, and you will discover that your cost for "participating" depends on your age. Generally, the younger you are, the more you are overcharged. For example, if you purchased a participating policy at age 20 from one of the largest insurance companies, you could have paid $13.60 per thousand. If you had purchased a nonparticipating policy from another large company using the same mortality table, you could have paid $9.04. The amount of your overcharge was $4.56 per thousand, or 50 percent. At age 35 your overcharge was 35 percent, and at age 50 it was 27 percent.

Mortality Tables

The mortality table is the base for calculating cost per thousand of a life insurance policy. Every year you live you are that more apt to die, and "funny banking" will never repeal that table, regardless of how many tantalizing names the advertising industry dreams up to call the various policies. The "insurance" factor is the likelihood of death and is listed by age per thousand.

The first table used by insurance companies was the American Experience Table. It was based on statistics gathered between 1843 and 1858. During that time, of 1000 men age 35, statistically 8.95 died during that year. This is the death rate in the days of Abraham Lincoln. The second table the insurance companies were required to use was the Commissioners' 1941 Standard Ordinary Table based on death statistics between 1930 and 1940—before penicillin. During that period, the death rate had dropped to 4.59 per thousand men aged 35. Later, in 1966, the insurance companies were required to go on to the Commissioners' 1958 Standard Ordinary Table based on death statistics between 1950 and 1954. Now woefully outdated, this is the last table regulatory agencies have required and is the one currently being used. On this table, the death rate has dropped to 2.51 per thousand. It is my understanding that sufficient statistics have been gathered for a later mortality table, on which the death rate should be in the neighborhood of 1.63 per thousand, or lower, at age 35.

If you are 35 years of age and have a policy on the American Experience Table, you may be paying 356 percent more than you would need to pay on the 1958 CSO Table. If you have a policy on the 1941 CSO Table and are healthy enough to pass a physical, you may be paying 180 percent more than you need to pay.

Table 13–1. Comparative Annual Whole Life Premiums (Par and Nonpar)

Issue Age	Whole Life (Par)	Whole Life (Nonpar)	Amount of Overcharge	Percentage Overcharge
20	$13.60	$ 9.04	$ 4.56	50%
21	13.99	9.40	4.59	49%
22	14.40	9.81	4.59	47%
23	14.82	10.23	4.59	45%
24	15.26	10.67	5.00	47%
25	15.72	11.09	4.63	42%
26	16.20	11.49	4.71	41%
27	16.70	11.88	4.82	41%
28	17.23	12.28	4.95	40%
29	17.77	12.70	5.07	40%
30	18.35	13.16	5.19	39%
31	18.95	13.71	5.24	38%
32	19.58	14.28	5.30	37%
33	20.24	14.87	5.37	36%
34	20.93	15.48	5.45	35%
35	21.67	16.11	5.56	35%
36	22.43	16.77	5.66	38%
37	23.24	17.46	5.78	33%
38	24.10	18.18	5.92	33%
39	24.99	18.94	6.05	32%
40	25.94	19.74	6.20	31%
41	26.93	20.59	6.34	31%
42	27.97	21.48	6.49	30%
43	29.07	22.42	6.65	30%
44	30.22	23.41	6.81	29%
45	31.45	24.45	7.00	29%
46	32.74	25.53	7.21	28%
47	34.10	26.68	7.42	28%
48	35.54	27.88	7.66	27%
49	37.07	29.15	7.92	27%
50	38.69	30.50	8.19	27%
51	40.40	31.93	8.47	27%
52	42.21	33.46	8.75	26%
53	44.14	35.08	9.06	26%
54	46.18	36.80	9.38	25%
55	48.35	38.61	9.74	25%
56	50.66	40.54	10.12	25%
57	53.12	42.59	10.53	25%
58	55.74	44.77	10.97	25%
59	58.53	47.08	11.45	24%
60	61.60	49.53	12.07	24%

It may surprise you to learn that insurance companies are not required to go back to old policyholders when a new mortality table becomes available. They continue year after year to charge on the old table.

Table 13–2 is a combination of all three mortality tables showing deaths per thousand at each age and life expectancy. Study it carefully.

WHOSE CASH VALUE?

If you presently own a policy in which there is cash surrender value, you may be under the impression that you are earning on "your" savings account. However, you do not receive any current economic benefit as income as the policy reserve in the hands of the insurance company earns for them. The policy provisions, if you'll take the time to study them, make this clear. There is no provision in the policy that says you own a part of the company reserves. The policy promises to pay benefits in certain events—usually upon death or upon living to a certain age or date. *Tax Facts*, published by the National Underwriters, states:

> The right to cash value upon surrender of the policy or the right to borrow against the cash value are, however, sometimes viewed as suggesting the ownership of a fund in the hands of the company upon which interest is being earned. Perhaps this misconception forms the basis of the conclusion that the policyholder is enjoying current interest income that should be taxed. It is true that in our sales talks and to some extent in our actuarial reasoning we have attributed to the cash value of a life insurance policy some of the characteristics of a savings account. But this popular notion is without legal foundation.

There is a good deal of confusion in the minds of insurance agents and the public as to the ownership of the cash values of insurance policies. This confusion has gone largely unchecked by any government agency such as the Securities and Exchange Commission, which regulates the securities industry. (However, when the Federal Trade Commission made its 1979 Life Insurance Cost Disclosure, the head of the commission was admonished by a Congressional Committee to keep hands off of the life insurance and funeral undertaker business.)

The fact of the matter is that the cash value in your insurance policy does not belong to you, as you may have supposed. It does, in fact, belong to the insurance company issuing the policy. Consequently, any increase in the cash values of your policies, either by interest earned

TABLE 13–2. DEATHS PER 1000 IN THREE STATUTORY MORTALITY TABLES

Age	American Experience Table	Commissioners' 1941 Table	Commissioners' 1958 Table	Expectation of Life 1958 Table in Years
20	7.80	2.43	1.79	50.37
21	7.86	2.51	1.83	49.46
22	7.91	2.59	1.86	48.55
23	7.96	2.68	1.89	47.64
24	8.01	2.77	1.91	46.73
25	8.06	2.88	1.93	45.82
26	8.13	2.99	1.96	44.90
27	8.20	3.11	1.99	43.99
28	8.26	3.25	2.03	43.08
29	8.34	3.40	2.08	42.16
30	8.43	3.56	2.13	41.25
31	8.51	3.73	2.19	40.34
32	8.61	3.92	2.25	39.43
33	8.72	4.12	2.32	38.51
34	8.83	4.35	2.40	37.60
35	8.95	4.59	2.51	36.69
36	9.09	4.86	2.64	35.78
37	9.23	5.15	2.80	34.88
38	9.41	5.46	3.01	33.97
39	9.59	5.81	3.25	33.07
40	9.79	6.18	3.53	32.18
41	10.01	6.59	3.84	31.29
42	10.25	7.03	4.17	30.41
43	10.52	7.51	4.53	29.54
44	10.83	8.04	4.92	28.67
45	11.16	8.61	5.35	27.81
46	11.56	9.23	5.83	26.95
47	12.00	9.91	6.36	26.11
48	12.51	10.64	6.95	25.27
49	13.11	11.45	7.60	24.45
50	13.78	12.32	8.32	23.63
51	14.54	13.27	9.11	22.82
52	15.39	14.30	9.96	22.03
53	16.33	15.43	10.89	21.25
54	17.40	16.65	11.90	20.47
55	18.57	17.98	13.00	19.71
56	19.89	19.43	14.21	18.97
57	21.34	21.00	15.24	18.23
58	22.94	22.71	17.00	17.51
59	24.72	24.57	18.59	16.81
60	26.69	26.59	20.34	16.13

or by your deposits, serves only one purpose—that is, the reduction of the insurance company's risk based on actuarial assumptions.

THE SIX-MONTH WAIT

Did you also know that most companies have a provision in their policies allowing them the privilege of waiting six months to make a loan to you or to let you have your cash surrender value? Did you ever wonder how the six-month waiting period happened to be a part of your policy if you carry the kind that has cash surrender value? It has a very interesting history. During the Depression, many people were cashing in their insurance policies, and many insurance companies were on the verge of bankruptcy. Around that time President Franklin Roosevelt declared a bank holiday, saying, in effect, "Sorry about that, but we cannot return to you the funds you have deposited in your bank checking and savings accounts." With this announcement, lights began flashing in the home offices of many insurance companies, and their executives said, "Oh, my goodness! Why didn't we think of that?" They got permission to suspend paying cash value, and ever since that date this six-month waiting period has been in most insurance policies. If you should ask an agent about this provision, the agent may assure you that his company would never make you wait. If he is so confident, why is the provision in the policy?

As a matter of fact, I feel that there is a real threat that insurance companies will invoke this provision during the 'eighties. This could be provoked by two causes. More and more people are becoming better informed about life insurance and how it works. At last count, over a million copies of the life insurance chapters excerpted from my latest two books are now in the hands of the buying public. This is causing many to examine their life insurance programs to see if they can obtain coverage at a lower cost per thousand. When they find that they can, they are replacing their old policies with new ones and claiming what cash surrender value has been accumulated.

Second, many existing policies allow the policyholder to borrow against the cash surrender value at rates that are now below current bank rates. This has caused a mass exodus of cash surrender value which, in turn, can cause liquidity and interest earning problems for many insurance companies. One major company has reported a 60 percent increase in loans. This, together with increased inflation, may very well create chaos and eventual bankruptcy or mergers of many of the less well-managed companies.

NET COST

Now let's look at another term that may be confusing to you. It's called "net cost," a term that is sometimes used to convince the unwary that life insurance is very inexpensive if bought the "permanent" way. Presentations I have seen go something like this:

Total premiums paid ages 35–65 ($200/yr)	$6,000.00
Minus cash value at age 65	5,000.00
Your Net Cost	$1,000.00
Your Average Cost Per Year	$ 33.33

Is this true?

If your death occurred at 65, your net cost was the total of the premiums you had paid to date, $200 x 30 years, or $6000. Your beneficiaries did not receive the face amount plus your savings account. They received $10,000, not $15,000.

Let's go a step further, and see if it can be proved that there is a way that you can receive your insurance free and still make a profit.

Net cost on a twenty-year endowment policy:

Total premiums, ages 35–55	$ 9,000
Maturity value at age 55	10,000 .
Net profit	$ 1,000

Isn't this great? $10,000 of insurance for twenty years, and you get all your money back, plus $1000. Does it appear that the insurance company is actually giving you free protection while paying you $1000? Can you afford to turn down this marvelous opportunity? If you truly care about your family's welfare, you had better turn it down. Remember the importance of the time-use of money, to say nothing of the destructive forces of inflation. (Some states now require an interest-adjusted cost index.) *

MINIMUM DEPOSIT

Minimum deposit insurance plans, affectionately called "mini-dip" by the salesmen who sell them, are whole life or limited-pay life policies (often "participating") that charge a very large premium to create artificially high early-cash-surrender values. If you have this type of insurance, it was your money that produced these high cash values. This type of policy is often presented to those in a 40 percent or above tax bracket,

---

* "It should be stressed that the interest-adjusted index is an index, and nothing more. The true cost of life insurance, if it can be calculated at all, obviously depends on when and how the policy is terminated."—Best Flitcraft

usually in the form of impressive computer printouts that show borrowing out most of the cash values as soon as possible and charging off the interest on their income tax returns. The impression is often given that the IRS is the one actually financing the insurance program. Even if the interest could be deductible in this plan (and there does seem to be some doubt about deducting all of it, especially if the policy was purchased after August 6, 1963), it is not brilliant economics to use after-tax dollars to substitute for insurance dollars that can be bought for pennies, pay a salesman to put those dollars into a savings account, and then pay an insurance company for the privilege of taking them out. No interest at all is better than tax-deductible interest. Only buy "mini-dip" if you have an insurance-agent friend whom you want to help prosper and become a member of the Million Dollar Round Table. If your first allegiance is to yourself and the welfare of your family, there is a better way.

COST PER THOUSAND GOES UP EACH YEAR

Regardless of what kind of policy you buy, your cost per thousand increases, because cost per thousand is based on likelihood of death. As you grow older, you are more likely to die.

Yet I find that many people have great difficulty grasping this concept. Figure 13–8 is a chart showing the insurance company's risk. I didn't add in the loss of earnings on your cash (which is a real loss), yet even without that you can get a picture of what is happening.

In the Event of Death

The direct cost of the insurance proceeds is the total input from the date of issue until the time of death.

Year	Annual Input	Cumulative Input
1	$190	$ 190
10	190	1,900
20	190	3,800
30	190	5,700
35	190	6,650

You cannot fool the mortality tables and the increasing cost of insuring an increasing risk. Remember, level premiums mean a decreasing Net Death Benefit; a Level Death Benefit means an increasing cost or premium.

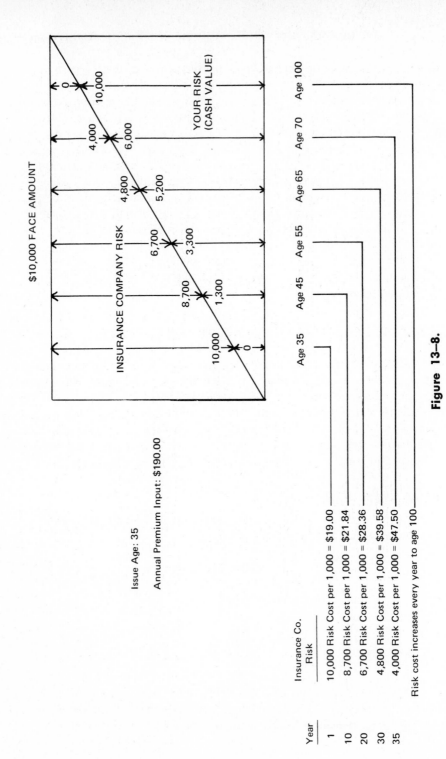

Figure 13—8.

430

REPOSITIONING

During my many years as a financial planner, I have found that the vast majority who come to me actually have some assets. The problem often lies in where these assets are positioned. Many times their assets are working much harder for others than they are for them.

Let me give you an example of a family man, age 35, with a wife and three children, who was carrying an $80,000 life paid up at 65, that contained $6258 in cash value and for which he was paying an annual premium of $1258. He was in a 33 percent tax bracket. The company for which he worked did not have a pension plan. He was eligible for an Individual Retirement Account, but after paying current expenses he did not have an additional $1500 to invest each year.

Let's take a look at how we greatly increased his living and death estate by just repositioning his assets without increasing his expenditures. We obtained a new $80,000 ten-year "deposit" term policy for $410 per year. We invested $1500 in an IRA account and used $800 for a deposit for his insurance. This left $3969 to put into the family's savings account. He also saved $495 in taxes because the $1500 he paid himself into his IRA account allowed him to deduct the $1500 (1500 × 33% tax bracket). If he had died immediately after we obtained the new policy, his estate would have been increased by $7612 just by repositioning.

Today

Age 35	$80,000 Policy $1258 premium
	$6269 c.v. 33% Bracket
80,000	Policy $410
800	Maturity ($800 Dep.)
1,500	IRA
495	Tax Savings
3,969	Sav. Acct. ($6269 − $1500 − $800 Dep.)
848	Prem. Sav. ($1258 − $410)
87,612	
80,000	
$ 7,612	Immediate Increase

Now let's look at ten years later. At the end of ten years he still has the option of retaining his $80,000 policy, since it is renewable and convertible at his option without evidence of insurability. At 6 percent, his IRA account would have grown to $20,957. He would actually have this amount in that it has been compounding tax-sheltered. Of course, we can't award him any gold stars if he only earns 6 percent on his money. If he had obtained 12 percent on his IRA account, it would have grown to $29,482.

As you can see, we increased his estate by $36,394 without his making any more expenditures.

Results in 10 Years

$ 80,000	Insurance	
$ 1,600	Maturity of deposit	
20,957	Value of IRA acct. at 6%	$29,482 at 12%
495	Tax Savings that year	
3,969	Savings acct. exclusive of interest	
848	Savings on premium that year	
$107,869	Total	$116,394
80,000	Previous Estate	80,000
$ 27,869	Increase in Estate	$ 36,394

COMPUTER PRINTOUTS

From time to time you may be tempted to be overly impressed by computer printouts. If you'll just remember the old warning "garbage in, garbage out," perhaps you can survive better in the true world of economic reality.

In the Appendix (Table 23) you'll find a copy of a computer printout presented to a prospective client by a major insurance company. I have blanked out the company's name to save them the embarrassment. Look over this printout and then carefully read the headings and the last line. It shows a proposal for a man age 40 for $25,000 face amount and tells him how super his finances will be at age 65. The premiums are $525.50 per year. The bottom line reads:

The total of your payments (column 4)	$13,137.50
The total savings portion of your insurance (5)	11,725.00
Therefore, your cumulative cost is only (7)	1,412.50

Is this true?

What has been the cumulative cost to the policyholder if he dies at age 65? Not $1,412.50, but $13,137.50! The company will not pay the beneficiary $25,000 plus $11,725.00, or $36,725. They will pay him $25,000 for which the man had paid $13,137.50.

Note also Column 8, which reads, "If you should die, your beneficiary will receive tax free," and the amount shown is $25,000. Is this true? Not necessarily, if his estate is over a certain amount and he is the owner of the policy. There is a little asterisk indicating "Federal income tax" at the bottom, but I find that most people have interpreted this to mean "free of estate taxes."

MY SEARCH FOR INFORMATION

Perhaps it would be helpful for me to share with you how I have developed such strong convictions about the insurance area of financial planning. Let me go back to the year 1958.

I began to have a gnawing feeling that there was something wrong with my family's life insurance program. (We had bought a policy from a friend some years before while we were still in college, struggling to earn enough money to finish, and had asked him for a policy with the lowest cost.)

I began my search for information by going first to a college library and then to a large public library. To my surprise, information about life insurance at that time was extremely scarce. This was puzzling. Millions of dollars were being spent annually on this commodity, but there was so little information available. I had heard of certain books about the subject, but they all seemed to be "out of print." Laboriously, I began to piece together bits of information in an effort to solve this puzzle of how the various types of insurance policies differed and how they were put together.

Decreasing Term Plus Banking

During this searching period, I awoke early one morning, and like a bolt out of the blue I felt I had solved the insurance mystery. All the policies that were being so aggressively sold by the life insurance community were either pure protection alone or pure protection plus "banking." Whole life, straight life, modified life, 20-pay life, 20-year endowment, executive life, presidential life, and various other golden titles created by the marketing departments of the life insurance companies were actually decreasing term plus a savings account.

I now remembered that the word "term" had come up when we had asked the agent for a low-cost policy. He had recoiled in horror when we asked and said that "term" is only "temporary" insurance, a poor substitute for "permanent" insurance. After all, you don't want to "rent" your insurance; you want to "own" it.

"Permanent" Insurance?

As I began to delve into how our policy was constructed, I began to question how "permanent" our "permanent insurance" really was. According to my understanding of the word "permanent," it is something that doesn't change; yet our insurance was decreasing each time we paid the premium and substituted some of our after-tax hard-earned dollars for a portion of our insurance protection. The company's risk was decreasing as the burden was shifted to us through "our" increasing savings account.

"Our" Savings Account?

Was it really ours? If it were "our" savings account, what were its characteristics?

First of all, we found, as you have already seen, that we were using after-tax dollars and substituting them for insurance dollars that we could buy for a few pennies. This did not seem to be brilliant economics. (And here I had a college degree in economics and finance!) Then we noticed from reading the cash surrender value table in the back of the policy that all of "our savings" the first few years had disappeared. (As I thought back over the explanation the agent had given us about the policy at the time of the sale, I couldn't remember his inserting the word "surrender" in his reference to the cash value. He referred to it as our "building up of cash for the future" so we could "get something back.")

We also discovered that as we continued to make deposits each year, we were being charged a commission to place money into our "savings account." Once the "savings" were deposited, we seemed to be losing all their earning power. I remember the agent saying we were getting 3 percent on the cash reserve, but as we examined the policy, it didn't seem too important what rate was being paid since, if death occurred, the insurance company planned to keep the "savings" and pay only the face amount of the policy.

We also found that if we wanted to borrow "our" savings, we would have to pay 5½ percent interest to borrow "our" own money. Really? Our own money? Again we asked, "Is it ours?"

We also found that if my spouse died with the "savings" there, the unilateral contract signed with the life insurance company specified that they got to keep "our" savings. The savings were part of the face amount, or death benefit of the policy—not an amount in addition to the face amount.

"Funny Banking"

It was then that we began asking ourselves questions. Suppose we had gone to our banker and said to him, "We want to open a savings account at your bank." And suppose he had said to us, "We're happy to have you, and these are the rules. First, we'll take everything you deposit into the account the first year. After that, we'll charge you to deposit money into your account. If you want to borrow from your savings, we'll charge you 5½ percent to borrow your own money. If you refuse to pay us for the privilege of borrowing your own money and withdraw your savings, you will have to give up your insurance policy." If he had said all of this, would we have opened the savings account?

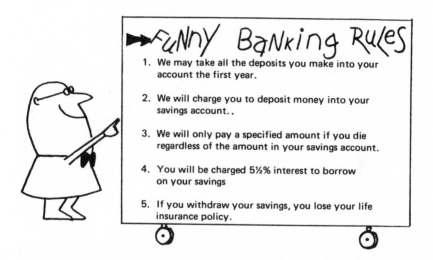

We then began to analyze our "banking." We examined four major areas: safety, yield, liquidity, and the cost of doing business.

The first thing we examined, as you should, was safety (stability). If your account isn't safe, none of the other characteristics is really all that important. Once you've established that it's safe, you will then want to know what rate of return you are obtaining on your money, because, as you've learned, the rate of return is vitally important to the success of any financial program. After that, you will want to know about liquidity—how readily accessible are your funds? Last, what is the cost of doing business? Much to my surprise, here is how I tallied the two "banks" with regard to the savings portion of our policy. (See Table 13–3.)

TABLE 13–3.   WITH WHOM SHOULD YOU
DEPOSIT "YOUR" SAVINGS?

	"Banking" tally savings with	
	Commercial National Bank	*Insurance Company*
Safety	Guaranteed by FDIC	Only as safe as the company *
Yield	5–7½%	2½%–3½% on cash reserve (perhaps) **
Liquidity	On demand	Could wait six months and then pay only if they had the money *
Cost of doing business:		
To deposit	0	10–55%
To withdraw	0	4½–8%

* Except in states with the Guaranty Association Act. The majority, but not all, of the states have now passed this act. This law guarantees any policy benefits stated in the policy issued by a company doing business in that state, or having domicile in that state. If a company is liquidated and owes more benefits than the liquidation of their assets provides, then all of the other insurance companies are assessed proportionate to their premium income to make up the deficit.
** Many experts agree that the interest return to the policyholder is always 0 percent (or negative interest) unless cash surrender value should exceed the face amount.

What is your reaction to this comparison? With whom do you feel you should be banking? With the life insurance company? With the bank? We chose the bank.

We had at last discovered that life insurance was for dying and investments were for living; the combining of the two under one insurance policy only built bigger and better life insurance companies. Even though one insurance company is still allowed, in most states, to come into your living room via "living color" television and through national magazines to tell you that you, too, can own a part of a jagged, porous piece of real estate guarding the gateway to the blue Mediterranean, it is not literally true. The state of Florida has now banned this ad, declaring that it is false advertising, and other states have required them to change the wording to "with a piece. . . ."

Buy When You Are Young

Have you heard, as we had, "Buy your insurance while you are young because it's cheaper"? We found that this is not true and that life insurance will cost more each year because it is based on a mortality table. We also found that the more recent the mortality table in use, the better the rates should be, because medical science is helping our population live longer.

Were you told when your policy was delivered, encased in leather or plastic and embossed in imitation gold, that it was sacred and should never ever be changed? We were. Our agent said it would cost us dearly if we ever changed. How many products can you think of that you have purchased during the last five to ten years that should not be replaced by another? You are living in a dynamic world of change, and this is especially true in the realm of money management.

As I look back now, this is rather ridiculous. This would mean that we found the most knowledgeable agent, that he had designed the best insurance package, that our needs would never change, and that no new mortality table would ever be used. In many states an agent can obtain a sixty-day temporary license to sell insurance before taking an exam. Perhaps your policy was sold to you by one of these people. It's just as binding a legal instrument as if he had had forty years of experience.

Our policy was sold to us by a fellow college student who was working part-time to help defray his college expenses. When we analyzed our policies, we found that changing them was much to our advantage.

How Did It Happen?

How did we even happen to agree to a policy with such a high premium and such low death protection? Would we have agreed to it if someone had told us about all the possible kinds of policies? Had we signed a contract without even reading it? We had asked the agent, who was a good friend of ours, for the lowest-cost policy with the maximum coverage. We later discovered he had not intentionally done us a disservice. He had sold us the kind of policy his company told him he should sell. (He was what is called a "captive salesman"—meaning that he could write insurance only for the company he represented.) His general manager had also assured him that this was the best policy for his client, for himself, and for the company. It was the best for him and for the company, but not for us.

It Made a Great Difference

In 1958, when we learned how life insurance policies are put together, we changed all our policies and were able to obtain a larger amount of protection for the same premium and to free our cash value for investments.

On September 29, 1959, my husband was a passenger on the Braniff Electra that crashed near Buffalo, Texas, killing all aboard. My whole world crashed around me.

When everything was settled, I realized that my benefits were much larger than they would have been if we had not made changes in our insurance program.

With intelligent investing of these proceeds since that time, I have moved along the road toward financial independence. I'm a financial planner today because I have chosen to dedicate my life to helping as many people as I can to become financially independent. I'm a financial planner because I want to be, and not out of economic necessity.

I have known how life insurance is packaged and sold since 1958, but it was not until 1971 that I finally had the courage to stand and publicly speak out about this vital subject. What took me so long? Frankly I was frightened. I was afraid that if I attacked the institution into which those attending my seminars had been pouring their life blood for years, my investment advice would be questioned. More important, I was afraid of the strong and powerful insurance lobby.

Before that time, when those attending the seminar would come in for counseling, as they were entitled to do, I would tell them how life insurance worked and if their program did not fit their needs, I would suggest that they go to their agent and set up the proper program. Many, many times when they went to their agent, he would again sell them the wrong kind of insurance. This happened just once too often.

A couple with five children who had attended one of my seminars came in for counseling. The man was a hard-working father, but did not earn a large salary. The mother had no vocational training at all. They wanted to start a $25 a month investment program. After spending a great deal of time on their budget, I asked about their life insurance program and found they had none. I told them that an adequate life insurance program must be their first priority. I then told them exactly what kind to buy and showed them that it could easily be fitted into their budget.

Three months later they called me about another matter, and it was then that I learned that an agent had sold them a $10,000 20-pay life for the same premium for which he could have sold them $100,000 of pure protection. If that father had died, his family would have been destitute. I was so furious that I swore this would never happen to a client of mine again. That is when I set up our life insurance agency.

I truly believe that we do more good in this area to help our clients become financially independent than any other of our programs.

WILL YOU LOSE IF YOU CHANGE YOUR POLICIES?

No more than my family did! The belief that you will lose if you change your insurance policies may have scared you away from the common-sense program of pure protection based on need. Your concern should not be how much you will lose by dropping an existing savings policy. This money has already been lost. A large portion of total commissions and other acquisition costs were taken out in the early years of your policy, and this money will never come back to you. Your real question is, "How much will I lose in the future by keeping a high-cost, low-protection policy?"

There is nothing sacred about those pieces of paper containing too much fine print glued or stapled together. Life insurance is a commodity like warehouses, pistachio nuts, or rice. You just get more emotional about something that is related to your life. Why should cash value life insurance be considered a sacred cow? Why is it as good today as it was a hundred years ago? Is our economy the same? Is our rate of inflation the same? Can you think of any other product or service that you can purchase today that was as good 100 years ago? Then why cash value life insurance? I repeat, economics, not emotion, should determine how you protect those dependent upon you.

Look at it this way. Assume that you are a pilot flying to Miami. On calculating your location, you find that you have overshot Miami and are over the Atlantic Ocean. You also find that you have just enough gas to get back to Miami. If you keep going, you'll run out of fuel and drop into the ocean. If you turn around now, you'll have enough fuel to make it back. Would you bury your error or rationalize it? You would change your course and head toward your destination as soon as possible, for every minute wasted could be costly and catastrophic. Successful financial planning is based on the same principle. If you are heading in the wrong direction, alter your course as soon as possible.

Costly Friendship

Not changing a poor policy can be a very expensive error. I remember a young single man, age 25, who was paying $130 per year for a $5000 whole life insurance policy he did not need. His employer provided in excess of the amount of protection he needed under a company group term insurance policy. I suggested that he might want to consider using this $130 more profitably in the form of a savings plan or investments.

The policy had been sold to him by a good friend who he felt had his best interest at heart. He did not want to upset his friend, and decided to continue the policy. He felt, after all, that he earned an above-average income and was not financially inconvenienced by paying a $130 per year premium. He told me he felt anyone could always use a little extra protection. He reasoned he had $5000 of insurance in case he died, and he would get back $6000 in cash when he was 65, if he lived, and that to him was a pretty good return on $130 per year. He obviously did not know how to measure what money must do, or he would not have been so complacent.

Here is what $130 per year for 40 years will become (exclusive of taxes) at various rates of return:

$130 per year for 40 years at 15% = $265,973.50
$130 per year for 40 years at 12% = $111,688.20
$130 per year for 40 years at 10% = $ 63,290.50
$130 per year for 40 years at 8% = $ 36,371.40
$130 per year for 40 years at 6% = $ 21,329.10

This particular young man did not need the protection, but he could have given his friend another reason for cherishing his friendship by having him replace his whole life policy with a level term policy, entitling his friend to another commission while saving himself $80 per year. His difference, exclusive of taxes, would have been:

$80 per year for 40 years at 15% = $163,676.00
$80 per year for 40 years at 12% = $ 68,731.20
$80 per year for 40 years at 10% = $ 38,948.00
$80 per year for 40 years at 8% = $ 22,382.40
$80 per year for 40 years at 6% = $ 13,125.60

In reality, his cost of friendship is greater than shown. His premiums were paid with after-tax dollars. In a 35 percent tax bracket, his cost is not $130, but $200 ($70 tax).

To carry this a step forward, let's say he was eligible for an IRA or Keogh Plan, and the investment could be increased to $200. $200 − $70 (35%) = $130. The IRS could subsidize his retirement.

$130 per year for 40 years at 15% = $265,973.50
$200 per year for 40 years at 15% = $409,190.00

A simple way to compute the tax is to divide the amount ($130) by the reciprocal of the tax bracket (.35 divide by .65).

$$\$130 \div .65 = \$200. \qquad \$200 \times .35 = \$70$$

In the second example, $80 becomes $123.

$$\$80 \text{ per year for 40 years at } 15\% = \$163,676.00$$
$$\$123 \text{ per year for 40 years at } 15\% = \$251,651.85$$

Remember this in your own planning.

THE $200,000 ESTATE

A minimum estate necessary to maintain a family today should be at least $200,000. At a 6 percent withdrawal, this is only $1000 per month, which is not particularly generous, I'm sure you'll agree, in these times of escalating living costs.

If you are a young family man just beginning your journey down the road toward financial independence, your accumulated assets will probably be small. For example, let's assume that you have accumulated $20,000. This is your "living estate"—meaning that no one has to die to make these funds available. If you need a $200,000 estate, you are $180,000 short. This will need to be provided by life insurance, which will be your "death estate" until you can substitute a "living estate" for it.

A diagram of your estate would look like Figure 13–9.

When your "living estate" has grown to $30,000, if your goal is still $200,000, you can reduce your "death estate" to $170,000. You then can keep substituting "living" for "death," "living" for "death," until when you are finished, you'll be self-insured and you and your wife can sit on the veranda and rock together. This—not the acquisition of life insurance policies—is your financial goal. Cash or its equivalent is far superior, I'm sure you'll agree, than a collection of life insurance policies.

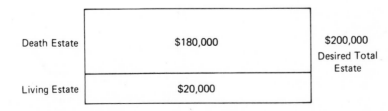

| Death Estate | $180,000 | $200,000 Desired Total Estate |
| Living Estate | $20,000 | |

Figure 13–9.

All life insurance premiums are money down a rat hole unless you die. When you have become self-insured and have no desire to help your heirs pay estate taxes, stop this waste.

WHICH LIFE INSURANCE COMPANY?

Does it make a difference from which legal reserve life insurance company you buy pure protection? No, generally it does not. But you should seek the one that offers the best features at the best rates, designed to help you build a living estate. It should offer policies that are renewable and convertible at your option to a variety of other policies, without evidence of insurability, to a ripe old age. This puts you in the driver's seat, and that's where you should be in designing and carrying out your financial plan.

WHICH LIFE INSURANCE AGENT— PLANNER OR SALESMAN?

From which agent should you buy your protection? Certainly one of the prerequisites is that he not be a member of a captive sales force —meaning that he can write only for the one company to which he is beholden. He cannot be impartial under these conditions. His company will not let him. Also, his company may not even have a policy that fits your needs, and if it does have one hidden away, his supervisor may severely reprimand him for not selling you the kind that makes him and the company the most profit.

In my opinion, you should plan your life insurance needs with a financial planner who is knowledgeable in investments to help you build a living estate and in life insurance to help you buy the time to build the estate. These two areas of financial planning are inseparable, since you don't know how long your life span will be. Your financial planner should be dually licensed to recommend both investments and life insurance.

Being dually licensed allows the professional to balance your financial program. I should warn you, however, that it does not make him impartial. In fact, some life insurance agents have obtained a securities license as a tool for selling more high-cost, low-protection policies. They maintain that it will not make any difference to them whether you invest in securities or put your investment dollar into your policy. Actually, it makes a whale of a difference in their compensation. If they sell you a whole life policy at a cost of $1000, they may receive as high as

110 percent of that first year's premium (or $1100) over a two-year period, plus some trail commission from the policy in the future. If they sell you "term" and invest the balance for you in a mutual fund, they would receive only a fraction of this amount.

"SAVING" AT THE RIGHT WINDOW

If you absolutely feel compelled to use the insurance industry for "banking" or saving, then be certain your dollars are deposited in the most beneficial accounts for you. You are aware that banks have different tellers or windows for different banking functions—checking, passbook savings, purchase of travel checks, certificates of deposit, etc. As far as the savings are concerned, the amount of interest you receive for lending the bank your money depends on which "window" you deposit your dollars through. At closing time it all goes into the same vault and all becomes available for the bank to use. Insurance companies also have different "windows" and interest rates they pay for the use of your savings.

Table 13–4 illustrates what a financial planner might recommend as compared to an insurance agent.

$100,000 WHOLE LIFE OR ORDINARY LIFE, ISSUE AGE 35
$1,711 GUARANTEED LIFE-TERM ANNUAL PREMIUM

End of Year	(1) Death Benefit	(2) Cash Surrender Value	(3) Insurance Death Benefit	(4) Annuity Value (9.75) *	(5) Total Death Benefit
5	$100,000	$ 4,300	$100,000	$ 6,243	$106,243
10	100,000	12,400	100,000	20,259	120,259
15	100,000	21,700	100,000	33,682	133,682
20	100,000	31,600	100,000	61,575	161,575
Age 65	100,000	50,400	100,000	150,425	250,425

* Assuming current rate level throughout the life of the contract.

Earlier in the chapter I referred to whole life or ordinary life as well as deposit term, and in Chapter 11, "Lending your Dollars," I discussed the new breed of annuities. Using exactly the same major insurance companies (over a billion of insurance in force) rates and contracts, look at the benefits to you of putting your dollars through the "right windows."

Columns 1 and 2 show death benefits and "bank account" of purchasing a whole life contract. Columns 3, 4, and 5 illustrate what happens using exactly the same dollar amount sent to the same company at the same time, *but* using ten-year "deposit term" and a flexible premium deferred annuity. Remember, with ordinary life, unless you can live and die at the same time, you get only the face amount of the contract or the cash value. Using this company's deposit term and their flexible premium annuity, they are separate contracts and you get the benefits of both—live or die.

LIFE INSURANCE IN QUALIFIED PLANS?

Should you ever include life insurance in qualified retirement plans? The answer is no. Never! It has been prohibited in IRA accounts, but there is still a large amount of insurance being sold for Keoghs, profit-sharing plans, and pension plans. Life insurance is completely contrary to the objectives of these plans.

The IRS code states that if you put life insurance into a qualified plan of any type, you are receiving an immediate economic benefit and the cost of that benefit must be passed on to you. For example, let's assume you work for a corporation with a qualified plan, and they make a contribution to your pension plan. This contribution is deductible to the corporation and is not taxable to you. However, if you or those making the decision on how it is funded have been induced to use part of these funds to buy life insurance, using as their pitch that you are paying for it with "before-tax" dollars, the amount paid for the life insurance becomes an immediate economic benefit and IRS's P.S. 58 table comes into play. This table tells you how much of the contribution is to be added to your taxable income. You will then be taxed on money you never received and are in reality turning your tax-sheltered benefit into a tax liability.

The agent may have convinced you that your cost would be "incidental." Look at Table 24 in the Appendix titled the "Incidental Cost of P.S. 58" and you will find the cost to be very much less than "incidental."

For example, let's assume that you have elected to take a $100,000 policy and that you are age 40. By the time you are 65, you will have had to pay taxes on an additional $35,302. If you have been in a 50 percent bracket during that time, you've had to pay additional taxes of $17,651 on money you never received. You may not feel that is an incidental amount. If you are younger, your expense at the beginning will be less, but by the time you are 65, you will find that your costs have grown considerably.

But the real thief in this scenario is the lost earnings that could have accumulated if this money had been put to work for you. The purpose of your qualified plan was to furnish you with as much capital as possible to retire on. Life insurance is a loss or cost item, thus reducing your ultimate retirement income. If you die, you have little use for income in or from the grave.

As you will remember from Chapter 4, "Letting the Pros Do Your Investing," $10,000 inside an insurance policy over a 46-year period grew to only $40,544 if all projected dividends occurred, while the same amount in the Seminar Fund grew to $1,907,061, or a difference of $1,866,517 exclusive of taxes.

If you own your own corporation and have more then ten employees, have your financial planner design for you a Section 79 plan. The first $50,000 is exempt and will not cause you any tax liability, and the Uniform Premium Table on the remaining $50,000 is approximately three-fourths of the P.S. 58 table. At age 45, the Uniform Premium Table is $4.80 per thousand that will be carried through to you as income on the second $50,000, while on the P.S. 58 table it is $6.30 per thousand beginning on the first dollar. In the Appendix you will find a P.S. 58 table (Table 25) and a Uniform Premium table (Table 26).

As you can see from the above analysis, never place life insurance inside your qualified plan because you will not only have the P.S. 58 cost, but you will have the premium cost as well as the lost earnings on those premiums. I repeat, do not combine living and dying. They are incompatible.

PAYING MORE WHILE YOU'RE YOUNG

Unfortunately, your family's need for protection is greatest at the time in your life cycle when your income probably has not reached its prime. Despite the fact that your mortality risk is low at that time, most policies are designed so that while you are young you are overcharged at the time your family needs maximum coverage so that you can begin "underpaying" at age 72, when your need for coverage should have diminished or become nonexistent because you have become self-insured.

Figure 13-10 is a diagram of the level premium method. Note how the policy is designed for coverage far beyond life expectancy.

If Ma Bell came to you at age 35 and asked you to overpay your telephone bill for the next 37 years so you could underpay it for the years you live after 72, what would you tell her? If your answer is "No way," then use the same good judgment regarding overpaying your life insurance premiums.

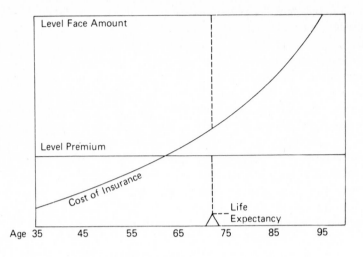

Figure 13–10. Level Premium Method

"SOMETHING BACK!"

When you buy term insurance on your life, you are doing so because you are concerned about the welfare of your family in the event of your death. You should not be asking, "What am I going to get back?" You know that term is pure protection and pays off only if you die while the policy is in force. You know that your beneficiaries will receive the payoff. You expect nothing in return other than the warm feeling that you have adequate protection for your family.

"Something back" appeals to your selfish instincts—and we all have them—but this is contrary to the purpose of life insurance.

A GOOD COMPULSORY SAVINGS PLAN?

Is insurance, in fact, a good compulsory savings plan? The previous analysis of this aspect of "permanent" insurance should indicate that you are much wiser to put savings in a bank, Series E government bonds, or preferably in good growth investments. You should save, but save for you and your family's benefit.

AN INEXPENSIVE WAY TO BORROW MONEY?

Sometimes a couple will proudly point out to me how very bright they have been to have figured out that they can borrow on their policy for 4½ to 8 percent instead of from the bank at a higher rate. If you are doing this, you are paying to borrow after-tax dollars that you placed there to begin with. Would you agree to the same arrangement with your bank? Also you are reducing the amount of your life insurance coverage when you borrow against your policy, because the loan is subtracted from the face amount if it is outstanding at the time of your death. Borrowing against your policies serves only to increase your cost and to reduce your coverage. If you are healthy enough to pass a physical, get pure protection. If you are not, by all means consider borrowing the cash value out and putting it to work, preferably in an investment with a tax-sheltered cash flow. Send the insurance company a check for the interest each year, and deduct the interest on your income tax return. You should be safe in deducting it if the policy was taken out before August 6, 1963.

LIFE INSURANCE FOR CHILDREN?

I'm amazed at the amount of money spent each year on premiums for life insurance for children. Let's reexamine the purpose of life insurance. Its purpose is to protect those dependent upon the policyholder in the event that he does not live long enough to build a living estate.

If you have a policy on the life of your child, ask yourself, "Who is dependent on my child for a livelihood?" You should never make a practice of protecting your liabilities, but only of protecting your assets. As much as you love your child or children, they are financial liabilities until they are old enough and sufficiently prepared to leave your nest.

Should you have enough for burial? You can if you want to, but it's a luxury I don't recommend. There are limited dollars in the family budget for life insurance, and every dollar spent on life insurance to cover the children means one dollar taken away from purchasing life insurance on the life of the breadwinner. You may shun such a somber thought, but a child's funeral expenses will be defrayed by the decrease in the cost of caring for the child, while the loss of a wage earner may be a near economic disaster to the family.

If you would feel more comfortable with a bit of insurance on the kids, you can obtain $1000 (called a unit) on each child, regardless of how many children you have, for about $8 per year total (not $8 for each) by adding this coverage as a rider on your policy. You can usually carry five of these units, and some companies offer ten or more. For example, five units would cost $40 and you would have $5000 insurance on each child. You can usually carry this coverage on each child until the child is 25 years of age. At that time, they have the privilege of obtaining five times the coverage carried without evidence of insurability. In other words, when each child reaches 25, he has the privilege of converting to $25,000 of coverage without having to take a physical to prove insurability and at the rate of his attained age, based on the current mortality table.

COLLEGE POLICIES

I've seen many endowment policies taken out at the time of a child's birth for the purpose of providing the expenses for four years of college that did not even cover the cost of the first semester. It makes me sad every time I see a billboard portraying a beaming youth with a mortarboard jauntily atop his head, proclaiming that his college endowment policy brought him to this happy occasion.

Although you certainly want to plan for your children's education, a college endowment policy is not an effective way to accomplish this worthwhile goal. Planning for this expense is covered in a later chapter.

DOUBLE AND TRIPLE INDEMNITIES

The question often arises about the amount of accidental death insurance a young family should carry. In our financial planning, we do not count accidental death policies when calculating the family's need for protection. Even though most young fathers are convinced that if they die, that's the way they'll go, it's not too likely—that's why the rates are low. It's more likely that they'll die from a heart attack while mowing their lawns. It doesn't really matter how you die; you are just as dead and the family's needs are just as real. Buy sufficient life insurance to cover full needs and don't worry about how you may die.

REPLACEMENT—BENEFIT OR BLASPHEMY?

As more and more people have became better informed about the potential earning power of their money and also more aware of inflation's devastation to its purchasing power, they have been searching for more productive ways to put their dollars to work. In an attempt to slow this tide of change, some companies have waged very successful campaigns to get regulations passed to require that agents complete and submit lengthy, detailed, and difficult replacement forms if they recommend the replacement of any cash value policy, regardless of which mortality table it was written on.

Replacement forms in some states have become so tedious and time consuming that many a conscientious financial planner has left his client's present insurance program alone, even when it was grossly inadequate and unnecessarily expensive, rather than spend the many hours required to complete these forms. There is an excellent company that employs full-time professionals to read existing policies and make the comparisons and complete all the necessary forms to comply. You can also send your policies to them without going through an agent. You'll find their name and address in the Appendix, plus a completed form taken from an actual case (Figure 13). See if you can calculate the owner's cost per thousand for his present coverage.

No "full disclosure" forms were required when you first started your life insurance program, and none were required when you bought additional insurance. Also, no replacement forms are usually required if the agent replaces a pure term insurance with a cash-value policy. If the "disclosure" forms help consumers know their true cost per thousand, shouldn't it be required for all policies?

Consider if you will for a moment the viability of the concept that any other financial decision made in this dynamic world in which we live should never be changed. Is it logical that the only exception is a cash surrender value life insurance policy? Should you ever be forced to make irreversible long-term financial decisions amidst economic uncertainty? Yet there are companies that teach their agents that cash surrender value policies are sacred.

You should have complete information about term policies and other policies that are term plus savings. We now have a "truth in lending law." A "truth in insurance law" was proposed by the late Senator Phillip Hart, but he died before seeing his proposal enacted.

TWISTING

Some cash value salesmen refer to a financial planner who recommends term insurance as a "termite," or, if the financial planner has replaced one of their policies, they may call him a "twister." This implies that all who recommend changing your insurance program are "twisters." This is not true. A cash value salesman *or* a term insurance salesman is said to be "twisting" if he uses misrepresentation or an incomplete comparison to induce a replacement to the detriment of the policyholder. If he provides an honest and complete explanation and reduces his cost per thousand, he is not a "twister."

Some insurance companies, when they receive a notice that one of their life policies is going to be replaced, send a dire warning letter and pamphlet to the policyholder, warning him of the serious mistake he is about to make. Often they include an old article from the 1961 publication of *Changing Times Magazine.*

I wrote to this magazine and asked if they had changed their thinking and if they realized how their article was being used. Mr. Jerome Oelbaum, Senior Editor, in a letter to me dated July 16, 1976, stated, "The article which you were given dates back to 1961, when conditions were quite different. I have enclosed a copy of a more recent article on the same subject." The article he enclosed from the August 1974 issue was titled "Trade One Life Insurance Policy For Another?" with a subtitle, "Sometimes switching makes sense, but don't be talked into it until you've examined all the angles." If you get a 1961 reprint, you may want to suggest that there is a later reprint.

Many of our large insurance companies have marshalled their forces to try to put an end to replacement of their policies. Figure 14 in the Appendix is a very strongly worded letter from their Chairman of the Board to their field forces.

SHOULD YOU REPLACE?

Your answer is probably "yes," if you are healthy enough to pass a physical and if any one of these four conditions applies:

1. You have more than one policy. There is an extra policy fee paid in addition, or already built in, each year for each policy to pay for administration, not for the mortality cost. This fee averages from $10 to $25 per year. If you are carrying six policies and you have a $20 policy fee per policy, you are spending $100 per year unnecessarily; that money could be used to provide additional coverage.

2. You have a savings program in your policy. You are probably "saving" with an insurance company under conditions that you would never save with your bank.

3. Your policies are not on a current mortality table.

4. It is a "participating" policy.

When Should You Not Replace?

Are there circumstances when you should not replace one or more of your insurance policies? Yes, and here are some of the reasons:

1. You are uninsurable.

2. You cannot lower your cost per thousand by obtaining a new policy.

3. You are planning to commit suicide within the next two years.

4. You are planning to give false information on your new insurance application. If you do, there will be a two-year contestability period that could result in your heirs receiving only the amount of coverage those premiums would have purchased had you told the truth.

5. If any of the nonforfeiture provisions of your present policies are important to your current financial planning. These provisions may include paid-up additions and extended-term provisions. Extended term provides that if you quit paying premiums, the company uses the cash surrender values in the policies to extend the period of your coverage. For example, let's say that your cash value was enough to buy you term coverage for ten years. You chose this option and died in the eleventh year. Your family would receive nothing. If you died the second year, they would receive only the extended term amount and the insurance company would keep the nine years of prepaid insurance premiums. There may be income options and annuity options in your present policies. Examine them. Determine if your financial planner can provide you with better alternatives.

6. If you bought your policies from a friend and you feel you would lose him as a friend if you replace them, and if a friendship based on *his* economic benefit is more important to you than the economic future of your family.

7. You cannot withstand the pressure that may be brought to bear on you by your present insurance company or its agent when you attempt to replace.

It's not, however, that it is not profitable for companies to be in the insurance business.

THOSE MARVELOUS MONEY MACHINES

An excellent article on this subject appeared in the September 1, 1974, issue of *Forbes* entitled "Those Marvelous Money Machines!" and states:

> While other businesses produce products, the insurance industry produces money, capital. The industry is a wonderful money machine. At a time when presidents of successful companies spend their sleepless hours wondering where to get capital, insurance company bosses worry only about where to invest it. That's a high-class worry.
>
> The numbers are not easy to come by, but FORBES has made some sensible estimates. We figure the industry took in about $91 billion in premiums last year [1973] and earned about $22 billion from investments and other income. Against this it paid out maybe $79 billion in benefits, operating expenses and taxes. The remaining $34 billion or so was added to the industry's capital base—either as plowed-back profits or as additional reserves. By the year's end the industry boasted $336 billion in assets—against, for comparison, 26.3 billion for the whole U.S. steel industry.*

The life insurance business can be very profitable. You should ask, "For whom?"

Possible profits become very evident when you recognize that the insurance companies have sizable sums to invest, sometimes at rates up to 13 percent. In recent years they have also demanded and received as much as one-half interest in the real estate developments they finance. These funds are available because their policyholders have been enticed to "invest" through them.

THE WIDOWS STUDY

How well is the industry doing the job of protecting the families of our nation? The Life Insurance Management Association conducted a survey of widows of men who were less than 65 years of age at the time of their death—men still in their earning years. Here are the results from The Widows Study:

---

* Reprinted by permission of *Forbes Magazine* from the September 1, 1974 issue. They have not done a study on the subject since this date.

1. Fifty-two percent of the widows received under $5000 in life insurance proceeds. This is less than half a year's income for most families. (The government classifies a family of four with an income of less than $5500 per year as being below the poverty level.)

2. In many cases the insurance money received is less than the final expenses connected with the husband's death. Fifty-two percent stated that the medical expenses amounted to $2000 or more.

3. After paying final expenses averaging $3900, the average widow ends up with about $8000 cash.

HOW TO ANALYZE YOUR POLICIES

Let's discuss how to take the first step in analyzing your own policies. First, you'll need to get them out of the safety deposit box or wherever you have them stored. Now read them. I'll bet you never have, even though you've been pouring some of your life blood into them.

After you have finished, look on the front of the policy. There you will find the date the policy was acquired. That's its birthdate. Take today's date, less the policy's birthdate, and this gives you the age of the policy. For example, if you acquired your policy in December 1969, and it is now December 1979, it is ten years old. Look toward the back of the policy if you have the "cash value" variety. Go down to the tenth year of the nonforfeiture section. Go across and you will find a "cash surrender" or "loan value." This amount will be for either the face amount or per thousand. It will state one or the other at the top of the chart. For example, if it's a $10,000 policy and your cash value table shows $350 opposite 10 years, and the table shows "per $1000," you would have a cash value of $3500.

Another group of facts were gathered by a large financial planning service company headquartered in Phoenix, Arizona. Here are the results of their study:

1. Within 18 months, 52 percent of all widows dissipate the insurance benefits of their husbands; within 60 days one out of four widows exhausts all of her insurance money.

2. The average of all death benefits left to a widow is only $12,000—including insurance, Social Security, VA benefits, pensions, etc.—against which the average cost of death expenses, including hospitals, doctors, funeral, etc. is $4000. And if you exclude accidental death and use only medical death, that average cost goes up to about $8000.

I've often had families tell me that they were insurance poor, but when I analyzed their programs, often I found them woefully under-insured. They were not insurance poor. They were premium poor.

It is a tragedy, in a society with workers with earnings as high as ours, that the widows of these workers do not have adequate protection because they are ignorant about how to obtain the proper coverage at costs well within their budgets.

To give you a better picture of your policy, you'll find worksheets in the Appendix. Worksheet I can be helpful for listing your policies. Worksheet II can be used to obtain a visual picture of them. Worksheet III will help in computing your present cost per thousand if you keep your policies. Worksheet IV will do so if you are replacing them.

HOW MUCH LIFE INSURANCE?

How do you calculate the amount of life insurance you should carry? First, take your present monthly salary. Let's assume that it is $3000. Multiply this amount by 70 or 75 percent, using 75 percent if you have three or more children. This is about what your family would need to maintain them at their present standard of living if you were not here to provide for them. At 70 percent, $2100 would be needed. Let's assume that your family would be eligible for maximum social security. Your wife may receive around $1200 per month until your children reach 18. Thus, $2100 less $1200 = $900. How much capital is required to provide $900 per month at 6 percent? Just multiply by 200 (12 ÷ .06) to determine how much capital is required at 6 percent to produce $900 per month. This gives you $180,000. Let's assume that you have accumulated $20,000, exclusive of home furnishings and nonliquid investments. Subtract this from the $180,000, leaving $160,000 of capital needed.

Calculate the amount you need using this method, adding other appropriate expenses that must be met, such as college costs, etc. Determine if the premiums for this amount can be fitted into your family's budget. If they can, fine. If they cannot, you must reduce the coverage to the amount you can afford and still live today.

An excellent financial planner I know uses a simpler method. Whatever your annual salary is, he just adds a zero to determine the coverage you'll need. He gives no credit for any "living" assets you have acquired. For example, if you earn $24,000 per year, he recommends $240,000. If inflation continues, as it appears it will, and if all our old established methods of investing keep changing, I think his method has merit.

LIFE INSURANCE, A VERY PERSONAL MATTER

Your life insurance program should be designed to fit your needs at this particular time. Your needs will change from year to year, so your policies should be reviewed constantly. They are not sacred instruments.

Your need for protection may be less, the same, or more each year. Is there a new mortality table now available? If so, you will want to apply for a new policy, probably at a lower rate. When you have the new policy safely secured (not before), then consider what should be done with your old policies. Policies can be changed, and riders can be dropped. Work with a creative financial planner to keep your insurance program finely tuned to your changing needs. A good insurance program should not be expensive, if properly designed, and should be well within your family's budget.

Let me re-emphasize—life insurance is a necessary umbrella until you've had time to accumulate a living estate. It should be purchased with these ten points in mind:

1. Determine your life insurance needs as if you were going to die today, but also include an extra amount to offset inflation.

2. Life insurance is based on a mortality table; therefore, it should cost you more each year, because you are more apt to die.

3. Every time there is a new mortality table, apply for a new policy. If you pass the physical and are granted a new policy at a lower rate, redeem or cancel the old one. A life insurance policy is no more sacred than a homeowner's policy.

4. The purpose of life insurance is to protect those dependent upon you in the event that you do not live long enough to accumulate a living estate. Your goal is to become self-insured by age 65 or sooner. You've either made it by then, or you'll probably never make it financially. (Yes, I know Col. Sanders did!) Life insurance is to protect an economic potential. After 65, your economic potential has greatly diminished. Yes, I also am aware that insurance proceeds can be used to pay estate taxes. If your heirs are in that enviable position, hurrah for you! Here we are speaking of bread on the table in the event that you are not here to provide for it. We can obtain pure protection to age 100, and that should take care of most situations, even including federal estate taxes.

5. Life insurance is for dying. Investments are for living. Never ever combine the two.

6. All life insurance is pure protection (term) or pure protection plus "banking." There is no other kind.

7. Only term insurance is "permanent" insurance. Those policies containing a "savings" element are decreasing insurance.

8. Do not "bank" with an insurance company under conditions that you would not accept with your bank.

9. Be sure that your policies are renewable and convertible without evidence of insurability. You should also consider waiver of premium.

10. Normally never have more than one policy (plus your group and unconverted GI term policy).

11. Don't buy a participating policy.

My wish for you is that you'll live a long and happy life and that all the life insurance premiums you'll ever pay will be pure waste!

APPLICATION

1. Complete Worksheet I in the Appendix. Circle in the left-hand column every policy after the first one. Then circle each cash surrender value in (2) and each time you have a policy that is not on the 1958 CSO mortality table. Then circle every time you show "a dividend." This will give you a rough idea of the places you can start lowering your cost per thousand. How many circles did you make?

2. Complete Worksheet II in the Appendix. You can obtain all this information from Worksheet I. Is this a picture of decreasing insurance and increasing savings?

3. Complete Worksheet III in the Appendix. What is your present cost per thousand?

4. What is the available cost per thousand at your age?

5. What action do you need to take?

14

PROTECTING AGAINST THE UNEXPECTED

You have now learned to buy time and have found that the cost can fit nicely into your budget if bought properly. You've also become familiar with the many excellent ways that are available to you today to build a living estate to substitute for the death estate that you do not want but must have until you've accumulated your living estate.

But what if you don't die, but rather become disabled before you have had time to accumulate a living estate—what if you and your family suffer economic death? Catastrophic long-term disability can destroy your most carefully laid plans. Statistics show that you are more likely to suffer long-term disability—lasting three months or longer—than you are to die during your working lifetime.

These studies also show that of every six men between the ages of 25 and 30, the probabilities are a near certainty that one of them will suffer a long-term disability during his working years. As a matter of fact, the probability is 97.5 to 99 percent. Table 27 in the Appendix summarizes these findings.

The best description I've ever read of the need for disability protection was written by the late Solomon S. Huebner, the noted insurance educator at the University of Pennsylvania's Wharton School of Commerce and Finance. He said, "He who becomes a living death totally and permanently is just as dead economically as he who is actually dead. He who becomes a living death totally but, as it may happen, not permanently, is also dead economically during the period of disability. The difference between the living death under conditions of permanency and the actual death is only six feet of sod."

I'm sure there is no question in your mind that if you have not yet accumulated a living estate, you will need some way to replace the income you are presently producing if you are not able to do so.

SOCIAL SECURITY

If you are covered by Social Security, you may be entitled to some disability benefits from that source. To qualify, you will have to have been covered for at least 20 of the 40 quarters preceding your disability; or if you are disabled before age 31, you must have coverage in at least half, but not less than six, of the quarters after attaining age 30.

To qualify for benefits, you would have to be unable to do "substantial gainful work" for at least five months, and then you would have to have your physician present a written statement that you will be disabled for at least one full year from the date of your disability. This would mean that you would probably not receive your first disability check until the thirteenth month after becoming disabled. Once the checks are started, however, they are paid retroactively to the fifth month of disability.

If you have not acquired sufficient funds to take care of your family and yourself for thirteen months and your company does not provide such insurance, you will certainly want to consider disability insurance.

NATIONAL SERVICE LIFE INSURANCE

If you are a veteran, you could have another source of disability insurance through your National Service Life Insurance. To be eligible for benefits, you must be totally disabled before your sixtieth birthday and remain disabled for six consecutive months. Your benefits will be $10 for each $1000 of the face amount of your policy.

Total disability is defined as any one of the following:

1. Any impairment of mind or body that continuously renders it impossible for you to follow any substantially gainful occupation.

2. The permanent loss of the use of both feet, of both hands, of both eyes, of one foot and one hand and one eye, or of one hand and one eye.

3. The total loss of hearing of both ears.

4. The organic loss of speech.

WORKER'S COMPENSATION

You may also live in a state that has enacted legislation that provides benefits for job-related disabilities. These benefits would be paid to you in addition to Social Security and other benefits. These vary from state to state but usually range between $100 and $200 per week. The waiting periods also vary, but there is usually a seven-day wait before benefits begin, and most benefits are paid for a maximum of 26 weeks. Your benefits are based on a percentage of your income. Eligibility for coverage usually follows the provisions of the unemployment or worker's compensation law.

AUTOMOBILE INSURANCE POLICIES

A personal injury endorsement on your automobile insurance policy could be another potential source of disability income. If you are injured in an accident, you could receive up to 85 percent of your gross income up to a maximum of $200 per week. The provisions vary from state to state. Some states also provide for coordination of benefits with other coverage you may have.

PRIVATE INSURANCE

You may or may not qualify for any of the sources of disability income discussed above, and even if you do, you should be aware that often the definitions of total disability may be very restrictive; benefits may be low; you may suffer loss of benefits if you have moved; and these benefits may be coordinated with other programs and only one may pay.

Various types of coverage are available through private insurance. These include group, association group, and individual policies. Here we will discuss only individual policies and encourage you to study carefully any group or association coverage for which you may be eligible.

Individual Policies

You will find a vast array of combinations available in individual disability policies. These will vary greatly from company to company, for there are no standard contracts. Clauses may vary widely, which can greatly affect the benefits you may receive and are difficult to interpret. You will probably need the assistance of a knowledgeable financial planner to fit the best policy to your particular needs and circumstances. Some of the most important provisions you'll want to investigate relate to renewal, accidents, sickness, and total disability, benefits if you return to work, age limitations, and qualification period.

Renewal Provisions. Five types of renewability clauses are used in the various disability policies. These are cancellable, optionally renewable, guaranteed renewable, conditionally renewable, and noncancellable. Guaranteed renewable and noncancellable are the two most preferable features.

Accident. How is this covered in the policy you are considering? The provision "bodily injury sustained through accidental means" is one that can deny disability claims in many cases regardless of the fact that you may be injured. The insurance company could be relieved of liability if you were injured performing an intended voluntary act. The provision "accidental bodily injury" is a more liberal clause, and the company would honor your claim so long as the claim resulted from any accidental injury.

Sickness.   Sickness is defined as "first contracted" or "first manifested." If the policy says "first contracted," the company could deny liability at a later date if they could prove you had this condition, even though you did not know it, at the time you applied for the policy. "First manifested" is a much more liberal clause.

Time Limit on Injury.   Following a specified period of time, 90 or 180 days, the insurance company could treat your claim resulting from an "accident" as a "sickness." If your policy has a lifetime accident benefit and a two-year sickness benefit, your insurance carrier would have greatly reduced its potential liability.

Relation-to-Earnings Clause.   This clause can reduce your insurance company's liability if there is other valid loss-of-time coverage.

Total Disability.   The definition of total disability is the single most important element in your disability policy. Definitions vary from policy to policy. To be considered totally disabled on some policies, you must be unable to engage in any gainful occupation. A more liberal definition would require that you be unable to engage in your own occupation for a specified period of time: five years, ten years, or to age 65.

Within the "own occupation" definition, variations exist from policy to policy. Some require that you be completely unable to engage in your "own regular occupation." This is a very restrictive definition of total disability. Historically, as periods of "own occupation" lengthened, the definition of total disability also improved. Today, the definition that has been interpreted by the courts to be the legal definition of total disability is "the inability of the insured to perform the material and substantial duties of his regular occupation." In selecting a disability policy, look for a policy with the most liberal definition possible—one using the terms "material and substantial" to define total disability.

Benefits If Insured Returns to Work. Over the past few years, several companies have introduced new benefits described as true residual, residual, partial, or proportionate. This means that if you are disabled and then return to your occupation but suffer a loss of income because of your disability, your insurance company will pay you benefits based on a percentage of the income you have lost.

You will want to check the disability policy to see if, in addition to the loss of income, there is a requirement that you be unable to perform all your duties or unable to engage in your profession full-time.

Age Limitations. Some companies reduce or eliminate income benefits after age 55.

Qualification Period. What qualification period is there for benefits? Some policies require one period of eliminated earnings to collect total disability benefits and yet another period to collect residual benefits.

How Is Income Measured? Is income measured on a cash basis or by accrual method? If you cannot tell from the policy, you may want to get a letter from the company.

Maximum Prior Earned Income. Is a maximum prior earned income considered? Some companies have none; others vary from $5000 to $10,000 per month. Companies expect to increase these limits in the future to cope with inflation.

In studying the various policies you will have to make some choices, for you probably will not find the ideal policy. Each will have limitations.

Your ability to produce an income is one of your most valuable assets. You will want to make adequate preparation to protect yourself and your family against economic death.

HEALTH INSURANCE

Although my discussion of health insurance will be brief, that does not mean that it is not an important aspect of being prepared for the unexpected.

There are five areas of coverage you will probably want to consider whether you have a family policy or you are under a group plan where you work.

Hospital Expense Insurance.   This is the most widely held form. It usually provides benefits for varying periods of time, ranging from 21 to 365 days. It is offered by commercial insurance companies and Blue Cross plans.

Benefits under these policies are used to pay for in-hospital services such as room and board, routine nursing care, and minor medical supplies.

Recently some Blue Cross plans began to offer coverage for such outpatient and out-of-hospital services as home care, preadmission testing, nursing home care, dental and vision care, prescription drugs, and a variety of diagnostic and preventive services.

Surgical Expense Insurance.   This coverage is used to defray the cost of operations. Policies contain listings of surgical operations and the maximum benefit they will pay for each.

Physicians' Expense Insurance.   This coverage is almost always combined with hospital and surgical expense insurance and is referred to as the "basic" coverage. Physicians' expense benefits usually cover a specific number of in-hospital visits to you by your doctor.

Major Medical Insurance.   This type of insurance picks up where your basic coverage leaves off. It pays for most types of care you may receive in or out of the hospital, with maximum benefits ranging to $250,000 and up. These policies use a deductible, which is the amount you must pay before benefits start, and a co-insurance factor, which is a percentage of the total bill you also must pay.

Disability Insurance.   This type of insurance is used to replace earnings lost because of disability. Maximum benefits during disability can go up to $1000 or more a month, although the maximum is usually about 60 percent of your gross earnings.

How Much Health Insurance Should You Carry?

Build your assets as quickly as you can so that you can insure yourself and family against losses that can result from illness or accident.

You should plan to cover your minor expenses from your accumulated assets. There are various rules of thumb after that, one being perhaps coverage for at least 75 percent of what you might expect as expense from an injury or illness. This dollar amount will be difficult to determine as medical costs rise—which occurs with inflation and increases in the minimum wage.

GROUP PROTECTION

Try to see if you are eligible for group protection. Group coverage may cost 15 to 40 percent less than individual coverage. Also, your coverage can't be cancelled until you leave the group. You don't have to take a physical, and pre-existing illness does not disqualify you. All policies express benefits in terms of days with benefit periods of 21 to 365 days. You should probably choose the shorter periods, in that statistics show the average length of stay in a hospital is just under eight days.

You will also want to check to see how much each policy pays per day and how the benefits are paid.

SUMMARY

Do prepare for the unexpected until you have acquired sufficient assets to become self-insured. Even then, you will probably want to carry some catastrophic medical insurance.

APPLICATION

1. Meet with several well-known and highly respected carriers and compare their policies or have a financial planner who is knowledgeable in the area do it for you.
2. Have your elimination period run as long as you feel your assets will carry you. This will reduce your premiums.
3. Inquire about hospital rates in your community.

15

YOU CAN
BECOME
A MILLIONAIRE

It is only fair to tell you I've never helped anyone become wealthy overnight. I've never helped someone with $10,000 turn it quickly into a million. The only people I've ever helped make a million dollars in a relatively brief period of time are those who brought me a million dollars to invest. Before you become too impressed, remember that it takes only an average return of 10 percent compounded to double your money in 7.2 years. At 12 percent it takes 6 years; and at 15 percent, 4.8 years.

I remember calling the office of Percy Foreman, the nationally known and brilliant criminal lawyer. I was calling to invite him to be my guest on my weekly television program, "Successful Texans."

When I asked to speak to him, the receptionist blurted out. "He's in jail." After chuckling over this literal response, I left word for him to call me when he "got out of jail." Later that afternoon he called, and I invited him to be my guest. He accepted my invitation; and just as I was about to say my goodbye, he said, "Aren't you that lady stock broker? Can you make me rich?" I answered, "Mr. Foreman, I understand you are already rich; but I believe I can make you richer."

Let's assume that you do not have the elusive million with which to start your high adventure. Is it still possible for you to become a millionaire? The answer is probably yes, if you have the discipline to save, the inclination to study, and a life span of sufficient length.

First, let me say that there are more desirable goals in life than becoming a millionaire. But if this is your desire, there are some very practical ways to approach your objective. To reach any goal, the first step is to divide it into its component parts so that it can be approached one step at a time.

COMPONENT PARTS OF A MILLION DOLLARS

What are the component parts of a million dollars? It's $1000 multiplied by 1000, isn't it? Trying to reach a million dollars in your lifetime may not be all that difficult to do.

How do you obtain the first $1000? The most obvious beginning is to save from current income. If you save slightly under $20 per week, you should have your $1000 in a year. Or if you do not want to wait until you have saved the $1000, you can start investing as you earn on a weekly or monthly basis from your current income. Another possibility is to borrow the $1000 from the bank at the beginning and pay the bank back on a monthly basis. This could give you a head start toward your goal.

Therefore, the first requirement for reaching your goal is the ability to set aside the relatively small amount of $20 per week.

MONEY, YIELD, TIME

The second requirement is to obtain a high return produced by adherence to aggressive but sound investment practices. These can be readily learned if your desire is strong enough.

Third, a life span of sufficient length.

So you see, the two most important things are time and yield. If you set your sights on a million dollars, you must keep these two factors in mind. Time is something over which you have very little control. But yield is different. I personally feel that anyone of good intelligence has the potential of earning a high return on his investment, and high returns are absolute musts if you ever expect to become a millionaire. When we speak of "yield," we ordinarily think of income (dividends or interest) as an annual return on the sum invested, expressed in the form of a percentage. For instance, if you receive $5 at the end of a year on a $100 investment, your yield is 5 percent. However, we shall broaden this definition for the purpose of this chapter and use "yield" to describe any distribution, plus any growth in market value. For example, if $100 grows to $318 in 10 years, we would say its "yield" is 12 percent.

One thing I think you must be fully aware of is the magic that comes from compounding the rate of return. This means that you are never to treat any income, capital appreciation, or equity buildup as spendable during the period you are building toward your million-dollar goal, but only as returns that are to be reinvested to increase your accumulation. In other words, don't eat your children. Let them produce more children, and before long you'll have a whole army of dollars working for you.

For the purpose of our calculations, any taxes that you must pay on your investments are deemed as having come from another source.

One of the most important things you must remember is how im-

Forward March!

portant the rate of return you receive on your investment is to your compounding. For instance, if you can put to work $1000 each year and average a compound rate of 10 percent per annum, you will be able to reach your goal in 48.7 years (taxes considered as coming from another source). However, if you can increase this compound rate to 20 percent per annum, you can reach your goal in 29.2 years. So you see, it does make a great deal of difference what return you obtain on your money.

DIVERISIFICATION—BASED ON DEMAND/SUPPLY

Risk in investing can be reduced by following some basic investment principles. As you have already become aware, one of the most important principles is diversification—spreading your risks.

After you've made that important decision, what investment media do you use? You stand back and determine where the demand is greater than the supply. You learned in Basic Economics 101 something that you must never forget: the law of supply and demand. Regardless of how diligently governments and economists have tried over the years, they have never been able to repeal it for any length of time. Russia has tried it and failed, as is evidenced by the millionaires now appearing on the scene in Communist Poland; England has attempted it and brought a once proud empire of plenty to its knees, and our own Congress continues to attempt to repeal this universal law. Their action has caused shortages and disruptions in energy, beef, housing, etc.

In making your determination of where the demand is greater than the supply, be an alert reader of the daily metropolitan newspaper; also read such papers and publications as *The Wall Street Journal, Time, Business Week, U. S. News and World Report, Fortune, Forbes,* and *Money Magazine.* Also begin to study the St. Louis Federal Reserve

Board reports. You'll begin to develop an awareness of demands and shortages.

AVOID THE BLUE CHIP SYNDROME

There are those who have the mistaken idea that all one has to do to make money in the stock market is to buy "blue chips" and throw them in the drawer and forget about them. In my opinion, this can be riskier than buying more aggressive stocks and watching them like a hawk. The "blue chips" of today may become the "red chips" or "white chips" or "buffalo chips" of tomorow. We live in a dynamic, thobbing, changing economy.

Just think back a few years. What car did the "man of distinction" drive? A Packard. I would have had difficulty convincing my father that only a few years later the manufacturers of the Packard automobile would be out of business. At the same time, what was the chief family home entertainment medium before television? It was radio, wasn't it? And who was the chief manufacturer of that half-egg-shaped wooden box in every home? Atwater-Kent. As you know, the Atwater-Kent Company no longer exists. You live in a world of constant change, and you must always be alert and ahead of this change if you want to become a millionaire through your investment know-how. You must sharpen your talents to predict trends before they happen, and move out before the trend has run its course.

If the money supply is being greatly restrained in our country, as you've already learned, you will want to develop a more conservative approach to the stock market. As the supply is even more diminished, move into money market funds so that you will have adequate liquidity to go back into the market as the money supply is accelerated and also to enjoy the higher yield that money will attract during this period of short supply.

DOLLAR-COST-AVERAGING

As discussed previously, dollar-cost-averaging is another approach. Timing can be difficult. Dollar-cost-averaging in large or small amounts can be done by anyone who has a regular amount to invest over a period of years. Using this plan, you invest the same amount of money in the same security at the same interval. This will always buy you more shares at a low cost than a high cost and give you an average cost for your securities. If the market eventually goes up (so far, it always has), you should increase your capital.

CAPITAL SHORTAGE

Shortage of capital probably will give you more opportunities for the triple-net leases we discussed in our chapter on investing in real estate. When money is tight, it is difficult for even major corporations to float bond issues at good rates, so they often sell their buildings and then lease them back. This gives them working capital and can also provide them with tax advantages. Triple-net leases of buildings of major corporations, I believe, offer a much safer investment than corporate bonds; in addition, they offer the investor some tax shelter and the opportunity for equity buildup and appreciation. Any court in the land will evict for nonpayment of rent, but not for nonpayment of interest on bonds.

HOUSING SHORTAGE

Another investment potential occurs when housing is in short supply. For example, if you read that the average family income of the nation is $15,800 and the average home is $64,000, then you know that a large number of families will not be able to qualify for a home loan even if they could be granted interest-free mortgages. So their only alternative is a garden-type apartment or trailer home. Often, if they want to live in the most desirable part of town and have access to a swimming pool and tennis court, they have no other alternative than to rent a garden apartment.

This national shortage of rentable units has created an excellent opportunity to invest in an area where rents should escalate, thereby increasing the value of the property. It also affords you a superior way to play the D.C. Game—Defer and Convert!

ENERGY

Another area is the shortage of energy that we have already described in the chapter on energy. Here is a product that everyone wants and needs that is in short supply. If you have the product to supply this need, this should indicate a good investment potential.

The list goes on. Suffice it to say that your role is to develop the sense of being able to unemotionally stand back from your money and the investment scene and determine the various areas where the demand exceeds the supply, and move your funds into those areas, so long as it appears that that situation will continue.

You can never rest on your laurels. We live in a dynamic world— that's why this book is entitled *Money Dynamics for the 1980s*—the world of money changes every day. That is what I love about my profession, financial planning. Every day is a new day! I must meet it with intelligence, energy, gusto, and enthusiasm, if I am going to help my clients and myself have our money in the right place at the right times. I'm convinced if you are doing anything the way you did it a few years ago, you are doing it wrong!

HISTORIC RETURNS

What skillfully selected investments have offered compound growth rates in excess of 20 to 30 percent in the past? There is no guarantee of what may occur in the future, but our study could shed some light on areas for you to explore. Those you will want to study are:

1. Carefully managed family businesses.

2. Well-located real estate: raw land, croplands, ranches, homes, residential and commercial income properties, always using leverage. For every $1 you invest, consider borrowing at least another $3 to put with it through long-term mortgages.

3. Carefully and aggressively selected growth common stocks in emerging industries.

4. Selected growth mutual funds.

5. Selected oil and gas income programs.

6. Investment-quality diamonds and precious jewels.

7. Antique furniture, art objects, and other collectibles.

8. Paintings and sculpture of gifted artists.

9. Rare stamps and coins.

10. Gold and gold stocks. Silver and silver stocks.

11. Commodities.

12. Tax-favored investments in cable television, video tapes and discs, equipment leasing, drilling for oil and gas, mining for coal and precious and strategic metals.

Be alert, pick a specialty that especially appeals to you, be imaginative, and see if you can turn it into a healthy profit.

REACHING A MILLION DOLLARS

Let's assume that you are 25 years of age, have saved $1000, can save $50 per month, can maintain an average of 15 percent performance on your investments, and can pay income taxes from another source. Your progress report should then look something like this:

Age 25	$1000 + $50 per Month
25	$ 1,000
30	8,663
35	18,054
40	40,967
45	87,052
50	179,745
55	466,185
60	741,183
65	1,495,435

If you are 30 years of age and fortunate enough to be able to make a lump-sum investment of $10,000 and can obtain an average return of 15 percent compounded annually, without adding new money to your investment but reinvesting all distributions and paying taxes from another source, your progress report should look something like this over a thirty-five-year period.

Age 30	$10,000
35	20,113
40	40,456
45	81,371
50	163,670
55	329,190
60	662,120
65	1,331,800

If you can move up the performance ladder to 30 percent (and we have outperformed this figure in our multifamily investments), your figures would be the following if you had started with $1000 and added $50 per month for forty years:

Age 25	*$1,000*
30	17,326
35	36,108
40	81,934
45	174,104
50	359,490
55	932,370
60	1,482,366
65	2,964,732

As you can see, at 30 percent you accomplished your goal in thirty years.

With a lump sum of $10,000 at 30 years of age and a 30 percent performance your progress report would look like this:

Age 30	*$10,000*
35	40,226
40	80,912
45	162,742
50	327,340
55	658,380
60	1,324,240
65	2,648,480

You've accomplished your goal here in less than twenty-five years.

Remember, we are not talking about "guarantees." All we are doing here is obtaining a visual picture of what compounding accomplishes over a period of years if you are able to maintain a 15 percent average and a 30 percent average.

We do not know what our future economy will be. Of one thing we can be certain, however: You will never reach your million dollar goal with this amount of savings using "guaranteed" dollars. As a matter of fact, you won't keep even after inflation and taxes. If you hope to reach your goal, you must save and let your money grow. Investing your money aggressively and intelligently in well-managed and strategically located American companies that are in the right industry at the right time, real estate expertly selected and intelligently leveraged, and natural resources that are in critical demand will not guarantee you growth of capital, but you will have provided your money with the opportunity to work as hard for you as you had to work to get it. The working dollar is an absolute necessity if your goal is to become a millinaire. Figure 15–1 shows how money compounds in a curve, not a straight line.

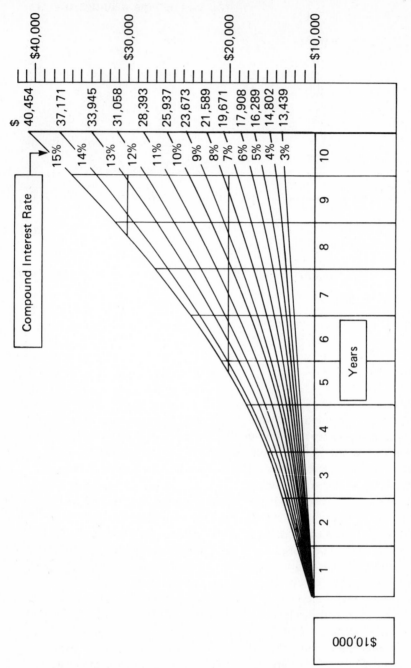

Figure 15–1. Potential Dollar Value of $10,000 Over a Ten-Year Period at Compound Interest

SITTING TIGHT

Do not be tempted to rationalize that because market conditions are unsettled now you should postpone starting your investment program or making investment decisions. When has the outlook been so obvious that you knew exactly what course to follow? If you take this attitude, you might as well dig a hole and bury your money. There is risk in any investment at any time. There is also a risk in a liquid position because of the steady erosion of fixed dollars due to inflation. As a matter of fact, I'll guarantee you at the present time you are going to lose.

As Figure 15–2 illustrates, there are always good reasons for investment inactivity, and our "sitting tight" friend was expert in discovering them. In doing so, he missed an entire lifetime of opportunities. Do the thing, and you will have the power!

THE COMMON DENOMINATOR OF SUCCESS

During my eight years as the moderator of the television show "Successful Texans" and my eighteen years as a financial planner, I've searched for the common denominator of success. In my search, one particular characteristic seems to run through each life. That characteristic is that the successful person has formed the habit of doing the things that failures do not like to do.

Perhaps you feel that you have certain dislikes that are peculiar to you, and that successful people don't have these dislikes but like to do the very things that you don't like to do. This isn't true. They don't like to do them any more than you do. These successful people are doing these very things they don't like to do in order to accomplish the things they want to accomplish. Successful people are motivated by the desire for pleasing results. Failures search for pleasing experiences and are satisfied with results that can be obtained by doing things they like to do.

Let's assume that your purpose is to become a millionaire—that your purpose is strong enough to make you form the habit of doing things you don't like to do in order to attain this goal.

To have maximum creativity, your body needs to have pure air, wholesome food, aerobic exercise, and creative thoughts. When you get home from work, do you grab a can of beer, light up a cigar, and sit in front of the tube to watch a wrestling match or the solving of one of the three to four murders that occur on television each night? Or do

476

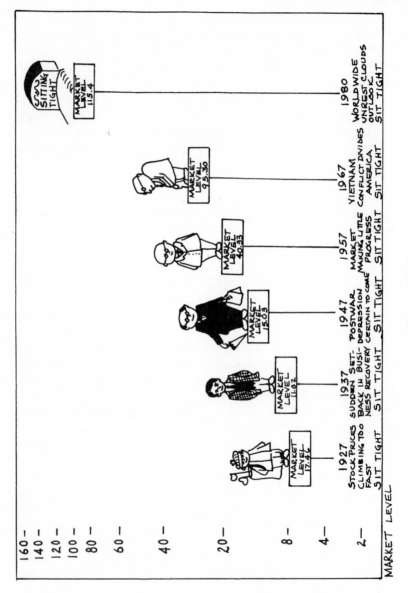

Figure 15–2.

you jog, ride a bicycle, exercise on a treadmill, walk a distance, eat a light nutritious dinner (sans large amounts of simple carbohydrates, sugar, salt, caffein, saturated fats, and alcohol, but high in proteins, vitamins, and minerals), and then read The *National Tax Digest*, The *Financial Planner* Magazine, *U.S. News & World Report*, The *U.S. News Washington Letter*, *Barrons*, The *Wall Street Journal*, *Newsweek*, and *Business Week*? The successful investor does these things not because he wants to, but because he must in order to accomplish his goal.

You must, too, if you desire to become knowledgeable. Then you must learn to act upon that knowledge. Failures avoid decision making. Successful people know they must act. They have no other choice if they want to reach their goal.

Time plus money plus American free enterprise may make you a millionaire. If it does, fine. If it makes you financially independent, that will be a major accomplishment of which you can be justly proud.

APPLICATION

1. What metropolitan newspaper will you subscribe to immediately?
2. What current affairs magazines?
   (1)
   (2)
3. What business publications and newsletters?
   (1)
   (2)
4. What period each week will you faithfully set aside to read and study financial publications?

5. What uninterrupted one-hour period will you set aside each week to contemplate where demand is greater than supply in our country?
   Day of week
   Time of day

6. What two-hour period will you spend driving around your city or a city nearby to observe building and land developments?
   Week of the month

7. What day each year will you take a financial inventory to see your progress dollarwise?
   Month
   Date

8. What self-improvement course will you take or what motivational tapes will you order to stimulate your thinking and improve your mental attitude?
   When?

9. Which books will you read to become better informed about nutrition? (You might start with *Pritikin's Program of Diet and Exercise.*)

10. What exercise program will you faithfully follow to become physically fit? (Dr. Kenneth Cooper's book, *The Aerobics Way*, is an excellent guide. I am on his aerobics program and heartily recommend it.)

16

PLANNING FOR THE LATER YEARS

As you have already learned, your financial life can be divided into three periods: the "Learning Period," the "Earning Period," and the "Yearning" or "Golden Period." Whether the third period will be your "Yearning Period" or your "Golden Period" will in all probability be determined by the financial decisions you have made during your "Earning Period." Unfortunately, as you learned in Chapter 1, 98 percent of your fellow citizens are making the wrong decisions, for of every 100 who are reaching 65 only 2 percent of them are financially independent; 23 percent must continue to work; and 75 percent are dependent upon friends, relatives, or charity. Of every 100 who are reaching 65, 95 are flat broke!

What a tragedy—a tragedy that need not happen. And as medical science gets more and more proficient at making us live longer, the number of years spent in this condition will be extended for a vast number of our older citizens. Being broke, especially when you are old, is not a lively or pleasant experience.

I've sincerely tried through my eighteen years of seminars, financial counseling, and two books to raise the level of comprehension of my fellow countrymen about these desperately important financial matters. I feel I've made a tiny dent in Houston and because of the wonderful financial planners and stockbrokers who have recommended my book in every state and abroad, I feel perhaps I've been able to make some impact nationally. More and more colleges and universities are using my book and the influence is growing, but this is just the tip of the proverbial iceberg—there are so many unreached, ignorant, and frightened people. They are frightened as they try to cope with a subject for which they have received absolutely no training.

Our educational system continues to send forth our young with so little information about financial matters that they are like time bombs about to destroy their own and their families' economic futures. We are equipping them to earn good incomes and to live the good life. Yet we are not preparing them to know what to do with the money they earn. There are no courses on how to manage their money, to invest their savings so that these savings can grow, or to protect these assets from the risks of casualty or inflation.

Perhaps you, too, have been a victim of this void in our educational system. The fact that you have reached this point in this book tells me you want to fill any void that may be there. Congratulations! Know that I'm delighted to be a channel for your learning. Know that you can fill any educational void you may have. To do this, you must first accept the reality of inflation and high taxes and then resolve to learn to put the former to work for you and avoid the latter. Neither of these will go away, but you do not need to sit and helplessly let them engulf you.

If you prepare yourself and develop a spirit of serendipity, opportunity will always present itself. Don't just sit and say "God will provide." God gave you talents, a mind, energy, and a strong body. You have all the tools you need to spade the productive loam, but God will not take your spade in hand. Don't sit and say "The government will provide." The government's efforts to provide are what have brought destructive inflation and higher and higher taxation.

I firmly believe that you owe it to yourself, to your family, and to the society in which you live to accumulate the financial means to take care of yourself for all the years you are on this earth. However, I'm equally convinced that you and your spouse, if you are married, do not have an obligation to pass on an estate to your heirs so long as they are physically and mentally fit and you have made an education available to them.

I'm also convinced that if you have at least an average ability to earn, an average ability to save a portion of what you earn, and will apply an average amount of intelligence to investing these savings, you will have sufficient assets to retire in financial dignity.

If you are male and retiring today at age 65, you can probably look forward to a life expectancy of another thirteen to fifteen years. If you are female you'll have an average of another eighteen to twenty years. So the sooner you begin, the better your chances are for reaching your retirement years and being financially able to retire in dignity.

As you learned in Chapter 1, there will only be three sources of income at retirement: you at work, your money at work, or charity. Which source do you want to depend on at age 65? Since you at work may not be an option open to you because the world may retire you, and charity will not be a fun way to go, that only leaves money at work.

Several means are available to you for preparing for retirement in financial dignity. Let's examine a few of them.

CORPORATE RETIREMENT PLANS

If you are incorporated or work for a corporation, one of the best tax-sheltered ways to prepare for your financial needs at retirement is either through a profit-sharing plan or a pension plan or a combination of both. It allows you to get before-tax dollars into the plan and then to compound them tax-sheltered. If you are the chief operating officer of a corporation, you will find it most advantageous to have a comprehensive study made by a specialist in the field. He can do a study to determine which type of plan is most advantageous to you while keeping within the IRS guidelines. If you are an employee, however, you may not be permitted to offer any input into that decision.

Technically, profit-sharing and pension plans are designed to attract and hold good employees, which they do if employees are kept adequately informed. However, let's assume you are the chief operating officer or head a closely held corporation. Your pay is probably higher than most of your employees', and the greatest advantage will usually accrue to you. An even greater advantage may accrue to you if you are older than your employees and set up a defined benefit pension plan.

Qualified pension and profit-sharing plans are undoubtedly the most attractive of all corporate fringe benefits. Certain specific details are beyond the scope of this book. Suffice it to say that more and more Americans will be receiving retirement benefits, and these benefits will become a more significant percentage of the average person's accumulated wealth. Total pension/profit-sharing assets now have a value of over $200 billion.

There are many variations of qualified pension and/or profit-sharing plans that can be tailored to the individual employer. However, the basic concept is simple.

1. The employer contributes dollars in a special account, taking a current tax deduction.

2. The employee is not taxed at the time of contribution, and assets are allowed to grow without taxation until retirement.

3. Death benefits paid to a named beneficiary or intervivos trust are estate-tax free, if the beneficiary chooses to accept distributions over more than one year.

4. Taxes on lump-sum distributions can be postponed and probably reduced by an IRA rollover.

THE TAX-SHELTERED DIFFERENCE

In order for you to obtain a visual picture of the enormous difference a qualified deferred compensation plan can make in your efforts to retire in financial dignity, let's assume you are a doctor with three choices: (1) incorporate, (2) don't incorporate but establish a Keogh Plan, or (3) don't incorporate and don't establish a Keogh Plan. Let's also assume the amount for investment is $20,000 per year. If you incorporate and your corporation contributes $20,000 in your behalf to your retirement program, the corporation can deduct the $20,000 and the funds can be invested. Let's assume you do not do a particularly outstanding job in your investment selections and only average 9 percent. In twenty years your accumulated benefits would total $1,115,000.

Let's say instead you do not incorporate and that you do not have any employees and that you contribute $7500 to a Keogh Plan (assuming $50,000 earnings from your practice), leaving $12,500 of the $20,000. In a 50 percent bracket after taxes, you would have $6250 left to invest outside of the plan. Your results in twenty years would be $623,000.

Let's assume instead you did not establish a Keogh Plan for yourself and paid your taxes. You would have $10,000 left after taxes to invest at 9 percent. Your results would be $328,000 in twenty years.

As you can see from Figure 16–1, deductible contributions that are permitted to compound tax-sheltered can make a tremendous difference in your net results in planning for your later years. If you have more than twenty years before retirement, the difference in your results should be even greater.

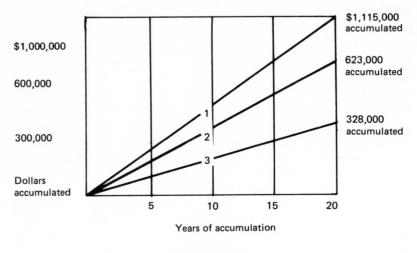

Figure 16–1.

SIMPLIFIED EMPLOYEE PENSION PLAN

Anytime any program or form designed by the government begins with "simplified," you can rest assured it will be complicated. To date there is still a great amount of confusion about the Simplified Employee Pension Plan, but as the IRS and the various branches of the government have an opportunity to study it more thoroughly, more detailed guidelines will no doubt be forthcoming. However, let's take a look at the plan as I understand it.

The "SEP-IRA," or "SEPP" as it is called, came into being with the Revenue Act of 1978. It is sort of a platypus of retirement plans in that it bears a resemblance to Keogh Plans, Individual Retirement Plans, and Corporate Pension Plans. The gist of the plan is that the employers can put up to $7500 into IRAs that employees establish, up to 15 percent of pay. Only the first $100,000 of total compensation counts. This contrasts with the $1500 lid on the amounts that employees can put into IRAs. Employers with SEPPs must make contributions for all employees, with three exceptions: those under age 25; some union members; and those who have not worked for the firm in three of the preceding five calendar years.

Other employees who have worked for part of three years out of the five must be covered, even if part-time or seasonal or for only a few days. All the eligible employees have to set up IRAs; otherwise it is possible that the IRS will disqualify the SEPP program.

Annual contributions are not required by the employer to

SEPPs; nor must the company have profits in any year for pay-ins to be deductible; nor will Social Security or unemployment taxes apply to SEPP set-asides. However, company pay-ins must be allocated uniformly via a written formula. Companies can have other tax-qualified plans in addition to SEPPs without losing their right to deduct pay-ins to employee IRAs. However, SEPP pay-ins by employers may reduce the deductions for pay-ins to other plans. An employer can cut SEPP pay-ins by its half of Social Security tax.

The employer cannot restrict withdrawals from IRAs by employees. SEPP pay-ins aren't taxable income to employees until withdrawn, but employees are subject to the usual tax penalties on early pay-outs. The employee sets up the IRA and the employee (not the employer) decides the type of IRA. The IRAs must specify that they can receive pay-ins exceeding $1500. There is a limit to what employees can add to IRAs under SEPP. In any year during which the employer fails to contribute at least the lesser of 15 percent compensation or $1500, the employee can make up the difference, bringing the total for the year to the 15 percent or $1500 maximum for a regular IRA account. Employees can have an IRA and be in other tax-qualified plans under the SEPP rules, but they cannot put in any amount themselves.

The administrative aspects of SEPPs are supposedly their main attraction. They are supposed to be less cumbersome than regular pension and profit-sharing plans. Although Congress told the Treasury to go easy on SEPP reporting requirements, it did not tell the Labor Department, nor did it say if fiduciary rules apply. I suspect that most interested employers will hold back on SEPPs to see if the S in SEPP truly stands for "simplified."

Your company's contribution, and yours, and the compounding return it produces are tax-sheltered. When you retire, all money distributed from your account will be taxed as ordinary income.

There are several ways to reduce the tax bite at that time. First, since you'll be retired, you may be in a lower tax bracket. Second, you may be able to use five-year income averaging. Third, most retirement programs permit you to draw income in several optional ways—in one lump sum, in regular periodic installments, or by conversion into an annuity.

IRA ROLLOVERS

When you retire, if you have been a participant in either a pension, profit-sharing, or Keogh plan, you will most likely need to make some choices that could vitally affect your finances for the remainder of your life. One of your options may be to receive a lump-sum distribution consisting of cash, stock, or a combination of the two. These funds will have come from the company's contribution and, if yours was a contributory plan, also from your contributions and the earnings that have compounded. If you take no action to shelter these proceeds, you will be liable for income taxes on the company's contribution and all the earnings on the company's and your contributions. No tax is due on your contribution because you contributed after-tax dollars. You are entitled to use a ten-year forward-average formula or to rollover all or a portion of your funds into an IRA rollover account. You will only have sixty days to make this decision from the date of the receipt of your distribution.

This provision for rolling over pension and profit-sharing benefits was primarily designed to give portability of accrued pension benefits to those who were moving from one company to another. Let's say that an engineer wants to move from one large company with a pension plan in which he has a vested interest (meaning that he can take it with him) to another firm. Under the new law he can move his funds into an IRA rollover account, not pay any current taxes, which he would have had to do formerly on all the company's contributions, and allow the funds to compound there without tax. Later, if he desires and it is agreeable to his new company, he can again roll it over into their pension plan, or if he prefers, he can just leave it in the account where he had originally rolled it.

However, those who are making the greatest use of this rollover provision are retirees who are rolling their pension proceeds into a rollover account that meets IRS custodian guidelines.

Let's say that after carefully weighing your alternatives, you choose to rollover. You will avoid current taxation on your lump-sum distribution, and, probably of equal importance, your funds will continue to compound tax-sheltered until you withdraw them.

If you have other assets, you may want to use them before you use the funds in your IRA account so that you can take advantage of this tax-sheltered compounding. You must wait until you are 59½ years of age or disabled, or you'll have a penalty for early withdrawal, and you must start withdrawing at 70½ an amount based on your life expectancy or the combined life expectancy of you and your spouse if you are married.

Formerly the law required that the recipient rollover his entire distribution in order to qualify for the tax-deferred treatment. In October of 1978, this all-or-nothing requirement was changed. Now you are permitted to retain a portion. This will be fully taxable as ordinary income. It will not be subject to the more favorable capital gains or ten-year averaging treatment that would otherwise be available.

You are not allowed to rollover your contribution. You wouldn't want to anyway, because those were after-tax dollars you contributed and for that reason they are not taxed when you withdraw them.

You will have several investment choices, but in most of the choices there must be a custodian that is acceptable to the government. Your choices are:

1. Mutual fund custodial account

2. Custodial account with a trust company

3. Commercial bank or savings and loan

4. Fixed and variable annuities provided by life insurance companies

5. Individual Retirement Plan Bonds from the Treasury Department.

Of the choices available to you, I would recommend 1 and/or 2. Let's consider 1. If you choose a mutual fund that is a part of a family of funds that has a money market fund, you can always have the choice whether to be in stocks or in a cash equivalent position. You can divide your funds between their growth funds, middle-of-the-road funds, special situation funds, bond funds, etc., and you can move from one to the other without commission and without tax..

If you choose option 2, you could use any investment that is acceptable to the trust company. This could lend itself to a wide array of limited partnerships in oil and gas, real estate, rare coins, gold, gold stocks, individual stocks, investment grade diamonds, certificates of deposit, etc. You could also direct the custodian to increase or decrease these areas as you saw fit.

If you choose a particular custodian and later want to change to another, you may do so. This is called a "Transfer of Assets" from one custodian to another. This is not a taxable transaction because no "constructive receipt" has occurred. For example, if you previously rolled over your pension plan into certificates of deposit at a bank or savings and loan, you do not have to leave it there. You need only have your financial planner prepare a transfer of asset form for your signature. He can do this easily if you'll give him a copy of one of your confirmations from your present custodian.

Before it's time to retire, I recommend that you consult with a competent financial planner and have him provide you with a computer printout showing past results with and without rollover.

An Actual Case Study

A couple who had attended one of my three-session financial planning seminars requested an appointment, as every attendee is entitled to do. When we sat down for our two-hour uninterrupted personal session in my office, I discovered that he had taken early retirement, had received his distribution fifty days previously, and was faced with a $14,056 tax bill on a $88,201 distribution. I quickly ordered the computer printout shown in Tables 28 and 29 in the Appendix, giving the past results if the funds had not been rolled over and if they had been using the Seminar Fund. I had the computer show a 9 percent withdrawal for eleven years, and, beginning in the twelfth year, use a 21-year self-liquidating program designed to exhaust the principal over their combined expected lifetimes. I had the program done this way even though the couple did not need to start withdrawal immediately. It was the only fair way to compare the two alternatives, because they planned to hold their Exxon stock if they did not choose to rollover.

In reality they had other funds that I recommended they use first if they decided to rollover so that their rolled-over funds could continue to compound tax-sheltered.

In the first printout we assumed that they did not rollover and paid the tax of $14,056, leaving a net of $74,154 to invest in the Seminar Fund. From the 9 percent monthly withdrawals of $556.09, we have deducted 20 percent in taxes on all dividends and 10 percent on capital gains.

As you can see, at the end of eleven years, their after-tax distributions were $73,403, and the remaining value was $115,034. The twelfth year begins a 21-year liquidation. During the 32-year period $388,331 after taxes would have been withdrawn.

Now let's turn and look at the past results, and I emphasize past, that would have resulted from rolling over their pension distribution. As you will note, they had $88,201 to rollover, because they did not owe the $14,056 in taxes that year. Again 9 percent is withdrawn, or $661.51 per month, for eleven years. From these distributions shown under "Annual Total" has been subtracted 20 percent for federal income taxes. By the end of the eleventh year $69,854 after taxes had been withdrawn and the balance of $167,258, shown under the column "Total Value," was still in the account. Again we started a 21-year self-liquidating program designed to exhaust principal. As you will note from the totals, $520,789 was withdrawn. (Incidentally, you are not limited to withdrawing just the annual amount shown. You can make larger withdrawals.)

In the period studied, they would have had $132,458 more distributions ($520,789–$388,331) by rolling over than if they had not rolled over. In reality, it could make an even larger difference because we anticipate their leaving their funds there to compound tax-sheltered for several years before making any withdrawals. I also recommend that you postpone withdrawals as long as you can comfortably do so.

A Hypothetical Example

Let's assume a hypothetical $100,000 distribution and a 25 percent federal tax liability. The value of the $25,000 that you would pay in federal taxes invested at 8 percent would be $53,950 in ten years and $79,302 in fifteen years. Your dividends and capital gains can compound tax-sheltered. For example, let's assume you receive dividends of $1000 each year and that you obtain only 8 percent on them:

	in 10 years	in 15 years
Without Rollover (25% federal tax)	$10,560	$18,722
With Rollover (No federal tax)	$17,200	$31,571

At a higher yield, which you can surely learn to obtain, your results would be greater.

Upon your death there are two other very important advantages to rollover. First, federal estate taxes on assets in your account at your death can be avoided if you have left the balance to a named beneficiary other than your estate and it is to be paid out over a period of at least 36 months. If the beneficiary is the spouse, the spouse also has the option to rollover, maintaining the tax shelter.

I hope you never have an occasion to use another feature of the IRA rollover: that your account is protected from assignment and cannot be attached in a law suit.

Disadvantages

Are there disadvantages? Yes.

1. Your distributions, when you do receive them, will be taxed as ordinary income.

2. If you should withdraw any funds before you reach 59½, there will be a 10 percent penalty unless you are disabled.

3. You cannot pledge your IRA account as collateral for a loan.

The other day we decided it was not advantageous for one of our clients to rollover. He was retiring while still relatively young in order to have leisure to do some writing. He wanted to use the money now. We obtained tax shelter by providing him with a tax-favored investment with a large write-off in that year.

In most of the cases I have studied, it was to my clients' advantage to rollover, but there have been some exceptions. Study all your options.

COMPANY TERMINATION OF RETIREMENT PROGRAMS

Perhaps you are not retiring, but your company decides to terminate its retirement plan and makes a lump sum distribution to you. (This has occurred at an alarming rate since the passage of the punitive ERISA bill.) Under this type of rollover, the requirements are exactly the same as above. However, unless you are 59½ or have also terminated your employment, your benefits do not qualify for special ten-year averaging; therefore, the use of a rollover would be even more valuable. Rollovers as a result of such decisions also may later be transferred into a new employer's retirement plan, if the employer's plan permits and is similar to the one from which the distribution was originally made.

INDIVIDUAL RETIREMENT ACCOUNTS

With the signing of the Employee Benefit Security Act of 1974, if you are not covered by any retirement plan other than Social Security, you may now set up one for yourself, tax deductible.

You may create an Individual Retirement Account, commonly referred to as an IRA. You may invest as much as 15 percent of your pay into IRA, up to $1500 a year, and take a tax deduction for that amount. If both you and your spouse receive taxable compensation and both are not covered by a retirement plan, you may each establish your own IRA. Together you may contribute up to $3000 annually ($1500 × 2). However, your individual deductible contribution may not exceed 15 percent of your compensation for that year. For example, if Mary and John Smith earn $8000 and $15,000, respectively, Mary can contribute up to $1200 and John $1500 to their individual IRA plans. This results in a total federal tax deduction on their joint 1040 return of $2700.

The Non-Working Spouse

In cases where one spouse works and contributes to an IRA but the other spouse receives no employment (or self-employment) compensation, an even larger tax-deductible contribution than $1500 is possible. The law now permits a working spouse to establish a similar IRA account for the nonworking spouse. However, certain requirements must be met. First, separate accounts must be established for each spouse. Second, the total yearly contribution to both accounts cannot exceed the lesser of 15 percent of the compensation of the working spouse or $1750. The total contribution must be equally divided between the two accounts if you want the full tax deduction.

Time for Making the Contribution

At present, the IRS will permit tax-deductible IRA contributions to be made if such action is taken within the time you have to file your 1040 return for that taxable year. The taxable year for most of us ends on December 31. Therefore, a deductible contribution can be made up to the following April 15, or the extension date for filing your return. Equally important is the fact that you can also establish your IRA during that 45-day period and still get the full deduction for the prior year. You may take the deduction even if you take only the "standard" deduction rather than itemizing when you file your income tax return.

If you do begin an IRA account using the Seminar Fund, what can you expect? I really don't know, but I can tell you what would have happened if you had started such a plan approximately forty years ago on December 31, 1939. Your results as of August 31, 1979, would have been as follows: amount of your yearly contributions $61,500. By August 31, 1979, you would have owned 137,975 shares with a market value of $1,196,245. Yes, over a million dollars! Again, the secret of financial independence is not brilliance or luck, but discipline—the discipline to save a part of all you earn and to put it to work in a good cross-section of American industry.

Again, you do not have to fight the battle alone. American industry will help you, as will the IRS by not taking away so much in taxes. Your IRA contribution is tax deductible. By making a $1500 contribution to your own retirement program, you saved $450 in taxes in a 30 percent bracket every year. Also, they did not tax your dividends and capital gains, so all of these compounded tax-sheltered. The dividends that were allowed to compound were $358,198, which grew to $519,785; and the capital gains were $370,245, which grew to $540,308. Your

$1,196,245 is taxable as ordinary income when and as you take it out. But you won't need all of it the day you retire, so only the portion you take out will be taxed and the remainder can continue compounding tax-sheltered. You will find a computer printout showing year-by-year results in Appendix Table 30.

The Cost of Not Having an IRA Account

Let's assume that you are in a 30 percent tax bracket and decide you really don't want the government to restrict when you can withdraw your funds or what method of funding you can use. So you take your $1500 of earnings and pay $450 to the IRS. This leaves you $1050. You now invest this amount yearly in the Seminar Fund for the same period of time as the person with the IRA account. You would have contributed a total of $43,050, and you would have left your dividends and capital gains in the account to be reinvested. The dividends would have come to a total of $121,324, and their value would have grown to $179,731 (you lost 30 percent of your dividends to taxes, remember). Your capital gains would have been $166,460 and would have grown to $247,465 (again there was loss to taxes), for a total number of shares on August 31, 1979, of 60,201 with a market value of $521,948. (See Appendix Table 31 for a computer printout.)

The Difference

With IRA	$1,196,245
Without IRA	521,948
Difference	$ 674,297

There would have been a difference of $674,297 on a contribution of $61,500. The tax advantages of IRA are worthy of your consideration. You should be aware that your withdrawals from your IRA account when you do make withdrawals will come out as ordinary income. Perhaps you'll be in a lower bracket at that time and, even if you are not, the balance left in the account is still compounding tax-sheltered.

KEOGH PLANS

Are you self-employed as a professional person, a proprietor, or a partner of an unincorporated business? If so, you probably work longer hours than your friend who works for a corporation, but you probably enjoy your freedom and independence. However, when you sit down at the beginning of each year to assess your financial progress and begin to make plans for the new year, you may become painfully aware that the tax bite left you with very little to invest for the golden years of retirement.

At that time, you may look with envy at your friend who works for a corporation with a pension and/or profit-sharing plan, or who has incorporated his business and set up such a plan. Contributions have been made for his benefit in a retirement plan with "before-tax" dollars, while you, if you are in a 30 percent tax bracket, had to earn $1.42 to have $1.00 left to set aside to invest for your retirement; and if that $1.00 produced income, you also lost 30 percent of that amount to taxes.

Congressman Keogh felt this was an inequitable arrangement, so in 1962, he was successful in getting Congress to enact the Self-Employed Individuals Tax Retirement Act, HR-10. With the passage of this legislation and later amendments, it became possible for you, if you are self-employed, to establish a Keogh Plan for your retirement.

Your Contributions

The plan allows you as a self-employed individual to set aside 15 percent of your earned income (after expenses and before income taxes) or $7500, whichever is the smaller of the two. These contributions are fully deductible, and all earnings accumulate over the years tax-sheltered.

If you have employees, you must also include all full-time employees who have been in your employ for three years. A full-time employee is defined as one who works for you at least 1000 hours per year (but may drop below this number without elimination).

If you have had your self-employed status less than three years and are setting up a plan for yourself, you must also do the same for each employee who has worked for you the same period of time. Here is a rule that may help you to answer questions you may have with regard to contributions you must also make for employees: "You must do for your employees what you are doing for yourself, if all conditions are the same."

The amount you must contribute for them must be the same percentage you contribute for yourself, with certain variations.

HR-10 Calculations

As an example: if your earned income from self-employment is $25,000 for the year, if you have been in business two years, if you have an employee who has worked for you for those two years, and if you pay him $6000 per year, you must include him. Your Keogh contributions would be

$25,000 × 15% = $3750 contribution for yourself
$ 6,000 × 15% = $ 900 contribution for your employee
$4650

In a 36 percent bracket Uncle Sam contributes $1674 of the $4650, and you contribute $2976, making it possible for you to invest $3750 for your benefit at a cost to you of $2076.

The Higher Your Income, the Greater Your Advantage

If, however, you are netting $50,000 annually, and have one employee whom you pay $6000, you may contribute $7500 on your behalf, and you must contribute 15 percent of the employee's income, or $900. Your net gains would be as follows:

Contribution for your Keogh	$7500
Contribution for employee	900
Total contribtuion deductible	8400
Your tax deduction ($8400 × 50%) =	$4200
Tax savings	4200
Investment you make for yourself	7500
Net gain in year contribution made	3300

If your income is above $100,000, you will not be permitted to count more than $100,000 of earnings in figuring the amount you may set aside. Therefore, you would use a set-aside factor of 7½ percent to invest the maximum of $7500. To meet the nondiscrimination rules, you must also contribute 7½ percent of your employees' pay, or $450 for an employee who earns $6000.

Do You Have a Large Payroll?

Not all self-employed persons, of course, can benefit equally from the law. Take the case of Dr. Williams, age 35, who has a taxable income of $22,000 and an eligible payroll of $12,000.

The law allows Dr. Williams to invest $3300, or 15 percent of his income. His tax saving on this amount would be $1056 in a 32 percent tax bracket. But he must also contribute 15 percent of his payroll, or $1800. This, of course, is classified as a business expense and gives him a further tax savings of $576. By adding the $1056 to the $576, we have a total tax saving of $1632. That means that the cost of the Keogh Plan to Dr. Williams is $168 a year ($1800 less $1632).

Remember, though, that's not the end of the story because of the tax-free accumulation feature. Over the years this could overshadow the small annual cost, since no taxes are payable until retirement, and the plan could also create considerable good will.

If Dr. Williams did not want to contribute to his employees' retirement program, he could set up his own individual retirement account and set aside $1500 tax-deductible.

Voluntary Contributions

If you have at least one participant in your plan who is not a greater than 10 percent owner (owner-employee), you may also make a $2500 voluntary contribution (or 10 percent, whichever is smaller). This must be made with after-tax dollars, but again, the dividends and capital gains compound tax-sheltered during the time that they are in the plan.

Your employees must also have the same privilege, and may also make voluntary contributions up to 10 percent of their salary, with no $2500 limit.

The principal in this account may be withdrawn without penalty. If you are in this position and have children whom you plan to send to college, this may be a good way to accumulate funds for that purpose. For example, let's assume that you have placed $2500 per year into your voluntary account. In ten years it's college time. You may withdraw the $25,000, leaving the earnings to continue compounding tax-free.

If you are an employer and have too many employees to make a maximum tax-deductible contribution economically feasible, you could make a 1 percent deductible contribution and a 10 percent voluntary contribution up to the $2500 limit. Under this arrangement, you would be required to contribute only 1 percent for each of your eligible employees. Then you could make your entire voluntary contribution and have all the earnings from it tax-sheltered.

If you have not established a Keogh Plan, you must do so before the end of your business fiscal year. I find a number of C.P.A.s and banks mistakenly tell clients that they have until they file their tax return to set up their Keogh plans. This is not true. The plan must be established before the end of the year. Once you have established your plan, you must make your contribution some time before you pay your federal income taxes.

The freedom to move from one investment to the other without tax consequences under that trusteeship gives you the flexibility needed for our dynamic world. You are allowed to place a wide variety of investments in the plan, such as registered oil and gas income limited partnerships and registered real estate limited partnerships, diamonds, certificates of deposit, etc.

Unlike IRA rollovers, where you may take receipt of the funds and within 60 days redeposit them in another IRA, Keogh assets must be carefully transferred from bank to bank. If you take receipt of the assets, they become fully taxable to you. You do have some limitations on moving from one fiduciary to another.

If you have chosen the mutual fund route, you may want to consider investing monthly as you earn. This gives you the possible benefits of dollar-cost-averaging. For example, if you are contributing $3600 to the plan, you might invest $300 per month.

You may also consider a lump-sum investment at the beginning of the year, so that your dividends and capital gains, if any, can be compounding throughout the year. Market conditions each year will determine which approach would have been best.

I find that most of my clients wait until we call to remind them that it's time to make their yearly Keogh contribution. We do this at the end of November and again in March. If you have not set up a Keogh, it must be done before December 31. If you have a Keogh, you must fund it by the time you file your tax return for the previous year.

I must warn you that I have never found a way to move a client out of the special U.S. Treasury bond into another Keogh investment. From all the interpretations I have been able to find, funds placed there must be left until you are 59½ years of age. If you don't want your IRA investment decisions written in stone, avoid this choice.

UNDERSTANDING YOUR BENEFITS

Both Keogh and IRA accounts allow you to invest at a discount. Uncle Sam is paying part of the cost of your retirement program. (At least, he is not taking his amount away from you, so you can have some to set aside.)

Second, the earnings compound tax-sheltered. We are so accustomed to paying taxes that we've forgotten what tax shelter can mean. You may begin withdrawing retirement benefits at 59½ years of age and must begin withdrawals at 70½.

Some self-employed professionals will not set up a Keogh Plan because they can't withdraw these funds until they are 59½ years of age without some penalties. It is usually a blessing that the funds cannot be withdrawn or pledged at the bank for collateral. You would be amazed at the number of professionals who arrive at what was supposed to be their golden years and find themselves scrimping to eke out an existence that is not so golden.

The Magic of Tax-Sheltered Compounding

When you add to the benefit of tax shelter the phenomenon of compounding, you have double forces working for you. Let's assume that you can afford to set aside $7500 per year and do so for 20 years. (If your contribution is less, just adjust by what percentage $7500 is of the amount you can invest.)

If you contribute $7500 per year from age 45 to age 65, you will have contributed $150,000. (Remember, these are before-tax dollars.) If you average 6 percent on your funds, this sum will grow to $292,443. If you move up to 10 percent, this amount will grow to $472,512.

Let's assume you used the Seminar Fund for your investment. As you will note from looking at Appendix Table 32, you would have contributed $157,500. Your dividends that were reinvested were $105,023, which grew to $140,638; and your capital gains were $85,022, which grew to $110,952, with a total result of 53,593 shares with a market value of $464,656. You contributed $157,500 to your retirement. American industry and the IRS contributed $307,156. Again, you don't have to fight the battle alone.

But let's assume you want to do so, and look at the difference it could make in your net results.

Without Tax Shelter

Let's assume you do not establish a Keogh account, are in a 50-percent tax bracket, and also invest in the Seminar Fund. To begin with, you will have only half as much to invest (if you don't shelter yourself in some other ways to lower your bracket). This leaves you $3750 to invest. From December 31, 1959, to August 31, 1979, you would have contributed $78,750. You would have reinvested $21,002 in dividends (50 percent of your dividends were lost to taxes) and $28,794 in capital gains (20 percent were lost to taxes). Your net results on August 31, 1979, would have been 19,733 shares with a market value of $171,086. (A computer printout may be found in Appendix Table 33.)

The Difference

With Keogh	464,656
Without Keogh	171,086
Difference	$293,570

These funds are tax-sheltered instead of tax-free, because at retirement you will have several choices as to how you will receive your benefits, and your tax will vary accordingly. These conditions seem to be changing so rapidly that it's difficult to give you any estimates about your tax status in the future. However, after retirement, you may be in a lower tax bracket. Also, the IRS presently allows the special ten-year income-averaging formula. Even if the funds were taxed as ordinary income, which can usually be minimized, just the privilege of compounding without taxes for twenty years will make a tremendous difference in your results.

Without Keogh, of course, you are free to withdraw anytime you desire without penalties, and your capital gains distributions enjoy the more favorable capital gains treatment.

With Keogh you cannot begin your withdrawal until 59½ without penalty unless disabled, and you must start withdrawing at 70½ if you are the owner of the business. If you are an employee who is not an owner, you may put off receiving Keogh benefits until you retire, even if that is beyond the time you have reached 70½. If you are the owner, you may continue to make contributions to your plan, but you must also start receiving benefits.

Don't ever be deceived into thinking tax laws are logical. They are not. The other day an engineer client began his comment about some tax consequence by saying "logically speaking," and I kiddingly told him he had made his first mistake. Tax laws are not logical. You learn them, apply them, and change when they change.

Following is a summary of the questions that I've been asked most often about Keogh plans.

COMMONLY ASKED QUESTIONS ABOUT KEOGH

1. Q: *How much can I contribute to a Keogh plan?*
   A: You can contribute up to 15 percent of your earned income with a maximum of $7500. However, under certain circumstances, contributions to defined benefit Keogh plans may exceed these limits.

2. Q: *Do I save federal taxes by contributing to a Keogh plan?*
A: Yes, you are allowed to deduct from your pre-tax earnings the total contribution made on behalf of yourself and your employees. For example, if your tax bracket is 33 percent and you make a $5000 contribution, you save $1650 in taxes in that your contribution is deductible.

3. Q: *Are there other tax benefits for the Keogh plan?*
A: Yes, all interest and all dividends and capital gains earned by your Keogh plan are accumulated free from current taxation.

4. Q: *Is a "silent partner" eligible for a Keogh plan?*
A: No. To be eligible for a Keogh plan, your income must be derived from personal services and be considered "earned income." An individual who has merely contributed his capital to an enterprise, but not his time, is not considered eligible for Keogh.

5. Q: *Can I be covered under a corporation or government retirement plan and also have a Keogh plan?*
A: Yes, if you have earned income from personal services, as well as corporate or government income, you are eligible for a Keogh plan.

6. Q: *What if my partners refuse to join the Keogh plan—may I have one?*
A: Yes, as long as the partnership establishes the Keogh plan, each partner who has a greater than 10 percent interest can elect not to participate.

7. Q: *Do I have to include my employees?*
A: Yes, but you may exclude all part-timers who work less than 1000 hours per year and employees with less than three years of service (with some exceptions).

8. Q: *Do I have to contribute 15 percent of my employees' pay?*
A: No, not necessarily—the "minimum" percentage that you may contribute is determined by what percentage of your personal income you are contributing to the plan. For instance, if you are earning $50,000 a year and contribute $2500 to a Keogh plan, you are contributing only 5 percent of your pay to the plan, and you may apply that same 5 percent figure to all of your employees.

9. Q: *Are there other tax advantages for my employees?*
A: Yes, your employees have the same advantage of employees covered by corporate retirement plans. For instance, they are not taxed currently on the plan contribution made in their behalf, and their earnings under the plan compound for them tax free.

10. Q: *Can I put my wife on the payroll so that she can qualify for Keogh benefits?*
A: Yes, if your wife is now an employee of yours, she'll be covered under the Keogh plan. If she works for you but is not formally recorded as an employee, you may place her on the payroll and she will become qualified for Keogh coverage.

11. Q: *Can my employees and I make voluntary contributions that are not tax deductible but have the same tax shelter on earnings?*
A: Yes, if your plan covers at least one participant who is not a greater than 10 percent owner (owner-employee) and you permit him to make voluntary contributions, you can contribute up to 10 percent of compensation to a maximum of $2500. Though you receive no tax deductions for these contributions, the money does compound tax free in the plan. You may withdraw from the plan, at any time, up to the amount you have contributed voluntarily without incurring any tax liability.

12. Q: *When may I receive distributions from my plan?*
A: Your retirement benefits may not ordinarily be withdrawn from the plan until you reach the age of 59½ years, and you must start withdrawing at age 70½ years. You may select any age within this range as your retirement age. Though you must start withdrawing at 70½, you may still contribute and get your tax deduction on your contribution.

13. Q: *How are my distributions taxed at retirement?*
A: You are entitled to treat as capital gains that portion of your taxable distribution which reflects your participation in the plan measured by the number of calendar years before 1974. You may elect to apply a ten-year averaging rule to that portion of your lump-sum distribution which reflects your participation in the plan for years beginning after 1973, and which is treated as the ordinary income portion of the distribution. You may also elect to calculate your entire lump-sum distribution under the ten-year averaging rule. If you choose periodic installments or any annuity, payments received over a period of time are taxed in the years received as ordinary income.

14. Q: *I have a Keogh plan with XYZ Fund. Is it possible to switch my plan to another fund?*
A: Yes, you have two possible choices: (1) Keep your Keogh plan with XYZ Fund and start a new Keogh plan with ABC Fund or (2) Establish a new plan in ABC Fund and have the custodian of your XYZ Fund transfer your total assets to your new plan.

THE PROFESSIONAL CORPORATION

In 1970 the IRS threw in the sponge in its long fight to keep incorporating professionals from being treated as corporations for tax purposes. By 1973, one-third of the physicians in the U.S. had incorporated, and it is estimated that at least half have now incorporated their practices. These can be one-man corporations.

The main advantage that you will have if you are self-employed and incorporated is that you will then be considered an employee as well as an owner. As an employee of a corporation, you may participate in retirement and insurance programs on a tax-deductible basis.

Let's assume that you are earning $50,000 as a physician and have incorporated. A comparison under Keogh and under a professional corporation would be as follows.

As a sole practitioner you may deduct $7500 annually and put it in your Keogh plan.

As a principal of Doctor, Inc., you draw a salary of $50,000 and set up a combined profit-sharing and pension plan. You may now contribute $12,500 (25 percent of $50,000) on a tax-deductible basis to your retirement plan. The corporate retirement plan may also have estate tax benefits if paid out in a non-lump-sum distribution.

As you can see, the corporate plan would allow you to set aside $5000 more than would a Keogh plan.

There are also insurance advantages under the corporate structure. You may also be eligible for substantial life, health, and disability insurance coverages, deductible to the corporation and not taxable as income to you.

Some of the extras you would be entiled to are:

1. Group life insurance—up to $50,000 tax free. Above that you would pay a nominal tax on term cost of insurance.

2. Group health insurance—hospital, surgical, major medical, and dental.

3. Disability—you would be eligible for long-term disability for life or up to age 65.

4. Key man insurance—the corporation could insure your life as a key employee.

5. You also may elect to set up a nonqualified deferred compensation plan and a medical expense reimbursement plan. The plan also permits a $5000 federal-income-tax-free death benefit.

You should weigh carefully the pros and cons of incorporation. Your attorney and certified public accountant should be consulted, and the financial and legal possibilities should be studied thoroughly before you take this step.

Do Get Started

While you are studying the pros and cons of incorporation, go ahead and start your Keogh plan. Even if you incorporate later, this money can be left in your Keogh plan to grow. If you skip this year, you can never make it up. When they blow the horn to signal a new year, you've passed up this year's tax savings forever.

Included in the Appendix (Figure 15) is a Keogh Worksheet. You may want to use it to determine whether it is to your advantage to have either an IRA account or a Keogh account.

NONQUALIFIED DEFERRED COMPENSATION PLANS

A nonqualified deferred compensation plan is a commitment by an employer to pay an employee a predetermined amount of money for a specified period of years upon his retirement or termination of employment.

Let's assume that you are a highly paid executive. You could choose to have your income reduced and have the amount of the reduction become the substance of a deferred compensation plan. You could also have additional amounts deferred in lieu of a salary increase. This would allow you to reduce your current income tax and have an investment compounding under a tax shelter.

When you reach retirement, you would begin to pay income taxes on your withdrawals. At that time you will no doubt be eligible for additional tax exemptions as a retiree, and you will probably be in a lower tax bracket.

The nonqualified plan can be installed without prior approval of the IRS. The rules for adoption and maintenance are few, and the plan can be discriminatory. You may have a deferred plan in addition to a qualified profit-sharing or pension plan.

Your corpration, however, cannot deduct its contributions from its federal income tax. As your taxes on this money come due, then the corporation begins to enjoy a corresponding tax deduction.

Deferred compensation is now a personal service income under the maximum tax law of 50 percent tax, and neither you nor the corporation has to pay the social security tax. Nor does the corporation have to pay federal unemployment tax. Deferred compensation does not reduce the Social Security benefits you are entitled to receive.

TAX-SHELTERED ANNUITIES FOR EMPLOYEES OF NONPROFIT INSTITUTIONS

If you work for a nonprofit institution such as a school, city, or hospital, you may also qualify for a tax-deferred retirement plan.

Let's assume that you are a school teacher. You may request that the school reduce your salary up to 16⅔ percent and have the school invest these funds in a qualified annuity program through a life insurance company or a mutual fund custodial account. You thereby avoid paying current taxes on the amount of the reduction. You may also reduce your income sufficiently to reduce the taxes on the remainder.

There are two types of annuities: (1) the fixed and (2) the variable. Many of the older fixed annuities still pay a very low rate of return—many under 3 percent annually. Even with tax shelter, that is not progress at our present rate of inflation.

The Consumer Price Index of the Bureau of Labor and the University of Chicago Center for Research project an average rate of inflation through the year 2000 of 6.2 percent. Whether one considers inflation a destructive force, real or pseudo-prosperity, or merely a normal way of life, one must recognize that it will forever be a part of the nation's economic environment.

Despite the foregoing, many people still feel that conservative investment requires a "riskless" savings device such as a fixed annuity, and that any nonguaranteed equity investment is automatically speculative. This attitude is dedicated to the proposition that the long-range economy will be deflationary rather than inflationary, and that the world's economy will stand still awaiting one's retirement.

History, however, has proved beyond any doubt that basing one's financial security on fixed-guaranteed savings vehicles is the ultimate in absurd speculation. In recent years a few progressive insurance companies have been offering fixed annuities in the 7 to 8 percent range and are also allowing you to move from a fixed to variable position for only a small transfer fee.

Variable Annuities

Another choice you may make is to use a variable annuity. I have examined a large number and find the performance of many of them discouraging. They are usually middle-of-the-road, which may or may not fit your needs. You may be relatively young and interested in growth, but your money may be pooled with a person who is about ready to retire and whose objective is income. Do considerable study of the pros and cons of establishing a tax-sheltered annuity. If you do decide to use one, spend considerable time and effort selecting the best one possible.

CUSTODIAN AND INVESTMENT CHOICES FOR YOUR RETIREMENT ACCOUNTS

Your custodian and investment choices are similar to the IRA rollover requirements.

I would especially recommend the consideration of a well-managed, high-quality mutual fund using their custodial account. It allows you to invest as you earn and offers you the potential advantage of dollar-cost-averaging and automatic dividend and capital gains reinvestment. You also have the flexibility of moving from one fund to another within the family of funds without commissions and without tax consequences. They keep the records for you and offer you the convenience of using a bank draft for adding to your account (in Keogh and IRA accounts, but not in IRA rollover accounts), and upon retirement you can establish a systematic withdrawal program. If you've chosen well, their past performance has been good.

Another choice you may want to consider is a trust company, as previously described under the IRA Rollover.

INVESTING YOUR PENSION AND PROFIT SHARING FUNDS

The same type of investments should be considered for these funds. Certainly a portion of your funds should be invested in stocks. I am not of the school that adds "and bonds." Bonds have been and, I feel, will continue to be a disappointing choice with our high level of inflation and fluctuating interest rates. If you are talented and agile and are the trustee of your own pension and profit-sharing plan, you might be able to win the discount bond race, but then if you miss you might have the government playing the hindsight game with you and declaring you were not "prudent." The government could even finance a suit against you brought by your employees.

You can select individual stocks yourself or you can let the professionals do it for you by using an investment advisor, the professional management of a mutual fund, a bank trust department, or an insurance company.

I have not been overly impressed by the results I've seen from banks and insurance companies. The study in Table 16–1 was done by

TABLE 16-1. COMPOUND ANNUAL RATES OF RETURN

Number of Years	1	2	3	4	5	6	7	8	9	10
Dates	1967	1967-68	1967-69	1967-70	1967-71	1967-72	1967-73	1967-74	1967-75	1967-76
S&P better than Dow	X	X	X	X	X	X	X	X	X	—
Funds better than S&P	X	X	X		X			X	—	X
Funds better than bank	X	X	X	X	X	X	X	X	X	X
Funds better than ins. co.	X	X	X	X	X	X	X	X	X	X
Bank better than S&P			X							
Ins. co. better than S&P					NONE					

Study includes 204 banks, 39 life insurance companies, 73 growth and income mutual funds.

A. S. Hansen, Inc., Actuaries & Consultants, and published in their report titled "Investment Performance Survey, 1966–1975." One of the areas the study included was a composite of the performance of 204 banks, 39 life insurance companies, and 73 growth and income mutual funds. If you are acting in a fiduciary capacity, making investment decisions regarding your pension plan, I recommend that you obtain a copy of this report and study the findings carefully.

A distillation of this information, as I interpret it, is as follows. The Standard and Poor's average outperformed the Dow in all but one of the periods in the study and was equal once. The growth and income mutual funds outperformed the Standard and Poor's in six of the ten periods studied, and was equal once. The mutual funds outperformed the bank management in each of the ten-year periods. They also outperformed the insurance companies in all of the periods studied. The banks outperformed the Standard and Poor's in one of the periods, and the insurance companies did not perform as well as the Standard and Poor's in any of the periods studied.

AVOID LIFE INSURANCE IN YOUR FUNDING

Do not place life insurance in your Keogh, pension, and profit-sharing plans. It has never been permitted in IRA accounts. Reread the portion in Chapter 13 regarding the "incidental" cost of P.S. 58. You will note from that discussion that if a $100,000 policy was placed in a retirement program at age 40, by age 65 the participant would have had to pay taxes on an additional $35,302 of income. When you place life insurance into your plan, you turn a portion of your tax shelter into taxable income.

WRAP-AROUND ANNUITIES

The dynamic growth of pension and profit-sharing fund assets, coupled with the investment experience of the last ten years, has caused money managers to turn their attention toward new avenues for diversification that could enhance the potential of attaining their investment objectives.

A new alternative investment vehicle that has appeared is one that has been designed to invest in real estate through a diversified mortgage portfolio comprised primarily of wrap-around mortgage loans (a form of junior loan), which are structured to provide equity build-up normally associated with equity ownership. Such loans are selected by a professional organization and serve as an investment medium for qualified pension and profit sharing trusts and other organizations intended to be exempt from federal income tax.

In a market abundant with under-leveraged properties, there is an ever-increasing demand for mortgage funds. In the past, the traditional sources of mortgage money for refinancing or providing second mortgage loans were able to keep pace with the increasing need for new sources of funds. Over the years, assets of pension funds have increased significantly, and money managers, aware of the investment potential of these vast assets, have responded to the increased demand for mortgage money by earmarking a portion of fund assets for investment in diversified real estate vehicles. Recognizing the potential for higher yields and anticipating the certain growth of real estate, money managers have come to realize that, because of these financial benefits and the diversification aspect, real estate deserves a place in their portfolios.

The objective of this investment is to generate a high current return with the enhancement of a higher total return over the life of the partnership. The higher total yield would be accomplished through the debt structuring to create a spread or differential in the principal reduction between the wrap-around and the underlying mortgage loans. These are structured as a partnership and the "equity build-up" will be realized by the partnership in later years and, therefore, will not be distributed on a current basis. It is usually planned that the loans will reach maturity in ten to fifteen years on the average.

Although the emphasis is on current yield, it is the equity build-up that sets this unique investment vehicle apart from other options.

The strategy is to provide financing for real estate properties that are several years into amortization, and requires that the borrower retain an equity interest which represents not less than 15 percent of the total value of the property.

Traditionally, plan managers have been looking for investment sources that will add further dimension to their various investment options; yet they remain somewhat reluctant to venture far beyond the familiar stock and bond market. While these still remain traditional investments for pension and profit-sharing assets, this type of investment provides added diversification.

The diversification requirements of the Employee Retirement Income Security Act (ERISA) have forced trustees and money managers to look for alternatives. Real estate, both from an equity and debt standpoint, is a viable alternative investment, which can provide competitive yields.

The real estate mortgages, if carefully selected by professionals, can offer an opportunity for pension and profit-sharing plans to obtain potentially higher yields and capital growth through equity build-up in the debt structuring of wrap-around mortgage loans.

In wrap-around financing, the borrower is offered a new mortgage loan on an existing property (the wrap-around loan); the principal amount of this new mortgage equals the balance outstanding on an existing prior mortgage loan on the property plus the amount of the new money loaned.

You may be wondering why the owner of a building would be willing to have his property wrapped in a new mortgage. There can be considerable advantages to the borrower and the lender. Let's assume the borrower is in the 50 percent tax bracket. As you know, interest payments are deductible and principal payments are not. The borrower's figures might look something like those in Table 16–2.

TABLE 16–2. WRAP-AROUND FINANCING

Borrower's Present Position First Mortgage		Position With a New Wrap-Around Mortgage
$ 567,528	Total debt service principal and interest	$702,000
460,786	Interest portion	702,000
106,742	Principal portion	–0–
230,393	50% of interest payment	351,000
337,135	Net after-tax cost to borrower	351,000
	Subtract first mortgage net cost	337,115
	Net cost after tax for $1,185,710	$ 13,885

Results for the Borrower

The borrower would now receive $1,185,710 of new money ($6,500,000 new mortgage minus $5,314,290 present mortgage) from the lender that is not taxable since it is borrowed money.

At a net after-tax cost of $13,885 or 1.17% interest (in the first year of the loan and reducing each year thereafter), the borrower also gives up an average of 13.6 percent equity build-up. Since equity build-up represents the principal portion of the mortgage payment and is not a current cash item, nor is it tax deductible, the trade-off is attractive to the borrower when compared to the current net after-tax cost.

In the fourth year (1983) of the wrap-around loan, the net after-tax effect on the borrower's cash flow is a positive one of $2089.

Through the nine years and eight months prior to the balloon payment, the borrowers will experience a $125,045 positive effect on after-tax cash flow. If the borrower is in the 70 percent tax bracket, the positive effect is $695,002 total over the nine years and eight months.

Results for the Lender

The lender's total return in this example equals 24.98 percent per year including accrued equity build-up of 13.6 percent. This high yield is motivation to the lender.

A registered limited partnership designed only for qualified retirement plans is now offered by real estate professionals; it has an excellent track record. It also is a qualified investment for Keogh and IRA accounts.

Figure 16 in the Appendix shows how the wrap-around mortgage works.

OTHER TAX-SHELTERED WAYS TO PREPARE FOR RETIREMENT INCOME

Earlier we discussed a number of ways that can provide cash flow, either all or partly tax-sheltered, that is not accumulated into qualified plans. Some of these also provide excess deductions. Most of these methods use the limited partnership approach. Many of them are ideal for accumulating the necessary funds for retirement. Let's enumerate a few that were covered earlier in more detail.

1. Oil and gas income limited partnership. In the past, they've provided excellent tax-sheltered cash flow which could be reinvested to produce a compounding effect. At retirement, instead of reinvesting, start taking the distributions in cash.

2. Limited triple-net leases of major corporate buildings. These have in the past provided excellent tax-sheltered cash flow and, though they usually do not offer reinvestment privilege, the distributions can be systematically reinvested in a growth mutual fund.

3. Multifamily housing limited partnerships have in the past produced excellent results. These results, as superior as they have been in the past, should accelerate as housing continues to get in shorter and shorter supply. This type of partnership usually produces tax-sheltered cash flow and excess deductions to shelter other income from taxes. These properties are usually sold after three to seven years. The profits will usually be taxed at the more favorable capital gains rates.

4. There are a wide variety of both registered partnerships and offerings exempt from registration. Some of them should fit very well into retirement programs both before and during retirement because of their tax advantages and generous cash flow. Marine containers, budget motels, model homes, and successful movies are only a few.

5. Single-premium deferred annuities are also a possibility in that they compound tax-deferred. Their disadvantage is that their rates are in a fixed range, but the principal is guaranteed and some have yields from 8 to 12½ percent.

Stocks

You can select growth stocks during your preretirement years; then when income is needed, either sell them and buy income stocks or sell a few shares as you need funds. If you have a large capital gain in a particular stock and little diversification, you may want to explore the installment sale; however this possibility is now under review by Congress.

Mutual Fund Withdrawal Programs

One of the best ways to plan for retirement income is to invest systematically in a well-managed growth mutual fund during your preretirement years, with or without superimposing a timing service. When retirement time comes, start a systematic withdrawal program so that the custodian of the fund will send you a check monthly. This provides undisturbed diversification, dollar-cost-averaging in reverse, a compounding of what you still have in your account, or an orderly use of capital if you do need to use a portion of it. Remember, we decided that there is nothing sacred about principal. The sacred thing is to make you and it come out together.

How Not to Prepare for Retirement

Annuities. Investments are for living. Insurance is for dying. Never combine the two. This is the lesson we learned in Chapter 13, "Life Insurance—the Great National Dilemma." Figure 17 in the Appendix shows four ads from magazines. The first, printed in 1935, proudly declares that you can live comfortably in the scenic beauty and healthy atmosphere of Hot Springs, Arkansas, for $100 a month. (Have you priced a hot bath there recently?) The 1939 ad declares, "Get $150 a month for life." The ad goes on to say, "You can guard against emergencies; you can avoid investment risks and uncertainties." The ad also said, "Let's assume you are 40 now." What about the uncertainty of what the purchasing power of the dollar will be when it's time to retire? The third ad is titled "How I retired in 15 years with $250 a month." The copy states "Sometimes I have to smile. It's hard to believe that I'm retired today—retired with a life income." It continues, "And I'm my own boss for keeps." There are some additional sentences that will be of interest: "And the income was guaranteed—whatever happened to the business world—each month, every month, from the day it began as long as I live." From the time I applied for my plan, "I've honestly felt like a rich man. Because I knew I wouldn't just simply live and work and die. I had a future I'd really enjoy. And that's what I'm doing today—with many, many thanks to my (*name of insurance company*) check for $250 a month that means financial independence for life." Incidentally, it shows the man fishing. I wonder why? The fourth, published in 1966, is titled "How we retired in 15 years with $300 a month." The script is similar. This couple is also fishing. Let's hope the catch is large so they can sell a few to pay for their Florida retirement.

Bonds.   Reread Chapter 11, "Lending Your Dollars," and you'll find that bonds have never been a good long-term investment.

Savings Accounts and Certificates of Deposit.   Your after-tax return today is less than the rate of inflation. Therefore, you are back to the little frog example of moving up one and sliding back two, making it ever so difficult to accomplish your retirement goal.

Social Security.   Do you really want to try to live on Social Security? Social Security payments to 65-year-old workers retiring in 1979 averaged around $265 a month for individuals and $400 a month for couples.

Social Security should be thought of as social insecurity. That way so many would not be deceived into thinking that it will take care of their retirement needs. It was never meant to provide financial independence. It was meant to prevent mass destitution. It was meant for a base, and you were to build on this base. Even though the Social Security system is for all practical purposes insolvent, you will, if you qualify, I believe, receive a check from the government. The question will be whether the proceeds of the check will be sufficient to keep body and soul together (see Table 16–3).

If they are not and you have to continue working, you could lose many of your benefits. If you are a Social Security beneficiary under 65, $3720 can be earned before benefits are reduced $1 for each $2 of excess earnings this year. If you are 65 or older, but not 72, the limit is now $5000. If you are over age 72, you won't lose any benefits no matter what you earn.

TABLE 16–3. PROJECTED BENEFITS FOR PERSONS RETIRING
AT AGE 65

Calendar Year of Retire- ment	Earnings in Previous Year *			Annual Benefit Amount for Workers with Following Earnings		
	LOW	AVERAGE	MAXIMUM	LOW	AVERAGE	MAXIMUM
1979	$ 5,271	$10,572	$17,700	$3,142	$ 4,932	$ 6,165
1980	5,682	11,396	22,900	3,375	5,315	6,699
1981	6,085	12,205	25,900	3,635	5,740	7,257
1982	6,475	12,986	29,700	3,485	5,438	6,809
1983	6,863	13,766	31,800	3,607	5,643	7,257
1984	7,258	14,557	33,900	3,841	6,010	7,798
1985	7,675	15,394	36,000	4,099	6,409	8,390
1990	10,150	20,359	47,700	5,451	8,519	11,509
1995	13,424	26,925	63,000	7,198	11,243	15,605
2000	17,753	35,609	83,400	9,519	14,870	21,427

* Low earnings are defined as $4,600 in 1976. Average earnings are $9,266 in 1976. Maximum earnings are defined as the top wages subject to Social Security taxes in a particular year. In each case it is assumed that the worker has had an unbroken pattern of earnings at the relative level indicated. The following increases in wages were assumed: 1977, 5.99 percent; 1978, 8.10 percent; 1979, 7.80 percent; 1980, 7.10 percent; 1981, 6.40 percent; 1982, 6.00 percent; 1983 and later, 5.75 percent.

If you retire at 62, your benefits will be reduced by 20 percent. The closer you are to 65, the smaller your reduction. At 63 you would receive 86⅔ percent, and at age 64 you would receive 93⅓ percent.

If you wait until after 65 to retire, you are entitled to an increase of 3 percent in your benefits for each year between 65 and 72. So if you wait until 70 to retire, you will get 15 percent more benefits. Here's a convenient table to use if you are considering retiring before 65:

Retirement Age	Percent of Full Benefit	Percent of Full Benefit Lost
62	80%	20%
63	86⅔%	13⅓%
64	93⅓%	6⅔%
65	100%	0%

If you take early retirement, your benefits do not go up when you reach age 65.

When you become entitled to Social Security benefits, your spouse can collect benefits equal to 50 percent of yours if your spouse is 65, or somewhat lower benefits as early as 62. (If the spouse, because of his or her own earnings, is entitled to an amount more than 50 percent of his or her spouse's benefit, then he or she gets the bigger benefit.)

There are also certain other extras. For example, if a wife is younger and has in her care dependent children under 18, she can collect the extra 50 percent. Also, unmarried children under 18 (or over 18 if disabled) or full-time students 18 to 22 are also eligible for the 50 percent of your full benefit. The maximum benefit payable to a family with the husband retiring at 65 is presently $880.70.

The provisions of Social Security benefits are extensive. For further information, call the Social Security Administration and ask them to send you some of the booklets they have on the subject.

SHOULD YOU TAKE EARLY RETIREMENT?

Your answer to the question of whether you should take early retirement depends on many things other than Social Security. If everything else is equal, and your income is sufficient with the lower benefits, then go ahead and take your benefits at 62. It will take you many years to make up the income you missed from age 62 to 65.

Make preparation for your retirement early so that if you receive Social Security it will only be the butter on your bread—not the bread itself. Becoming financially independent will not be an unattainable goal if you begin early, use your intelligence, and don't allow yourself to be enticed by the words "guaranteed" and "no risk" when it comes to investments. Those that seem to have the least risk are often those that guarantee your losses.

The least you can do—not that I consider this enough—is to begin an Individual Retirement Account if you are eligible. I believe one of the reasons that the Individual Retirement Account provisions were set up in our tax laws was an admission by Congress that you had better take some steps to fend for yourself if you want your golden years to have any semblance of sparkle and not depend on Social Security.

YOUR WILL

You should have a current will drawn by a competent attorney in the state in which you think you are most likely to die. You should have one drawn while you are still young and you should keep it updated. It should certainly be kept current as our laws change.

I'm a financial planner and do not practice law. Do obtain the services of an attorney with whom you are compatible and in whom you have confidence. If your estate is in excess of $500,000, you should also look into the possible tax advantages of trusts.

If you intelligently combine the three ingredients of financial independence, time, money, and American free enterprise, you can surely reach retirement age with sufficient assets to retire in financial dignity. Time is your powerful ally, so take an inventory now and get started.

APPLICATION

1. How many years before you retire? _____
2. How much income would you need per month to maintain your present standard of living if you were retiring today? _____
3. What do you think the rate of inflation will be? _____
4. How much will you need by then? _____
5. Look at the chart below. Choose your income and years. _____

TOTAL EARNINGS

Average Monthly Income	5 Years	10 Years	15 Years	20 Years	25 Years	30 Years
800	48,000	96,000	144,000	192,000	240,000	288,000
900	54,000	108,000	162,000	216,000	270,000	324,000
1,000	60,000	120,000	180,000	240,000	300,000	360,000
1,200	72,000	144,000	216,000	288,000	360,000	432,000
1,500	90,000	180,000	270,000	360,000	450,000	540,000
2,000	120,000	240,000	360,000	480,000	600,000	720,000
3,000	180,000	360,000	540,000	720,000	900,000	1,080,000

6. Your age? _____
7. How many years have you worked? _____
8. What were your total earnings for those years? _____
9. What are your assets now? _____
10. Are your assets sufficient? _____
11. If not, what action do you plan to take this week?
    1. _____
    2. _____
    3. _____
    4. _____
    5. _____

17

FINANCING COLLEGE COSTS

Earlier we discovered that there are three financial periods in most every life: "The Learning Period," "The Earning Period," and the "Golden" or "Yearning Period." Let's discuss how you might finance the "learning" period if you have children who want to go to college.

Is a college education a good investment? There are discussions about this matter from time to time, but from the studies I have seen, it appears that a college degree can add another $200,000 to $250,000 in earning power. Of course, it adds much more. It adds a greater dimension to life and establishes frienships that lend themselves to business activities later (especially if you are a Texas Aggie), and reportedly there are fewer divorces among college graduates.

THE NEW ELITE

The major feature and front cover of the February 25, 1980, issue of *U.S. News & World Report* was devoted to discussing the tremendous influence that those who are the product of the mass college education that has occurred since 1940 are having on America. This new elite of articulate, educated graduates with skills honed by technology and rapid change are permeating every facet of American life, affecting our opinions, our policies, our pleasures, and even our way of life.

Every day their influence is becoming more evident in government, business, industry, marketing, and research. "Think tanks" are producing studies for both government and industry. They especially affect the media, which in turn affects a vast number of people through news shows and documentaries.

Figure 18 in the Appendix gives a visual picture of how the number of college graduates has increased since 1940. In 1940, only 4.6 percent of adults over 25 were college graduates. By 1978, the number had increased to 15 percent. Also shown is the increase in technical and professional jobs since 1940—from 3.9 million to 15.3 million in forty years.

An even more interesting picture is Figure 19, which shows the increase in pay gap between college graduates and high school graduates. In 1956, the median income for high school graduates was $4413 and for college graduates $6038. By 1978, the high school graduates' income had reached a median $14,286 and the college graduates' $20,189; thus the gap grew from $1625 to $5903, or since 1956 the median income of high school graduates has fallen from 73 to 71 percent of that of college graduates.

COSTS TO JOIN THE "ELITE"

If your son or daughter asked you for $15,000 to $50,000 for college expenses, would you be able to make the college of his or her choice a reality instead of a dream? Costs for a year of college today range from $3000 to $8300, or a median figure in the neighborhood of $5700. Future costs are unknown; however, if the present trend of escalation continues, this cost could run as high as $10,200 per year by 1995. Appendix Figure 20 provides a comprehensive study of present costs, scholarships and financial aid information, and requirements for military academies, which you will find extremely helpful.

Figure 17–1 is a graphic projection of costs if they continue to increase as they have in recent years. Using these projected cost figures, let's assume that you have two children. One will start to college in 1989 and the second in 1992. Their college-cost picture might look something like this.

	Child No. 1	Child No. 2
1987	$ 7,800	
1988	8,100	
1989	8,400	
1990	8,700	$ 8,700
1991		9,000
1992		9,300
1993		9,600
	$33,000	$36,600
		$33,000
		$69,600

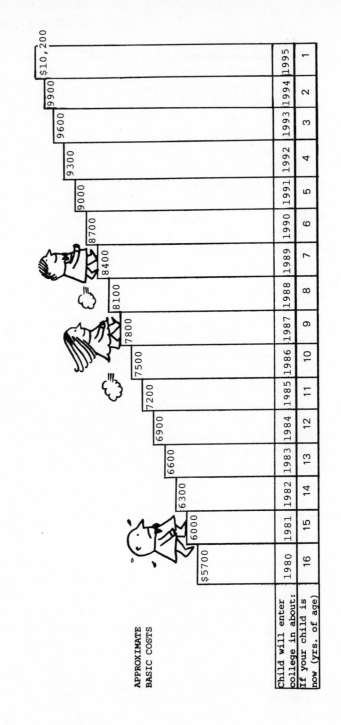

Figure 17–1. Anticipated Annual College Costs

APPROXIMATE BASIC COSTS	$5700	6000	6300	6600	6900	7200	7500	7800	8100	8400	8700	9000	9300	9600	9900	$10,200
Child will enter college in about:	1980	1981	1982	1983	1984	1985	1986	1987	1988	1989	1990	1991	1992	1993	1994	1995
If your child is now (yrs. of age)	16	15	14	13	12	11	10	9	8	7	6	5	4	3	2	1

COLLEGE FINANCING FORMULA

Let's now change our basic formula to read: Time plus money plus American companies equals opportunity for a college education.

Often I'm counseling a couple who have stated that their financial goal is to provide the funds to send their children to college. After I have outlined a plan, one of them will ask, "Is it 'guaranteed'?"— meaning every hour of every day. Of course, it's not "guaranteed" on a daily basis. Their goal is to have the necessary college funds in ten to fifteen years. They may not be able to afford a "guaranteed" investment.

For example, let's assume that they can save $150 a month toward building a college fund to educate their two children. One will be going to college in ten years and the other in fourteen years.

THE GUARANTEED ROUTE vs. THE UNGUARANTEED

At 5 percent compounded annually, $150 a month in ten years will be $23,778. In fourteen years, it's $37,044. This brings them up short for Child No. 1, to say nothing of Child No. 2.

At 12 percent, on the other hand, $150 per month would be $35,370 in ten years and $65,304 in fourteen years. You may be concerned with the fact that if Child No. 1 is taking from the kitty, funds will not be there to compound. This is true. However, Child No. 1 does not need the total amount of $33,000 the day he enters the vine-covered portals. He just needs the funds for one semester, which allows the remainder to grow until it is needed.

A plan that I have used successfully to accomplish this objective has been a check-a-month withdrawal from a fund similar to the Seminar Fund. While the student has been taking out funds, American industry has been putting funds back in.

Don't worry about the short-term fluctuations of the market. If you want to have enough money in the college fund using the "guaranteed" route, you will have to increase your savings to such a huge amount that you will have to drastically reduce your present standard of living. The "guaranteed" dollar in many cases becomes an academic discussion rather than a workable plan.

DON'T FIGHT THE BATTLE ALONE

Don't try to fight the battle for college funds alone. Give American industry a chance to help. You may find that American industry will contribute more to your child's educational funds than you do, if you'll give it a chance through proper investing.

On March 21, 1965, I was interviewed by Patricia Shelton, who was then a reporter in the women's department of the *Houston Chronicle*. She is now a well-known syndicated fashion writer. Her question to me in her interview was how to go about financing a college education. At that time we estimated that if parents had a child who would be entering college in 10 years, they would need to save $5400 at $45 per month. If they had 15 years, they would need to save $3600 at $20 per month. (See how important time is to the accomplishment of any financial objective?)

This would not be sufficient if they used the guaranteed route, but we found that it should be if they had used a specific local mutual fund. We arrived at these figures by working backward using the bank's computer. We wanted to be able to withdraw $3000 a year or $250 per month each month for four years. Working backward, we found that if the account had $9565 in it at registration time and $250 a month had been drawn out each month for four years, a total of $12,000 would have been withdrawn and there would have been $440 left.

Again, here is an example to encourage you not to fight the battle alone, but to let American industry help you. In this case American industry had contributed $7040, and the parents had contributed $5400 (at $45 per month). These parents had placed their money in a position to let American industry pay more of their child's college costs than they had contributed.

College costs have skyrocketed since this article was published, and stock market performance has been erratic; however, it seems evident that American industry can provide a very helpful hand to you if you are a parent desiring to send your child to college.

UNIFORM GIFTS TO MINORS

If you are in a fairly high tax bracket, you should consider setting up custodial accounts for each child and registering the stock in this manner:

> John E. Jones, Custodian for
> John E. Jones, Jr., under the
> _____ Uniform Gifts to
> (State)
> Minors Act.

This should allow most of the dividends and capital gains to compound tax-free. You should use your child's Social Security number for the account. You will still be able to claim the child as a deduction if you supply over 50 percent of his support. I should caution that you may not use any of these funds for things that you are legally obligated to provide for your child—items such as food and clothing. But you can use the funds for college education.

If your estate is large, you may want to name as custodian someone other than yourself. In the event of your death, the value of the account could be considered a part of your estate for estate tax purposes if you are the custodian. You may also want to investigate the Clifford Trust and interest-free loan possibilities discussed in Chapter 12, "Avoiding the One Way Trip to Washington."

DON'T PROCRASTINATE

Time plus money—both are essential to combine with American free enterprise. The sooner you start, the easier it will be to reach your goal. By starting five years earlier, you can usually reduce the amount you must invest by one-half. A college education can add a new dimension to a life. If you have children, help them to reach their maximum potential.

TAX-FAVORED INVESTMENTS

You may also want to consider investing in a tax-favored investment now, taking the deduction, and later giving the asset to your children. A good example is the one discussed under "Cattle Feeding" in Chapter 12, "Avoiding the One-Way Trip to Washington." Remember the example? You invested $10,000 and wrote off $10,000, leaving you an after-tax savings cost of $5000 in a 50 percent bracket or $6000 in a 40 percent bracket. Assuming that it did grow to $25,000 (no guarantees) in seven years, it would have cost you $5000 to provide your child with $25,000. If you wait the seven years and you are still in a 50 percent bracket, you will have to earn $50,000 to give your child $25,000. As your child needs funds for college, portions of the partnership can be liquidated as they are needed.

COLLEGE EXPENSE WORKSHEET

Table 17–1 is an actual worksheet prepared by a financial planner for a client in 1976. The client had four children, all of whom he hoped

TABLE 17-1. ASSUMED 5% INFLATION RATE
AVERAGE COST $2650
INCLUDES TUITION & RELATED EXPENSES

Entrance Year	Child: Age:	Jim 14		Janis 13		Jeff 12		Charles 8		Total	
		1976 DOLLARS	FUTURE NEEDS	1976 DOLLARS	FUTURE NEEDS	1976 DOLLARS	FUTURE NEEDS	1976 DOLLARS	FUTURE NEEDS	1976 DOLLARS	FUTURE NEEDS
1980		$ 2650	$ 3222							$ 2650	$ 3222
1981		2650	3381	$ 2650	$ 3381					5300	6762
1982		2650	3551	2650	3551	$ 2650	$ 3551			7950	10,653
1983		2650	$ 3728	2650	3728	2650	3728			7950	11,184
1984				2650	3914	2650	3914			5300	7828
1985						2650	4110			2650	4110
1986								$ 2650	$ 4316	2650	4316
1987								2650	4531	2650	4531
1988								2650	4759	2650	4759
1989								2650	4997	2650	4997
Total		10,600	13,882	10,600	14,574	10,600	15,303	10,600	18,603	42,400	62,362

to send to college. Before the planner did this worksheet, the father had not realized how the children's needs for college funds would overlap. The client only wanted to use a 5 percent inflation factor and an average cost per year of $2650 (much too low at today's inflation rates). When the chart was completed, the total cost was calculated to be $62,362. In a 26 percent tax bracket, this meant that he would have to earn $84,272.97.

Because the planner made him aware of his approaching problem, the client not only established an investment program with him, but also realized the necessity of holding a family financial strategy meeting to encourage his four children to do their very best in school so that they might qualify for scholarships and grants. The oldest son is ready for college this year and has been accepted at Annapolis and also was offered a scholarship at Duke University.

Begin now with financial preparation and an investigation of available scholarships, grants, and federal loan programs. Your child may even choose Harvard, which I understand presently costs $10,000 per year.

In the Appendix (Table 34), you will find a blank college expense worksheet for your convenience, plus the addresses of scholarship sources and various other ideas to help your children meet their college expenses.

APPLICATION

1. Complete the worksheet in the Appendix.
2. Do your expected expenses and expected funds mesh?
3. If not, what investment program will you begin?
4. How much will you need to invest if you average 12 percent a year on your money?
5. Should you call a family counsel meeting to discuss college expenses and how they can be met?

HOW TO READ
A PROSPECTUS

18

The first rule is—Don't! At least, don't try to read the prospectus from cover to cover as you would a mystery novel. Use the prospectus as you would a handy reference guide. It can be horribly long, confusing, and worthless unless you know beforehand what to look for and who wrote the prospectus.

A prospectus is usually very long and contains many things to which you may not be able to relate. The Securities and Exchange Commission has many bright young men (some in training for top corporate or legal jobs) and many dedicated career servants, but the information that it usually requires a company to transmit to potential investors can at times be extremely confusing, with great emphasis on all the negative aspects, all the possible risks of the offering, and rarely, if ever, any of the possible positive aspects.

If a company wants to offer shares to you and the general public, it must submit a "registration statement" to the SEC, together with a copy to each state in which shares are to be sold. Nine-tenths of the information called for by the registration statement constitutes the prospectus. It contains information required by a checklist compiled by the SEC. There are about fifteen different forms, each pertaining to a different kind of company. Each form is designed to cover every conceivable type of information about the company. And each time the checklist is revised it gets longer. This has been going on since 1934. By now, the average prospectus contains thirty to fifty pages of fine print, which may cause you to miss seeing the forest because of the many mesquite trees. I hope in the not-too-distant future the prospectus can be shortened to no more than ten pages, free of "legalese." As it is now, it usually takes the proverbial Philadelphia lawyer to make heads or tails of all that mass of fine print, and I suspect he often has difficulty with it, too.

UNDULY LONG

The undue length of the prospectus does serve one very practical purpose, however. Past experience has shown that small enterprises have a much higher mortality rate than do the larger and older ones. It does cost a great deal of money to gather all the financial data and other information required by the SEC for the prospectus. Small companies are often presented with insurmountable expense hurdles to overcome if they intend to offer their shares publicly. A few have actually gone bankrupt in the attempt. If the SEC wants the company to change the terms of its offering, if it's a new concept, or if it believes the company to be weak, it can delay the offering, require new audits, and increase the burden of expenses. The final draft of the prospectus may, for all intents and purposes, have been edited by SEC examiners to such an extent that it may bear little similarity to the original document presented to them.

The SEC rarely makes any field investigation of a company. Their primary function is to determine that the prospectus contains information required by its rules. Their rules do not relate to merits or fairness of the offering (as do the rules of some states) nor the value of the securities, and the SEC does not check out or investigate the accuracy of the information contained in the prospectus; hence, the disclaimer that appears in bold type on the face of every SEC prospectus:

> **THESE SECURITIES HAVE NOT BEEN APPROVED OR DISAPPROVED BY THE SECURITIES AND EXCHANGE COMMISSION NOR HAS THE COMMISSION PASSED UPON THE ACCURACY OF THIS PROSPECTUS. ANY REPRESENTATION TO THE CONTRARY IS A CRIMINAL OFFENSE.**

This legend must be placed on every prospectus, regardless of the size or quality of the offering, to emphasize the fact that the Commission has not approved or disapproved the securities, and that it is a criminal offense to make a representation to the contrary. The reference "criminal offense" relates to someone's making a representation that the Commission has passed upon the merits of the offering. This applies to any company, whether it be General Motors or a new company offering its stock for sale. Even the most conservative of investment company trusts have this caption in bold, frightening print on the front. As I mentioned earlier, I recommended to a prospective woman client a particular mutual fund that has a portfolio of such high quality that the fund invests exclusively in common stocks and/or securities convertible into common stocks that are legal for the investment of trust funds in the District of Columbia. In keeping with what registered representatives are legally required to do, I gave her the prospectus of the fund with the above in bold print on the front. She called me the next day, absolutely incensed that I dared recommend to her something that the Securities and Exchange Commission had not approved. I explained the reason, but I was never able to really satisfy her, and she did not make the investment. This caption has frightened away a host of people who should have become investors. The SEC no doubt is fully aware of the problems of the length and complicated nature of the prospectus. Their theory is that they require detailed information so that the professionals in the investment community can analyze and interpret it for the less sophisticated investor. Unfortunately, it usually does not work out that way. Many brokers have never even read the prospectuses and, even if they have, are not sufficiently knowledgeable to discuss such diverse areas in real estate as debt financing, gross rent multipliers, equity buildup, etc.; or in oil and gas, such things as depletion, restored liquidity, intangible drilling costs, tax preference items, investment tax credit and depreciation; or in agriculture as crop loan reduction, unamortized loan fees, and prepared cultural costs.

I truly believe in having all my clients completely informed of the nature of the investment they are about to make, the risks involved, and what they may reasonably hope to accomplish if they do decide to invest; but the prospectus as it is presently required can be a serious deterrent. My sincere hope is that the Securities and Exchange Commission will make the simplification of the prospectus their top priority for the near future.

INVESTOR LOSSES

Most investors' losses occur from factors that never appear in the prospectus. The number one factor is the market system itself. It is a mechanism that favors the large institutional investor over the small investor. The reason is simple. Many small investors tend to buy when everything looks great. For example, they tend to buy common stocks when they are performing well, and they tend to sell them when things are gloomy. Hence, the tendency for small investors is to buy a stock near its peak price and sell it near its low. It is the large investors who more often do just the opposite. Fortunes were made in common stocks by those investors who bought in 1931 to 1933, not those who bought in 1929. The same story holds true for all the peaks and valleys in share prices since then. Small investors have their best chance by buying into the large investment funds or large individual companies at a time when most people regard them with disfavor and think the country is at an all-time economic or political low. If history repeats itself, they will then participate in their subsequent rise.

DEMAND/SUPPLY

In the area of limited partnerships, the investments made may be especially attuned to supply and demand and tax advantage. However, that would be difficult to determine from looking at the weighty prospectus—if the prospective investor ever gets beyond all the RISK warnings on the first two pages.

FINANCIAL ILLITERATES

I have found that the majority of prospective investors are financial illiterates. If they look at a real estate offering, for example, depreciation shows up as an expense even though no checks were sent. Without a financial planner there explaining that the "loss" is good (meaning it can shelter his quarterly cash flow from taxes, and the excess can shelter a portion of his salary from taxes), the client wonders how the planner dares to recommend an investment that is operating at a loss. Most prospective investors do not have the vaguest idea of how the depreciation pass-through may be equivalent in many instances to an 8 percent after-tax yield with no cash distributions being sent to him.

MANAGEMENT IS THE KEY

The other major factor that doesn't appear in the prospectus is the honesty, integrity, and ability of company management. Management is a vital ingredient of success, yet most investors fail to make any independent investigation of the company in which they are investing.

MAKE A CHECKLIST

Let's say you are trying to reach a decision as to whether to buy shares in a new offering. Your checklist for determining whether a company is a good investment is short and simple. If your research is competent and your timing is good (which is vastly important), then you may be able to make money on new stock issues by making the following determinations, in order of their importance.

1. Who is really running the business? Find out which persons are actually in day-to-day charge of company affairs. It is usually no more than a handful. Try to determine if the outside directors are "window dressing" or are making a worthwhile contribution to the company by watching over the activities of management. Then independently check out in detail the reputation for honesty, integrity, and ability of those persons who are in charge. You won't find this in the prospectus. But it is worth more than ten prospectuses. Check on these corporate officers as if they were filling out an employment application. After all, if you buy shares in the company they run, they should be working for *you*. If you find any lack of good character, don't invest.

2. Are shares owned by management? If they don't own any, why should you? If they own a bunch, you should make a serious study of the company. Be careful about "dilution." If management owns a lot of shares, that's great. But did they pay 20¢ two years ago for shares they are offering to you for $20? If so, this usually is picked up in the prospectus under a separate paragraph headed "Dilution." It will give you the details.

3. Look at the *size* of the company. This appears in the balance sheet. The smaller the size, usually the more risk involved. For every large company that fails, a hundred small ones go under. You will find the size of the company in the balance sheet. If there are less than seven figures in assets, the company has a high risk. Of course, if you are looking for a long shot that could pay off handsomely, such a company might be for you. Otherwise, pass.

4. Look at the *debt* of the company. This is also in the balance sheet. If shareholder equity is less than 30 percent of total assets, watch out!

5. Age. Time often cures all. The first five years are the biggest risk. Over ten is usually over the hump.

6. Management take. Compare management compensation with other similar companies. Think in terms of percentage of company income. The president of General Motors can be paid an enormous sum (which he is) without hurting the percentage. But when a small company pays an enormous sum, then double-check who runs the business and the number of shares they own.

7. Preferred stock and debentures. The safest policy is to put your money in a company with little or no "senior" securities. This is

just another form of debt. Take senior securities into account when figuring debt risk.

8. Earnings. Why does this come last? Because management will think of every accounting possibility to show high earnings during a stock offering. Go back over the past five years and see what the trend has been.

THE "RED HERRING"

Most brokers mail to prospective investors a preliminary or "red herring" prospectus in advance of a company's offering. This prospectus is used to solicit preliminary orders called "indications of interest." The "red herring" prospectus has not been finally reviewed by the SEC. Use the "red herring" to do your homework on the kind of people who are running the business and how many shares they own. On the basis of your preliminary investigation you may decide to place a preliminary "order." You are under no obligation to place the actual purchase order even after you have received the final prospectus unless you decide to do so. Don't send in your check until you have reviewed the final prospectus carefully as to each of the above eight points.

PRIVATE PLACEMENTS

In 1974, the SEC adopted Rule 146 to the Securities Act of 1933. The rule states that it is "designed to provide more objective standards for determining when offers or sales of securities by an issuer would be deemed to be transactions not involving any public offering within the meaning of Section 4 (2) of the Act, and thus would be exempt from the registration provision of the Act."

In May of 1978, Rule 146 was amended to require an issuer to notify the SEC when an offering was made that relied on this exemption from registration, excluding offerings of less than $50,000 during any twelve-month period. One of the stated purposes of this filing was "the need to be able to perceive misuses of the rule and, thus, to become aware of, and prevent, frauds in their incipient stages." No explanation is given about how they can prevent fraud in its "incipient stage" by legislation or regulation.

One area that causes a great deal of difficulty for those who try to abide by the rules is that the Rule prohibits any offering to be made by any form of general solicitation or general advertising.

The honest and bona fide issuers go to great lengths to live by the letter of the rules. The result is that the smaller and honest entrepreneur often has great difficulty reaching viable investors in the marketplace. Not so with those who try to mislead or defraud.

I am convinced that Rule 146, if permitted to work effectively in the marketplace, can be a much needed source of capital for worthwhile business undertakings. We are at a critical position in the economic life of our nation. We have tremendous needs for capital formation. It is vital that we encourage investments in capital goods to provide employment for the new batch of youth who want to join the work force but cannot find employment. Let us hope that the SEC will try less in the future to "protect" us and place the burden for financial responsibility back on our individual shoulders where many of us think it belongs. Financial responsibility can never be legislated.

Private placement offerings can be, and often are, superior to those offered by public registration. Many of them need only relatively small amounts of money, and the enormous legal and registration costs piled on to the offering would destroy its economic feasibility. Some of the best investments I've seen have been offered by private placement, and some of the worst have been, too.

Offering memorandums provide the offeree with the same information that a full registration would disclose. They contain all relevant and material facts. Unfortunately, these documents are written by lawyers who anticipate that the document may be reviewed by other lawyers; therefore they emphasize the risks while usually ignoring any potential rewards. This results in an offering memorandum that the average investor is not able to understand. The investor may take it to an advisor to interpret. Unfortunately, these advisors are often inexperienced in the particular field and are unable to comprehend totally the nature of the investment and its risks and rewards. Also, the memorandum is often an inch thick, and who wants to plow through all that? So, they recommend against it. C.P.A.s and attorneys can be helpful, but only if they understand the offering and the potential benefits, as well as the risks.

To me, one of the sad parts of Rule 146 is that the suitability requirements for a potential offeree are so high that if your taxable income is $44,000 instead of $45,800 (plus a certain net worth), I have to let you just pay your taxes, while I can cut the 50 percent bracket clients' taxes down very low. Or if a client has $100,000 in taxable income but only $50,000 in net worth, and the suitability requirements state $150,000 net worth, again I'm not allowed to show it to him.

Private placements also limit the number of purchasers. Currently this is a total of thirty-five. However, a $150,000 investor is not counted in determining the thirty-five.

If you are a "knowledgeable" and "experienced" person with the necessary assets, you should definitely consider private placements. The exemption saves the general partner considerable legal and administrative expenses, which can run into hundreds of thousand of dollars, and allows flexibility in timing and tax considerations. Some offerings have been drawn up and placed within ten to thirty days. This flexibility could allow an investor group to take advantage of special situations offering temporary opportunities which would be unavailable by the time the public offering registration was completed.

The reduction in costs and the flexibility and speed of private placements can also allow investors to take advantage of smaller opportunities. This can be particularly important with regard to certain real estate opportunities.

Most private offerings place emphasis on tax-sheltered investments, but do avoid the offerings that emphasize only "write-offs" and do not offer sound economic investment potential. There are legitimate opportunities under the tax code to partially shelter your income. Congress created these opportunities in order to funnel investment funds into high risk areas. There are reputable general partners who will utilize your investment funds in an honest and capable manner that should provide you with not only tax advantages but economic gain.

Seek out a competent financial planner who is a specialist in tax-sheltered investments. Tax shelters are very complex and require the attention of a very knowledgeable individual. Begin early in the year. Study tax laws yourself, and learn to apply them to your own particular needs. You'll find the investment of time and energy very rewarding.

A GREAT NEED

It has not been my intent to be unduly critical of the Securities and Exchange Commission. They do an admirable job with dedicated and limited personnel. I am, however, keenly aware of the great need for a simpler, more understandable prospectus that a person who has not had the benefit of legal training can read and grasp in order to make an informed investment decision.

There are indications that this may occur in time. In a speech given by the former SEC Chairman Ray Garrett, and reported in *The Wall Street Journal*, he was quoted under the caption "Prospectus Parodies" as having said:

"We all know the somber, liturgical disclaimers that appear in corporate prospectuses," says Ray Garrett. "There can be no assurance that a heavier-than-air machine can be made to fly, or that if it can, anyone will want to buy one, or if someone wants to buy one, he will be willing to pay enough to make production profitable."

"Or suppose General Eisenhower's D-Day order had to be filled with the SEC," says Mr. Garrett. "The officers who planned this assault, including myself, have never before planned anything like this. In fact, I have never commanded any troops in combat. The airborne and other methods being employed have never before been tried by our Army. The weather forecast is only slightly favorable, and such forecasts have a high degree of unreliability. Therefore, there is no assurance that any of you will reach Normandy alive, or, if you do, that you can secure the beach."

Go to a financial planner and obtain a prospectus and then answer the questions.

APPLICATION

Registered Stock Offering

1. What industry is involved?
2. Is this an ascending industry?
3. What products or services are produced?
4. What is the demand/supply situation today regarding these products or services?
5. How many years experience does the chief executive officer have in this field?
6. How many shares are owned by management?
   What is their compensation?

	Shares owned	Compensation
President	_____	$_____
Vice President	_____	$_____
Secretary	_____	$_____
Treasurer	_____	$_____

7. Total net worth of the company?
8. What is the debt/equity ratio of the company?
9. What other alternative investments can you find that offer as much potential for the same or less risk?
10. Is it feasible to make an on-the-spot investigation of the company and their facilities?

Registered Limited Partnership Offering

1. Industry?
2. Demand/supply situation?
3. Years of experience of the general partner? Is the general partner a corporation or an individual or both? What is their net worth?
4. Is this their first offering? If not, how many previous offerings have been made?
5. Answer 9 and 10 above.

Rule 146—Private Placement Limited Partnerships

1. Do the tax provisions fit your needs?
2. Are the tax opinions well documented?
3. How many gray areas are there, and will they bother you enough to make you forego the investment?
4. Are the deductions presented overly aggressive?
5. What is the demand/supply ratio in this area of investment?
6. What is the performance record and experience of the general partner?
7. Is the program assessable?
8. Does the investment require additional investments over a period of years? If so, do you anticipate being in a sufficiently high bracket over that period of time to benefit?
9. If your tax return is audited, will it upset you? Which will upset you more—being audited or paying the tax?

19

TAKING
A FINANCIAL
INVENTORY

Financial planning is like navigation. If you know where you are and where you want to go, navigation isn't such a great problem. It's when you don't know the two points that it's difficult.

To find out where you are, take an in-depth financial inventory. Figure 19–1 is the personal planning data sheet that I hand out at the first session of my three-session financial planning seminars.

We require each person in attendance who wants an appointment to complete and return it to us together with all his life and disability insurance policies before our consultation. This gives us time to map out tentative recommendations and do an analysis of any stocks in the portfolio. If we should grant an appointment to someone who has not completed it, we complete one together. Without this information, we are flying blind. If an individual does not choose to give us this information, we usually do not accept him as a client. It would be as if he had gone to his family doctor in pain and refused to tell him where the pain was located. Please stop now and complete your personal planning data sheet.

FINANCIAL PLANNING DATA SHEET

DATE _____

NAME _____ AGE _____

ADDRESS _____ ZIP CODE _____

HOME PHONE NO. _____ BUSINESS PHONE NO. _____

EMPLOYER _____ OCCUPATION _____

NAME OF SPOUSE _____ AGE _____

EMPLOYER _____ SPOUSE'S BUSINESS PHONE NO. _____

OCCUPATION _____

DO YOU HAVE A CURRENT WILL? _____

ARE YOU COVERED UNDER A PENSION PLAN?

_____IRA_____KEOGH_____

My financial resources

I. LOANED DOLLARS:

   A. Checking Account $_____

   B. Amounts in Passbook Savings Accounts:

Institution	Amount
1. _____	_____
2. _____	_____

$_____

   C. Certificates of Deposit:

Institution	Rate %	Maturity	Amount
1. _____	_____	_____	_____
2. _____	_____	_____	_____
3. _____	_____	_____	_____

$_____

   D. Credit Union_____% $_____

   F. Government Bonds & Instruments

Type	Rate %	Maturity Date	Current Value
_____	_____	_____	_____
_____	_____	_____	_____
_____	_____	_____	_____

$_____

   F. Bonds—Corporate and Municipals

Name of Company or Municipality	No. of Bonds	Rate %	Maturity Date	Cost	Market Value
_____	_____	_____	_____	_____	_____
_____	_____	_____	_____	_____	_____
_____	_____	_____	_____	_____	_____
_____	_____	_____	_____	_____	_____

$_____

G. Mortgages You Carry $_____

H. Loans Receivable $_____

I. Cash Value of

   Insurance Policies (see Worksheet) $_____

                        TOTAL LOANED DOLLARS $_____(1)

II. WORKING DOLLARS:

A. Stocks and Mutual Funds

No. of Shares	Name of Company	Date of Purchase	Cost	Market Value
_____	_____	_____	_____	_____
_____	_____	_____	_____	_____
_____	_____	_____	_____	_____
_____	_____	_____	_____	_____
_____	_____	_____	_____	_____
_____	_____	_____	_____	_____
_____	_____	_____	_____	_____
_____	_____	_____	_____	_____
_____	_____	_____	_____	_____
_____	_____	_____	_____	_____

                                      $_____

                 Total Market Value $_____(2)

Real Estate

Home (Market Value Less Mortgage) $_____

Other Real Estate (Net After Mortgages):

_____ $_____

_____ $_____

_____ $_____

_____ $_____ $_____

540

Limited Partnerships:

_____ $_____

_____ $_____

_____ $_____ $_____

Total Loaned and
Working Dollars $_____

Financial Objective numbered in order of Importance:

_____ Income now

_____ Income at retirement

_____ Maximum tax advantage

_____ Educate children

_____ Travel

_____ Other _____
                        (specify)

Estimated Gross Income this year $_____

Estimated taxable income $_____

Tax Bracket   _____%

Taxable Income last 3 years:

$_____ $_____ $_____

Taxes Paid:

$_____ $_____ $_____

No. of Dependents_____

Amount you could save each month $_____

Retirement Data:

    No. of years before: _____years

    Desired monthly income $_____

        Possible Sources:

        Social Security $_____

Pensions $_____

Investments $_____

Other $_____

                                    Total $_____

                    Additional needed if retiring today $_____

                    Anticipated inflation rate per year _____%

Children Educational Cost Data:

| | | Years Before | |
Name of Child	Age	College	Estimated Cost
_____	____	_____	_____
_____	____	_____	_____
_____	____	_____	_____

                    Total   _____

                    Amount set aside   _____

                    Additional needed   _____

Present Life Insurance, & Annuities Work Sheet
(to complete item I-H)

Company	Type	Face Amount	Cash Value	*Net Insurance	Annual Premium
_____	____	_____	_____	_____	_____
_____	____	_____	_____	_____	_____
_____	____	_____	_____	_____	_____
_____	____	_____	_____	_____	_____
_____	____	_____	_____	_____	_____
_____	____	_____	_____	_____	_____

TOTAL ____ ____ ____ ____ ____

* Face Amount less Cash Value = Net Insurance

Disability Insurance

Company	Monthly Coverage	Premium
_____	$_____	$_____

Figure 19–1.

YOUR WILL

You will note that I ask if you have a will. This is a very important part of your financial planning. In reality, everyone has a will. It will be the one that you have written to fit your own wishes or the one that the state writes for you after your death. However, the state's will most likely will not bear any resemblance to the way you would have written it, had you done so during your lifetime.

I urge you to obtain a properly drawn will prepared by a competent lawyer in the state where you are living. I won't go into details about all the will should contain. However, let me make this one suggestion as to what you should *not* do. Do not, for example, will so many shares of XYZ company to your daughter Sally, nor your credit union account to your son Johnny. If you do, every time you change your investments (which you will need to do often in the world of change in which we live) you'll also need to alter your will. If you plan for all the disbursement of your assets equally among your four children, specify that 25 percent of your assets should go to each. If you want a portion to go to charity, reduce these percentages in order to have some left for this purpose.

In making these suggestions, I'm not trying to practice law. A competent lawyer in the state in which you reside should prepare your will. I'm a financial planner, and I should and will stick to recommending financial plans that can fulfill your needs. How often I've wished that lawyers would do likewise and stick to their profession and let me practice mine. The temptation to give financial advice seems at times to be just too great for some of them. This may be especially true when a woman has lost a husband on whom she was very dependent. The lawyer may be the only man she knows to depend on at a time when she is very lonely and insecure. Unfortunately, many times her lawyer will take the easy way out and tell her just to put her funds where they will be "safe," meaning a savings account. Here the ravages of inflation will destroy the only value the money has —purchasing power—and she may have to lower her standard of living each year.

Men, prepare your wives to be widows. Most of them will be. Women live longer than men. You've worked together a lifetime to accumulate your assets. The shock will often be so great to your widow that she can't make rational decisions about money or many other things. Yet, some of her most crucial financial decisions must often be made at a time when she may be least prepared emotionally to make them.

If you are a woman who has been raised in the South you may have been taught that it's "not nice to talk about money." It is "nice" to talk about money. It is dumb not to be savvy about it!

Many a large law firm has very strong ties with a particular bank in its city. The firm secures clients for the bank's trust department by drawing up the will in such a way that the bank becomes the trustee. This may be a good arrangement if the heirs have a spendthrift nature and little or no knowledge of money management. It may be a very poor arrangement otherwise. Many bank trust departments are woefully understaffed—often with less than knowledgeable people. They may also be forced by regulations to choose investments based on what will please the bank examiners rather than what might be most advantageous to the beneficiaries.

LOANED DOLLARS

We have already listed many of the ways that you can loan money. I've covered these in detail in Chapter 11, "Lending Your Dollars" and will not repeat them here.

All of these ways of "lending" money offer you a reasonably good guarantee of return of principal and a stated rate of return, with the exception of the cash surrender value of your life insurance policies.

Checking Account. This item is self-explanatory. Add up all your checking accounts and list here, or if you have several make a separate list.

Passbook Savings Account. List these by institutions and amounts. Then total.

Credit Union. List this amount.

Government Bonds and Instruments. If you have a variety of them, be sure and give a description, the interest rate, how much you paid for them, and their current value.

Bonds—Corporate and Municipal. Be sure to describe the bonds fully, or your financial planner will not be able to get a current quote for you. List the bonds, their rates, maturities, cost, and, if you know, their current value.

Mortgages You Carry. Have you carried back a mortgage when you sold some real estate? If so, list it here along with the payment schedule.

Loans Receivable. Have you loaned money that you anticipate will be paid back to you? If so list in H.

Cash Surrender Value of Life Insurance. In the Appendix you will find a worksheet for calculating your cash surrender value. These funds do not technically belong to you. They belong to the life insurance company as a part of its reserve. However, you can obtain that portion designated as cash surrender value by borrowing it from the insurance company and paying interest to do so, or by surrendering your protection. If it is left with the insurance company and death occurs, the beneficiary receives only the face amount of the policy, regardless of how much you have "saved" using this method.

HOW MUCH IN CASH RESERVES?

As you make a total of your "loaned dollars" you may be asking, "How much should I keep in cash reserve?"

As I mentioned earlier, when I first started giving investment seminars, I suggested three months' expenses in cash reserve.

Now I suggest that my clients leave as much money idle as it takes to give them peace of mind, for peace of mind is a good investment. I don't seem to have peace of mind with any of my money idle, with the exception of a checking account. You may not have any peace of mind without a lot in a "guaranteed" savings account where you can give it a comforting pat every now and then.

If you need cash and have your funds invested in good stocks, mutual funds, oil and gas income limited partnerships, and commercial income real estate limited partnerships, you can sell the first two any time you desire. However, it may not be the right time in the market, or you may not want to destroy this goose that is laying the golden eggs. If not you can take your stock certificates to the bank and use them for collateral for a loan.

You can rent a lot of time for a reasonable amount of rent (interest) and deduct the rent on your income. Therefore, I don't feel I need to keep money idle working for someone else while waiting for an emergency. I have cash any time I need it.

WORKING OR "OWNED" DOLLARS

The four main categories in this area are stocks, real estate through individual ownership or through limited partnerships, energy, and other areas of high demand through the same form.

Stocks

Under "stocks" you should list your common stocks, preferred stocks, convertible bonds, and any warrants or rights you may own. List the number of shares, the cost basis, date of purchase, and today's market value.

Knowing your cost basis is very important in doing good financial planning for two reasons. First of all, you need to unemotionally take a good hard look at your performance in the market. For example, let's say that you purchased 100 shares of XYZ Corporation five years ago for $10 per share. Today's market value is 14⅝. Your average gain per year has been 8 percent compounded. If the stock pays a significant dividend that you are reinvesting, add this to your return after adjusting for your tax loss.

Is 8 percent gain per year within your investment results guideline? If you have calculated that you must have a result of 12 percent a year to reach your goal and your investments are not reaching this objective, you will need to consider making some changes in your investment program.

Another important reason for knowing your cost basis is that you need to know how much capital gains would be realized if you were to sell at a profit or capital loss if selling at a loss You need to weigh how much you will have to gain from another investment to overcome the tax loss if you are selling at a profit, to come out ahead. On the

other hand, if you have a loss, you may need to know how much you could save on your income taxes by establishing the loss.

Many have difficulty figuring cost basis. This is because of poor record keeping or because they become confused by stock splits. It only takes a small amount of time to keep good records if done as the transactions are made. In the Appendix I have a stock record sheet that you may want to consider using. I like to use this sheet in a looseleaf notebook, and then pull and file the sheets after the stock has been sold. Both the buy and sell confirmations that you receive from your broker should be kept in your permanent files.

Figuring the effect of stock splits and dividends is not difficult if done as they are made. Let's look at an example. You purchased 100 shares of XYZ Corp. at $50 per share, or $5000, in 1970. You received a stock dividend of 2 percent or two shares in 1971, and a two for one stock split in 1972, which gives you a total of 204 shares. You have added no new money. Your cost basis is still $5000. Your cost basis per share, however, has changed. You now have 204 shares. Your original 100 plus 2 =102 × 2 = 204 shares. You paid $5000, and you have 204 shares, so your new cost basis per share is $24.51. If you should sell 50 shares, your cost basis would be 50 × $24.51 or $1225.50, and the cost basis for your remaining shares would be $3774.50

Real Estate

Real estate can also be a good variable-dollar investment. First, list your home (its current market value less the mortgage). Then list your equity in other real estate holdings. Others: limited partnerships in oil and gas, tax-favored investments of various kinds, commodity accounts, silver and gold bullion and coins, gold jewelry, art works, antiques bought as investments, rare coins and stamps, etc. Now, total your assets and subtract any liabilities. This should give you your net worth.

YOUR FINANCIAL OBJECTIVES

The last section of the personal data sheet is designed to help you determine your financial objectives. Number these in the order of their priority to you.

_____ Income now

_____ Income at retirement

_____ Maximum tax advantage

_____ Educate children

_____ Travel

_____ Other _____
                                (specify)

Estimated Gross Income

Determine early in the year what you estimate your income from all sources will be. The reason this is so necessary is that you will want to do your tax planning earlier.

Estimated Taxable Income

Now list all the deductions you will be entitled to. Study last year's tax return. This will help you list many that you may otherwise overlook. What is your estimated taxable income? Do you want to be taxed on this amount? If not, start early to select tax-favored investments with good economic potential so that you can lower your taxable income. Always strive to turn your tax liabilities into assets. You don't increase your net worth through tax receipts. You increase it by avoiding the one-way trip to Washington.

Your Tax Bracket

Look in the Appendix (Table 20) at the tax schedule. I find that many do not understand what is meant by tax bracket. For example, it does not mean that if you earned $45,800 on a joint return you lost 49 percent, or $22,442, to taxes. Your tax would be $12,720. It means that if you have taxable income of $45,801, you lose 49¢ of that last $1.00. If you have a combination of "earned" (by your expertise or the sweat of your brow) and "unearned" (from investments) income to calculate your exact tax payable, you'll need to use the more detailed worksheet. We have a progressive tax system beginning at 14 percent and going to 70 percent. Your income is taxed at these various levels.

Your tax bracket is a very important item, for it should influence your selection of investments. If you are in the lower brackets, you can afford to invest for income that is taxable. The higher your bracket, the more you should consider tax-sheltered and tax-favored investments.

Amount You Can Save Monthly

Sit down with your family and determine how much you can comfortably save each month—not too comfortably, or you won't save anything. However, don't set the amount too high, but establish an amount you can actually save. If you set it too high, you may become discouraged, abandon the plan, and fail to reach your goal of financial independence.

Taxable Income Last Three Years

I ask this question for two reasons. I often find that estimates of current taxable income are too high or too low. This gives me a picture of what it has been and gives me an opportunity to inquire about what has caused the change. Also, there are investments that contain Investment Tax Credit that under certain conditions can be carried back three years to allow us to recoup taxes already paid.

Number of Dependents

This, of course, is a number each of us can calculate. However, if you are using some tax-favored investments with good write-offs, you may want to fill out a W-4 form and claim a deduction for each $1000 of write-off. You are only required to send the IRS the taxes you owe. If it won't be owed, why send it to them and wait for them to send it back? Remember, money has fantastic earning power. It will either work for the IRS or for you. Which do you choose?

IF RETIREMENT IS YOUR OBJECTIVE

Determine when you plan to retire and map your plan accordingly. Sometimes I'll be counseling a couple age 50 who solemnly tell me that they plan to retire at age 55. When I look at their assets, I realize that there is just no way. They are not being realistic. Regardless of how much they may want to retire in five years, they will not be able to do so with only the income from the assets they have accumulated. They didn't begin combining the three ingredients of time, money, and free enterprise soon enough.

Desired Monthly Income

Decide what you feel would be an adequate or desired monthly income and adjust for inflation. Use the inflation factor you feel is realistic. Do learn to look at circumstances the way they truly are rather than the way you wish they were.

Sources of Monthly Income

Social Security.   I suggest that you call your local Social Security office and request their latest booklet to determine your projected income from Social Security. You may want to consider whether you think Social Security will be solvent when it is time for you to retire.

Pension.   If your company has a pension and/or profit-sharing plan, find out how much your pension will be and what has been credited to your profit-sharing account. Also find out how much is vested (meaning how much you could take with you if you should leave).

Be sure to read about the possible tax advantages of an IRA rollover in Chapter 16, "Planning For the Later Years."

COLLEGE FINANCING NEEDS

The chapter on college education will be helpful in calculating how much you are going to need for your dependents' college expenses.

HOW DID YOU DO?

You've now completed your personal planning data sheet. You have, haven't you?

How did you do? How many years have you worked? How much

have you earned? How much have you saved? How many years before retirement? What do you plan to do about your financial situation beginning today? Write down specific steps that you are going to take to reach your goal. Have a family council and plan your attack.

Financial planning should be a joint endeavor if a couple is involved and a family matter if there are children. When it comes to financial planning, I find that love is not so much looking into each other's eyes as looking in the same direction. If both have the financial vision, the chances for attaining financial goals are vastly improved.

APPLICATION

1. Complete the Financial Data Sheet.
2. Are you pleased with your results?
3. How many dollars do you have idle in a "guaranteed" position?
4. Should you have more of them idle?
5. Do you feel that these dollars are safe? (Safety means that you will be returned the same amount of purchasing power at a point of time in the future that you have today.)
6. Should you have more dollars working for you?
7. In what areas today is demand greater than supply?
8. Do these areas lend themselves to convenient and prudent investing?
9. Which are best for you?
10. What yield are you averaging on your fixed-dollar investments?

Fixed Dollar	*Yield*
_____	_____
_____	_____
_____	_____

11. What rate of return are you averaging on your working dollars?

Investment	*Rate of Return*
_____	_____
_____	_____
_____	_____

12. What date each year have you set aside to update your analysis and consider alternative courses?_____

20

HOW TO
CHOOSE
A FINANCIAL
PLANNER

Reaching your predetermined worthwhile goal of financial independence will require from you creativity, determination, willingness to change courses often and with agility, sublimation of ego, reduction of prejudices, an open mind, and the ability to act quickly.

If you are a success in your chosen profession, you are no doubt devoting many hours to keeping thoroughly informed and to implementing that knowledge. This leaves little time for the very specialized and demanding area of financial planning. Therefore, to obtain the maximum performance on your investable dollars you will need to search out and use the services of a dedicated, creative, knowledgeable, and caring financial planner who is backed up by a team of professionals.

You may not have heard of the profession of financial planner before or, if so, only for the last few years. The profession as such is only about fifteen years old. Their national organization, the International Association of Financial Planners, was formed only eleven years ago. It is a growing profession because the world of investment is growing more dynamic, the tax bite more oppressive, the laws more complex, the inflation rate more destructive, the rapidity of change in economic events nationally and internationally more intense, and individual professions more specialized.

The other day I heard this example of specialization. Two men were discussing the Nabisco factory out on Almeda in Houston and how each department was organized. One of the men said, "They are so organized they have a vice-president of Fig Newton cookies." The other replied, "Oh, you're just talking." They decided to call the company and see. When the operator answered, they asked for the vice-president of Fig Newtons, and she replied "bulk or packaged?" Perhaps your area of expertise is not that specialized, but the world of money is, so you will need to procure the best investment advice you can.

Many of the large Fortune 500 corporations provide personal financial planning with the services of an expert consultant paid for by the employer. This is becoming more and more entrenched as an executive perk. It is good for the corporation as well as the executive, because it allows their officers to devote more of their time to the corporation rather than taking the time required to do their own financial planning. If they are worrying about the proper utilization of their money, they are being distracted from the maximum utilization of their concentration on corporate matters.

If you are not so fortunate as to have this service provided for you, you will need to select a financial planner for yourself.

WHERE TO OBTAIN FINANCIAL ADVICE

Lawyers

Do not go to a lawyer for financial advice. It is not his area of expertise. He usually has little or no training in this area, yet he will have difficulty admitting to his lack of expertise. He will usually be knowledgeable in only one small segment of the law, and you may have trouble finding even what that is.

There is a growing concern by many who observe our society that it is being overburdened with lawyers and that their encouragement of law suits is miring our courts in litigation and causing our medical bills to soar as the cost of malpractice insurance premiums is passed on to each of us. I will not pronounce judgment on this matter but will leave that appraisal to you. If this is the situation, it will not be remedied soon, because our law schools continue to pour more and more graduates on to the scene each new spring. Even though there is no other profession from which you'll have such a vast number to choose, you will probably find it most difficult to find the right attorney with the knowledge you need. Be prepared also to pay while he "researches" your question. Be as informed as you can before asking advice. Always ask his fees before the consultation begins and as you go along. If you do not, you may find your coffers diminished more than you had planned.

Bankers

For banking advice go to your own banker if he is well informed in the area in which you need advice. Your banker may be competent to make loans effectively enough to make a profit for the bank, and he may or may not have sufficient expertise to determine whether your ideas for a particular business will yield a profit. However, investments are not his specialty. If you deposit your dollars in his bank through checking, savings accounts, and certificates of deposit his expertise is to lend your money out again at a higher rate. Always develop a close relationship with a very good banker who heads up or is a ranking officer of a bank which has sufficient funds to handle your bankable· ideas. He can make a very important contribution toward your goal of financial independence.

Certified Public Accountants

It is essential that you have an extremely sharp, creative, diligent, industrious, and accessible Certified Public Accountant. You should go to him for tax advice—on certain points in the tax law or to see if the tax portion of a certain tax-favored investment fits your circumstances. Do not go to him for investment advice. You are not paying him for this. It's not his field, and if you place this burden on him, he will reject almost any tax-favored investment you present to him. If he should encourage you and the investment does not perform to your expectations, you will hold him responsible, and he may lose you as a client. He therefore won't take that risk. It's much safer for him to say No. In that way, he doesn't have to run the risk of losing you as a client, and he also doesn't have to read the private placement offering memorandum that is probably an inch thick written in legalese by lawyers for other lawyers to read. In this way he is never wrong. Of course, he is never right either, and it's the IRS that wins. But you lose!

Accountants are by nature "conservative." They do not handle financial products such as securities, insurance, and tax shelters, and they generally don't much trust those who do. Therefore, don't expect accountants to go out on a limb. Most of the Big 8 firms have a few toes in the water, but their planning usually consists of elaborate analysis and little "implementation" of plans. Some of the smaller, more aggressive firms have taken a more active interest in helping to guide the complete planning process.

For advice on a legal question, go to a competent lawyer; for advice on taxes, go to a C.P.A.; for advice on banking, go to a banker. But don't expect good money management advice from any of them. Yes, I did intend to include the banker. Many bankers are trained to be money changers, money counters, and money lenders, but few are trained to be money managers. I say this even though I am a director of a national bank.

WHY I BECAME A FINANCIAL PLANNER

For many years I was a stockbroker for a large brokerage firm that was a member of the New York Stock Exchange. However, I found myself frustrated by the feeling that I was not doing enough for my clients. I found that what most people needed was not someone to tout them on a stock that they felt might go up a few points; what they really needed was someone to sit down with them and help them analyze where they were, where they wanted to be at a certain period in their lives, and to give them some directional help as to how to arrive at their desired destination and to buy the time to acquire this desired living estate.

I found that the broker was trying to get all of his clients' money into securities, and the insurance agent was trying to get it all into the cash surrender value of whole life insurance policies and was recommending this as the solution for all his money problems. If they had a C.P.A., he was only telling the client how much tax he owed on April 15, when it was 3½ months too late to do anything about reducing his tax liabilities. Most of them did not have an attorney, and if they did, they did not even have a properly drawn will, to say nothing of any provision for reduction of estate taxes. There seemed to be a great need for a person or team that was competent and caring to pull these torn people together into a coordinated, guided, functioning whole. It also seemed that the client should be free to leave and to return as he saw fit.

I became convinced that this was a calling worthy of my life and talents. So, in 1968, at a very low spot in the stock market and at a time when nearly all the small brokerage houses were merging into the large ones, I left a large one to set up a small one. This was a scary move. You have no idea of the mass of regulations that entangle a stock brokerage firm, and the regulatory agencies make it especially difficult for smaller firms. But the need was so great and my dedication so strong that I made the move. It has gone well over these past twelve years, and I have the satisfaction of knowing that I've made a truly worthwhile contribution to the financial future of thousands. Our seminars have grown and grown in attendance and so have the number of our clients. I feel we've done our bit to raise the level of financial independence in Houston and the surrounding cities.

At one of these regular three-session seminars, an editor of Reston Publishing, a subsidiary of Prentice Hall, was in the audience. The next day he wrote me a letter that said, "You have the ability to make a difficult subject simple. Have you considered writing a book?" I had indeed thought of writing a book, but probably would never have done so if they had not signed me to a contract and kept after me until it was completed.

After my first book, *Money Dynamics*, came out, a marvelous thing happened. Stock brokers and financial planners across the country began to recommend and give it to their clients and use it in their investment seminars. Colleges began using it in their classrooms, financial writers began to praise the book, and bookstores began to have brisk sales. The sales increased with my second book, *The New Money Dynamics*, and it became a top seller. This has been a gratifying experience for me because I now feel I've helped raise the level of financial independence across our nation—and abroad.

There are a number of reasons why I feel my books have filled such a great need. First, most of the people in this country are financial illiterates. Even the basic rudiments of money management are not taught in our schools. We continue to spend millions teaching our youth how to earn a dollar, but not what to do with it once it has been obtained. There is a real dearth of knowledge about money. Second, my books are written in lay language from experience, not theory. These are the problems I've seen during my daily counseling with clients in my office. These are my observations of solutions from eighteen years of experience. I have been able to see what these clients need and to appraise their temperaments and coordinate their investments with them in order to match their needs to their tax brackets, the amount of money they have to work with, and the time they have to accomplish their goals. This book is a how-to book from experience, plus a motivational book to get you to act on your new-found knowledge. You can glowingly say, "I can be financially independent. "But unless you act, I will have left you right where I found you.

This is my third book on this subject, because the world of money changes so rapidly that I must keep writing to keep you current. Also Congress keeps changing our tax laws, which in turn change the rules of the money game.

Newsletter

If you would like to keep current on financial events, new investments as they arrive on the scene, and changes in and applications of our tax laws, write to me and let me know. If enough of you express an interest, I'll begin publishing a Financial Update Newsletter. I presently send my clients a Financial Update Letter about every other month and also present to them Financial Update Seminars. My address is: Venita VanCaspel, VanCaspel & Co., Incorporated, 5051 Westheimer, Suite 1540, Houston, Texas 77056. Telephone: (713) 621-9733.

The other day I spoke for a Success Rally, and during the question and answer portion of the program I was asked why I felt our firm had been so successful. I believe there are many reasons, but one that I feel has been important is that we've always tried to visualize how the business will be done in ten years and do it that way now. It's very interesting to me to see some of our major brokerage houses begin to set up Financial Planning Departments. Most of them are floundering, but they are trying. How we welcome them! The country needs more and more really top-quality financial planners.

CHARACTERISTICS YOU'LL WANT IN YOUR FINANCIAL PLANNER

"Sixth Sense"

You will want him to have a sixth sense about money. I used the pronoun him, but remember that I'm using it as a neutral pronoun, with no reference to sex. As a matter of fact, your financial planner can be either female or male. God was very fair. He handed out brains fairly equally between the sexes. The female planner, however, may be superior because she has had to become accepted in what has been un- til recently a male domain. I remember back when I was a broker with a large firm and my desk was out in front of the board like all the other male brokers. A man dropped into the office and selected me to open his account with. He told me the reason he had done so was that he felt I must be good or they would not have let me stay since I was a woman.

You'll want your planner to have the ability to stand back and analyze where demand is greater than the supply. This is a talent that can only be developed from being in the thick of financial undertakings and having contacts with some of the handful of people in this country who make the major decisions or influence those who do. You'll want your planner to be well-informed about the economy here and abroad and to have the talent to predict trends before they occur, the acute perception to detect when the trends have changed, and the ability to act.

Questioning Technique

Your planner should be one who asks you a lot of in-depth ques- tions, similar to the ones you've just completed in the data sheet. Then he'll want to talk to you to learn of your preferences, fears, prejudices, values, and goals. After I have the data and learn about a person's goals, I usually know what will be the best investments for him, but translating and applying my recommendations to fit his temperament is my great challenge. And even though one investment would be better for him from a money-making standpoint than others, it will not be the best investment if it does not provide him with sufficient peace of mind.

Investment Recommendations

Your financial planner should recommend investments that will help you accomplish your financal goals after he has become thoroughly familiar with your tax bracket, your time schedule, your assets, your diversification, and current events as he interprets them.

Tax Savings Techniques

He should be familiar with our tax laws as they apply to investments. He should be constantly attuned to each change and be cognizant of the IRS Letter Rulings. But he should not come unglued if one of them should occur that pertains to an investment you've already made. A ruling is really nothing more than the opinion of the IRS. Only Congress and the tax courts can determine or give the parameters of the law.

Every investment you make must be coordinated with your tax bracket or you are making the wrong investment.

HOW IS A PLANNER COMPENSATED?

Fee-Only Planners

Your planner may be a fee-only planner, meaning he will charge you a fee for gathering all your financial data, analyzing it, and recommending a plan of action. He will receive his compensation whether you implement your plan or not. His role is to recommend objectively what he believes will accomplish your financial objectives. His fee may well range from $500 to $10,000. Many of them set the meter running at $50 an hour. Fee-only planners tend to be thorough and conscientious. Many of them are accustomed to dealing with the well-to-do and do not do cut-rate work. One planner I know has a rather unique fee schedule. He has his clients put him on their payroll and pay him monthly whatever he pays his lowest-paid employee. Some planners charge annual retainer or review fees to keep all of your documents updated and to keep you current on your performance. If yours is good (and do replace him if he is not), his fees should be insignificant compared to the potential value you will receive. Your fee to him is also tax deductible, so the IRS gets to share in his cost.

Fee and Commission Planners

Some financial planners charge both a fee and a commission when you implement your plan. Some fee-only planners have the mistaken opinion that a planner cannot be objective if he is receiving a commission. This is not true, because the planner cannot keep the client unless he performs very well, nor will he receive any referrals from that client. Referrals are the greatest source of clients for a good planner.

It is perfectly acceptable for the planner to receive both a fee and a commission. It is quite costly to gather your data, process it, and make suitable recommendations. He deserves a fee for doing this. However, unless you implement your plan, it will not enhance your net worth. Most people prefer to have the planner, in whom they have already developed confidence and who has all their information, implement their plan. Because he receives a commission, he can usually afford to charge you a smaller fee than the fee-only planner can. Also the offerer of some of the investments pays the planner similar to the way a travel agent is compensated.

Whether they do or not, accept the fact that there is no free lunch and that the commission is there—either built-in or in addition to.

Commission-Only Planners

Your planner may charge only a commission. This is how the planners of our company receive their compensation. It is not superior to either of the other plans. It is just the way we've chosen to do our business. We may start charging a fee in the future, but we do not at present. However, our tax laws are becoming more and more complex, and many of our tax-favored investments require investments over three- and four-year periods with write-offs over even longer periods of time; so the need for very sophisticated calculations are mushrooming and will eventually require more and more computer time. Computer time is expensive, so sooner or later at least a portion of that cost will and should be passed on to the client. Always remember your concern is not what something costs, but what it pays!

Seek out a financial planner who has an excellent reputation and in whom you truly have confidence. Then follow his advice. Don't make the mistake of going from person to person asking their opinions. This will only serve to confuse you, causing you to make poor decisions. You'll always find those eager to give free advice about your money. Often the more readily they give advice, the more miserable the job they have done with their own money.

Your financial planner should be experienced in investments, life insurance, tax shelters, and estate planning, and have a close working relationship with a creative CPA and a competent attorney.

All of these areas must be skillfully meshed in the complex money arena you will find yourself in today.

INTERNATIONAL ASSOCIATION OF FINANCIAL PLANNERS (IAFP)

Your planner, in my opinion, should definitely be a member of the International Association of Financial Planners, headquartered in Atlanta. Their address is 2150 Parklake Drive, N.E., Suite 260, Atlanta, Georgia 30345. Their telephone number is (404) 934-0533.

The IAFP has grown into an internationally prominent organization representing 6300 individual members, many of them the leading financial planners in the world. (There is interest in financial planning in western Europe, South Africa, and Canada. Otherwise, it is an American phenomenon.) Among its services, the IAFP will provide you with information about a financial planner in your area. I'm very pleased to have the privilege of serving on the board of the IAFP. They are making a tremendous contribution to the field of financial planning. Their study modules are very effective educational programs, and their magazine, *The Financial Planner*, makes a major contribution toward keeping its members updated on new investments and pertinent national and international events.

CERTIFIED FINANCIAL PLANNER

Many of the IAFP members have also received the accreditation of Certified Financial Planner. I'm proud to say I have been awarded this very valued accreditation from the College for Financial Planning, headquartered in Denver.

The College for Financial Planning has graduated more than 1500 Certified Financial Planners who hold the CFP designation. While this designation is not yet as well recognized by the public as C.P.A. (Certified Public Accountant), it is rapidly gaining such respect in the industry. For information about their code of ethics and for Certified Financial Planners in your area, contact the College for Financial Planning, 9725 East Hamptden Avenue, Suite 200, Denver, Colorado 80231. Their telephone number is (303) 755-7101.

Both of these organizations—the IAFP and the College for Financial Planning—were originally formed by men and women who were mutual-funds and life-insurance oriented. Many of them were "dually licensed," meaning they held licenses to sell both insurance and securities. Most of the truly qualified financial planners you will find today were trained in these two areas, but that does not mean they offer only insurance and securities services.

It might be helpful to take a look at some of the strengths and weaknesses of the different backgrounds you will find in the financial planning industry.

Insurance. More than any other financial industry, insurance has done an excellent job of teaching its salesmen to listen to people and answer their questions. Unfortunately, many insurance salesmen were trained to give the same answer to every question: "Buy whole life insurance." Whole life has been the insurance industry's big blind spot in financial planning, not only because it is an inferior product (see Chapter 13), but also because it has been billed as one easy solution to a host of problems and goals. Of course, we know financial planning is not that easy.

Most financial planners from the insurance industry now recommend term insurance. They also may recommend annuities as savings and retirement vehicles. Unfortunately, some of them recommend only the mutual funds sponsored by their own insurance company, and many such funds have had relatively dismal performance records in recent years.

A good test of an insurance-financial planner is to ask how many insurance companies he represents. If he says, "Why, I represent only the finest, Gibraltar Life," you can be almost sure he is not a real financial planner. A creative insurance-financial planner should be free to select the best products available from a variety of companies.

Securities. You may have read in the newspaper that such and such large brokerage house has established a financial planning subsidiary, called by a name such as Personal Capital Planning. However, if you call their local office and say, "Financial planning department, please," the switchboard operator will invariably ask, "Do you have a broker?" "No," you say, "I want a financial planner." "Just a second," she says, "I'll connect you with a broker." Don't blame the operator. She doesn't know the firm has a financial planning subsidiary and neither do some of their brokers, believe it or not. Right now, financial planning is a quiet experiment for a number of the major stock exchange member firms.

Securities brokers, unfortunately, don't receive much training listening to people, except in thirty-second snatches over the telephone. Some of them have never met their best clients face-to-face. The reason is that if they leave their phone to meet people, they are not "writing tickets" (taking orders), and therefore, in the eyes of many securities firms, they are failing at their jobs.

This is unfortunate, because the securities industry has the best range of financial planning services to offer—including insurance, tax shelters, asset management programs, and even pension planning. They also have recognized images and "storefronts" so that people can walk in off the street and receive help quickly.

There are some praiseworthy bright spots in the recent financial planning efforts of stock exchange firms. Several firms now make relatively inexpensive financial plans available through their branch-office broker networks. Several regional firms have begun to more or less promote financial planning. If you already have a good broker, you may want to ask him about his interest in financial planning. Many of them "caught the bug" and are moving ahead to help and listen to clients, whether their firm's officers are interested or not.

Independent Planners.   Most real planning to date has been done by the smaller professional groups. In effect, they work for their clients, negotiating for them with many of the largest financial service companies in America. A good planner is neither a wholesaler nor a retailer. He will be representing you. You usually do not need to worry about whether he has a large amount of corporate assets and high capitalization, because most of the independent financial planners do not take possession of client securities or act as fiduciaries.

Everything depends on personal integrity and performance in accordance with your objectives. Therefore, you should not feel the least bit shy about doing some personal investigation of the independent planner before you hire him. What do other clients think of him? How is he viewed in the community? If your investigation turns up a bad egg, don't let that destroy your faith in all financial planners. The industry is still working on a system for keeping incompetent practitioners out of the business.

A good financial planner is like a good growth investment that keeps paying for a lifetime yet keeps growing in value. He should be one of your most valuable assets in projecting you progressively down the road to financial independence.

APPLICATION

1. Contact the International Association of Financial Planners and get the name of members in your area.
2. Contact the College for Financial Planning and do likewise.
3. Look in your telephone directory for a listing of Financial Planners, Certified. Some cities now permit such a listing in the yellow pages.
4. Attend a financial planning seminar. Try to appraise the speaker's knowledge and personality, and determine if you should be able to work together.
5. Ask your associates if they have a good financial planner.

21

THE DIAGRAM FOR FINANCIAL INDEPENDENCE

We've come a long way together, and it is now time to tie everything together and map your financial plan. To help you accomplish this I want to share with you my Diagram for Financial Independence. It is a diagram that I have designed, refined, tested, and embraced during my eighteen years as a financial planner. The diagram has served my clients well. When we've diversified their assets over the diagram in correlation with their tax bracket, they have remained financially whole, with repositioning within the diagram, regardless of economic changes. I first published my diagram in the *Financial Planner Magazine* in February of 1977. Since that time it has come into common use by many financial planners.

Figure 21–1 is my Diagram for Financial Independence. Study it, look at how it ties together many of the areas you have studied, and then let's look at implementation. All the knowledge that ever existed will not benefit you if you do not apply it to your own particular situation.

THE UMBRELLA OF TIME

Across the top of the diagram you will find "Life Insurance—the Umbrella of Time." You learned in Chapter 13 that the great mystery of life is the length of it and that you need a plan whether you live a "normal" lifetime or not. Since you do not know which it will be, you will want to provide an umbrella over your dependents in order to protect them until you have had time to substitute a living estate for a death estate. You have already discovered that the cost of buying time is not expensive if done properly and that the expense can be conveniently covered in the average budget.

We also agreed that you want a living estate rather than a death estate. Once you have provided this living estate, you have fulfilled your obligation to those dependent upon you and are free to stop wasting your hard after-tax dollars on life insurance premiums. (We also determined that if you wanted to pass on your estate intact, we could continue to carry sufficient life insurance for that purpose.)

After you have provided this umbrella or have become self-insured, you are free to devote your attention to making your assets grow. We've already concluded that although money will not bring you happiness, neither will poverty. Money *will* give you options in life that you will not have without it. No person is free, regardless of race or creed, until he is financially independent.

566

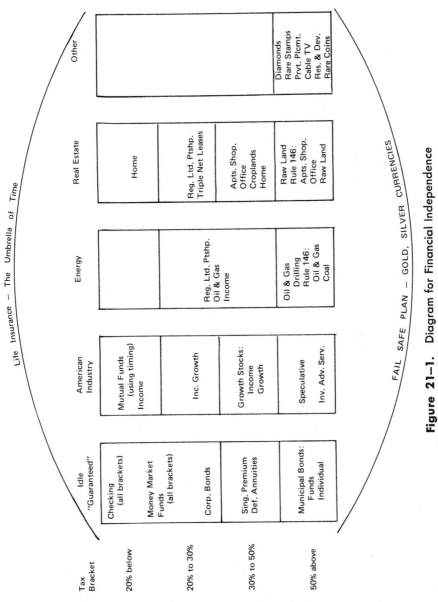

Figure 21–1. Diagram for Financial Independence

TAX BRACKET

Now that we have bought you time, let's proceed with the building of your living estate, or if you've already acquired sufficient assets, let's plot where they are located on the diagram and then see if some of them should be repositioned for greater growth, tax advantage, safety, diversification, or increased spendable income.

Every investment you will ever make should be carefully correlated with your tax bracket. If it is not, you are probably making the wrong investment. The only money you'll ever spend is what the government lets you keep; therefore you must learn to think in terms of "keepable" income or "after-tax" income, not pre-tax income.

TAX EQUIVALENTS

You must learn to think in tax equivalents: What would you have to earn on a taxable instrument, such as a certificate of deposit, to be equivalent to the after-tax, tax-sheltered, or tax-free return on an alternative investment? For example, if you are in the 30 percent tax bracket, you must earn $1428 to have $1000 left after taxes. You calculate this by taking 1.00 minus .30 (your bracket), which gives you .70, your reciprocal ($1000 ÷ .70 = $1428). If you are in a 40 percent bracket you would need to earn $1666 ($1000 ÷ .60).

TAX CATEGORIES

You will note that the diagram has four tax categories: below 20 percent, 20 to 30 percent, 30 to 50 percent, and above 50 percent. Because we have a progressive tax schedule you will have some of your income in all of these brackets, beginning at 17 percent. By now you should have determined your top tax bracket. If not, look at Appendix Table 20 and do so now.

The next column in the diagram is for Idle "Guaranteed" Dollars. You need some liquid assets. We all do. As a matter of fact, I encourage you to keep as much money there as it takes to give you peace of mind. You may need what I call "patting" money. Some people do, and you may be one of them, so you should keep some money in that position. Peace of mind is a good investment. However, throughout this book I've tried to educate you to the point where you will not have any peace of mind if you leave *too many* of your funds idle. The assets that you have in this column are "guaranteed" as to principal on maturity and rate of return. Unfortunately, today they are guaranteed to lose! After inflation and taxation you cannot win! You are like the little frog we've already learned about who is trying to get out of the financial well by hopping up one and sliding back two—you are losing the money game on all the funds you have positioned in this column.

Let's now analyze each category in the diagram in a general way, and then I'll go through the diagram using two hypothetical cases. I'll diagram where they are now and see if some of their assets could be repositioned to maximize their growth and safety.

Checking Accounts

Our first category under "guaranteed" dollars is a checking account. You will need one or more accounts for convenience and for a strong banking connection. Develop a superb relationship with the top people in the bank of your choice. Choose a bank large enough and progressive enough to fund any good bankable project that you may present to them. Your banking connections will be of immeasurable help to you in winning the money game. You will find that the wise use of leverage will be indispensable to you in the inflationary world in which we live. In addition, our tax laws subsidize a portion of its expense.

You may need more than one checking account to allocate your spending and investments properly. You will certainly need an account for the payment of your bills, whether for necessities or luxuries, but do not keep too large an amount there not earning interest. On the other hand, always keep enough there so that you can write a check whenever you want to. It's psychologically bad for you to feel poor. You won't feel like a winner. You won't feel that you have options in life. You want to think, feel, and act like a winner at all times—because you are!

Money Market Funds

In my opinion, there are only two places to have "idle" dollars. These are in a checking account and in one of the mutual fund money market funds. There will be times when you need liquid assets, such as when you're waiting for the right investment to become available, or have set aside funds to pay taxes (not too many, I hope), or have temporarily withdrawn from the stock market and are waiting to return when conditions become more favorable. There are a number of money market funds from which to choose. Their rates will vary slightly, but most will be fairly comparable. They give you the convenience of opening an account for $1000 or more with no cost to deposit the funds, no cost to take it out, and the privilege, if you request it, of writing checks for $500 or more. Your dollars even earn while your check is on its way to the fund. Any time you need money in your checking account, just write a check on the fund and deposit it into your checking account. If the amount you need is $500 or more, you can write a check on the fund itself. I personally transfer funds from my money market fund to my checking account for ease of record keeping.

Certificates of Deposit

I know of no occasion when you should buy a certificate of deposit. Why tie up your money for a long period of time at a fixed rate and suffer a penalty if you should desire to withdraw it early? You also run the risk of the bank or savings and loan company refusing to allow you to withdraw it all. Withdrawal is at their option—read the fine print. Over a period of a few years you can usually obtain a higher rate on your money in money market funds than in certificates of deposit, and you'll have flexibility, which is very important in this world of constant change.

Corporate Bonds

I do not recommend that you ever invest in corporate bonds, with perhaps the exception of short-term investments in selected discount corporate bonds. I have placed them in the guaranteed column. However, they are not guaranteed as to principal before their maturity date. If you should need your funds or find more attractive investments before that date and sell them, you will have a loss if interest rates have risen above the rate your bonds carry. On the other hand, you may obtain a premium if interest rates have dropped below the rate of your bond. As you learned in Chapter 11, "Lending Your Dollars," corporate bonds have been a financial disaster over any of the past 26 ten-year periods.

Single-Premium Deferred Annuity

There can be some uses for single-premium deferred annuities if you feel that for your peace of mind you just have to have your funds guaranteed, yet you are in a 30-percent tax bracket or higher and would like to defer taxes. This type of "loaned" dollar fits this requirement. Another use for them that you may want to consider is when you have invested in an aggressive tax shelter that has used accelerated depreciation, which creates a negative cost basis. When the property is sold or a foreclosure takes place, you may owe a capital-gains tax. Therefore, you should invest these tax dollars you have saved (you would not have had them anyway if you had not invested in the tax-favored investment and paid the tax) into an annuity where they can compound tax-deferred. When and if the tax is due, you'll have the funds with which to pay the taxes, and because the annuity has been earning interest on interest without the dilution of taxes, you should have funds left over. Remember that until you withdraw from the annuity more than your original investment, there is no tax due.

Another use for the annuity that is worthy of your consideration is that of refinancing your home and placing the funds in the annuity. (Unfortunately, you can't do this if you live in Texas.) You should definitely not leave idle capital in the equity of your home. Your home doesn't know whether it has a small or large mortgage on it. It will inflate just as much with a large mortgage or a small one. Having a large equity in your home is like having that much money in a checking account not drawing interest.

If you need the peace of mind of knowing that money is available and guaranteed if you should ever desire to pay on or off the mortgage, you could place these funds into the annuity and let them compound tax-deferred. You can always withdraw them whenever you choose to pay off the mortgage or to use for expenses such as college education, starting a business, participating in an investment, etc.

Cash is severely hurt by inflation. Debt is the beneficiary. Also, you are entitled to deduct the interest while using the funds in alternative investments, and when you pay off the principal, you can do so with cheaper dollars. Again, I emphasize that inflation rewards those who owe money, not those who pay cash.

However, you must remember unless your annuity rate is greater than the inflation rate, you are still not winning the money game.

Municipal Bonds

On the diagram under "idle" guaranteed dollars in the 50 percent bracket and above, I have placed municipal bonds. These can be municipal bond funds, municipal bond trusts, or individual municipal bonds that you have selected. Regardless of which you choose, under present conditions you are not winning the race with inflation. The bonds also decline in market price when interest rates exceed the rates of the bonds. You are guaranteed to receive back at maturity each dollar of face amount, but it will be a dollar that has lost its purchasing power. In a 43 percent bracket or above, you may have more keepable income from a municipal than a corporate or a certificate, but your purchasing power is shrinking rather than growing.

Also remember that there is no such thing as a "tax free" bond. The spread between the corporate rate and the municipal rate is your tax.

AMERICAN INDUSTRY

We now move into the area of putting your dollars to work for you as hard as you had to work to get them. You'll definitely want to consider stock of American corporations and, if you have developed sufficient expertise, that of foreign corporations.

Equities in stocks should be a viable part of your asset distribution, however you should probably never have more than 25 percent of your assets in that position, and there will be periods of time when none should be there. The only reason you should ever have money invested in the stock market is to make money. When you can't make money, and there will be times when this will be extremely difficult to do, get out and sit on the sidelines in money market funds. This will usually be the time these funds are paying their highest yields.

If you have the three Ts and an M and find the time spent selecting stocks is more enjoyable and more profitable than some leisure pursuits, select and manage your own portfolio. You'll remember that the Ts are: Time to study the market and the information about current companies and national and international affairs; Training to interpret and decipher financial reports; and the Temperament to make rational decisions quickly. The M is for sufficient funds to diversify in order to spread your risks and broaden your base for profits.

Mutual Funds

If you do not have the three Ts and an M, don't take an ego trip. Let the professionals help you through either *private* professional management, using an investment advisory service if you have sufficient funds to obtain an excellent one, or *public* professional management, using the best-managed mutual funds.

You'll note that I have placed the income funds in the 20 percent or below category (if you are warm, you are in at least a 20 percent bracket). If you are in that bracket you usually need income and will not be sacrificing as much to taxes. As you move up the bracket, you will want to move more and more toward growth.

If you use a family of funds that has a money market fund, you can move in and out of the market freely without commission. This gives you a safe harbor to run to and stay in until the storm has passed. (You could have a capital-gains tax if you do not have it inside an annuity.)

Speculation

In the 50-percent-or-above category there is nothing wrong with speculating with money you can afford to lose. Approach this area intelligently, and you may find it to be extremely rewarding. Be a strategist—try to predict a trend before it happens, and move out of it before it runs out. Some of my most productive investments (meaning I made money rapidly) were in the lower priced silver, gold, and oil stocks in 1979.

ENERGY

Energy is a hard tangible asset. To me it is black gold. It's a product everyone wants and needs that is in short supply. If you can supply it, that's certainly a possibility worthy of your consideration.

Registered Oil and Gas Income Limited Partnerships

I would not recommend the use of this type of an investment in the below-20-percent tax bracket. Not that you wouldn't enjoy the income (presently tax-sheltered) in this bracket, but you may need quicker access to your funds than these provide.

In the 20 to 50 percent bracket, these can be an excellent choice for your "serious" after-tax dollars. In the past we have done extremely well for our clients in this area, and they have been extremely pleased. I'm even more enthusiastic about this type of investment today. When I first presented this program in the early 1970s, I told my clients what I hoped to have this investment do for them. The results have far exceeded this hope, but I still use the same presentation as I did then. (I didn't know we would do so well, and OPEC certainly added its bit.) I told them then, as I still do now, that I hoped that they would receive a 7 to 9 percent cash flow the first twelve months with a write-off of 13 to 15 percent of their investment. The first year the general partner would be acquiring the properties. The second year and thereafter I had hoped to have them receive a cash flow of 10 to 12 percent. In reality we have moved up to 12 percent by the fifth quarter after their investment and have surpassed our hoped-for results each year thereafter.

As you will remember, you'll have three options regarding your cash flow if you use this type of investment. First, you may reinvest your distributions. This is an especially good choice if you are investing for growth or will be retiring in a few years and want to build your assets. At retirement you could choose option two or three. In option two you may withdraw a certain percent and reinvest the remainder in order to preserve your capital. The third option is to take everything in cash. Technically you should be receiving a return *on* capital as well as a return *of* capital when you choose this option, but as the price of energy has escalated, your balance would have grown rather than diminished.

If the OPEC alliance holds together, if there continues to be some semblance of deregulation, and if the demand for oil and gas keeps increasing, this type of investment should benefit. Also, the limited partnerships will have a definite advantage over the oil companies in acquiring properties, because the first 1000 barrels a day of oil for each partner in the partnership will be taxed at a lower "windfall-profits tax" than will the oil of larger producing companies. This should place the limited partnership programs in a very advantageous position when it comes to acquiring future production. It now appears that the windfall-profits tax will be very burdensome to many oil companies and will be an administrative and computer nightmare.

As you are already aware, corporate earnings bear the burden of double taxation. First, corporate earnings are taxed. A portion of what is left is then paid out to shareholders and is taxed again. This added tax burden is causing stock in many corporations to sell near a 25 percent discount on assets.

The limited partnership escapes this double taxation. All the tax advantages flow through to the investor as an individual. To date, not only has there been no double taxation, but very little or no taxation has been due on the cash flow.

Registered Oil and Gas Drilling Programs

If you are in the 50 percent bracket or above you may want to consider investing in a drilling program. You will usually have a wide range of programs to choose from (exploration, development, royalty, etc.), as you learned from the last half of Chapter 8, "Energizing Your Investments." For this approach to energy you should use as much "tax cash" as you can, rather than "cash cash," meaning you should consider using some of your "soft" dollars—those that will be making that one-way trip to Washington if you dont invest in some tax-favored investment. Most registered programs will have little or no leverage in them, so for each $1 you put up you'll write off nearly $1. This means that if you are in a 50-percent bracket, half of the money you invest will be yours and one half will be the IRS's.

Private Placement Drilling Programs

I've seen some of the best *and* worst drilling programs structured as private offerings. These offerings can usually be more creatively financed to offer write-offs in excess of 100 percent. This is usually accomplished by using recourse financing. This means that you would be signing recourse notes which you will be required to pay if they are not paid off out of production. Even if they are, any money paid on your loan is taxable to you.

Some programs have been structured with leverage, plus mining prospects for precious metals. This combination can be very favorable tax-wise if properly financed and structured with a general partner who has outstanding know-how. If the program is structured with a 2 for 1 write-off you would be using, for the present, only tax dollars. You would hope to be able to turn your tax liabilities into assets in the future. At the same time you could have the satisfaction of knowing that you have put some of your funds to work productively to improve your and your fellow Americans' quality of life.

REAL ESTATE

In the next column you will find real estate. There is no question that our tax laws favor commercial and residential income-producing real estate. Nonrecourse financing can still be used (meaning the lender looks to the value of the property rather than to you for his collateral). You receive the appreciation on the total value of the buildings, not just on your cash contribution. You are permitted to deduct the interest while at the same time you are allowed to take depreciation on the total cost basis of the property, not just on your down payment. There are a number of possibilities in real estate you will want to investigate.

Home

Your first consideration may be the purchase of your own home. I have positioned your home at the top of the real estate column. This is not because I think that you should consider the purchase of your own home only if you are in the lower brackets. As a matter of fact, it may be cheaper for you to rent if you are in a lower bracket, because your tax advantage will not be as great as it would be if you were in a higher tax bracket. Housing is one of the necessities of life and can also be an "investment in living" if it fits your lifestyle. A home in most instances has also been an excellent financial investment over the past few years.

Triple-Net Leases of Registered Limited Partnerships

If you are in the 20 to 30 percent bracket, you may want to consider investing in registered limited partnerships that put your money to work in triple-net leases of the buildings of our major corporations. These are conservative nonoperating partnerships that provide capital for business expansion. As you will remember from Chapter 6, "The Real Rewards of Real Estate," in times of tight and/or expensive money, major corporations such as J. C. Penney, General Motors, Sears, and Safeway sell their buildings and then lease them back. This allows them to continue their program of growth unhampered by a shortage of funds, and it also provides them with some financing and tax advantages. Under this arrangement, they make a lease payment each month and pay all other expenses. I much prefer these to the bonds of the same corporations, because the corporation must pay the rent or it will have to move. Their objective is an 8 to 9 percent cash flow with 50 to 75 percent of it tax-sheltered. Presently we are obtaining shelter on nearly all of the cash flow. You should consider this as your "now" benefit. Your "later" potential benefits could be equity build-up of perhaps 4 percent a year (mortgage paydown) and appreciation (as much as inflation, one hopes) on both your investment and the mortgaged portion. As properties have been sold from these partnerships, the appreciation on these buildings has far exceeded what we had hoped for.

Registered Limited Partnerships in Multifamily Housing

If you are in the 30 to 50 percent bracket, you should consider registered limited partnerships that invest in multifamily housing. There are a number of excellent ones available.

The housing shortage of the 'eighties will probably be the worst we've ever had in the U.S. As we enter this decade, vacancy rates of multifamily garden-type apartments are below 4½ percent, and the number of units under construction is declining. This is occurring when the average family cannot qualify for a home loan and will have no choice but to rent housing or to buy or rent a mobile home.

Investments in this type of already-occupied housing should offer you an excellent potential for gain as rents increase, construction costs for new units escalate, and family units rise in number. I feel that housing is one of the most viable investments that you should be considering today, and it certainly should have a priority position on your diagram. Your "now" benefits will be greater in the 30 to 50 percent bracket because of the excess deductions to which you will be entitled. Your "later" benefits should be excellent as rents and replacement costs increase. This provides a possibility for deferring taxes and converting to capital gains. It's an excellent way to play the D.C. game—defer and convert.

Tax Equivalent

In deciding which is best for you currently—the triple-net lease or the multifamily partnership—remember to use tax equivalents. (You may, however, want to use both investments.) If you invested $10,000 in triple-net-lease partnerships and received an 8 percent cash flow (we are receiving more) and all of it is tax-sheltered, your keepable cash distribution would be $800 for your "now" benefit. If, on the other hand, you had invested $10,000 in the multifamily housing partnership, and they paid out a 5 percent cash flow tax-sheltered, you would receive $500. Let's also assume that you have an excess deduction of 9 percent because of additional depreciation and interest expense. This would entitle you to save $360 in taxes in a 40 percent bracket ($900 × .40). You would then have $500 plus $360 of taxes saved, or a total of $860. Your net keepable cash flow would be $60 more, even though the cash distribution sent to you was $500 instead of $800. I often find that my clients forget about the $360 they didn't have to send to Washington, and I have to remind them that if they didn't have to send it to Washington they still have it in their pockets.

There is a wide range of registered limited partnerships offered by general partners who have excellent past performance records. Some of these will have larger write-offs and larger cash flow. They may invest in office buildings and shopping centers in addition to apartments. Even those that invest primarily in apartments will often add an office building or a shopping center to give the program added diversification.

Real Estate Private Placements

You should consider real estate private placements if you have some of your income in the 50 percent bracket. If these are properly and fairly structured with the right general partner and the right real estate, they can offer you tremendous investment potential while at the same time providing write-offs going in and tax shelter on cash flow during your holding period. You will give up the wide diversification of the registered program, for there will usually be only one property in the program. You will also not have the watchful eye of the SEC or the expense of registration costs. These offerings are usually structured so that you can take mostly or all "tax cash"! Your write-off could run from 30 to 150 percent of your investment and as high as 260 percent in certain two-tier partnerships. The properties may be apartment buildings, shopping centers, motels, hotels, or office buildings. They may be new construction or second- or third-owner properties. If you invest in new construction you could have more risk because you could have building cost overruns, have interim financing rates escalate while the buildings are under construction, and have rent-up lag time. I have personally found investments in partnerships that invested in new construction and those investing in second-owner properties extremely profitable.

We have done the equity financing for a number of office buildings and shopping centers for a particular Houston builder and our clients have been very pleased with the results that they have received.

Suitability requirements on private placements usually run very high. You always have to be in a 50 percent tax bracket or are required to have a substantial net worth if you are not in that bracket.

Raw Land

Raw land for investment purposes may not be a viable investment for you unless your bracket is very high and you anticipate having sufficient future income to service the mortgage and pay the taxes. You must be in a position to support it over a period of time rather than the reverse situation.

If you purchase a small bit of acreage in the country as a get-away retreat, you should consider that as an investment in living, rather than an investment for increasing your net worth. It may do the latter, but that's not your main purpose.

Tangibles

Diamonds, Rare Coins, Rare Stamps, and Collectibles. These are hard assets that are viable investment choices. Diamonds have been a special joy to our clients, and I feel they will continue to be. They are portable, passable, scarce, in demand, beautiful, desirable, and an excellent store of value that requires a minimum of space and servicing.

Rare coins and rare stamps have many of the same characteristics. The demand for them is great and the supply is limited, which fits our first criterion for a good investment.

Look at the various collectibles we've already discussed and if one or more attracts your attention and you develop an expertise in that area, they may also find a place in your portfolio. You can use these types of investments from the 30 percent bracket up.

Tax-Favored Investments

If you are in the 50 percent bracket or above, you will definitely want to consider one or more of the tax-advantaged investments discussed in Chapter 12, "Avoiding the One-Way Trip to Washington." This type of investment, properly structured with economic viability, is difficult for your financial planner to find. He will have to spend much time and money doing his "due diligence" before recommending one to you.

When he does find one or more—and you should diversify—they will usually be complex, high risk, and often in areas unfamiliar to you. But they can be well worth the search and can do much toward lowering your greatest expense—your taxes. Tax-advantaged favorites of mine are cable television, real estate, drilling, mining, and various forms of agriculture such as cattle feeding, fig ranches, etc. These types of investment can often be structured to use only tax dollars. You should not be investing in this type of offering if you are not using some 50¢ to 70¢ dollars.

Gold, Silver, Currencies

As I've discussed earlier, I have used gold as my "fail-safe fire insurance" program in case my other areas of investing ran into difficulties. I do believe that a portion of your funds should be in this type of hard asset. The more that inflation increases and the world's stability is threatened, the more you should look at gold and silver. I believe that gold, for all practical purposes, will be remonetized in the 'eighties.

APPLICATION

I hope you have received some practical guidance for tying your financial plan together and will plot your assets on the diagram in order to determine if you have sufficient diversification and if their location fits your tax bracket and your financial objectives.

It may now be helpful for you to examine the finances of two hypothetical families to see how their assets are positioned and to consider whether or not they should be repositioned to accomplish their financial goals.

THE JONES FAMILY

Figure 21–2 is their data sheet. Look it over at this time.

Now that you've studied Jack and Jill Jones's data sheet, what suggestions would you make? First, you'll note that if Jack should die, Jill could probably continue working; but her income would not be sufficient to enable the family to continue living at their present standard of living. With Jack's present coverage his family would receive $95,000. Of this, $9790 is cash value, and $85,210 is insurance for which they are paying premiums of $1572. Jack's present income is $30,000. If we allow a generous $5000 for deductions and $5000 for taxes, this would leave a net amount of $20,000 per year, or a net amount of $200,000 that he will contribute over a ten-year period, with no provision for cost-of-living increases. If we estimate that 40 percent of that is needed for Jill and 10 percent for each of their children, a minimum of 60 percent of that amount would be needed (plus Social Security), or $120,000.

Another method that can be used is to take his present net income of $20,000 and divide by 12, which equals $1666. Subtract around $666 for Social Security benefits, which leaves $1000. Multiply this amount by 200, which gives you an amount of $200,000—the amount of capital required to produce $1000 a month at 6 percent. (Widows can become very conservative.) From this amount subtract $84,241, the amount of their already-accumulated estate less their home and lot. They will need the home to live in and from their description of the recreational lot it seems nonliquid at the present. This leaves a $115,759 difference. As you can see, the $120,000 is a bare minimum and should probably be increased to a minimum of $150,000 to provide for the added expenses of college and inflation.

The family will need this coverage for at least ten years, therefore they may want to consider a ten-year deposit level term policy for Jack in the amount of $150,000. The premium on this amount will be $750 per year (a savings of $822 per year or $68.50 per month compared to his present cost), plus an increase in coverage from $95,000 to $150,000, or $55,000. This also releases $9790 for repositioning. After using $1500 for the deposit (which is returned to them doubled in ten years), he would have $8290 to invest.

Disability Income

Jack is much more likely to be disabled than he is to die. He should also obtain a disability income policy that would pay the family $1200 per month. If he uses a 91-day elimination period, he could obtain a sickness and accident policy for $478 per year.

Figure 21–2.

FINANCIAL PLANNING DATA SHEET

DATE _____

Jack T. Jones   35
NAME   AGE

1234 Briar Lane, Houston, TX 77027
ADDRESS   ZIP CODE

123-4567   891-2345
HOME PHONE NO.   BUSINESS PHONE NO.

self   Architect
EMPLOYER   OCCUPATION

Jill B.   33
NAME OF SPOUSE   AGE

Texas Corp.   678-9101
EMPLOYER   SPOUSE'S BUSINESS PHONE NO.

Secretary
OCCUPATION

DO YOU HAVE A CURRENT WILL? _____no_____

ARE YOU COVERED UNDER A PENSION PLAN?

_____no_IRA_no__KEOGH__no__

My financial resources

I. LOANED DOLLARS:

A. Checking Account $___2,000___

B. Amounts in Passbook Savings Accounts:

	Institution	Amount	
1.	Gibraltar S&L	3,000	
2.	Capital Nat'l	4,000	$ 7,043

581

C. Certificates of Deposit:

	Institution	Rate %	Maturity	Amount	
1.	Gibraltar	7-3/4	1/1/85	10,000	
2.	Home S&L	7-1/2	1/1/84	10,000	
3.	Am. S&L	7-1/2	1/1/81	5,000	$ 25,000

D. Credit Union____% $ 8,100

F. Government Bonds & Instruments

Type	Rate %	Maturity Date	Current Value
Series E	6 various		5,000+

$ 5,000

F. Bonds—Corporate and Municipals

Name of Company or Municipality	No. of Bonds	Rate %	Maturity Date	Cost	Market Value
AT&T	2	7-1/8	2003	1960	1178
Putnam Mun.					
Bd. Fund				21,000	14,700

$ 15,878

G. Mortgages You Carry $_____

H. Loans Receivable $_____

I. Cash Value of

Insurance Policies (see Worksheet) $ 9,790

TOTAL LOANED DOLLARS $ 72,811 ___(1)

II. WORKING DOLLARS:

A. Stocks and Mutual Funds

No. of Shares	Name of Company	Date of Purchase	Cost	Market Value
200	Southern Co.	1977	3600	2180
200	Houston Ind.	1977	7220	5550
70	AT&T	1978	4248	3700

$ 15,068

Total Market Value $ 11,430 _____(2)

Real Estate

Home (Market Value Less Mortgage) $ 40,000
   $70,000 mkt. $30,000 mtg.
Other Real Estate (Net After Mortgages):

Lake Lot _____ $ 10,000 ____

_____ $_____

_____ $_____

_____ $_____ $_____

Limited Partnerships:

_____ $_____

_____ $_____

_____ $_____ $_____

Total Loaned and
Working Dollars $ 134,241

Financial Objective numbered in order of Importance:

_____ Income now

___3____ Income at retirement

___2____ Maximum tax advantage

___1____ Educate children

___4____ Travel

_____ Other _____
                    (specify)

Estimated Gross Income this year $__45,000__

Estimated taxable income $__35,200__

Tax Bracket   __43__ %

Taxable Income last 3 years:
$__28,129__ $__29,900__ $__32,246__

Taxes Paid:
$__5,634__ $__6,201__ $__7,069__

No. of Dependents____3____

Amount you could save each month $__$200__

Retirement Data:

    No. of years before: _____30_____ years

    Desired monthly income $__8,000__

        Possible Sources:

        Social Security $____?____

        Pensions $____--____

        Investments $____?____

        Other $_____

                    Total $_____

Additional needed if retiring today $_____

Children Educational Cost Data:

Name of Child	Age	Years Before College	Estimated Cost
Jim	10	7	30,000
Jan	8	9	35,000
	Total		65,000
	Amount set aside		25,000
	Additional needed		40,000

Present Life Insurance, & Annuities Work Sheet
(to complete item I-H)

Company	Type	Face Amount	Cash Value	*Net Insurance	Annual Premium
Blessed Assurance	WL	80,000	6280	73,720	1258
"	WL	5,000	1455	3545	93
"	WL	5,000	1040	3960	125
"	WL	5,000	1015	3985	98
TOTAL		95,000	9790	85,210	1572

* Face Amount less Cash Value = Net Insurance

Disability Insurance

Company	Monthly Coverage	Premium
none	$	$

Jack has one employee who has worked one year. He has had his own firm for 7 years.

Jill works for a corporation with no pension plan.

Now that we've placed the umbrella of time over the family in case the main breadwinner should die or become disabled, let's turn our attention to the family's other assets and see if they are positioned in the best way to accomplish the family's financial goal. Let's examine their data sheet item by item.

Checking Account. $2000 is a reasonable average amount to keep in this position and should be left there.

Savings Account.   The account at Gibraltar Savings of $3000 could be left for emergencies, travel, etc. The Capital National account of $4000 could be moved to our reposition list.

Certificates of Deposit.   There are three. Let's leave his American Savings and Loan certificate of $5000 in place until it matures and then move it to a money market fund. Since neither their Gibraltar Savings and Loan account of $10,000 or their Home Savings and Loan account of $10,000 are keeping up with inflation and taxes, and both have a long time before maturity, they should take their "hickie" (penalty) on them and redeem them.

Series E Bonds.   There has never been a period of time when Series E bonds have been a good investment, so these should be repositioned. Since there would be taxes due on the interest, they should redeem $2500 of them this year and $2500 in January of the next year.

Bonds.   Bonds do not fit their financial objective, and they are vulnerable to inflation, taxes, and increasing interest rates. They have a loss of $782 on their AT&T bond. This should be sold and the loss realized, freeing $1178 to be put to work more productively.

Municipal Bond Fund.   This couple, in my opinion, should never have been sold a municipal bond fund. They should redeem it and put the funds to work more productively. A sale would release $14,700 and establish a loss of $6,300.

Cash Value of Insurance. $9790 will be released to be put to work for the Joneses while obtaining $55,000 more coverage, at a savings of $68.50 per month.

Stocks.   The Joneses had been reading a particular financial writer for several years and had followed his advice to buy utilities. This was poor advice, for a utility is composed basically of two things— raw materials and money, both of which are expensive and could continue to be so. Add to this an angry consumer, and you have an industry with reduced opportunity for growth. These funds should be repositioned. This would release $11,430 and establish a loss of $3638.

Home. The Joneses are looking for a new home. If they should decide to buy one for $80,000, I would advise them to make the minimum down payment. If they can obtain 80 percent financing, this would require $16,000 down and release another $24,000 for investment to help make the added payments and enable the asset to grow.

Recreational Lot. Since the lot was bought as an investment and not as a recreational spot, they might consider placing it on the market.

Retirement Program. Jack is self-employed and has been for seven years. He has one employee who has worked for him for one year. I recommend that he establish a Keogh Plan. He will be allowed to contribute $4500 (15 percent of $30,000). This now becomes a deductible item on his income tax return, and the funds are allowed to compound tax-sheltered. Jill is eligible for an Individual Retirement Account and can contribute $1500 per year, which can also be deducted.

Will. They both should have wills prepared by a competent attorney practicing in the state in which they reside.

Now let's tally up the assets they would have to reposition:

Amount	Source	Gain or Loss
4,000	Capital National	
10,000	Home S&L	
10,000	Gibralter S&L	
2,500	Series E Bonds	
1,178	AT&T Bond	(782)
14,700	Municipals	(6300)
9,790	Cash Value	
11,430	Stocks	(3638)
63,598	Total	(10,720)

(plus $24,000 if they buy a new home)

Recommended Allocation of Funds

$ 1,500	Deposit for $150,000 of life insurance
750	Premium for one year
4,500	Keogh account to be invested in a growth mutual fund
1,500	IRA account in a growth mutual fund
15,348+	In the same growth mutual fund under a $25,000 Letter of Intent

20,000	In an oil and gas income program
20,000	In a multifamily real estate limited partnership
$63,598	

Tax Deductions Resulting From Repositioning

$ 4,500	Keogh contribution is totally deductible
1,500	IRA contribution is deductible
2,800	Oil and gas program @ 14 percent deductibility the first 12 months
2,800	Assuming 14 percent write-off on the real estate program
3,000	$6000 of long-term capital losses can be used against $3000 of ordinary income. $4700 of the loss can be carried forward to be used the next year
$14,600	Total Deductions

Taxable Income

35,200	Taxable income before repositioning
14,600	Additional deductions after repositioning
20,800	New taxable income

Taxes Saved

$ 8,162	Taxes due before repositioning
3,441	Taxes due after repositioning
$ 4,721	Tax savings per year plus no taxes at present on the limited partnership distributions, as compared to the taxable interest they had been receiving from their savings and certificates of deposit earnings.

Savings to be added to their mutual funds investment:

822	Insurance premium savings
4,721	Tax savings
5,543	Total

They began their mutual fund account with $15,348, $4500 Keogh, $1500 IRA (set up in separate accounts but qualifying for the quantity discount under the Letter of Intent), and the $5543 tax savings, for a total of $26,891. They also estimate that they can save $200 per month, or $2600 in a thirteen-month period, that can be added to their mutual fund account. Their multifamily housing could also pay out $1000 during the year, which can be added to their mutual fund in addition to all the reinvestment of any dividends and capital gains that may occur. They should have over $30,000 in their account by the end of thirteen months (the period of the Letter of Intent) depending on market conditions. They should also superimpose a timing device on their open account and their Keogh account (when it reaches $10,000).

After they have accumulated this amount in the growth fund, they could open an account that invests in South African gold stocks. They can build that account with their premium savings and the $200 per month they can save.

Next January they can redeem the remainder of their Series E bonds, and this amount (plus their tax savings) could be used to invest in investment-grade diamonds. This should be placed in their safety deposit box to appreciate until needed for college expenses. It could be placed in a custodian account for the oldest child. Assuming the diamond cost around $6000, there would be no taxes due when the account was established and no taxes due during the appreciation period—if it appreciated, which they have done in the past.

If the Joneses buy a new home, paying down 20 percent on a $80,000 home, they would also free $24,000. If they will need additional funds to make house payments, they could place these funds into an excellent growth mutual fund and begin with a withdrawal program for the amount of their additional house payments. If they will have sufficient funds by using only $12,000, they may want to consider an investment-grade diamond for the second child.

Results of Repositioning

1. Their life insurance protection has been increased from $95,000 to $150,000; their cost has been reduced by $822 per year; and $9790 of earning power has been released.

2. By placing $30,000 into the growth sector of American industry, their assets will have an opportunity to grow. In addition, they will qualify for a write-off against taxable income of $6000 on their IRA and Keogh accounts and $3000 on realized losses.

3. Their tax savings should be over $5000 a year.

4. Their energy and real estate investments should appreciate with (and one hopes ahead of) the cost of living and produce tax-sheltered income.

5. Their diversification is vastly improved.

6. Their liquidity is lessened. The real estate partnership funds could be tied up for six to eight years. The oil and gas program does have liquidity, the amount depending on the partnership's value at the time it is redeemed.

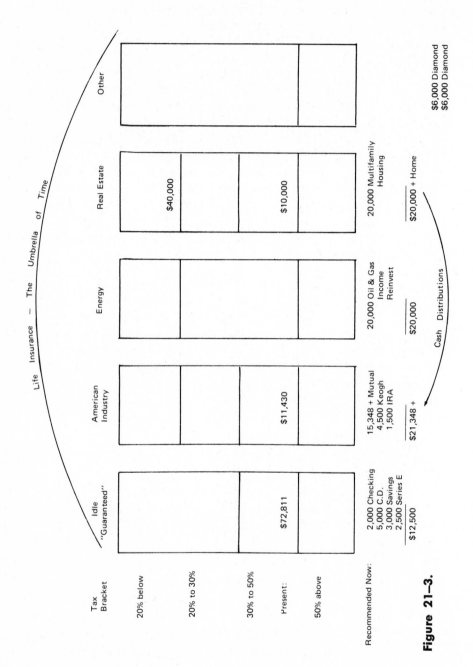

Figure 21-3.

590

7. Their ability to educate their children, obtain tax advantage and prepare for income at retirement is greatly enhanced.

Where will the Joneses be in ten years? I really don't know. I would be disappointed in the results of my plan for them if they had not accomplished at least the following:

$ 90,000+	Mutual funds
80,000	Oil and gas program
85,000	Multifamily housing
58,000	Gold stock mutual fund
48,000	Diamonds
108,000	Keogh
36,000	IRA
10,000	Recreational lot
48,000	Home equity
3,000	Insurance policy deposit
10,000	Miscellaneous
$532,000	Estimated assets in 10 years

In ten years Jim will be 20, and Jan will be 18 years old. There should be sufficient assets to pay for their college expenses and provide Jill with a cushion in the event of Jack's death. His $150,000 of life insurance is renewable and convertible at his option without evidence of insurability if he wants to renew for that amount of coverage at the end of the ten-year period. Jack and Jill may, however, decide they are self-insured or that a smaller amount seems more appropriate and thus reduce or eliminate their coverage and quit this waste.

THE SMITHS

Let's examine the data sheet of Bob and Jane Smith (Figure 21–4). Their two children are both married and self-sufficient. Bob is taking early retirement and setting up a consulting firm. His close friend did so three years ago and is now earning more than when he worked for the corporation. Bob has already received offers of more assignments than he feels he can handle.

Checking Account. $2500 could be a reasonable amount in checking, for they may be doing some personal and business travel.

Savings Account. The Smiths could consider leaving $8000 in the Spring Branch Savings and Loan since it is near their home, and they could reposition the $7000 in the Pasadena Savings and Loan.

Figure 21–4.

FINANCIAL PLANNING DATA SHEET

DATE
_____

Robert A. Smith   55
_____
NAME   **AGE**

5678 Roaring Brook   Houston, TX   77012
_____
ADDRESS   **ZIP CODE**

891-2345   678-9123
_____
HOME PHONE NO.   **BUSINESS PHONE NO.**

Ho-Tex Energy   Engineer
_____
EMPLOYER   **OCCUPATION**

Jane B. Smith   55
_____
NAME OF SPOUSE   **AGE**

housewife
_____
EMPLOYER   **SPOUSE'S BUSINESS PHONE NO.**

_____
OCCUPATION

DO YOU HAVE A CURRENT WILL? _____ yes _____

ARE YOU COVERED UNDER A PENSION PLAN?

_____X_ IRA____KEOGH_____

My financial resources

I. LOANED DOLLARS:

   A. Checking Account $ 2,500

   B. Amounts in Passbook Savings Accounts:

Institution	Amount	
1. Pasadena S&L	7,000	
2. Spring Br. S&L	8,000	$ 15,000

C. Certificates of Deposit:

	Institution	Rate %	Maturity	Amount	
1.	Am. S&L	7-3/4	1/1/85	15,000	
2.	Home S&L	7-1/2	1/1/84	17,000	
3.	1st City Bk	7-1/2	1/1/81	5,000	$ 37,000

D. Credit Union____% $____5,000

F. Government Bonds & Instruments

Type	Rate %	Maturity Date	Current Value
____	____	____	____
____	____	____	____
____	____	____	____
			$_____

F. Bonds—Corporate and Municipals

Name of Company or Municipality	No. of Bonds	Rate %	Maturity Date	Cost	Market Value
Exxon	5	8-1/4	2001	5200	3262
RCA	10	9-1/4	1990	10,020	7875
____	____	____	____	____	____
____	____	____	____	____	$ 11,137

G. Mortgages You Carry $ 10,500

H. Loans Receivable $_____

I. Cash Value of

Insurance Policies (see Worksheet) $ 18,209

TOTAL LOANED DOLLARS $ 99,346 ___(1)

II. WORKING DOLLARS:

A. Stocks and Mutual Funds

No. of Shares	Name of Company	Date of Purchase	Cost	Market Value
300	Am. Elec. Pwr.	1977	7725	4875
400	Gen. Pub. Ut.	1977	8640	2400
300	Gulf States Ut.	1977	4470	2970
400	AT&T	1978	25,890	18,800
200	Safeway	1978	9200	5740
200	Gen. Motors	1977	15,700	9500
300	Exxon	1978	16,080	17,475
			$ 87,615	

Total Market Value $ 61,760 (2)
Pension Funds 189,000
250,760

Real Estate

Home (Market Value Less Mortgage) $ 130,000
$150,000 - $20,000 mtg.
Other Real Estate (Net After Mortgages):

Commercial lot	$ 50,000	
	$_____	
	$_____	
	$_____	$_____

Limited Partnerships:

	$_____	
	$_____	
	$_____	$_____

Total Loaned and
Working Dollars $ 530,106

Financial Objective numbered in order of Importance:

_____ Income now

___2___ Income at retirement

___1___ Maximum tax advantage

_____ Educate children

___3___ Travel

_____ Other _____
                        (specify)

Estimated Gross Income this year	$ 75,000
Estimated taxable income	$ 65,000
Tax Bracket	54 %

Taxable Income last 3 years:

$ 57,123 $ 61,291 $ 63,210

Taxes Paid:

$ 18,268 $ 20,375 $ 21,411

No. of Dependents___1___

Amount you could save each month $_____

Retirement Data:

No. of years before: ___0___ years

Desired monthly income $_____

Possible Sources:

Social Security $_____

Pensions $ have 189,000 in acct.

Investments $_____

Other $_____

Total $_____

Additional needed if retiring today $_____

Anticipated inflation rate per year _____%

Children Educational Cost Data:

Name of Child	Age	Years Before College	Estimated Cost
_____	_____	_____	_____
_____	_____	_____	_____
_____	_____	_____	_____

	Total	_____
Children ages 30 and 32; married, self-sufficient	Amount set aside	_____
	Additional needed	_____

Present Life Insurance, & Annuities Work Sheet
(to complete item I-H)

Company	Type	Face Amount	Cash Value	*Net Insurance	Annual Premium
Group	_____	70,000	0	70,000	---
XYZ	_____	10,000	4025	5975	100
ABC	_____	28,000	14,184	13,816	464
_____	_____	_____	_____	_____	_____
_____	_____	_____	_____	_____	_____
TOTAL		108,000	18,209	89,791	564

* Face Amount less Cash Value = Net Insurance

Disability Insurance

Company	Monthly Coverage	Premium
_____	$_____	$_____

Is taking early retirement and setting up a
consulting practice. He expects to earn as
much or more than he does now.

Certificates of Deposit.   They should reposition the $15,000 and $17,000 certificates due in 1985 and 1984. They could leave the $5000 certificate until it matures and then reposition it.

Corporate Bonds.   Corporate bonds, regardless of the fact that many financial writers advise them for retirement, just won't make it in a world of high inflation and high taxes. They should reposition the proceeds from their bonds. This frees $11,137 to work for them and establishes a $4083 capital loss to be charged off at tax time.

Cash Value of Life Insurance.   Bob's group policy will be carried by his company with reduced coverage. This could be sufficient for Jane's needs, since they already have a living estate of $530,106. If, however, they would like to continue carrying a $50,000 policy, this could be for a ten-year level premium of $21.74 per thousand, or $1107 including policy fee, and a $500 deposit. This would free $18,209 to be put to work while increasing their coverage by $12,000 and only increasing their cost by $45.25 per month. (The $18,209 of cash value invested at only 8 percent would earn $1457 or $121   per month.)

Mortgage Receivable.   This asset is locked in and all they can do is to accept the monthly payment of principal and interest. They sold some land that was appreciating, so in reality they traded an appreciating asset for one that is depreciating in purchasing power.

Stocks.   Again we find a couple who believed the financial writers who advised their readers to invest in high-quality corporate bonds and utility stocks for income at retirement. Don't be lured into this trap, for the same reasons that I pointed out in the Jones case. The Smiths have a quality portfolio of utilities and three "blue chips," only one of which shows a profit.

The Smiths do not enjoy studying and investing in the market, so it was decided that it would be best to put their portfolio under professional management by repositioning these funds. This would release $61,760 and establish a loss of $25,855.

Home.   The Smiths live in a large home in the suburbs. Bob does not want to commute, and Jane and Bob are both tired of yard work. There is a very high-quality high-rise being built near the office complex where Bob will establish his new office. The condominium will cost $120,000 and can be obtained for a 25 percent down payment of $30,000. If they sell their home, which cost them $50,000, they will have a capital gains of $100,000. Under our new law, this gain will not be taxable, because they owned and used their home as their principal residence for over five years, and they are 55 years of age. (Only one of them needed to be to qualify.)

Commercial Lot. The Smiths bought the commercial lot ten years ago for $21,000. They have an offer to sell it for $50,000. They feel the property has matured and that this is the maximum amount they can obtain for several years. They should sell the lot. This will establish a $29,000 long-term capital gain. There should not be any tax due, since they have also established a $29,938 long-term capital loss from the sale of their stocks and bonds.

Pension Fund. Bob will receive $189,000 from his pension upon retirement. He should roll this over into an IRA rollover for all the reasons I have discussed in Chapter 16, "Planning For the Later Years." A convenient program would be to use a mutual fund rollover account or he could split it and put a portion of it into an oil and gas income program using a trust company as the custodian.

Taxes. The Smiths should attempt to lower their taxes using tax-favored investments. A cable television investment that requires an investment of $25,000 over a three-year period could be a consideration. If $10,000 was required for this year and it carried a 200 percent write-off, it would provide them with a write-off of $20,000. This would bring his taxable income down to $45,000.

Several other types of tax-favored investments are also worthy of his consideration. One that carries a small write-off of around 38 percent the first year is marine containers, and it also should produce a generous sheltered income. An oil and gas drilling program would provide a 90 percent write-off, and a cattle feeding program a 100 percent deferral. A private placement of an apartment building could also provide from 100 percent to 150 percent write-off.

Assets to be Repositioned

7,000	Pasadena S&L
15,000	American S&L
17,000	Home S&L
11,137	Bonds
18,209	Cash value of insurance
61,760	Stocks
189,000	Pension Funds
100,000	Home
50,000	Commercial lot
$469,106	
19,777	Tax savings
$488,883	

Repositioning Recommendations

Amount	Investment	Write-Off
$100,000	IRA Rollover—Mutual Fund #1	
89,000	IRA Rollover—Mutual Fund #2	
11,000	Mutual Fund #2	
18,883+	Gold stock mutual fund and add $400 per month	
100,000	Oil & Gas Income Fund	(14,000)
30,000	Down payment on Condo	
50,000	Triple-Net Lease Real Estate Ltd. Pt.	
60,000	Multifamily Housing Ltd. Pt.	(6,000)
10,000	Cable Television	(20,000)
20,000	Marine Containers	(7,600)
$488,883		($47,600)

Tax Results of Repositioning

	Taxable Income	Taxes Due
Before:	$65,000	$22,378
After:	17,400	2,601
Tax Savings		$19,777

Results of Repositioning

1. The rollover of Bob's pension plan (which he must do within 60 days of receipt of the check) will avoid present taxation on the proceeds and allow his investment to compound tax-sheltered. Had he not chosen to do the roll over, his funds would have been diluted by a substantial tax (even with averaging). Since he is now free to move around inside the family of funds without tax consequences, he will want to superimpose a timing device to move in and out of the market without commission or present tax consequences.

I have used two funds for his rollover in order to give him added diversification of stocks *and* diversification of brains. By investing $100,000 in Fund #1 they obtain the $100,000 discount, and by investing $89,000 from the rollover in Fund #2 and $11,000 in an open account, they will qualify for the $100,000 discount on the second $100,000. (Bob will need to leave the $189,000 rollover inside a shelter until he reaches 59½ years of age, 4½ years hence.)

I have placed $18,883 in a mutual fund that invests in South African Gold stocks under a $25,000 Letter of Intent. By adding the $400 a month that they have indicated they can invest, they should be able to add another $5200 in thirteen months, for a total of $24,083, to which they can add $917 or more from their cash flow from their

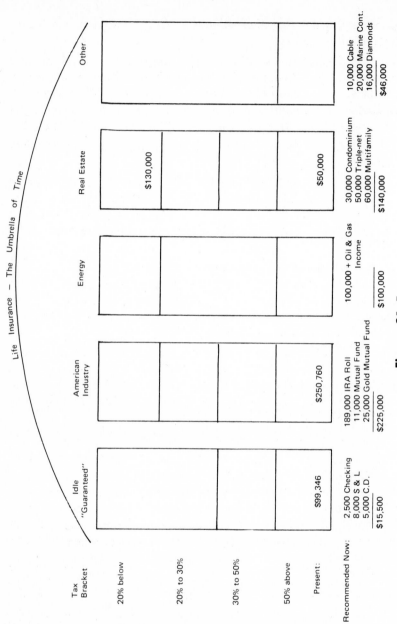

Figure 21–5.

600

limited partnership investment in marine containers, triple-net leases, and multifamily housing.

2. $100,000 in an oil and gas income fund should produce around a $14,000 write-off the first twelve months. If they want income, they can have the distributions sent to them in cash. If they do not, they can have them reinvested. If the cash flow averages 12 percent and if it is reinvested, this could grow to $200,000 in six years (Rule of 72).

3. $30,000 can be used as a down payment on a condominium high-rise.

4. $50,000 could be invested in a triple-net lease registered limited partnership. Instead of having taxable income as in the certificates, they can now hope to receive tax-sheltered income. I haven't shown a write-off, but this could be around $4000, with income of $4000.

5. $60,000 could be invested in multifamily housing. This should provide more growth than the triple-net lease, but I've used both to give added safety and the option for Bob to quit consulting and obtain a higher cash flow. I've only used a write-off of $6000 for both of the real estate limited partnerships.

6. $10,000 could be invested in a cable television limited partnership, with a commitment to invest $10,000 next year and $5000 the following year. Tax-sheltered cash flow is projected by the third year, plus a write-off for three more years after he ceases investing. This should provide a write-off of $20,000 for the year.

7. $20,000 could be invested in marine containers. He should receive a write-off equivalent to around 38 percent the first year of the investment, or $7600.

8. An investment of $16,000 could be considered in investment-grade diamonds.

9. These investments should provide the Smiths with write-offs their first year of around $47,600 and a tax savings of around $19,777.

10. Their taxable income should also be reduced the following years from their write-offs on the cable television, the marine containers, and excess deductions on their multifamily housing. Their cash flow from their oil and gas income programs should be tax-sheltered in comparison to the taxable income they had been receiving on their bonds and certificates.

11. If Bob desires, he can also establish a Keogh plan, since he will be self-employed as a consultant. He can contribute 15 percent of his net earnings. If he earns $50,000 per year, he will be allowed to

contribute $7500 and deduct the amount from his taxable income. Since he is 55 years of age, he only has to wait 4½ years before being eligible to start withdrawing from this account, or if he wishes, he can wait until he is 70½ years of age. Even then, he is allowed to add to his account while he is taking from it and still receive a deduction for his contribution.

12. Their added insurance premiums are incidental and can easily be met from the cash flow from their real estate limited partnership. The remainder of their cash flow can be added to their mutual fund open account.

13. If the Smiths decide they really want to retire, they should have sufficient income after taxes to do so, plus sufficient liquidity in the meantime for travel or emergencies.

Assets at 65.   What will Bob and Jane's assets be at 65? I have no idea. I do know that I will be very disappointed if they have not grown to well in excess of $1 million.

THE DECADE OF THE 'EIGHTIES

What will happen in our economy in the decade of the 'eighties? It is difficult to tell. However, I feel you must accept the fact that changes will occur and often very rapidly. Agility on your part will be the order of each day. Remember that no decision is a decision!

To review what we've already covered you will remember that our world of economic stability changed in 1966 when the Great Society was attempted without paying for it. That is when the Era of Pendulum Economics was launched with the government manipulating the money supply and the printing presses working at full capacity. Remember our example of the pendulum on the grandfather clock. If you are with the pendulum you can fare very well. If you are not, you can be knocked to the floor. To add to this disruption came 1973, when the world as we had known it changed radically. Cheap and abundant energy, capital, raw materials, labor, housing, and food are all things of the past. With OPEC there began a series of events that will bring shortages in not only oil, but also in strategic metals, chemicals, and food supplies. These shortages will change our economic world as we have known it. If free enterprise were allowed some latitude, some of these shortages might be corrected, but they come at a time when government is growing and interference and taxation are at the highest point ever.

These changes need not diminish your wealth and can enhance it if you truly understand the dynamic world in which you are living and finely tune your investments to take advantage of change.

SUMMARY

The first thing you must do to survive is to accept change. Agility continues to be the order of the day. If you are abiding by the "prudent man's rule" of yesteryear, you will lose. The "prudent man's rule" during times of super inflation and high taxation becomes the "stupid man's rule." Do not expect this scenario to change during the decade of the 'eighties. It will not.

For inflation to subside, government spending and costly regulations must be reduced. Neither of these desirable happenings is on the horizon. There will be token speeches made in the halls of Congress about reducing government spending, but the Congressmen do not mean cuts in their own districts. They mean that spending should be reduced in someone else's district. Our greatest need today is for statesmen who are more concerned about the future of America than about re-election. We must fill the void that presently exists in our education system and at least teach personal finance, the rudiments of capitalism, basic economics, and some of the virtues of the free-enterprise system. Only when we educate our people and elect men and women in Congress who understand and love our free-enterprise system will our strangling bureaucracy be diminished and free people be allowed to rise to their highest levels of potential.

My creed, which is also that of some of our leading financial planners, is as follows:

I DO NOT CHOOSE TO BE A COMMON MAN. It is my right to be uncommon—if I can.

I seek opportunity—not security. I do not wish to be a kept citizen, humbled and dulled by having the State look after me. I want to take the calculated risk: to dream and to build, to fail and to succeed.

I refuse to barter incentive for a dole. I prefer the challenges of life to the guaranteed existence and the thrill of fulfillment to the stale calm of Utopia.

I will not trade freedom for beneficence, nor my dignity for a handout. I will never cower before any master, nor bend to any threat. It is my heritage to stand erect, proud and unafraid; to think and act for myself; to enjoy the benefits of my creations; and to face the world boldly and say, "This, I have done."

As you lay down this book and go forth to implement your plan, remember that the world can be your oyster. All you'll need to do is approach it with enthusiasm, intelligence, a willingness to change, and true gusto. If you implement what you have learned, you should have the financial means by which to live the good life, enjoy the beautiful world around you, and someday be able to retire in financial dignity.

If you accomplish this worthy predetermined goal you will say, "It was good that Venita passed my way." God bless!

GLOSSARY
OF INVESTING

ACCRUED INTEREST Interest accrued on a bond since the last interest payment was made. The buyer of the bond pays the market price plus accrued interest.

ACCUMULATION PLAN A plan for the systematic accumulation of mutual fund shares through periodic investments and reinvestments of income dividends and capital gains distributions.

AGENT One who acts for another. The broker/dealer acts as an agent when he buys or sells for the account of someone other than himself.

AMORTIZATION Accounting for expenses or charges as applicable rather than as paid. Includes such practices as depreciation, depletion, write-off of intangibles, prepaid expenses, and deferred charges.

ANNUAL REPORT The formal financial statement issued yearly by a corporation. The annual report shows assets, liabilities, earnings, standing of the company at the close of the business year, performance of the company profit-wise during the year, and other information of interest to shareowners.

ARBITRAGE Dealing in differences. Example: buying on one exchange while simultaneously selling short on another at a higher price.

ASKED PRICE The price asked for a security offered for sale. Quoted, bid, and asked prices are wholesale prices for interdealer trading, and do not represent prices to the public.

ASSET On a balance sheet, that which is owned or receivable.

AUCTION MARKET Dealings on a securities exchange where a two-way auction is continuously in effect.

AUTHORIZED STOCK The total number of shares of stock authorized for issue by a company's shareholders.

AVERAGES Various ways of measuring the trend of stocks listed on exchanges. Formulas, some very elaborate, have been devised to compensate for stock splits and stock dividends and thus give continuity to the average. In the case of the Dow-Jones Industrial Average, the prices of the 30 stocks are totaled and then divided by a figure that is intended to compensate for past stock splits and stock dividends and that is changed from time to time.

BALANCE SHEET A condensed financial statement showing the nature and amount of a company's assets, liabilities, and capital on a given date. The balance sheet shows in dollar amounts what the company owned, what it owed, and its stockholders' ownership in the company.

BALANCED FUND A mutual fund that is required to keep a specified percentage of its total assets invested in senior securities.

BEAR One who believes the stock market will decline.

BEAR MARKET A declining stock market.

BEARER BOND A bond that does not have the owner's name registered on the books of the issuing company and that is payable to the holder.

BID AND ASKED Often referred to as a *quotation* or *quote*. The bid is the highest price anyone has declared that he wants to pay for a security at a given time; the asked is the lowest price anyone will take at the same time.

BIG BOARD   A popular term for the New York Stock Exchange, Inc.

BLOCK   A large holding or transaction of stock, popularly considered to be 10,000 shares or more.

BLUE CHIP   A company known nationally for the quality and wide acceptance of its products or services, and for its ability to make money and pay dividends.

BLUE SKY LAWS   A popular name for laws enacted by various states to protect the public against securities frauds. The term is believed to have originated when a judge ruled that a particular stock had about the same value as a patch of blue sky.

BOND   Basically an IOU or promissory note of a corporation, usually issued in multiples of $1000. A bond is evidence of a debt on which the issuing company usually promises to pay the bondholders a specified amount of interest for a specified length of time, and to repay the loan on the expiration date. In every case, a bond represents debt—its holder is a creditor of the corporation and not a part owner, as is the shareholder.

BOND FUND   A mutual fund invested completely in bonds.

BOOK VALUE   An accounting term for the value of a stock determined from a company's records by adding all assets and then deducting all debts and other liabilities, plus the liquidation price of any preferred issues. The sum arrived at is divided by the number of common shares outstanding, and the result is book value per common share. Book value of the assets of a company or a security may have little or no significant relationship to market value.

BROKER   An agent who handles the public's orders to buy and sell securities, commodities, or other property. A commission is charged for this service.

BULL   One who believes the stock market will rise.

BULL MARKET   An advancing stock market.

BUSINESS CYCLE   The long-term boom–recession cycle that has been characteristic of business conditions not only nationally, but on a worldwide basis.

CALL   An option to buy a specified number of shares of a certain security at a definite price within a specified period of time.

CALLABLE   A bond issue, all or part of which may be redeemed by the issuing corporation under definite conditions before maturity. The term also applies to preferred shares, which may be redeemed by the issuing corporation.

CAPITAL GAIN or CAPITAL LOSS   Profit or loss from the sale of a capital asset. A capital gain, under current federal income tax laws, may be either short-term (six months or less) or long-term (more than six months). A short-term capital gain is taxed at the reporting individual's full income tax rate. A long-term capital gain is subject to a lower tax.

CAPITAL MARKET   The market that deals in long-term securities issues of both debt and equity.

CAPITAL SHARES   When referring to a dual- or leveraged-type closed-end investment company, those shares to which all gains or losses accrue and which have no claim on dividends.

CAPITAL STOCK   All shares representing ownership of a business, including preferred and common.

CAPITALIZATION   Total amount of the various securities issued by a corporation. Capitalization may include bonds, debentures, preferred and common stock, and surplus.

CERTIFICATE   The actual piece of paper that is evidence of ownership of stock in a corporation. Loss of a certificate may cause, at least, a great deal of inconvenience; at worst, financial loss.

CLOSED-END INVESTMENT COMPANY.   An investment company that issues a fixed number of shares and does not redeem them. It may also issue senior securities and/or warrants.

COLLATERAL   Securities or other property pledged by a borrower to secure repayment of a loan.

COMMISSION   The broker's basic fee for purchasing or selling securities or property as an agent.

COMMON STOCK   Securities that represent an ownership interest in a corporation. If the company has also issued preferred stock, both common and preferred have ownership rights. Claims of both common and preferred stockholders are junior to claims of bondholders or other creditors of the company. Common stockholders assume the greater risk, but generally they also exercise the greater control and may gain the greater reward in the form of dividends and capital appreciation.

COMMON STOCK FUND   A mutual fund that has a stated policy of investing all of its assets in common stocks. The term is also applied to funds that normally invest only in common stocks, though are not restricted to them by charter.

CONFIRMATION   A written description of the terms of a transaction in securities supplied by a broker/dealer to his customer or to another broker/dealer.

CONGLOMERATE   A corporation that has diversified its operations, usually by acquiring enterprises in widely varied industries.

CONSTRUCTIVE RECEIPT   A doctrine of the Internal Revenue Service that requires the reporting of income (including capital gains) in the year in which it could have been received had the taxpayer so wished. Thus, dividends of a mutual fund automatically reinvested are taxable in the year in which reinvested on the basis that the taxpayer could have received them by check and then reinvested them or not at his option.

CONVERTIBLE   A bond, debenture, or preferred share that may be exchanged by the owner for common stock or another security, usually of the same company, in accordance with the terms of the issue.

CORPORATE BOND   An evidence of indebtedness issued by a corporation, rather than by the U.S. government or a municipality.

CORPORATION   An organization chartered by a state government. When the term is used without qualification, it generally refers to an organization carrying on a business for profit. However, there are nonprofit corporations and municipalities, which differ from corporations organized for profit in that they do not issue stock.

COUPON BOND   Bond with interest coupons attached. The coupons are clipped as they come due and are presented by the holder for payment of interest.

CUMULATIVE PREFERRED   A stock with a provision that if one or more dividends are omitted, the omitted dividends must be paid before dividends may be paid on the company's common stock.

CUMULATIVE VOTING   A type of shareholder voting in which the number of shares held is multiplied by the number of directors to be elected to determine the number of votes a shareholder may cast. He may cast all votes for one director or may allocate them in any way he sees fit.

CURRENT ASSETS   Those assets of a company that are reasonably expected to be realized in cash, or sold, or consumed during the normal operating cycle of the business.

CURRENT LIABILITIES   Money owed and payable by a company, usually within one year.

CUSTODIAN   The corporation, usually a bank, charged with the safekeeping of an investment company's portfolio securities.

DEALER   An individual or firm in the securities business acting as a principal rather than as an agent. Typically, a dealer buys for his own account and sells to a customer from his own inventory. The dealer's profit or loss is the difference between the price he pays and the price he receives for the same security. The dealer's confirmation must disclose to his customer that he has acted as principal. The same individual or firm may function, at different times, as either a broker or dealer.

DEBENTURE   A promissory note backed by the general credit of a company and usually not secured by a mortgage or lien on any specific property.

DEPLETION   Natural resources, such as metals, oils and gas, and timber that conceivably can be reduced to zero over the years, present a special problem in capital management. Depletion is an accounting practice consisting of charges against earnings based upon the amount of the asset taken out of the total reserves in the period for which accounting is made. A bookkeeping entry, it does not represent any cash outlay, nor are any funds earmarked for the purpose.

DEPRECIATION   Normally, charges against earnings to write off the cost, less salvage value, of an asset over its estimated useful life. A bookkeeping entry, it does not represent any cash outlay, nor are any funds earmarked for the purpose.

DIRECTOR   A person elected by shareholders to establish company policies. The directors elect the president, vice president, and all other operating officers. Directors decide, among other matters, if and when dividends will be paid.

DISCOUNT   The amount by which a preferred stock or bond may sell below its par value.

DISCRETIONARY ACCOUNT   An account in which the customer gives the broker or someone else discretion, either complete or within specific limits, as to the purchase and sale of securities or commodities, including selection, timing, amount, and price to be paid or received.

DIVERSIFICATION   Spreading investments among different companies in different fields. Another type of diversification is also offered by the securities of many individual companies because of the wide range of their activities.

DIVERSIFIED INVESTMENT COMPANY   An investment company which, under the Investment Company Act of 1940, must invest 75 percent of its total assets so that not more than 5 percent of total assets are invested in the securities of any one issuer. Also, the company may not own more than 10 percent of the voting securities of any one issuer.

DIVIDEND   The payment designated by the board of directors to be distributed pro rata among the shares outstanding. On preferred shares, it is generally a fixed amount. On common shares, the dividend varies with the fortunes of the company and the amount of cash on hand, and it may be omitted if business is poor or the directors determine to withhold earnings to invest in plant and equipment. Sometimes a company will pay a dividend out of past earnings even if it is not currently operating at a profit.

DIVIDEND REINVESTMENT PLAN   A mutual fund share account in which dividends are automatically reinvested in additional shares. With this type of account, capital gains distributions are also automatically reinvested. Dividends (but not capital gains) may be invested at offering price (i.e., with a sales charge), but are more commonly reinvested at asset value.

DOLLAR-COST-AVERAGING   A system of buying securities at regular intervals with a fixed dollar amount. Under this system the investor buys by the dollars' worth rather than by the number of shares. If each investment is of the same number of dollars, payments buy more when the price is low and fewer when it rises. Temporary downswings in price thus benefit the investor if he continues to make periodic purchases in both good times and bad, and the price at which the shares are sold is more than their average cost.

DOUBLE TAXATION   The federal government taxes corporate profits once as corporate income; any part of the remaining profits distributed as dividends to stockholders may be taxed again as income to the recipient stockholder.

DOW JONES AVERAGE   Widely quoted stock averages computed regularly. They include an industrial stock average, a rail average, a utility average, and a combination of the three.

DOW THEORY   A theory of market analysis based upon the performance of the Dow-Jones industrial and transportation stock price averages. The theory says that the market is in a basic upward trend if one of these averages advances above a previous important high, accompanied or followed by a similar advance in the other. A dip in both averages below previous important lows is regarded as confirmation of a basic downward trend. The theory does not attempt to predict how long either trend will continue, although it is widely misinterpreted as a method of forecasting future action.

DUAL FUND   A closed-end investment company with two classes of shares: income and capital-outstanding. Also designated as a *leveraged fund.*

EQUITY   The ownership interest of common and preferred stockholders in a company. Also refers to excess of value of securities over the debit balance in a margin account. Also, the value of a property which remains after all liens and other charges against the property are paid. A property owner's equity generally consists of his or her monetary interest in the property in excess of the mortgage indebtedness. In the case of a long-term mortgage, the owner's equity builds up quite gradually during the first several years because the bulk of each monthly payment is applied, not to the principal amount of the loan, but to the interest.

EX-DIVIDEND   A synonym for "without dividend." The buyer of a stock selling ex-dividend does not receive the recently declared dividend. Every dividend is payable on a fixed date to all shareholders recorded on the books of the company as of a previous date of record. For example, a dividend may be declared as payable to holders of record on the books of the company on a given Friday. Since five business days are allowed for delivery of stock in a "regular way" transaction on the stock exchange, the exchange would declare the stock "ex-dividend" as of the opening of the market on the preceding Monday. That means anyone who bought it on or after Monday would not be entitled to that dividend. When stocks go ex-dividend, the stock tables include the symbol "x" following the name.

EX-RIGHTS   Without the rights. Corporations raising additional money may do so by offering their stockholders the right to subscribe to new or additional stock, usually at a discount from the prevailing market price. The buyer of a stock selling ex-rights is not entitled to the rights.

EXTRA The short form of "extra dividend." A dividend in the form of stock or cash in addition to the regular or usual dividend the company has been paying.

FACE VALUE The value of a bond that appears on the face of the bond, unless the value is otherwise specified by the issuing company. Face value is ordinarily the amount the issuing company promises to pay at maturity. Face value is not an indication of market value. It is sometimes referred to as par value.

FIDUCIARY One who acts for another in financial matters.

FLOOR The huge trading area of a stock exchange where stocks and bonds are bought and sold.

FLOOR BROKER A member of the stock exchange who executes orders on the floor of the exchange to buy or sell any listed securities.

FULLY MANAGED FUND A mutual fund whose investment policy gives its management complete flexibility as to the types of investments made and the proportions of each. Management is restricted only to the extent that federal or blue sky laws require.

GILT-EDGED High-grade bond issued by a company that has demonstrated its ability to earn a comfortable profit over a period of years and pay its bondholders their interest without interruption.

GOOD DELIVERY Certain basic qualifications must be met before a security sold on the exchange may be delivered. The security must be in proper form to comply with the contract of sale and to transfer title to the purchaser.

GOOD 'TIL CANCELLED ORDER (GTC) OR OPEN ORDER An order to buy or sell that remains in effect until it is either executed or cancelled.

GOVERNMENT BONDS Obligations of the U.S. government, regarded as the highest grade issues in existence.

GROWTH FUND A fund whose rate of growth over a period of time is considerably greater than that of business generally. An average rate of 10 percent per year is used by some analysts as definitive.

GROWTH STOCK Stock of a company with a record of relatively rapid growth in earnings.

HOLDING COMPANY A corporation that owns the securities of another, in most cases with voting control.

INCOME FUND A mutual fund with a primary objective of current income.

INDENTURE A written agreement under which bonds and debentures are issued, setting forth maturity date, interest rate, and other terms.

INSTITUTION An organization holding substantial investing assets, often for others. Includes banks, insurance companies, investment companies, and pension funds.

INTEREST   Payments made by a borrower to a lender for the use of his money. A corporation pays interest on its bonds to its bondholders.

INVESTMENT   The use of money for the purpose of making more money: to gain income or increase capital or both.

INVESTMENT BANKER   Also known as an *underwriter*. The middleman between the corporation issuing new securities and the public. The usual practice is for one or more investment bankers to buy outright from a corporation a new issue of stocks or bonds. The group forms a syndicate to sell the securities to individuals and institutions. Investment bankers also distribute very large blocks of stocks or bonds (perhaps held by an estate).

INVESTMENT COMPANY   A company or trust that uses its capital to invest in other companies. There are two principal types: the closed-end and the open-end, or mutual fund. Shares in closed-end investment companies are readily transferable in the open market and are bought and sold like other shares. Capitalization of these companies remains the same unless action is taken to change, which seldom occurs. Open-end funds sell their own new shares to investors, stand ready to buy back their old shares, and are not listed. Open-end funds are so named because their capitalization is not fixed; they issue more shares as people want them.

INVESTMENT COMPANY ACT OF 1940   An act passed by the Congress for the specific purpose of empowering the SEC to regulate investment companies.

INVESTMENT COUNSEL   One whose principal business consists of acting as investment adviser, and a substantial part of whose business consists of rendering investment supervisory services.

INVESTOR   An individual whose principal concerns in the purchase of a security are regular dividend income, safety of the original investment, and, if possible, capital appreciation.

ISSUE   Any of a company's securities, or the act of distributing such securities. Upon the death of a joint tenant, his interest passes, not to his heirs, but to his co-owner.

LEGAL LIST   A list of investments selected by various states in which certain institutions and fiduciaries, such as insurance companies and banks, may invest. Legal lists are often restricted to high-quality securities and, if possible, capital appreciation.

LEVERAGE   The effect on the per-share earnings of the common stock of a company when large sums must be paid for bond interest or preferred stock dividends or both before the common stock is entitled to share in earnings. Leverage may be advantageous for the common stock when earnings are good, but may work against the common stock when earnings decline. Leverage also refers to mortgage funds used in financing of real estate and oil limited partnerships.

LIABILITIES   All the claims against a corporation. Liabilities include accounts and wages and salaries payable, dividends declared payable, accrued taxes payable, fixed or long-term liabilities such as mortgage bonds, debentures, and bank loans.

LIEN   A claim against property that has been pledged or mortgaged to secure the performance of an obligation. A bond may be secured by a lien against specified property of a company.

LIMITED ORDER   An order to buy or sell a stated amount of a security at a specified price, or at a better price.

LIQUIDATING VALUE   When referring to the shares of an open-end investment company, the value at redemption. Usually the net asset value.

LIQUIDATION   The process of converting securities or other property into cash. The dissolution of a company, with cash remaining after sale of its assets and payment of all indebtedness being distributed to the shareholders.

LIQUIDITY   The ability of the market in a particular security to absorb a reasonable amount of buying or selling at reasonable price changes. Liquidity is one of the most important characteristics of a good market.

LISTED STOCK   The stock of a company that is traded on a securities exchange.

LOCKED IN   An investor is said to be locked in when he has a profit on a security he owns, but does not sell because his profit would immediately become subject to the capital gains tax.

MANAGEMENT   The board of directors, elected by the stockholders, and the officers of the corporation, appointed by the board of directors.

MANAGEMENT FEE   The fee paid to the investment manager of a mutual fund. It is usually about one-half of one percent of average net assets annually. Not to be confused with the sales charge, which is the one-time commission paid at the time of purchase as a part of the offering price.

MANIPULATION   An illegal operation. Buying or selling a security for the purpose of creating false or misleading appearance of active trading or for the purpose of raising or depressing the price to induce purchase or sale by others.

MARGIN   The amount paid by the customer when he uses his broker's credit to buy a security.

MARGIN CALL   A demand upon a customer to put up money or securities with the broker. The call is made when a purchase is made or when a customer's equity in a margin account declines below a minimum standard set by the exchange or by the firm.

MARKET ORDER   An order to buy or sell a stated amount of a security at the most advantageous price obtainable.

MARKET PRICE   In the case of a security, market price is usually considered the last reported price at which the stock or bond sold.

MATURITY   The date on which a loan or a bond or a debenture comes due and is to be paid off.

MEMBER FIRM   A securities brokerage firm organized as a partnership or corporation and owning at least one seat on the exchange.

MORTGAGE BOND   A bond secured by a mortgage on a property. The value of the property may or may not equal the value of the so-called mortgage bonds issued against it.

MUNICIPAL BOND   A bond issued by a state or a political subdivision, such as a county, city, town, or village. The term also designates bonds issued by state agencies and authorities. In general, interest paid on municipal bonds is exempt from federal income taxes and from state and local income taxes within the state of issue.

MUTUAL FUND   An open-end investment company that continuously offers new shares to the public in addition to redeeming shares on demand as required by law. While in common use, the term mutual fund has no meaning in law.

NASD   The National Association of Securities Dealers, Inc. An association of brokers and dealers in the over-the-counter securities business. The Association has the power to expel members who have been declared guilty of unethical practices. NASD is dedicated to, among other objectives, "adopt, administer and enforce rules of fair practice and rules to prevent fraudulent and manipulative acts and practices, and in general to promote just and equitable principles of trade for the protection of investors.

NASDAQ   An acronym for National Association of Securities Dealers Automated Quotations. An automated information network that provides brokers and dealers with price quotations on securities traded over the counter.

NEGOTIABLE   Refers to a security, title to which is transferable by delivery.

NET ASSET VALUE   A term usually used in connection with investment companies, meaning net asset value per share. It is common practice for an investment company to compute its assets daily by totaling the market value of all securities owned. All liabilities are deducted, and the balance is divided by the number of shares outstanding. The resulting figure is the net asset value per share.

NET CHANGE   The change in the price of a security from the closing price on one day to the closing price on the following day on which the stock is traded. The net change is ordinarily the last figure on the stock price list. The mark +2⅛ means up $2.125 a share from the last sale on the previous day the stock traded.

NEW ISSUE   A stock or bond sold by a corporation for the first time. Proceeds may be issued to retire outstanding securities of the company, for new plant or equipment, or for additional working capital.

NONCUMULATIVE   A preferred stock on which unpaid dividends do not accrue. Omitted dividends are, as a rule, gone forever.

NYSE COMMON STOCK INDEX   A composite index covering price movements of all common stocks listed on the "Big Board." It is based on the close of the market December 31, 1965, as 50.00 and is weighted according to the number of shares listed for each issue. The index is computed continuously and printed on the ticker tape each half hour. Point changes in the index are converted to dollars and cents to provide a meaningful measure of changes in the average price of listed stocks.

ODD LOT   An amount of stock less than the established 100-share unit or 10-share unit of trading: from 1 to 99 shares for the great majority of issues, 1 to 9 for so-called inactive stocks. Odd-lot prices are geared to the auction market. On an odd-lot market order, the odd-lot dealer's price is based on the first round-lot transaction that occurs on the floor following receipt at the trading post of the odd-lot order. The differential between the odd-lot price and the "effective" round-lot price is 12½ cents a share. For example: You decide to buy 20 shares of ABC common at the market. Your order is transmitted by your commission broker to the representative of an odd-lot dealer at the post where ABC is traded. A few minutes later there is a 100-share transaction in ABC at $10 a share. The odd-lot price at which your order is immediately filled by the odd-lot dealer is $10.125 a share. If you had sold 20 shares of ABC, you would have received $9.875 a share.

OFFER   The price at which a person is ready to sell. Opposite of bid, the price at which one is ready to buy.

OPEN ACCOUNT   When referring to a mutual fund, a type of account in which the investor may add or withdraw shares at any time. In such an account, dividends may be paid in cash or reinvested at the account holder's option.

OPEN-END INVESTMENT COMPANY   By definition under the 1940 Act, an investment company that has outstanding redeemable shares. Also generally applied to those investment companies which continuously offer new shares to the public and stand ready at any time to redeem their outstanding shares.

OPTION   A right to buy or sell specific securities or properties at a specified price within a specified time.

OVERBOUGHT   An opinion as to price levels. May refer to a security that has had a sharp rise or to the market as a whole after a period of vigorous buying which, it may be argued, has left prices "too high."

OVERSOLD   An opinion, the reverse of overbought. A single security or a market that, it is believed, has declined to an unreasonable level.

OVER-THE-COUNTER   A market for securities made up of securities dealers who may or may not be members of a securities exchange. Over-the-counter is mainly a market made over the telephone. Thousands of companies have insufficient shares outstanding, stockholders, or earnings to warrant application for listing on an exchange. Securities of these companies are traded in the over-the-counter market between dealers who act either as principals or as brokers for customers.

PAPER PROFIT   An unrealized profit on a security still held. Paper profits become realized profits only when the security is sold.

PAR   In the case of a common share, par means a dollar amount assigned to the share by the company's charter. Par value may also be used to compute the dollar amount of the common shares on the balance sheet. Par value has little significance so far as market value of common stock is concerned.

PENNY STOCKS   Low-priced issues, often highly speculative, selling at less than $1 a share. Frequently used as a term of disparagement, although a few penny stocks have developed into investment-caliber issues.

POINT   In the case of shares of stock, a point means $1. If ABC shares rise three points, each share has risen $3. In the case of bonds, a point means $10, since a bond is quoted as a percentage of $1000. A bond that rises three points gains 3 percent of $1000, or $30 in value. An advance from 87 to 90 would mean an advance in dollar value from $870 to $900 for each $1000 bond. In the case of market averages, the word point means merely that and no more. If, for example, the Dow-Jones Industrial Average rises from 870.25 to 871.25, it has risen a point. A point in this average, however, is not equivalent to $1.

PORTFOLIO   Holdings of securities by an individual or institution. A portfolio may contain bonds, preferred stocks, and common stocks of various types of enterprises.

PREFERRED STOCK   A class of stock with a claim on the company's earnings before payment may be made on the common stock and usually entitled to priority over common stock if the company liquidates. Usually entitled to dividends at a specified rate, when declared by the board of directors and before payment of a dividend on the common stock, depending upon the terms of the issue.

PREMIUM   The amount by which a preferred stock or bond may sell above its par value. In the case of a new issue of bonds or stocks, premium is the amount the market price rises over the original selling price.

PRICE–EARNINGS RATIO   The price of a share of stock divided by earnings per share for a 12-month period. For example, a stock selling for $100 a share and earning $5 a share is said to be selling at a price–earnings ratio of 20 to 1.

PRIMARY DISTRIBUTION   Also called *primary offering*. The original sale of a company's securities.

PRINCIPAL   The person for whom a broker executes an order, or a dealer buying or selling for his own account. The term "principal" may also refer to a person's capital or to the face amount of a bond.

PROFIT-TAKING   Selling stock that has appreciated in value since purchase to realize the profit that has been made possible. The term is often used to explain a downturn in the market following a period of rising prices.

PROSPECTUS   The document that offers a new issue of securities to the public. It is required under the Securities Act of 1933.

PROXY   Written authorization given by a shareholder to someone else to represent him and vote his shares at a shareholders' meeting.

PROXY STATEMENT   Information required by the SEC to be given to stockholders as a prerequisite to solicitation of proxies for a security subject to the requirements of Securities Exchange Act.

PRUDENT MAN RULE   An investment standard. In some states, the law requires that a fiduciary, such as a trustee, may invest the fund's money only in a list of securities designated by the state—the so-called legal list. In other states, the trustee may invest in a security if it is one that a prudent man of discretion and intelligence, who is seeking a reasonable income and preservation of capital, would buy.

PUT   An option to sell a specified number of shares at a definite price within a specified period of time. The opposite of a call.

QUOTATION   Often shortened to *quote*. The highest bid to buy and the lowest offer to sell a security in a given market at a given time. If you ask your broker for a quote on a stock, he may come back with something like "45¼ to 45½". This means that $45.25 is the highest price any buyer wanted to pay at the time the quote was given on the floor of the exchange, and that $45.50 was the lowest price any seller would take at the same time.

RALLY   A brisk rise following a decline in the general price level of the market, or in an individual stock.

RECORD DATE   The date on which you must be registered as a shareholder on the stock book of a company to receive a declared dividend or, among other things, to vote on company affairs.

RED HERRING   A preliminary prospectus used to obtain indications of interest from prospective buyers of a new issue.

REDEMPTION PRICE   The price at which a bond may be redeemed before maturity, at the option of the issusing company. Redemption value also applies to the price an open-end investment company must pay to call in certain types of preferred stock. It is usually the net asset value per share—it fluctuates with the value of the company's investment portfolio.

REGISTERED BOND   A bond that is registered on the books of the issuing company in the name of the owner. It can be transferred only when endorsed by the registered owner.

REGISTERED REPRESENTATIVE A full-time employee who has met the requirements of an exchange as to background and knowledge of the securities business. Also known as an *account exchange* or *customer's broker*.

REGISTRAR Usually a trust company or bank charged with the responsibility of preventing the issuance of more stock than authorized by a company.

REGISTRATION Before a public offering may be made of new securities by a company, or of outstanding securities by controlling stockholders, through the mails or in interstate commerce, the securities must be registered under the Securities Act of 1933. Registration statement is filed with the SEC by the issuer. It must disclose pertinent information relating to the company's operations, securities, management, and purpose of the public offering. On security offerings involving less than $300,000, less information is required.

Before a security may be admitted to dealings on a national securities exchange, it must be registered under the Securities Exchange Act of 1934. The application for registration must be filed with the exchange and the SEC by the company issuing the securities. It must disclose pertinent information relating to the company's operations, securities, and management.

REGULATION T The federal regulation governing the amount of credit that may be advanced by brokers and dealers to customers for the purchase of securities.

REGULATION U The federal regulation governing the amount of credit that may be advanced by a bank to its customers for the purchase of listed stocks.

REIT Real estate investment trust, an organization similar to an investment company in some respects, but concentrating its holdings in real estate investments. The yield is generally liberal, since REITs are requested to distribute as much as 90 percent of their income.

RETURN Another term for *yield*.

RIGHTS When a company wants to raise more funds by issuing additional securities, it may give its stockholders the opportunity, ahead of others, to buy the new securities in proportion to the number of shares each owns. The piece of paper evidencing this privilege is called a right. Because the additional stock is usually offered to stockholders below the current market price, rights ordinarily have a market value of their own and are actively traded. In most cases they must be exercised within a relatively short period. Failure to exercise or sell rights may result in actual loss to the holder.

ROUND LOT A unit of trading or a multiple thereof. On most exchanges the unit of trading is 100 shares in the case of stocks and $1000 par value in the case of bonds. In some inactive stocks, the unit of trading is 10 shares.

SEAT   A traditional figure of speech for a membership on an exchange. Price and admission requirements vary.

SEC   Securities and Exchange Commission, established by Congress to help protect investors. The SEC administers the Securities Act of 1933, the Securities Exchange Act of 1934, the Trust Indenture Act, the Investment Company Act, the Investment Advisers Act, and the Public Utility Holding Company Act.

SECONDARY DISTRIBUTION   Also known as a *secondary offering*. The redistribution of a block of stock some time after it has been sold by the issuing company. The sale is handled off the exchange by a securities firm or group of firms, and the shares are usually offered at a fixed price that is related to the current market price of the stock. Usually the block is a large one, such as might be involved in the settlement of an estate. The security may be listed or unlisted.

SINKING FUND   Money regularly set aside by a company to redeem its bonds, debentures, or preferred stock from time to time as specified in the indenture or charter.

SPECIAL OFFERING   Occasionally a large block of stock becomes available for sale that, due to its size and the market in that particular issue, calls for special handling. A notice is printed on the ticker tape announcing that the stock will be offered for sale on the floor of the exchange at a fixed price. Member firms may buy this stock for customers directly from the seller's broker during trading hours. The price is usually based on the last transaction in the regular auction market. If there are more buyers than stock, allotments are made. Only the seller pays a commission on a special offering.

SPECIALIST   A member of an exchange who has two functions. The first is to maintain an orderly market, insofar as reasonably practicable, in the stocks in which he is registered as a specialist. The exchange expects the specialist to buy or sell for his own account, to a reasonable degree, when there is a temporary disparity between supply and demand. The specialist also acts as a broker's broker. When a commission broker on the exchange floor receives a limit order, say, to buy at $50 a stock then selling at $60, he cannot wait at the post where the stock is traded to see if the price reaches the specified level. So he leaves the order with the specialist, who will try to execute it in the market if and when the stock declines to the specified price. The specialist must put his customers' interests above his own at all times.

SPECULATOR   One who is willing to assume a relatively large risk in the hope of gain. His principal concern is to increase his capital rather than his dividend income. The speculator may buy and sell the same day or speculate in an enterprise he does not expect to be profitable for years.

SPLIT   The division of the outstanding shares of a corporation into a larger number of shares. A 3-for-1 split by a company with 1 million shares outstanding results in 3 million shares outstanding. Each holder of 100 shares before the 3-to-1 split would have 300 shares, although his proportionate equity in the company would remain the same; 100 parts of 1 million are the equivalent of 300 parts of 3 million.

SPREAD   The difference between the bid price and the offering price. Also, the combination of a put and a call "points away" from the market.

STATEMENT OF POLICY   The SEC's statement of its own position as to those things considered "materially misleading" in the offer of shares of open-end investment companies.

STOCK   Ownership shares of a corporation.

STOCK CERTIFICATE   A certificate that provides physical evidence of stock ownership.

STOCK EXCHANGE   An organization registered under the Securities Exchange Act of 1934 with physical facilities for the buying and selling of securities in a two-way auction.

STOCK DIVIDEND   A dividend paid in securities rather than cash. The dividend may be additional shares of the issuing company or shares of another company (usually a subsidiary) held by the issuing company.

STOCK POWER   An assignment and power of substitution separate from a stock certificate authorizing transfer of the stock on the books of the corporation.

STOCKHOLDER OF RECORD   A stockholder whose name is registered on the books of the issuing corporation.

STOP ORDER   An order to buy at a price above or to sell below the current market. Stop buy orders are generally used to limit loss or protect unrealized profits on a short sale. Stop sell orders are generally used to protect unrealized profits or limit loss on a holding.

STREET NAME   Securities held in the name of a broker instead of his customer's name are said to be carried in a street name. This occurs when the securities have been bought on margin or when the customer wishes the security to be held by the broker.

SUITABILITY RULE   The rule of fair practice that requires a member to have reasonable grounds for believing that a recommendation to a customer is suitable on the basis of his financial objectives and abilities.

TENANTS IN COMMON   A form of registration of property, frequently used with securities. An undivided estate in property where, upon the death of the owner, the undivided estate becomes the property of his heirs or divisees and and not of his surviving co-owner.

TENANTS BY THE ENTIRETY   A form of registration of property, usually real estate.

TIPS   Supposedly "inside" information on corporation affairs.

TRADER   One who buys and sells for his own account for short-term profit.

TRANSFER   This term may refer to two different operations. For one, the delivery of a stock certificate from the seller's broker to the buyer's broker and legal change of ownership, normally accomplished within a few days. For another, to record the change of ownership on the books of the corporation by the transfer agent. When the purchaser's name is recorded on the books of the company, dividends, notices of meetings, proxies, financial reports, and all pertinent literature sent by the issuer to its securities holders are mailed directly to the new owner.

TRANSFER AGENT   One who keeps a record of the name of each registered shareowner, his or her address, and the number of shares owned, and sees that certificates presented to his office for transfer are properly cancelled and that new certificates are issued in the name of the transferee.

TREASURY BILL   Short-term U.S. Government paper with no stated interest rate. It is sold at a discount in competitive bidding and reaches maturity in 90 days or less.

TREASURY BOND   U.S. government bonds issued in $1000 units with maturity of five years or longer. They are traded on the market like other bonds.

TREASURY NOTE   U.S. government paper, not legally restricted as to interest rates, with maturities from one to five years.

TREASURY STOCK   Stock issued by a company but later reacquired. It may be held in the company's treasury indefinitely, reissued to the public, or retired. Treasury stock receives no dividends and has no vote while held by the company.

UNDERWRITER'S FEE   In the sale of mutual funds shares, the difference between the total sales charge and the underwriter's reallowance to the dealer.

UNLISTED   A security not listed on a stock exchange.

VOTING RIGHT   The stockholder's right to vote his stock in the affairs of his company. Most common shares have one vote each. Preferred stock usually has the right to vote when preferred dividends are in default for a specified period. The right to vote may be delegated by the stockholder to another person.

WARRANT   A certificate giving the holder the right to purchase securities at a stipulated price within a specified time limit or perpetually. Sometimes a warrant is offered with securities as an inducement to buy.

WHEN ISSUED   A short form of "when, as, and if issued." The term indicates a conditional transaction in a security authorized for issuance but not yet actually issued. All "when issued" transactions are on an "if" basis, to be settled if and when the actual security is issued and the exchange or National Association of Securities Dealers rules that the transactions are to be settled.

WITHDRAWAL PLAN   A mutual fund plan that permits monthly or quarterly withdrawal of specified dollar amounts, usually involving the invasion of principal. Alternately, a plan may permit varying withdrawals based on the liquidation of a fixed number of shares monthly or quarterly.

WORKING CONTROL   Theoretically, ownership of 51 percent of a company's voting stock is necessary to exercise control. In practice—and this is particularly true in the case of a large corporation—effective control sometimes can be exerted through ownership, individually or by a group acting in concert, of less than 50 percent.

YIELD   Also known as *return*. The dividends or interest paid by a company expressed as a percentage of the current price. A stock with a current market value of $20 a share that has paid $1 in dividends in the preceding 12 months is said to return 5 percent ($1.00/$20.00). The current return on a bond is figured the same way.

APPENDIX

TABLE 1. $10,000 LUMP SUM AT VARYING RATES COMPOUNDED ANNUALLY—END OF YEAR VALUES

	5th Yr.	10th Yr.	15th Yr.	20th Yr.	25th Yr.	30th Yr.	35th Yr.	40th Yr.
1%	10,510	11,046	11,609	12,201	12,824	13,478	14,166	14,888
2%	11,040	12,189	13,458	14,859	16,406	18,113	19,998	22,080
3%	11,592	13,439	15,579	18,061	20,937	24,272	28,138	32,620
4%	12,166	14,802	18,009	21,911	26,658	32,433	39,460	48,010
5%	12,762	16,288	20,789	26,532	33,863	43,219	55,160	70,399
6%	13,382	17,908	23,965	32,071	42,918	57,434	76,860	102,857
7%	14,025	19,671	27,590	38,696	54,274	76,122	106,765	149,744
8%	14,693	21,589	31,721	46,609	68,484	100,626	147,853	217,245
9%	15,386	23,673	36,424	56,044	86,230	132,676	204,139	314,094
10%	16,105	25,937	41,772	67,274	108,347	174,494	281,024	452,592
11%	16,850	28,394	47,845	80,623	135,854	228,922	385,748	650,008
12%	17,623	31,058	54,735	96,462	170,000	299,599	527,996	930,509
13%	18,424	33,945	62,542	115,230	212,305	391,158	720,685	1,327,815
14%	19,254	37,072	71,379	137,434	264,619	509,501	981,001	1,888,835
15%	20,113	40,455	81,370	163,665	329,189	662,117	1,331,755	2,678,635
16%	21,003	44,114	92,655	194,607	408,742	858,498	1,803,140	3,787,211
17%	21,924	48,068	105,387	231,055	506,578	1,110,646	2,435,034	5,338,687
18%	22,877	52,338	119,737	273,930	626,686	1,433,706	3,279,972	7,503,783
19%	23,863	56,946	135,895	324,294	773,880	1,846,753	4,407,006	10,516,675
20%	24,883	61,917	154,070	383,375	953,962	2,373,763	5,906,682	14,697,715
21%	25,937	67,274	174,494	452,592	1,173,908	3,044,816	7,897,469	20,484,002
22%	27,027	73,046	197,422	533,576	1,442,101	3,897,578	10,534,018	28,470,377
23%	28,153	79,259	223,139	628,206	1,768,592	4,979,128	14,017,769	39,464,304
24%	29,316	85,944	251,956	738,641	2,165,419	6,348,199	18,610,540	54,559,126
25%	30,517	93,132	284,217	867,361	2,646,698	8,077,935	24,651,903	75,231,638

TABLE 2. $1200 PER YEAR AT VARYING RATES COMPOUNDED ANNUALLY—END OF YEAR VALUES

	5th Yr.	10th Yr.	15th Yr.	20th Yr.	25th Yr.	30th Yr.	35th Yr.	40th Yr.
1%	6,182	12,680	19,509	26,686	34,231	43,359	50,492	59,250
2%	6,369	13,402	21,168	29,739	39,205	49,654	61,192	73,932
3%	6,561	14,169	22,988	33,211	45,063	58,803	74,731	93,195
4%	6,760	14,983	24,990	37,162	51,974	69,993	91,917	118,592
5%	6,962	15,848	27,188	41,662	60,135	83,713	113,803	152,208
6%	7,170	16,766	29,607	46,791	69,787	100,562	141,745	196,857
7%	7,383	17,740	32,265	52,638	81,211	121,287	177,495	256,332
8%	7,603	18,774	35,188	59,307	94,744	146,815	223,322	335,737
9%	7,827	19,872	38,403	66,918	110,788	178,290	282,150	441,950
10%	8,059	21,037	41,940	75,602	129,818	217,131	357,752	584,222
11%	8,295	22,273	45,828	85,518	152,398	265,095	454,996	774,992
12%	8,538	23,586	50,103	96,838	179,200	324,351	581,355	1,030,970
13%	8,786	24,976	54,806	112,164	211,020	397,578	741,298	1,374,583
14%	9,043	26,454	59,976	124,521	248,799	488,084	948,807	1,835,890
15%	9,304	28,018	65,660	141,372	293,654	599,948	1,216,015	2,455,144
16%	9,572	29,679	71,910	160,609	346,905	726,194	1,560,032	3,286,173
17%	9,848	31,440	78,778	182,566	410,115	909,004	2,002,792	4,400,869
18%	10,130	33,306	86,326	207,625	485,126	1,119,982	2,572,378	5,895,109
19%	10,419	35,284	94,620	236,216	574,117	1,380,464	3,304,696	7,896,595
20%	10,716	37,380	103,730	268,831	679,652	1,701,909	4,245,610	10,575,154
21%	11,019	39,601	113,736	306,021	804,759	2,098,358	5,453,622	14,156,310
22%	11,330	41,954	124,722	348,416	952,998	2,587,006	7,003,256	18,939,087
23%	11,649	44,446	136,779	396,727	1,128,558	3,188,884	8,989,333	25,319,371
24%	11,976	47,085	150,013	451,758	1,336,360	3,929,683	11,532,334	33,820,458
25%	12,310	49,879	164,530	514,417	1,582,186.	4,840,641	14,666,342	45,132,982

TABLE 3. APPROXIMATE ANNUAL INVESTMENT REQUIRED TO EQUAL
$100,000 AT THE END OF A SPECIFIED PERIOD—VARYING RATES

	5 Yrs.	10 Yrs.	15 Yrs.	20 Yrs.	25 Yrs.	30 Yrs.	35 Yrs.	40 Yrs.
1%	19,380	9,464	6,151	4,497	3,506	2,768	2,378	2,026
2%	18,841	8,954	5,669	4,036	3,061	2,417	1,961	1,624
3%	18,290	8,470	5,220	3,613	2,663	2,041	1,606	1,288
4%	17,751	8,009	4,802	3,229	2,309	1,714	1,306	1,011
5%	17,236	7,572	4,414	2,880	1,966	1,433	1,054	788.39
6%	16,736	7,157	4,053	2,565	1,720	1,193	846.59	609.58
7%	16,254	6,764	3,719	2,280	1,478	989.39	676.08	468.14
8%	15,783	6,392	3,410	2,024	1,267	817.36	537.34	357.42
9%	15,332	6,039	3,125	1,793	1,083	673.06	425.31	271.52
10%	14,890	5,704	2,861	1,587	924.37	552.66	335.43	205.40
11%	14,467	5,388	2,618	1,403	787.41	452.67	263.74	154.84
12%	14,055	5,088	2,395	1,239	669.64	369.97	206.41	116.40
13%	13,658	4,805	2,190	1,070	568.67	301.83	168.00	87.29
14%	13,270	4,536	2,001	963.69	482.32	245.86	126.47	65.36
15%	12,898	4,283	1,828	848.82	408.64	200.02	98.68	48.88
16%	12,537	4,043	1,669	747.16	345.92	165.25	76.92	36.52
17%	12,185	3,817	1,523	657.30	292.60	132.02	59.92	27.27
18%	11,846	3,603	1,390	577.97	247.36	107.14	46.65	20.36
19%	11,517	3,401	1,268	508.01	209.02	86.93	36.31	15.20
20%	11,198	3,210	1,157	446.38	176.56	70.51	28.26	11.35
21%	10,802	3,030	1,056	392.13	149.11	57.19	22.00	8.48
22%	10,591	2,860	962.14	344.42	125.92	46.39	17.13	6.34
23%	10,301	2,700	877.33	302.48	106.33	37.63	13.35	4.74
24%	10,020	2,549	799.93	265.63	89.80	30.53	10.41	3.55
25%	9,749	2,406	729.35	233.27	75.84	24.79	8.18	2.66

TABLE 4. LUMP SUM REQUIRED TO EQUAL $100,000 AT THE END OF A SPECIFIED PERIOD—VARYING RATES

	5 Yrs.	10 Yrs.	15 Yrs.	20 Yrs.	25 Yrs.	30 Yrs.	35 Yrs.	40 Yrs.
1%	95,147	90,529	86,135	81,954	77,977	74,192	70,591	67,165
2%	90,573	82,348	74,301	67,297	60,953	55,207	50,003	45,289
3%	86,261	74,409	64,186	55,367	47,761	41,199	35,538	30,656
4%	82,193	67,556	55,526	45,639	37,512	30,832	25,341	20,829
5%	78,353	61,391	48,102	37,689	29,530	23,138	18,129	14,205
6%	74,726	55,839	41,727	31,180	23,300	17,411	13,011	9,722
7%	71,299	50,835	36,245	25,842	18,425	13,137	9,367	6,678
8%	68,058	46,319	31,524	21,455	14,602	9,938	6,763	4,603
9%	64,993	42,241	27,454	17,843	11,597	7,537	4,899	3,184
10%	62,092	38,554	23,940	14,864	9,230	5,731	3,558	2,209
11%	59,345	35,218	20,900	12,403	7,361	4,368	2,592	1,538
12%	56,743	32,197	18,270	10,367	5,882	3,340	1,894	1,075
13%	54,276	29,460	15,989	8,678	4,710	2,557	1,388	753.12
14%	51,937	26,974	14,010	7,276	3,780	1,963	1,019	529.43
15%	49,718	24,718	12,289	6,110	3,040	1,510	750.89	373.32
16%	47,611	22,683	10,792	5,139	2,447	1,165	554.59	264.05
17%	45,611	20,804	9,489	4,329	1,974	900.38	410.67	187.31
18%	43,711	19,107	8,352	3,651	1,596	697.49	304.88	133.27
19%	41,905	17,560	7,359	3,084	1,292	541.49	226.91	95.10
20%	40,188	16,151	6,491	2,610	1,048	421.27	169.30	68.04
21%	38,554	14,864	5,731	2,209	851.85	328.43	126.62	48.82
22%	37,000	13,690	5,065	1,874	693.43	256.57	94.93	35.12
23%	35,520	12,617	4,482	1,592	565.42	200.84	71.34	25.34
24%	34,112	11,635	3,969	1,354	461.80	157.52	53.72	18.33
25%	32,768	10,737	3,512	1,153	377.78	123.79	40.56	13.30

TABLE 5. ONE DOLLAR PRINCIPAL COMPOUNDED ANNUALLY

End of Year	2½%	3%	5%	6%	8%	10%	12%	15%
1	$ 1.0250	$ 1.0300	$ 1.0500	$ 1.0600	$ 1.0800	$ 1.1000	$ 1.1200	$ 1.1500
2	1.0506	1.0609	1.1025	1.1236	1.1664	1.2100	1.2544	1.3225
3	1.0769	1.0927	1.1576	1.1910	1.2597	1.3310	1.4049	1.5209
4	1.1038	1.1255	1.2155	1.2625	1.3605	1.4641	1.5735	1.7490
5	1.1314	1.1593	1.2763	1.3382	1.4693	1.6105	1.7623	2.0114
6	1.1597	1.1941	1.3401	1.4185	1.5869	1.7716	1.9738	2.3131
7	1.1887	1.2299	1.4071	1.5036	1.7138	1.9487	2.2107	2.6600
8	1.2184	1.2668	1.4775	1.5938	1.8509	2.1436	2.4760	3.0590
9	1.2489	1.3048	1.5513	1.6895	1.9990	2.3579	2.7731	3.5179
10	1.2801	1.3439	1.6289	1.7908	2.1589	2.5937	3.1058	4.0456
11	1.3121	1.3842	1.7103	1.8983	2.3316	2.8531	3.4785	4.6524
12	1.3449	1.4258	1.7959	2.0122	2.5182	3.1384	3.8960	5.3503
13	1.3785	1.4685	1.8856	2.1329	2.7196	3.4523	4.3635	6.1528
14	1.4130	1.5126	1.9799	2.2609	2.9372	3.7975	4.8871	7.0757
15	1.4483	1.5580	2.0789	2.3966	3.1722	4.1772	5.4736	8.1371
16	1.4845	1.6047	2.1829	2.5404	3.4259	4.5950	6.1304	9.3576
17	1.5216	1.6528	2.2920	2.6928	3.7000	5.0545	6.8660	10.7613
18	1.5597	1.7024	2.4066	2.8543	3.9960	5.5599	7.6900	12.3755
19	1.5987	1.7535	2.5270	3.0256	4.3157	6.1159	8.6128	14.2318
20	1.6386	1.8061	2.6533	3.2071	4.6610	6.7275	9.6463	16.3665
21	1.6796	1.8603	2.7860	3.3996	5.0338	7.4002	10.8038	18.8215
22	1.7216	1.9161	2.9253	3.6035	5.4365	8.1403	12.1003	21.6447
23	1.7646	1.9736	3.0715	3.8197	5.8715	8.9543	13.5523	24.8915
24	1.8087	2.0328	3.2251	4.0489	6.3412	9.8497	15.1786	28.6252
25	1.8539	2.0938	3.3864	4.2919	6.8485	10.8347	17.0001	32.9190

End of Year	2½%	3%	5%	6%	8%	10%	12%	15%
26	$ 1.9003	$ 2.1566	$ 3.5557	$ 4.5494	$ 7.3964	$ 11.9182	$ 19.0401	$ 37.8568
27	1.9478	2.2213	3.7335	4.8223	7.9881	13.1100	21.3249	43.5353
28	1.9965	2.2879	3.9201	5.1117	8.6271	14.4210	23.8839	50.0656
29	2.0464	2.3566	4.1161	5.4184	9.3173	15.8631	26.7499	57.5755
30	2.0976	2.4273	4.3219	5.7435	10.0627	17.4494	29.9599	66.2218
31	2.1500	2.5001	4.5380	6.0881	10.8677	19.1943	33.5551	76.1435
32	2.2038	2.5751	4.7649	6.4534	11.7371	21.1138	37.5817	87.5651
33	2.2589	2.6523	5.0032	6.8406	12.6760	23.2252	42.0915	100.6998
34	2.3153	2.7319	5.2533	7.2510	13.6901	25.5477	47.1425	115.8048
35	2.3732	2.8139	5.5160	7.6861	14.7853	28.1024	52.7996	133.1755
36	2.4325	2.8983	5.7918	8.1473	15.9682	30.9127	59.1356	153.1519
37	2.4933	2.9852	6.0814	8.6361	17.2456	34.0039	66.2318	176.1246
38	2.5557	3.0748	6.3855	9.1543	18.6253	37.4043	74.1797	202.5433
39	2.6196	3.1670	6.7048	9.7035	20.1153	41.1448	83.0812	232.9248
40	2.6851	3.2620	7.0400	10.2857	21.7245	45.2593	93.0510	267.8635
41	2.7522	3.3599	7.3920	10.9029	23.4625	49.7852	104.2171	308.0431
42	2.8210	3.4607	7.7616	11.5570	25.3395	54.7637	116.7231	354.2495
43	2.8915	3.5645	8.1497	12.2505	27.3666	60.2401	130.7299	407.3870
44	2.9638	3.6715	8.5572	12.9855	29.5560	66.2641	146.4175	468.4950
45	3.0379	3.7816	8.9850	13.7646	31.9204	72.8905	163.9876	538.7693
46	3.1139	3.8950	9.4343	14.5905	34.4741	80.1795	183.6661	619.5847
47	3.1917	4.0119	9.9060	15.4659	37.2320	88.1975	205.7061	712.5224
48	3.2715	4.1323	10.4013	16.3939	40.2106	97.0172	230.3908	819.4007
49	3.3533	4.2562	10.9213	17.3775	43.4274	106.7190	258.0377	942.3103
50	3.4371	4.3839	11.4674	18.4202	46.9016	117.3909	289.0022	1083.6574

TABLE 6. ONE DOLLAR PER ANNUM COMPOUNDED ANNUALLY

End of Year	3%	5%	6%	8%	10%	12%	15%
1	$ 1.0300	$ 1.0500	$ 1.0600	$ 1.0800	$ 1.1000	$ 1.1200	$ 1.1500
2	2.0909	2.1525	2.1836	2.2464	2.3100	2.3744	2.4725
3	3.1836	3.3101	3.3746	3.5061	3.6410	3.7793	3.9934
4	4.3091	4.5256	4.6371	4.8666	5.1051	5.3528	5.7424
5	5.4684	5.8019	5.9753	6.3359	6.7156	7.1152	7.7537
6	6.6625	7.1420	7.3938	7.9228	8.4872	9.0890	10.0668
7	7.8923	8.5491	8.8975	9.6366	10.4359	11.2297	12.7268
8	9.1591	10.0266	10.4913	11.4876	12.5795	13.7757	15.7858
9	10.4639	11.5779	12.1808	13.4866	14.3974	16.5487	19.3037
10	11.8078	13.2068	13.9716	15.6455	17.5312	19.6546	23.3493
11	13.1920	14.9171	15.8699	17.9771	20.3843	23.1331	28.0017
12	14.6178	16.7130	17.8821	20.4953	23.5227	27.0291	33.3519
13	16.0863	18.5986	20.0151	23.2149	26.9750	31.3926	39.5047
14	17.5989	20.5786	22.2760	26.1521	30.7725	36.2797	46.5804
15	19.1569	22.6575	24.6725	29.3243	34.9497	41.7533	54.7175
16	20.7616	24.8404	27.2129	32.7502	39.5447	47.8837	64.0751
17	22.4144	27.1324	29.9057	36.4502	44.5992	54.7497	74.8364
18	24.1169	29.5390	32.7600	40.4463	50.1591	62.4397	87.2118
19	25.8704	32.0660	35.7856	44.7620	56.2750	71.0524	101.4436
20	27.6765	34.7193	38.9927	49.4229	63.0025	80.6987	117.8101
21	29.5368	37.5052	42.3923	54.4568	70.4027	91.5026	136.6316
22	31.4529	40.4305	45.9958	59.8933	78.5430	103.6029	158.2764
23	33.4265	43.5020	49.8156	65.7648	87.4973	117.1552	183.1678
24	35.4593	46.7271	53.8645	72.1059	97.3471	132.3339	211.7930
25	37.5530	50.1135	58.1564	78.9544	108.1818	149.3339	244.7120

End of Year	3%	5%	6%	8%	10%	12%	15%
26	$ 39.7096	$ 53.6691	$ 62.7058	$ 86.3508	$ 120.0999	$ 168.3740	$ 282.5688
27	41.9309	57.4026	67.5281	94.3388	133.2099	189.6989	326.1041
28	44.2189	61.3227	72.6398	102.9659	147.6309	213.5828	376.1697
29	46.5754	65.4388	78.0582	112.2832	163.4940	240.3327	433.7451
30	49.0027	69.7608	83.8017	122.3459	180.9434	270.2926	499.9569
31	51.5028	74.2988	89.8898	133.2135	200.1378	303.8477	576.1005
32	54.0778	79.0638	96.3432	144.9506	221.2515	341.4294	663.6655
33	56.7302	84.0670	103.1838	157.6267	244.4767	383.5210	764.3654
34	59.4621	89.3203	110.4348	171.3168	270.0244	430.6635	880.1702
35	62.2759	94.8363	118.1209	186.1021	298.1268	483.4631	1013.3757
36	65.1742	100.6281	126.2681	202.0703	329.0395	542.5987	1166.4975
37	68.1594	106.7095	134.9042	219.3158	363.0434	608.8305	1342.6222
38	71.2342	113.0950	144.0585	237.9412	400.4478	683.0102	1545.1655
39	74.4013	119.7998	153.7620	258.0565	441.5926	766.0914	1778.0903
40	77.6633	126.8398	164.0477	279.7810	486.8518	859.1424	2045.9539
41	81.0232	134.2318	174.9505	303.2435	536.6370	963.3595	2353.9969
42	84.4839	141.9933	186.5076	328.5830	591.4007	1080.0826	2708.2465
43	88.0484	150.1430	198.7580	355.9496	651.6408	1210.8125	3115.6334
44	91.7199	158.7002	211.7435	385.5056	717.9048	1357.2300	3584.1285
45	95.5015	167.6852	225.5081	417.4261	790.7953	1521.2176	4122.8977
46	99.3965	177.1194	240.0986	451.9002	870.9749	1704.8838	4742.4824
47	103.4084	187.0254	255.5645	489.1322	959.1723	1910.5898	5455.0047
48	107.5406	197.4267	271.9584	529.3427	1056.1896	2140.9806	6274.4055
49	111.7969	208.3480	289.3359	572.7702	1162.9085	2399.0182	7216.7163
50	116.1808	219.8154	307.7561	619.6718	1280.2994	2688.0204	8300.3737

TABLE 7.

If you're interested in growth

Summaries of assumed $10,000 investments

Here's what would have happened if you had invested $10,000 in The Seminar Fund and taken all income dividends and capital gains distributions in additional shares . . .

10-Year Periods

Jan. 1-Dec. 31	Income Dividends Reinvested	Total Investment Cost	Ending Value of Shares	Capital Gain Distributions Taken in Shares*
1934-1943	$6,367	$16,367	$34,334	$6,853
1935-1944	6,038	16,038	33,734	6,640
1936-1945	3,801	13,801	25,192	5,337
1937-1946	3,005	13,005	16,853	3,598
1938-1947	5,545	15,545	27,612	6,993
1939-1948	5,273	15,273	21,577	5,779
1940-1949	6,006	16,006	23,416	6,297
1941-1950	7,002	17,002	28,746	7,154
1942-1951	8,421	18,421	36,562	9,256
1943-1952	8,026	18,026	35,134	9,383
1944-1953	6,783	16,783	26,579	7,691
1945-1954	6,106	16,106	33,648	7,482
1946-1955	5,072	15,072	30,844	6,976
1947-1956	5,805	15,805	34,995	9,056
1948-1957	6,351	16,351	30,558	10,432
1949-1958	6,935	16,935	44,084	11,638
1950-1959	6,959	16,959	46,002	13,339
1951-1960	6,404	16,404	40,139	13,026
1952-1961	5,938	15,938	41,912	12,831
1953-1962	5,801	15,801	32,421	12,945
1954-1963	6,286	16,286	39,662	13,821
1955-1964	4,407	14,407	29,537	10,119
1956-1965	3,834	13,834	29,872	9,225
1957-1966	3,870	13,870	27,238	9,741
1958-1967	4,968	14,968	39,877	12,382
1959-1968	3,956	13,956	32,214	9,400
1960-1969	3,985	13,985	25,196	9,333
1961-1970	4,334	14,334	24,736	9,495

. . . here's how you would have done in any of these 37 periods:

BEST PERIOD 16.5 % # (1950-1959)

MEDIAN PERIOD 11.4 % # (1955-1964)

15-Year Periods

Jan. 1-Dec. 31	Income Dividends Reinvested	Total Investment Cost	Ending Value of Shares	Capital Gain Distributions Taken in Shares*
1934-1948	$15,397	$25,397	$57,089	$20,336
1935-1949	14,332	24,332	49,772	17,919
1936-1950	9,162	19,162	32,569	10,739
1937-1951	7,149	17,149	26,303	7,323
1938-1952	12,808	22,808	47,929	13,854
1939-1953	11,428	21,428	37,573	11,524
1940-1954	12,638	22,638	58,174	13,894
1941-1955	14,538	24,538	74,744	19,262
1942-1956	17,453	27,453	89,365	27,177
1943-1957	16,695	26,695	67,439	27,353
1944-1958	13,996	23,996	73,532	23,037
1945-1959	12,569	22,569	68,078	22,827
1946-1960	10,263	20,263	52,022	18,862
1947-1961	11,563	21,563	65,590	22,118
1948-1962	12,512	22,512	56,391	24,019
1949-1963	13,557	23,557	69,051	26,499
1950-1964	13,540	23,540	73,362	28,102
1951-1965	12,370	22,370	77,732	27,859
1952-1966	11,723	21,723	66,593	28,299
1953-1967	11,794	21,794	76,532	28,446
1954-1968	13,422	23,422	89,115	31,288
1955-1969	9,820	19,820	50,985	23,062
1956-1970	8,844	18,844	41,685	19,525
1957-1971	8,935	18,935	44,049	17,770
1958-1972	11,265	21,265	57,963	21,332
1959-1973	8,654	18,654	33,301	15,298
1960-1974	8,864	18,864	23,928	12,795
1961-1975	9,615	19,615	30,992	11,927

. . . here's how you would have done in any of these 32 periods:

BEST PERIOD 15.7 % # (1942-1956)

MEDIAN PERIOD 11.6 % # (1946-1960)

WORST PERIOD 6.0 % # (1960-1974)

WORST PERIOD 4.1%#

Period				
1962-1971	3,966	13,966	23,508	7,660
1963-1972	5,102	15,102	31,400	9,352
1964-1973	4,645	14,645	21,257	7,795
1965-1974	4,734	14,734	14,994	6,177
1966-1975	4,260	14,260	16,002	4,411
1967-1976	4,646	14,646	20,523	3,986
1968-1977	3,949	13,949	15,523	2,972
1969-1978	3,682	13,682	15,215	2,209
1970-1979	4,583	14,583	20,299	2,060

20-Year Periods

...here's how you would have done in any of these 27 periods:

Period				
1934-1953	$31,576	$41,576	$99,201	$35,435
1935-1954	28,345	38,345	123,418	33,970
1936-1955	17,651	27,651	84,521	24,379
1937-1956	13,615	23,615	64,174	20,149
1938-1957	24,579	34,579	91,846	38,256
1939-1958	21,625	31,625	103,944	33,217
1940-1959	23,815	33,815	117,703	40,426
1941-1960	27,120	37,120	126,064	48,064
1942-1961	32,157	42,157	167,493	60,535
1943-1962	30,292	40,292	124,450	57,336
1944-1963	25,040	35,040	115,177	47,824
1945-1964	22,306	32,306	108,571	44,673
1946-1965	17,996	27,996	100,743	38,084
1947-1966	20,616	30,616	104,215	46,325
1948-1967	22,934	32,934	133,109	51,763
1949-1968	25,980	35,980	155,150	56,909
1950-1969	26,986	36,986	126,637	60,252
1951-1970	25,406	35,406	108,473	54,662
1952-1971	24,105	34,105	107,694	47,929
1953-1972	23,878	33,878	111,244	45,624
1954-1973	26,417	36,417	92,123	47,606
1955-1974	19,692	29,692	48,421	30,068
1956-1975	17,741	27,741	52,228	23,623
1957-1976	17,710	27,710	61,116	21,606
1958-1977	22,171	32,171	67,632	25,334
1959-1978	16,921	26,921	53,573	17,181
1960-1979	16,609	26,609	55,905	15,008

BEST PERIOD 15.1%#

MEDIAN PERIOD 12.4%#

WORST PERIOD 8.2%#

Period				
1962-1976	8,649	18,649	32,616	9,707
1963-1977	11,010	21,010	36,636	11,520
1964-1978	9,923	19,923	34,198	8,997
1965-1979	9,588	19,588	35,032	7,563

25-Year Periods

...here's how you would have done in any of these 22 periods:

Period				
1934-1958	$58,378	$68,378	$274,006	$ 92,456
1935-1959	51,959	61,959	249,340	90,027
1936-1960	31,827	41,827	142,370	56,830
1937-1961	24,140	34,140	120,145	44,024
1938-1962	43,042	53,042	169,326	78,968
1939-1963	37,238	47,238	162,816	68,257
1940-1964	40,650	50,650	187,710	78,196
1941-1965	45,860	55,860	244,133	94,648
1942-1966	55,276	65,276	266,129	122,350
1943-1967	53,293	63,293	293,762	118,563
1944-1968	45,761	55,761	258,788	98,548
1945-1969	42,202	52,202	187,411	92,252
1946-1970	34,891	44,891	140,585	72,821
1947-1971	39,993	49,993	168,537	77,045
1948-1972	43,951	53,951	193,484	81,640
1949-1973	48,604	58,604	160,386	85,318
1950-1974	51,507	61,507	120,265	77,652
1951-1975	48,559	58,559	135,906	65,323
1952-1976	45,560	55,560	149,420	57,308
1953-1977	44,809	54,809	129,796	53,306
1954-1978	49,288	59,288	148,202	52,814
1955-1979	35,366	45,366	113,131	34,544

BEST PERIOD 14.5%#

MEDIAN PERIOD 12.0%#

WORST PERIOD 10.2%#

46 Years

ICA's Lifetime 12.1%#

Period				
1934-1979	$631,334	$641,334	$1,907,061	$624,538

*The value of the shares acquired with these capital gain distributions is reflected in "Ending Value of Shares."

THE ANNUALIZED RATE OF RETURN FOR THIS SPECIFIED TIME PERIOD.

TABLE 8. THE SEMINAR FUND

DATE	INITIAL INVESTMENT	OFFERING PRICE	SALES CHARGE INCLUDED	SHARES PURCHASED	NET ASSET VALUE PER SHARE	INITIAL NET ASSET VALUE
1/ 1/50	10000.00	10.84	8.50%	922.509	9.920	9151

MONTHLY INVESTMENTS OF $ 100.00 -- SAME DAY AS INITIAL INVESTMENT
DIVIDENDS AND CAPITAL GAINS REINVESTED

CUMULATIVE VOLUME DISCOUNT REFLECTED WHERE APPLICABLE IN THIS ILLUSTRATION

	--------COST OF SHARES--------					--------VALUE OF SHARES--------					
DATE	CUM INV'M'T	CURRENT INCOME DIVS	CUM. INCOME DIVS	TOTAL INVM'T COST	CURRENT CAP GAIN DISTRIB'N	FROM INV'M'T	FROM CAP GAINS REINV'D	SUB-TOTAL	FROM DIVS REINV'D	TOTAL VALUE	SHARES HELD
12/31/50	11100.	484.	484.	11584.	354.	11238.	360.	11598.	506.	12104.	1098.380
12/31/51	12300.	567.	1051.	13351.	660.	13273.	1057.	14330.	1120.	15450.	1295.005
12/31/52	13500.	632.	1683.	15183.	807.	14843.	1907.	16750.	1796.	18546.	1505.347
12/31/53	14700.	747.	2430.	17130.	540.	15025.	2323.	17348.	2434.	19782.	1711.321
12/31/54	15900.	822.	3252.	19152.	1500.	23007.	4882.	27889.	4441.	32330.	3881.146
12/31/55	17100.	1065.	4317.	21417.	2870.	27203.	8497.	35700.	6118.	41818.	4439.231
12/31/56	18300.	1197.	5514.	23814.	3399.	28323.	11885.	40208.	7294.	47502.	5037.284
12/31/57	19500.	1361.	6875.	26375.	2629.	23722.	12075.	35797.	7080.	42877.	5656.579
12/31/58	20700.	1464.	8339.	29039.	2181.	33506.	18725.	52231.	11266.	63497.	6182.857
12/31/59	21900.	1597.	9936.	31836.	4819.	36029.	24373.	60402.	13332.	73734.	6897.506
12/31/60	23100.	1884.	11820.	34920.	4180.	35795.	27769.	63564.	14744.	78308.	7624.848
12/31/61	24300.	1968.	13788.	38088.	5038.	42010.	36788.	78798.	18838.	97636.	8337.824
12/31/62	25500.	2171.	15959.	41459.	3817.	35161.	33221.	68382.	17479.	85861.	9047.431
12/31/63	26700.	2320.	18279.	44979.	4389.	41600.	42684.	84284.	22498.	106782.	9796.593
12/31/64	27900.	2609.	20888.	48788.	7165.	45728.	52957.	98685.	26683.	125368.	10733.543
12/31/65	29100.	2977.	23865.	52965.	9626.	54537.	71644.	126181.	34291.	160472.	11790.770
12/31/66	30300.	3842.	27707.	58007.	12345.	50968.	77145.	128113.	35112.	163225.	13120.914
12/31/67	31500.	4577.	32284.	63784.	9975.	62262.	102681.	164943.	46714.	211657.	14205.188
12/31/68	32700.	5675.	37959.	70659.	8958.	69090.	122835.	191925.	56945.	248870.	15333.912
12/31/69	33900.	6381.	44340.	78240.	15045.	57296.	113526.	170822.	52563.	223385.	16910.266

TOTAL $ 100296.

DATE	INITIAL INVESTMENT	OFFERING PRICE	SALES CHARGE INCLUDED	SHARES PURCHASED	NET ASSET VALUE PER SHARE	INITIAL NET ASSET VALUE
1/ 1/70	223385.00	13.21	0.0 %	16910.296	13.210	223385.

SYSTEMATIC WITHDRAWAL PLAN
DIVIDENDS AND CAPITAL GAINS REINVESTED
MONTHLY WITHDRAWALS OF $ 1116.93 (6.0% ANNUALLY) BEGINNING 1/16/70

| | -------AMOUNTS WITHDRAWN------- | | | | | ===VALUE OF REMAINING SHARES==== | | | |
DATE	FROM INCOME DIVS	FROM PRINCIPAL	CURRENT TOTAL	CUM. TOTAL	CURRENT CAP GAIN DISTRIB'N	REMAINING ORIGINAL SHARES	CAP GAIN SHARES	TOTAL VALUE	SHARES HELD
12/31/70	6648.	6755.	13403.	13403.	9705.	204447.	9815.	214262.	17099.918
12/31/71	6533.	6870.	13403.	26806.	4300.	221123.	15330.	236453.	16901.596
12/31/72	6467.	6936.	13403.	40209.	7703.	234871.	24628.	259499.	16949.636
12/31/73	6803.	6600.	13403.	53612.	5406.	178209.	24860.	203089.	16938.206
12/31/74	9862.	3541.	13403.	67015.	0.	135127.	19215.	154342.	16667.624
12/31/75	8726.	4677.	13403.	80418.	1115.	168875.	25834.	194709.	16348.398
12/31/76	7694.	5709.	13403.	93821.	3651.	202173.	35613.	237786.	16186.961
12/31/77	7774.	5629.	13403.	107224.	4399.	180682.	37232.	217914.	16105.956
12/31/78	8207.	5196.	13403.	120627.	0.	194580.	41222.	235802.	15741.148
12/31/79	9661.	3742.	13403.	134030.	2820.	215311.	49819.	265130.	31191.747
TOTALS	78375.	55655.	134030.		39099.				

TABLE 9.   INVESTING IN COMMON STOCKS REQUIRES SKILL

The difficulty of selecting individual stocks is illustrated by the wide variation in the results of assumed investments made 46 years ago in each of the 30 stocks now in the Dow Jones Industrial Average.*

	Market Value of Investment *		
DOW JONES INDUSTRIAL STOCKS	DEC. 31, 1933	DEC. 31, 1979	% CHANGE
Minnesota Mining & Manufacturing	$10,000	$6,030,000	60,200%
Merck	10,000**	3,392,612	33,826
International Business Machines	10,000	3,060,807	30,508
The Seminar Fund	10,000	462,959	4,530
International Paper	10,000	459,517	4,495
Eastman Kodak	10,000	385,361	3,754
United Technologies	10,000	275,127	2,651
Procter & Gamble	10,000	231,134	2,211
Texaco	10,000	216,476	2,065
Sears, Roebuck	10,000	207,380	1,974
Exxon	10,000	198,856	1,889
Standard Oil Co. of California	10,000	170,645	1,606
General Electric	10,000	155,769	1,458
Aluminum Company of America	10,000	133,464	1,235
Goodyear Tire & Rubber	10,000	105,271	953
Westinghouse Electric	10,000	90,040	800
General Motors	10,000	84,507	745
General Foods	10,000	82,769	728
duPont	10,000	79,532	695
Bethlehem Steel	10,000	68,513	585
International Harvester	10,000	58,688	487
INCO	10,000	53,977	440
Union Carbide	10,000	53,053	431
Johns-Manville	10,000	47,851	379
American Brands	10,000	40,222	302
Owens-Illinois	10,000	40,000	300
United States Steel	10,000	32,984	230
Allied Chemical	10,000	30,424	204
American Telephone & Telegraph	10,000	28,018	180
Woolworth, F.W.	10,000	17,428	74
American Can	10,000	14,394	44

* It was assumed that the entire $10,000 was invested in each stock and that fractional shares were purchased where required to use up the full amount. No brokerage charges were included in the cost. Adjustments were made for all stock splits and stock dividends.
** This $10,000 investment was made one year later, December 31, 1934, when stock of the company was first available for purchase by the public.

TABLE 10. SEMINAR FUND VS. LEADING STOCK MARKET INDEXES

	Seminar	S&P 500	DJIA	NYSE		Seminar	S&P 500	DJIA	NYSE
1934	+ 14.8%	− 5.9%	+ 4.1%	na	1957	− 14.5%	− 14.3%	− 12.8%	− 13.3%
1935	+83.1	+41.4	+38.5	na	1958	+40.8	+38.1	+34.0	+36.7
1936	+43.4	+27.9	+24.8	na	1959	+11.5	+ 8.5	+16.4	+11.4
1937	−40.9	−38.6	−32.8	na	1960	+ 1.9	− 3.0	− 9.3	− 3.8
1938	+28.0	+25.2	+28.1	na	1961	+20.4	+23.1	+18.7	+24.1
1939	− 1.4	− 5.4	− 2.9	na	1962	−15.5	−11.8	−10.8	−11.9
1940	− 6.1	−15.3	−12.7	−12.9%	1963	+20.0	+18.9	+17.0	+18.1
1941	−12.3	−17.9	−15.4	−18.0	1964	+13.8	+13.0	+14.6	+14.4
1942	+11.0	+12.4	+ 7.6	+12.5	1965	+24.3	+ 9.1	+10.9	+ 9.5
1943	+28.5	+19.4	+13.8	+20.4	1966	− 1.4	−13.1	−18.9	−12.6
1944	+19.6	+13.8	+12.1	+14.0	1967	+26.0	+20.1	+15.2	+23.1
1945	+33.6	+30.7	+26.6	+31.1	1968	+14.1	+ 7.7	+ 4.3	+ 9.4
1946	− 5.3	−11.9	− 8.1	−11.5	1969	−13.2	−11.4	−15.2	−12.5
1947	− 3.4	0	+ 2.2	− 2.0	1970	− 0.7	+ 0.1	+ 4.8	− 2.5
1948	− 4.1	− 0.6	− 2.1	− 2.8	1971	+13.8	+10.8	+ 6.1	+12.3
1949	+ 4.5	+10.3	+12.9	+10.2	1972	+12.8	+15.6	+14.6	+14.3
1950	+14.5	+21.8	+17.6	+21.2	1973	−19.5	−17.4	−16.6	−19.6
1951	+13.2	+16.5	+14.4	+13.2	1974	−22.8	−29.7	−27.6	−30.3
1952	+ 8.1	+11.8	+ 8.4	+ 6.5	1975	+29.4	+31.5	+38.3	+31.9
1953	− 3.5	− 6.6	− 3.8	− 6.1	1976	+25.3	+19.1	+17.9	+21.5
1954	+51.3	+45.0	+44.0	+42.6	1977	− 6.0	−11.5	−17.3	− 9.3
1955	+21.9	+26.4	+20.8	+22.2	1978	+10.7	+ 1.1	− 3.1	+ 2.1
1956	+ 7.8	+ 2.6	+ 2.3	+ 2.7					

† Seminar Fund's results are based on the assumption that the current maximum sales charge was paid, while results for the indices were computed without sales charge.

* Figures reflect change in net asset value per share, adjusted for reinvested capital gain distributions. They differ slightly from the figures shown on pages 10 and 11 under "Capital Return," which reflect the effect of reinvested income dividends in prior years.

** Prior to June 1964 this index was calculated weekly. Therefore, some of the "years" before 1964 actually represent periods of 52 or 53 weeks.

na index not computed for this period.

641

TABLE 11.

If you're interested in a retirement program

Many shareholders who reinvest all of their income dividends and capital gain distributions while they are accumulating shares find it helpful to begin taking these dividends and distributions in cash when they retire.

Such was the case with John and Martha. This couple began a Seminar Fund accumulation program by investing $250 on January 1, 1944. They added $100 each month thereafter until John retired 15 years later at the end of 1958. By this time, the value of their investment (as shown by the circled number below) had grown to $60,401.

Now John and Martha began to take all their dividends and capital gain distributions in cash. The right-hand table shows what they would have received each year and the fluctuations in the year-end value of their shares for the past 20 years. As you can see, over the past two decades they would have received $43,639 in dividends and $59,226 in capital gain distributions — a total of $102,865 in cash. And by the end of 1978 the value of their holdings would have grown to $88,102.

15-Year Share Accumulation Illustrations
Total Investments: $18,150

Jan. 1-Dec. 31	Dividends Reinvested	Total Cost (including dividends)	Capital Gain Distributions Taken in Shares*	Ending Value of Shares
1934-1948	$8,784	$26,934	$10,959	$39,668
1935-1949	8,613	26,763	9,989	37,673
1936-1950	8,592	26,742	9,107	39,599
1937-1951	9,153	27,303	9,737	43,433
1938-1952	9,928	28,078	10,915	46,488

20-Year Use of Investment
$60,401 — Net asset value of shares accumulated as of December 31, 1958†

Year Ended Dec. 31	Dividends in Cash	Capital Gains in Cash	Value at Year End
1959	$1,470	$4,411	$62,871
1960	1,529	3,470	60,401
1961	1,470	3,764	68,870
1962	1,470	2,647	55,814
1963	1,470	2,764	64,106

Period				
1939-1953	9,942	28,092	10,359	41,889
1940-1954	9,949	28,099	11,599	59,097
1941-1955	9,997	28,147	14,336	65,869
1942-1956	9,810	27,960	16,509	63,802
1943-1957	9,238	27,388	16,166	47,725
1944-1958	8,918	27,068	15,423	(60,401)
1945-1959	8,656	26,806	16,787	60,688
1946-1960	8,623	26,773	17,254	56,702
1947-1961	8,712	26,862	18,326	63,549
1948-1962	8,513	26,663	17,724	49,139
1949-1963	8,164	26,314	17,008	53,243
1950-1964	7,600	25,750	16,754	53,147
1951-1965	7,090	25,240	16,916	57,799
1952-1966	6,896	25,046	17,577	50,661
1953-1967	6,718	24,868	16,846	56,274
1954-1968	6,525	24,675	15,277	55,876
1955-1969	6,334	24,484	14,817	42,582
1956-1970	6,404	24,554	13,891	39,104
1957-1971	6,486	24,636	12,380	41,325
1958-1972	6,437	24,587	11,505	42,886
1959-1973	6,225	24,375	10,017	31,431
1960-1974	6,695	24,845	8,279	23,664
1961-1975	6,865	25,015	6,889	29,207
1962-1976	6,889	25,039	6,124	34,631
1963-1977	6,755	24,905	5,435	30,531
1964-1978	6,584	24,734	4,155	31,470

Year			
1964	1,529	4,176	68,694
1965	1,588	5,117	80,045
1966	1,823	5,999	73,163
1967	2,000	4,352	87,631
1968	2,235	3,705	95,454
1969	2,294	5,764	77,692
1970	2,294	3,411	73,693
1971	2,29.	1,529	82,279
1972	2,294	2,764	90,043
1973	2,411	1,941	70,517
1974	3,529	—	54,461
1975	3,176	412	70,046
1976	2,823	1,353	86,396
1977	2,882	1,647	79,574
1978	3,058	—	88,102
Totals:	$43,639	$59,226	

†If all the shares had been purchased at offering price (which includes the sales commission as described in the prospectus) on December 31, 1958, instead of accumulated in the shareholder account, the cost would have been $63,224.

*The value of the shares acquired with these capital gain distributions is reflected in "Ending Value of Shares."

TABLE 12.

If you're interested in investing monthly

Here's what would have happened if you had invested $250 in The Seminar Fund and added $100 every month . . . .

...for 10 Years

(Total Investments: $12,150)

Here's how you would have done in every 10-year period in the Fund's history:

Jan 1-Dec. 31	Dividends Reinvested	Total Cost (including dividends reinvested)	Capital/Gain Distributions Taken in Shares*	Ending Value of Shares
1934-1943	$2,832	$14,982	$2,138	$19,954
1935-1944	2,719	14,869	2,111	21,129
1936-1945	2,526	14,676	3,061	24,980
1937-1946	2,776	14,926	3,938	22,630
1938-1947	3,328	15,478	4,550	22,023
1939-1948	3,540	15,690	4,312	19,783
1940-1949	3,653	15,803	4,248	19,770
1941-1950	3,744	15,894	4,069	21,297
1942-1951	3,704	15,854	4,129	22,083
1943-1952	3,425	15,575	3,940	21,057
1944-1953	3,311	15,461	3,490	18,667
1945-1954	3,209	15,359	3,827	25,890
1946-1955	3,275	15,425	4,979	29,026
1947-1956	3,427	15,577	6,261	29,355
1948-1957	3,437	15,587	6,530	23,022
1949-1958	3,353	15,503	6,275	29,393
1950-1959	3,120	15,270	6,686	28,533
1951-1960	2,921	15,071	6,460	25,378
1952-1961	2,748	14,898	6,367	26,913
1953-1962	2,554	14,704	5,717	20,136
1954-1963	2,292	14,442	5,018	21,003
1955-1964	2,067	14,217	4,747	20,747
1956-1965	2,011	14,161	5,025	23,435
1957-1966	2,068	14,218	5,530	21,302
1958-1967	2,126	14,276	5,498	24,422
1959-1968	2,151	14,301	5,017	24,725
1960-1969	2,265	14,415	5,242	19,841
1961-1970	2,361	14,511	4,863	18,394
1962-1971	2,303	14,453	4,191	19,524
1963-1972	2,212	14,362	3,763	20,096
1964-1973	2,384	14,534	3,120	14,844
1965-1974	2,466	14,616	2,262	11,231
1966-1975	2,479	14,629	1,665	14,139
1967-1976	2,521	14,671	1,431	17,050
1968-1977	2,626	14,776	1,335	15,618
1969-1978	2,841	14,991	1,018	16,991
1970-1979			968	19,195

...for 20 Years

(Total Investments: $24,150)

Here's how you would have done in every 20-year period in the Fund's history:

Period				
1934-1953	$20,836	$44,986	$22,279	$ 76,561
1935-1954	19,967	44,117	23,135	103,655
1936-1955	19,635	43,785	27,075	113,533
1937-1956	20,533	44,883	32,583	116,063
1938-1957	22,022	46,010	36,166	96,643
1939-1958	21,860	46,172	35,720	124,788
1940-1959	21,782	45,932	39,722	128,003
1941-1960	21,555	45,705	40,827	118,964
1942-1961	20,772	44,922	41,451	128,247
1943-1962	19,302	43,452	38,360	94,830
1944-1963	18,394	42,544	36,623	101,930
1945-1964	17,742	41,892	37,189	104,552
1946-1965	17,455	41,605	39,302	118,599
1947-1966	17,924	42,074	43,082	109,020
1948-1967	18,047	42,197	43,149	124,915
1949-1968	18,207	42,357	41,487	128,493
1950-1969	17,814	41,964	41,043	98,650
1951-1970	17,257	41,407	37,648	87,183
1952-1971	16,780	40,930	33,092	88,925
1953-1972	16,068	40,218	30,012	89,317
1954-1973	15,153	39,303	25,994	63,756
1955-1974	15,176	39,326	20,983	45,341
1956-1975	15,385	39,535	17,956	55,258
1957-1976	15,367	39,517	16,215	64,995
1958-1977	15,187	39,337	14,755	57,235
1959-1978	14,728	38,878	11,993	58,273
1960-1979	15,037	38,187	10,666	63,355

...for 25 Years

(Total Investments: $30,150)

Here's how you would have done in every 25-year period in the Fund's history:

Period				
1934-1958	$42,130	$72,280	$67,588	$220,655
1935-1959	40,340	70,490	71,529	218,130
1936-1960	39,206	69,356	71,911	199,360
1937-1961	40,089	70,239	77,023	226,244
1938-1962	41,949	72,099	80,109	185,151
1939-1963	41,010	71,160	78,633	202,859
1940-1964	40,501	70,651	81,734	211,977
1941-1965	39,647	69,797	85,896	239,262
1942-1966	38,919	69,069	90,097	211,896
1943-1967	37,286	67,436	86,276	232,838
1944-1968	37,200	67,350	82,555	237,963
1945-1969	37,380	67,530	84,016	187,449
1946-1970	37,823	67,973	81,006	172,096
1947-1971	38,665	68,815	75,806	183,375
1948-1972	38,342	68,392	71,728	189,186
1949-1973	37,431	67,581	65,505	138,898
1950-1974	37,522	67,672	54,918	98,659
1951-1975	36,510	66,660	46,443	115,598
1952-1976	35,155	65,305	41,077	131,154
1953-1977	33,566	63,716	36,472	111,512
1954-1978	31,691	61,841	29,801	110,394
1955-1979	30,544	60,694	25,378	114,106

*The value of the shares acquired with these capital gain distributions is reflected in "Ending Value of Shares."

Note: 15-year illustrations are on page 13.

TABLE 13.

All it takes is $250 to start your investment program now

If you had invested $250 in The Seminar Fund and then added $100 every month through the 45-year lifetime of the Fund, here's how you would have done . . . .

Total Invested since January 1, 1934	$ 54,150
Income Dividends (reinvested)	464,886
Total Cost (including dividends reinvested)	$ 519,036
Value of Investment on December 31, 1978	$1,351,233*

*Includes value of shares taken as capital gain distributions

This table covers the period from January 1, 1934 through December 31, 1978. While this period, on the whole, was one of generally rising common stock prices, it also included some interim periods of substantial market decline. Results shown should not be considered as a representation of the dividend income or capital gain or loss that may be realized from an investment made in the Fund today. A program of the type illustrated does not ensure a profit or protect against depreciation in declining markets.

COST OF SHARES

Year Ended Dec. 31	Monthly Investments (cumulative)	Dividends Reinvested Annually	Dividends Reinvested Cumulative	Total Cost (including dividends)
1934	$1,350	—	—	$ 1,350
1935	2,550	—	—	2,550
1936	3,750	$ 99	$ 99	3,849
1937	4,950	275	374	5,324
1938	6,150	57	431	6,581
1939	7,350	206	637	7,987
1940	8,550	379	1,016	9,566
1941	9,750	591	1,607	11,357

VALUE OF SHARES ACQUIRED

Monthly Investments	Capital Gain Distributions (cumulative)	Dividends Reinvested (cumulative)	Total Value	Annual Capital Gain Distributions Taken in Shares*
$ 1,416	—	—	$ 1,416	—
4,379	—	—	4,379	—
6,495	$ 1,219	$ 129	7,843	$ 972
4,490	755	290	5,535	73
6,755	1,393	420	8,568	324
7,620	1,613	610	9,843	241
8,153	1,645	957	10,755	152
8,144	1,472	1,404	11,020	35

Year									
1942	10,950	613	2,220	13,170	10,158	1,753	2,209	14,120	120
1943	12,150	612	2,832	14,982	14,082	2,452	3,420	19,954	221
1944	13,350	730	3,562	16,912	17,409	3,750	4,692	25,851	900
1945	14,550	727	4,289	18,839	22,894	7,196	6,620	36,710	2,501
1946	15,750	1,123	5,412	21,162	21,251	8,730	6,914	36,895	2,409
1947	16,950	1,570	6,982	23,932	20,678	9,815	7,920	38,413	1,788
1948	18,150	1,802	8,784	26,934	20,256	10,338	9,074	39,668	1,223
1949	19,350	1,836	10,620	29,970	21,616	11,973	11,068	44,657	1,538
1950	20,550	2,234	12,854	33,404	25,224	14,931	14,632	54,787	1,605
1951	21,750	2,452	15,306	37,056	28,460	19,002	18,316	65,778	2,806
1952	22,950	2,598	17,904	40,854	30,563	22,933	21,548	75,044	3,276
1953	24,150	2,932	20,836	44,986	29,811	23,592	23,158	76,561	2,095
1954	25,350	3,108	23,944	49,294	44,354	39,745	36,903	121,002	5,621
1955	26,550	3,920	27,864	54,414	51,375	55,885	45,765	153,025	10,543
1956	27,750	4,322	32,186	59,936	52,549	68,095	50,036	170,680	12,225
1957	28,950	4,832	37,018	65,968	43,218	63,671	44,537	151,426	9,319
1958	30,150	5,112	42,130	72,280	59,948	94,516	66,191	220,655	7,601
1959	31,350	5,507	47,637	78,987	63,563	115,181	74,434	253,178	16,585
1960	32,550	6,422	54,059	86,609	62,265	125,517	78,105	265,887	14,268
1961	33,750	6,642	60,701	94,451	72,217	160,401	95,897	328,515	16,989
1962	34,950	7,258	67,959	102,909	59,664	141,405	85,110	286,179	12,789
1963	36,150	7,686	75,645	111,795	69,766	177,394	105,783	352,943	14,520
1964	37,350	8,581	84,226	121,576	75,921	213,800	121,821	411,542	23,538
1965	38,550	9,734	93,960	132,510	89,733	281,588	152,410	523,731	31,444
1966	39,750	12,496	106,456	146,206	83,154	295,324	151,564	530,042	40,177
1967	40,950	14,817	121,273	162,223	100,832	386,998	196,619	684,449	32,280
1968	42,150	18,298	139,571	181,721	111,121	457,035	233,712	801,868	28,933
1969	43,350	20,505	160,076	203,426	91,522	415,587	210,191	717,300	48,412
1970	44,550	22,147	182,223	226,773	88,090	426,043	223,261	737,394	31,493
1971	45,750	23,207	205,430	251,180	99,582	491,581	273,061	864,224	15,635
1972	46,950	24,338	229,768	276,718	110,203	568,155	324,110	1,002,468	29,619
1973	48,150	27,170	256,938	305,088	87,359	467,808	279,812	834,979	22,096
1974	49,350	42,583	299,521	348,871	68,484	361,293	256,423	686,200	—
1975	50,550	40,694	340,215	390,765	89,316	470,040	370,927	930,283	5,327
1976	51,750	37,988	378,203	429,953	111,430	598,685	496,795	1,206,910	18,440
1977	52,950	40,809	419,012	471,962	103,792	575,216	498,013	1,177,021	23,630
1978	54,150	45,874	464,886	519,036	116,151	636,861	598,221	1,351,233	—

The total cost column represents the initial investment of $250, plus the cumulative total of monthly investments of $100, plus the cumulative amount of dividends reinvested. A sales charge, as described in the prospectus, was included in the price of the shares purchased through periodic investments with right of accumulation reflected where applicable. There is no sales charge on shares acquired through reinvestment of dividends and capital gain distributions.

*Capital gain distributions taken in shares totaled $493,763.

Table 14
Hypothetical Illustration
THE SEMINAR FUND

Prepared for: Sam Steady

	Initial Investment	Offering Price	Sales Charge Included	Shares Purchased	Net Asset Value Per Share	Initial Net Asset Value
1/1/50	$100.00	$2.71	8.50%	36.900	$2.480	$92

MONTHLY INVESTMENTS OF $100.00 -- SAME DAY AS INITIAL INVESTMENT
DIVIDENDS AND CAPITAL GAINS REINVESTED

CUMULATIVE VOLUME DISCOUNT REFLECTED WHERE APPLICABLE IN THIS ILLUSTRATION

==========COST OF SHARES==========   ==========VALUE OF SHARES==========

DATE	CUM INV'M'T	ANNUAL INCOME DIVS	CUM INCOME DIVS	TOTAL INV'M'T COST	ANNUAL CAP GAIN DISTRIB'N	FROM INV'M'T	FROM CAP GAINS REINV'D	SUB-TOTAL	FROM DIVS REINV'D	TOTAL VALUE	SHARES HELD
12/31/50	1,200	37	37	1,237	35	1,173	36	1,209	39	1,248	452
12/31/51	2,400	86	123	2,523	113	2,376	152	2,528	128	2,656	890
12/31/52	3,600	130	254	3,854	178	3,576	337	3,913	265	4,178	1,356
12/31/53	4,800	189	443	5,243	143	4,443	458	4,901	438	5,339	1,847
12/31/54	6,000	239	683	6,683	449	7,731	1,118	8,849	903	9,752	2,341
12/31/55	7,200	336	1,019	8,219	910	9,898	2,207	12,105	1,366	13,471	2,860
12/31/56	8,400	399	1,417	9,817	1,144	10,976	3,347	14,323	1,758	16,081	3,410
12/31/57	9,600	474	1,891	11,491	919	9,760	3,573	13,333	1,837	15,170	4,002
12/31/58	10,800	530	2,422	13,222	794	14,558	5,701	20,259	3,094	23,353	4,547
12/31/59	12,000	598	3,019	15,019	1,808	16,280	7,766	24,046	3,822	27,868	5,213
12/31/60	13,200	723	3,743	16,943	1,597	16,803	9,123	25,926	4,414	30,340	5,908
12/31/61	14,400	773	4,515	18,915	1,980	20,332	12,417	32,749	5,829	38,578	6,588
12/31/62	15,600	869	5,384	20,984	1,522	17,572	11,422	28,994	5,609	34,603	7,292
12/31/63	16,800	946	6,330	23,130	1,795	21,373	14,970	36,343	7,430	43,773	8,031
12/31/64	18,000	1,080	7,410	25,410	2,973	24,022	19,036	43,058	9,028	52,086	8,918
12/31/65	19,200	1,248	8,657	27,857	4,040	29,222	26,351	55,573	11,860	67,433	9,909
12/31/66	20,400	1,626	10,283	30,683	5,217	27,809	29,013	56,822	12,435	69,257	11,134
12/31/67	21,600	1,953	12,237	33,837	4,261	34,503	39,142	73,645	16,882	90,527	12,151
12/31/68	22,800	2,439	14,676	37,476	3,840	38,835	47,347	86,182	20,994	107,176	13,207
12/31/69	24,000	2,761	17,437	41,437	6,489	32,664	44,380	77,044	19,776	96,820	14,658
12/31/70	25,200	3,012	20,448	45,648	4,264	32,226	46,408	78,634	22,007	100,641	16,063
12/31/71	26,400	3,187	23,635	50,035	2,154	37,189	54,005	91,194	27,837	119,031	17,016
12/31/72	27,600	3,370	27,006	54,606	4,113	41,902	63,293	105,195	33,965	139,160	18,178
12/31/73	28,800	3,792	30,798	59,598	3,093	33,851	52,768	86,619	30,227	116,846	19,490
12/31/74	30,000	6,002	36,800	66,800	0	27,140	40,753	67,893	29,029	96,922	20,933
12/31/75	31,200	5,784	42,584	73,784	759	36,119	53,179	89,298	43,181	132,479	22,246
12/31/76	32,400	5,434	48,017	80,417	2,644	45,789	68,305	114,094	58,880	172,974	23,549
12/31/77	33,600	5,873	53,891	87,491	3,408	43,308	66,345	109,653	60,052	169,705	25,085
12/31/78	34,800	6,641	60,531	95,331	0	49,156	73,455	122,611	73,267	195,878	26,151
12/31/79	36,000	8,349	68,881	104,881	2,355	57,031	85,897	142,928	91,780	234,708	27,612
TOTAL					62,996					234,708	

Hypothetical Illustration

THE SEMINAR FUND

Prepared for: George Genius

| | COST OF SHARES | | | | | VALUE OF SHARES | | | | | |
DATE	CUM NET INV'M'T	ANNUAL INCOME DIVS	CUM INCOME DIVS	TOTAL INV'M'T COST	ANNUAL CAP GAIN DISTRIB'N	FROM INV'M'T	FROM CAP GAINS REINV'D	SUB-TOTAL	FROM DIVS REINV'D	TOTAL VALUE	SHARES HELD
12/31/50	1,200	35	35	1,235	38	1,292	38	1,330	36	1,366	495
12/31/51	2,400	108	144	2,544	123	2,572	166	2,738	148	2,886	967
12/31/52	3,600	148	292	3,892	195	3,833	369	4,202	303	4,505	1,462
12/31/53	4,800	188	480	5,280	156	4,784	501	5,285	472	5,757	1,992
12/31/54	6,000	276	756	6,756	498	8,471	1,231	9,702	995	10,697	2,568
12/31/55	7,200	382	1,138	8,338	1,026	10,864	2,457	13,321	1,518	14,839	3,150
12/31/56	8,400	451	1,588	9,988	1,273	12,049	3,725	15,774	1,960	17,734	3,761
12/31/57	9,600	501	2,089	11,689	965	10,814	3,919	14,733	2,022	16,755	4,420
12/31/58	10,800	601	2,690	13,490	893	16,140	6,279	22,419	3,428	25,847	5,033
12/31/59	12,000	673	3,363	15,363	2,024	17,997	8,586	26,583	4,244	30,827	5,767
12/31/60	13,200	805	4,168	17,368	1,760	18,530	10,081	28,611	4,904	33,515	6,526
12/31/61	14,400	864	5,032	19,432	2,210	22,424	13,744	36,168	6,482	42,650	7,284
12/31/62	15,600	959	5,991	21,591	1,674	19,479	12,634	32,113	6,230	38,343	8,080
12/31/63	16,800	1,051	7,042	23,842	1,985	23,675	16,558	40,233	8,253	48,486	8,896
12/31/64	18,000	1,205	8,247	26,247	3,303	26,571	21,070	47,641	10,033	57,674	9,875
12/31/65	19,200	1,378	9,625	28,825	4,467	32,328	29,161	61,489	13,170	74,659	10,971
12/31/66	20,400	1,791	11,415	31,815	5,763	30,858	32,099	62,957	13,794	76,751	12,339
12/31/67	21,600	2,177	13,592	35,192	4,741	38,340	43,333	81,673	18,738	100,411	13,478
12/31/68	22,800	2,710	16,302	39,102	4,246	43,215	52,410	95,625	23,304	118,929	14,655
12/31/69	24,000	3,040	19,341	43,341	7,181	36,364	49,124	85,488	21,927	107,415	16,262
12/31/70	25,200	3,348	22,689	47,889	4,716	36,005	51,365	87,370	24,410	111,780	17,842
12/31/71	26,400	3,553	26,242	52,642	2,392	41,505	59,782	101,287	30,897	132,184	18,896
12/31/72	27,600	3,754	29,996	57,596	4,566	46,690	70,077	116,767	37,712	154,479	20,180
12/31/73	28,800	4,185	34,181	62,981	3,402	37,788	58,400	96,188	33,537	129,725	21,638
12/31/74	30,000	6,651	40,832	70,832	0	30,422	45,103	75,525	32,201	107,726	23,266
12/31/75	31,200	6,451	47,284	78,484	844	40,585	58,858	99,443	47,935	147,378	24,748
12/31/76	32,400	6,063	53,347	85,747	2,942	51,474	75,617	127,091	65,395	192,486	26,206
12/31/77	33,600	6,518	59,865	93,465	3,791	48,621	73,465	122,086	66,691	188,777	27,904
12/31/78	34,800	7,393	67,258	102,058	0	55,212	81,338	136,550	81,385	217,935	29,096
12/31/79	36,000	9,305	76,562	112,562	2,619	64,012	95,128	159,140	101,981	261,121	30,720
TOTAL					69,794						

TABLE 15. HYPOTHETICAL ILLUSTRATION—$48,000 INVESTMENT IN THE SEMINAR FUND

DATE	INITIAL INVESTMENT	OFFERING PRICE	SALES CHARGE INCLUDED	SHARES PURCHASED	NET ASSET VALUE PER SHARE	INITIAL NET ASSET VALUE
1/1/50	$48,000.00	$2.64	5.00%	18,181.820	$2.480	$45,091

SYSTEMATIC WITHDRAWAL PLAN
DIVIDENDS AND CAPITAL GAINS REINVESTED
MONTHLY WITHDRAWALS OF $512.29 (12.8% ANNUALLY) BEGINNING 1/31/50

DATE	AMOUNTS WITHDRAWN				ANNUAL CAP GAIN DISTRIB'N	VALUE OF REMAINING SHARES			SHARES HELD
	FROM INCOME DIVS	FROM PRINCIPAL	ANNUAL TOTAL	CUM TOTAL		REMAINING ORIGINAL SHARES	CAP GAIN SHARES	TOTAL VALUE	
12/31/50	2,038	4,110	6,147	6,147	1,410	45,710	1,433	47,143	17,111
12/31/51	1,933	4,210	6,147	12,294	2,122	45,301	3,697	48,598	16,428
12/31/52	1,791	4,356	6,147	18,441	2,170	45,324	6,011	48,335	15,693
12/31/53	1,741	4,407	6,147	24,588	1,192	35,344	6,820	42,164	14,589
12/31/54	1,587	4,560	6,147	30,735	2,765	44,530	12,656	58,186	14,970
12/31/55	1,773	4,374	6,147	36,882	4,731	46,922	19,230	66,152	14,044
12/31/56	1,768	4,380	6,147	43,029	4,896	42,753	24,113	66,866	14,181
12/31/57	1,791	4,357	6,147	49,176	3,420	40,668	22,653	53,321	14,068
12/31/58	1,704	4,444	6,147	55,323	2,497	36,298	33,413	59,711	13,575
12/31/59	1,662	4,485	6,147	61,470	4,951	33,299	39,796	73,095	13,675
12/31/60	1,768	4,379	6,147	67,617	3,991	27,452	42,393	69,845	13,601
12/31/61	1,668	4,479	6,147	73,764	4,244	26,698	52,659	79,357	13,553
12/31/62	1,664	4,484	6,147	79,911	2,992	17,269	45,339	62,608	13,194
12/31/63	1,595	4,553	6,147	86,058	2,961	15,092	55,135	70,227	12,885
12/31/64	1,627	4,520	6,147	92,205	2,395	11,736	63,507	75,243	12,884
12/31/65	1,701	4,447	6,147	98,352	5,434	8,981	79,617	88,598	13,019
12/31/66	2,028	4,119	6,147	104,499	6,588	4,262	78,998	83,250	13,384
12/31/67	2,242	3,905	6,147	110,646	4,851	1,076	99,612	100,688	13,515
12/31/68	2,593	3,555	6,147	116,793	4,211	0	110,958	110,958	13,673
12/31/69	2,734	3,414	6,147	122,940	5,637	0	93,225	93,225	14,114
12/31/70	2,764	3,383	6,147	129,087	4,046	0	88,798	88,798	14,173
12/31/71	2,698	3,449	6,147	135,234	1,771	0	97,363	97,363	13,918
12/31/72	2,654	3,494	6,147	141,381	3,153	0	106,175	106,175	13,870
12/31/73	2,772	3,375	6,147	147,528	2,197	0	82,462	82,462	13,755
12/31/74	2,978	3,169	6,147	153,675	0	0	62,022	62,022	13,395
12/31/75	3,493	2,655	6,147	159,822	447	0	77,447	77,447	13,005
12/31/76	3,045	3,103	6,147	165,969	1,440	0	93,694	93,694	12,756

CONTINUED ON PAGE 2

DATE	AMOUNTS WITHDRAWN				ANNUAL CAP GAIN DISTRIB'N	VALUE OF REMAINING SHARES			SHARES HELD
	FROM INCOME DIVS	FROM PRINCIPAL	ANNUAL TOTAL	CUM TOTAL		REMAINING ORIGINAL SHARES	CAP GAIN SHARES	TOTAL VALUE	
12/31/77	3,046	3,101	6,147	172,116	1,717	0	84,975	84,975	12,560
12/31/78	3,181	2,967	6,147	178,263	0	0	90,979	90,979	12,146
12/31/79	3,719	2,429	6,147	184,410	1,093	0	101,725	101,725	11,967
TOTALS	68,763	115,647	184,410		92,320				

TABLE 16.   DIAMONDS VS. OTHER TYPES OF INVESTMENT
(10-YEAR RECORD)

	Compounded Annual Rate of Return, 1969–1979
Chinese Ceramics	18.0%
Rare Books	16.5%
Gold	16.3%
Stamps	15.4%
Coins	13.0%
Diamonds	12.6%
Oil (crude, at the wellhead)	11.8%
Paintings (old masters)	11.6%
Farmland	10.6%
Housing	9.2%
Consumer Price Index	6.1%
Bonds	6.1%
Stocks	2.9%

Source: U.S. News & World Report, Aug. 13, 1979.
Note: Bonds measured by Salomon Brothers index; stocks by Standard & Poor's composite index.

SELECTED SOURCES OF INFORMATION ON DIAMONDS AND GOLD

Arem, Joel. *Gems and Jewelry.* (New York: Bantam, 1975).

Bruton, Eric. *Diamonds.* (Radnor, Pa.: Chilton Book Co., 1970).

Copeland, Lawrence L. *Diamonds, Famous, Notable and Unique.* (Gemological Institute of America, 1974).

The Economist Intelligence Unit (EIU): "Inflation Shelters" EIU Special Report No. 65 (London: The Economist Intelligence Unit, Ltd., 1979).

Moyersoen, Jean-Francois. *Executive Report on Investment Diamonds.* (Thousand Oaks, Ca.: Precious Stones Newsletter, 1979.)

Precioustones Newsletter, P.O. Box 4649, Thousand Oaks, California 91359.

TABLE 17. TAX-FREE VS. TAXABLE BONDS

INTEREST ON A TAX-EXEMPT BOND YIELDING

IS EQUAL TO THE TAXABLE YIELD (%) SHOWN BELOW

MARRIED PERSONS FILING JOINTLY

Taxable Income Bracket (in $1,000's)	Tax Bracket %	5%	5.25%	5.5%	5.75%	6%	6.25%	6.5%	6.75%	7%	7.25%	7.5%	7.75%	8%	8.25%	8.5%	8.75%	9%
7.6-11.9	18	6.10	6.40	6.71	7.01	7.32	7.62	7.93	8.23	8.54	8.84	9.15	9.45	9.76	10.06	10.37	10.67	10.98
11.9-16.0	21	6.33	6.65	6.96	7.28	7.59	7.91	8.23	8.54	8.86	9.18	9.49	9.81	10.13	10.44	10.76	11.08	11.39
16.0-20.2	24	6.58	6.91	7.24	7.57	7.89	8.22	8.55	8.88	9.21	9.54	9.87	10.20	10.53	10.86	11.18	11.51	11.84
20.2-24.6	28	6.94	7.29	7.64	7.99	8.33	8.68	9.03	9.38	9.72	10.07	10.42	10.76	11.11	11.46	11.81	12.15	12.50
24.6-29.9	32	7.35	7.72	8.09	8.46	8.82	9.19	9.56	9.93	10.29	10.66	11.03	11.40	11.76	12.13	12.50	12.87	13.24
29.9-35.2	37	7.94	8.33	8.73	9.13	9.52	9.92	10.32	10.71	11.11	11.51	11.90	12.30	12.70	13.10	13.49	13.89	14.29
35.2-45.8	43	8.77	9.21	9.65	10.09	10.53	10.96	11.40	11.84	12.28	12.72	13.16	13.60	14.04	14.47	14.91	15.35	15.79
45.8-60.0	49	9.80	10.29	10.78	11.27	11.76	12.25	12.75	13.24	13.73	14.22	14.71	15.20	15.69	16.18	16.67	17.16	17.65
60.0-85.6	54	10.87	11.41	11.96	12.50	13.04	13.59	14.13	14.67	15.22	15.76	16.30	16.85	17.39	17.93	18.48	19.02	19.57
85.6-109.4	59	12.20	12.80	13.41	14.02	14.63	15.24	15.85	16.46	17.07	17.68	18.29	18.90	19.51	20.12	20.73	21.34	21.95
109.4-162.4	64	13.89	14.58	15.28	15.97	16.67	17.36	18.06	18.75	19.44	20.14	20.83	21.53	22.22	22.92	23.61	24.31	25.00
162.4-215.4	68	15.63	16.41	17.19	17.97	18.75	19.53	20.31	21.09	21.88	22.66	23.44	24.22	25.00	25.78	26.56	27.34	28.13

SINGLE PERSONS

(in $1,000's)	%	5%	5.25%	5.5%	5.75%	6%	6.25%	6.5%	6.75%	7%	7.25%	7.5%	7.75%	8%	8.25%	8.5%	8.75%	9%
6.5-8.5	19	6.17	6.48	6.79	7.10	7.41	7.72	8.02	8.33	8.64	8.95	9.26	9.57	9.88	10.19	10.49	10.80	11.11
8.5-10.8	21	6.33	6.65	6.96	7.28	7.59	7.91	8.23	8.54	8.86	9.18	9.49	9.81	10.13	10.44	10.76	11.08	11.39
10.8-12.9	24	6.58	6.91	7.24	7.57	7.89	8.22	8.55	8.88	9.21	9.54	9.87	10.20	10.53	10.86	11.18	11.51	11.84
12.9-15.0	26	6.76	7.09	7.43	7.77	8.11	8.45	8.78	9.12	9.46	9.80	10.14	10.47	10.81	11.15	11.49	11.82	12.16
15.0-18.2	30	7.14	7.50	7.86	8.21	8.57	8.93	9.29	9.64	10.00	10.36	10.71	11.07	11.43	11.79	12.14	12.50	12.86
18.2-23.5	34	7.58	7.95	8.33	8.71	9.09	9.47	9.85	10.23	10.61	10.98	11.36	11.74	12.12	12.50	12.88	13.26	13.64
23.5-28.8	39	8.20	8.61	9.02	9.43	9.84	10.25	10.66	11.07	11.48	11.89	12.30	12.70	13.11	13.52	13.93	14.34	14.75
28.8-34.1	44	8.93	9.38	9.82	10.27	10.71	11.16	11.61	12.05	12.50	12.95	13.39	13.84	14.29	14.73	15.18	15.63	16.07
34.1-41.5	49	9.80	10.29	10.78	11.27	11.76	12.25	12.75	13.24	13.73	14.22	14.71	15.20	15.69	16.18	16.67	17.16	17.65
41.5-55.3	55	11.11	11.67	12.22	12.78	13.33	13.89	14.44	15.00	15.56	16.11	16.67	17.22	17.78	18.33	18.89	19.44	20.00
55.3-81.8	63	13.51	14.19	14.86	15.54	16.22	16.89	17.57	18.24	18.92	19.59	20.27	20.95	21.62	22.30	22.97	23.65	24.32
81.8-108.3	68	15.63	16.41	17.19	17.97	18.75	19.53	20.31	21.09	21.88	22.66	23.44	24.22	25.00	25.78	26.56	27.34	28.13

HEADS OF HOUSEHOLD

(in $1,000's)	%	5%	5.25%	5.5%	5.75%	6%	6.25%	6.5%	6.75%	7%	7.25%	7.5%	7.75%	8%	8.25%	8.5%	8.75%	9%
6.5–8.7	18	6.10	6.40	6.71	7.01	7.32	7.62	7.93	8.23	8.54	8.84	9.15	9.45	9.76	10.06	10.37	10.67	10.98
8.7–11.8	22	6.41	6.73	7.05	7.37	7.69	8.01	8.33	8.65	8.97	9.29	9.62	9.94	10.26	10.58	10.90	11.22	11.54
11.8–15.0	24	6.58	6.91	7.24	7.57	7.89	8.22	8.55	8.88	9.21	9.54	9.87	10.20	10.53	10.86	11.18	11.51	11.84
15.0–18.2	26	6.76	7.09	7.43	7.77	8.11	8.45	8.78	9.12	9.46	9.80	10.14	10.47	10.81	11.15	11.49	11.82	12.16
18.2–23.5	31	7.25	7.61	7.97	8.33	8.70	9.06	9.42	9.78	10.14	10.51	10.87	11.23	11.59	11.96	12.32	12.68	13.04
23.5–28.8	36	7.81	8.20	8.59	8.98	9.38	9.77	10.16	10.55	10.94	11.33	11.72	12.11	12.50	12.89	13.28	13.67	14.06
28.8–34.1	42	8.62	9.05	9.48	9.91	10.34	10.78	11.21	11.64	12.07	12.50	12.93	13.36	13.79	14.22	14.66	15.09	15.52
34.1–44.7	46	9.26	9.72	10.19	10.65	11.11	11.57	12.04	12.50	12.96	13.43	13.89	14.35	14.81	15.28	15.74	16.20	16.67
44.7–60.6	54	10.87	11.41	11.96	12.50	13.04	13.59	14.13	14.67	15.22	15.76	16.30	16.85	17.39	17.93	18.48	19.02	19.57
60.6–81.8	59	12.20	12.80	13.41	14.02	14.63	15.24	15.85	16.46	17.07	17.68	18.29	18.90	19.51	20.12	20.73	21.34	21.95
81.8–108.3	63	13.51	14.19	14.86	15.54	16.22	16.89	17.57	18.24	18.92	19.59	20.27	20.95	21.62	22.30	22.97	23.65	24.32
108.2–161.3	68	15.63	16.41	17.19	17.97	18.75	19.53	20.31	21.09	21.88	22.66	23.44	24.22	25.00	25.78	26.56	27.34	28.13

ESTATES AND TRUSTS

(in $1,000's)	%	5%	5.25%	5.5%	5.75%	6%	6.25%	6.5%	6.75%	7%	7.25%	7.5%	7.75%	8%	8.25%	8.5%	8.75%	9%
2.1–4.25	18	6.10	6.40	6.71	7.01	7.32	7.62	7.93	8.23	8.54	8.84	9.15	9.45	9.76	10.06	10.37	10.67	10.98
4.25–6.3	21	6.33	6.65	6.96	7.28	7.59	7.91	8.23	8.54	8.86	9.18	9.49	9.81	10.13	10.44	10.76	11.08	11.39
6.3–8.4	24	6.58	6.91	7.24	7.57	7.89	8.22	8.55	8.88	9.21	9.54	9.87	10.20	10.53	10.86	11.18	11.51	11.84
8.4–10.6	28	6.94	7.29	7.64	7.99	8.33	8.68	9.03	9.38	9.72	10.07	10.42	10.76	11.11	11.46	11.81	12.15	12.50
10.6–13.25	32	7.35	7.72	8.09	8.46	8.82	9.19	9.56	9.93	10.29	10.66	11.03	11.40	11.76	12.13	12.50	12.87	13.24
13.25–15.9	37	7.94	8.33	8.73	9.13	9.52	9.92	10.32	10.71	11.11	11.51	11.90	12.30	12.70	13.10	13.49	13.89	14.29
15.9–21.2	43	8.77	9.21	9.65	10.09	10.53	10.96	11.40	11.84	12.28	12.72	13.16	13.60	14.04	14.47	14.91	15.35	15.79
21.2–28.3	49	9.80	10.29	10.78	11.27	11.76	12.25	12.75	13.24	13.73	14.22	14.71	15.20	15.69	16.18	16.67	17.16	17.65
28.3–41.1	54	10.87	11.41	11.96	12.50	13.04	13.59	14.13	14.67	15.22	15.76	16.30	16.85	17.39	17.93	18.48	19.02	19.57
41.1–53.0	59	12.20	12.80	13.41	14.02	14.63	15.24	15.85	16.46	17.07	17.68	18.29	18.90	19.51	20.12	20.73	21.34	21.95
53.0–79.5	64	13.89	14.58	15.28	15.97	16.67	17.36	18.06	18.75	19.44	20.14	20.83	21.53	22.22	22.92	23.61	24.31	25.00
79.5–106.0	68	15.63	16.41	17.19	17.97	18.75	19.53	20.31	21.09	21.88	22.66	23.44	24.22	25.00	25.78	26.56	27.34	28.13

TABLE 18.

Accumulation Program
$100,000 single premium—$94,000 net premium payment [1]

Year End	Minimum guaranteed interest rate values		Current interest rate values [2]		
	Surrender Amount	Annuity Amount	Surrender Amount	Annuity Amount	Annuity Amount Applied as 120 month payout
1	$ 94,707	$ 99,170	$100,991	$105,750	$1,234
2	99,616	104,624	111,090	116,325	1,358
3	105,412	110,379	122,199	127,958	1,493
4	111,209	116,450	134,419	140,753	1,643
5	117,326	122,854	147,861	154,829	1,807
6	123,779	129,611	162,647	170,311	1,988
7	134,279	136,740	183,970	187,343	2,186
8	141,664	144,261	202,367	206,077	2,405
9	149,455	152,195	222,604	226,685	2,645
10	157,675	160,566	244,865	249,353	2,910
11	169,397	169,397	274,288	274,288	3,201
12	178,714	178,714	301,717	301,717	3,521
13	188,543	188,543	331,889	331,889	3,873
14	198,913	198,913	365,078	365,078	4,260
15	209,853	209,853	401,585	401,585	4,687
16	221,395	221,395	441,744	441,744	5,155
17	233,571	233,571	485,918	485,918	5,671
18	246,418	246,418	534,510	534,510	6,238
19	259,971	259,971	587,961	587,961	6,862
20	274,269	274,269	646,757	646,757	7,548

Monthly annuity rates for each $100,000 of annuity value

Sex	Age[3]	Guaranteed		Current [2]	
		Life	Life 10 C & L	Life	Life 10 C & L
	60	$620	$596	$ 837	$801
M	65	707	662	920	860
	70	830	743	1,041	932
	60	$556	$545	$ 770	753
F	65	627	607	836	808
	70	733	689	939	882

TABLE 19.

Withdrawal Program
$100,000 single premium—$94,000 net premium payment[1]

Year End	$6,000 Annual Withdrawal Program [2] Non-qualified Deferred Annuity				
	Amount [4] Withdrawn	Taxable Income For Year	Total Withdrawn	Remaining Cash Value [5]	Combined Values
1	$6,000	$ -0-	$ 6,000	$ 99,750	$105,750
2	6,000	-0-	12,000	103,725	115,725
3	6,000	-0-	18,000	108,098	126,098
4	6,000	-0-	24,000	112,907	136,907
5	6,000	-0-	30,000	118,198	148,198
6	6,000	-0-	36,000	124,018	160,018
7	6,000	-0-	42,000	130,420	172,420
8	6,000	-0-	48,000	137,462	185,462
9	6,000	-0-	54,000	145,208	199,208
10	6,000	-0-	60,000	153,728	213,728
11	6,000	-0-	66,000	163,101	229,101
12	6,000	-0-	72,000	173,411	245,411
13	6,000	-0-	78,000	184,753	262,753
14	6,000	-0-	84,000	197,228	281,228
15	6,000	-0-	90,000	210,951	300,951
16	6,000	-0-	96,000	226,046	322,046
17	6,000	2,000	102,000	242,650	344,650
18	6,000	6,000	108,000	260,915	368,915
19	6,000	6,000	114,000	281,007	395,007
20	6,000	6,000	120,000	303,107	423,107

[1] No allowance has been made for any applicable state premium taxes.

[2] The Company's current interest rate and the current monthly income payout rates are subject to change. Actual rates may be more or less, but never less than the Guaranteed Rates. If the Contract is annuitized while this contract series is still being offered, then the Current Annuity Rates listed will be used.

[3] Assumes year of birth prior to 1916.

[4] A $2.50 processing fee will be deducted from each partial withdrawal.

[5] This amount is subject to the surrender penalty provision.

TABLE 20. TAX RATE SCHEDULES
SCHEDULE I. SINGLE TAXPAYERS WHO DO NOT QUALIFY FOR RATES IN SCHEDULES II OR III

If the Amount of Taxable Income Is		The Tax Is		
OVER—	BUT NOT OVER—			OF EXCESS OVER—
$ 2,300 —	$ 3,400.........	$ 0 plus 14%	—	$ 2,300
$ 3,400 —	$ 4,400.........	$ 154 plus 16%	—	$ 3,400
$ 4,400 —	$ 6,500.........	$ 314 plus 18%	—	$ 4,400
$ 6,500 —	$ 8,500.........	$ 692 plus 19%	—	$ 6,500
$ 8,500 —	$ 10,800.........	$ 1,072 plus 21%	—	$ 8,500
$ 10,800 —	$ 12,900.........	$ 1,555 plus 24%	—	$ 10,800
$ 12,900 —	$ 15,000.........	$ 2,059 plus 26%	—	$ 12,900
$ 15,000 —	$ 18,200.........	$ 2,605 plus 30%	—	$ 15,000
$ 18,200 —	$ 23,500.........	$ 3,565 plus 34%	—	$ 18,200
$ 23,500 —	$ 28,800.........	$ 5,367 plus 39%	—	$ 23,500
$ 28,800 —	$ 34,100.........	$ 7,434 plus 44%	—	$ 28,800
$ 34,100 —	$ 41,500.........	$ 9,766 plus 49%	—	$ 34,100
$ 41,500 —	$ 55,300.........	$13,392 plus 55%	—	$ 41,500
$ 55,300 —	$ 81,800.........	$20,982 plus 63%	—	$ 55,300
$ 81,800 —	$108,300.........	$37,677 plus 68%	—	$ 81,800
$108,300	....	$55,697 plus 70%	—	$108,300

SCHEDULE II. MARRIED TAXPAYERS FILING JOINT RETURNS, AND CERTAIN WIDOWS AND WIDOWERS

If the Amount of Taxable Income Is		The Tax Is		
OVER—	BUT NOT OVER—			OF EXCESS OVER—
$ 3,400 —	$ 5,500.........	$ 0 plus 14%	—	$ 3,400
$ 5,500 —	$ 7,600.........	$ 294 plus 16%	—	$ 5,500
$ 7,600 —	$ 11,900.........	$ 630 plus 18%	—	$ 7,600
$ 11,900 —	$ 16,000.........	$ 1,404 plus 21%	—	$ 11,900
$ 16,000 —	$ 20,200.........	$ 2,265 plus 24%	—	$ 16,000
$ 20,200 —	$ 24,600.........	$ 3,273 plus 28%	—	$ 20,200
$ 24,600 —	$ 29,900.........	$ 4,505 plus 32%	—	$ 24,600
$ 29,900 —	$ 35,200.........	$ 6,201 plus 37%	—	$ 29,900
$ 35,200 —	$ 45,800.........	$ 8,162 plus 43%	—	$ 35,200
$ 45,800 —	$ 60,000.........	$12,720 plus 49%	—	$ 45,800
$ 60,000 —	$ 85,600.........	$19,678 plus 54%	—	$ 60,000
$ 85,600 —	$109,400.........	$33,502 plus 59%	—	$ 85,600
$109,400 —	$162,400.........	$47,544 plus 64%	—	$109,400
$162,400 —	$215,400.........	$81,464 plus 68%	—	$162,400
$215,400	....	$117,504 plus 70%	—	$215,400

Schedule III.   Unmarried (Or Legally Separated) Taxpayers Who Qualify as Head of Household

If the Amount of Taxable Income Is		The Tax Is	
OVER—	BUT NOT OVER—		OF EXCESS OVER—
$ 2,300 —	$ 4,400	$ 0 plus 14% —	$ 2,300
$ 4,400 —	$ 6,500	$ 294 plus 16% —	$ 4,400
$ 6,500 —	$ 8,700	$ 630 plus 18% —	$ 6,500
$ 8,700 —	$ 11,800	$ 1,026 plus 22% —	$ 8,700
$ 11,800 —	$ 15,000	$ 1,708 plus 24% —	$ 11,800
$ 15,000 —	$ 18,200	$ 2,476 plus 26% —	$ 15,000
$ 18,200 —	$ 23,500	$ 3,308 plus 31% —	$ 18,200
$ 23,500 —	$ 28,800	$ 4,951 plus 36% —	$ 23,500
$ 28,800 —	$ 34,100	$ 6,859 plus 42% —	$ 28,800
$ 34,100 —	$ 44,700	$ 9,085 plus 46% —	$ 34,100
$ 44,700 —	$ 60,600	$13,961 plus 54% —	$ 44,700
$ 60,600 —	$ 81,800	$22,547 plus 59% —	$ 60,600
$ 81,800 —	$108,300	$35,055 plus 63% —	$ 81,800
$108,300 —	$161,300	$51,750 plus 68% —	$108,300
$161,300		$87,790 plus 70% —	$161,300

TABLE 21.

PROJECTED INVESTMENT PERFORMANCE FOR A LIMITED PARTNER IN A 50% TAX BRACKET
FOR A $57,250 INVESTMENT (1/35th OF TOTAL OFFERING AMOUNT)

YEAR	INVESTMENT	ANNUAL (TAX LOSSES) OR TAXABLE INCOME	RATIO OF TAX LOSSES TO INVESTMENT	ANNUAL TAX SAVINGS OR (TAX LIABILITY)	ANNUAL SHELTERED CASH DISTRIBUTION	TOTAL ANNUAL BENEFITS	CUMULATIVE AFTER TAX BENEFITS
1979	$ 6,500	$(7,193)	111%	$ 3,597		$ 3,597	$ 3,597
1980	15,500	(25,589)	165%	12,794		12,794	16,391
1981	13,000	(19,946)	153%	9,973	$ 2,096	12,069	28,460
1982	12,000	(16,783)	140%	8,392	2,739	11,131	39,591
1983	10,250	(14,873)	145%	7,436	3,384	10,820	50,411
1984		(3,869)		1,935	4,104	6,039	56,450
1985		402		(201)	4,782	4,581	61,031
1986		1,222		(611)	5,383	4,772	65,803
1987		2,040		(1,020)	6,014	4,994	70,797
1988		2,861		(1,431)	6,676	5,245	76,042
	$57,250	$ 81,728		$40,864	$35,178	$76,042	

PROJECTION OF RESALE ON JANUARY 1, 1989

ASSUMPTIONS	PRETAX RESALE PROCEEDS		RESALE TAX LIABILITY		YEAR OF RESALE AFTER TAX BENEFITS		PREVIOUS AFTER TAX BENEFITS		CUMULATIVE AFTER TAX BENEFITS THROUGH RESALE
A. Abandonment on 1/1/89	None	-	$19,243	=	$(19,243)	+	$76,042	=	$ 56,799
B. Resale of property at the Partnership's original purchase price	$44,544	-	30,379	=	14,165	+	76,042	=	91,042
C. Resale of property at estimated market value	87,186	-	41,040	=	46,146	+	76,042	=	122,188

THE ACCOMPANYING NOTES AND ASSUMPTIONS ARE AN INTEGRAL PART OF THIS STATEMENT.

(The above represents a mere prediction of future events based on assumptions which may or may not occur and may not be relied upon to indicate the actual results which may be obtained.)

TABLE 22.

Marine Containers

Hypothetical Example of Limited Partner's Share of Distribution,
Taxable Income or Loss, and Investment Tax Credit
For a $10,000 Investment

PARTNERSHIP TAX CALCULATIONS

YEAR	1. CASH* DISTRIBUTIONS TO LIMITED PARTNER	2. ADD REPAYMENT of PRINCIPAL on LOANS	3. DEDUCT DEPRECIATION	4. TAXABLE INCOME (loss) REPORTED TO LIMITED PARTNER	5. INVESTMENT TAX CREDIT	6. LIMITED PARTNER'S AFTER-TAX CASH FLOW ***	7. UNRECOVERED INVESTMENT	8. ENDING BALANCE of REINVESTMENT FUND
1979	$ ---	$ ---	$ 400	$ (400)	$400	$ 600	$ 9,400	$ 600
1980	1,200	---	3,400	(2,200)	600	2,900	6,500	3,623
1981	1,588	350	2,150	(212)	---	1,694	4,806	5,585
1982	1,680	400	1,800	280	---	1,540	3,266	7,506
1983	1,777	450	1,450	777	---	1,389	1,877	9,387
1984	1,879	550	1,150	1,279	---	1,240	637	11,227
1985	1,986	600	800	1,786	---	1,093	---	13,026
1986	2,098	650	350	2,398	---	899	---	14,734
1987	2,216	800	---	3,016	---	708	---	16,347
1988	2,839	---	---	2,839	---	1,420	---	18,790
1989	2,968	---	---	2,968	---	1,484	---	21,446
1990	3,104	---	---	3,104	---	1,552	---	24,331
1991	3,247	---	---	3,247	---	1,624	---	27,464
1992	5,898*	---	---	5,898**	---	3,549	---	32,767
1993	6,517*	---	---	6,517**	---	3,559	---	38,400
TOTAL	38,997	3,800	11,500	31,297	1,000	25,251		

* Includes Limited Partner's share of sales proceeds -- $2,500 in 1992 and $3,000 in 1993.

** Taxable income is reallocated to General Partners to eliminate their capital account deficits -- $1,200 in 1992 and $175 in 1993. In addition, $925 of commissions and organizational expenses are deducted in 1993.

*** For the other key assumptions, see Explanatory Footnotes which accompany this example. Assumes a 50% investor tax bracket.

TABLE 23. ANALYSIS OF PRESIDENTIAL 100 LIFE INSURANCE PLAN

AGE 40M — AMOUNT OF POLICY $25000

	ANNUAL RESULTS			CUMULATIVE RESULTS					
	(1) Your Annual Payment	(2) The Savings Portion of Your Insurance Will Increase By	(3) Therefore, Your Annual Cost Is Only	(4) The Total of Your Payments	(5) The Total Savings Portion of Your Insurance	(6) You May Elect Paid-Up Insurance in the Amount of	(7) Therefore, Your Cumulative Cost Is Only	(8) If You Should Die, Your Beneficiary Will Receive Tax Free *	INSURANCE YEAR
	$525.50	$ NONE	$525.50	$ 525.50	$ NONE	$ NONE	$ 525.50	$25000	1
	525.50	250	275.50	1051.00	250	600	801.00	25000	2
	525.50	450	75.50	1576.50	700	1600	876.50	25000	3
	525.50	475	50.50	2102.00	1175	2600	927.00	25000	4
	525.50	475	50.50	2627.50	1650	3575	977.50	25000	5
	525.50	475	50.50	3153.00	2125	4475	1028.00	25000	6
	525.50	500	25.50	3678.50	2625	5400	1053.50	25000	7
	525.50	475	50.50	4204.00	3100	6250	1104.00	25000	8
	525.50	500	25.50	4729.50	3600	7075	1129.50	25000	9
	525.50	500	25.50	5255.00	4100	7900	1155.00	25000	10
	525.50	500	25.50	5780.50	4600	8650	1180.50	25000	11
	525.50	500	25.50	6306.00	5100	9400	1206.00	25000	12
	525.50	525	.50	6831.50	5625	10150	1206.50	25000	13
	525.50	500	25.50	7357.00	6125	10825	1232.00	25000	14
	525.50	525	.50	7882.50	6650	11500	1232.50	25000	15
	525.50	500	25.50	8408.00	7150	12125	1258.00	25000	16
	525.50	525	.50	8933.50	7675	12750	1258.50	25000	17
	525.50	525	.50	9459.00	8200	13350	1259.00	25000	18
	525.50	500	25.50	9984.50	8700	13900	1284.50	25000	19
	525.50	525	.50	10510.00	9225	14475	1285.00	25000	20
	525.50	525	.50	10510.00	9225	14475	1285.00	25000	AGE 60
	525.50	500	25.50	13137.50	11725	16875	1412.50	25000	AGE 65

* Federal Income Tax

This Column Shows The Most That You Could Lose If You Surrendered This Plan

661

TABLE 24.   INCIDENTAL COST OF P.S. 58

The Incidental Cost of P.S. 58 when Life Insurance is included in a Pension or Profit Sharing Plan just may not be so incidental.

The following shows the cumulative Income Tax Liability passed through to the Insured "For the Premature Death Benefit" when it is included in a Pension or Profit Sharing Program.

TAX LIABILITY PER $100,000 INSURANCE FACE AMOUNT

Issue Age	P.S. 58
65	$ 3,151
64	6,049
63	8,712
62	11,162
61	13,415
60	$15,488
59	17,396
58	19,152
57	20,770
56	22,261
55	$23,635
54	24,902
53	26,071
52	27,150
51	28,147
50	$29,069
49	29,922
48	30,711
47	31,443
46	32,121
45	$32,751
44	33,336
43	33,880
42	34,387
41	34,860
40	35,302

TABLE 25.   P.S. No. 58 RATES

The following rates are used in computing the "cost" of pure life insurance protection that is taxable to the employee under: qualified pension and profit-sharing plans (Q&A 179); split-dollar plans (Q&A 76); and tax-sheltered annuities (Q&A 123). Rev. Rul. 55–747, 1955–2 CB 228; Rev. Rul. 66–110, 1966–1 CB 12.

ONE YEAR TERM PREMIUMS FOR $1,000 OF LIFE INSURANCE PROTECTION

Age	Premium	Age	Premium	Age	Premium
15	$ 1.27	37	$ 3.63	59	$ 19.08
16	1.38	38	3.87	60	20.73
17	1.48	39	4.14	61	22.53
18	1.52	40	4.42	62	24.50
19	1.56	41	4.73	63	26.63
20	1.61	42	5.07	64	28.98
21	1.67	43	5.44	65	31.51
22	1.73	44	5.85	66	34.28
23	1.79	45	6.30	67	37.31
24	1.86	46	6.78	68	40.59
25	1.93	47	7.32	69	44.17
26	2.02	48	7.89	70	48.06
27	2.11	49	8.53	71	52.29
28	2.20	50	9.22	72	56.89
29	2.31	51	9.97	73	61.89
30	2.43	52	10.79	74	67.33
31	2.57	53	11.69	75	73.23
32	2.70	54	12.67	76	79.63
33	2.86	55	13.74	77	86.57
34	3.02	56	14.91	78	94.09
35	3.21	57	16.18	79	102.23
36	3.41	58	17.56	80	111.04
				81	120.57

The rate at insured's attained age is applied to the excess of the amount payable at death over the cash value of the policy at the end of the year.

TABLE 26.   UNIFORM PREMIUM TABLE
UNIFORM PREMIUMS FOR $1,000 OF GROUP-TERM
LIFE INSURANCE PROTECTION *

5-Year Age Bracket	Cost per $1,000 of Protection for 1-Month Period
Under 30	8 cents
30 to 34	10 cents
35 to 39	14 cents
40 to 44	23 cents
45 to 49	40 cents
50 to 54	68 cents
55 to 59	$1.10
60 to 64	$1.63

* In using the above table, the age of the employee is his attained age on the last day of his taxable year. However, if an employee has attained an age greater than age 64, he shall be treated as if he were in the 5-year age bracket 60 to 64.

Up to $50,000 of group-term life insurance coverage is tax-exempt to an employee. IRC Sec. 79(a). This exemption is not available, however, unless (1) the coverage is on the life of an *employee,* and is provided as compensation for personal services rendered by the insured as an employee; (2) the coverage is *group-term life insurance* under the regulations; and (3) the insurance is carried directly or indirectly by the insured's employer. Reg. §1.79–1(a) and (b).

No part of the cost of group-term insurance on the life of a self-employed person, whether he is the employer or someone who performs services for the employer as an independent contractor, is exempt. Reg. §1.79–1(b)(2). Thus, the cost of group-term insurance for a partner or sole proprietor is not exempt to the self-employed individual even though he is included in the coverage for his employees. And group term insurance provided for an individual in his capacity as a corporate owner or as a director does not qualify for the exemption.

TABLE 27. DISABILITY PROBABILITY COMPARED WITH DEATH PROBABILITY FOR 1,000 LIVES EXPOSED

Attained Age	Probability of Disability of 90 Days or More at Age Indicated	Probability of Indicated	Ratio of Disability Probability to Probability of Death
22	6.64%	.89%	7.46
27	6.57%	.98%	6.70
32	7.78%	1.18%	6.59
37	9.81%	1.68%	5.84
42	12.57%	2.95%	4.26
47	16.76%	4.91%	3.41
52	22.39%	8.21%	2.73
57	31.10%	13.22%	2.35
62	44.27%	21.22%	2.10

Source: O. B. Dickerson Health Insurance, Third Edition.

PROBABILITY OF AT LEAST ONE LONG TERM DISABILITY (90 DAYS OR MORE) IN GROUPS OF ONE TO SIX MEN

AGE	PERIOD OF YEARS	ONE	TWO	THREE	FOUR	FIVE	SIX
25	40	53.7%	78.6%	90.1%	95.4%	97.9%	99.0%
30	35	52.2%	77.1%	89.1%	94.8%	97.5%	98.8%
40	25	47.7%	72.7%	85.7%	92.5%	96.1%	98.0%
45	20	44.3%	69.0%	82.7%	90.4%	94.6%	9%
50	15	39.4%	63.2%	77.7%	86.5%	91.8%	95.0%
55	10	32.1%	53.8%	68.6%	78.7%	85.5%	90.2%
60	5	20.4%	36.6%	49.5%	59.8%	68.0%	74.5%

Source: 1964 Commissioners' Disability Table.

Almost half of all disability claims are paid to people 55 and over, according to separate studies by the Social Security Administration and a private disability insurer. This dramatically illustrates the need for non-cancellable insurance which does not eliminate benefits as an insured person grows older.

Age Group	Insurance Co. Study	Social Security Claimants
18–39	7.3%	13.9%
40–44	9.6%	8.2%
45–49	9.6%	11.9%
50–54	22.9%	18.4%
55–59	26.7%	26.2%
60–64	23.9%	21.5%
	100.0%	100.0%

TABLE 28. WITHOUT IRA ROLLOVER

$88,201 distribution   January 1, 1944 - December 31, 1954

$14,056 taxes due   Self-Liquidating for the next 21 years

$74,145 Balance Invested in The Seminar Fund   January 1, 1955 - January 1, 1976

9% withdrawal for first 11 years

DATE	INITIAL INVESTMENT	OFFERING PRICE	SALES CHARGE INCLUDED	SHARES PURCHASED	NET ASSET VALUE PER SHARE	INITIAL NET ASSET VALUE
1/ 1/44	$74,145.00	$4.75	4.50%	15,609.470	$4.532	$70,742

SYSTEMATIC WITHDRAWAL PLAN
DIVIDENDS AND CAPITAL GAINS REINVESTED
MONTHLY WITHDRAWALS OF $556.09 (9.0% ANNUALLY) BEGINNING 1/31/44

DATE	=======AMOUNTS WITHDRAWN=======					====VALUE OF REMAINING SHARES=====			
	FROM INCOME DIVS	FROM PRINCIPAL	ANNUAL TOTAL	CUM TOTAL	ANNUAL CAP GAIN DISTRIB'N	REMAINING ORIGINAL SHARES	CAP GAIN SHARES	TOTAL VALUE	SHARES HELD
12/31/44	1,920	4,753	6,673	6,673	2,536	76,330	2,609	78,939	15,116
12/31/45	1,640	5,033	6,673	13,346	6,235	89,410	9,567	98,977	15,245
12/31/46	2,243	4,430	6,673	20,019	5,407	75,400	13,751	89,151	15,509
12/31/47	2,869	3,804	6,673	26,692	3,446	65,696	16,086	81,782	15,448
12/31/48	2,854	3,819	6,673	33,365	2,108	57,444	17,047	74,491	15,152
12/31/49	2,556	4,117	6,673	40,038	2,311	53,652	19,522	73,174	14,752
12/31/50	2,715	3,958	6,673	46,711	2,134	55,373	23,854	79,227	14,378
12/31/51	2,668	4,005	6,673	53,384	3,327	55,971	29,189	85,160	14,276
12/31/52	2,550	4,123	6,673	60,057	3,514	53,577	33,694	87,271	14,167
12/31/53	2,637	4,036	6,673	66,730	1,956	46,278	33,551	79,829	13,811
12/31/54	2,526	4,148	6,673	73,403	4,844	61,744	53,290	115,034	13,809
TOTALS	27,178	46,225	73,403		37,818				

NOTE: 20.0% SUBTRACTED FROM DIVIDENDS AND 10.0% SUBTRACTED FROM CAPITAL GAIN DISTRIBUTIONS AS PAID TO REFLECT LIABILITY FOR FEDERAL INCOME TAXES.

SYSTEMATIC WITHDRAWAL PLAN
DIVIDENDS AND CAPITAL GAINS REINVESTED

DATE	INITIAL INVESTMENT	OFFERING PRICE	SALES CHARGE INCLUDED	SHARES PURCHASED	NET ASSET VALUE PER SHARE	INITIAL NET ASSET VALUE
1/ 1/55	$115,034.00	$8.33	0.00%	13,809.600	$8.330	$115,034

MONTHLY WITHDRAWALS BEGINNING 1/31/55 BASED ON A 21-YEAR SELF-LIQUIDATING PROGRAM DESIGNED TO EXHAUST PRINCIPAL

	=====AMOUNTS WITHDRAWN=====					=====VALUE OF REMAINING SHARES=====			
DATE	FROM INCOME DIVS	FROM PRINCIPAL	ANNUAL TOTAL	CUM TOTAL	ANNUAL CAP GAIN DISTRIB'N	REMAINING ORIGINAL SHARES	CAP GAIN SHARES	TOTAL VALUE	SHARES HELD
12/31/55	2,875	3,313	6,188	6,188	8,659	126,629	8,995	135,624	14,397
12/31/56	2,958	4,240	7,198	13,386	9,286	122,702	18,229	140,931	14,945
12/31/57	3,080	4,083	7,164	20,550	6,642	95,234	21,012	116,246	15,335
12/31/58	3,035	4,692	7,727	28,277	5,028	123,528	33,939	157,467	15,332
12/31/59	3,034	6,923	9,956	38,233	10,188	121,668	45,649	167,317	15,651
12/31/60	3,265	6,917	10,182	48,415	8,273	109,723	52,479	162,202	15,793
12/31/61	3,110	9,242	12,352	60,767	8,904	115,628	68,904	184,532	15,758
12/31/62	3,113	8,187	11,300	72,067	6,286	85,837	61,439	147,276	15,519
12/31/63	3,015	9,746	12,761	84,828	6,304	88,472	77,080	165,552	15,188
12/31/64	3,055	12,318	15,373	100,201	9,260	82,725	91,923	174,648	14,952
12/31/65	3,116	14,800	17,916	118,117	11,159	80,791	118,649	199,440	14,653
12/31/66	3,563	16,289	19,852	137,969	13,120	58,249	120,820	179,069	14,394
12/31/67	3,739	20,086	23,825	161,794	9,038	49,174	154,042	203,216	13,638
12/31/68	3,992	22,827	26,819	186,613	7,572	28,944	177,080	206,024	12,694
12/31/69	3,815	23,521	27,336	215,949	10,930	1,893	153,972	155,865	11,798
12/31/70	3,483	20,319	23,802	239,751	5,988	0	131,831	131,831	10,521
12/31/71	2,957	25,919	28,876	268,627	2,044	0	122,503	122,503	8,756
12/31/72	2,386	30,509	32,895	301,522	2,899	0	105,567	105,567	6,895
12/31/73	1,862	28,842	30,704	332,226	1,447	0	58,008	58,008	4,838
12/31/74	1,582	24,489	26,071	358,297	0	0	23,515	23,515	2,539
12/31/75	414	29,620	30,034	388,331	14	0	0	0	0
TOTALS	61,451	326,880	388,331		143,040				

NOTE: 20.0% SUBTRACTED FROM DIVIDENDS AND 10.0% SUBTRACTED FROM CAPITAL GAIN DISTRIBUTIONS AS PAID TO REFLECT LIABILITY FOR FEDERAL INCOME TAXES.

TABLE 29. WITH IRA ROLLOVER

$88,201 Invested in The Seminar Fund

9% withdrawal for 11 years

Self-Liquidating for the next 21 years

January 1, 1955 through January 1, 1976

DATE				NET ASSET VALUE PER SHARE	INITIAL NET ASSET VALUE
1/ 1/44	$88,201.00	$4.75	4.50%	18,566.630	$4.532	$84,153

SYSTEMATIC WITHDRAWAL PLAN
DIVIDENDS AND CAPITAL GAINS REINVESTED
MONTHLY WITHDRAWALS OF $661.51 (9.0% ANNUALLY) BEGINNING 1/31/44

DATE	=====AMOUNTS WITHDRAWN=====				ANNUAL CAP GAIN DISTRIB'N	====VALUE OF REMAINING SHARES====			SHARES HELD
	FROM INCOME DIVS	FROM PRINCIPAL	ANNUAL TOTAL	CUM TOTAL		REMAINING ORIGINAL SHARES	CAP GAIN SHARES	TOTAL VALUE	
12/31/44	2,864	5,074	6,350	6,350	3,367	91,396	3,464	94,860	18,165
12/31/45	2,471	5,467	6,350	12,701	8,365	107,664	12,790	120,454	18,554
12/31/46	3,425	4,513	6,350	19,051	7,346	91,560	18,498	110,058	19,147
12/31/47	4,451	3,487	6,350	25,402	4,766	80,893	21,769	102,662	19,392
12/31/48	4,506	3,432	6,350	31,752	2,969	71,941	23,185	95,126	19,350
12/31/49	4,112	3,826	6,350	38,102	3,319	68,577	26,728	95,305	19,214
12/31/50	4,459	3,479	6,350	44,453	3,126	72,437	32,869	105,306	19,111
12/31/51	4,469	3,469	6,350	50,803	4,980	75,002	40,618	115,620	19,383
12/31/52	4,363	3,575	6,350	57,154	5,375	73,777	47,378	121,155	19,667
12/31/53	4,621	3,317	6,350	63,504	3,064	65,961	47,488	113,449	19,627
12/31/54	4,527	3,411	6,350	69,854	7,764	90,907	76,351	167,258	20,078
TOTALS	44,267	43,051	69,854		54,442				

NOTE: 20.0% SUBTRACTED FROM TOTAL AMOUNTS WITHDRAWN TO REFLECT LIABILITY FOR FEDERAL INCOME TAXES.

DATE	INITIAL INVESTMENT	OFFERING PRICE	SALES CHARGE INCLUDED	SHARES PURCHASED	NET ASSET VALUE PER SHARE	INITIAL NET ASSET VALUE
1/ 1/55	$167,258.00	$8.33	0.00%	20,076.990	$8.330	$167,258

SYSTEMATIC WITHDRAWAL PLAN
DIVIDENDS AND CAPITAL GAINS REINVESTED
MONTHLY WITHDRAWALS BEGINNING 1/31/55 BASED ON A 21-YEAR SELF-LIQUIDATING PROGRAM DESIGNED TO EXHAUST PRINCIPAL

DATE	=AMOUNTS WITHDRAWN= FROM INCOME DIVS	FROM PRINCIPAL	ANNUAL TOTAL	CUM TOTAL	ANNUAL CAP GAIN DISTRIB'N	=VALUE OF REMAINING SHARES= REMAINING ORIGINAL SHARES	CAP GAIN SHARES	TOTAL VALUE	SHARES HELD
12/31/55	5,248	3,797	7,236	7,236	14,050	185,168	14,592	199,760	21,205
12/31/56	5,462	5,180	8,514	15,750	15,259	180,421	29,767	210,188	22,289
12/31/57	5,762	4,972	8,587	24,337	11,050	140,959	34,508	175,467	23,148
12/31/58	5,744	5,975	9,376	33,713	8,466	183,947	55,963	239,910	23,360
12/31/59	5,796	9,447	12,194	45,907	17,312	182,044	75,792	257,836	24,119
12/31/60	6,320	9,472	12,633	58,541	14,201	165,071	87,615	252,686	24,604
12/31/61	6,076	13,249	15,461	74,002	15,462	174,631	115,644	290,275	24,788
12/31/62	6,146	11,712	14,286	88,288	11,005	130,332	103,523	233,855	24,642
12/31/63	6,001	14,332	16,266	104,554	11,161	134,828	130,432	265,260	24,335
12/31/64	6,134	18,581	19,772	124,326	16,541	126,264	156,428	282,692	24,203
12/31/65	6,324	22,786	23,288	147,614	20,138	123,137	203,093	326,230	23,969
12/31/66	7,324	25,342	26,133	173,748	23,910	88,313	208,183	296,496	23,834
12/31/67	7,762	31,838	31,680	205,428	16,683	73,127	266,570	339,697	22,798
12/31/68	8,387	36,714	36,081	241,509	14,064	40,049	307,617	347,666	21,421
12/31/69	8,103	38,361	37,171	278,679	20,493		266,168	266,168	20,148
12/31/70	7,475	33,447	32,737	311,417	11,362		227,621	227,621	18,166
12/31/71	6,395	43,606	40,001	351,418	3,937		213,107	213,107	15,232
12/31/72	5,198	52,185	45,907	397,324	5,625		185,164	185,164	12,094
12/31/73	4,091	49,925	43,213	440,537	2,832		102,684	102,684	8,564
12/31/74	3,513	42,802	37,052	477,588	0		42,129	42,129	4,549
12/31/75	929	53,073	43,201	520,789	27		0	0	0
TOTALS	124,190	526,796	520,789		253,578				

NOTE: 20.0% SUBTRACTED FROM TOTAL AMOUNTS WITHDRAWN TO REFLECT LIABILITY FOR FEDERAL INCOME TAXES.

TABLE 30. HYPOTHETICAL ILLUSTRATION—$1500 INVESTMENT IN THE SEMINAR FUND

DATE	INITIAL INVESTMENT	OFFERING PRICE	SALES CHARGE INCLUDED	SHARES PURCHASED	NET ASSET VALUE PER SHARE	INITIAL NET ASSET VALUE
1/ 1/39	$1,500.00	$2.30	8.50%	652.174	$2.108	$1,375

ANNUAL INVESTMENTS OF $1,500.00 -- SAME DAY AS INITIAL INVESTMENT
DIVIDENDS AND CAPITAL GAINS REINVESTED

CUMULATIVE VOLUME DISCOUNT REFLECTED WHERE APPLICABLE IN THIS ILLUSTRATION

| | =====COST OF SHARES===== | | | | | =====VALUE OF SHARES===== | | | | | |
DATE	CUM INV'M'T	ANNUAL INCOME DIVS	CUM INCOME DIVS	TOTAL INV'M'T COST	ANNUAL CAP GAIN DISTRIB'N	FROM INV'M'T	FROM CAP GAINS REINV'D	SUB-TOTAL	FROM DIVS REINV'D	TOTAL VALUE	SHARES HELD
12/31/39	1,500	30	30	1,530	37	1,313	43	1,356	30	1,386	688
12/31/40	3,000	99	128	3,128	41	2,480	82	2,562	130	2,692	1,448
12/31/41	4,500	210	339	4,839	13	3,366	85	3,451	316	3,767	2,319
12/31/42	6,000	270	609	6,609	54	5,209	155	5,364	641	6,005	3,366
12/31/43	7,500	308	917	8,417	113	8,361	311	8,672	1,123	9,795	4,322
12/31/44	9,000	396	1,313	10,313	485	11,213	857	12,070	1,702	13,772	5,274
12/31/45	10,500	418	1,731	12,231	1,421	15,667	2,506	18,173	2,568	20,741	6,389
12/31/46	12,000	664	2,395	14,395	1,419	15,099	3,608	18,707	2,897	21,604	7,516
12/31/47	13,500	960	3,355	16,855	1,085	15,183	4,399	19,582	3,617	23,199	8,764
12/31/48	15,000	1,134	4,489	19,489	764	15,388	4,849	20,237	4,441	24,678	10,039
12/31/49	16,500	1,188	5,677	22,177	986	16,952	5,881	22,833	5,718	28,551	11,512
12/31/50	18,000	1,477	7,154	25,154	1,055	20,395	7,606	28,001	7,898	35,899	13,030
12/31/51	19,500	1,652	8,806	28,306	1,880	23,607	10,135	33,742	10,218	43,960	14,739
12/31/52	21,000	1,777	10,582	31,582	2,230	25,836	12,720	38,556	12,353	50,909	16,528
12/31/53	22,500	2,029	12,612	35,112	1,444	25,584	13,365	38,949	13,625	52,574	18,191
12/31/54	24,000	2,179	14,790	38,790	3,927	38,934	23,275	62,209	22,110	84,319	20,244
12/31/55	25,500	2,766	17,557	43,057	7,436	45,649	34,038	79,687	27,849	107,536	22,831
12/31/56	27,000	3,068	20,625	47,625	8,666	47,146	42,686	89,832	30,876	120,708	25,600
12/31/57	28,500	3,448	24,073	52,573	6,645	39,060	40,682	79,742	27,899	107,641	28,401
12/31/58	30,000	3,673	27,745	57,745	5,456	54,882	61,042	115,924	42,002	157,926	30,754
12/31/59	31,500	3,971	31,716	63,216	11,950	58,633	75,643	134,276	47,711	181,987	34,048
12/31/60	33,000	4,645	36,361	69,361	10,327	57,720	83,428	141,148	50,607	191,755	37,342
12/31/61	34,500	4,820	41,181	75,681	12,325	67,465	107,666	175,131	62,667	237,798	40,614
12/31/62	36,000	5,278	46,459	82,459	9,308	55,847	95,560	151,407	56,163	207,570	43,744
12/31/63	37,500	5,605	52,063	89,563	10,582	65,806	120,676	186,482	70,361	256,843	47,127
12/31/64	39,000	6,273	58,337	97,337	17,199	72,081	146,637	218,718	81,588	300,306	51,422

CONTINUED ON PAGE 2

670

	===========COST OF SHARES===========				ANNUAL CAP GAIN DISTRIB'N	===========VALUE OF SHARES===========					SHARES HELD
DATE	CUM INV'M'T	ANNUAL INCOME DIVS	CUM INCOME DIVS	TOTAL INV'M'T COST		FROM INV'M'T	FROM CAP GAINS REINV'D	SUB-TOTAL	FROM DIVS REINV'D	TOTAL VALUE	
12/31/65	40,500	7,131	65,468	105,968	23,029	85,697	194,640	280,337	102,732	383,069	56,292
12/31/66	42,000	9,169	74,636	116,636	29,488	79,666	205,756	285,422	102,893	388,315	62,430
12/31/67	43,500	10,890	85,527	129,027	23,721	97,171	270,895	368,066	134,326	502,392	67,435
12/31/68	45,000	13,462	98,988	143,988	21,304	107,445	321,211	428,656	160,694	589,350	72,624
12/31/69	46,500	15,100	114,088	160,588	35,675	88,647	293,566	382,213	145,497	527,710	79,895
12/31/70	48,000	16,330	130,418	178,418	23,234	85,478	301,951	387,429	155,622	543,051	86,680
12/31/71	49,500	17,130	147,548	197,048	11,533	97,079	348,860	445,939	191,312	637,251	91,101
12/31/72	51,000	17,982	165,530	216,530	21,871	107,845	404,070	511,915	228,045	739,960	96,663
12/31/73	52,500	20,087	185,617	238,117	16,327	85,609	333,337	418,946	197,804	616,750	102,877
12/31/74	54,000	31,505	217,122	271,122	0	67,251	257,439	324,690	182,596	507,286	109,565
12/31/75	55,500	30,150	247,272	302,772	3,945	88,388	335,078	423,466	265,318	688,784	115,664
12/31/76	57,000	28,177	275,449	332,449	13,671	110,831	427,325	538,156	356,388	894,544	121,789
12/31/77	58,500	30,288	305,738	364,238	17,530	103,433	411,242	514,675	358,265	872,940	129,037
12/31/78	60,000	34,071	339,808	399,808	0	116,145	455,314	571,459	431,446	1,002,905	133,899
8/31/79	61,500	18,389	358,198	419,698	12,069	136,152	540,308	676,460	519,785	1,196,245	137,975
				TOTAL	370,245						

TABLE 31. HYPOTHETICAL ILLUSTRATION—$1050 INVESTMENT IN THE SEMINAR FUND

DATE	INITIAL INVESTMENT	OFFERING PRICE	SALES CHARGE INCLUDED	SHARES PURCHASED	NET ASSET VALUE PER SHARE	INITIAL NET ASSET VALUE
1/ 1/39	$1,050.00	$2.30	8.50%	456.522	$2.108	$962

ANNUAL INVESTMENTS OF $1,050.00 -- SAME DAY AS INITIAL INVESTMENT
DIVIDENDS AND CAPITAL GAINS REINVESTED

CUMULATIVE VOLUME DISCOUNT REFLECTED WHERE APPLICABLE IN THIS ILLUSTRATION

	=======COST OF SHARES=======					=======VALUE OF SHARES=======					
DATE	CUM INV'M'T	ANNUAL INCOME DIVS	CUM INCOME DIVS	TOTAL INV'M'T COST	ANNUAL CAP GAIN DISTRIB'N	FROM INV'M'T	FROM CAP GAINS REINV'D	SUB-TOTAL	FROM DIVS REINV'D	TOTAL VALUE	SHARES HELD
12/31/39	1,050	14	14	1,064	23	918	27	945	15	960	477
12/31/40	2,100	48	62	2,162	25	1,737	50	1,787	63	1,850	994
12/31/41	3,150	101	163	3,313	8	2,357	52	2,409	152	2,561	1,576
12/31/42	4,200	129	292	4,492	33	3,647	94	3,741	307	4,048	2,269
12/31/43	5,250	146	438	5,688	67	5,852	188	6,040	537	6,577	2,902
12/31/44	6,300	186	624	6,924	286	7,849	511	8,360	810	9,170	3,512
12/31/45	7,350	195	819	8,169	831	10,955	1,477	12,432	1,218	13,650	4,205
12/31/46	8,400	306	1,125	9,525	821	10,548	2,111	12,659	1,366	14,025	4,880
12/31/47	9,450	436	1,561	11,011	618	10,608	2,558	13,166	1,689	14,855	5,612
12/31/48	10,500	508	2,070	12,570	429	10,754	2,804	13,558	2,053	15,611	6,351
12/31/49	11,550	526	2,596	14,146	546	11,829	3,377	15,206	2,620	17,826	7,187
12/31/50	12,600	645	3,241	15,841	578	14,221	4,339	18,560	3,585	22,145	8,037
12/31/51	13,650	713	3,954	17,604	1,017	16,445	5,726	22,171	4,601	26,772	8,976
12/31/52	14,700	758	4,711	19,411	1,191	18,003	7,116	25,119	5,520	30,639	9,947
12/31/53	15,750	854	5,566	21,316	761	17,817	7,431	25,248	6,036	31,284	10,824
12/31/54	16,800	908	6,473	23,273	2,050	27,103	12,805	39,908	9,729	49,637	11,917
12/31/55	17,850	1,137	7,610	25,460	3,841	31,783	18,468	50,251	12,173	62,424	13,253
12/31/56	18,900	1,245	8,855	27,755	4,412	32,821	22,872	55,693	13,402	69,095	14,654
12/31/57	19,950	1,378	10,234	30,184	3,337	27,188	21,583	48,771	12,004	60,775	16,035
12/31/58	21,000	1,449	11,683	32,683	2,704	38,194	32,179	70,373	17,922	88,295	17,194
12/31/59	22,050	1,551	13,234	35,284	5,860	40,799	39,432	80,231	20,214	100,445	18,792
12/31/60	23,100	1,787	15,020	38,120	5,009	40,170	43,100	83,270	21,255	104,525	20,355
12/31/61	24,150	1,835	16,855	41,005	5,897	46,957	55,145	102,102	26,125	128,227	21,900

CONTINUED ON PAGE 2

	=====COST OF SHARES=====					=====VALUE OF SHARES=====					
DATE	CUM INV'M'T	ANNUAL INCOME DIVS	CUM INCOME DIVS	TOTAL INV'M'T COST	ANNUAL CAP GAIN DISTRIB'N	FROM INV'M'T	FROM CAP GAINS REINV'D	SUB-TOTAL	FROM DIVS REINV'D	TOTAL VALUE	SHARES HELD
12/31/62	25,200	1,984	18,840	44,040	4,414	38,877	48,628	87,505	23,193	110,698	23,329
12/31/63	26,250	2,089	20,929	47,179	4,952	45,815	60,963	106,778	28,821	135,599	24,880
12/31/64	27,300	2,314	23,243	50,543	7,967	50,179	73,350	123,529	33,168	156,697	26,831
12/31/65	28,350	2,598	25,841	54,191	10,540	59,653	96,352	156,005	41,440	197,445	29,014
12/31/66	29,400	3,289	29,130	58,530	13,342	55,450	100,667	156,117	41,103	197,220	31,707
12/31/67	30,450	3,861	32,991	63,441	10,566	67,628	131,466	199,094	53,162	252,256	33,859
12/31/68	31,500	4,703	37,693	69,193	9,424	74,780	154,762	229,542	62,932	292,474	36,041
12/31/69	32,550	5,204	42,897	75,447	15,595	61,698	140,008	201,706	56,288	257,994	39,060
12/31/70	33,600	5,554	48,451	82,051	10,008	59,495	142,921	202,416	59,380	261,796	41,787
12/31/71	34,650	5,769	54,220	88,870	4,869	67,569	164,525	232,094	72,212	304,306	43,503
12/31/72	35,700	5,999	60,219	95,919	9,148	75,066	189,373	264,439	85,258	349,697	45,682
12/31/73	36,750	6,628	66,847	103,597	6,753	59,590	155,293	214,883	73,108	287,991	48,038
12/31/74	37,800	10,254	77,101	114,901	0	46,813	119,934	166,747	66,167	232,914	50,305
12/31/75	38,850	9,657	86,758	125,608	1,584	61,512	155,849	217,361	94,862	312,223	52,430
12/31/76	39,900	8,917	95,675	135,575	5,419	77,131	197,789	274,920	126,227	401,147	54,615
12/31/77	40,950	9,478	105,153	146,103	6,870	71,984	189,092	261,076	125,653	386,729	57,166
12/31/78	42,000	10,533	115,686	157,686	0	80,831	209,357	290,188	149,875	440,063	58,753
8/31/79	43,050	5,638	121,324	164,374	4,664	94,752	247,465	342,217	179,731	521,948	60,201
TOTAL					166,460						

NOTE: 30.0% SUBTRACTED FROM DIVIDENDS AND 12.0% SUBTRACTED FROM CAPITAL GAIN DISTRIBUTIONS AS PAID TO REFLECT LIABILITY FOR FEDERAL INCOME TAXES.

TABLE 32. HYPOTHETICAL ILLUSTRATION—$7500 INVESTMENT IN THE SEMINAR FUND

DATE	INITIAL INVESTMENT	OFFERING PRICE	SALES CHARGE INCLUDED	SHARES PURCHASED	NET ASSET VALUE PER SHARE	INITIAL NET ASSET VALUE
1/ 1/59	$7,500.00	$5.61	8.50%	1,336.898	$5.135	$6,865

ANNUAL INVESTMENTS OF $7,500.00 -- SAME DAY AS INITIAL INVESTMENT
DIVIDENDS AND CAPITAL GAINS REINVESTED

CUMULATIVE VOLUME DISCOUNT REFLECTED WHERE APPLICABLE IN THIS ILLUSTRATION

	=====COST OF SHARES=====					=====VALUE OF SHARES=====					
DATE	CUM INV'M'T	ANNUAL INCOME DIVS	CUM INCOME DIVS	TOTAL INV'M'T COST	ANNUAL CAP GAIN DISTRIB'N	FROM INV'M'T	FROM CAP GAINS REINV'D	SUB-TOTAL	FROM DIVS REINV'D	TOTAL VALUE	SHARES HELD
12/31/59	7,500	171	171	7,671	515	7,146	521	7,667	172	7,839	1,466
12/31/60	15,000	374	545	15,545	832	13,529	1,367	14,896	549	15,445	3,007
12/31/61	22,500	558	1,104	23,604	1,428	23,337	3,012	26,349	1,202	27,551	4,705
12/31/62	30,000	763	1,867	31,867	1,346	24,625	3,642	28,267	1,751	30,018	6,326
12/31/63	37,500	994	2,861	40,361	1,876	36,377	6,119	42,496	3,050	45,546	8,357
12/31/64	45,000	1,280	4,141	49,141	3,509	46,652	10,092	56,744	4,531	61,275	10,492
12/31/65	52,500	1,617	5,758	58,258	5,222	62,700	17,151	79,851	7,017	86,868	12,765
12/31/66	60,000	2,242	8,000	68,000	7,210	63,852	22,486	86,338	8,613	94,951	15,265
12/31/67	67,500	2,855	10,855	78,355	6,219	85,141	33,343	118,484	13,223	131,707	17,678
12/31/68	75,000	3,712	14,567	89,567	5,875	100,625	43,526	144,151	18,368	162,519	20,026
12/31/69	82,500	4,339	18,905	101,405	10,250	87,791	44,657	132,448	19,175	151,623	22,955
12/31/70	90,000	4,902	23,808	113,808	6,975	90,142	49,412	139,554	23,476	163,030	26,022
12/31/71	97,500	5,356	29,164	126,664	3,606	108,729	58,836	167,565	31,701	199,266	28,486
12/31/72	105,000	5,814	34,978	139,978	7,071	126,907	71,595	198,502	40,732	239,234	31,252
12/31/73	112,500	6,678	41,656	154,156	5,428	105,057	61,684	166,741	38,286	205,027	34,199
12/31/74	120,000	10,817	52,473	172,473		86,728	47,639	134,367	39,811	174,178	37,619
12/31/75	127,500	10,751	63,224	190,724	1,407	120,852	62,687	183,539	62,068	245,607	41,243
12/31/76	135,000	10,324	73,548	208,548	5,009	158,078	82,461	240,539	87,232	327,771	44,625
12/31/77	142,500	11,327	84,875	227,375	6,556	152,333	82,554	234,887	91,571	326,458	48,256
12/31/78	150,000	13,005	97,880	247,880		176,752	91,402	268,154	114,662	382,816	51,110
8/31/79	157,500	7,143	105,023	262,523	4,688	213,066	110,952	324,018	140,638	464,656	53,593
					TOTAL 85,022						

TABLE 33. HYPOTHETICAL ILLUSTRATION—$3750 INVESTMENT IN THE SEMINAR FUND

DATE	INITIAL INVESTMENT	OFFERING PRICE	SALES CHARGE INCLUDED	SHARES PURCHASED	NET ASSET VALUE PER SHARE	INITIAL NET ASSET VALUE
1/ 1/59	$3,750.00	$5.61	8.50%	668.449	$5.135	$3,432

ANNUAL INVESTMENTS OF $3,750.00 -- SAME DAY AS INITIAL INVESTMENT
DIVIDENDS AND CAPITAL GAINS REINVESTED

CUMULATIVE VOLUME DISCOUNT REFLECTED WHERE APPLICABLE IN THIS ILLUSTRATION

| | =======COST OF SHARES======= | | | | | =======VALUE OF SHARES======= | | | | | |
DATE	CUM INV'M'T	ANNUAL INCOME DIVS	CUM INCOME DIVS	TOTAL INV'M'T COST	ANNUAL CAP GAIN DISTRIB'N	FROM INV'M'T	FROM CAP GAINS REINV'D	SUB-TOTAL	FROM DIVS REINV'D	TOTAL VALUE	SHARES HELD
12/31/59	3,750	42	42	3,792	204	3,572	207	3,779	43	3,822	715
12/31/60	7,500	91	133	7,633	325	6,730	537	7,267	134	7,401	1,441
12/31/61	11,250	134	267	11,517	549	11,587	1,171	12,758	291	13,049	2,228
12/31/62	15,000	180	448	15,448	512	12,202	1,405	13,607	420	14,027	2,956
12/31/63	18,750	233	681	19,431	703	17,998	2,339	20,337	726	21,063	3,864
12/31/64	22,500	296	977	23,477	1,296	23,004	3,813	26,817	1,070	27,887	4,775
12/31/65	26,250	369	1,346	27,596	1,902	30,915	6,407	37,322	1,643	38,965	5,725
12/31/66	30,000	501	1,846	31,846	2,590	31,478	8,302	39,780	1,993	41,773	6,715
12/31/67	33,750	628	2,475	36,225	2,188	41,924	12,199	54,123	3,026	57,149	7,671
12/31/68	37,500	802	3,276	40,776	2,054	49,567	15,808	65,375	4,153	69,528	8,567
12/31/69	41,250	920	4,197	45,447	3,532	43,259	16,046	59,305	4,276	63,581	9,626
12/31/70	45,000	1,023	5,220	50,220	2,359	44,426	17,606	62,032	5,160	67,192	10,725
12/31/71	48,750	1,107	6,327	55,077	1,187	53,602	20,864	74,466	6,896	81,362	11,631
12/31/72	52,500	1,190	7,517	60,017	2,305	62,581	25,182	87,763	8,783	96,546	12,612
12/31/73	56,250	1,349	8,866	65,116	1,746	51,844	21,528	73,372	8,168	81,540	13,601
12/31/74	60,000	2,149	11,015	71,015	0	42,805	16,626	59,431	8,342	67,773	14,637
12/31/75	63,750	2,097	13,113	76,863	437	59,659	21,823	81,482	12,849	94,331	15,840
12/31/76	67,500	1,986	15,098	82,598	1,532	77,998	28,490	106,488	17,902	124,390	16,935
12/31/77	71,250	2,149	17,248	88,498	1,978	75,173	28,232	103,405	18,618	122,023	18,037
12/31/78	75,000	2,431	19,679	94,679	0	87,236	31,258	118,494	23,096	141,590	18,903
8/31/79	78,750	1,323	21,002	99,752	1,396	105,169	37,716	142,885	28,201	171,086	19,733
				TOTAL	28,794						

NOTE: 50.0% SUBTRACTED FROM DIVIDENDS AND 20.0% SUBTRACTED FROM CAPITAL GAIN DISTRIBUTIONS AS PAID TO REFLECT LIABILITY FOR FEDERAL INCOME TAXES.

TABLE 34. ASSUMED — INFLATION RATE
AVERAGE COST
(INCLUDES TUITION & RELATED EXPENSES)

Entrance Year	Child: Age:								Total	
	1976 DOLLARS	FUTURE NEEDS	1976 DOLLARS	FUTURE NEEDS	1976 DOLLARS	FUTURE NEEDS	1976 DOLLARS	FUTURE NEEDS	1976 DOLLARS	FUTURE NEEDS
1980	$	$							$	$
1981			$	$						
1982					$	$				
1983										
1984										
1985										
1986							$	$		
1987										
1988										
1989										
TOTAL										

676

STOCKS

Company _____

Date Bought	No. of Shares	Price Per Share	Total Cost	Date Sold	No. of Shares	Price Per Share	Total Net Proceeds

Figure 1.

DIVIDEND RECORD

Company_____

Date Dividend Paid	Number of Shares	Rate per Share	Total Amount of Dividend

Figure 2.

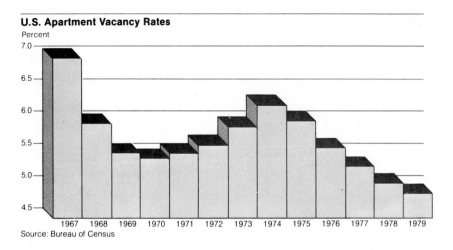

U.S. Apartment Vacancy Rates

Percent

Source: Bureau of Census

Figure 3.

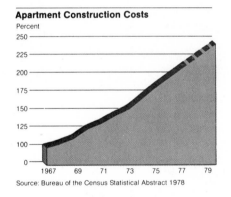

Apartment Construction Costs

Percent

Source: Bureau of the Census Statistical Abstract 1978

Figure 4.

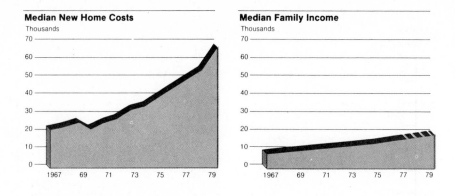

Median New Home Costs

Thousands

Median Family Income

Thousands

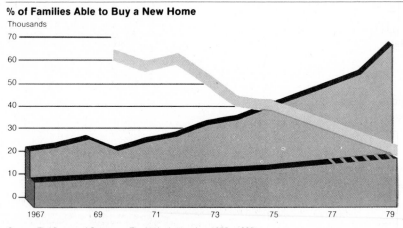

% of Families Able to Buy a New Home

Thousands

Source: The Bureau of Census — The Nation's Housing, 1975 - 1985

Figure 5.

INDEX OF U.S. FARM REAL ESTATE VALUE PER ACRE
Percent of March 1, 1967

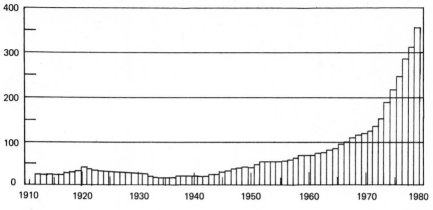

PERCENT CHANGE IN PER-ACRE VALUE FROM PREVIOUS YEAR

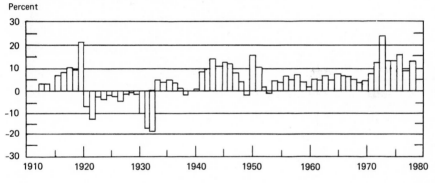

Reported as of March 1, 1912–75, and February 1, 1976 to date.
Excludes Alaska and Hawaii. Data unavailable prior to 1912.
USDA

Figure 6.

681

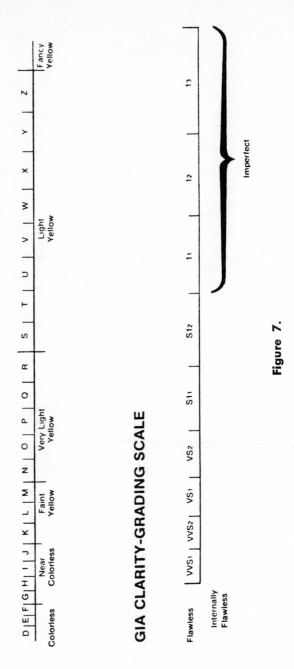

Figure 7.

APPROXIMATE COMPARISON CHART OF COLOR GRADING SYSTEMS FOR POLISHED DIAMONDS

* Reflectance Spectrophoto-meter Units	C.M.	P.M.	Original Name Terms	U.K.	G.I.A.	A.G.S.	Deutsche RAL560QA5 Scan.D.N. 0.50 Ct. & Above	Scan.D.N. Less Than 0.50 Ct.	
0 - 50	0.25		Jager	Blue White					
51 - 80					D	0			
81 - 120	0.75		River	Top Fine White			River	Rarest White	Color-less
121 - 160					E				
161 - 200	1.25	0.90							
201 - 275					F	1			
276 - 350									
351 - 425				Fine White					
426 - 500							Top Wesselton	White	
501 - 750	2.25	0.95	Top Wesselton		G				Nearly Color-less
751 - 1000						2			
1001 - 2000	2.75	1.00	Wesselton	White	H		Wesselton		
2001 - 3000		1.03	Top Crystal	Commercial White	I	3	Top Crystal		
3001 - 4000	3.25	1.10	Crystal	Crystal	J	4	Crystal	Tinted White	
4001 - 5000	3.75		Top Cape		K	5			
5001 - 6000	4.25	1.15	Cape	Top Cape	L	6	Top Cape		Slightly Tinted
6001 - 7000	4.75		Low Cape		M		Cape	Yellow-ish	
7001 - 8000	5.25	1.20	Lt. Yellow	Cape	N	7			
8001 - 9000	5.75				O				
9001 - 10000	6.25		Yellow	Light Yellow	P	8	Light Yellow		Very Light Yellow
10001 - 11000	6.75				Q				
11001 - 12000	7.25	1.30			R				Light Yellow
12001 - 18000	7.75 10.00	1.50		Yellow	S - Z	9-10	Yellow	Yellow	Light Yellow

All the systems on this chart are based on master stones and opinion and are, therefore, open to different interpretations within each system. This means that they are not precisely comparable with each other

* Reflectance Spectrophotometer PMQ II using grating monochromator M20; System covers 0 to 18,000+ points for Cape series stones only.

G.I.A. - Gemological Institute of America
A.G.S. - American Gem Society
C.M. - Colorimeter

P.M. - Photometer
Scan.D.N. - Scandinavian Diamond Nomenclature
U.K. - United Kingdom

Figure 8.

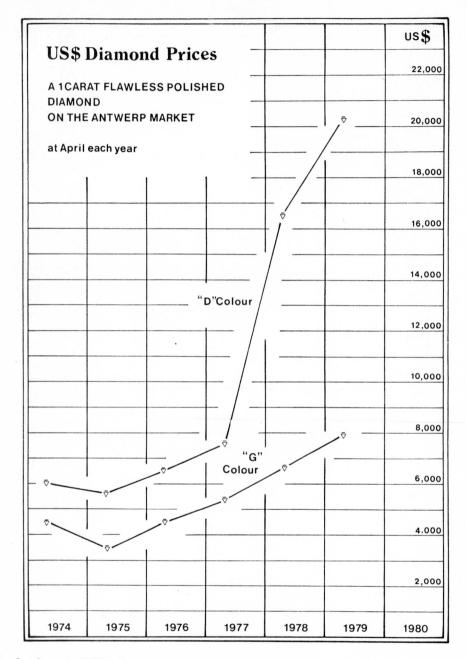

Note: By the end of 1979 the cost of a D-Flawless was $40,000.   Source: EIU

Figure 9.

	Amount
Carryovers From Prior Years	
Net Taxable Income (For income averaging purposes if applicable)	
19	
19	
19	
19	
Short Term Loss from 19	
Long Term Loss from 19	
Extimated Gross Income — 19	
Personal Service Income (Salary, bonus, pensions, annuities, deferred comp. (from W-2)	
Dividends (Specify allocation between joint, taxpayer or spouse)	
Interest From Federal Obligations Treasury Notes and Bills, etc.	
Interest From State & Municipal Obligations Issued by cities, counties, towns, school districts, etc.	
All Other Interest From banks, corporate bonds, etc.	
Partnership Income (or loss) Please indicate source: Prior tax shelter investment, real estate syndication, etc.	
Rental Income Net Income (after expenses and depreciation)	
Income From Estates or Trusts Please identify source	
Sole Proprietor Profit (or loss) (Unincorporated Personal Business)	
Short Term Capital Gain (or loss)	
Long Term Capital Gain (or loss)	
Adjustments to Gross Income-Moving, overnight travel, local transportation, outside sales expense, alimony paid	
Estimated Itemized Deductions 19 (Best obtained by reviewing last year's tax return	
Real Estate Primarily taxes paid on all personal residences	
State Income Tax Paid Prepayments this year — Include Estimates and Withheld Amounts	
Total Charitable Contributions Both cash and fair market value of donations	
Investment Interest Expense Margin or other interest paid on loans to make investments	
Non-Investment Interest Expense Personal loan charges, home mortgage	
Miscellaneous (include T & E) Professional fees, publications, non-reimbursed office expenses, travel & entertainment	
Sales taxes paid for any large purchases	
Medical Deductions Doctors, medical transportation, hospital bills (Net of Insurance)	
Keogh and/or IRA Deductions Personal contribution to pension plan	
Credit to Tax	
Cost of Business Equipment Include only depreciable equipment purchased in 1979 for use in business	
Useful Life of Business Equipment (Number of years used to depreciate property)	
Tax Preference Items —	
Preference Items Subject to Minimum Tax Total estimated amount of preferences for 1979 Excess depletion, excess accelerated depreciation, excess intangible drilling costs, etc.	
Amount(s) of tax write-off you wish us to calculate in the equation	
Enter tax preference amount generated by "K14"	

Figure 10.

685

ALTERNATIVE MINIMUM TAX

Taxable Income   _____

Excess Adjusted Itemized Deductions*   _____

60% (Excluded Portion) of Net LTCG   _____

Less Exemption   __(20,000)__

TOTAL   _____

First $40,000 of Total   _____ X10% = _____

Next $40,000 of Total   _____ X20% = _____

Excess over $80,000 of Total   _____ X25% = _____

           TOTAL ALTERNATIVE MINIMUM TAX   _____

*Those itemized deductions which exceed 60% of AGI.

Figure 11.

Program:

Investment Schedule: _____ _____ _____   TOTAL _____

<u>TAX SAVINGS WORKSHEET</u>

WITHOUT INVESTMENT:

1. Taxable Income $_____   Bracket _____%

2. Tax Due $_____

WITH INVESTMENT:

3. Amount of Investment $_____ $_____ $_____

4. Write-off   _____   _____   _____

5. Net Taxable Income After Investment   _____   _____   _____

6. Tax Due   _____   _____   _____

7. Net Tax Savings $_____ $_____ $_____

8. Investment Tax Credit   _____   _____   _____

9. TOTAL TAX SAVINGS   _____   _____   _____

10. Amount Invested $_____ $_____ $_____

11. Less Tax Saved   _____   _____   _____

12. Net Cost of Investment   _____   _____   _____

Figure 12.

687

COMPARISON STATEMENT

NAME OF APPLICANT	STREET	CITY	STATE	ZIP CODE
John W. Doe				

NAME OF INSURED IF OTHER THAN APPLICANT	DATE OF BIRTH OF INSURED

1. COMPARATIVE INFORMATION	†Existing Life Insurance	†Existing Life Insurance	†Existing Life Insurance	Total Existing Life Insurance	Proposed Life Insurance
Policy Number					XXXXXXXXXXXX
Insurance Company					
Amount of Basic Insurance					
Currently	$ 15,000	$ 15,000	$ 16,000	$ 46,000	$ 46,000
10 Years Hence	$ 15,000	$ 15,000	$ 16,000	$ 46,000	$ 46,000
20 Years Hence	$ 15,000	$ 15,000	$ 16,000	$ 46,000	$ Ren & conv
At age 65	$ 15,000	$ 15,000	$ 16,000	$ 46,000	$ at client opt
Basic Plan of Insurance	Adj W.L.	Adj W.L.	Adj W.L.	Adj W.L.	10-yr deposit
Present Amount of Term Rider(s)	$	$	$	$	$ level term
Issue Age	30	30	34	Various	51
Issue Date	4-25-56	4-25-56	6-1-60	Various	XXXXXXXXXXXX

Premium For:	Premium / Age / Payable To Age / Cov. Ceases	Premium / Age / Payable To Age / Cov. Ceases	Premium / Age / Payable To Age / Cov. Ceases	Premium / Age / Payable To Age / Cov. Ceases	Premium / Age / Payable To Age / Cov. Ceases
Basic Policy	$316.20 Life	$316.20 Life	$384.00 Life	$1,016.40 Life	$649.40 '88 at [1]
*Accidental Death Benefit	$ — —	$ — —	$ — —	$ — —	$ cl opt
*Waiver of Premium Benefit	$ — —	$ — —	$ — —	$ — —	$ Ren &
*Disability Income Benefit	$ — —	$ — —	$ — —	$ — —	$ conv
Family Income or Increased					
Protection Rider	$	$	$	$	$
Option to Purchase Additional					
Insurance	$ — —	$ — —	$ — —	$ — —	$ — —
Other Benefits (Explain)	$	$	$	$	$ [1]
Total Current Premium	$316.20	$316.20	$384.00	$1,016.40	$649.40 [1]
Frequency of Premium Payment	Annual	Annual	Annual	Annual	Annual
Tabular Cash Values:					
At Present	$ 5,145	$ 5,145	$ 4,832	$ 15,122 [2]	$ 0
1 Year Hence	$ 5,415	$ 5,415	$ 5,136	$ 15,966	$ 0
5 Years Hence	$ 6,489	$ 6,489	$ 6,352	$ 19,330	$ 0 [2]
10 Years Hence	$ 7,800	$ 7,800	$ 7,850	$ 23,450	$ 1,610 [2]
At age (Highest age shown in Cash Value Table of existing policy) Age 65	$ 8,820	$ 8,820	$ 8,976	$ 26,616	$ 0 [3]
Cash Value of any existing Dividend Additions or Accumulations (if available from applicant)	$	$	$	$	$
Amount of any Loan Now Outstanding	$	$	$	$	$
Amount of Annual Loan Interest	$ 5%	$ 5%	$ 5%	$ 5%	$
Date Contestable Period Expires	Expired	Expired	Expired	Expired	1980
Date Suicide Clause Expires	Expired	Expired	Expired	Expired	1980
Dividends**					
Is Policy Participating?	Yes	Yes	Yes	Yes	No
Annual Dividend (current scale)					
1 Year Hence	$ 196	$ 196	$ 207	$ 599	$
2 Years Hence	$ 204	$ 204	$ 217	$ 625	$
5 Years Hence	$ 236	$ 236	$ 257	$ 729	$
10 Years Hence	$ 276	$ 276	$ 304	$ 856	$
Total 10 Years	$ 2,405	$ 2,405	$ 2,595	$ 7,405	$

[1] Excluding premium deposit of: $621.00 -- Maturity Value is: $1,610

[2] Plus value of investments of $14,501 ($15,122 - $621) plus value of annual premium savings at end of 10 years.

[3] Above at end of 14 years.

Figure 13. These are samples of comparison forms of disclosure. They may vary from state to state.

688

*If Premium for Benefits: (A) is not separable from basic policy premium, insert "Included in Basic Policy Premium," or (B) is an aggregate premium, show the aggregate premium.

**Dividends are based on the 19_____ dividend scale. The dividends shown are not to be construed as guarantees or estimates of dividends to be paid in the future. Dividends depend on mortality experience, investment, investment earnings and other factors, and are determined each year in the sole discretion of the Company's board of directors.

The agent is responsible for furnishing required dividend information. It is recommended that he obtain this for the policy being replaced from the Company issuing the original insurance. As an alternative, however, he may show dividends on closest comparable policy, amount, age and duration from current statistical manuals. (Interpolating where necessary). It is to be recognized that dividend information under this alternative method, with respect to existing insurance is not likely to be as accurate as dividend information obtained directly from the Company issuing the original insurance.

Source of dividend information used: _____

†If more than one existing life insurance policy is to be affected by a transaction included within the definition of a replacement contained in the Regulation, (1) the existing life insurance column of a separate signed Comparison Statement form must be completed for each such policy providing the information required by the form with respect to existing policies, and (II) a separate signed Comparison Statement form must be completed for the proposed policy. The latter form must summarize, to the extent possible, the information concerning the existing policies set forth on the separate forms, and must include the information required in Sections 2 through 5 of the Comparison Statement:

2. Advantages of Continuing the Existing Life Insurance:

3. Advantages of the Proposed Replacement of the Existing Life Insurance:

4. Additional information:
     (A)   The Existing Life Insurance Cannot fulfill Your Intended Objectives for the Following Reason(s):

     (B)   Under the Proposal, the Existing Insurance Policy Will be Treated as Follows:

5. The Primary Reason for the Proposed Replacement of the Existing Life Insurance by New Insurance is as Follows:

_____   _____
           (DATE)   (SIGNATURE OF AGENT)

                                   _____
                                       (ADDRESS)

   I hereby acknowledge that I received the above "Comparison Statement" and the "Notice to Applicants Regarding Replacement of Life Insurance" before I signed the application for the proposed new insurance.

_____   _____
           (DATE)   (SIGNATURE OF APPLICANT)

From: _____ Life Insurance Company

By: _____
     Chairman of the Board

To the Field Force in the United States,
Canada, and Puerto Rico:

I am pleased to announce the creation of the Office of Insurance Conservation. Vice-President _____ will be in charge of the new Office, in
addition to carrying out his other marketing responsibilities. He will continue
to report to the Senior Vice President in charge of Marketing.

This new Office is designed to give renewed force and direction to the
Company's long-standing policy opposing any sales approach that is generally
based upon borrowing on or cashing in existing policies to finance the purchase of new ones.

The regulations of 34 states, Canada, and Puerto Rico, and the statutes of
most others make it clear that the replacement of existing life insurance
policies is generally not in the best interest of the policyowners. We firmly
believe that "twisting" and other such unwarranted practices have no place in
the life insurance business.

Vice President _____ will move constructively and aggressively against
all such practices from both outside and inside the Company.

OUTSIDE REPLACEMENTS

He will help us fight back against outside replacements and will:

- help our agents conserve business, marshaling legal and actuarial
resources on their behalf;
- prepare protest to high officers of replacing companies whether in the
insurance industry or the securities industry;
- prepare cases against outside abuses for presentation to State Insurance
Departments, assisted by the Office of the General Counsel, the Actuarial
Department, and the Governmental and Legislative Affairs Department;
- determine how our agents can be advised more quickly of twisting of
their business;
- utilize data already available in the Home Office concerning companies
that are replacing our business, agents who are to blame, and the geographical
areas in which this replacing is occurring;
- consult with our Field Force concerning twisters who are evading state
regulations.

INSIDE REPLACEMENTS

_____ intends to resist at every turn any and all unwarranted
attempts to replace business by those outside our Company. And the standards
we raise must be, and will be, applied equally to practices inside our Company.

To maintain these standards, Vice President _____ will:

- study and evaluate present Company rules designed to discourage replacement of our own business by our own agents to determine if such rules are
realistic and whether new ones need to be developed;
- recommend to the Senior Vice President in charge of Marketing any new
replacement rules;
- enforce all rules with the help, if necessary, of experts in the Electronics,
Actuarial, and Auditing Departments and in the Office of the General Counsel;
- consult with the Senior Vice President in charge of Marketing about agents
whose practices may be questionable and recommend to him any disciplinary
action for those who do not comply with the rules;
- continually research ways to prevent all types of replacement of our business and that of other companies, and cooperate directly with companies whose
business has been placed in jeopardy or has been replaced by our agents.

_____ and its agents enjoy an enviable reputation for professionalism
in the service of our policyowners. At all times--and particularly in this age
of the consumer--we must take whatever constructive actions we can to protect
and enhance that reputation by assuring excellence and quality performance on
behalf of our own consumers. The creation of the Office of Insurance Conservation is another important step designed to help achieve this essential objective.

Figure 14.

CONTRIBUTIONS FOR EMPLOYER

	Example	Your Figures
1. Annual Earned Income (Schedule C, Line 21 of Federal Tax Return)	$ *30,000*	$ _____
2. Standard Deduction and Personal Exemptions	$ *3,500*	$ _____
3. Taxable Income (Form 1040, line 48)	$ *26,500*	$ _____
4. Percentage Tax Rate on Top Dollar (See table below)	*36* %	_____ %
5. Deductible Keogh Contribution (Up to 15% of Line 1 or $7,500, whichever is less)	$ *4,500*	$ _____
6. Tax Savings (Line 5 x Line 4)	$ *1,620*	$ _____

CONTRIBUTIONS FOR EMPLOYEE

	Example	Your Figures
7. Eligible Employees' Earnings	$ *8,000*	$ _____
8. % Contributions for Employees (Must be same percentage as used by employer in Line 5)	*15* %	_____ %
9. Deductible Contribution for Employee	$ *1,200*	$ _____
10. Tax Savings (Line 9 x Line 4)	$ *433*	$ _____
11. Cost of Employee Contribution (Line 9 less Line 10)	$ *767*	$ _____

SUMMARY

	Example	Your Figures
12. Total Keogh Contribution (Line 5 plus Line 9)	$ *5,700*	$ _____
13. Net Tax Savings (Line 6 less Line 11)	$ *853*	$ _____

Figure 15.

Wrap-Around Loan

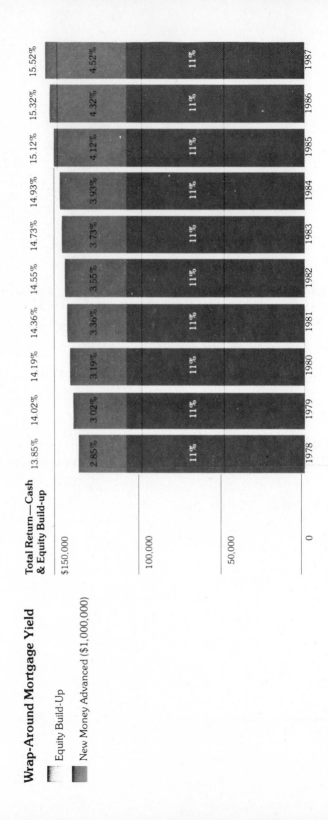

Wrap-Around Mortgage Yield

Total Return—Cash
& Equity Build-up

Equity Build-Up

New Money Advanced ($1,000,000)

$150,000

100,000

50,000

0

	1978	1979	1980	1981	1982	1983	1984	1985	1986	1987
	13.85%	14.02%	14.19%	14.36%	14.55%	14.73%	14.93%	15.12%	15.32%	15.52%
	2.85%	3.02%	3.19%	3.36%	3.55%	3.73%	3.93%	4.12%	4.32%	4.52%
	11%	11%	11%	11%	11%	11%	11%	11%	11%	11%

Hypothetical Wrap-Around Loan Schedule

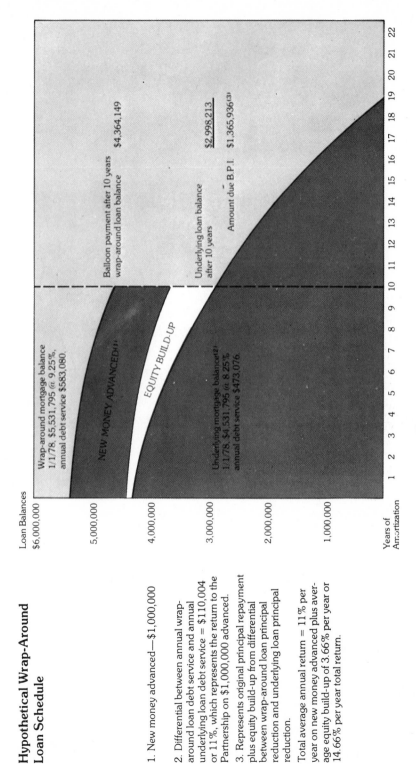

1. New money advanced—$1,000,000

2. Differential between annual wrap-around loan debt service and annual underlying loan debt service = $110,004 or 11%, which represents the return to the Partnership on $1,000,000 advanced.

3. Represents original principal repayment plus equity build-up from differential between wrap-around loan principal reduction and underlying loan principal reduction.

Total average annual return = 11% per year on new money advanced plus average equity build-up of 3.66% per year or 14.66% per year total return.

Loan Balances
$6,000,000

5,000,000

4,000,000

3,000,000

2,000,000

1,000,000

Years of Amortization

1 2 3 4 5 6 7 8 9 10 11 12 13 14 15 16 17 18 19 20 21 22

Wrap-around mortgage balance 1/1/78, $5,531,795 @ 9.25%, annual debt service $583,080.

NEW MONEY ADVANCED[1]

EQUITY BUILD-UP

Underlying mortgage balance[2] 1/1/78, $4,531,795 @ 8.25% annual debt service $473,076.

Balloon payment after 10 years wrap-around loan balance $4,364,149

Underlying loan balance after 10 years $2,998,213

Amount due B.P.I. $1,365,936[3]

Figure 16.

 On $100 a Month

You can live in the famous

HOT SPRINGS *Region*

● Of the many attractive localities, where it is possible to live on $100 a month, Hot Springs, Ark., has a special appeal. By the time you are ready to retire from active work, its famous hot spring baths might prove a great boon to you physically.

Here in a land of scenic beauty— a favorite playground of the American people—and where there's just enough cold weather to make it welcome—you could have a cozy home, and live comfortably on a very moderate income.

That's the kind of life you can lead, when you're ready to retire. Whether it's Hot Springs, or another of the nation's wonder spots—

or perhaps your own home town —it would be possible to live comfortably on $100 a month. And what a great satisfaction it is to know that at 55, or later, you can have that income, or more, for the rest of your life! That's what you can do if you own ▮▮▮▮▮▮▮ ▮▮▮▮▮ *retirement insurance.*

Decide now that you will have a worry-proof income for your less productive years . . . a sure, dependable check every month from one of America's oldest, strongest life insurance companies. Mail us the coupon below for the booklet— "EARNED LEISURE." Play safe with your future!

Without obligation, please send me your booklet "EARNED LEISURE."

Name ....

Address ....

City.................................... Age...........

T-2- -25-35

The assets of the ▮▮▮▮▮▮▮ *as reported to state insurance departments, now total a billion dollars—a great estate administered for the mutual welfare and protection of more than 600,000 policyholders.*

694

Figure 17.

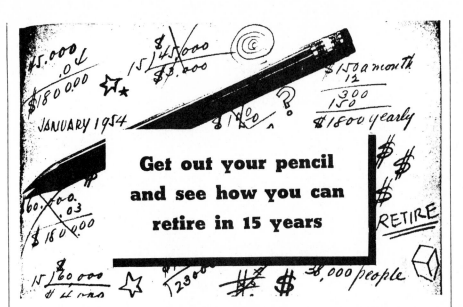

Get out your pencil and see how you can retire in 15 years

An advertisement that will help you get the things you want

IF YOU WANT an income for life — that will support you after you reach 55 or 60 — here are facts you should know.

Let's assume you are 40 now. Perhaps you are saving regularly — hoping you will have enough money some day to let you retire.

But will you? Let's see. In order to retire on $150 a month, you will have to save $45,000 and invest it at 4%. If you can get only 3%, you must save $60,000 to get the same income! Can you set aside that much in the next 15 years? It's a good way to retire, but it takes too much money for most of us.

That's why the ■■■■■■■■■ Retirement Income Plan was started. It is now being used by over 38,000 people. Through this Plan, you can get a guar-anteed income for life, you can guard against emergencies, you can avoid investment risks and uncertainties. And you can do all this with much less money than other investment plans require.

Get $150 a Month for Life

Here's how it works. Suppose you are 40 now, and you qualify for the following ■■■■■■■■ Plan which pays you $150 a month for life, beginning at age 55. Here is what the Plan provides:

1. A check for $150 when you reach 55, and a check for $150 every month thereafter as long as you live.

2. A life income to your wife in case of your death before age 55, and

3. A monthly Disability Income to you if, before age 55, total disability stops your earning power for six months or more.

Of course, you need not be 40 now. You may be older or younger. The income need not be $150 a month. It can be any amount from $10 to $200 a month or more. And you can have it start at any age: 55, 60, 65 or 70. Similar Plans are available to women.

You don't have to be rich to retire this way. Since you start the Plan 15 years or more before you need the retirement income, you receive all the benefits of compound interest, long-range invest-ments and *mutual* operation. You get a retirement income for far less money than ordinary investments require.

Send for Free Booklet

Let us mail you an important book-let giving the complete facts about the Retirement Income Plan. In a simple, illustrated way, this booklet shows you exactly how thousands of people are providing their own life incomes, tells you how the Plan protects against such emergencies as death or disability. Send the coupon below and we will mail you this booklet without cost or obligation. Discover for yourself the secret of get-ting your own life income!

How I retired in 15 years with $250 a month

"Sometimes I have to smile. It's hard to believe that I'm retired today—retired with a life income. You see, I never had more than my salary, never inherited a dime, or even had luck in business! Yet a check for $250 a month arrives on the dot. And I'm my own boss for keeps!

"I left the office two years ago. And when I explained how I was doing it, though I was only 55, more than one of my friends said he only wished I'd told him years before. He'd be retiring, too.

"There's only one secret. Seventeen years ago, back in 1938, I had saved a little money. So I went into partnership with a friend. We thought it was going to pay off very well.

"Well, it didn't. But it was the most profitable investment I ever made. It showed me that there was no easy way for *me*, with *my* limited experience, to make a lot of money.

"I had to find a way that was systematic and sure. I was 40 then.

"It was shortly after that that I read an advertisement that told of a modern way for people of moderate means to retire. It didn't call for any great capital. It simply required fifteen or twenty working years ahead. One thing I liked particularly was that my family was protected with life insurance from the first day I took out my plan. (This, surely, was better than any ordinary savings method!) And the income was guaranteed—whatever happened to the business world—each month, every month, from the day it began as long as I live. The plan was called the ▮▮▮▮▮ Retirement Income Plan.

"The ad offered more information. So, I mailed in the coupon. It brought a booklet describing the various plans.

"Soon after, I applied and qualified for a ▮▮▮▮▮ Plan. And from that day on I've honestly felt like a rich man. Because I knew I wouldn't just simply live and work and die. I had a future I'd really enjoy. And that's what I'm doing today—with many, many thanks to my ▮▮▮ ▮▮▮▮ check for $250 a month that means financial independence for life."

Send for Free Booklet

This story is typical. Assuming you start at a young enough age, you can plan to have an income of $10 a month to $3,000 a year or more—beginning at age 55, 60, 65 or older. Send the coupon and receive, by mail and without charge, a booklet which tells about ▮▮▮▮▮ Plans. Similar plans are available for women—and for employee pension programs. Don't put it off. Send for your copy now.

696

"How we retired in 15 years with $300 a month"

"Look at us! We're retired and having the time of our lives. A fish story? It sure isn't! Let me tell you about it.

"I started thinking about retiring in 1950. Nancy thought I was silly. It all seemed so far away. 'And besides,' she said, 'it makes me feel old.' It didn't seem silly to me, though. We'd just spent the afternoon with Nancy's aunt and uncle. Uncle Will had turned 65 during the war, and, by 1945, his working days were over.

"Now, life seemed to be standing still for them. They couldn't take even the short weekend trips that their friends could easily afford; they couldn't visit their children as often as they'd like.

"A pretty grim existence, I thought. But why? He'd had a good job. Then Nancy reminded me . . . they'd never planned ahead. During her uncle's working years, his paycheck was spent almost as soon as it arrived.

"Fortunately, they had put some money aside for a rainy day. But they hadn't planned ahead enough to make those retirement days sunny!

"Not for me, I decided. When it's time for me to retire, I want to be able to do the things we've always dreamed of doing instead of counting every penny.

"I showed Nancy a ▊▊▊▊▊▊▊▊ advertisement I'd seen in Life magazine a week or so before. It described their retirement income plan, telling how a man of 40 could retire in 15 years with a guaranteed income of $300 or more for life!

"Nancy agreed it was a great idea. The thought of retiring at 55 didn't make her feel old at all! So I filled out the coupon that day and sent it right off.

"A few days later the booklet describing the ▊▊▊▊▊▊▊▊ Plans arrived. I picked the right one for us and signed up right away. Three months ago my first check arrived—right on time.

"Last month we moved down here to Florida, and we love it. Nancy looks great with her tan, and she's thrilled at the thought of keeping it all year long!

"My tan suits me fine, but I'm really hooked on the fish. Whether I catch one a day or ten (or none), I'm having the time of my life, because we saved for a sunny day with ▊▊▊ o ▊▊▊."

Send for free booklet

This story is typical. Assuming you start early enough, you can plan to have an income of from $50 to $300 a month or more—beginning at age 55, 60, 65 or older. Send the coupon and receive by mail, without charge or obligation, a booklet which tells about ▊▊▊▊▊▊▊▊ Plans. Similar plans are available for women—and for Employee Pension Programs. Send for your free copy now. In 15 years you'll be glad you did!

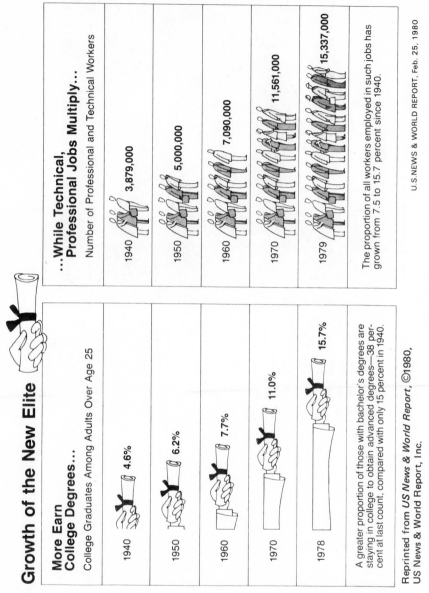

Growth of the New Elite

More Earn College Degrees...

College Graduates Among Adults Over Age 25

1940   4.6%

1950   6.2%

1960   7.7%

1970   11.0%

1978   15.7%

A greater proportion of those with bachelor's degrees are staying in college to obtain advanced degrees— 38 percent at last count, compared with only 15 percent in 1940.

Reprinted from *US News & World Report,* ©1980, US News & World Report, Inc.

...While Technical, Professional Jobs Multiply...

Number of Professional and Technical Workers

1940   3,879,000

1950   5,000,000

1960   7,090,000

1970   11,561,000

1979   15,337,000

The proportion of all workers employed in such jobs has grown from 7.5 to 15.7 percent since 1940.

U.S.NEWS & WORLD REPORT, Feb. 25, 1980

Figure 18.

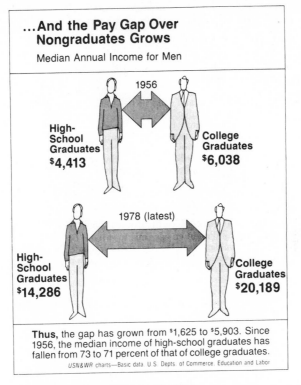

...And the Pay Gap Over Nongraduates Grows

Median Annual Income for Men

1956

High-School Graduates $4,413

College Graduates $6,038

1978 (latest)

High-School Graduates $14,286

College Graduates $20,189

Thus, the gap has grown from $1,625 to $5,903. Since 1956, the median income of high-school graduates has fallen from 73 to 71 percent of that of college graduates.

 USN&WR charts—Basic data U.S. Depts. of Commerce. Education and Labor

U.S.NEWS & WORLD REPORT, Feb. 25, 1980

Figure 19.

Figure 20. RESEARCH STATISTICS REGARDING COSTS OF UNDERGRADUATE EDUCATION IN U.S., SCHOLARSHIPS, AND APPOINTMENTS TO MILITARY ACADEMIES

Costs of State Schools

(Undergraduate costs of state and land grant public colleges and universities.)

Source: National Association of State Universities and
Land Grant Colleges
One Dupont Circle, Suite 710
Washington, D.C. 20036
Mr. Garven Hudgins
Director, Office of Communications Services
(202) 293-7120

Median Undergraduate costs for state universities and land-grant colleges.

1979–80:	Tuition & Fees	Room & Board	Total Costs
For resident student of home state	$ 781	$1589	$2333
1979–80 For non-resident student (out-of-state)	$1,877	$1589	$3667

Costs of Community and Junior Colleges

(*Two-year public and two-year private colleges*):

Source: American Association of Community and Junior Colleges
One Dupont Circle Suite 410
Washington, D.C. 20036
Mrs. Fontelle Gilbert

Median costs of 2 year public community/junior college:
(With no boarding facilities; a community commuter college.)

1979:	Tuition & Fees	Total
	$410	$410

Median costs of 2 year private community or junior college:

Tuition & Fees	Room & Board	Other (Books, etc.)	Total
$2043	$1780	$1096	$4919

Costs of Private Schools

(Independent Colleges and Universities, i.e., Ivy Leagues and Other U.S. Private Universities, i.e., Stanford University)

Source: Association of Independent Colleges and Universities
1717 Massachusetts Avenue, N.W.
Washington, D.C. 20036
Ms. Nancy Carter
(202) 387-7623

Year of Data: 1979–80
Median Costs of Private College Expenses per year (for on-campus student)

Tuition and Fees:	$2923
Room & Board	$1754
Other Expenses:	$1056
Total:	*$5733*

Median Costs of Private College Expenses per year (for off-campus student)

Tuition & Fees:	$2923
Room & Board:	$ 963
Other Expenses:	$1091
Total:	*$4977*

Costs of Selected Private Universities per Year

(Total costs included)

Stanford University Palo Alto, California:	$5595
M.I.T. Cambridge, Massachusetts:	$5265
California Institute of Technology:	$4708
Duke University:	$4535

Costs of the Ivy League Schools and Seven Sisters Women's Colleges

Ivy League Costs per Year (Undergraduate tuition & fees available only):

Cornell:	$5306
Yale:	$5550
Brown:	$5615
Columbia:	$5150

Harvard:	$5300
Dartmouth:	$5289
University of Pennsylvania:	$5270
Princeton:	$5585

Note: For a total per year costs for the above colleges, estimate another $3000 more for room and board and other expenses. For example, Harvard's total cost per year would be approximately $8300.

Seven Sisters Women's Colleges (*Undergraduate Tuition & fees available only*):

Barnard:	$5150
Vassar:	$4733
Mt. Holyoke:	$4620
Smith:	$5150
Bryn Mawr	$5325
Wellesley:	$4710
Radcliffe:	$5300

Note: For full college year expenses, estimate the same $3000 more for the costs of room and board and other expenses for total one year costs. For example, Smith's estimated one year costs would be $8150.

Scholarship Information

General Information: There are literally thousands of universities, colleges, institutions, organizations, foundations and corporations which provide scholarships to the undergraduate student entering college. Most of these scholarships provide a substantial portion of the full costs per year for undergraduate education, but do not furnish the student with the complete costs which cover tuition, room and board, books, student union fees, athletic fees, and other necessary costs for the normal undergrad college student. However, there are three areas of scholarship funding which *do* cover *all* expenses, and they are the following:

1. Merit Scholarships
2. Athletic Scholarships
3. Students of Employees of the College or University.

Campus Financial Aid Departments: A vital resource made available to the student and his parents is the Student Financial Aid Office on most every campus today. These counselors chart a plan for the student who needs financial assistance. A "package" plan of financial aid from the institution itself, federal grants, state grants, student

702

loans (at very low interest rates), and the campus "work-study" program are components of the plan. Financial aid departments are of real assistance and understanding and have the expertise to arrange for the most beneficial plan for the student in need of financial assistance for undergraduate education.

Source Books on Scholarships Available in the United States

You Can Win a Scholarship
By: Samuel C. Brownstein &
   Mitchell Weiner
Barron's Education Series
113 Crossways Park Drive
Woodbury, New York

Student Aid Annual
Chronicle Guidance Publications,
   Inc.
Moravia, New York 13118

Scholarships, Fellowships and Loans
By: S. Norman Feingold
   National Director
B'nai Brith Vocational Service
Washington, D.C.

Bellman Publishing Company
Arlington, Massachusetts 02174

*How to Get the Money to Pay for
   College*
Gene R. Hawes
(author of New American Guide to
   Colleges)

and
David M. Brownstone
David McKay Co., Inc.
New York
A Hudson Group Book

*Directory of Financial Aids for
   Women*
By: Gail Ann Schlacter
Reference Service Press
Los Angeles, California

Money for College! How to Get It
By: Donald R. Moore
Barron's Education Series, Inc.
Woodbury, New York

A Guide to Money for College
An Up-To-Date Listing of Over 300
   Assistance Programs for the
   Undergraduate
By: Louis T. & Joy W. Scarringi

*Financial Aids for Higher Education,
   1978–79*
By: Oreon Keeslar
William C. Brown Co. Publishers
Dubuque, Iowa

Requirements for Appointment to the U.S. Military Academies

General Information: To be considered for admission to a service academy an applicant must have a nomination. Title 10, United States Code, establishes two nomination categories—Congressional and Military-Service-Connected. Applicants who meet eligibility requirements may apply for and receive nominations in both categories. Members of the United States Senate and House of Representatives may nominate applicants who meet basic eligibility requirements established by law. Senators nominate from applicants in their entire state. Representatives nominate from applicants domiciled in their Congressional district. Applicants may apply for and receive nominations from both their United States Senators and from their Representative.

Basic Eligibility Requirements. Each applicant for a nomination must meet the following basic eligibility requirements on July 1 of the year of entry to a service academy:

1. *Age*: Be at least 17 years old, but not have passed the 22nd birthday.

2. *Citizenship*: Be a United States citizen

3. *Marital Status*: Be unmarried, not pregnant, and have no legal obligation for child support of a former spouse.

Selecting the Nominees: An applicant who meets *basic* eligibility requirements should also measure up in other areas. Thus, nominees must fulfill requirements in academics, physical aptitude, and medical fitness to qualify for admission. The overall qualification and selection process also involves an evaluation of the nominee's character and leadership potential. Careful evaluation of an applicant's overall potential for qualification and selection for admission plays an important part in determining which applicant should receive a nomination. Each service academy has its own method of determining a candidate's qualification for admission.

The Whole Person Is Evaluated. All factors for nomination are a part of the "whole-person" evaluations used by each of the Academies. The evidence of scholarship, stamina, character, leadership, motivation, and pride of accomplishment—qualities which are required to meet the challenges encountered at the Academies and, following graduation, as officers in the armed forces.

Figure 20.

My Life Insurance & Annuity Worksheet
(Use separate sheet for Term, Term Riders & Family Plan Riders)

NAME _____

BIRTHDATE _____ AGE _____

DATE _____

Company	Type Policy	Mortality table	(1) Face amt. Basic policy	(2) Cash value	(3) Rate to borrow	(4) Actual ins	(5) Annual premium	(6) Last year's refund (dividend)	(7) Net premium	(8) Lost earnings @ —% on cash value	(9) Total cost	(10) Cost per thousand
TOTALS												

Example:

Company	Type Policy	Mortality table	(1) Face amt. Basic policy	(2) Cash value	(3) Rate to borrow	(4) Actual ins	(5) Annual premium	(6) Last year's refund (dividend)	(7) Net premium	(8) Lost earnings @ —% on cash value	(9) Total cost	(10) Cost per thousand
Blessed Assurance Company	Whole Life	1941 CSO	$10,000	$4,000	5½%	$6000 (1) − (2)	$245	$40	$205	$240 (2) × 6%	$445 (7) + (8)	$74.16 (9) ÷ (4) ($445÷6= $74.19)

Worksheet 2.

A Picture of My Present Life Insurance Program

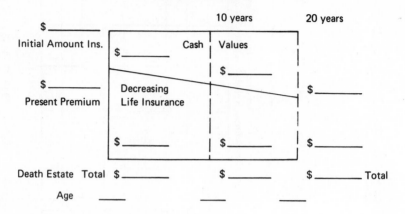

Worksheet 3.

My age: _____

My Life Insurance Cost Worksheet

Present Plan

Face amount of policies	$_____	
Less cash surrender value	$_____	
Net insurance		$_____(1)
Present premium	$_____	
Less dividend	$_____	
(last year)		
Net premium		$_____
Plus lost earnings on		
cash value of $_____		$_____
@ _____ %		
TOTAL COST		$_____(2)
Cost per thousand @ age _____		$_____(3)
[(2) ÷ per thousand of (1)]		

Recommended Plan

Plan _____

Cost per thousand @ age _____ $_____

Worksheet 4.

Replacement Cost Index Worksheet *

Present Program:

   (1) Face amount $_____

   (2) Less cash surrender value $_____

   (3) Net insurance $_____

   (4) Present Premium $_____

   (5) Less cash value increase
           for the year $_____

   (6) Plus lost earnings on $_____
           @ _____ %   (2) $_____

   (7) Less current dividend $_____

   (8) Total cost $_____

   (9) Replacement cost per thousand $_____
        @ _____ age [(8) ÷ no. of thousand in (3)]

Recommended Program:

   Plan _____

   Cost per thousand @ age _____ $_____

* If you are calculating replacement cost use IV. If you want to calculate your cost if you continue to hold your present policies use Worksheet III.

ADDRESSES YOU'LL NEED TO KNOW

American Birthright Trust Management
247 Royal Palm Way, Palm Beach, FL 33480. (305) 655-3481, also (800) 327-4508.

American Funds Distributors, Inc.
333 South Hope Street, Los Angeles, CA 90071. (213) 486-9651.

Anchor National Life Insurance Co.
2202 E. Camelback Rd., Phoenix, AZ 85016. (602) 263-0363.

Angeles Realty Corp.
1888 Century Park East, Los Angeles, CA 90067. (800) 421-4374.

The Balcor Company
The Balcor Building, 10024 Skokie Boulevard, Skokie, IL 60077. (312) 677-2900.

The Brennan Reports
P.O. Box 882, Valley Forge, PA 19482. (215) 783-0647.

Brigham Young University
1222 SFLC, Provo, UT 84602. (801) 374-1211.

College for Financial Planning
9725 East Hamptden Ave., Suite 200 Denver, CO 80231 (303) 755-7107

Consolidated Capital Equities Corp.
Suite 701, 333 Hegenberger Road, Oakland, CA 94621. (800) 227-1870; in California (800) 772-2443.

Continental Trust Company
P.O. Box 367, Plano, TX 75074. (214) 422-1075

The Financial Planner
2150 Parklake Drive N.E., Suite 260, Atlanta, GA 30345. (404) 934-0533. Editor: Rich White

Fireman's Fund American Life Insurance Company
1600 Los Gamos Road, San Rafael, CA 94911. (415) 492-6953.

IAFP Training Institute
2150 Parklake Drive, N.E., Suite 260, Atlanta, GA 30345. (404) 934-0533.

Institute for Business Planning, Inc.
IBP Plaza, Englewood Cliffs, NJ 07632. (201) 592-2022.

Institute of Certified Financial Planners
P.O. Box 6097, West Palm Beach. FL 33405. (305) 964-8729.

Integrated Marketing, Inc.
660 Newport Center Dr., Suite 1420, Newport Beach, CA 92660. (714) 759-0451, national toll free (800) 854-3891, California toll free (800) 432-7203.

Investment Company Institute
1775 K Street, N.W., Washington, D.C. 20006. (202) 293-7700.

Investment Timing Services, Inc.
1568 Banksville Road, Pittsburgh, PA 15216. (412) 341-5795.

Investors Guaranty Life Insurance Company
9611 Sunset Highway, Mercer Island, WA 98040. (206) 232-2800.

Johnny Reb Farms, Inc.
Route #2, Box 445, Staunton, VA 24401. (703) 337-1880.

Jones Intercable, Inc.
880 Continental National Bank Bldg., Englewood, CO 80110. (303) 761-3183.

Kershaw Distributors, Inc.
600 "B" St., Suite 2200, San Diego, CA 92101. (714) 442-6695, also (714) 236-0505.

Life Insurance RX Corporation
P.O. Box O, Sausalito, CA 94965. (415) 332-2266.

Lincoln Trust Company
P.O. Box 5831 T.A., Denver, CO 80217. (303) 771-1900.

Magnetic Video Corp.
23434 Industrial Pak Court, Farmington Hills, MI 48024. (313) 477-6066.

Massachusetts Financial Services
Company
200 Berkeley St., Boston, MA 02116.
(800) 343-2829, also (617) 423-
3500.

National Tax Shelter Digest
1720 Regal Row, Suite 242, Dallas,
TX 75234 (214) 630-0684
David Goark

New England Rare Coin Galleries
89 Devonshire Street, Boston, MA
02109. (800) 225-6794. In Massachusetts: (617) 227-800.

New York Institute of Finance
70 Pine Street, 2nd Floor, New York,
NY 10005. (212) 344-2900.

John Nuveen & Co., Inc.
61 Broadway, New York, NY 10006.
(212) 668-9500.

Oppenheimer Management
Corporation
One New York Plaza, New York,
NY 10004, (212) 825-8260.

Pacific Investments
2855 Campus Drive, San Mateo, CA
94403. (415) 572-0660, also (800)
227-6709.

The Pioneer Group, Inc.
60 State Street, Boston, MA 02109.
(617) 742-7825, also (800) 225-
6292.

Pioneer Western Corporation
P.O. Box 5068, Clearwater,
FL 33518, (813) 585-6565, ext. 212.

Public Storage
94 So. Los Robles, Pasadena,
CA 91101. (213) 681-6731.

Putnam Fund Distributors, Inc.
265 Franklin St., Boston, MA 02110.
(617) 423-4960, ext. 405-406.

Reston Publishing Company, Inc.
11480 Sunset Hills Road, Reston,
VA 22090. (703) 437-8900.

Universal Stamp Corp.
12 Richmond St. E, Suite 324, To-
ronto, Ontario, Canada, M5C 1N1.
(416) 862-1018.

Warren, Gorham & Lamont
210 South St., Boston, MA 02111.

INDEX